W9-CDV-140

THE INCARNATION OF GOD

B
2949
.R3
.K8313

HANS KÜNG

THE INCARNATION OF GOD

An Introduction to Hegel's Theological Thought
as Prolegomena to a
Future Christology

Translated by
J. R. Stephenson

Crossroad · New York

APR 1 0 1989

478070

The Crossroad Publishing Company
370 Lexington Avenue, New York, N.Y. 10017

Originally published as *Menschwerdung Gottes*
Copyright © Herder KG, Freiburg im Breisgau, 1970

Authorised English translation
Copyright © T. & T. Clark Ltd, 1987

All rights reserved. No part of this publication may be reproduced, stored in a retrieval system, or transmitted, in any form or by any means, electronic, mechanical, photocopying, recording or otherwise, without the written permission of The Crossroad Publishing Company.

Library of Congress Cataloging in Publication Data
Küng, Hans, 1928-
  The Incarnation of God.

  Translation of: Menschwerdung Gottes.
  Bibliography: p.
  Includes index.
  1. Hegel, Georg Wilhelm Friedrich, 1770-1831—
Contributions in theology. 2. Jesus Christ—History of
doctrines—19th century. 3. God—History of doctrines—
19th century. I. Title.
B2949.R3K8313   1987   230'.092'4   86-23262
ISBN 0-8245-0793-2

Printed in the United Kingdom
Typeset by Print Origination, Liverpool,
Printed by Billings Ltd, Worcester.

Publisher's Note

The translation of Hans Küng's magisterial book, *Menschwerdung Gottes*, has been a lengthy, difficult but richly satisfying task. The final text is the result of the hard work of many scholars who have brought their expertise to this project. The publishers would like to express their thanks to the Reverend Dr. J. R. Stephenson, of the University of Durham, who translated the German original; to the Reverend Dr. J. A. Williams, of the University of Durham, who supplied the references to English translations, where they exist, of the primary and secondary literature to which the author refers in his text, notes and bibliographies; to the Reverend Canon B. L. Hebblethwaite, Fellow & Dean of Chapel of Queens' College, Cambridge, who read through the complete text of the English version, and made very helpful suggestions on the translation; and to the Reverend P. D. Eaton, assistant curate of the Collegiate Church of All Saints, Maidstone, Kent, who revised and corrected the proofs.

CONTENTS

Publisher's Note   v
Contents   vii
Preface to the English Edition   ix
Preface   xiii

INTRODUCTION   1

CHAPTER ONE: CHRIST IN OBLIVION
1. A Man of the Enlightenment's Religion   23
2. Theology at odds with itself   31
3. Revolution of the Spirit   40
4. Religion and Society   46

CHAPTER TWO: CONCENTRATION ON JESUS
1. Jesus or Socrates?   59
2. Critique of Religion   67
3. The Life of Jesus according to Kant   74
4. From Proclaimer to Proclaimed   90
5. Representations of Christ in the Modern Age   96

CHAPTER THREE: THE GOD-MAN
1. Forward into Unity   102
2. Alien God and Alienated Man   112
3. Life Reconciled in Love   117
4. God in Jesus   122
5. Christ and Faith   127
6. True to the New Testament?   131

CHAPTER FOUR: TURNING TO PHILOSOPHY
1. Changing, yet the Same   143
2. Christ in Eclipse   156
3. The Death of God   162
4. The Drive toward a System   174
5. The Career of God   181

CHAPTER FIVE: SPECULATIVE CHRISTOLOGY
1. Via Consciousness to Spirit   190
2. The Religion of the Incarnation of God   206

3. Christology in the Context of the Community   212
4. Christ Sublated in Knwoledge   220

CHAPTER SIX: THE SYSTEM
1. God before the World   243
2. Christ Sublated in Knowledge   254
3. God in the World   267
4. Christ Sublated in the System   279
5. God through the World   289
6. Christ Sublated in 'Light'   259

CHAPTER SEVEN: JESUS CHRIST IN HISTORY
1. Old Age as Return   312
2. Christ in World History   318
3. Christ in Art   333
4. Christ in Religion /   348
5. Christ in Philosophy   374
6. God of the Future?   382

CHAPTER EIGHT: PROLEGOMENA TO A FUTURE CHRISTOLOGY
1. Hegel sub judice   413
2. The Historicity of God   430
3. The Historicity of Jesus   460

EXCURSUSES
Excursus   I : The Road to Classical Christology   509
Excursus   II : Can God Suffer?   518
Excursus   III : The Dialetic of the Attributes of God   525
Excursus   IV : Immutability of God?   530
Excursus   V : Recent Attempts at a Solution of the Old Problems   538

ABBREVIATIONS   559

BIBLIOGRAPHY
I.   Works by G. F. W. Hegel   560
II.   Literature on Hegel   561
III.   Further Philosophical Literature   573
IV.   Literature on Christology   576

INDEX OF NAMES   588

Preface To The English Edition

I am happy that the publishers Messrs. T. & T. Clark have ventured to publish a translation of one of my more difficult books, which demands of the reader a good deal of mental effort in the areas of theology and philosophy. After already appearing in Italian (1972), French (1973) and Spanish (1974) translations, with this English edition all my larger publications are now available in the English language. Above all, I am cordially grateful to my translators and all those involved in the editorial processes for undertaking the infinitely backbreaking labour of transposing such complicated philosophical thinking as that of Hegel into the sphere of the English language.

When *The Incarnation of God* appeared in the German language in 1970, it did so in what was a decisive phase for both my ecclesiological and christological thinking. The simultaneous appearance of such heterogeneous books as *Infallible?* and *The Incarnation of God* is even today a symbol of the seemingly grotesque dissonance of contemporary Catholic theology. What is at stake in this book? It has two goals.

This book is not intended to be a charter for some movement 'back to' or 'away from' Hegel, nor will it pronounce some last word 'upon' him; rather it will endeavour to provide theologians with an *introduction to Hegel's theological and christological thought*. In doing so it will at the same time provide an introduction to that section of the history of theology which Hegel's thought embodies and which has determined the whole future of the subject. What then do we have in mind? Not only a presentation of Hegel's statements about Jesus Christ all neatly strung together, but a many-levelled *'initiation'* into Hegel's life and thought, with particular reference to his religious world, and thence into his theology and Christology. In the case of Hegel too, truth is the whole that becomes transparent in detail. The Introduction's historical layout is intended to demonstrate the fact that Hegel of all philosophers did not drop down from heaven as a ready-made master. This placing of him in his context will facilitate the understanding of his philosophy without watering it down. Thus it is proposed to offer an 'initiation', not an 'explication' that would pay more heed to the philosophical detail and shed further light on the endless problems arising over individual points. It will be an 'initiation' into Hegel which will automatically turn into a *'discussion'* with Hegel, above all for the theological reader. Hegel the 'theologian' deserves to be taken seriously as a partner in dialogue. Just why it is so important for us today to engage in discussion with Hegel is to be demonstrated formally in the Introduction, although it can only be materially substantiated in the body of the book.

Since Hegel is so much invoked and so little read by so many theologians at the present time, it would seem appropriate in these pages to let him state his own case as much as possible. The almost thirty volumes of Hegel's works are not available to every reader, so that critical scrutiny of the sources themselves is almost impossible. By means of extensive quotation, the reader can be spared the ordeal of perpetually consulting them, while at the same time retaining some control over the interpretation given here. In this respect longer books are often shorter.

The subtitle makes plain the scope and objective of this study. It is 'an introduction to Hegel's theological thought by way of *'prolegomena to a* had to dispense with discussion of many philosophical questions, as with analysis and further development of presuppositions and conclusions of varying importance, and even with much internal criticism of the Hegelian system. This was decided in favour of a specifically theological initiation and discussion, whose *criterion is supplied by the pristine Christian message* to which Hegel too appealed, albeit in his own way. Moreover, this book is an introduction to Hegel's theological thought by way of *'prolegomena* to a future Christology'. In these pages we endeavour to return not a final and all-embracing answer to the question of Christ, but a provisional reply that will take us some way in the right direction.

The necessarily wide scope of this book has meant that it has had to steer a middle path between theology and philosophy for much of its course. On this account it is doubly exposed to criticism from the specialists on both sides, and can only half-satisfy the demands made by the very immensity of the material and of the problems stemming from it. But perhaps for these reasons it can hope for a double measure of understanding. The whole work remains an endeavour, and just as much can be learned from its shortcomings as from its accomplishments. Since the subject of our present efforts is Hegel himself, we trust that the reader will not think it presumptuous if we put the book into his hands with the wish with which Hegel himself set the second edition of his *Logic* on its way a week before his unexpected demise: that for this book also 'leisure might have been granted to work through it seventy-seven times. Yet as the author views his work in relation to the immensity of the task, he must rest content with what it was pleased to become' (III, 22).

This book was advertised as 'prolegomena', and, with it as my basis, I attempted, during the 1970s, to draw out the wider implications of the substantive issues involved. This had to be done, first of all, with respect to *Christology*. Actually, *The Incarnation of God* was itself already set between two fronts. On the one side, it made it clear that 'classical Christology', that is, the speculative ontological-*cum*-metaphysical doctrine of the Trinity, along with the two natures Christology (cf. Excursuses I-V), was forced into ever more abstruse hypotheses and speculations, whereby it had rendered itself increasingly remote from the biblical witness. And, on the other side, it also made it clear that Hegel's modern philosophical-*cum*-speculative Christology was not a genuine solution to the historico-critical questions concerning the person of Jesus Christ posed by the New Testament. This was why the Tübingen figure of D. F. Strauss had to be contrasted with Hegel as his antipode. He it was who, in a decisive way, connected the question of the historicality of God in the Hegelian speculative sense with the question of the historicality of Jesus in the historico-critical sense, so that the latter has, in the intervening period, become one of the great but still unresolved issues of nineteenth and twentieth-century theology.

Beginning with Jesus' proclamation, Jesus' conduct, and Jesus' fate, and pushing forward to the question of Jesus' significance, *The Incarnation of God* strove on an historico-critical basis to produce a 'Christology from below', which was then worked out in greater detail and placed before the public four years later in *On Being a Christian*. Hegel was now obliged to withdraw completely from view, and there was no small element of intellectual adventure involved when, quite apart from Hegel and consistently taking my point of departure 'from below' with the Jesus of history, I sought to see how far I would get in defining a *conception of God* that would be appropriate to our age. The result? Even for me, it was surprising to see that, as far as content goes, the 'God with attributes' proclaimed by Jesus of Nazareth is not so very far removed from the God whose historicality Hegel had sought to think through in a modern, philosophical way. Admittedly, with Jesus the 'dialectic of the attributes of God' is no philosophical, abstract problem, but a personal, historical experience. With Jesus, the concrete meaning of the eternity, omnipresence, spirituality, goodness, immutability, righteousness and incomprehensibility of God turns into a matter of living proclamation and concrete action. Nevertheless, in the final analysis Hegel was spiritual godfather to *On Being a Christian* also. For the intention of this book was precisely not to play off the 'God of Israel and Jesus' in a naive, biblicistic manner against the 'God of the philosophers', but, on the contrary, to be on the lookout for dialectical connecting links. It entered a plea for the 'sublation', in the best Hegelian sense of the word, of the 'God of the philosophers' in the 'God of Israel and Jesus'.

Here, then, in the definition of an adequate conception of God for our age – corrected by the specifically Christian conception of God – lies the enduring significance of Hegel's thinking for theology. Here he set irrevocable standards. Hence the problem of the worldliness and historicality of God, that is, the relationship of transcendence and immanence, can no longer be fittingly defined without reference to Hegel's thought. Hegel has here produced distant effects culminating in philosophical-*cum*-theological blueprints of the twentieth century such as those of Teilhard de Chardin and A. N. Whitehead. Hegel had once again to play a central role in my own thought also as I attempted, four years after *On Being a Christian*, to give a 'reply to the question of God in the modern age' in the book *Does God Exist?* In company with Descartes and Pascal, Feuerbach, Marx, Nietzsche and Freud, Hegel here receives a chapter to himself. And the 'theses on the worldliness and historicality of God' developed here make the actuality and enduring significance of Hegel for theological thought as clear as can be. Here too, notwithstanding all the criticism levelled at Hegel's conception of God, I was on the lookout for convergences and dialectical connecting links. In this book the thesis was yet again clearly outlined that the biblical message concerning a God who is by no means separated from the world but rather operates within it, and who is by no means stuck immovable and immutable in an unhistorical or suprahistorical realm but rather performs living acts in history, can be better understood in terms of the worldliness and historicality of God conceived along these lines than in terms of the metaphysics of either classical Greece or the middle ages.

The English-speaking reader can now survey these three books which are decisive for my own thinking, and he can – and indeed is meant to – read them as a unity. Looking back, I can, not without a certain satisfaction, state that, even though I have during this whole period been learning new things, the decisive basic intentions of my theological thought since *The Incarnation of God* have remained constant.

Tübingen, July 1984   *Hans Küng*

Preface

'Let it be put away for nine years'[1] (Horace: *Ars poetica*)

The first draft of the manuscript of this book was completed more than nine years ago but its issue has been delayed until now by the treatment of ecclesiological questions rendered necessary by the Second Vatican Council. The whole manuscript was completely revised for publication, but the point of departure of the study, along with the methods employed, the central questions and the appraisal of the issues involved have remained constant throughout. It may be that as a result of this delay a situation has arisen in contemporary theology which makes this work of even more immediate interest now than when the first draft was written. For at that time man, world and Church stood in the forefront of theological concern, whereas today, for the first time in half a century, the question of God, the definitive object of *theo*logy, is once more its principal theme. The observer of this new concern for the question of God, and even of the most radical projects for a 'theology after the death of God', is struck by two factors. In the first place, whether the question of God is faced more with western secularism or with eastern Marxism, theology today is picking up the threads at the very point where, before the advent of dialectical theology, this issue last stood at the centre of interest, namely in German Idealism, and particularly in *Hegel,* the thinker who has so much to say both to secular bourgeois society and to Marxist socialism. Secondly, whether the object of discussion is more the dead or the living, the present or the future God, theology today, like German Idealism, is concerned not so much with the 'wholly other', unworldly God, as was early dialectical theology (the theology of diastasis), but rather with the God of the here-and-now. Precisely in this concern contemporary theology is forging fresh links between theology and *Christology*. It may then be that a work dealing with the incarnation in Hegel's thought, a theme where all these points of view intersect, will, in virtue of a renewed concentration upon the

---

[1] *Nonumque prematur in annum*'.

xiii

question of God, seem less out of date to the reading public of today than it appeared premature to the author when he first wrote it.

Consequently, our study has a twofold aim: as a reply to the question of *Christ* in *Hegel's* thought it is meant to be a contribution at once to Christology in general and to the theological understanding of Hegel's philosophy in particular. The idealist tradition from Kant to Hegel has, of course, faded into insignificance as far as theologians are concerned; the terminology of post-Kantian Idealism is far removed from our time, and Hegel himself is commonly reckoned to be one of the most difficult authors of the history of thought. Regrettably, this latter judgment is neither unjust nor peculiar to theologians. Hegel's dialectical and speculative thought offers tough resistance to any attempt to come to grips with it and calls for an exceptional measure of intellectual exertion. But thinking never hurt anybody! Even so, there is no intention here of offering either a 'renewal' or a 'confutation' of Hegel: Hegel renaissances were always a purely academic affair, and thoroughgoing internal criticism of the Hegelian system, necessary though this is, is best left to the philosophers. Finally, there is no attempt here, either, to produce an 'appreciation' of Hegel, an undertaking tantamount to making the pretentious claim that the interval of time separating us from him already permits a superior, conclusive verdict upon him.[2]

This study is appearing in the series *Ecumenical Investigations* not only because a debate with Hegel is at the same time a debate with a type of Protestant theology which has exerted a powerful influence, but also because the classical issues of dispute in the field of soteriology (especially the doctrines of grace and justification) are not to be separated from the conceptions of God and Christ under discussion here.

Along with the rest of the literature Hegel's works are cited in the text in the most abbreviated form possible. The reader will find the full titles in the Index.

My belated thanks are due to all those without whose stimulation, help and correction, not to mention their faithful friendship, encouragement and forbearance, not only this book but my entire theological work would not have been possible. In particular I cordially thank my honoured teachers at the *Collegium Germanicum Hungaricum* in Rome, including my great friend Wilhelm Klein, who has given me so much stimulation, along with Emerich Coreth and Walter Kern. I wish to thank likewise Alois Naber at the *Gregoriana*, Maurice de Gandillac and Jean Wahl at the *Sorbonne*, finally Hermann Volk in Münster (Westphalia) and – last but not least – Karl Barth,

---

[2] The paragraphs of the original German Preface omitted here are repeated *verbatim* in the Preface to the English edition.

Hans Urs von Balthasar and Karl Rahner, who have made a decisive contribution to my theology in general and to my theological understanding of Hegel in particular. I am indebted to my colleagues in Tübingen, both Catholic and Protestant, for continuous and manifold intellectual stimulation. When I started this work in Paris about fifteen years ago with a chapter on the Tübingen Hegel, I had no idea that I should some day be permitted to bring it to a close in Tübingen, where, by my own choice, I am thankful to live.

I have much cause for gratitude toward my fellow-workers. I do not of course have any 'research assistants' at my beck and call, as a reviewer from the *New York Times* wrote on my book *The Church*; it is to be hoped that his ignorance was limited to this! I take pleasure in writing my books on my own down to the last sentence, albeit largely at night and during the vacations, though not without the accompaniment of classical music and a seemly amount of aquatic sport. However, at a time when it is becoming ever harder at universities actually to write books, the fact that I may continually receive counsel, criticism and not least technical help from like-minded fellow-workers represents an invaluable support. At an earlier stage of revision of the manuscript Frl. Christa Hempel was a considerable help, and Josef Nolte, Dr. theol., accompanied me throughout the last decisive revision with his encouragement and criticism. Margret Gentner, Dr. phil., took care of the production of a manuscript which was complicated in many ways with expertise and wholehearted devotion. Herr Hans-Josef Schmidt, Dip. theol., took over responsibility for all the proof-reading, for the verification of the countless Hegel quotations and finally for the Index of Persons, and gave me several pieces of relevant advice in the process. My cordial thanks go to Frau Annegret Dinkel, who attended to correspondence with libraries, and to the occasional helpers at the *Institute for Ecumenical Research,* Ulrich Hinzen, Ruth Sigrist, and Walter Tietze.

I owe Walter Kern a second grateful mention of his name; for after his brilliant and highly pertinent reports on the most recent Hegel literature had considerably assisted the orientation of my work, I was not a little encouraged that he kept pace with the development of the manuscript in its last draft. This he did with precision, correcting it in not a few places, in particular kindly checking the bibliographical data.

Tübingen, January 1970   *Hans Küng*
The year of the 200th anniversary of the birth
of G. W. F. Hegel

Introduction

'God has died, God is dead – this is the most appalling thought,
that everything eternal and true is not, and that negation itself is
in God; bound up with this is the supreme pain, the feeling of the
utter absence of deliverance, the surrender of all that is higher.
However, the course of events does not grind to a halt here; rather
a reversal now comes about, to wit, God maintains himself in this
process. The latter is but the death of death. God arises again to
life.'[1]

'Without Hegel there would have been no Darwin,' says Nietzsche,[2] and he
could have said this of himself too; for as he put it so waspishly a decade
earlier, 'whoever once succumbs to the disease of Hegelitis never fully
recovers'.[3] And what would Feuerbach's and Marx's critique of religion be
without Hegel? What indeed that of Ernst Bloch and Georg Lukács today?
That their critique of religion did not turn out so trite as so many other
attempts – especially that of vulgar materialism – is to be attributed to the
extraordinary refinement of the Hegelian conception of God which sparked it
off. Furthermore, notwithstanding numerous other influences, what would
the theology of the following be without Hegel: Kierkegaard and F. C. Baur,
Karl Barth and Paul Tillich, Karl Rahner and Jürgen Moltmann, a good
many Frenchmen and particular American and German God-is-dead theologians? For all their conscious dissociation, their proximity to him cannot be
overlooked. As Ernst Bloch rightly says, '[t]here is little past history that
seems to come at us from the future so full of problems as his does'.[4]

The question of God is always also at the same time a question about man;
but again, whether this is accepted or denied, the question of man is always a
question about God. Meanwhile the question of the relationship between
theology and anthropology, and *vice versa,* is posed in an acute fashion when
it is asked in close connection with that of a Christology. For those thinkers
who stemmed from Hegel, be they atheistic critics of religion or even Christian

---

[1] G. F. W. Hegel: *Religionsphilosophie* XIV, 167.
[2] *Die fröhliche Wissenschaft* V, 357; *Werke* II, 226. Vol. X, 306.
[3] *Unzeitgemässe Betrachtungen* I, 6; *Werke* I, 165. Vol. 1, 46.
[4] *Subjekt-Objekt,* 12.

1

theologians, God's becoming man was at stake, and consequently at the same time man's becoming human. In very different ways to be sure: for the theologians, God's becoming man in man's becoming human manifests God's life, while for the atheistic critics the same process manifests God's death. In these differing judgments, however, both groups appealed to Hegel, who for his part stands in the great tradition of classical Christology. To anticipate the conclusions of this study we may say that it was of fundamental importance for Hegel that, in worldly thought, the world does not become godless, and that, in religious thought, God does not become unworldly. This seems to him to be evidently set forth in the overt Christian religion of God's incarnation. It becomes plain to him here what must be asserted about God's life and death, and consequently about man's life and death too. It was not modern atheism, nor was it Feuerbach or Nietzsche, least of all was it the modern God-is-dead theologians, who coined the slogan 'death of God'. Hegel did it before them, and he for his part took it over from Luther. Precisely at this point, then, Hegel stands in the great Christian tradition, and it was he who, more profoundly than all his successors, pondered this slogan in the context of the death of Christ: 'The death of Christ is, however, the death of this very death, the negation of negation' (XIV, 167).

Let us open our consideration of Hegel's Christology with this central text, where theologically responsible discourse about God threatens to topple over into mysticism or intellectual filibustering. If anywhere, it is at this point of intersection of theology and anthropology that man has always failed to press his enquiry through to its due conclusion. This will presently become clear as, by way of introduction, we cast a brief glance over the Christology of the modern period, the Catholic first and then the Protestant.

The *Catholic Christology* of the Counter-Reformation period sailed in calm waters. The storms lay far back, a thousand years and even more: Ephesus, Chalcedon, Constantinople – far distant lands these, but still continually present in men's consciousness, at once luminous trophies of battles won and eternally valid landmarks pointing onwards. From these vantage-points, so it seemed, the dogma of Christ stood firm and unshakeable like the polar star. A millenium of successive generations of theologians did not risk any quibbling on this matter; the course was well-known and it was adhered to. And what did those obstinate souls – as they were soon reckoned – amount to by way of exception, men desirous of pointing to unknown, dangerous waters, be they Eriugena, Gerloh of Reichersberg, Eckhardt, Nicholas of Cusa or whoever? Was there not after all still sufficient to discover and to ponder, even on the 'safe' journey?

The formula of Chalcedon was indeed crystal clear: true God and true man, one person in two natures; but there remained sufficient mystery in which one could immerse oneself. And thus the greatest minds of late antiquity and of the middle ages (themselves 'modern' at the time) already achieved much in the way of reflection upon the mystery of Christ, working with new categories and changing systems. Now this was undertaken with painstaking scrupulousness and matchless concentration, and perhaps precisely for this reason with a certain narrowing of perspective and shift of emphasis. Why should this occasion surprise? The concentration was given through the great christological discussions of the Greeks on the subject of the 'person' of Christ; at a later date the further, western set of problems to do with the 'redemptive work and office' of Christ was added. By force of necessity concentration was focussed on certain aspects of the Christ-event. The others were neither denied nor forgotten – they stood too clearly in Scripture for that – but passed over. They were still a truth of faith, but no longer a challenge directed to faith. And even in the case of those aspects of the Christ-event that were subjected to examination, shifts of emphasis set in. These were scarcely noticed, however, and since the fundamental christological problems were commonly regarded as solved, Catholic Christology, even in the modern period, moved within the prescribed limits of an already charted systematic plan. This was possible, moreover, in spite of the Reformation, in which not so much Christ as created grace, justification, Church and sacraments seemed to be at stake. Controversial theology (and exegesis), as embodied by, say, Cardinal Bellarmine, left Christology out of consideration except in so far as it impinged upon certain specialist issues (among these, though, was the important question of the *communicatio idiomatum*). Even scholasticism, which enjoyed its Indian summer around 1600, opened up no decisively new christological horizons, notwithstanding the phenomenal achievements of such men as Suarez, Vasquez, Bañez and Molina. Nor can the validity of this judgment be seriously called into question by the fair vistas that were disclosed in the work of Petavius and Thomassinus, scholars who delved back to the riches of the Bible and the Fathers. The Schools were engaged in vigorous internecine disputes on such questions as the best way to demonstrate the sinlessness of Christ; but even if our gaze is directed elsewhere it is only to find that the deep devotion to Christ characteristic of the Spanish mystics – a phenomenon which was often the object of suspicion in those days – had a negligible influence upon systematic theology. Not only did such figures as Teresa and John of the Cross have little influence, but the same was true even of Ignatius Loyola, Bérulle in France, and Friedrich von Spee and Angelus Silesius in Germany. The theologians, wedded to their system as they were, looked on them as rather dangerous outsiders.

Even so the Counter-Reformation renewal did furnish *devotion* to Christ with some positive impulses. The abolition of not a few abuses gave it some

3

fresh air after the theology *and* popular piety of the late middle ages had threatened to smother it with peripheral and secondary matters. Christ was now celebrated in baroque splendour, with all the expedients at the disposal of art and music. But 'what the baroque had in mind in its enthusiastic endeavour to "bring heaven down to earth" was not so much the mediatorship located in the humanity of Jesus as it was the notion, overwhelmingly connected with the Divine in Christ, of the enthroned *Triumphator* transfigured with divine radiance, the eternal *Rex coelorum* whose image was now reproduced on all sides in the form, largely taken over from pagan antiquity, of a worldly and cheerful apotheosis'.[5] The divine pomp of the baroque mass, a theatrical performance which the people were permitted to look at and listen to in silent awe without understanding the texts, fitted in with this triumphalistic Christ-piety; as did the supper table of the divine-human mediator which, as a high altar replete with tabernacle, was enhanced to become the heavenly throne of the Most High. In keeping with this form of piety were the triumphal processions at Corpus Christi (*Fête-Dieu!*), and the exposition and adoration of the Lord's Body, which was received ever more infrequently in holy communion.

The clear but icy winter of the Enlightenment was meanwhile succeeding the Indian summer of baroque scholasticism. The stripping away of a decadent scholasticism and a superstitious piety admittedly did Christology no harm; but even in Catholic theology questions of belief were neglected in favour of the education of a moral humanity, doubt was cast upon things supernatural and suprarational, and the gospel of salvation was inappropriately rationalised. All this froze solid any reflection upon the mystery of the God-man. It was a situation in which the warmth that was lacking could be supplied as little by the marriage of convenience between theology and philosophy characteristic of Descartes, Leibniz and Wolff as by the zeal of orthodoxy against the English and French enlighteners.

A fresh consideration of Christology came only in the nineteenth century in the Tübingen School, which endeavoured to combine historical and speculative thought. This was prior to the labours of Scheeben and C. von Schäzler in the province of neo-scholasticism. Of especial significance were Staudenmaier's doctrine of ideas and, albeit in a different way, the work of Anton Günther. It is worthy of note in this connection that these two abovementioned theologians, who most decisively led the way in the re-examination of christological questions, grew up in dialogue with the philosophy of Hegel. But with these remarks we have already hurried on beyond the milestone that was to be the goal of this Introduction.

---

[5]F. X. Arnold: *Das gottmenschliche Prinzip*, 311.

Now if in the Protestant sphere calm had meanwhile been so swiftly overtaken by storm, this did not happen in isolation from the all too sluggish and superficial tranquillity that reigned in the forecourts of Catholic theology. It could easily be demonstrated that the christological revolution had already been prepared in many ways in the final part of the patristic period and in the middle ages. Already in those times 'natural' man and the order of creation had been brought less and less into a living and theologically existential relationship to the Christ-event. This was in marked contrast to the tendency displayed in the New Testament and in the masterpieces of patristic thought. The upshot was to narrow down the import of the Christ-event and to bring into being that striking *complexio oppositorum* of reason and faith, philosophy and theology, order of grace and order of nature, which in the mediating masterpieces of scholastic theology remained a thoroughly *Christian* synthesis. Be this as it may, however, this unity in tension was frankly overloaded, and in the dynamic of historical development was forced to play its part in unleashing that liberation movement writ large, the Enlightenment. The latter was certainly anything but a merely retrogressive movement, but in spite of this it finally made itself felt – against the will of those who set it loose – as an insurrection on the part of the now independent 'natural' substructure against the 'supernatural' christological superstructure. Without any doubt the many-levelled process whereby a neutral order of reason and nature attained its independence – a development rendered possible in terms of the history of thought with the aid of Greek philosophy – liberated enormous intellectual forces. It is hard to underestimate the consequences of the emergence of autonomous man, his science and philosophy, his rights and his ethics! Yet with all this new reference to reason and nature, and then, more and more, in the wake of nominalism and the Renaissance, to feeling, will, freedom, individuality, humanity etc., that which in the original Christian synthesis was a matter of out and out affirmation turned, later on, into indifferent self-reliance and anti-Christian denial. This transformation followed more quickly than anyone envisaged at the time.

The *Reformation* was, like the Renaissance, a liberation movement away from the mediaeval synthesis of Christian religion and Greek philosophy. In contrast to the Renaissance, however, it intended to set free not the pure *ancient* but the pure *Christian* spirit. Hence the theology of all the Reformers was indisputably distinguished by a powerful vivification of the personal relationship to Christ. *Luther,* whose devotion to Christ was stamped by the New Testament and dependent upon German mysticism, had an extraordinarily stimulating effect in this area too. Precisely in the questions of justification and the Church he was concerned with Christ. As he says in the preface to his great *Commentary on Galatians* (1535), '[t]his one article of faith in Christ rules in my heart. From him, through him and to him flow all my theological thoughts night and day' (*WA* 40 I. 33, 7-9). With these words he certainly did not mean scholastic speculations, but taking the living and historic Jesus as the point of departure, especially as he was manifested in the the crib and on the cross. An old Franciscan concern, if you like (Francis of Assisi, Bernardino of Siena); but at the time of the Reformation a theologian could come under suspicion with the Roman Inquisition, *perchè ha sempre in bocca Cristo,* because Christ was always on his lips. Nevertheless Luther by no means neglected the divine in Jesus. On the contrary, his principal concern was the *God* who deals graciously and justifies in Christ, at the cost of cross and death. For him, *theologia* was essentially *theologia crucis.* Even so, when seen as a whole the Christology of the Reformation, for example that of Melanchthon, was more concerned with the benefits of Christ than with the mysteries of his divinity and person. The failure of Calvin's Christocentrism in the doctrine of predestination was fraught with the gravest consequences. Moreover, Melanchthon, Zwingli and Calvin were themselves humanists and, although the Reformers' own anthropology was theologically controlled, precisely in the Reformation a further step was taken in the direction of autonomous man. Man would come to be regarded as a self-confident subject of faith, secure in grace and independently inquiring into Scripture, a religious individual free from subjection to the mediaeval universal Church.

Be that as it may, Lutheran and Reformed *orthodoxy* now reigned in the Protestant world for a good century and a half as a counterpart to Spanish scholasticism. The result of this development was a rapid cooling of the originally luminous fire of the Gospel. It was smothered by systematisation and specialist questions, by literalism and by inter-Protestant and anti-Catholic polemics. The enthusiasm of the previous age was maintained only in the intensified subjective religion of the *collegia pietatis.* Geared to practical devoutness, pietism produced a characteristic fruit of christological meditation at this time. This was not so much evident in the father of pietism, Philipp Jakob Spener's, 'theology of the twice-born', as in the anti-dogmatic 'heart and lamb theology' of Count Nicholas von Zinzendorf, for whom the person of Christ is the 'compendium of theology'. Bearing in mind, however, Zinzendorf's view that it is in the hearts of believers that Christ is born, dies and rises again with salvific effect, we find that his Christ-piety is interiorised, subjectivised and humanised in such a way that the distance and distinction between Christ and the devout soul is no longer plainly preserved. Zinzendorf even visualises Christ without hesitation as the 'Elder-General' of his Moravian Brotherhood. It was thus not surprising that, for all its positive attributes, pietism to a great extent fell victim to that very movement to which, in virtue of a certain 'humanisation' of the Christian faith, it was only too closely related; the movement which it had itself helped to prepare, by means of the ethicisation and individualisation of religion along with the consequent unchurching of the pious and the 'softening' of orthodoxy: namely the Enlightenment.

For by now *modern science and philosophy,* and with them the whole new world-consciousness, had covered vast expanses with giant strides. With the Renaissance the irrevocable dissolution of the Greek world-picture had set in. By means of their use of the *potentia dei absoluta* the Occamists had skilfully cast radical doubt on Aristotle's propositions in the field of natural science and on his superstitions. In the second book of the *Docta ignorantia* Cusanus had been the first to perceive in the *machina mundi* a structureless infinity without centre or circumference, an insight in which he was followed by Marsilio Ficino, Giordano Bruno and Pascal. With his discovery Cusanus had overturned the ancient Greek world-hierarchy, according to whose topography the Father is enthroned above in heaven, while the Word descends into the centre of the world (earth), indeed beneath the earth (hell), in order to journey upwards again on the day of his Ascension. In his third book he could look upon the two infinite entities with joyful assurance as cosmologically reconciled by the *copula universi,* the God-man. By way of contrast Pascal is struck with dread and dismay when confronted with the loneliness of the universe unveiled by the new physics, with its inconceivable, mute and empty expanses. This universe no longer declares the glory of God. (In the same seventeenth century the discovery of the microscope was to open up the abysses of the microcosm.) Furthermore, Pascal no longer appeals to the God-man as a *copula* to be cosmologically understood, which even at this stage should secure for the earth its cosmic centrality. Instead he calls upon the Jesus who, forsaken in the Garden of Olives, pours out his blood drop by drop for every sinner.[6]

The point of connection between Christology and the new world-consciousness was mankind, which, emerging from long neglect, now stood in the forefront of interest not only for the philosophy of the day but also for Protestant Christology. The well nigh monophysite over-exposure of Christ's Godhead characteristic of Fathers and Schoolmen had cried out for a reaction. Individualistic modern man, set on his own self-sure feet in the face of all scepticism by Descartes' *cogito,* began his long journey in reliance on his *ratio.* From this starting-point a systematic interpretation of Being steadily gained ground, an interpretation of its transparent laws and proportions, in the spirit of mathematics and geometry, of mechanics and engineering. Copernicus, Galileo, Newton, Leibniz and Laplace demonstrated what

---

[6]On this development, cf. M. de Gandillac: *Pascal et le silence du monde.*

7

imposing feats the human spirit can perform, and the awe-inspiring newly arisen sciences conspired with the rapidly ensuing technical inventions to change the face of the earth. Descartes had spoken much of man, his world and his 'method', less and in more general terms of God, hardly at all of Christ. But let none be deceived: the age was thoroughly devout. Descartes, Newton, Pascal and Leibniz were convinced Christians, indeed apologists for their faith. Even the Jew Baruch de Spinoza found fair words for the man Jesus Christ, whom he termed 'the Voice of God', 'the Wisdom of God', 'the Way of Salvation', placing him above all other men.[7] Spinoza's ontological and ethical pantheism looked upon the individual ego and all finite things as modes of the one divine substance, which was perceptible under the twin attributes of 'extension' and 'thought'. He was a solitary man, too far ahead of his time to have been able to found a school. In the aftermath of Lessing, however, 'Spinozism' was in the age of Goethe and Hegel to become the more or less covert refuge of those who longed for 'unity'. Indeed the being and activity of God are already understood, amongst the Cartesians, in the occasionalism of Malebranches, and especially in the thought of Berkeley, as a being within the human spirit. The God *within* man makes a mediator between God and man (*extra nos!*) appear ever more problematic and superfluous.

Next to the philosophy of the state it was nature and the problems of its knowability that received most attention in the England characterised by the empiricism of Hobbes, Locke and Hume. The Christ-event was without constitutive significance for the 'religion of nature' that was developed in this context. Subsequently English deism and freethinking also formed the precondition for the rapid anti-Christian development on the continent. In Descartes' own country opinion was considerably more radical than in England; Voltaire's visit thither had borne fruit for France. Here the change to undisguised sensualistic and materialistic atheism quickly ensued. The Cartesian Left – Diderot, d'Holbach, Helvetius, La Mettrie – founded that vulgar materialism which Feuerbach and Marx, following in Hegel's footsteps, were to criticise so sharply. The *'homme-Dieu'* was no longer an entity patient of discussion; he must step down in favour of the *'homme-machine'*.

In Germany the debate took longer to get under way, and it was here, where the 'enlightened' were neither atheists nor materialists, that the decisive argument was to be conducted on the subject of Christology. In Germany the problem was not bypassed. Men neither held their peace about Christ in well-

---

[7] *Tract. theol. polit.* I (éd. Pléiade, 680f); ET *Theologico-Political Treatise*; *Chief Works*, vol. 1, 19.

meaning indifference, nor did they deny him with malevolent aggressiveness. The philosophy which dominated the German Enlightenment was that of the Cartesian Right, and it was intent upon safeguarding the Christian faith, which it hoped to serve by providing a rational justification for it. The *Theodicy* published in 1710 by the brilliant Gottfried Wilhelm Leibniz, who was at once philosopher, theologian, historian, philologist, natural scientist, lawyer and politician, himself indeed an admirable 'monad' of knowledge reflecting the entire universe, was popularised in Enlightenment style in the German vernacular by the work of Christian Wolff: *Rational Thoughts concerning God, the World and the Soul of Man, also concerning All Things in general, communicated to the Lovers of Truth by Christian Wolff* (1720). Wolff's tidy separation of two partly overlapping but thoroughly autonomous planes of reason and revelation has been compared with Thomas Aquinas's conception, and the rumour of his conversion was not entirely accidental. He came under vigorous attack from the orthodox and especially from the pietists over a number of particular questions, such as, among other things, human freedom, the temporal beginning of the world and the relationship between body and soul. But since this polemic never touched on the basic starting-point provided by his definition of the relationship between faith and reason, the attacks on Wolff petered out. He founded a school and became *the* philosopher of the Enlightenment. Given its 'exposed position', Christian theology was basically glad to receive such a modern support. At least on the basis of this rational philosophy an almost equally rational theology could be worked out to form a second – essential, useful or perhaps even superfluous – storey. Over and above this the positive elements in the thought of the great Leibniz were unmistakable. Not only did he busy himself with mission to the heathen and the union of the Churches.[8] At the same time he penned 'replies' to 'objections against the Trinity and against the Incarnation of the Most High God',[9] while Wolff accounted for the necessity of the incarnation along the lines proposed by Anselm in the *Cur Deus homo*. 'So I was desirous to learn mathematics *methodi gratia,* in order that I might occupy myself with bringing theology to irrefutable certitude,' wrote Wolff in his *Autobiography*.[10] But this largely rationalistic demonstration was *either* a success *or* a failure, so that Christianity was proved to be *either* rational and hence in the end of the day superfluous to reason, *or* irrational and hence unacceptable to reason. Although Leibniz could maintain elsewhere that 'the best way to

---

[8] *Opera* I, 507-737.
[9] *op. cit.* I, 10-27.
[10] *Eigene Lebensbeschreibung,* 121.

9

achieve the best of all possible worlds was for Christ to be the God-man',[11] in the *Theodicy* he was still able to derive the world *a priori* from the concept of God as the best of all possible worlds – *sicut in mathematicis* – without discussing the world and its evil in christological terms.[12] As time went on, emphasis on the simplicity of God was directed against the dogma of the Trinity; and the entirely rational, almighty principle of contradiction was applied against the Christ dogma, where it is alleged that God is not God and man is not man, but rather that God *is* man.

Dogmas in general – how unpopular they had become! And was this not perfectly understandable in the wake of the wars of 'religion' along with the unfruitful and loveless interconfessional strife and the general weariness with religion that ensued? Indifferentism became a religious concern. Nathan the Wise was not needed to demonstrate this: 'It was not possible to prove which was the right ring . . . That was almost as elusive as the right faith is now for us.'[13] No more needed were the newly discovered peoples beyond the ocean, who with their religions surely could not all be worthy of damnation just because they had the world-historical hard luck to have heard nothing of Christ for 1500 years. Enough then of the fruitless *odium theologicum,* and of theories and doctrines continually at odds with one another! In place of controversy, tolerance; of theory, practice; of doctrine, life; of dogma, morality! True Christian faith is action, it is working to the advantage of man and his felicity!

Certainly, the men of the Enlightenment did not speak in these plain terms from the start. The 'theologians of transition', who lived between the late orthodoxy of the seventeenth century and the enlightened modern era, wanted to have dogma neither set aside nor eroded. Such worthy men as the Lutherans J. F. Buddeus and C. M. Pfaff, the church historian J. L. von Mosheim and his pupil J. P. Miller, the two Walchs and even the Swiss Reformed divines S. Werenfels, J. F. Osterwald and the younger Turrettini had no greater ambition that to be 'rational' orthodox. They shifted the accents a little, and, quite without noticing it, began to put reason and revelation on the same level and hence to all intents and purposes to elevate reason to the position of criterion of revelation. This took place quite openly and systematically, though still without an attack upon dogma, with Christian Wolff and the theologians who followed him. These included I. G. Canz, J.

---

[11]'*optimae autem seriei rerum – nempe huius ipsius – eligendae maxima ratio fuit Christus theanthropos': Opera* I, 482 (*Causa Dei adserta per iustitiam eius, cum caeteris eius perfectionibus cunctisque actionibus conciliatam*).

[12]*op. cit.* I, 126-130 (*Theodicea* I, 7-10); ET *Theodicy,* 127-129.

[13]G. E. Lessing: *Werke* III, 304; cf. Henry Chadwick: *Lessing's Theological Writings* (London, 1956), 27 (Introduction).

Carpov and S. J. Baumgarten; and many a Catholic must be numbered among them. The assault upon dogma was ushered in by the theologians known as 'neologians', a term fraught with implications of heresy. We think especially of J. F. W. Jeremias, J. J. Spalding, Friedrich Nicolai and C. F. Bahrdt, with whom, albeit with some nuances, the historians J. S. Semler, J. A. Ernesti and I.D. Michaelis saw fit to associate themselves. The neologians did not deny revelation as such. Instead they kept quiet on this or that dogma, attacked a second and reinterpreted a third. In short, dogma was pruned and its core located in the religion of reason, based on God, freedom (i.e. mortality) and immortality. Surreptitiously, by this process, much that already at an earlier stage was no longer very important became unimportant and superfluous-for example, the Godhead and virgin birth of Christ, his death understood as a satisfaction, his resurrection, ascension and second advent. The neologians did not relinquish these things for the sake of any great theories, such as a consistent Wolffianism. All this simply no longer made any sense for modern practical piety and for the better life. Enlightened modern man felt no emotional 'need' for such things. On the contrary many of them (original sin, for example) had become cumbersome and inconvenient to an honest moral endeavour.[14]

We must remember, even with regard to future development in Germany, that, several years before Jeremias published his *Considerations on the Noblest Truths of Religion* in 1768 and Bahrdt his *Biblical Dogmatics* in 1769, another more radical and profound thinker had already spoken. This was Jean-Jacques *Rousseau,* who, for all his pessimism about society, optimistically rounded off and overcame the Enlightenment. His Vicar of Savoy extols enthusiastically the *'douceur, pureté, grace, sagesse, finesse (et) justice'* of Jesus[15] and praises his death as the *'mort d'un Dieu',*[16] only to grind to a halt in a *'scepticisme involontaire'* in face of the *'contradictions'* of the Gospel.[17] The Vicar of Savoy spurns orthodox religion in favour of a religion of nature which is not only perceived by the intellect but 'felt' by a heart and conscience themselves by nature good, and in favour of a *'religion civile'* which, while necessary for the state, is nevertheless minimalistic and tolerant.[18]

In the meantime the theology of 'enlightenment' prevailed in Protestant Germany to an extent impossible in Catholic theology, which was bound to ecclesiastical dogmas in a quite different manner. The new theology was right

---

[14]cf. Karl Barth: *Protestant Theology in the Nineteenth Century,* 136-173.
[15]J.-J. Rousseau: *Émile,* 271.
[16]*op. cit.,* 272.
[17]*ibid.*
[18]cf. J.-J. Rousseau: *Contrat social,* 220-229.

11

to combat all possible obscurantism in theology, piety and church practice. Its major preoccupations were thereby vastly simplified to a clearly rational and tritely natural religion of Everyman, which, humane, neutral, optimistic and eudaemonistic, builds upon the inborn consciousness of God, the natural moral law, the freedom of the will, the immortality of the soul and the dignity of man. Its goal was good morality, that is to say the cultivation of a noble humanity. Man was thought to be by nature good, and the moral virtues the precondition for the happiness of the individual! Religion was less a service for God's sake than a service to mankind! Against Luther's 'exaggerated' consciousness of sin was set the optimism of the great century! Revelation was a supplement of reason and Christianity the most advantageous of religions! Christ or, better, Jesus, who was a wise teacher of morality, brought to awareness in a new and plausible fashion what humanity had always known, namely, what it was to live a natural human life in accord with the dictates of reason!

The following factors belong to the background of this theology, which filled the orthodox of all camps with increasing alarm: the growing influence of English deism, Voltaire, and the Encyclopaedists; a new sense of history; and the aspirations of national Churches, along with the Enlightenment-style absolutist Church policies of monarchs of the stamp of Louis XIV, Frederick II and Joseph II. What was sown in nominalism and humanism had come up. The summons back to the sources had been raised afresh, softly at first but then loudly; and this call was directed not only against the symbolic books of the Reformation period – they had been deprived of their magic by men like Gottlieb Jakob Planck with the help of the pragmatic understanding of history and a certain idealised image of primitive Christianity – but also against Holy Scripture itself. And just as the humanist claim to understand classical literature once more in its original sense had led to the development of a philological hermeneutic, even so in connection with this the claim of the Reformers to understand the Bible once more in its original literal sense was carried through. The development of a theological hermeneutic was achieved. The Reformers had indeed adhered to the unity of the whole of Scripture in a strict dogmatic fashion and were therefore able to give a unified interpretation to the individual texts from the perspective of the total biblical context. Enlightenment exegesis on the other hand now attempted to understand the texts in their own terms, undogmatically, as it claimed, but in fact using the key supplied by a basically Cartesian rationality. This rationalistic biblical criticism – prepared by Erasmus, Grotius and Hobbes, established by Spinoza in accordance with scientific-mathematical cognition, and then consolidated by Bayle and Hume – now set off on its triumphal advance right through Protestant theology, albeit against the opposition of the people and of many

12

pastors: pietism often had to join forces with orthodoxy. However this did not disturb the new scholarship very much. In many ways it had a thoroughly sound point of departure in the newly founded Greek and Semitic philology, in the study of the ancient codices and biblical versions and of the literature of the Jewish synagogue, in the historical thought which was now slowly establishing itself, and even in its unmythological rationality. Of what use against this was unhistorical and reactionary Protestant biblicism with its verbal inspiration? Or, for that matter, what use was Catholic exegesis, which had run aground in confessional polemics or citation and imitation of the Fathers? The brilliant Richard Simon, who around 1700 was far ahead of his time and was opposed by the mighty Bossuet, found no successor. The process could no longer be held up; so that even the history of Jesus had to be illuminated through reason in the face of all dogmatism. The struggle was no longer about the Church, as had been the case in the sixteenth and seventeenth centuries; in the century of impartiality the controversial issue was Jesus the Christ himself. The tendency of the ancient and mediaeval Church towards a docetic dissolution of the historical Jesus had been turned on its head. 'The historical investigation of the life of Jesus did not take its rise from a purely historical interest; it turned to the Jesus of history as an ally in the struggle against the tyranny of dogma. Afterwards when it was freed from this πάθος it sought to present the historic Jesus in a form intelligible to its own time.'[19]

Johann Salomo Semler, the most significant and, as a scientific historian, the most original of the neologians, took the decisive step in rationalist textual criticism in Germany with his *Treatise on the Free Examination of the Canon* (1771-1775). (He was not without predecessors, especially among the English deists, who are often overlooked in this connection.) This founder of the modern undogmatic study of the history of Church and dogma wants to understand Holy Scripture itself in the same undogmatic terms: the given is not some purported unity of Holy Scripture, but rather the diversity of the individual writings and their authors. And the old hermeneutical principle of the Reformation, that the parts should be understood in terms of the whole, is significantly widened and precisely by that process overcome: the context in which the individual elements are to be understood is no longer the (dogmatically conceived) totality of Scripture, but the (historically conceived) totality of history in general. In other words, Holy Scripture becomes a collection of historical sources which can only be correctly understood, exactly like profane writings, in historical terms. Philosophical and theological hermen-

---

[19]A. Schweitzer: *The Quest of the Historical Jesus,* 4. On the further development, cf. esp. 13-47 (on Reimarus); see also E. Günther: *Entwicklung der Lehre von der Person Christi,* esp. 119-126.

eutics are encompassed by an historical hermeneutic now in process of development.

In all this and with total consistency Semler at the same time attacks the authority of the biblical canon. In doing so he attacks the previous equation of Scripture and revelation, the inspiration of the sacred text and the equality of both Testaments. Semler's own canon for the clarification of the canon of Scripture is compounded of Enlightenment rationality (i.e. moral usefulness) and primitive Christianity (i.e. the pure religion of reason) minus the supernatural or 'positive' residue. The distinction, important for Kant as for Hegel, between 'natural' and 'positive' was introduced. But Semler escaped the radical practical consequences of his views by drawing the distinction between free private religion (i.e. the real essence of Christianity or the religion of ethical piety) and public ecclesiastical religion, underwritten by the state, which despite its low quality is to be kept up for the people.

Nevertheless, at that very time another was ready to go further. He had toiled for thirty years on his *Defence of the Rational Worshippers of God,* a manuscript of approximately four thousand pages. But apart from a first part which, being Wolffian in tone, was inoffensive to his contemporaries (*The Most Noble Truths of Natural Religion in Ten Discourses*, published in 1754), he resolutely held his peace. The pioneering genius of the German classical period, Gotthold Ephraim Lessing, only published *Anonymous Fragments* six years after the writer's death. It was a systematic piece of work. The anonymous Hermann Samuel Reimarus, a highly honourable professor of oriental languages in Hamburg, illuminated the received religion with a mixture of Wolffian reason and historical instinct, but without bothering his head with Semler's distinction between private and public religion. Thus he uncovered a wealth of inconsistencies in the sources, along with things human and indeed all too human in the disciples and even in Jesus himself. Did this mean disintegration of the Christ-event? In the century before Reimarus it was still possible, in the interesting *Life of Jesus* written in the Persian language by the Indian missionary Xavier, a nephew of the great Francis Xavier, to set a glorious divine Christ before the eyes of the Mongol Emperor Akbar of Hindustan. This was achieved with the aid of omissions and apocryphal additions, and by simply putting on one side all that was humanly offensive about Christ. Now with Reimarus the 'disintegration' takes place in the opposite direction.

Reimarus displays an indisputably brilliant perception of the genuine issues involved in gospel research in the fragment *The Goal of Jesus and His Disciples.* (The fragment already published by Lessing *On the Resurrection Narrative* forms part of this.) As a point of method, it was clever of him to eliminate the apostolic 'doctrine' of the New Testament epistles from his historical survey (Part I, Section 3). For him the entire gospel of Jesus is reduced to the message, 'Repent, for the kingdom of heaven is at hand' (Section 4). In this he had hit upon the core of the message of Jesus with unerring aim. He continually cautions against reading the catechism of today back into the gospels. The biblical message must be seen in its original straightforwardness and simplicity. With his 'Repent!' Jesus taught genuine morality against the Pharisees, and nothing but genuine morality (Sections 5-7). This moral teaching receives Reimarus' sincere praise. With Jesus himself there is no trace of the revelation of new supernatural mysteries, such as divine Sonship in the strict sense, Holy Spirit, Trinity (Sections 8-18), nor even of the abolition of the ceremonial law of Moses. Baptism and holy communion are not new ceremonies, and Jesus himself expressly rejected an extension of the kingdon of heaven to the Gentiles (Sections 19-28). Jesus stands not at the beginning of a new Christian religion, but at the end of the old Jewish one. He had in mind things quite other than the foundation of a new religion. His whole morality of repentance was directed to the single point, 'The kingdom of heaven is at hand!' Jesus paraphrased in parables, but never explained what the 'kingdom of heaven' is. This means that he took the concept over from contemporary Judaism. In this he was politically understood as intending to be the political liberator of Israel and the messiah of a worldly kingdom of heaven. That led to the notorious fiasco of his death on the cross (Sections 29-30). Only with difficulty could the disciples get over this great disappointment of their life. They fell back in their anguish on the second form of the Jewish hope of the messiah cherished in apocalyptic circles at that time, according to which the messiah makes a two fold appearance: first in lowliness (the death of Jesus being reinterpreted as the expiatory death of a spiritual redeemer from sin), then in glory (on the clouds of heaven). As a religion of apocalyptic imminent expectation primitive Christianity was born, and all the gospels are written, retrospectively, from that perspective (Section 31).

In the second part Reimarus then gives detailed examination to the two 'patterns' of the story of Jesus: the original political-worldly pattern of which only traces are still present in the gospels (Part II, Sections 2-8); and the new spiritual pattern of the apostles, which almost completely conceals the old one, and which was no less successful than it was profoundly unbelievable. For even apart from the miracles and prophecies and heroic deeds of the apostles, which prove nothing as far as the reason is concerned (Sections 46-60), the two principal pillars of the Christian religion tumble down on closer inspection. For one thing the resurrection of Jesus is unproven and probably a deception on the part of the disciples; the Old Testament prophecies of it are a *petitio principii*, i.e. they beg the question, and the contradictions in the New Testament testimonies are blatant (Sections 9-36). Furthermore, the imminently expected return of Jesus has patently failed to materialise. Reimarus, the style of whose reporting is for the most part superior and dry, cannot conceal his triumph at this point. He realises only too well that he thereby opens up a problem no longer taken seriously since the days of primitive Christianity (though traceable in the English deists): the delay of the parousia! And he pours out all the scorn of which he is capable over the apostolic consolations that seek to explain this delay. (With the Lord a thousand years are as but a day, so we have just been waiting for a day and a half, and we only need to wait 365,000 human years until a divine year comes to an end! [Sections 37-45]).

In Germany the eyes of theologians and learned men in general now opened with consternation to the extent to which the Christian message had become problematic – the confession of faith of Rousseau's Vicar of Savoy had already caused a similar shock in France several years previously. While some made merry and scoffed, others protested and shouted for civil protection or censorship; preachers were at a loss and many students of theology gave up their studies. Men were simply not prepared for all this, nor were they a match for this radical denial of the Christian revelation, undertaken for the first time with the resources of historical and exegetical scholarship and buttressed by a rational 'religion of nature'. It was sufficiently paradoxical (and there was already astonishment on this score at the time) that it was precisely a neologian, a man whose thought moved basically on the same lines as that of Reimarus himself, who now appeared on the scene and undertook the concerted attack on Reimarus – none other than Semler! Despite his 'private religion', he now defended the 'church religion' that had been so intensely called in question by Reimarus. His *Reply to the Fragments of an Unknown Writer* confuted the dead author sentence by sentence. It was not hard to detect inner absurdities and errors in the detail of Reimarus' deistical polemical tract. At the time Semler almost completely finished Reimarus off by means of a war of attrition. But it was a pyrrhic victory. The great historian Semler came in the following years to despair of his own historical scholarship. The great tragedy of this 'neological' theologian, who did not wish to pursue to its end the path on which he had once set out, was shown in his turning away from theology in his old age. Not only did he devote himself to natural history, but to theosophy and alchemy and even to the fabrication of artificial gold and like enterprises.

At the end of his retort Semler attacked Lessing too, the half guilty, half innocent fire-raiser: *On the Aim of Mr. Lessing and his Unknown Writer. A few Fragments of an Unknown Writer from my Library. Published from A – Z.* Without doubt Lessing came away in better shape from the whole dispute. Not only was this greatest polemicist of German classical literature (Voltaire was his master!) vastly superior in verbal debate to opponents like Chief Pastor Goeze of Hamburg, who first achieved fame through him; Lessing, by nature an enlightener and yet already far beyond the Enlightenment, instictively ferreted out the storm centres of the controversy. With the publication of the *Fragments* and the ensuing debate he wanted to arouse the theologians and at the same time do the Church a service: 'I simply will not be shouted down by you as one who means less well by the Lutheran Church than you do',[20] he writes against Goeze.

---

[20]*Werke* VI, 273 (*Eine Parabel*).

Lessing by no means identifies himself with Reimarus. According to the latter, the resurrection of Christ is unworthy of belief, for the reports of the evangelists on this matter contradict each other. According to the orthodox, on the other hand, the resurrection of Christ is worthy of belief, for the evangelists' reports do *not* contradict each other. Lessing maintains against both that the resurrection of Christ is worthy of belief, *although* the reports contradict each other.[21] Lessing's questions are these: At the time of Christ there were 'demonstrations of spirit and of power'; but how is the Christian truth to enlighten me today, when I no longer have demonstrations of the spirit and of power but only reports about them? How am I to be able to jump across the 'ugly, broad ditch', so that I may come from the accidental truth of history to the necessary truth of reason?[22] In company with Reimarus against orthodoxy, Lessing rejects the doctrine of inspiration (*theopneustia*) as a theological device, for it is obvious that Scripture contains contradictions and errors. At the same time Lessing rejects – against the orthodox and Reimarus – historical proofs for Christian truth: the whole of eternity should not be hung upon a spider's thread.[23] Does Lessing perhaps intend to take a radical stand upon faith? On the contrary, what matters for him is that revelation be understood by reason on the basis of its own inner truth, in which case historical proofs are superfluous. Religion is not true because the evangelists and apostles taught it; they taught it because it is true.[24] The New Testament revelation is therefore basically capable of being superseded. According to Lessing's last writing *The Education of the Human Race*[25] (of which he might well in reality be more than just the editor) in the loosening of that revelation which Christ, the 'better instructor' (Section 53) and 'the first reliable, practical teacher of the immortality of the soul' (58-60), brought, we have to hope for 'perfect illumination' (80-84), 'the time of consummation' (85), 'the time of a new eternal Gospel' (86), the 'third Age' (89). The last sentence of this work ran: 'And what have I then to lose? is not the whole of eternity mine?'(100).

The next year Lessing was dead, and in the same year a work appeared which was afterwards looked on as the beginning of a new epoch: Immanuel Kant's *Critique of Pure Reason* (1781). But others succeeded Reimarus; for example, Karl Friedrich Bahrdt, whose *Letters on the Bible in the Popular Idiom* (1782) saluted Jesus as the great enlightener and exponent of a secret order, and Karl Heinrich Venturini with his 2,700-page *Natural History of the Great Prophet of Nazareth* (Bethlehem-Kopenhagen, 1800-1802). These were indeed novels about Christ, and the theory of Reimarus was only to make itself fully felt in the nineteenth century. However the apologists of the supernatural could not arrest the development. They took their stand too much upon their opponents' ground. They were themselves indebted to the Enlightenment, as can be read from the title of Franz Volkmar Reinhardt's

---

[21]*op. cit.* VI, 200-203 (*Eine Duplik*).
[22] *Lessing's Theological Writings,* 51-56 (*On the Proof of the Spirit and of Power*).
[23]*Werke* VI, 202-210 (*Eine Duplik*).
[24]cf. esp. *op. cit.* VI, 294-305 (*Axiomata* IX-X).
[25]*Lessing's Theological Writings,* 82-98.

book: *An Attempt to set out the Plan which the Founder of the Christian Religion drew up for the Advantage of Mankind* (1781). Reinhardt presupposes the divinity of Christ, but his Life of Jesus aims only at the conclusion that 'the founder of Christianity is to be considered as an outstanding divine teacher'. And he gives as his opinion that the 'rights of the human reason cannot be more conscientiously esteemed and tenderly respected than was done by Jesus'.[26] The revolution of thought was now well-nigh complete: Holy Scripture, and with it dogmas, had become historically contingent period documents, and divine inspiration had turned into human rationality; the Gospel had become general teaching on nature and morality, and the God-man Jesus Christ had turned into the teacher of wisdom Jesus of Nazareth – and even in this restricted role doubt was soon cast upon him. Reflection on primitive Christianity (often misunderstood as it was) and historico-critical exegesis, deficient understanding of the development of ecclesiastical doctrine and the nascent study of the history of religions, English and French freethinking and the Wolffian system that had sunk to the level of a trite popular philosophy, the re-emergence of ancient heresies and mechanical natural science, pragmatism and indifferentism in theology and a scarcely contestable nadic in living popular piety – all this along with other things had consummated what had slowly developed in various phases and at various levels from foundations laid centuries beforehand: the revolt of reason against faith, of history against dogma, of philosophy against theology, of nature against grace, of natural law against the Sermon on the Mount. In concrete terms this amounted to the banishment of God from the world, the exclusion of the world from the mystery of God; the separation of the two natures; the elimination of the God-man!

But let us say once more quite plainly: we are not concerned with maligning what is positive in this negative development! Who today could honestly wish that all of the following (and more besides) had not taken place: the process – brought about not least by the good spirit of the middle ages – whereby the nation-states, the sciences and the different spheres of life attained to maturity and autonomy; man's reflection on himself and on his world; the implementation of individual rights of toleration; the formation and cultivation of personality; the triumphal march of reason in the face of every form of obscurantism and mental indolence; the triumph of philosophy, mathematics, the natural sciences and political economy, and their alliance with technology; the intoxication with freedom and with worldly art; the whole optimism of the modern age, indeed even the luminaries of the Enlightenment itself (against the various systems of terror and absolutisms, against superstition, trials of

---

[26]Quoted in Schweitzer: *The Quest of the Historical Jesus*, 31ff.

INTRODUCTION

witches, torture, serfdom of the peasants and the numerous arbitrary acts of the *ancien régime*; the majority of the German Enlighteners were sincere and morally earnest men!); and, finally, historico-critical exegesis, whose enduring results – first and foremost the authentic historicity of the man Jesus and the historical context and the complex development of the sources – are at last being used by Protestants and Catholics alike as a matter of course? The catchphrase 'progress of the modern era' can by no means be eclipsed by the catchphrase 'decline of the West', and the notion of the 'Christian' middle ages is, as is well known, more than problematic. There is, then, every reason to ask whether, even in the history of modern times – and perhaps precisely in this movement towards humanity – there is, notwithstanding a certain ambiguity, a manifold and pressing realisation of demands inherent in the Christian message. While for many the path away from mainstream Christology led through deistic Christology to an atheistic Christology, for others it was precisely the new understanding of history and humanity that created the conditions for a new, more wide-ranging Christology. The christological debate that has persisted since the dawn of the modern age has not yet been resolved. It merely entered the consciousness of people in the course of the Enlightenment and became capable of formulation.

In the course of the Enlightenment – it was into this time that Hegel was born. It is worth pursuing more closely the history of these fifty years between the death of Lessing and the publication of Kant's *Critique of Pure Reason* (1781) and the deaths of Hegel and Goethe (1831-32) by running through the life-history of this one man as it were in slow motion. For these years were characterised by a breathtaking speed of development and by a profusion of problematic issues seldom observed in the history of human thought, perhaps not even in the similarly compressed history of Greek philosophy.[27] But why precisely Hegel?

1. Hegel brings German Idealism, and with it in a certain sense, the whole of modern philosophy, to systematic completion; so that Karl Barth, for example, correctly says this: 'Fundamentally the astonishing thing is not that

[27]On Hegel's *biography* in general see especially the *Dokumente zu Hegels Entwicklung* (*Documents on Hegel's Development*), edited by J. Hoffmeister, and referred to in these pages as *H*. Also the *Briefe von und an Hegel* (*Letters from and to Hegel*); XXVII, 1-265: Stuttgart – Tübingen – Bern – Frankfurt – Jena – Bamberg; XXVII, 267-430 and XXVIII, 1-144: Nuremberg; XXVIII, 145-200: Heidelberg; XXVIII, 201-368; XXIX, 1-356: Berlin; XXX, 3-35: *Nachträge und Ergänzungen* (*Addenda and Amendments*). In addition there is the classical, 'orthodox' biography by K. Rosenkranz (1844), and the more politically oriented presentation of his critical, liberal counterpart, R. Haym (1857). The latter work is a complement and corrective of the former, and Rosenkranz replied to it in 1858 and finally yet again in 1870. Next to K. Fischer the studies on the young Hegel offer much biographical material (cf. the index of literature for ch. 1, 1). On the individual periods of Hegel's career cf. the detailed information given in the chapters following. On the criticism levelled at Hegel cf. the footnotes of ch. 8, 1.

Hegel believed his philosophy to be an unsurpassable climax and culmination. It is that he was not right in thinking [this to be the case] ... Why did Hegel not become for the Protestant world something similar to what Thomas Aquinas was for Roman Catholicism?'[28] Whether in other respects Schelling should not be designated the climax of Idealism, is not under discussion in these pages. At any rate it is in keeping with the intentions of this book that special attention has recently been devoted to the earlier, theological Schelling – the Schelling of *The Ages of the World* and the *Philosophy of Mythology and Revelation.*[29]

2. Now, as hitherto, the after-effects of Hegel are immense, despite the conflicts of the Diadochi and the scorn about the 'process of decay of the Absolute Spirit'. They are discernible to begin with and above all in what has everywhere been taken over tacitly from him. T. Adorno has justly stated: 'At the present day hardly any theoretical thought of any importance does justice to the experience of consciousness, and indeed not only of consciousness but of the bodily aspects of man as well, that does not have Hegel's philosophy stored up within it.'[30] But Hegel also has a direct effect through the various more or less critical Hegel revivals which follow upon one another at periodic intervals.[31] In England there were J. H. Stirling, E. Caird, F. H. Bradley, B. Bosanquet, W. Wallace and J. McTaggart; in Italy the early adherents of Hegel's philosophy A. Vera and B. Spaventa, and at a later date B. Croce, G. Gentile and E. de Negri; in the French-speaking countries J. Wahl, J. Hyppolite, A. Kojève and H. Niel, along with the Hegel studies of G. Fessard, A. Peperzak, A. Chapelle, C. Bruaire, and R. Vancourt; from Holland G. J. P. J. Bolland merits first mention and then B. Wigersma and R. F. Beerling. And finally – to say nothing of Hegel's influence even in South America and the Far East – the understanding of Hegel was promoted in Germany by the textual editions of G. Lasson, J. Hoffmeister, H. Glockner and H. Nohl. There are also the introductions to the history of Hegel's youth written by, among others, W. Dilthey and T. Haering. Then there are the fresh interpretations of the philosopher given by R. Kroner, N. Hartmann, T. Litt and I. Iljin (also F. Heer's *Introduction*). Finally there remains to be mentioned the positive debate with Hegel on the part of philosophically oriented Protestant theologians of the first third of the century (F. Brunstäd, K. Leese, E. Hirsch and K. Nadler, and at a later date on these lines J. Flügge and E. Schmidt), and on the part of Catholic theologians or philosophers (E.

---

[28] *Protestant Theology in the Nineteenth Century,* 384.
[29] cf. esp. the works of W. Schulz, H. Fuhrmans, W. Kasper, K. Hemmerle.
[30] *Drei Studien zu Hegel,* 14.
[31] cf. the Proceedings of the Hegel Congresses.

Przywara, T. Steinbüchel, C. Nink, J. Möller, E. Coreth, W. Kern, P. Henrici and J. Splett), and finally on the part of recent Protestant theologians (G. Rohrmoser, H. Schmidt, W.-D. Marsch and T. Koch). After the period of neo-Kantian subjectivism ill-disposed towards metaphysics, in the wake of Husserl's phenomenology a 'turn towards the object' slowly came about, a 'turn towards realism' and therefore a 'turn towards metaphysics, towards ontology'. This movement of thought also brought about an overt 'turn towards Hegel', which set in in Germany especially during the thirties and which with one voice no longer emphasised the purely idealistic character of his philosophy, but its realistic, empirical, down to earth attributes, indeed its metaphysical-ontological sides.[32] The complex of problems concerning the relation of religion and society was of special importance for the most recent discussion. Hegel's significance today is attested by two international scholarly associations (the *International Hegel Society* and the *International Hegel Association*), by the regular *Hegel Congresses* and above all by the astonishing number of publications devoted to him.[33]

3. Hegel's influence is no less considerable when exercised indirectly through his foes. The greatest anti-Hegelians, Kierkegaard and Marx, drew upon him the most. Although liberalism and inductive science dethroned him after his death, Hegel's name has been invoked by monarchy and revolution, relativism and historicism, nationalism and totalitarianism, Taine and Renan, pan-Slavists and the anarchist Bakunin, the Tübingen School both Catholic and Protestant, and dialectical materialism along with world Communism. Thus in the article on Hegel in the *Large Soviet Encyclopaedia* we read the characteristic sentence: 'All the same, "a *grain* of profound truth" (Lenin) lay embedded in the mystical shell of Hegelianism', namely, 'dialectic as the "algebra of the Revolution"'.[34] One group of currently influential interpreters of Hegel either stems directly from dialectical materialism (E. Bloch, G. Lukács, W. R. Beyer and R. Garaudy, along with the most recent Italian exponents of Hegel's youthful writings etc.) or else tends in that direction (H. Marcuse, H. Lefebvre).

By contrast with all these writers, the particular motive behind this book is as follows. Although it is unnoticed by many, in Hegel the debate about Christ, in close connection with the question of God, presses towards a dramatic climax. Taking the Enlightenment and its notion of Jesus as his

[32]cf. E. Coreth: *Das dialektische Sein,* 7-12.
[33]W. Kern points out 75 books in his excellent report on the literature of the years 1958-1960 alone! For the years 1961-1965 he reports about more than 200 titles, which are all to be found in the fourth volume of *Hegel-Studien* (1967).
[34]E. Coreth: *op. cit.*, 16, 17.

point of departure, Hegel goes on to discover the full measure of the God-man Christ. And he was not the man to proceed carelessly at this point. His brilliant mind wrestled with the significance of the incarnation, for God himself, and for the process of man's attaining to humanity. He thought through his whole system from the perspective of Christ – or was it the other way around?[35] We have now posed enough preliminary questions and, to use an image of Hegel's, sufficiently sharpened the knives to get down to the incision, i.e. to the matter in hand.

---

[35]*General presentations* of Hegel's philosophy: we leave out of account here *Introductions* of the kind to be found in general works on the history of philosophy (such as recently F. Copleston and J. Chevalier). Of fundamental importance are the mainly systematic works by K. Rosenkranz, *Kritissche Erläuterungen des Hegelschen Systems,* (*Critical Explanations of Hegel's System*) 1840, and his *Hegel als deutscher Nationalphilosoph,* (*Hegel as the National Philosopher of Germany*) 1870. The same can be said of the presentation written by the theologian F. A. Staudenmaier in the initial period. Then there is Kuno Fischer's general presentation, written after a long period marked by a lack of interest in Hegel, and remarkable as the hitherto most comprehensive work and the one which sums up the research of the nineteenth century. This was followed after World War I by three significant works marking the Hegel renaissance: R. Kroner, N. Hartmann and H. Glockner (editor of the *Jubilee Edition*). For our purposes the presentations written at the same time by the following are of importance: J. Wahl, H. Marcuse, T. Steinbüchel, W. Schultz.

Important for the post-World War II period are: from the standpoint of theological critique, K. Barth and E. Hirsch; from that of a liberal approach to the history of thought, T. Litt; from the Marxist perspective, E. Bloch. Far and away the most thorough *Introduction* to Hegel's thought process and theology was penned by I. Iljin, appearing as early as 1916 in a Russian edition. Amongst the most recent *Introductions* are some of lesser scope and pretensions: P. Touilleux, E. Weil, G. A. van den Berg van Eysinga, T. I. Oiserman and A. Marietti. The following are outstanding: W. T. Stace (now in a new edition), J. N. Findlay, R. Heiss, R. Garaudy, W. Kaufmann, G. R. G. Mure, and in a more popular vein G. E. Müller. And cf. the *Dictionary* articles by W. Anz (*EKL*), W. Wieland (*RGG*) and W. Kern (*LThK*).

Apart from works devoted to Hegel's youthful writings, to his proofs of the existence of God and to the debate between German Idealism and Christianity, the recent publications by the following are to be mentioned: C. Hötschl, H. Niel, G. Dulckeit, J. Möller, E. Schmidt, J. Flügge, F. Heer and T. Koch. On the doctrine of the Trinity, after J. Hessen, now J. Splett. On the problems to do with religion and society, G. Rohrmoser, H. Schmidt and W.-D. Marsch. On the Christology of the young Hegel, J. W. Schmidt-Japing. On individual published and unpublished works of Hegel, cf. the specialist literature in the pertinent chapters. In spite of various preliminary works, the judgment of P. Henrici will find consent, when he writes that it is 'to be regretted that we still do not possess a solid work on Hegel's Christology' (*Hegel und die Theologie,* 729).

Chapter One: Christ in Oblivion

'Thy kingdom come, and may our hands not rest idle in our lap.'[1]

1. A Man of the Enlightenment's Religion

The young Hegel did not think much of Jesus Christ.[2] Or did he simply fail to express himself fully? How, at a remove of almost two hundred years, should one wish to pry into the lad's heart anyway? The sources flow sparingly, and are more appropriately to be termed general reports, a schoolboy's copied extracts, short insignificant essays, a scanty diary which covers a year and a half with long breaks in between. What kind of basis is this on which to assess eighteen years of a human life? Even so, while we may well err in our judgment, the impression remains inescapable that the young Hegel does not set great store by Christ. This is not to imply that he was not what in those days was commonly dubbed a good Christian. He was good, very good, a model pupil whose parents 'molly-coddled him, so to speak . . . as the first-born, and because he studied diligently' (from the report of Hegel's sister Christiane; *H*, 394). He was often awarded prizes for coming top of the class,

---

[1]To Schelling, 1795 (XXVII, 18).

[2]For our account of Hegel's youth we rely above all on the documents on Hegel's development published by J. Hoffmeister and referred to in these pages as *H*; and on T. M. Knox's translation of H. Nohl's edition of *Hegels Theologische Jugendschriften,* referred to here as *N*. There is no English translation of the *Dokumente zu Hegels Entwicklung.* A selection of letters in ET is found in *Hegel: A Reinterpretation, Texts and Commentary*, by W. Kaufmann, London 1966, reprinted by Anchor Books (Garden City, NY), 1978 to which page references are made where possible. On chronology, with reference to the new edition of the collected writings, cf. G. Schuler: *op. cit.,* 111–159 (chart 127–133).

The nineteenth century had an almost exclusively biographical interest in the young Hegel and was wont to emphasise the continuity with the later writings: in this vein see K. Rosenkranz, R. Haym and also K. Fischer, who at once summed up and concluded nineteenth century research. (In Italy cf. B. Croce's *Saggio* of 1907.)

W. Dilthey's account of Hegel's youth opened up a new period in that he subjected the *Theologische Jugendschriften* (*Early Theological Writings*) to thorough scrutiny. These were subsequently published under this problematic title by his pupil Nohl. After a Kantian period in Hegel's development, Dilthey detected a 'mystical pantheism', with the upshot that the element of discontinuity *vis-à-vis* the later writings stood out in bold relief (along the same lines as Dilthey see also J. Wahl and G. della Volpe). This onesidedly theological interpretation of the young

and was accordingly once exhorted by the headmaster 'to warn our school-fellows not to get involved in those despicable, dissolute gambling clubs etc.' (The names of the classmates in this 'curs' club' are carefully noted in the diary; *H*, 8). And in the solemn speech that he delivered upon leaving the grammar school in 1788, he assured his peers that 'it may be too late as far as the past is concerned, but already now we are to understand at least in part what detrimental consequences stem from every form of inattentiveness to the warnings of our teachers and superiors; we shall continually become more convinced of this as we grow in experience and riper knowledge' (*H*, 53). So Hegel was good, betook himself to church and had dealings with pastors; 'the father confessor in his confirmation instruction, who afterwards became Prelate Griesinger, was uncommonly well satisfied with his religious knowledge' (Christiane; *H*, 392). He read the Bible and heard sermons, and more than once he even sat before a Catholic pulpit, 'which so pleased me that I would have visited that congregation more frequently'[3] (*H*, 21). His background and upbringing were thoroughly Protestant. The ancestor of the family, the soap-box politician Johannes Hegel, had migrated 'as an exile from Carinthia to Swabia, on account of his Protestant confession';[4] and the

---

Hegel was corrected and complemented already by F. Rosenzweig's study on Hegel and the state, in which he elaborated upon the political elements of Hegel's thought (cf. the important study by J. Ritter on Hegel and the French Revolution). At a later date these elements were acutely but in many ways onesidedly analysed, especially by the largely Marxist interpreters G. Lukács, E. de Negri, A. Negri, A. Massolo and M. Rossi. One group of these 'leftists' understand Hegel as himself a 'leftist' and thus reach conclusions sympathetic to him (e.g., Lukács, Massolo, Negri), while the others deem him a 'rightist' and come to correspondingly anti-Hegelian conclusions (e.g., della Volpe in company with his pupils L. Coletti and N. Merker, and Rossi).

The leading minds of the Hegel renaissance were concerned with Hegel's system and either did not bother their heads with the early writings at all (R. Kroner emphasises the historically necessary development from Kant via Fichte and Schelling to Hegel, N. Hartmann above all the romantic, irrational and concrete elements), or only considered them later and then with qualifications (as, e.g., Glockner in his second volume).

It was the historico-genetic analysis which T. Haering executed with meticulous respect for minute detail that provided the first comprehensive vision of the personality and work of the young Hegel. Haering radically corrected Dilthey's conclusions and set forth the continuity of the later with the earlier writings with great discrimination. Haering's work was confirmed by G. Aspelin and J. Hyppolite; neither H. Wacker nor J. Schwarz refuted it; it was then documented by J. Hoffmeister (especially in the extensive footnotes of *H*); and, finally, its scope was significantly enlarged and delimited by C. Lacorte.

The recent studies by P. Asveld, A. T.B. Peperzak, K. Wolf, G. Rohrmoser, H. Schmidt and H. J. Krüger are important for the set of problems dealing with the philosophy of religion that occur in the early writings. On the doctrine of the Trinity in the early writings, cf. J. Splett, and on Chrstology, cf. J. W. Schmidt-Japing and W.-D. Marsch.

On the cultural milieu and climate of opinion, especially in Tübingen, cf. further the works of J. Klaiber, W. Betzendörfer, E. Staiger, R. Schneider, E. Müller and W. Axmann.

[3] '*quae mihi ita placuit, ut saepius hanc concionem adire statuerim*'.
[4] K. Rosenkranz: *op. cit.*, 3.

parson Hegel, who baptised Schiller, was but one of the sundry clergymen from the Hegel clan. And he himself, the young Georg Wilhelm Friedrich, son of a middle-ranking civil servant of the State of Württemberg, was he not destined to become a theologian?

Yes, he was intended for this profession; but despite all the Christian activity that goes with the Christian milieu as a matter of course, we fail to notice in him any sign of special religious zeal. We do not mean by this a pious cast of mind (and bound up with this the 'lofty sensation' on hearing the funeral bell and the trumpets in church; *H*, 16), but any sober believing emotion. Let us not require too much of a grammar school boy; let it not be laid to his charge that, on the feast day, 'he did not go to church, but . . . went walking in Bopser Wood' (*H*, 9), or that, on the occasion of a sermon on the Confession of Augsburg ('then there was a sermon'), he deemed worthy of record only the enlargment of his 'historical knowledge' by jotting down the relevant dates (*H*, 6f). Let us not reproach him (as did Schopenhauer, who preferred the *Iliad*!) for the fact that he was able totally to forget himself in *Sophia's Journey from Memel to Saxony* (6 volumes and *circa* 4000 pages: 'one of the sorriest and most boring pieces of work of our literature at that time'[5]), and that among Shakespeare's works it was the *Merry Wives of Windsor* which first spoke to him (*H*, 392). All this is understandable and not to be accorded disproportionate significance. Of greater moment, however – and this is something one might well look to find in a grammar school boy and future theologian, especially where this development runs in such uninterruptedly linear fashion as in Hegel's case – is that nowhere in these documents, which reach back into Hegel's earliest youth, does there appear a living relationship to the Christian message and particularly to the person of Christ himself.

But is this so surprising? How could the Christian spark have been kindled so easily under the ice-sheet of the Enlightenment? It is no mere labelling to declare that, even as a grammar school boy, for all his individualities, Hegel was decisively on the side of the Enlightenment.

'As far as principle is concerned, Hegel's education belonged entirely to the Enlightenment; as far as the actual course of study is concerned, it belonged entirely to classical antiquity.' So one can read in the encyclopaedia article of 1827. It is a view which can be traced back indirectly to Hegel himself. With interests spanning a universal range, he speaks in his diary, written largely *'latino idiomate'*, though briefly and fragmentarily (cf. *H*, 6-41), of Socrates and Roman history, the course of the sun and playing chess, geometry, music and religion, classical languages and copying extracts, childbirth and eating cherries, and paying visits to concerts and libraries. The

---

[5]K. Fischer: *op.cit.*,9.

Greek tragedies were his favourite reading, and physics and botany were his favourite subjects in the upper forms of the grammar school (*H*, 393). His extensive and carefully indexed extracts (cf. the examples to be found in *H*, 54-166; and further 398-400) deal with philosophy and the history of literature (amongst ancient authors especially Sophocles), aesthetics (Lessing, Wieland, Klopstock, Schiller's *Fiesko*; conversely, there are no references to the epoch-making dramas penned at that time: *Emilia Galotti, Nathan the Wise, Götz von Berlichingen, Iphigenia, Egmont, The Robbers*), travel journals and arithmetic, geometry, and applied mathematics, psychology, ethics and pedagogics, the history of philosophy, and theology. In all his assiduity, however, the young Hegel does not appear as an infant prodigy, but rather as a somewhat precocious and dutiful model pupil, narrow mindedly and pedantically accumulating knowledge, but otherwise good-natured and well-liked by his schoolfellows.

Stuttgart was for Hegel a period devoted to the quiet accumulation of knowledge, which, while certainly fragmentary and disconnected, was not devoid of inner unity and purposeful direction. His far-flung field of knowledge, which greatly surpassed the compulsory contents of the school curriculum, shows for all its diversity a concentration on psychological and, above all, historical and cultural-historical phenomena. His ideal was neither pure factual history in the sense appropriate to specialised historical scholarship, nor an abstract-theoretical philosophy of history, but, as he defines it at the beginning of his diary, under the influence not so much of Montesquieu as of the church historian Schröckh, a 'pragmatic history'. 'I believe it is to be termed pragmatic history when one does not merely relate *facta,* but also sets forth the character of a celebrated man, of an entire nation, its manners, customs, religion etc., and the various fluctuations and deviations between it and other peoples on these scores, when one subjects the fortune and rise of great empires to investigation, when one demonstrates, *inter alia,* what consequences this or that event or alteration in the order of the state has had for the constituion of the nation, for its character etc.' (*H*, 9f.) It is the same as what Hegel has in mind at the end of his diary with the notion of a 'philosophically studied' history (*H*, 37): a pragmatic-didactic history, a *historia* whose usefulness resides in its being *magistra non scholae sed vitae.* In this way the Enlightenment had taught men how to understand history afresh.

Because of the circumstances of the times and under the influence of his teachers and his reading, Hegel must already during his grammar school days have arrived at the conviction that he was living in a transitional period, out of which would emerge more perfect forms of culture and community – in the political system, in ethics, art, science and religion. And for this reason he was concerned not only with the mental acquisition of 'individual fields', but at the same time to acquire a comprehensive grasp of human and cultural history. Therefore he also had an interest in religion. But his interest was not so much

26

in religion *qua* religion – just as little as in aesthetics *qua* aesthetics or even in history *qua* history; rather it comprehended all these things to the extent that they were embedded in a more general historical interest in the development of mankind, an interest oriented toward the accomplishment of a better future. And it is in precisely this perspective that religion, among the various mental structures, enjoys such vast importance for Hegel. *In fine,* religion reflects most directly and completely mankind's condition and progress, the degree of enlightenment that a people has achieved. Thus Hegel sees religion ever more clearly in a wider social and cultural-historical context, a procedure which certainly does not need to be at odds with his own personal religiosity. ('Religiosity' is used here quite generally in the sense of a subjective religion understood as a personal relationship to God, in which man gets involved with God in a positive way.)

The overall perspective of the young Hegel's reflection upon religion has been minutely worked out in an outstanding study by C. Lacorte, whose examination of the Stuttgart period is more thorough than that of any other scholar.[6] We must concur with his conclusions, especially against Dilthey and his excessive stress upon the problematic nature of religion in the young Hegel. We may oppose his judgment, however, when he casts doubt upon Hegel's personal religiosity on the basis of this conception of religion. As if on account of this conception of religion the grammar school boy could not have been a 'practising and convinced Lutheran', as that was understood *at the time.*[7] Just as Lacorte overinterprets an early distinction drawn by Hegel (*H,* 122f) between understanding (*Verstand*) and reason (*Vernunft*),[8] he likewise reads too much into an entirely jutified remark on the superstition to be found in the Catholic Church (*H,* 36) or on the Roman mass (*H,* 21), the latter remark being combined with high praise of a Catholic sermon (*H,* 21). For Hegel it is by no means a question of an ardent 'root and branch condemnation' (*condanna complessiva*) of the 'ceremonial apparatus' or of the rites and practices of the various Christian Churches.[9]

We have equally little cause to overinterpret the absence of any manifestation of religious zeal in the diary, as if for precisely this reason we may conclude that Hegel was in no way a religious man, or that (as A. Negri baldly asserts without stating his grounds[10]) the problematic nature of religion had been impressed upon him by a fanatical upbringing. Whoever expects religious confessions in this diary of a few months and scarcely forty pages of print, fails to grasp its character. It has absolutely nothing to do with any of those journals of 'fair souls' which were proliferating at this time, and which even at a later date had no particular place in Hegel's affection. It is the sober diary of a diligent seventeen year-old schoolboy, composed of book bills, regurgitations of school material and suchlike things, and written for long stretches in Latin for the sake of practice. There are throughly objective observations taken from

---

[6]*op. cit.,* 59-116; esp. 85f; 111-116.
[7]*op. cit.,* 81.
[8]*op. cit.,* 94f; 115.
[9]*op. cit.,* 83.
[10]*op. cit.,* 111.

school life and only dry psychological remarks that seldom refer to his own person. How many a person could be said to have had no religious convictions, if he were judged exclusively on the basis of such journal entries, some school essays and copied extracts!

Why is it impossible that a predominantly intellectual interest in religion (in the objective sense) should go hand in hand with a genuine religiosity (in the subjective sense)? Any questioning of Hegel's religiosity comes to grief not only through placing too much weight on the sources at our disposal and through reading too much into individual texts. It also flies in the face of incontestable facts which deserve to be taken seriously in their concreteness: that Hegel was brought up in a Protestant family and grew up in a Protestant milieu; that several of his teachers, some of whom were his personal friends, were pastors; that not only his religious knowledge but also his religious practice were the object of praise. Lastly, it is attested that Hegel intended to be a theologian.

The false or at least undiscriminating judgments on the religiosity of the young Hegel, which by no means tally with the sources, have their root in the unhistorical prejudice that religiosity and Enlightenment were not to be associated with one another in the Germany of those days. Yet it is a characteristic of the *German* Enlightenment – and on this point Asveld is to be defended against Lacorte's polemic[11]
that it intended to be pronouncedly religious and to some degree even Christian. And so, alongside 'orthodox' Lutherans and 'pietistic' Lutherans, there were also numerous 'enlightened' Lutherans, whose Lutheran conviction and practice we should not dispute, however their Lutheranism be assessed against the yardstick of Martin Luther and the pristine Christian message. As happened to Christ, Luther too was understood *in terms of the Enlightenment.*

That a conflict is latent in Hegel's religiosity and Christian profession is incontestable from the privileged vantage-point of our current understanding of religion and especially of Christianity. This rift can conclusively be explained in terms of the fact that Hegel's religiosity, when looked at as a whole, is, like that of so many of his contemporaries, the typical religiosity of a man of the Enlightenment, a characterisation which we intend, not as a loose-fitting label, but as a sharply contoured definition. The religiosity of a man of the Enlightenment was intended to be Christian precisely in its aridity and intellectuality; and it may not, in unhistorical fashion, be measured against a 'romantic' or 'mystical' or even 'orthodox' religiosity. It can be at once rational *and* Christian for the very reason that, as we saw in our Introduction, the Christian message itself, when viewed through 'enlightened' spectacles, as a matter of fact coincides with the rational religion of nature: a religion of rationality provided by nature in the context of human society and of the state, geared towards education and utility, virtue and felicity, protesting against obscurantism and every form of superstition. In the journal we read the amusing exclamations concerning those who – *'pudendum dictu'* – still

---

[11]*op. cit.,* 112f.

believe in the fable of Muthe's army: 'Ha! Ha! Ha! *O tempora! O mores!* Occurred *Anno* 1785. O! O!' (*H,* 14). In those days Hegel did not think much of the religious customs of the time and of the 'rabble' – cf. in this context the celebrated Enlightenment theme of Socrates' sacrifice of a cock (*H,* 10; cf. 86f and 47f). He did, however, have a high regard for religious tolerance, which was why he so greatly appreciated the Catholic sermon he heard that he determined to go to that church more often (*H,* 21; cf. 48). He moralised about the sundry passions to be encountered in public life (*H,* 22), and in a school paper *Concerning the Religion of the Greeks and Romans* (1787), he explained the rise of religion on the basis of the 'notion of a Divinity' which is 'natural to man', whereby in time, with the assistance of 'men of illuminated reason', the ignorance of natural law, the despotic conditions of society and the craving for power of the priestly caste would be overcome. The inference that he drew from this was 'to test' all 'our inherited and received opinions' (*H,* 43-48). Rational critique of society – critical scrutiny of everything that had become conventional in Church, religion and society – in this too Hegel turns out to be a typical man of the Enlightenment.

So at length, aged eighteen, Hegel quitted the grammar school, 'fully conversant with ... the so-called philosophical point of view concerning religious dogmas' (*H,* 395) and, like his territorial prince, 'persuaded of the importance of education, and of the universal and widespread advantage of science' (from his farewell speech; *H,* 52). His enlightened Christianity, which (despite occasional polemic against excessive ratiocination and purely theoretical religion) was identical with the natural religion of reason, was totally open to the influence of ancient Greece. At an early age imbued with a sense of the nobility and beauty of Hellenism, Hegel was never able to recognise genuine Christianity in any form which would bar the solemnity of that ancient serenity.[12] This enlightened Christianity was less open to the person of Christ himself. It is nowhere demonstrable that this person had made an enduring impression upon him. It would appear that such an impression had not been transmitted to the lad by his family, just as little as it had by his enlightened teachers. Apart from the mention of the feast of the '*nativitas*' (*H,* 25), the name of Christ hardly crops up at all in Hegel's papers from his grammar school days. Jesus turns up only in the extract on true felicity from Wünsch's *Discourses on Cosmology for Young People* (*H,* 87-100) as a teacher of wisdom, who reveals what all people already know 'by means of an oral, more simple and appropriate instruction'. 'When we sin in haste', we take refuge in his merits; faith in him consists in 'enlightenment of the understanding and in the exercise of virtue'. These then are *les lumières du*

---

[12]K. Rosenkranz: *op. cit.,* 12.

29

siècle which light upon the figure of Christ – one might well say, somewhat too pallidly to awaken religious enthusiasm.

As his diary demonstrates, the young Hegel had a flair for exact, detailed observation. He was not what one might perhaps suspect: he was no abstract speculator! And just as little as he could abide superstition, no more did he esteem religion as abstract pure theory. Already at this early stage he saw religion as embedded in other structures of the spirit in social life, in the wide context of history and of peoples. One realises somewhat vaguely (but even so distinctly enough) that the supra-individual-*cum*-inclusive status was of greater moment for him than was the individual status of this one man Jesus of Nazareth. There may be something hidden here which could become significant later on. Notwithstanding all this, let us repeat: had not positive Christian seeds been planted in the young Hegel? Did he not, as a lad and as a grammar school boy, live in a family which was filled with the Protestant spirit? Had he not enjoyed a thorough instruction in Holy Scripture? Did he not harken to Holy Scripture in preaching and teaching, did he not read a great deal in the Greek New Testament during the private coaching he received from Preceptor Löffler, a closer friend than any other? According to Hegel's own account in his diary, he read with his teacher the Epistles to the Romans and to the Thessalonians and even some Hebrew from the Psalms (*H*, 12). Let us then not overlook the fact that, however much he behaved in the manner of the Enlightenment, the young Hegel had gone through the school of the Bible! Quotations from Scripture were to accompany him and his philosophy from start to finish.

In addition, there developed a basic doubt about the Enlightenment, which far surpasses the detailed points of criticism of the Enlightenment that can be found in his writings. At the end of his diary he gives an account of this. It had occurred to the young student that 'enlightenment through the sciences and arts' was restricted to 'the caste of the learned'. And then: 'to draw up a blueprint for the enlightenment of the common man is something that I deem very hard, in part even for the most learned persons, in part especially for myself, for whom indeed it is much more onerous, since I have not yet made a philosophical and thorough-going study of history. Besides, I also believe that this enlightenment of the common man has always been contingent upon the religion of his time, and that its range extends only so far as enlightenment through artisans and the physical comforts of life' (*H*, 37). So then, there resides here in the rational framework of Hegel's enlightenment the worm of doubt. The question will never again let him go: how is the enlightenment of the as yet unenlightened common man possible? This is at once a socio-political and a religious question! Moreover, Hegel will not in fact forget religion. He lived too much with and among the people – and this he did until his life's end – to have been able to abandon himself to any illusions on the subject of life as the common man saw it. He took this thoroughly practical question of his with him into the seminary.

2. Theology at Odds with Itself

And what did the young theologian feel like in Tübingen? For a theologian he now was, notwithstanding all his far-flung interests in the provinces of history and philosophy. In the autumn of 1788, aged eighteen, he had moved into the celebrated Evangelical seminary, which had been an Augustinian monastery until the time of the Reformation. In company with Hölderlin he had passed the university entrance examination. In the apt and pious idiom of the time, he was 'consecrated to theology'. *Consacrum*: according to this formulation the theologian was meant to have to do with what is holy. Were men still aware, at a time when everything was being enlightened by reason, that theology, being the *logos* concerned with *theos,* has to do with the holy, with an 'object' of a special kind? As a theologian Hegel first studied for two semesters in the Faculty of Philosophy as the regulations of study prescribed. Then, after taking the Master's examination in philosophy in 1790, he studied for three years in the Faculty of Theology; but his attitude to *theologia sacra* during his time in Tübingen is an enigma.

Should we wish to probe this enigma somewhat – and it cannot be cracked open with pincers – we shall come up against a number of difficulties.
1. At first glance Hegel's writings from this period appear to be numerous, but on closer inspection they quickly dwindle away. For the Master's examination in philosophy in 1790 he did indeed write scholarly essays: 'On the Judgment of Common Sense about Objectivity and Subjectivity of Ideas', and 'On the Study of the History of Philosophy'. However, we know no more than the titles of these works (*H,* 436). Furthermore – at least according to Rosenkranz, who gives a short statement of their contents[13] – Hegel wrote for the same Master's examination a dissertation *'De limite officiorum humanorum seposita animorum immortalitate',*[14] and another for his examination by the Consistory in 1793, *'De ecclesiae Wirtembergiae renascentis calamitatibus'.*[15] This is a mistake, however, for these dissertations were in fact composed by professors to serve the students as disputation fodder (*H,* 436, 438), so that in this respect Hegel did have to occupy himself with the problems that they raised. For his own part he did at least write an essay for the seminary, 'On some Advantages afforded us by the Reading of the ancient classical Greek and Roman Authors' (1788; *H,* 169-172). Howbeit the latter is nothing but the grammar school oration from the

---

[13]*op. cit.,* 35, 39.
[14]'Concerning the limits of human duties when the notion of the immortality of the soul has been laid aside'.
[15]'On the calamities that befell the resurgent Church of Württemberg'.

same year, slightly altered and padded out to meet the changed requirements (*H,* 48-51, and cf. 440-445).

2. As regards the second difficulty, the outward evidence of the theologian's activity is self-contradictory. Did he do a lot of work, or only a little? Did he principally occupy himself with philosophy, or with theology? Was he acquainted with modern authors, or was he not? Hegel's fellow-student Leutwein, who claimed 'to enjoy an intimacy' with him 'of the kind not shared with the others' (*H,* 428), speaks in his later report, which Rosenkranz appraised as 'on the whole not incorrect',[16] of 'a certain joviality' (which, according to Schwegler, even went so far as 'a propensity to pub-crawling'), and of 'convivial drinking bouts . . . at which Bacchus received his customary sacrifice'. On these occasions Hegel would conduct himself 'somewhat brilliantly', though, according to an interpolation by Schwegler, 'he was otherwise regarded in the seminary as a *lumen obscurum*'. Leutwein goes on to remark that 'as far as his academic diligence and his regular attendance at lectures were concerned, he did not exactly commend himself', that 'in Tübingen he was not even properly acquainted with father Kant', and that 'discussions on Kant, Reinhold and Fichte' could 'find little in the way of a favourable response' with him. At this period of his life 'Hegel was an eclectic, still roving cavalierly in the domain of knowledge'. It took a setback in his doctoral work to bring about a change of heart in him. Leutwein could report nothing about Hegel's last year of studies, since he left the seminary at that time. A further report by Fink (*H,* 431-433) tends in the same direction: rambles into the surrounding countryside and adventures that occurred on these occasions, Hegel's first romance, and the special role that the club for revolution enthusiasts played for him. Add to this the pessimistic report of Professor Schnurrer (*H,* 434) and Rosenkranz's remark that the 'acquaintances of his Swabian youth were amazed when he later surprised them with his fame: "We should never have expected it of Hegel."'[17] And finally there are the official testimonials with their twice-repeated observation '*mores languidi*', and the reference in the final testimonial, '*in discursu mediocres in theologia commonstravit progressus*' (*H,* 439).[18] But all this is only *one* side of the theologian. The other is made up of his participation along with Hölderlin and others in a circle where Plato, Kant and Jacobi were read; there are, moreover, various positive statements about Hegel, and there is his close friendship, discernible especially in the letters from Bern, with the leading lights from among that generation of seminarians. Not only was he a close friend of Hölderlin, but also of Schelling who, aged only fifteen, had entered the seminary as an '*ingenium praecox*'[19] two years after Hegel. In his last year of residence Hegel shared a room with these two. Finally, there is the significant first theological fragment that comes down to us from this period.

3. And there is a third difficulty, namely that Hegel's pieces of written work appear to contradict each other. The difference between the sermons and the theological fragment is blatant. On top of this, it is difficult to assess the extent to which other authors, and especially Kant, exercised a positive influence upon Hegel.

---

[16]*op. cit.,* 29. But cf. the discrepancies between the letter transmitted by Schwegler, which to some extent contains tendentious variations and additions, and the original letter by Leutwein on Hegel, which was recently edited with a commentary by D. Henrich (66f, 75-77).
[17]*op. cit.,* 30.
[18]'sluggish behaviour' and 'has displayed average progress in disputation in theology'.
[19]'infant prodigy'.

Notwithstanding these caveats, the few documents and the scanty biographical data from this period (not to forget in retrospect Hegel's Bern correspondence) must suffice for us to sketch a makeshift portrait of the Tübingen theology student, of his religious world and his Christian profession. This small amount of material in fact speaks volumes, if only we understand how to listen properly to what it says. We shall beware of touching up one side of his character in favour of another. Out of the clumsy but honest pub-crawler roving through neighbourhood and scholarship, we shall not fashion a seeker after God thirsting exclusively for the Absolute. Just as little shall we be tempted by all those anecdotes and diary entries about liberty, love, wine and impassioned kisses to come up with the conclusion that the gist of the matter resides simply in a convivial student way of life and in a philistine, day-to-day bourgeois existence. Hegel's profound mind stood out in sharp contrast to the kind of intellectual smugness which goes its own optimistic and problem-free way, complacently content with itself and the world in true bourgeois style and unaffected by all the anguish of the times and indeed of its own heart, inspecting all that sped tormentedly by, whether drily or in high spirits, whether from a pinnacle of lofty eminence or with condescending contempt. Hegel was certainly not, like his fellow idealist Schelling, an 'abysmal lake of fire', full of ardent passion and disposed at all times to erupt at white heat. Nor was he the magnificent, sombre thundercloud earmarked, along with all the glittering light that it contained, to be emptied out and to meet its ruin: this was Hölderlin. Hitherto Hegel had gone through no 'storm and stress', nor had he undergone any romantic catastrophe. On the other hand, his thoroughly commonplace adolescence had not been spared from affliction. We know from his sister's letter (*H*, 392f; Kaufmann, 299f) that at the age of six he had such a severe bout of smallpox that the physician thought him lost; he was blind for several days. At thirteen he was once more near death, suffering this time from 'bilious dysentery'. Subsequently he had to endure an operation to remove a large ulcer behind his ear. Then in Tübingen he had tertian fever and was obliged to return home to Stuttgart for a few months. His mother died during his sickness at the age of thirteen, an event which remained strongly present in his consciousness (cf. its mention in his letter to his sister at so late a date as 1825; XXIX, 96). Moreover, his fellow seminarians conferred upon him the nickname 'the old man', an odd piece of nomenclature for the genial socialite. He was portrayed in the register by his friend Faltot as furtively slouching along, head bowed and supported by crutches. Subjoined is the dictum 'God be at the old man's side!' (*H*, 431). Some deep-lying seriousness must have been latently present in him. It was only in his fifth year of studies, however, after the departure of that mischief-making fellow Leutwein, that this aspect of his character became more noticeable. We are indebted to Dilthey's pioneering arguments,[20] to Haering's minutely executed analyses[21] and to Lacorte's exact examination of the sources[22] for the fact that, in spite of the difficulties noted above, so much light has been thrown on Hegel's basic attitudes in Tübingen that we can now pursue our own line of approach further.

Looking back in a letter from Bern on his Tübingen days, Hegel formulated for Schelling what had been his secret motivation: 'May the kingdom of God come, and may our hands not rest idle in our lap!' (January 1795, XXVII, 18; cf. the letter to Hölderlin, XXVII, 9). This is an astonishing formulation, and it is moreover biblical. How are we to understand it?

The renewal of society: how is enlightenment possible, not only of the educated classes, but the common man and the people? What is the function of religion in all this, without which such enlightenment is not possible? Hegel had taken this question with him to the seminary. He ought to have found an answer there; after all, he might have expected something from theology.

Unfortunately, however, he could not expect much enlightenment on his question from *this* theology.[23] That is not to say that the Tübingen theology was bad theology. Hegel had good, and to some extent very open-minded, professors. The celebrated orientalist and theologian, C. F. Schnurrer, for example (like A. F. Bök, a representative of an Enlightenment-style rationalism) was not only in contact with Eichhorn and Ernesti, but also knew Rousseau personally. The church historian, F. C. Rösler, had been first and foremost preoccupied with Mosheim and Semler. And C. G. Storr above all, the head of the older Tübingen school and the founder of its 'biblical supernaturalism', was a potent theological force.[24]

In earlier times Lutheran orthodoxy, which Storr represented in a new way, had pursued a *via media* between deism and pietism, the latter being also thought to hold out dangers for the Lutheran doctrinal system. In the first half of the century the ideas of Spener, the father of pietism, had made an impression even on the Tübingen professors C. M. Pfaff[25] and C. E. Weismann.[26] This pietistic influence had soon been overcome at the hands of

---

[20]*op. cit.*, 8-16.
[21]*op. cit.*, 1, 35-115.
[22]*op. cit.*, 117-315.
[23]*op. cit.*, 127-172.
[24]*op. cit.*, 154-172.
[25]Especially in his early work *De praejudiciis theologicis (1718).*
[26]*Institutiones theologiae exegetico-dogmaticae* (1739).

Wolff's pupil B. Bilfinger[27] and of J. G. Canz,[28] the teacher of Ploucquet, by means of a rationalism redolent of Leibniz and Wolff, in which enterprise they received support from the orthodox Lutherans J. F. Cotta and C. F. Sartorius.[29] In Hegel's day Storr used Sartorius' *Dogmatics* in his lectures, students being examined on Sartorius, while he delt with the New Testament writings in his seminars. But the battle fronts had shifted once again in the last third of the century: so all-powerful had the Enlightenment become, that pietism and Lutheran orthodoxy had for the most part joined forces in a defensive manoeuvre. Storr's teacher J. F. Reuss had already beaten a strategic retreat from defending orthodox Lutheran doctrine to vindicating the New Testament writings, in order then to be able indirectly to advance an all the more effective vindication of the Lutheran position precisely on the basis of the absolute priority of the Bible.

But at this juncture Semler's massive assault had interposed, immediately to meet with resolute opposition from Reuss,[30] and, a decade later, from Storr.[31] Reuss withstood Semler by dint of a forceful vindication of the authenticity and authority of that part of the New Testament canon which had suffered sharpest attack and seemed most vulnerable, namely, the Apocalypse. So Semler, early on, became the chief enemy of the older Tübingen school, as this was represented by Storr.

Semler's historical investigations had ascertained an historical development not only in the provinces of ecclesiastical history and doctrine, but also in the Bible itself. This discovery seemed to him to render impossible the practice of setting all the scriptural writings and, if possible, even all their parts and propositions, on the same level, in order to let them all count as dogmatic proofs in a similar mechanical fashion. As far as Storr was concerned, this approach was tantamount to a denial of the theory of verbal inspiration. It dealt a dangerous blow to the dogmatic authority of the Bible in all its parts. This stands out even more clearly when Semler's recourse to a rationalistic 'private religion' and to an attitude of tolerance *vis-à-vis* the various Christian confessions is borne in mind. Consequently Storr was bound to be vitally concerned with the vindication of the authority of Scripture (as against every form of criticism of the canon) and therefore of the religion of revelation (as against every form of the rationalistic religion of nature). He carried out this defence skilfully, through a combination of various methods. With the assistance of the historical research that had been used by his opponent he proves the *authenticity* of the Holy Scriptures. In the case of the Apocalypse, for example, he examines and demonstrates with complete

---

[27]Who, from a Wolffian position, falls back, critically, on Leibniz: *Dilucidationes philosophicae* (1725); *Varia* (1743).
[28]*Philosophiae Leibnitianae et Wolffianae usus in theologia* (1733-1735).
[29]*Compendium theologiae dogmaticae* (1777).
[30]*Verteidigung der Offenbarung Johannis gegen ... Semler* (1772).
[31]*Neue Apologie der Offenbarung Johannis* (1783).

historical and philological precision the writing's authorship, unity and integrity. He sets about proving the *credibility* of the Holy Scriptures with the aid of the apologetic method, which rests upon the basic assumption of the Wolffian-scholastic 'storey theory': *religio naturalis – religio revelata, lumen naturale – lumen fidei.*[32] He has recourse to supernatural factors located in the upper storey – for example, to fulfilled prophecies and miracles – in order to establish the reliability of the Bible; for the trustworthiness of Scripture may not be subjected to any other criterion. In order to render the supernatural authority and the divine inspiration of the whole of Holy Scripture in all its parts unassailable by the rationalists – those who would challenge any mandatory, positive, revealed and supernatural elements in religion – Storr brings a third factor to bear upon his argument. While the Lutheran orthodoxy of the previous century, along with Catholic baroque scholasticism, had availed itself of the philosophy of Aristotle, and while the enlightened divines Bilfinger and Canz, in the company of so many Catholic theologians of this period, had sought refuge in the arms of Leibniz and Wolff, Storr, astonishingly, devoted himself to Kant and, to a lesser extent, to Fichte. According to Storr, we need only see Kant's transcendental critique of pure reason in the correct perspective for it to become clear that pure reason is incompetent and is indeed overstepping its appointed limits, when it wishes to make any statements, negative or positive, concerning the truth-content of revealed religion. Pure reason can only remain silent on the subject of the authority of Scripture. The certainty of this authority proceeds from another source, to wit, from the fact of its divine origin, as this is vouched for by the words of Jesus and the apostles, and confirmed by fulfilled prophecies and miracles. Faith alone, therefore, and not pure reason, is competent in this sphere – a faith, however, which has every reason to believe.

By means of Kant's critique of reason Storr secures the positive character of revealed religion against every form of Enlightenment-style rationalism. Belief in the Trinity, divine providence, the resurrection of Christ and of the dead in general, along with the supernatural origin of the Church and the efficacy of baptism and the Lord's Supper – all this can be neither affirmed nor denied by pure reason, but can only be accepted on the basis of the divine revelation witnessed and attested in Scripture and proved by Storr through innumerable *loca probantia.*[33]

The year 1793 was the last Hegel spent in Tübingen, and on the personal level it was highly significant for him. In this very year the representative work of 'biblical supernaturalism' appeared; and, upon its immediate translation into German, it was adopted forthwith as the official textbook in dogmatics in the state schools of Württemberg. This book was Storr's *Doctrinae christianae pars theoretica e sacris litteris repetita.*[34] The subject-matter of this dogmatics, which was as modern as it was traditional, had doubtless found its

[32]'natural religion – revealed religion, the light of nature – the light of faith'.
[33]'proof texts'.
[34]*The Theoretical Part of Christian Doctrine, Derived from Holy Scripture.*

way into Storr's lectures. It is accordingly all the more astonishing that Hegel appears to have been utterly unaffected by it. His personal writings reveal no sign of any concentrated study of the lectures, nor do they yield any trace of Storr's theology, not even of its distinct concentration upon Jesus' person and teaching, upon Jesus as mediator and reconciler. Maybe the core of this theology was altogether too soft, maybe, precisely as a supernatural theology, its foundation was altogether too natural for it to have been able to command Hegel's respect?

This is not to say that Hegel learned nothing from Storr's theology, but that, if he did learn from it, it was *per oppositionem*. That this was an opposition right across the board would soon be demonstrated – in presuppositions, in method, in purpose and in perspective. He wanted nothing to do with this lukewarm compromise between tradition and the modern age, between dogmatics and criticism, between faith and reason. In keeping with the student's time-honoured right, Hegel skipped a great number of lectures. It must have been no small measure of annoyance that rankled within his breast when later on, in 1794 in Bern, he could write to Schelling in the following malicious vein: 'Until a man of the ilk of Reinhold or Fichte sits upon a chair there [in Tübingen], nothing solid will emerge' (XXVII, 12); and that 'orthodoxy cannot be shaken so long as its profession, itself entailing temporal benefits, is woven into the totality of a state' (XXVII, 16). It goes without saying that the then students at the seminary did not all think along these lines. There also two tendencies were to be discerned, reducible in Hegel's terminology to 'good' and 'mechanical' minds: 'Nowhere is the old system transmitted so staunchly as it is there – and even if this has no influence upon a few good minds, orthodoxy stands its ground among the majority, among the mechanical minds' (to Schelling, XXVII, 12). In the next letter he refers once more to 'the whole gang, always the most numerous, of parrot-like repeaters and copyists, folk without a single thought or higher concern in their head' (XXVII, 16). Schelling of course thought like Hegel, and in a subsequent letter to him he sneered at the pseudo-Kantian culinary arts of these theologians, in whose work '*tamquam ex machina*' such strong philosophical broths are being prepared on *quemcunque locum theologicum* that theology, which was beginning to get over-excited, will presently be striding along in healthier and stronger condition than ever before'[35] (XXVII, 14).

Kant's *Critique of Practical Reason* being employed to rehash reactionary theology! But, Storr would possibly have objected, what should one do as a theologian in a difficult time? Revelation – must it not be vindicated? And in a 'reasonable' vindication must one not occupy the opponents' ground and

---

[35]'as by machine' and 'upon whatever theological topic'.

strike them with their own (i.e. in this context, Kantian) weapons? This all added up to a defensive rational theology, carried out with the assistance of practical reason and of 'a few ingredients of Kant's system' (XXVII, 14). Revelation is drained harmlessly away into glasses of thin concepts, themselves all too transparent to provoke a response of faith. Hegel's criticism is radical. He pours out derision upon the backwardness of this theology: 'Nowhere is the old system transmitted so staunchly as there [in Tübingen]' (to Schelling, XXVII, 12). Again he scorns its bogus modernity, because it 'attempts to conduct the water of new ideas over its own ancient, clattering mills' (XXVII, 12). In some such way this theology continues upon its somnolent course: 'It says, "Yes, that is certainly true", and then it dozes off. In the morning one drinks one's coffee and pours it out for the others as though nothing had happened' (XXVII, 16). But the fact remains that, for good or ill, Hegel had been confronted with theology, and for all his opposition to it, a debate was getting under way here on the subject of Christianity, which was to be of the greatest consequence. (On the lectures to which Hegel went, cf. H, 435).

A certain double-standard was hardly to be avoided in this whole process, and it is noticeable that a different, more feeble, spirit pervades Hegel's sermons from the one that reigns in his theological fragments (H, 175-192: the seminarians preached practice homilies in the refectory to the accompaniment of potato-eating and spoon-clattering). Already Rosenkranz[36] voiced the conjecture that the sermons were *opera operata*.[37] They seem at all events to have been compulsory pieces of work required by the teaching regulations and a replica, moreover, of the customary school-theology. We find here a mixture of lame and flabby orthodoxy (weak presentations of the divinity and resurrection of Christ) with an arid theological version of shallow rationalism; and we encounter a tendency toward general moralising discourse on the subjects of virtue, felicity, duties and the general good of the human race. There is a thoroughly tasteless form of naturalism and eudaemonism here in the following argument: 'When he [man] gives himself up excessively to carnal enjoyment, he ruins his own equipment and renders himself unfit and unserviceable for further and more noble pleasures ... !' (H, 177). But how could one censure this student, when he was praised by his own teachers? It was not indeed on account of his slight and halting pulpit discourse that he found praise ('*in recitando non magnus orator visus*'[38]), but in virtue of his

---

[36]*op. cit.*, 26.
[37]'works performed irrespective of the disposition of the agent'.
[38]'he did not seem to be a great orator in the manner of his delivery'.

organisation of the sermon ('*orationem sacram non sine studio elaboravit*',[39] says Hegel's graduation certificate, *H*, 439).

The cool and official tone of Hegel's sermons may also partially be explained in terms of the less than satisfactory condition of the seminary. By this we do not simply mean the bad living conditions; and, besides, the preacher used to get better food.[40] Rather we mean the extremely critical spiritual state of the seminary, which was viewed with great alarm in the Stuttgart Consistory. Almost everything was in a state of turmoil: the relationship of the students toward authority, toward discipline and order, and toward theology, Church and state, though Haering is surely right when he cautions against painting things too black.[41] At all events the grammar school boy, accustomed as he was to his former freedom, did not feel exactly at ease in the seminary. In his schooldays he had managed to dodge the 'little seminar' and its 'eccentricity'.[42] But now he had got himself thoroughly caught up in 'the monastic temper and the pedantry of the theological seminary'.[43] The strict rules pertaining to discipline and punishment, which could easily lead to servile obedience and hypocrisy, was felt by many seminarians to be a form of pedantry and repression. Schelling speaks expressly of a 'moral despotism' which reigned in the seminary (XXVII, 27f). That Hegel found himself time and again at loggerheads with the house regulations, is attested by his fellow students (*H*, 429ff), by his teachers (434) and finally by himself (apparently he stayed on at home for a longer period than his illness necessitated, *H*, 434).

We may not assume, however, that the seminarians were virtually subjected to spiritual coercion. Their teachers were too deeply influenced by the *Zeitgeist* for that. And there were abundant possibilities for them to engage in 'extra-curricular' activities: they pursued 'unofficial' theology in reaction against what was delivered in the lectures. If they read the Bible in public, then in private they read Voltaire. Hegel was especially drawn to the study of Rousseau, 'believing through such reading to be emancipated from certain widespread prejudices and tacit presuppositions or, as Hegel would put it, to be divested of chains' (*H*, 430). In addition to this there was a theological circle, in which Hegel, Hölderlin and others read and discussed Plato, Kant, Jakobi's Spinoza letters and Hippel's biographies. And then above all there was the 'political club', where Hegel got to know Schelling, who was five years his junior.

---

[39]'he applied himself with diligence to working out his sermon'.
[40]*ibid.*
[41]*op. cit.*, I, 49.
[42]K. Rosenkranz: *op. cit.*, 6.
[43]*ibid.*

In the face of the princely absolutism that had intruded into the regulations and administration of the seminary and against the establishment in Church and theology, enthusiasm for liberty dominated the club. The ideas of 1789, which met with such a response among the students of Tübingen, were spread around the seminary not least by a small group of students from Mömpelgard (Montbeliard) which, although French-speaking, belonged to Württemberg. With some of these students Hegel was on good terms. In this way the ideas of the Revolution were animatedly discussed and French newspapers were devoured. Written on the leaves of the register were such sentiments as '*In tyrannos!*' '*Vive Jean-Jacques!*' and '*Vive la liberté!*' (*H*, 433). Hegel was 'the most fervent speaker in the cause of liberty and equality' and he is said to have planted a liberty tree in or around Tübingen along with Hölderlin, Schelling and others (*H*, 430).[44] Schelling was accused of having translated the *Marseillaise* and Hölderlin composed hymns to liberty and humanity in the spirit of Rousseau. In 1793 an inspection was carried out in the seminary on the orders of the Consistory, in order to suppress the extremely revolutionary spirit and to check whether in fact French anarchy and regicide were defended there. A seminarian was sent down. The territorial prince, the Elector of Württemberg, delivered an address in person in the refectory. Schelling had to present his apologies, and this he did by means of the prudent quotation from Scripture: 'Majesty, we all make many mistakes!'[45]

The result was disarray. Even if thinking and reading remained duty-free, nevertheless a schizophrenic double-standard was inevitable: lectures, examinations and sermons were one thing; circle, club, reading and personal ideas were another. Only after his departure from the theological college does Hegel, now in Switzerland, declare: 'I believe the time has come when one should speak more freely, indeed that one already may do so and that in fact people are already doing it' (to Schelling, 1794, XXVII, 11).

3. Revolution of the Spirit

Thus, for all his outward simplicity, Hegel followed his own ideas and pursued his private theology – increasingly so, as time went on. But he certainly did not take this path as a precocious speculative genius reflecting upon being as such. Hegel's thought had practical motives and developed out of the very concrete experiences of the social situation at that time. Hegel and his Tübingen friends stood under the spell of three powerful movements. In

---

[44] cf. D. Henrich: *op. cit.*, 74.
[45] '*wir fehlen alle mannigfach*'; cf. the *Lutherbibel* rendition of Jas. 3:2,'*Denn wir feilen alle manchfeltig*'.

the first place there was the revolution in the way of thinking heralded and launched by Kant, by which he had at once criticised and consummated the Enlightenment. Secondly, there was the politico-social or 'great Revolution', which had exploded in France with elemental force a year after Hegel's admission to the Tübingen seminary, and which had seen its gruesome climax in the Jacobin dictatorship towards the end of Hegel's student days. Lastly, and in reaction against the two foregoing, was the early Romantic movement, now set to gain very rapidly in strength. Hegel's exertions must be seen against this exceedingly complex and highly explosive intellectual and social horizon.

The problem that he had brought with him from Stuttgart and which gained an added urgency in Tübingen through the unfruitful orthodox school-theology, was that of the relationship of the Enlightenment to the person in the street and, bound up with it, that of religion. How much was decadent in Church, state and people! The key to all doors was furnished as little by the rational Enlightenment as by traditional orthodoxy. A general renewal of society was called for, a renewal which would go beyond the enlightenment of the educated classes and penetrate into the ranks of the people! Toward the end of his time at the theological college this became ever clearer in the minds of Hegel and his friends. How should they not have read the manifold signs of the times, pointing to stormy weather? Was not everything striving after a radical new orientation? Indeed, were there not already powerful signs of its appearance? Had it not begun with the Copernican Revolution in natural science (mathematics, geometry and astronomy) against all reactionaries, temporal and ecclesiastical? And was it not implemented by Kant with a powerful consistency in the realms of philosophy and the human sciences in the triumph of reason over empiricism, authority and tradition? And the great Revolution of liberty and fraternity – had it not, in a neighbouring country, completed the new orientation with gruesome straightforwardness in the province of politico-social life? And was there not amid the contemporary tumult – this too should not be forgotten – a sturdy signpost toward the future in the form of Hellenism (joy, harmony, vivacity, humanity, friendship and silent greatness)? That which was already present, yet which precisely in Germany ran up against stiff opposition, must not go down the drain, but had to become universal. The bright day must emerge from the womb of the dawn! As Schelling afterwards wrote to Hegel from Tübingen, with reference to Kant as the 'originator': 'No, friend, we have not become strangers to one another, but are still side by side on the old paths. If they have taken a turning which perhaps neither of us suspected, yet things still remain the same with us two. We both desire to go further, each of us desires to prevent the greatness brought forth by our age ending up once again with the mendacious leaven of past times. This greatness shall remain pure among us, just as it proceeded from its originator's mind. It shall be handed on by us if possible to posterity, without being reduced by disfigurements and modifications to the ancient, conventional form, but in its entire perfection, in its most exalted state. And we shall hand it on loudly proclaiming that battle to the finish – to victory or defeat – is being offered to the whole previous ordering of the world and of science' (XXVII, 20f).

This then was the great concern of the hour, and for the theology student Hegel it was a socio-political and at the same time an essentially religious concern, as he himself put it, referring both to Scripture and to Kant's *Critique of Practical Reason:* 'May God's kingdom come!' (XXVII, 18). In Kant's *Critique of Practical Reason* the biblical expression 'kingdom of God' is syonymous with the highest good, the realm of liberty, the realm of ethics and ethical community.[46] With the 'coming of the kingdom of God' Hegel and his friends did not have a political revolution in mind. Marxist interpreters have very much held it against them that they did not cause their revolutionary theories to take effect in revolutionary praxis, in order not only to interpret the world but to change it. In the end of the day this may well be a case of falling into the trap of thinking unhistorically.[47] They too, and Hegel in particular, wanted to change the world. But the small-scale German world of princely states was definitely not ripe for the 'great Revolution' in the same way as the French Kingdom, which was centrally governed and politically much further advanced. Only if one took the step of emigration was direct revolutionary action actually feasible at that time. This step was in fact taken by an acquaintance of Hegel, the seminarian C. F. Reinhardt, under the inspiration of Rousseau and Schiller and after what had been for him an oppressive time at the seminary. He was charged with official diplomatic missions as early as the outbreak of the Revolution from 1791 onwards; in 1799 he was even Foreign Minister for a short time, and he went on to receive the confidence of Napoleon and to die in Paris in 1837. In a memorial address before Parliament Talleyrand described him as 'Tübingen's gift to France' Even so, Reinhardt remained the exception.

At first Germany's leading minds were certainly heavily biassed in favour of the French Revolution: not only Kant, Jacobi and Fichte, but also Klopstock, Herder, Wieland, Schiller, Novalis and Friedrich Schlegel. The enthusiasm displayed by the Tübingen club for the ideas of 1789 was not a mere 'playing at Revolution', as Haym and Lukács suppose, measuring Hegel against the

---

[46]See *Critique of Practical Reason and Other Writings in Moral Philosophy* (tr. L. W. Beck, Chicago, 1949), 229-236. On recent concepts of the kingdom of God, cf. E. Hirsch: *Geschichte der neueren evangelischen Theologie.*
[47]cf. the apposite comments of C. Lacorte: *op. cit.,* 175-180.

yardstick of later programmes. Hegel held fast to the ideas of the French Revolution his whole life long. But just toward the end of his stay in Tübingen the revolutionary dictatorship of the Jacobins was getting under way. The September murders of 1792 had already damped down sympathy for the Revolution abroad, Louis XVI had been executed in January 1793, and the frightful time of the Committee of Public Safety under Robespierre was beginning, with mass executions running into thousands. All this came as an endorsement of the influential book by the liberal English statesman Edmund Burke, *Reflections on the Revolution in France* (1790), which appeared in German translation in that year of terror 1793, and which spoke up for the freedom of the individual and for justice in the state, while setting its face against violent political upheaval. It was a fundamental book as far as the early Romantic movement was concerned. The Jacobin terror was condemned by Hegel, Schelling and Hölderlin, as it was by Herder, Schiller, Klopstock and others, yet without abandoning the aims of the Revolution.

More was at stake in this for our Tübingen men than mere political revolution. As far as they were concerned the crux of the matter was a revolution of the spirit. What they had in mind was not simply a revolutionary political programme, which had small prospect of realisation at that time anyway; rather, they set out to formulate a humanitarian programme encompassing all fields and branches of knowledge: literature and art, politics and philosophy, and, above all, religion.[48] It was to be in this sense a thoroughly concrete and fundamental renewal of society, its revitalisation in the light and in the power of the ideas of the new age. Here was the vision that held the three room-mates together. 'Their intention was once more to activate the torpid state of life to be found in every field, above all in Church (religion), state and ethics, and hence, according to the idiom of the day, in every "positive ordinance". This they sought to reanimate from the inside. They expected this rebirth to arise primarily from the dissemination and consolidation of the novel ideas of the time.'[49] So, as Hölderlin reports, they afterwards took leave of each other 'with the catchphrase "kingdom of God"' (XXVII, 9). This is the basis of their 'hopes' (XXVII, 25), of 'the cosmopolitan

---

[48]cf. the oldest systematic programme of German Idealism in Hölderlin: *Werke* IV, I, 297-299.
[49]T. Haering: *op. cit.*, I, 38. The accurate original text of the poem quoted here is given at the end of Haering's book (cf. also *H*, 380f):

> 'Bliss of assurance,
> Faith of ancient bond,
> Bond that no oath did seal,
> To find it firmer and more ripe,
> "To live unto free truth alone",
> Ne'er to make peace with the law
> That rules both heart and mind.'

ideas' (XXVII, 18) concerning which Hegel later wrote; and, indeed, looking back, he had already expressed himself on this subject in the poem 'Eleusis' of August 1796, addressed to Hölderlin.

Each in his own way, the three seminarians struggled for this 'kingdom of God'. Schelling forged well into the lead, elegant and yet with something unearthly about him, titanic and revolutionary. With sympathetic understanding and brilliant fantasy, rapidly surveying the whole field, always finding new paths, believing in the omnipotence of man and his science, he shone brightly ahead of his friend – and dazzled him. Hegel, who was five years older than Schelling, tramped along behind him, as always straightforward, circumspect and somewhat clumsy, but for all that steady and upright, sober and down to earth. Sure in what he was doing, indefatigable with his calm rationality and steady pace, he was like a mountain guide in the Alps. And Hölderlin, was he at the rear or really out in front? In fact, a pure soul full of love and feeling, of nostalgia and dreams, he was hovering gently over his friends, lost in thought but, in a childlike way, open to all that is. More deeply affected at an emotional level than the other two, he burned his waxen wings in the sun he reached too soon. Everything was still at the beginning, they were still close to one another, their ways had not yet diverged. As Hegel put it, 'the invisible church' united them as their 'point of union' (to Schelling, January 1795, XXVII, 18; Kaufann, 301). 'The power of feeling that inspires them in the seminary is nothing less than the desire to mould the world anew from top to bottom. It is hard to transpose ourselves into the eschatological hope of that generation, where such determination outlasts the first youthful ecstasy.'[50]

In this way they had set out on their journey, without as yet a fixed destination and without a proper plan; only the direction was clear. They took with them only what they could use there and then. They were subject to influence from many quarters: from Rousseau and Kant, Schiller and Lessing, Spinoza, Jacobi, Mendelssohn and Shaftesbury. Beyond all differences they saw in these thinkers the single set of ideas that they too had espoused. An important catalytic function seems to have been exercised by the young Schiller, in whose periodical *Thalia* Hegel's best friend Hölderlin had published some poems and the *Fragment of Hyperion* (1794), a first draft of his epistolary novel. Schiller's principal concern was not religion and the philosophy of history, as Hegel's was, but rather the fields of aesthetics and ethics. Even so, he had sought to subject the philosophy of Kant to a critical reconstruction in a manner similar to Hegel's subsequent attempt. This he did by taking up Winckelmann's idealisation of classical Hellenism, along with Klopstock's, von Gerstenberg's and Herder's revaluation of Germanic folk-

[50]E. Staiger: *Der Geist der Liebe,* 13.

tradition and folk-culture, and Rousseau's ideal of the renewal of humanity. By this means he meant to emphasise against Kant the unity of understanding and fantasy, of moral law and inclination. However, a detailed appraisal of the influence of these modern minds (especially of Kant) upon the three seminarians is a difficult task; many ideas, for example those of Rousseau, were simply in the air. The three were undoubtedly more concerned with basic attitudes than with questions of detail. At issue were the renewal and quickening of the numbed spirit in Church, state and society. The great catchwords beloved of the friends, which have been pertinently analysed by Haering,[51] are to be understood from the perspective of this shared basic mood. *Freedom*: understood not only as the *liberté* of the Revolution, but also in the sense of Schiller's *Räuber* and *Don Carlos,* and of Kant's notions of ethical autonomy (*Critique of Practical Reason,* 1788) and creative personality (*Critique of Judgment,* 1790). *Love*: the power of fellowship in Schiller's hymn *Blessed through Love,* the primal force in Spinoza's world, Plato's *eros* and the love of Eckhart, Böhme and Shaftesbury, the *fraternité* of the Revolution and finally, all else notwithstanding, the *agape* of St John's Gospel. *Hen kai pan*:[52] not without qualification, as when, in temporary dependence upon Spinoza, it became an antitheistic, pantheistic slogan in Hölderlin and in the young Schiller of the *Theosophie des Julius* (as has been demonstrated in the case of the Tübingen Hegel by Haering[53]), but probably understood with greater reticence as an expression for the 'universe's immense liveliness and inner unity of life', as a sign of the 'living universal connection and unity of all being with God'. It was a piety and spirituality that embraced God, man and nature.

All of this goes far beyond Kant's conception of the 'kingdom of God': 'Christian ethics', says Kant, 'present a world wherein reasonable beings single-mindedly devote themselves to the moral law; this is the Kingdom of God, in which nature and morality come into a harmony, which is foreign to each as such, through a holy Author of the world, Who makes possible the derived highest good.'[54] Here we come upon that old sore in the modern world, at first pasted over in many ways. We referred to it in the Introduction as the unreconciled world. This sore was like a fissure wrought by a multiplicity of contrary forces and unfolding in numerous twists and turns and complicated retrogressive steps. Reality itself had as it were come unstitched at the seams, leading to an alienation of the world from God and of God from the world, to a worldless God and to a godless world. In the furthest

---

[51]*op. cit.,* I, 40-47.
[52]'one and all'.
[53]*op. cit.,* I, 45-47.
[54]*Critique of Practical Reason* (tr. Beck), 231.

depths of this fissure is to be found the potential, indeed the actual, dissolution of Christology into an undiluted God and a mere man. According to classical incarnational theology the Incarnate Word was the locus of the event of mediation between God and man. Now, in the Enlightenment, however, there stood on the one side the divine *logos asarkos,* the Word that has nothing to do with the flesh, and on the other the human *sarx alogikos,* the flesh that neither can nor will know anything of the Word. The *true God and true man,* which according to the Christian proclamation is concretely manifest in the Incarnate Word, appears to have been relinquished, on the one hand in favour of a *Verbum Dei purum,* an ideal God, a *Deus deisticus,* and on the other in favour of a *homo Jesus purus,* an ideal man, a *homo humanisticus.* On the periphery of this vigorous and at times even violent development which reached its climax in the Enlightenment there had always been novel, comprehensive attempts at mediation. These can be found as early as the dawn of the modern age, stimulated by mediaeval undercurrents, in Giordano Bruno and then in Spinoza. And now the counter-movement against the rationalist-deistic Enlightenment and even against the critical philosophy of Kant had begun, taking its point of departure from Hamann's religious thought, Jacobi's philosophy of feeling and Herder's philosophy of history. Even so, all these essays in mediation seemed to get stuck on one of the two sides without quite managing to reach the other. Even if reference was made, as in the case of Kant's 'kingdom of God' to the 'Christian doctrine of morals',[55] the theological question remains: What recognisable middle term is there between God and man when a mediatory salvation-event had been and remained excluded from the field of vision? Was it not inevitable under these conditions that thinking people would once more come perilously close to an acosmic panteism or even to an atheistic pancosmism? Did not these alternatives represent unintended sham mediations for the very reason that the middle term (*terminus medius*) was incompetent to integrate and able only to eliminate one or the other extreme? Were they not in the last resort unhistorical attempts at mediation because they sought reconciliation of the world with God in an imaginary X and not in the historical event of the cross? The problem of mediation remained on the agenda. Was there, in this thoroughly muddled intellectual situation, any ground to hope for a *Christian* mediation?

4. Religion and Society

In his grammar school days Hegel had not bothered his head a great deal with Christ and Christianity. The great significance of his time in Tübingen,

---

[55]*ibid.*

however, lay in the fact that the theological student was obliged to busy himself with these issues. Although his head was full of the Enlightenment and of relics of orthodoxy, nevertheless, alongside every form of Hellenism, he became increasingly absorbed in the significance of Christianity. And while, during his first years in the seminary, he had sauntered cavalierly through the domains of philosophy and theology, towards the end of his time there his occupation with Christianity took on a serious aspect. This development had its roots in the hidden reorientation effected within the group of friends. Yet even at this stage, Hegel's interest was by no means of a theoretical and speculative sort. Continually collecting materials and meditating on them, he was rather disposed to be stimulated and carried along than to take the lead and become productive himself. But his concern with Christianity was serious and concentrated; it penetrated to the roots of the matter, and, characteristically, it had above all a practical and social objective. The critical situation of society, the condition of the Church joylessly fossilised in dogma and fixed structures, the tattered, authoritarian and decadent state, the superstition and sluggishness that characterised the body of the nation – these factors were not considered by Hegel to be summoning him, as with Hölderlin, to prophetic and arousing poetry, nor, as with Schelling, to far-reaching speculation, but rather to practical and reforming thought. He did not permit his brilliant friends and his wide reading to encourage him to erect his own system, but to think through the practical, social tasks of the day. How could fresh life be breathed into these fossilised forms and movement be injected into their structures? Hegel deemed religion of decisive importance precisely from his humanitarian and socio-political standpoint. And it was in this social dimension that his reflections now centred on Christianity. Already at the grammar school it had seemed to him that the person in the street could only share in the new age by means of religion (*H*, 37). The problem on which Hegel now begins to work intensively, in Tübingen and then supremely in Bern, can be more precisely formulated as that of religion in its social dimension, and of Christianity as a folk religion (a concept which, together with that of the spirit of a people, originates above all with Montesquieu and Herder).

This socially vigorous, lively folk religion, which was meant to be the model of Christianity – what does it look like? We give consideration here to the first of the fragments published by Nohl under the title *Folk Religion and Christianity*,[56] which is dated by its editor to the end of Hegel's time in

---

[56]Knox' translation of the *Early Theological Writings* specifically *excludes* these fragments, unfortunately. The ET available is in H. S. Harris: *Towards the Sunlight: Hegel's Development 1770-1801*, Oxford, 1972, 481-516. I have referred to page numbers as 'Harris' throughout this section. (The translation differs, of course, from that made in the text above).

Tübingen (*N*, 1-29, 335-359[57]). When all due allowance is made for its provisional character and for the varied influences at work in the framing and solution of the problems with which it deals, it is an astonishingly original and unified product.

This first fragment, which in its turn consists of partly unfinished minor fragments, begins with the statement that '[r]eligion is one of the most important concerns of our life'. It describes the vast importance of religion in daily life from a thoroughly practical angle: 'already as children we were taught to stammer prayers to the Deity, already our little hands were folded together so that we might raise them to the Supreme Being, and our memory was burdened with a collection of sentences then as yet incomprehensible to us, for future use and comfort in our life' (*N*, 3; Harris, 481). The 'we' is significant. The whole fragment confirms how right it was to defend Hegel's personal religiosity in his Stuttgart and Tübingen days against repeatedly expressed doubts. A certain measure of religiosity, albeit in the manner of the Enlightenment, cannot be denied the young Hegel. There is corroboration of what was said above especially on the subject of his diary. Even if not practicable without further ado for the masses, Hegel maintains that the following is of central importance for the wise man: 'belief in a wise and kindly providence and, if the belief is a living one and of the right kind, total submissiveness to God as well'. For Hegel this belief in providence is 'the chief doctrine of the Christian Church . . . in that all that is recited there amounts in a nutshell to the unmeritable love of God – and furthermore that, year in, year out, God is represented as always near and present, and as bringing about everything that takes place around us' (*N*, 22; Harris, 500). In addition to the religion that embraces man's whole life from his youth up there remains man's reflection 'when he grows older, on the nature and attributes of this Being, in particular on the relationship of the world to this Being toward which all his feelings are directed' (*N*, 3; Harris, 481). Hegel's critical attitude to the religion of his day is an argument not against, but for his own religious commitment, which in fact typified that of many a German of the Enlightenment. His critique of religion is aimed not at the abolition, but at the renewal of religion in a modern enlightened society.

Onesided quotation and arbitrary interpretation are the customary means whereby interpreters whose dearest wish is to make of the young Hegel at the very least a potential Feuerbach bring their pet scheme into disrepute. Against this it is well to bear in mind how Hegel defines the essence of *religion* and how, already at this juncture, he is prepared to pass beyond a sophistical kind of Enlightenment: 'Implicit in the concept

---

[57]On the dating see *N*, 404; for confirmation of this view see G. Schuler: *op. cit.*, 128, no. 32.

of religion is that it is not mere knowledge concerning God, his attributes, the relationship of ourselves and the world to him and the continued existence of our souls after death. After all, these are things that at a pinch can be apprehended by reason alone or be made known to us by other means. Religion is not mere historical or reasoned knowledge. Instead it concerns the heart, and it has an influence on our feelings and on the determination of our will. This is the case partly because our duties and the laws receive stronger emphasis by dint of being presented to us as the laws of God; and partly because the notion of the grandeur and the loving-kindness of God toward us inspires our heart with awe and with feelings of humility and gratitude. Religion therefore gives morality and its motives a fresh and more noble impetus, it furnishes a new and stronger barrier against the power of the sensual urges' (*N*, 5; Harris, 483).

Hegel's concern was the revivification of personal religion: 'All that matters is subjective religion' (*N*, 8; Harris, 485). Hegel's reforming zeal is demonstrated in his polemic against an objectified and arid religion of the understanding, and in his espousal of a lived subjective religion, which nevertheless does not exclude, but includes religious belief of a purified, simplified and universally human sort, related to ethical practice. There is room for a *fides quae creditur* (*N*, 6; Harris, 484) and 'some few fundamental propositions' (*N*, 8; Harris, 485). Subjective religion is much the same among good people; its objective aspect can have almost whatever colour it pleases – what makes me a Christian to you makes you a Jew to me, says Nathan – for religion is a matter of the heart, which often deals inconsistently with the dogmas accepted by the understanding or the memory. The most honourable men are certainly not always those who have speculated the most about religion, those who often transform their religion into theology, i.e. often exchange the abundance and sincerity of religion for cold knowledge and verbal display' (*N*, 10; Harris, 488).

Hegel's subjective religious commitment is always most clearly in evidence when, with his eye to the Greeks, he stands up for the qualities of humanity, joy, courage, cheerfulness, gracefulness, determination, liberty and love, against a joyless and gloomy form of Protestant Christianity (*N*, 8f, 22f, 26-29; Harris, 485f, 500f, 504-7). Precisely from this standpoint Hegel can then vigorously advocate a purified and realistic belief in providence, in which pain and misfortune remain pain and misfortune throughout (cf. *N*, 22f; Harris, 500f). 'The only true comfort in suffering (there is no consolation for pain; one can only set spiritual strength against it) is trust in God's providence; everything else is empty chatter that glances off the heart' (*N*, 20; Harris, 499).

For all the accentuation of subjective religion, however, we discern no 'root and branch condemnation' of the 'ceremonial apparatus'.[58] On the contrary, Hegel emphasises that religion consists of 'three things': 'a) concepts; b) essential customs; c) ceremonies' (*N*, 24; Harris, 502). In this classification he places baptism and the eucharist – when correctly, i.e. for him morally, understood – in the second category, and he regards ceremonies too as necessary for folk religion, even when they are erroneously taken by many for the very essence of religion (*N*, 24; Harris, 502).

Thus this first cluster of fragments mirrors the Enlightenment and the

---

[58]C. Lacorte: *op. cit.*, 83.

things that paved its way, while at the same time leading emphatically beyond it. The texts cited are in the first instance, without their author needing always to be aware of it in detail, a good recapitulation of the while modern development within Christianity. It almost seems as though all the spirits of the past, frequently unrecognised by the one who conjures them up, were having a secret rendezvous. Here is the spirit of nominalism: in religion Hegel attaches great importance to 'experience' (*N*, 12, 15; Harris 489-90, 492-3), to the will (Kant's 'postulate of practical reason' crops up here; *N*, 8; Harris, 485-6), to individuality (in everything that Hegel calls 'subjective religion'; *N*, 9), and to 'liberty' (with which folk religion goes 'hand in hand'; *N*, 27). And here is the spirit of humanism: religion should exist primarily for man; it should be conducive not only to 'putting hands together' and 'bowing knees and heart before the Holy One', but also to 'cheerful delight in human joys', 'to the expression of human powers, whether of courage or of humanity, and to being glad, to the enjoyment of life' (*N*, 8f; Harris, 486). There is not a serious word on the subjects of sin and redemption, but on the contrary much praise for bright and cheery Hellenism in contrast to dark Christianity (*N*, 23, 26-28; Harris 501, 504-7). Christ is spoken of in the same terms as Socrates and many pious pagans (*N*, 10f; Harris 487-8). Here is also in shadowy form the spirit of the late Reformation; the individual loosed from ecclesiastical ties constructs for himself his religion and church; freely enquiring and assured of grace, he is now so certain of the latter that he no longer needs to talk of it. And here finally is the spirit of modern philosophy: the 'lofty demand reason makes upon mankind, whose validity we so often recognise with a full heart' (*N*, 4; Harris, 481) is presupposed as a matter of course; bound up with this, alongside the implicit deism, we find Leibniz's optimism (*N*, 22f; Harris, 500f) and Wolff's rational proof of dogma (*N*, 13; Harris, 490-1). We find too Reimarus' rationalisation of the Bible (*passim*; and cf. the secularised biblical texts to do with the salt of the earth and the light of the world; *N*, 4; Harris, 482) and Planck's demystification of the creeds (*N*, 5f, 14; Harris 483, 491-2), Lessing's parable of the ring and his doctrine of tolerance (*N*, 10; Harris 487-8), along with Semler's distinction between the natural that is binding and the positive that is not binding, between private and public religion (*N*, 19ff, 26; Harris 496-8, 504; cf. the line of development Semler-Rousseau-Gibbon-Mendelssohn). The names are assuredly not found in Hegel; he only quotes Lessing along with Fichte and Mendelssohn. Nor ought we to maintain any direct genetic dependence right across the board, as we may with reference to Schiller, Kant, Rousseau and Herder. Even so the spirits of these dead men are alive. Accordingly, in reaction against theological speculation and ethical casuistry that have become unworthy of belief (*N*, 11, 12f, 16f; Harris 489-91, 493-5), we encounter, as the result of a long development, the religion of the new age. It is objectively grounded in the consciousness of God, in the natural moral law and in the immortality of the soul (*N*, 3, ;5 Harris 481-3), and it is vigorously activated by self-produced virtue (*N*, 20, 22; Harris 497-8, 500). This religion is the same for all people (whether they call their Jehovah 'Jupiter' or 'Brahma'; *N*, 107f), and its principal importance resides in its being a form of morality designed to educate man to humanity (*N*, 5, 16, 20, 26; Harris 483, 493-4, 497-8, 504).

Yet this résumé of the past, at once reflecting unbroken Enlightenment and washed out orthodoxy, depicts but *one* side of Hegel's 'folk religion'. We must even say that this is the less important side. According to Hegel the real emphasis patently lies elsewhere. Steps are taken which point clearly beyond the Enlightenment and even beyond Kant to the future; this was well worked out by Haering.[59] An unquestionable and above all practical Kantianism is certainly to be found in this fragment, although Haering[60] vigorously disputes at least any *direct* marked influence of Kant's *theoretical* writings on the young Hegel. Evidence of Kantian influence is to be found in the concept of the ethical as unconditioned but free subordination to a law transcending the individual, in a dualism (albeit limited to the plane of abstract systematics) between reason and the senses in morality (*N*, 4; Harris, 482), and then in formulas such as 'idea of holiness' (*N*, 17; Harris 495), 'moral motives' (*N*, 18; Harris 495), 'legality' (*N*, 18; Harris, 495) and 'esteem for the law' (*N*, 18; Harris, 496). But just as Hegel at that early stage was not an unreserved disciple of the Enlightenment, even so he was not an uncompromising Kantian. On the contrary! He holds that Kant's high morality could mean nothing to the masses. The actual object of his own remarks is compromise! We deliberately do not yet use the word dialectic at this juncture. To begin with, Hegel has in mind an often vague compromise between reason and the senses (the senses woven through with reason; *N*, 4; Harris, 482), between individuality and the spirit of community, between an abstract religion of reason and the Church's faith or, rather, a religion of feeling based solely on the emotions. And what purpose was all this meant to serve? Its practical aim is expressed throughout the whole essay and particularly in the last part: to oppose the 'partition between life and doctrine' (*N*, 26; Harris, 504), to uphold an alliance between religion and life, a folk-life vibrating with religion but also embracing other spheres as well. This is to be achieved, not through revolutionary political subversion, but through a spiritual transformation. Folk religion is not regarded as the object of some philosophy of religion or history, but as the best means for educating the people! From the perspective of his

---

[59]*op. cit.*, 1, 62-115.
[60]*op. cit.*, 1, 55.

entirely practical concern for the folk-life that was to be fashioned, and in a polemically anti-Enlightenment and anti-Kantian manner, Hegel places emphasis on two points: on the importance of heart and feeling in religion (against all forms of theological rationalism; e.g., *N,* 12ff; Harris, 489-92); and on love and altruism (against an exclusive private religion and any individualistic or egotistical mentality; *N,* 18f; Harris 496f).

Toward the end of the fragment everything is summarised into a kind of programme answering the question: 'How must folk religion be constituted?' The reply is as follows:

'A. I. Its doctrines must be founded upon universal reason.

II. Fantasy, heart and the senses must not come away empty-handed.

III. It must be so constituted that all needs of life and the public acts of state are bound up with it.

B. What does it have to avoid? Fetishism – in the form, particularly prevalent in our verbose age, of the belief that one has satisfied the demand of reason through tirades on Enlightenment and the like; men are for ever at loggerheads with one another about dogmatic doctrines, and in the meantime doing less and less to improve themselves or others.'(*N,* 20; Harris, 498-9; and cf. the remarks to be found in *N,* 21-29; Harris 499-507).

We shall doubtless detect a host of influences behind Hegel's new emphasis. We shall think, for example, of the folk-spirit (*Volksgeist*) in Montesquieu and Herder (hence the German word folk religion, *Volksreligion,* that possibly originated with Hegel himself), of Shaftesbury's altruism, of the importance of feeling in Mendelssohn, of the idealisation of Hellenism in Winckelmann, Wieland, Herder and Schiller, and of the difference between a pure religion of reason and true religion in Fichte etc. Certainly much in Hegel has been taken from books and then independently reworked. He has often adopted a certain terminology and immediately given it another, personally determined, content. It was a studied collection, and more than this. This treatment of the theme of folk religion is altogether the first of its kind and in terms of arrangement and intention it is clear and independent. It appears here as a summary of Hegel's previous personal studies and as a first original and spontaneous formulation of his own philosophical and theological perspective, responding to all the contemporary streams of thought with disciplined reflection and clever reserve, but without identifying itself with any of them. Alongside Schiller's already mentioned methodological and formal influence there appears an inward kinship between Hegel and Rousseau, whom he was forever being caught reading in Tübingen. He has indeed nothing to do with Rousseau's unbalanced character or with certain radical aspects of his teaching (cultural pessimism, opposition to property law and science). Even so, in addition to every aspect of the Enlightenment, to which Rousseau too is heavily committed, the following factors connect them with each other: the living alliance of reason and the senses; the authority of heart, fantasy and feeling; natural altruism (sympathy, friendship, love); the pedagogical and anti-authoritarian tendency (let grow!); the sense for supra-individual unity (*volonté generale – Volksgeist*); the desire to renew society in every sphere, from art to politics and religion; and finally also the confession of faith of the Vicar of Savoy.

Some caution is appropriate on the other hand in face of the oft repeated claim that Hegel was dependent on '*Swabian spiritual ancestors*'. After J. Klaiber, in the *Festschrift* for the 400th anniversary of the University of Tübingen in 1877, had already delineated the political, cultural and religious aspects of the common Swabian homeland of Hegel, Hölderlin and Schelling, and after W. Betzendörfer had carried out a precise examination of life in the Tübingen seminary in Hegel's day in 1922, the time was perhaps especially ripe in 1938 to give a comprehensive explanation of Hegel from the viewpoint of 'nationality' (*Volkstum*). R. Schneider's research into spiritual ancestry went back from Storr, Gottfried Ploucquet and the general 'mood of the time', via Oetinger, Hahn, Bengel and Swabian pietism, to Jokob Böhme, Paracelsus and the Renaissance, demonstrating pantheistic or pantheising factors and parallels for concepts such as life, spirit, love, Logos, totality etc. in these 'Swabian spiritual ancestors' of Hegel and Schelling. All of this is doubtless important for local Swabian history; but beyond an interesting account of some analogies in the history of thought, which in the last analysis are not of unshakeable validity, Schneider was nowhere able to show from the sources any direct dependence of the young Hegel on these 'ancestors'. In particular no direct relationship of Hegel to the Bengel pupil F. C. Oetinger, 'the Wizard of the South', can be proved, nor to Gottfried Ploucquet, who, in the last phase of his development, taking Leibniz and Wolff as his point of departure, had turned his attention to Oetinger. Ploucquet, however, was no longer teaching during Hegel's time in Tübingen. (Against Schneider cf., above all, C. Lacorte.[61])

We can already discover in isolation, in these few pages of fragments, elements which Hegel afterwards brings to a grandiose systhesis. For example, the unity of religion, morality, history and political freedom (*N*, 27; Harris, 505), the significance of sacrifice (*N*, 24f; Harris, 503-4) and the spirit of a people (*Volksgeist*; *N*, 26; Harris, 504), religion as centre and pivot of inclinations and thoughts (*N*, 3; Harris, 481). Although more on the margin here, the statements about love were to be important for the future. Love unites people among themselves and with God; it 'has something in common with reason' (*N*, 18; Harris, 496) and, as the 'unmeritable love of God', it is what 'everything boils down to' in belief in providence (*N*, 22; Harris 500f).

[61]*op. cit.*, 128-134, 150-153.

53

Despite some basic differences, from this perspective we see more of a personal nature even in the sermons (e.g., the emphasis on love, *H*, 180, 184-192; on the kingdom of God, *H,* 179-182; and on the spirit of forgiveness, *H,* 184-192), just as we notice, on the other hand, the connection between Hegel's basic tendency of thought and particular compulsory academic essays (e.g., the essay on the resurgence of the Church or the other on morality and belief in immortality).

Of greater importance from the viewpoint of Christian theology, however – and the young Hegel was at the end of the day a student of Christian theology – is the fact that it nowhere appears that Hegel was seized in a lively and inward fashion by the Christian faith, by the figure of Christ himself, during this time in Tübingen. Certainly Hegel had been brought in Tübingen to an encounter with theology, certainly also to an encounter with Christianity; and this is truly a fact full of significance for the future. On the other hand, the converse is also true: on the basis of all that we know not only from this first theological fragment but from Hegel's time in Tübingen as a whole – and this is something which ought not to surprise us overmuch against the background of the situation in Tübingen that we have described (theological college, university, the general circumstances obtaining at the time) – Hegel does not actually seem to be existentially affected by the Christian faith, at any rate if we are to mean by this faith in the New Testament sense. Hegel hardly speaks of Christianity at all and, when he does speak of it, then it is mostly in a critical vein, indeed with extreme dislike and joylessness (cf. *N,* 26f, 256f; Harris 504-5). His sermons are 'of astonishingly average quality' (*H,* 446), being more academic papers than addresses, insipid and devoid of any religious fire. Neither the uplifting formulas at the beginning nor the hymns he quotes at the end (these are not Lutheran psalmic hymns!) can dispel this impression. Holy Scripture is certainly quoted, but the sermon itself does not grow out of Scripture; the latter is used as a peg on which to hang the theme to be treated or as a source for arguments.

And Christ himself? It seems that he is hardly *persona grata* with the young theologian. In the sources that lie before us he is conspicuous by being almost entirely kept from view. His name is invoked twice in the fragment in contexts of secondary importance and he is accorded roughly the same dignity as Socrates. Even in Hegel's correspondence immediately after his sojourn in Tübingen the person of Christ plays no role. The effect of the assertion of Christ's divinity in the sermons is conventional, that of the picture of the man Jesus drawn there without colour or vigour.

From our theological viewpoint we may no longer suppress the theological questions that we have stifled hitherto. Does Christ say anything at all to the young theologian? Does he say anything to him in the way of a decisive event of salvation? Is the young Hegel a believer in the New Testament sense or is he, when all is said and done, only a religious fellow without any strict ties? Is the theology which shapes his thought and which he reproduces aware of any serious talk of revelation? Is not the religion of revelation for him only a special case of a universal religion of humanity, making itself felt only on the periphery of the fragment? And when we look at Hegel's programme for the structure of a folk religion in modern society (*N*, 20f; Harris, 499), we find no serious word on the subjects of grace, sin, man's creatureliness and wretchedness . . . There is talk of faith, particularly in the sense of faith in providence (e.g., *N*, 6, 8, 9, 10, 23; Harris 484, 486-7, 501). But looked at theologically, the question is: What tips the scales: faith that trusts or autonomous reason? the grace that comes as a gift or nature under its own steam?

In the first sentence of the programme for a folk religion the primacy of reason is unequivocally stated; 'its doctrines must be founded upon universal reason' (*N*, 20; Harris, 499). Already at the beginning of the fragment Hegel speaks with emphasis of the 'ideas of reason' which 'animate the whole tissue of his feelings' (*N*, 4; Harris, 482), and of the 'lofty demand reason makes upon mankind, whose validity we so often recognise with a full heart' (*N*, 4; Harris, 481). In explanation of the first sentence of his programme he specifies that 'even when their authority reposes on a divine revelation, doctrines must necessarily be constituted in such a way that they are actually authorised by the universal reason of men, and that every man perceives and feels their obligatory character on becoming aware of them' (*N*, 21; Harris, 499). From the fact of religion's rational basis Hegel infers that it has to be as practical as possible (no 'intolerant creeds'), simple (devoid of the 'apparatus of learning' and of the 'luxury of laborious proofs') and humane ('commensurate with the level of morality . . . on which a people stands'). Looked at as a whole this is a religion with a meagre and vague substance. It has some few truths and principles, but their content is left completely undefined.

At stake here is a 'a pure religion of reason, which worships God in spirit and in truth, and which places its service in virtue alone' (*N*, 17). Nietzsche once remarked with malicious irony that 'among Germans I am immediately understood when I say that philosophy is ruined by the blood of theologians. The Protestant minister is the grandfather of German philosophy, Protestantism itself is the latter's *peccatum originale*. Definition of Protestantism: the partial paralysis of Christianity – *and* of reason . . . One needs only to pronounce the words "Tübingen Seminary", in order to understand *what* German philosophy really is at bottom, i.e. theology *in disguise*.'[62] Might we

---

[62] *The Antichrist,* sec. 10; quoted from *Collected Works,* vol. 16 (tr. A. M. Ludovici, Russell & Russell Inc., New York, 1964), 135f.

not by the same token pointedly ask the Tübingen Hegel whether this theology of his is not in fact perhaps a *philosophy* in disguise?

It is important to set out and to interpret this problem aright. We recall how already as a grammar school boy Hegel had stated in programmatic form his intention 'to examine our inherited and received opinions, even those concerning which neither the doubt nor the suspicion ever crossed our minds that they might be utterly false or only half true' (*H*, 47f), and how in the seminary he intended 'to be emancipated from certain widespread prejudices and tacit presuppositions or, as Hegel would put it, to be divested of chains' (*H*, 430). And we remember how later on, in the poem from which we quoted above, he pledged 'to live unto free truth alone, "Ne'er to make peace with the law, That rules both heart and mind"' (*H*, 380f), and finally how in the fragment he emphasises the necessity of the Enlightenment (*N*, 12-20; Harris, 489-99). Despite all this, however, Hegel in no way naively shared the basic prejudice of the Enlightenment: 'This basic prejudice of the Enlightenment is prejudice against prejudices in general and is thereby tantamount to depriving tradition of its power.'[63]

Hegel takes as his starting-point the insight that 'the understanding is a courtier who willingly complies with the whims of his master: it knows how to find excuses for every passion and for each venture. It is preeminently a servant of self-love, which always has the great subtlety to bestow a pretty colour on the mistakes that have been or are to be committed. Self-love often indulges in self-praise for having found such a good excuse for itself'(*N*, 12; Harris, 490). And thus Hegel perceives the limits of the Enlightenment: 'Enlightenment of the understanding certainly makes men shrewder, but not better ... That evil inclinations do no well up nor reach a greater intensity cannot be achieved by any published moral code nor by any enlightenment of the understanding' (*N*, 12; Harris, 490). Hegel is a man of the Enlightenment to the extent that he wishes 'to free the people from their prejudices and to enlighten them, and to the extent that he distinguishes among "folk prejudices" between those which are real errors and those whose truth is discerned not by reason but only in virtue of faith' (*N*, 13; Harris, 491). On the other hand, he is decidedly convinced that 'it is impossible for a religion which is intended universally for the people to consist of universal truths' (*N*, 14; Harris, 491). Hegel the theology student is certainly anything but a supranaturalistic school theologian, but neither is he a rationalistic freethinker. In wanting no unreasonable tradition he is a man of the Enlightenment; but – and here he leaves the Enlightenment behind him – neither does he want

---

[63]H.-G. Gadamer: *Wahrheit und Methode*, 255 (ET *Truth and Method, 239f*).

56

any reason without tradition. For him it is obvious 'that folk religion (and whatever is bound up with the concept of religion in itself) absolutely cannot be built on reason alone, if its doctrines are to be effective in the spheres of life and action. Positive religion must be based on faith in the tradition by means of which it is transmitted to us. Therefore we can find its religious rites convincing only on the basis of a binding obligation to them and of the belief that God requires them as well-pleasing in his sight and as a duty on our part' (*N*, 14; Harris, 492). Accordingly Hegel criticises with remarkable vehemence the Enlightenment-style 'conceit' of certain 'men and youths', who, on account of recent books and often out of vanity, 'begin to give up their previous faith', and who make disparaging remarks on the subject of the faith and 'prejudices' of the people. 'Whoever knows how to hold forth at length about the inconceivable stupidity of the people, whoever can meticulously demonstrate that it is the greatest folly for a people to have such and such a prejudice, showing off the while by bandying about such words as "Enlightenment", "human knowledge", "history of humanity", "felicity" and "perfection" – such a man is nothing more than a chatterbox of the Enlightenment, a marketplace quack offering stale panaceas for sale' (*N*, 16; Harris, 494). According to Hegel one may well ask, with regard to religion in general, 'how far reasoning may intrude before it ceases to be religion' (*N*, 14; Harris, 492). Religion in his sense is to be neither mere rational speculation nor a mere system of morality (or only preparing the ground for the latter); but no more is it to be a mere matter of feeling. In the end of the day it cannot be a question of Enlightenment, only one of wisdom. 'Wisdom is something other than Enlightenment and reasoning. But wisdom is not science. Wisdom is an uplifting of the soul ... it reasons little; it did not take its starting point in mathematical fashion[64] from concepts and come to what it takes for truth by way of a series of syllogisms, like Barbara and Barocco; it has not purchased its conviction on the universal market where knowledge is handed over to everyone who pays the correct price, as if wisdom did not also know how to count out again onto the table in shining coins and in valid currency; rather wisdom speaks from the fullness of the heart' (*N*, 15; Harris, 492f). In a rationalistic religion of reason 'a universal spiritual Church' remains 'only an ideal of reason' (*N*, 17; Harris 495). Hegel, on the other hand, would like to take men seriously in his entirety, that is, in the entirety of his nature as reason and sentiment and in the totality of his history; not as an abstract individual or as an abstract human race, but in the history of the people as a personification of humanity. In order that religion might be a lively folk religion and a sign of

---

[64]*methodo mathematica.*

human progress as well as a stimulus toward it, Hegel, in critical and constructive vein, wants fantasy, sentiment and heart together with intellect and memory. He wants tradition and faith along with reason and, when it is correctly understood, he even wants to combine a positive religion of revelation with a natural religion of reason. But to combine is not the same thing as to mediate. In Hegel's folk religion all these elements simply exist side by side at this stage. It is more a question of addition than of mediation. As we have already observed above, he did not get beyond a compromise.

Thus in the thought of the young Hegel all the questions are still basically open. Now twenty-three years old, he stands at the threshold of his development. Much about his criticism and his demands is frankly justified, much is as yet immature. What changes will occur as he goes on his further way in the coming years! But is it really the case that all that at least today Christian theology deems to be missing is absent? May not these things be already present, though not yet visible? Had not Hegel, for good or ill, carefully studied the New Testament in Tübingen (and perhaps rather for good than for ill), and had he not heard Storr's lectures on dogmatics, whose starting-point was precisely the trustworthiness of the person of Jesus? And was Hegel able in this fragment to express everything that moved him? Will he not come back in greater detail to Jesus the Christ in the following fragments? And does not this first fragment in fact represent but a preamble for a whole series of fragments, perhaps just a preliminary observation before he comes to the heart of the matter? These fragments in fact form an inner unity, and so it is a mere formality that we now start a fresh chapter with Hegel's move to Bern.

Chapter Two: Concentration on Jesus

'For the believer therefore it is no longer a virtuous person who
has appeared here, but virtue itself' (*N*, 57).

1. Jesus or Socrates?

Hegel had not gone to Switzerland as a tourist,[1] although tourism was just
then starting to come into fashion and indeed to become an element of
'education'. In the summer of 1796, shortly before his departure from Bern,
Hegel too went on a hiking tour through the uplands of Bern, but without any
great enthusiasm. 'In the idea of the duration of these mountains or in the kind
of grandeur that is ascribed to them, *reason* finds nothing to impress, nothing
to command awe and admiration. The sight of these eternally dead masses
gave me nothing but the uniform and eventually boring idea: *it is so*' (*H*, 236
Kaufmann, 307). There are many more observations in this vein on the
ugliness of the Alps and of the crags and glaciers and on the 'inevitability of
nature' (*H*, 234) in Hegel's travel diary (*H*, 221-244; extracts in Kaufmann,
305-7). These judgments were influenced by the artistic taste for symmetry
characteristic of the last phase of the age of absolutism, and especially by
Lessing's criticism, in his *Laokoon*, of A. von Haller's classical landscape
description in *Die Alpen* of 1729. But at the sight of a waterfall there forced
itself upon Hegel's experience something fundamental, something that was to
be a central thought in his later understanding of Spirit and in the flowing
terms which he used to define it: 'No power or great force is seen, and *the idea
of the constraint or inevitability of nature* remains *remote*; rather the *image of
a free game* is produced by our perception of *what is alive,* continually
disintegrating and bursting asunder, not merged into *one* mass, but *eternally
active and restless*' (*H*, 224; Kaufmann, 307). On another and later occasion
Hegel again writes: 'its image, its shape is continually disintegrating, in each
moment being superseded by a new one; *in this waterfall one sees eternally the
same spectacle and sees at the same time that it is never the same*' (*H*, 231;

---

[1]On Hegel's period in Bern cf. the literature on Hegel's youth specified at the beginning of ch. 1.

Kaufmann, 308); he writes too of its *eternal life, the stupendous vitality* in the same' (*H*, 232; Kaufmann, 308).

In addition to acquiring swollen feet on those long stony and often rainy hikes over the numerous Alpine passes (he did not climb any mountain peaks!), Hegel found that his last shred of pleasure in the eudaemonistic natural theology of the Enlightenment was fading away. 'Educated men might perhaps have invented all other theories and sciences in these desolate wastes, but hardly that part of *physico-theology* which proves to man's pride how nature has spread forth all things with a view to his enjoyment and pleasure. This pride is characteristic of our age in being more disposed to find satisfaction in the idea of all that has been done for it by an alien Being than it would be to find satisfaction in the knowledge that it has itself imposed all on nature' (*H*, 235; Kaufmann, 309). Even so, the 'calm resignation' of the mountain inhabitants is to his liking, and he avails himself of the shepherds' saga of the devil's bridge to make a derogatory remark on the subject of Christianity: 'But, as ever . . . the Christian imagination has given rise to nothing but an *absurd legend*' (*H*, 241; Kaufmann, 309). How completely different were the myths of the Greeks!

But this tiresome bout of Alpine tourism was only a holiday pastime. Hegel's everyday life was filled with the duties of a family tutor, which added up to a truly drab workaday routine. Nearly all the leading minds of German Idealism went through this frequently uncomfortable school of 'employment as a servant of higher rank':[2] Kant, Fichte, Schiller and then, along with Hegel, Hölderlin and finally Schelling. Here too Hegel made slower progress than Schelling, for his period of teaching and travel from Tübingen to Bern and then to Frankfurt lasted seven years, until in 1801 at the age of thirty-one he was able to take his second doctorate (*Habilitation*) in Jena, while his friend had become a professor at twenty-three. But Hegel needed time; it was only slowly and with painful effort that he made headway.

After a short sojourn in his home-town Hegel had moved to Bern in the autumn of 1793 as *'Gouverneur des enfants de notre cher et féal Citoyen Steiguer de Tschougg'* (*H*, 447). Fichte, and at a later date Herbart too, had previously been domestic tutors in Switzerland, and the democratic freedoms enjoyed especially by the original peasant cantons had not gone unnoticed. But on this score Hegel was disappointed. Trouble was brewing in Bern; for the Revolution was casting its shadow over this not so much democratic as aristocratic-oligarchical state as well. Many a citizen of Bern did not return home from the massacre of the Tuileries, which took place a year before Hegel's arrival in the city. Toleration had been accorded neither to Voltaire in

---

[2]W. Dilthey: *Die Jugendgeschichte Hegels*, 16.

Lausanne nor to Rousseau in Geneva. Unrest was on the increase in the subject territories, especially in the Pays de Vaud. The Bernese political system was decadent, the government being thrown back upon censorship and brute force. Hegel sent Schelling a report on the subject of the nepotism displayed at the re-election of the *Conseil souverain* (XXVII, 23). He could not reconcile himself to these corrupt political conditions. He does not seem to have felt very much at home even in his closest surroundings among the aristocratic Steiger family in old Bern, for he complains about a lack of time and about his 'remoteness from the chief centres of literary activity' (XXVII, 11).

In spite of these drawbacks Hegel used his time in Bern strenuously, so that he might 'gather in' what he had 'previously omitted, and even set about a piece of work here and there' (XXVII, 11). And what was there to be gathered in? The still extant written works and the correspondence that have come down to us from this period give us the relevant information and show us his persistent interest in socio-political developments. Thus it can also be said of his time in Bern that Hegel's theological endeavours have to be seen against the total historical, cultural, social, ethical and political horizon.

Among Hegel's Bernese writings we find first of all some material for a philosophy of the subjective spirit (*H*, 195-217[3]). Two short extracts (*H*, 217-219) follow these psychological compilations, along with the transcript of an outline of Schelling's system (*H*, 219-221; 455). Finally there are the following political writings: an essay on 'the changes wrought in the art of war by the transition from a monarchical to a republican form of government' (no longer extant); and a commentary (likewise lost) on James Stewart's book on political economy (cf. *H*, 280, 466f); and, lastly, Hegel's first (anonymous!) publication, on which he worked in Bern and which was published at Frankfurt in 1798. It was a translation of and commentary on Cart's *Confidential letters on the former constitutional relationship of the Pays de Vaud to the City of Bern. A complete exposure of the previous oligarchy of the State of Bern* (the commentary in *H*, 247-257; 457-465).

This anonymously published treatise demonstrates that the theologian who was already an enthusiastic adherent of the French Revolution during his days at the Tübingen seminary, still stands on the left, democratic wing of the German intelligentsia. Even so, a sharp rejection of the revolutionary excesses of the Jacobin reign of terror is now clearly visible in his thought as in that of many of his intellectual associates, notwithstanding the fact that he always stood by his conviction of the historical necessity and significance of the French Revolution. At Christmas 1794 he writes to Schelling that '[t]hese proceedings [i.e. the execution of Carrier] are highly important and have laid bare all the shamefulness of Robespierre's faction' (XXVII, 12). The Bernese Hegel cannot be dubbed a Jacobin (as Lacorte, Rossi and Peperzak correctly maintain against Lukács and Negri).

Our analysis of Hegel's fundamental outlook during his time in Tübingen is

---

[3]Dated Bern 1794 as No. 43 by G. Schüler against *H*, 452f (cf. 140f.)

confirmed by the information from the period he spent in Bern. Here too we are *not* faced with a stark choice between a 'religious view' of Hegel, as elaborated, more or less exclusively, by Dilthey, Nohl, Schneider, Asveld, Wolf and Peperzak, and a 'political view', as emphasised, to some extent against these interpreters (especially Dilthey), in the school of Rosenzweig above all by Lukács, Massolo, Negri and Rossi. The overall tendency of Hegel's thought, a mixture of Enlightenment and post-Enlightenment influences, is *at once socio-political and religious,* as has been shown comprehensively in the school of Haering especially by Lacorte, Rohrmoser, H. Schmidt, Marsch and, with a negative evaluation of the religious factor, also by Krüger. In his account of the literature about the young Hegel, W. Kern, after an extensive comparison of the various recent interpretations, correctly states with reference to the narrowly construed political interpretation, 'that the political factor, in the sense of the intention to pursue social reform, is overstressed in the books of Massolo, Negri and Rossi, although by no means so grossly as in Lukács. Where political philosophy becomes the special theme of a survey, a kind of methodological ambiguity easily creeps in: on the one hand, the scope of the enquiry is legitimately and necessarily extended to include the entire literature under discussion (thereby gaining the appearance of an exhaustive presentation), while on the other hand, the specialist theme urges abstinence from due assessment of the non-political aspects, theological, metaphysical etc.'[4]

Just as Hegel was not developing into a 'mystical pantheist' in Bern, as we shall presently see, so he was not at this early stage a potential materialistic atheist. As a representative of dialectical materialism, Lukács has elaborated on the significance of the economic-social problematic in a one-sided polemical thrust against Dilthey and others, thereby turning Hegel into a precursor of dialectical materialism.[5] But even he concedes 'that Hegel gave a moral slant to all the social and historical problems that confronted him', and 'that in these debates on the philosophy of history, religion plays a decisive role'.[6] And even if Hegel engages in vigorous polemic against the Christianity of his day, he does not seek a controversy with religion as such. On the contrary, in the words of Lukács: 'His critique of Christianity never reaches the point of materialistic atheism. Quite the reverse, the core of his work here is religious . . .'[7]

We do not wish to dispose of Hegel in a facile way by 'pigeon-holing' and labelling him as a philosopher, theologian or political scientist; for while he is certainly all of these things, he is none of them exclusively. To avoid this pitfall, we shall hold fast to three factors which are characteristic of Hegel's time in Bern. First, he is not concerned with theory and speculation. Almost our sole source of information on this side of things is Hegel's correspondence with Schelling (in this context see *N,* 361f); and what we find said of him here demonstrates that his chief interests lie elsewhere.[8] Secondly, his concern is of a practical and socio-political nature. Thirdly, in their range, significance and originality, religious questions stand in the forefront of this concern.

Hegel's central concern lay where it had already been situated in his last year in Tübingen, that is, with religion, or rather, with the renewal of society

---

[4]*Neue Hegel-Bücher,* 113.
[5]For a critique of this position see R. Garaudy: *Dieu est mort.*
[6]G. Lukács: *Der junge Hegel,* 34; see the ET *The Young Hegel* (Merlin Press, London, 1975), 8.
[7]*op. cit.,* 35 (ET, 9).
[8]On the correspondence with Schelling see Haering: *op. cit.* I, 196-214.

and people by means of religion. Since his change of locality did not disturb the inner continuity of the fragments on *Folk Religion and Christianity,* it is of secondary importance to determine which new insights dawned on him in Tübingen and in Bern respectively. Something decisive certainly becomes *visibly* perceptible in Bern in that the concentration on religion in general that characterised Hegel's time in Tübingen is followed by a conspicuous concentration on Christianity in particular and, finally, on Christ himself. This last development was at most indirectly prepared for by Storr's lectures on dogmatics, which, for all their tedious orthodoxy, were at least biblically focussed on Christ and his trustworthiness.

But in what way does the figure of Jesus now confront Hegel? He found this figure by no means mysterious in his first, somewhat incoherent Bernese fragment (*N,* 30-35). Apart from the fact that here too the point at issue was not directly Jesus himself, but rather the significance of great popular educators for living folk religion and especially for the right kind of instruction, we can say that in this fragment Jesus stood before Hegel's eyes as 'so good a man' (*N,* 33). He was this and no more than this; indeed, he was not even this absolutely, for at all events even 'so good a man' had a serious rival in one no less good: Socrates. For in a comparison of this kind Jesus of Nazareth had always had some difficulty in coming off as well as Socrates. This tendency already crops up in the Italian humanists. Indeed, it is interesting to find spectacular praise being heaped on Socrates as the first and greatest teacher of moral philosophy[9] as early as the beginning of the scholastic period in Abelard[10] (following Augustine and Plato), and very much earlier still in Justin, Athenagoras, Tatian and others.[11] This veneration of Socrates was well-nigh universal, reaching from the early Christian apologists and many Church Fathers, through scholasticism, the Italian Renaissance and Erasmus, right up to the Enlightenment, Rousseau and Hegel. And it is fitting to observe that the problems bound up with a Christian humanism are already plainly manifested in this veneration.[12]

Jesus was certainly an honourable and exemplary man. But according to Hegel he lacked the humane and universal scope of the distinguished sage and republican Socrates, this lofty paradigm of a free, good and humane Hellenism and of harmony with nature, world and state.[13] Here with Socrates we find dialogue: 'graceful urbanity . . . devoid of the didactic tone, without the

---

[9]*primus et maximus philosophiae moralis doctor.*
[10]Abelard: *Opera* II, 686; and cf. 31ff, 410ff.
[11]Adolf von Harnack: *Sokrates und die alte Kirche.*
[12]On the vast importance of Socrates in the eighteenth century cf. the study by B. Böhm, which does not, however, go on to include Hegel.
[13]*physis, kosmos* and *polis.*

appearance of wanting to give instruction . . . led in the most elegant way to a doctrine which spoke with its own authority and which could not seem obtrusive even to a Diotima' (*N*, 30). There with Jesus we find confrontation: 'moralistic sermons and a direct schoolmasterly tone . . . such a form of address as, "Ye serpents and generation of vipers"' (*N*, 30f). To be sure, excuses can be made for this severity by reference to the Jewish national character, to which Christ was obliged to adjust himself. But even so, 'Christ was not satisfied with having disciples such as Nathaniel, Joseph of Arimathea, Nicodemus and the like – that is, to have had intellectual affinity with intelligent men of superior spirit, and perhaps to have cast some new ideas, some sparks into their souls, which are lost anyway, if the place where they fall does not contain combustible matter. Such men – happy and content of an evening in the bosom of their family and useful and active in their sphere of activity, yet familiar with the world and its prejudices and hence tolerant toward it though strict toward themselves – such men would not have been responsive to the demand to become some kind of adventurers' (*N*, 32). How was folk religion to be possible under these circumstances?

Socrates was completely different; for no 'preaching down at folk from a *cathedra* or a mountain' accompanied the 'midwifery' that he performed in an understanding and questioning spirit. His sole aim was 'to apprise men of that which should arouse their supreme concern – to enlighten them, and to invigorate them for it'. Socrates, 'notwithstanding his wisdom, remained a husband and a father without any repugnance' (*N*, 33). And with regard to his disciples, he did not stick to any outward number. His custom was to educate them 'so that each remained what he was; Socrates was not to live in them nor to be the head from which they as members would receive the sap of life'. 'He was not anxious to fashion for himself a small corps of bodyguards with the same uniform, drill and password, who would have only one Spirit in common, and who would bear his name for ever'; 'each of his pupils was a master for himself . . . they were to be heroes not in martyrdom and suffering, but in action and in life'; 'moreover, whoever was a fisherman remained a fisherman, no one was meant to leave house and home' (*N*, 33f).

Socrates: a *citoyen* among *citoyens*! Such was the manner of his life: 'He offended no one by boastfulness about his importance or by using mysterious, high-flown expressions which can only impress the ignorant and the gullible – had he done so, he would have become an object of derision among the Greeks' (*N*, 34). And thus he also died, talking to his companions, full of hope in immortality, so that 'it was not necessary for him to fortify them with the idea of resurrection': that sort of thing is only needful for 'paltry spirits' (*N*, 34). Socrates's own person was not the decisive issue: 'He left no freemasonic signs behind him, no command to proclaim his name, no spiritual method for mounting the roof of the soul and pouring morality into it. The "good"[14] is born with us, and is something that cannot be preached into us. To bring men to proficiency in the good Socrates indicated no detour (across fragrant flowers that impair the judgment) leading via him – a detour where he would be the focus of attention, the capital as it were to which with difficulty men would have to travel, and from which they would have to carry the graciously distributed provender home and then raise interest on it. Nor did Socrates teach any "ordered path of salvation" (*ordo salutis*), in which each character, each social class, each age group, each temperament would have to endure certain stages of suffering and certain spiritual conditions. Instead of this he immediately knocked at the right door – without a mediator – and simply brought men to themselves . . .' (*N*, 34f).

In this process of educating a harmonious humanity – 'working away uninterruptedly at its intellectual and moral perfection' (*N*, 31) – no 'mediator' is required! Christ is a 'diversion' for those who are good by nature. Man must simply enter into himself relying on his own resources: Know thyself! Socrates undoubtedly renders better service in pursuit of this end than does Christ. Man's becoming human must take place through the agency of man himself! There must be no salvation from without, whereby man 'should prepare a dwelling for a completely alien guest Spirit from a far country' (*N*, 35). Instead there must be a coming to oneself: 'he should rather make light and room for his old landlord, whom the crowd of violinists and pipers had forced to take refuge in an old attic' (*N*, 35). The image Hegel uses here recalls a remark which he had jotted down in Tübingen. Understandably criticising the edifice of a purely objective and enlightened intellectual religion, he had urged a subjective interiorisation in its stead: 'The human intellect is flattered when it reflects on its own work – a great, high edifice made up of the knowledge of God, of human duties and of nature. The intellect itself has procured the requisite building materials and, after fashioning a structure out of them, it goes on to embellish and adorn it. But the more this building, at which the whole of mankind labours, is piled up and the more complex it becomes, the less does it belong to each one personally. Whoever only copies this universal structure, gathering the stuff of his thoughts from it alone, and whoever does not build a little house of his own to dwell in, with roof and framework, in himself and from himself – a house in which he is fully at home and whose every stone he has, if not actually hewn from the bare rock, at least prepared himself and turned over in his hands – such a man is of the letter, he has not lived and woven himself . . .' (*N*, 16f). We perceive here a contraction to the realm of private subjectivity, in order by this very step to render possible

---

[14] *to agathon*.

the expansion of this subjectivity. We perceive a tactical withdrawal on the part of the subject which makes it possible to transcend both the Enlightenment's reason and religion's abstract feeling from the vantage-point of subjectivity. With reference to this programmatic subjectivisation of objective religion (and its recourse to the existential aspects of faith[15]) H.-J. Krüger, writing from a Marxist point of view, underlines the fact that 'whatever does not fit into this petty philistine scheme is rigorously deleted'.[16] His words provide food for thought, even for theologians.

Hegel holds the disciples responsible for some of the negative features of Christianity (*N*, 32); for Christ too only intended to found a private religion (*N*, 360). But despite all the qualifications that can be made, his first theological encounter with Christ revolves unequivocally around an ironical and aggressive opposition to him. Is this the fault of the person and message of Jesus himself? Is it the fault of a particular understanding of his message and person? The opposition may have many a source, and there is much that might have stood between the true figure of Christ and the young Hegel: the prim and joyless Christianity of his home background, the superficial, Enlightenment-style religiosity of the Tübingen seminary, and the lifeless, rationalistically constricted Christology of the teachers at the university. Perhaps a part could also have been played by the historico-critical approach to the person of Jesus that had come on the scene with Reimarus, by the influence of Lessing's Nathan, who was always being quoted, and by the influence of Kant and Fichte, whose works on the philosophy of religion had just appeared (Fichte's *Critique of all Revelation,* 1792; Kant's *Religion Within the Limits of Reason Alone,* 1793).

Finally we must also bear in mind the general social structures of the petty Church-state establishments that obtained in princely, absolutist Württemberg and in aristocratic, oligarchic Bern, with their amalgamation of politics and 'Christianity'. Hegel himself says that 'religion and politics have conspired together in the *same* cause, the former teaching what despotism wanted it to teach, namely, disdain of the human race, its incapacity to perform any sort of good work or to be anything through its own efforts' (to Schelling 1795; XXVII, 24). All of these things may well have played a part in shaping Hegel's attitude. But be that as it may, this fragment reinforces our earlier impression that the young Hegel shows no sign of a living relationship to Christ in the sense of a positive, existential relationship of faith. Or at least he has shown no such sign until now. But can we not perhaps detect the first stirrings of something positive, albeit under highly negative auspices? At all

---

[15] *fides qua creditur.*
[16] *Theologie und Aufklärung,* 45.

events it is conspicuous that Hegel, now that he is able freely to shape his own course of study, begins to occupy himself increasingly with the figure of Christ.

2. Critique of Religion

The critical attitude that Hegel has adopted hitherto is maintained in the next fragment (*N*, 36-47; cf. the draft in *N*, 359f). Not all of it is original by a long chalk. Personal concerns and even expressions of grievance are interspersed with enlightened platitudes. We may say that Hegel is as yet little inclined toward the historical fairness that characterised his later years. But we must bear in mind that this fragment is only a collection of detached thoughts casually jotted down, and not a carefully revised essay destined for publication. A critique of religion is pursued by means of a series of arguments developed in rapidly changing directions. Hegel analyses the Christian religion from the point of view of its social usefulness. But however much this critique of religion, which is to be found in all his early writings, may anticipate the arguments of his disciples Feuerbach and Marx (and also Nietzsche's derivation of Christian ethics from resentment), at no time is religion for Hegel himself simply the opium of the people, but rather, when accompanied by a good political constitution, it has the potentiality of becoming a living element for the people. He has no quarrel with religion in general, but only with dead religion. In this fragment he praises the primitive and childlike religion (of antiquity) lived by the entire people, not so much over against a one-sided religion of reason, but over against the externalised, fossilised and untrue religion of a segregated, hypocritical and power-hungry priesthood (*N*, 37f). Setting his face against an ecclesiastical state and a state-owned Church, Hegel espouses a cooperation of state and religion in the service of folk religion. Thus he expresses himself in favour of a democratisation of religion and in favour of a religion in which the people's 'heart is stirred and its reason satisfied' (*N*, 39). Therefore Hegel desires not an objective and dead religion taking outward form in a rational theory or in a secularised ecclesiasticism, but an inward, subjective and living religion!

Christianity undergoes severe criticism supported by historical, socio-psychological and theological arguments. As witnesses of his indictment Hegel invokes: the historical failure of Christianity and of priestly politics (*N*, 39f); violation of conscience wrought by the various ecclesiastical institutions and by the Reformers (*N*, 42); asceticism of the pietistically egocentric, psychologising and tormentingly negative variety (*N*, 43); and the authoritarianism and moral censoriousness of ecclesiastical leaders (*N*, 45). The argument against Christianity is provided by Christians themselves! The question forces itself upon us: which is humankind's better achievement, Christianity or the Enlightenment? 'Their excuse is always that the Christian religion has been misconstrued, but after all they had the Bible just as we do. And if this is let out of the bag, they give us to understand that their copy was simply missing. Were this not so, the outcome would surely have been different. Has religion opposed despotism? For how long then has it been opposing the slave trade? Their priests go on the ships to Guinea. Or wars? After all, chaplains are sent to accompany armies. Or despotism of all kinds? The arts and the Enlightenment have improved our moral condition, but afterwards they say that the Christian religion has done this, for without it philosophy would not have found its basic principles' (*N*, 360). Thus the Church, according to Hegel, has had a ruinous effect both on free human personality and on living human fellowship. In this attack on the Church, both Catholic and Protestant, Hegel is not so much advancing the usual rationalist criticisms concerning the irrationality of the articles of faith, but rather arguments of a practical, psychological and political kind.

The fragment ends with a comparison between the Greeks' cheery this-worldly religion of life and the Christians' gloomy other-worldly religion of death (*N*, 45-47). Although for Christians the whole of life is meant to be a meditation on death, in fact they understand death as badly as they do life. Precisely because they depreciate this life and drain it of significance in favour of the next, they need every possible outward spiritual luxury to help them face their deaths. While the Greeks used to die unaffected and valiant deaths, Christians die uttering laments and in an unmanly fashion. While for the Greeks death is the fair guardian angel and the brother of sleep, for Christians it is the skeletal figure whose ghastly skull decorates every coffin. The remembrance of death causes the Greeks to enjoy life, for Christians it spoils the enjoyment of life: 'For them it had the odour of life, for us the odour of death' (*N*, 47).

On the whole we can say that Hegel's point of departure at this juncture in his life was not an ideal concept of Christianity, but an ideologised form of it, interwoven with many-sided superstitions and with the facts of political domination. But precisely on this score it is conspicuous that, even if the anti-Christian criticism has not diminished, at least its emphasis has shifted from Christ to Christianity. Hegel at least in part exonerates the person of Jesus Christ by transferring the blame onto contemporary Christianity. Were not the virtues in which the rulers of the Church were deficient those demanded by the teaching of Jesus? And 'which vice has not become fashionable among them? And which was not in fact forbidden by their Lord and Master?' (*N*, 40). Certainly the religion of Christ was ill-suited to mould public life: at least the literal application of his ethics would mean the disintegration of civil society (just think of the application of the Sermon on the Mount to the ownership of property and the legal system). Therefore the ministry of Jesus issued in conflict with the Jewish establishment. But due allowance must be made in Jesus' case for the fact that he did not intend to create any form of public religion; he wanted not a folk-religion, but a private religion. Ecclesiastical religion and the state-owned Church are a product of the disciples and of the later generation. 'From all the evidence it appears that the doctrines and principles of Jesus were only suitable for the education of individual men and had this end in view' (*N*, 41). It can be abundantly illustrated 'that, when the apparatus and rules of a small society, in which every citizen has the freedom to decide whether or not to be a member, are extended to embrace civil society at large, they never fit the bill, nor can they coexist with civic liberty' (*N*, 44).

The seed of a positive appraisal of the historical figure of Jesus lies hidden here under a thick layer of Enlightenment-style polemic. Notwithstanding the belligerent tone, it is remarkable how in what follows the figure of Jesus is more clearly outlined, coming into our purview in a more kindly light, and how this process is now increasingly discernible almost from fragment to fragment. The next piece consists in fact of three fragments (*N*, 48-69), which mesh together as outline, first draft and more mature form. (We can consider the small sheet *N*, 70f along with these.) We are afforded a glance into Hegel's workshop which reveals the incomplete and provisional nature of much of these materials, and how wrong it would be to take them for definitive finished products. In many respects an experiment is taking place here, an experiment vague in its detail but with a clear-cut objective. The old question of the significance of religion for man and society is at stake. 'The supreme end of man is morality, and his religious bent is preeminent among his aptitudes for promoting that end' (*N*, 48). Thus the 'chief end' of religion is precisely not 'propagation of the name and glory of Christ' or 'glorification of God's name'. Were this the case, then it would be true that 'the Pope at the great mass in St Peter's Church would be a worthier object of God's good pleasure than the corporal (Woltemar) who saved thirteen persons from shipwreck at the risk of sacrificing his own life, and then, together with the fourteenth, died in the service of humanity' (*N*, 49). Nevertheless not only hostile bellicosity but also apathy toward the figure of Christ has subsided.

Here too the question at issue is, to use a distinction Hegel adopted from Fichte, how objective religion (the orthodox doctrinal system) can become subjective, that is, engaged, emotionally felt, lived religion (subjective piety); and what can be done by state and individual respectively to achieve this. The relationship of religion and state engrosses Hegel to an exceptional extent in this fragment: 'To make objective religion subjective must be the great concern of the state' (*N*, 49). The influence of Mendelssohn's *Jerusalem: A*

Treatise on Religious Power and Judaism (1783) makes itself felt here. Even so, Hegel's central question is: 'What, from these points of view, are the prerequisites of a folk religion? Do we find them in the Christian religion?' (*N*, 62) Is Christianity qualified to overcome the gulf between the theology of the understanding and the religion of the heart? Is it suited to the task of healing the inner strife of the man who is not in his right mind? For Christianity and especially for the Church the outcome of this enquiry is very negative. Its unpolitical character is alleged as the reason for Christianity's illfittedness for these tasks: 'The Christian religion is originally a private religion, modified in accordance with the requirements of the circumstances of its emergence, and with those of human beings and their prejudices' (*N*, 49). On the negative side the following factors are of importance: truths of history which, if miraculous, are exposed to unbelief; further, doctrines which are not aboriginal but oriental, cheerless and devoid of feeling; and, finally, ceremonies which have been emptied of meaning with the passage of time (cf. the survey in *N*, 49f and the examples that follow later).

In Hegel's view there are no grounds for objection to simple, humane, reasonable dogmas in a folk religion. There are such grounds, however, against incomprehensible 'mysterious, theoretical doctrines' (*N*, 50) which exist neither for the understanding nor for the reason nor for the fantasy but solely for the memory (*N*, 51). These doctrines are superfluous in practice (*N*, 51f), and to them belong the doctrines of the Trinity, the atonement and original sin (*N*, 58). It is quite otherwise with the 'practical, moral doctrines' (*N*, 58). Even many opponents of what is specifically Christian have 'been inspired by the ethics of Christianity' (*N*, 58). And now in this perspective 'the history of Jesus, not merely his doctrines or those ascribed to him, is of very great practical importance' (*N*, 56).

In order that people may perform the good and acquire principles, they need more than a virtuous man. 'Were virtue, says Plato, visibly to appear among men, then all mortals would be constrained to love it. Plato indeed believed in virtue; but, in order to inspire men to zealous admiration, he demanded virtue itself' (*N*, 56f). And it is precisely at this point that Socrates cannot help. Jesus now stands *above* Socrates for Hegel in two respects. First, there is in his case 'the admixture, the addition of the divine': 'Without the divinity of his person we should have only the man, but we have here a true, superhuman ideal; an ideal which is not alien to the human soul even though the latter must think of itself as far removed from it' (*N*, 57). Secondly, there is the 'advantage of not being a cold abstract noun, but rather his individuation': 'For the believer therefore it is no longer a virtuous person who has appeared here, but virtue itself. In the case of the former, we are always inclined to presume that there are some hidden shadows or that there was a struggle in times past (as we assume in the case of Socrates purely on the basis of his physiognomy); but in the latter case faith has as its object unblemished, though not disembodied, virtue' (*N*, 57).

Thus Hegel appeals to the earthly Jesus as an ideal of virtue. He is persuaded, however, that precisely this aspect of Jesus is imperilled by faith in the post-Easter Christ (he makes no terminological distinction between Jesus and Christ), and by the 'worship of Christ and God', bound up with which are mission to the heathen, piety, charity etc. (*N*, 59). All these things are simply 'detours' on the road to morality, which is in fact upstaged by faith in Christ as the decisive condition of salvation (*N*, 62). 'The hinge around which the entire hope of our salvation turns, is faith in Christ as the reconciler of God with the world, as the one who bore retribution in our stead' (*N*, 68). The presupposition of this pivotal doctrine of Christianity is on the one hand the doctrine of the original sinfulness of human nature and of man's consequential inability to perform the good, and on the other hand the doctrine of the divinity of Christ. These are doctrines that mutually condition and complement each other. 'In comparison with this storey in the edifice of the Christian faith, the other doctrines are to be taken as but so many supporting buttresses. Therefore it was necessary, in propounding the worthlessness of man and his inability to gain any worth by natural means, to maintain the divinity of Christ, for only the suffering of such a one could offset the guilt of the human race. Thence too comes the doctrine of the free grace of God, because that history to which our salvation is tied could remain unknown to half the world through no fault of its own. And so it was necessary to develop many another doctrine that is bound up with this central notion' (*N*, 68f; and cf. 63).

Hegel's christological position has consequently become clearer. In formulations redolent of Feuerbach he rejects the notion that, on account of the natural corruption of man, moral goodness is to be 'imputed solely to a faraway Being' and therefore 'cannot form a part of our own being'; so that we cannot 'recognise ourselves in virtuous men', but require instead 'a God-man for such an ideal which would be an image of virtue for us'. The truly divine fact about Christ is precisely not 'that he is the second person of the Godhead, that he is eternally generated by the Father etc.' (*N*, 67). On the other hand, Hegel accepts that 'the admixture, the addition of the divine, qualifies the virtuous man Jesus to be an ideal of virtue' (*N*, 57). What is truly divine about Christ consists in the fact 'that his Spirit and his way of thinking coincided with the moral law. Of course, we must in the end take the idea of the moral law from ourselves, even though its letter can be given in signs and words' (*N*, 67f).

Even though the Christian theologian cannot recognise this divine Sonship understood in moral terms as a faithful translation of the New Testament message, he will not be able to overlook the fact that theological errors played a part in shaping it, errors which may perhaps be laid at the door of the Tübingen theology. At any rate they may not be held against Hegel personally without further ado. To name but three of these: first, there are the problems that arise in connection with the (basically Augustinian) doctrine of original sin. Without any biblical authority this doctrine utises the notion of biological transmission (cf. *N*, 63). These problems are widely recognised today, but at that time had only just become a topic of discussion. Secondly, the orthodox Protestant assertion of human nature's total depravity on account of sin, unchecked by divine grace (cf. *N*, 63), must, in its unbiblically systematised onesidedness, have seemed incomprehensible in the eyes of the men of the Enlightenment, with their conviction of the good in man and of the needfulness of human activity, themes which are surely not simply anti-Christian. Thirdly, the question of the salvation of the heathen before and after Christ gave rise to the dilemma that *either* faith in Christ was not absolutely essential *or* there was no universal possibility of salvation for all people (cf. *N*, 64f). Given the recent discovery of whole continents and the universal enthusiasm for Greek paganism, this problem had taken on an acute urgency not only for Voltaire and Rousseau but also for Christian theologians. Protestant theology particularly, from the Reformation on, made little effort to tackle positively the problem of the religions (and of mission!). However, the truly questionable aspect of all this lies at a deeper level. The decisive question regarding the understanding of Christ is whether Hegel understood what *faith* is, faith, that is to say, in the New Testament sense, Christian faith, faith in Christ. This question must be posed in two directions, concerning faith's relation to reason and to works.

1. The New Testament demands a faith which is certainly meant to include understanding and, in this sense, to be a thoroughly reasonable faith. There is not a whiff of the *credo quia absurdum* about it. Yet it is to be a faith which does not make its own preconceptions, which it inevitably brings in tow, into the decisive criterion of the message. In his whole existence man may rely with confidence on the Christian message, in the same way as he relies on love – certainly not blindly or unreasonably, indeed thoroughly critically, yet also without any stringent rational proof. On the contrary, it is more like confidently taking a risk, the appropriateness of which only becomes apparent in the performance of the act. Does not Hegel (and with him of course many a contemporary theologian) remain, in comparison with this New Testament faith, tied to a form of rationalism – a rationalism which scarcely reflects sufficiently on the fact that its reason does not approach the Christian message without prejudice, but stands itself in need of enlightenment and hermeneutical reflection? Hegel legislates 'for the dogmas of a folk religion,

that they are to be as simple as possible, that they are to contain nothing that is not recognised by universal human reason – nothing to permit some belief exceeding the bounds of reason to be defined or dogmatically maintained, even if the warrant for it should be said to have its origin in heaven itself'(*N*, 50). For 'reason is the supreme judge of its faith' (*N*, 53f). And where trustful faith in Jesus Christ is concerned, 'in the end reason still dares to test that faith out of its own resources, and to draw out of itself the principles of possibility and probability. It does this regardless of that artificial historical edifice, which on historical grounds claims a primacy over conviction by truths of reason. This it puts on one side' (*N*, 66).

2. The New Testament demands a faith which is certainly meant to be an efficacious faith active in human works. It is to be no sluggish, quietistic faith. Nevertheless, it is to be a faith prey to no illusions about the true nature of man. Now man, in actuality, is by no means simply that superior free man following the law of reason, that he likes to pose as being. If he is honest, he sees himself as continually threatened by himself, because he finds himself in bondage to the things, desires, goods and powers of this world and, at the very deepest level – precisely in his ethical activity – in bondage to himself, to the self that he has hitherto made out of himself. Plainly then he is a man who in every respect needs freedom; but this is a freedom which he can as little confer on himself as he can pull himself out of a bog by his own bootstraps. Does not Hegel (and with him many a contemporary theologian) remain, in comparison with this New Testament faith, tied to a form of optimism – an optimism which does not sufficiently bear in mind that the greatest enemy of man's true humanity is man himself? Hegel might well be failing to appreciate the profundity of human existence and of the Christian faith (which is by no means simply reducible to accepting the truth of certain propositions), when he delivers himself of the opinion that 'faith in Christ' would necessarily and in a bad sense be a 'substitute for morality', and when he then maintains that 'activity in good works may be required as a necessary element of faith, but yet, according to the dictum of the theologians, in the end of the day faith takes the precedence over works; otherwise works might be meritorious for us, or give us some peculiar value that might bring upon us God's good pleasure. And then faith in general depends on a conviction of the intellect or of the fantasy that is supposed to deem things true which partly rest upon historical credibility, and partly are of such a kind as to be incompatible with the intellect' (*N*, 64).

Nevertheless it should not be overlooked that, even if Hegel's critique did not touch the faith of the New Testament, it did deal a blow to a passive and fideistic type of Protestant piety. On the other hand, it is indeed true that a deepened understanding of Christ would be possible from the perspective of a faith conceived in New Testament terms. Intimations of such an approach on Hegel's part appear in the fact that he now unequivocally places Jesus above Socrates and seeks to understand him as not only, like the latter, a 'model' and examplar, but, for 'faith' – in opposition to the 'reasoning of the cold intellect' – as a substantial 'ideal of virtue', as a 'superhuman ideal' and as 'virtue itself'. In brief, the change is beginning to occur when Hegel attempts to understand 'the divine element of his person' (cf. *N*, 57). Even so, for the time being Hegel does not think of taking these impulses more seriously. He takes great pains to understand the figure of Christ, but sets about this task by going in a different direction, namely by writing a *Life of Jesus*.

3. The Life of Jesus According to Kant

Are the life and teaching of Jesus at all useful for the task of shaping a future folk religion? But let us postpone this question for a while. At all events the prologue and epilogue of this *Life of Jesus* (*N*, 75-136) are most informative concerning Hegel's intentions. Hegel's description of the life of Jesus starts with the teaching of the Johannine Prologue about the Logos, that is to say, about reason, the promotion of whose development in man was Christ's chief merit. 'Pure reason knowing no limits is the Godhead itself. The layout of the world as a whole is ordered in accordance with reason, and it is reason that acquaints man with his vocation, an unconditional purpose for his life. Reason has often been obscured, yet never entirely extinguished; even in the darkness a faint glimmer of it has been preserved. Among the Jews it was John who once more drew men's attention to this their dignity. This dignity was not meant to be something alien to them, but something they should seek in themselves, in their true self, not in birth, nor in the impulse towards happiness, nor in being servants of a highly respected man, but in the development of the divine spark which has been bestowed on them, and which gives them testimony that they are descended in a more sublime fashion from the Deity itself. Cultivation of reason is the sole source of the truth and reassurance which John purported to possess – not exclusively, nor as a rarity, but as something which all men can develop in themselves. We are more indebted to Christ for his work in improving the corrupt maxims of men and in promoting the knowledge of genuine morality and of a purified worship of God' (*N*, 75).

Hegel's description of the life of Jesus ends with a sentence concerning Jesus' death. 'Joseph, along with Nicodemus, another friend, therefore took the dead man down, embalmed him with myrrh and aloes, wrapped him in linen and buried him in his family tomb. This rock-hewn tomb was in his own garden and close to the place of execution. They were therefore able to carry out these preparations there all the earlier, before the beginning of the feast itself, on which it would not have been permitted to have anything to do with the dead' (*N*, 136). We shall scarcely be able to avoid the assumption that, so far as this *Life of Jesus* is concerned, we have to do with a man who is quite simply dead and gone. Nohl's footnote confirms that 'the date of completion – 24 July 95 – given in the margin shows that the manuscript ends here'.

Between this rational beginning and the melancholy end we find an exegesis, undertaken with the aid of a harmony of the gospels, concerning which even Rosenkranz had to confess, that it is at times 'reasonable and intelligible to the point of triviality'.[17] It amounts to a version of rational morality, full of duty and virtue, eternal law, ethics and the dignity of man, directed in the light of contemporary problems against heteronomous authority, against outward ceremonies and statuary religion, and with an eye to the kingdom of the ethically good as the kingdom of God. In our context it is not necessary to go into the details of this moralistic exegesis of Jesus' discourses and recorded deeds, an interpretation which refrains from every attempt at a pragmatic causally connected narrative. Christ's parents are quite simply Joseph and Mary (*N*, 75); the testimony given in his baptism to his 'great talents' is given not by heaven, but by John (*N*, 76); and the tragic conflict of his life, which led to his death, is nothing but the struggle of rational faith against the ecclesiastical faith of the Pharisees. Everything mysterious and miraculous – we are now post-Reimarus! – is here tacitly eliminated by a preconceived set of ideas whose most remarkable feature is the unconcerned matter of fact way in which it is applied. What is not simply eliminated (e.g., miraculous birth, resurrection and ascension) is reinterpreted. This process is taken so far that, out of the narrative of Jesus' temptation, temptation becomes the temptation 'to convert, through the study of nature, less noble elements into nobler ones, more directly useful to man, such as, for example, stones into bread' (*N*, 77). But whatever may be said about such enlightened piquancies and about all the details with which Hegel deals so carefully, of much more decisive importance is the fact that throughout this work we hear out of the mouth of Jesus of Nazareth the clearly perceptible tones of none other than Immanuel Kant: in the conversation with Nicodemus (*N*, 79f) as in that with the Samaritan woman (*N*, 80f), in the Sermon on the Mount (*N*, 82-88) as in the parables of the kingdom of God (*N*, 92-94; 108-113), and in the polemical discourses against the Pharisees (*N*, 88-92; 94-99; 102-107; 117-121) as in the addresses to the disciples and the farewell discourses. Let us hear, by way of example, the paraphrase of Mt. 7:12: 'Whatever you can will to be a universal law among men should also apply to you. Behave in accordance

---

[17]*op. cit.*, 45.

75

with such a maxim, for this is the fundamental law of morality, the content of all legislation and of the sacred books of all peoples. Enter through this door of right into the temple of virtue. This door is indeed narrow, the way to it fraught with peril; and your companions will be few, for the palace of vice and corruption is more sought after; its gates are wide and its streets are smooth' (*N*, 87). What is this Jesus concerned with? According to Hegel it is absolutely clear: 'Do I then require respect for my person or faith in myself? Or do I want to impose on you a yardstick invented by myself for estimating the value of men and for judging them? No, respect for yourselves, faith in the sacred law of your reason, and attention to the inner judge in your bosom, to conscience, a yardstick which is also the yardstick of the Deity – this is what I wanted to awaken in you' (*N*, 119).

There is therefore no doubt that *Kant* stands behind Hegel's *Life of Jesus*. And Hegel sets himself to be more Kantian than Kant – for example in the rejection of every kind of substitution. The *Philosophy of Religion* of the great Königsberg scholar, which had been eagerly awaited on all sides, had appeared in 1793, and Hegel had studied it forthwith in Bern. Given that at this time Hegel had long since gone beyond Kant in many respects, his motives in writing this work will merit our investigation. Hegel's *Life of Jesus* is, at all events, a consistent interpretation of Jesus' life and teaching in the light of Kant's philosophy of religion. Here less than anywhere can we understand Hegel without Kant, to whom we must therefore devote our concentrated attention for a while.

'What can I know? What ought I to do? What may I hope?' According to Kant the whole concern of human reason is concentrated in these three questions.[18] While it is above all the *Critiques* of Pure and Practical Reason that answer the first two questions, the third is answered by Kant's writing on the *philosophy of religion*. Kant was educated in the Leibnizian-Wolffian 'school' philosophy, but Hume, Rousseau and the natural sciences summoned him to critical self-reflection. As in the case of most areas of his philosophy, for his *Religion within the Limits of Reason Alone*[19]

---

[18]*Critique of Pure Reason* (tr. N. Kemp Smith, London, 1929), 635.
[19]The author has used the second, enlarged edition of 1794. Quotations in this translation have been taken from *Religion with the Limits of Reason Alone* (tr. Greene and Hudson, Illinois, 1934; repr. Harper & Row, 1960). On Kant in our context cf, among recent works especially F. Delekat's historico-critical analysis of Kant's writings; cf. moreover the chapter on Kant and Barth's *History of Protestant Theology in the Nineteenth Century*, and the chapter on Kant and Schiller in vol. IV of Emmanuel Hirsch's *Geschichte der neueren evangelischen Theologie*. The best and most thorough essay on Kant's philosophy of religion was written by J. Bohatec. See also on Kant's Christology, H. Vogel; on Kant and the question of the gracious God, H. Blumenberg; on Kant and prayer, W. A. Schulze; and on the theology of the pre-critical Kant, H.-G. Redmann. In the whole of the literature on Hegel's youth (cf. the bibliography at the beginning of ch. 1), opinions are frequently expressed about the relationship between Kant and Hegel (in greatest detail by A. T.B. Peperzak). Important monographs on the relationship of the young Hegel to Kant include those by H. Wacker and I. Görland (cf. also W. Burian).

Kant availed himself of prior models. While his *Critique of Pure Reason* acquired its content through a transposition of the theistic metaphysics of A. G. Baumgarten into anthropology (cf. F. Delekat), his philosophy of religion follows the *loci dogmatici* of the theological textbooks penned by moderate men of the Enlightenment, above all the Reformed *Dogmatics* of J. F. Stapfer (cf. J. Bohatec). In addition Kant meticulously read through a Königsberg Catechism of the year 1732-33, presumably the catechism of his own youth. Kant's writing on religion deals with four problematic areas of traditional theology: original sin, the person and work of Christ, the Church, the ministerial office and the means of grace. But it deals with these topics under headings which sound remarkably different. Even so, he managed to unite in a quite sensational way biblical theology (which was taught in the Faculty of Theology) and natural theology (which was taught in his own Faculty of Philosophy). This overlap between the two disciplines had always been unavoidable in practice. Now, however, it was carried out by Kant in terms of his trenchantly expressed programme: theology as the handmaid of philosophy. And this overlap furnished the subject-matter of his *Conflict of the Faculties,* an essay which, although written at the same time as the *Philosophy of Religion,* for political reasons only appeared in 1798. All in all, the question that Kant sought to answer had not only a scholarly and theoretical character but also at the same time a practical and political one: what in fact pertains to the state religion (*religion civile*) which is obligatory for all its citizens? Kant's personal religious background was pietism, from which he acquired not only the tendency to subordinate grace to morals, but also many an argument against the theory and practice of the orthodox ecclesiastical world, though not without colouring these arguments with a rationalistic hue.

'Man so conceived, alone pleasing to God, "is in Him through eternity"; the idea of him proceeds from God's very being; hence he is no created thing but His only-begotten Son, "the *Word* (the *Fiat!*) through which all other things are, and without which nothing is in existence that is made" (since for him, that is, for rational existence in the world, so far as he may be regarded in the light of his moral destiny, all things were made). "He is the brightness of His glory." "In him God loved the world," and only in him and through the adoption of his disposition can we hope 'to become the sons of God"; etc.' In this modern theology long neglected texts reach our ears: from *Religion within the Limits of Reason Alone!*[20] We should not become suspicious on this score. Was it not Kant who, as a great son of the Enlightenment, irrevocably overcame it in his *Critiques?* Did he not help the best men of his time to understand more deeply what they themselves were feeling and striving after in the great upheaval of the modern age? Did he not take up once more in a constructive fashion the old problem of faith and knowledge, and did he not, by means of his *Critique,* impose sharp limits on the naive omnipotence of reason? And did he not show himself thereby, all in all, to be certainly a bold but, at the same time, a careful rethinker, one who held

---

[20]*op. cit.,* 54.

everything 'romantic' (*genialisch*) and precipitate in abhorrence? Did he not locate his life's task as that of patiently and doggedly thinking through the problems, and assimilating the most diverse stimuli? Did he not prove, precisely in his philosophy of law and of religion, that, for all his open approbation of the French Revolution, his deep interest in this epochal new orientation was certainly not bound up with politico-religious restoration or with politico-seditious revolution? These works much rather prove that he was concerned with a rational and critical reform and development in the field of religion that would be tantamount to a revolution in men's disposition. Did he not cut the ground from under the feet of the Enlightenment's shallow eudaemonism by way of his appeal to the moral consciousness and to the manly and austere ethic of duty, obedience and motive (doing good for its own sake)? This kind of ethic outstrips by far every kind of eudaemonistic ethic of desire and every kind of utilitarian ethic of function, and even compels the respect of its oponents. Did not Kant plainly bring before the eyes of Enlightenment optimism the evil principle, man's radical propensity to evil? And was not the upshot of this that he put unselfcritical freethinking and all contempt of religion firmly in its place, and that he made Christianity relevant in a new way? Indeed, did he not speak once more in a fresh and significant way about sin and satisfaction, about justification and rebirth and, as we have just heard, even about the eternal Logos and his significance for the world?

But just this text about the Logos plainly discloses the fact that Kant is looking in another direction than that of traditional Christianity. From the point of view of the New Testament it is astonishing how Kant here applies the Johannine Prologue and the language about 'Logos' and 'only-begotten Son' to '*Mankind* (rational earthly existence in general) in its complete moral perfection' (p. 54)! *Mankind* is 'that which alone can render a world the object of a divine decree and the end of creation' (p. 54). Accordingly, the title of Kant's second chapter does not read, as in the case of his traditional theological models, 'Doctrine of the Person and Work of Christ', but 'Concerning the Conflict of the Good with the Evil Principle for Sovereignty over Man'. Kant speaks not of an antithesis, but of a conflict of principles; yet while we may concede that a person can engage in conflict, we may well ask whether this can be said of principles. This raises the basic christological problem: what is the relationship of the 'Logos' and the 'only-begotten Son' to the historical Jesus of Nazareth?

Kant certainly does not remain silent on the subject of Jesus of Nazareth in his philosophy of religion. It is obviously Jesus who is meant when Kant speaks of him who 'had given men in his own person, through his teaching, his conduct and his sufferings, an example of a man well-pleasing to God' and who had 'through all this, produced immeasurably great moral good upon

78

earth by effecting a revolution in the human race' (p. 57). To explain this, however, we require neither the hypothesis of a supernatural generation, which is of no practical value (p. 57), nor the hypothesis of his sinlessness: 'his distance from the natural man would then be so infinitely great that such a divine person could no longer bee held up as an example to him' (p. 57). For with reference to the 'disposition which he makes the rule of his actions, but which he places before their eyes only through his teachings and actions, the same godly-minded teacher, even though he was completely human, might nevertheless truly speak of himself as though the ideal of goodness were displayed incarnate in him' (p. 59).

Yet it is remarkable that this whole passage is founded upon unreality: 'Now if it were indeed a fact that such a truly godly-minded man at some particular time had descended, as it were, from heaven to earth . . .' (p. 57). This is not to say that Kant doubted the historical existence of Jesus. In the second section of his chapter on Christology, where he speaks not of the idea of the good principle but of the conflict of the two principles, he comes once more to speak of the life and death of Jesus: 'Now there suddenly appeared among these very people, at a time which was ripe for a revolution, a person whose wisdom was purer even than that of previous philosophers, as pure as though it had descended from heaven. This person proclaimed himself as indeed truly human with respect to his teachings and example, yet also as an envoy from heaven who, through an original innocence, was not involved in the bargain with the evil principle into which, through their representative, their first father, the rest of the human race had entered, and "in whom, therefore, the prince of this world had no part"' (p. 74f). Kant here adopts a contrary position to that of the novel about Jesus by C. F. Bahrdt (according to which Jesus himself sought death and was therefore the author of his death) and to that of Reimarus (according to whom Jesus strove to bring about not a moral, but a political, revolution). He can assert in an unambiguous historical indicative that 'this death (the last extremity of human suffering) was therefore a manifestation of the good principle, that is, of humanity in its moral perfection, and an example for everyone to follow' (p. 77). Kant sketches Jesus' life and teaching in accordance with this perspective, so that Jesus appears as a lofty ideal of virtue and as the founder of that historically formed religion of Christianity which, on account of man's natural propensities, is, as a matter of fact (i.e. historically), necessary for the inauguration of the universal, pure religion of reason, of the ideal and invisible Church, of the kingdom of God (cf. pp. 55-60, 74-78, 94-100, 118-120, 146-151). Even if everything to do with miracle, mystery and grace in Jesus' existence is not directly denied, it is completely ruled out, with a canny, indeed detrimental, scepticism, as uncertain, unknowable and unimportant. 'Faith in miracles', 'faith in mysteries' and 'faith in means of grace' are but 'three kinds of illusory faith' (p. 182); and even the resurrection and ascension cannot 'be used in the interest of religion within the limits of reason alone without doing violence to their historical valuation' (p. 119).

The reason for the aura of unreality is that it is entirely possible for Kant's interpretation to work even *without* Jesus. It is important for him to maintain: 'We need, therefore, no empirical example to make the idea of a person morally well-pleasing to God our archetype' – the reason being: 'this idea as an archetype is already present in our reason' (p. 56). Or as Kant put it with even greater clarity in the second section of his Christology: 'Yet the good principle has descended in mysterious fashion from heaven into humanity not at one particular time alone but from the first beginnings of the human race' (p. 77).

What is here taking place in Kant's thought is that salvific importance is being accorded to the idea of humanity as Logos and Son of God rather than to the historical person of Jesus, whose absence would basically make no difference and whose very name, moreover, Kant avoids where possible. What Paul, John and Scripture in general say about Jesus, Kant transfers with astonishing unconcern to the 'personified idea of the good principle'. The figure of Christ has evaporated into an idea, and the biblical Christ appears in secular guise as the idea of humanity. If the Gnostics of old had transferred the myth of the primal man on to Jesus, the same thing is taking place in the other direction in this modern, rational *gnosis*. For Jesus becomes here a temporarily necessary imaginative aid for the idea of humanity, for the 'ideal of a humanity pleasing to God' (p. 55). Almost docetically, Kant portrays the history of Jesus in a grossly mythical form, for example, in terms of contract and conflict with the devil. Even so, '[o]nce this vivid mode of representation, which was in its time probably the only *popular* one, is divested of its mystical veil, it is easy to see that, for practical purposes, its spirit and rational meaning have been valid and binding for the whole world and for all time ... Its meaning is this: that there exists absolutely no salvation for man apart from the sincerest adoption of genuinely moral principles into his disposition' (p. 78).

Accordingly Kant's Christology is at its root anthropology. Here more than ever before, on the basis of a vigorous system which compels admiration, man's free self-determination, even with regard to religion itself, is translated into reality. Kant's system in its unalloyed sublimity is auto-nomy: legislating oneself in theory and practice. Reason as freedom! In this ahead of the Enlightenment, he sets at the side of the autonomous pure reason, which accepts no laws apart from the pure forms which it carries within itself, the autonomous practical reason, which is only bound to its own unconditional, universal and formal principles and maxims. In this way Kant authoritatively solves the age-old problem of freedom and law, by positing man, in the freedom of his rational being, as a law unto himself, in both the logical and the practical spheres, and in the spheres of scholarship, morality and aesthetics. The Copernican Revolution is here resolutely thought through to the end as man moves into the centre of things, with his reason and with his free moral consciousness, in terms of which not only morality but also faith and all religion are explained. Religion is conceived as 'morality in relation to God'; it is deduced from morality and is at once reduced again to morality. Religion is the handmaid of autonomous morality, in which man creates an ethical ordering of his life by his own strength. And he does this in terms of the slogan with which Kant brings his work to a close: 'not . . . from grace to virtue, but rather . . . from virtue to pardoning grace' (p. 190).

Could not Kant rightly claim to have discovered and preserved the essential element of Christianity in this way? God, freedom and immortality, these foundations of the Christian religion, he unshakeably secured in face of all hair-splitting criticism and of all destructive doubt. This he did in the first place by propounding an exhaustive doctrine of original or primal sin, 'concerning the indwelling of the evil principle with the good, or, on the readical evil in human nature' (pp. 15-49). For Kant original sin was not a natural predisposition, as it was for Manichaeism or, say, Flacius Illyricus. It was in fact a propensity toward evil (in three grades: frailty, impurity, wickedness), which in the end of the day is unfathomable and inexplicable as far as reason is concerned, and which is, in actuality, to be understood as a wicked deed. Furthermore, Kant offers a much more profound interpretation of conversion and regeneration than we find in the neological men of the Enlightenment, one in terms of a revolution of the disposition. This revolution is to prove itself in an unremitting effort undertaken with a view to moral perfection and therefore to justification and reconciliation. Morality, duty, virtue and conscience are emphasised more strongly than ever, so that the libertines' mockery is silenced in face of this ethical earnestness. Could the Christian revelation be assigned a more worthy task than was assigned it here, namely, the proclamation of what is eternally latent in man? Thus not only the temporary halt called to the freethinkers' assault on Christianity, but also the awakening of a new, positive interest in Christ within the bounds of idealistic philosophy, is to be attributed above all to Kant's philosophy of religion. His idea of humankind in its moral perfection seems like a reflection of the historical portrait of Christ. The christological speculation of German Idealism took its point of departure from Kant; and where the Enlightenment theologians had displayed an unadulterated misunderstanding of Christ, there was discovered in the wake of Kant a deep concentration of truth, which led people into ultimate questions about man and God.

Nevertheless, we may not overlook the fact that Kant thereby introduced a new biblical hermeneutic into German philosophy. This entails a rational demystification ('divested of its mystical veil', p. 78) and dehistoricisation (detachment from historical forms of representation) and in essence a speculative ideologisation of the Bible and, in particular, of Christology. Since reason is the ultimately decisive authority in this speculative hermeneutic, Kant appears as an Enlightenment rationalist to a greater extent in his philosophy of religion than in his three *Critiques.* The demystifying and dehistoricising speculative ideologisation of Scripture means for Kant neither simply lumping together the irrational along with the rational elements without any connection, nor the elimination of the irrational elements in favour of the rational. Semler did the first and Reimarus the second. Kant knew these two options but himself wanted to pursue a third, namely, the reinterpretation of the Bible on the basis of idealistic philosophy in accordance with the principles of a natural religion of reason, and hence the interpretation or reinterpretation of the incomprehensible elements in terms of the philosophically comprehensible ones. The ecclesiastical interpretation of the Bible, which busies itself with the historical aspects of Scripture, he abandons to the 'biblical theologians' as unimportant. For him as a philosopher the authentic interpretation of Christianity is solely the interpretation of the faith of the Church in the sense of the pure moral faith of religion. The scope of this interpretation, however, extends far beyond the Bible to encompass all ecclesiastical doctrines, institutions and constitutions. Thus it becomes a dangerous weapon *vis-à-vis* established theology and the Church in general. Thus whatever in the end of the day stands in the way of the adoption of this interpretation must be looked on as servile faith, superstition and pseudo-service. In making these charges Kant is not sparing of cutting words.

Already in the Foreword to his *Religion within the Limits of Reason Alone* Kant was honest enough to express his hermeneutical tendency with all the clarity that could be desired. The neological theologians prior to Kant still believed in good faith that they had hit on the true original sense of the biblical text. Here too Kant brings the Enlightenment to an end by claiming for himself, as a philosopher devoid of any illusions, the right violently to rationalise the Bible, if necessary without regard for the original intention of the writers. Such a procedure only becomes mischievous in his view when the philosopher *imports* something alien into Scripture, but not when he '*borrows* something, in order to use it for his purpose' (p. 9). Later, in the *Conflict of the Faculties,* he made the sarcastic observation: 'If the biblical theologian will stop using reason for his own ends, then the philosophical theologian will cease to use the Bible for the confirmation of his own propositions.'[21] Hence the hermeneutical principle of the philosophy of religion must be 'a thoroughgoing interpretation of it [the revelation which has come into our possession] in a sense agreeing with the universal practical rules of a religion of pure reason . . . Frequently this interpretation may, in the light of the text [of the revelation], appear forced – it may often really be forced; and yet if the text can possibly support it, it must be preferred to a literal interpretation which either contains nothing at all [helpful] to morality or else actually works counter to moral incentives' (p. 100f; cf. p. 102f). Such had been the conduct of all civilised peoples with their Holy Scriptures: they had 'kept on interpreting them until . . .' (p. 101)! Kant carried out this rational transformation for Christianity on the basis of a moral idealism, in order thereby to transpose the faith of the Church into the pure faith of religion or reason. Hence he has not the slightest inhibitions about accomodating himself to a very great extent to ecclesiastical language and theological terminology. It is consequently easy to understand that he too sees no difficulties in reinterpreting the 'Son of God' and the 'Logos' in terms of the idea of mankind, and in ascribing to this 'Son of God' pre-existence, humiliation and satisfaction (pp. 54ff).

Thus Kant too achieved what theologians and philosophers of that age desired: a harmony between the faith of revelation and the faith of reason came about. He did so, however, not from the standpoint of the Christian revelation, as had been the case with the theologians of the Enlightenment, but from the standpoint of rationalist philosophy. The result of this is in fact a radical destruction of the christological dogma, and not only of the christological. In his treatise Kant touches on the following topics: Trinity (p. 133); sin (pp. 34-39); revelation (pp. 102f, 122f); grace (pp. 19, 70, 109); redemption (pp. 66ff, 106ff); justification (pp. 70ff); judgment (pp. 136ff, 173ff); and the mystery of faith (pp. 136-138). Kant's hermeneutical approach is the key to our understanding how these notions can at once play a large part in his system and at the same time be cut adrift from their original biblical context, how they can be 'borrowed, to be used for his purpose'. This purpose amounts to the promotion of a moral religion of reason ('pure faith of religion'), for which the religion of revelation ('statutory ecclesiastical faith') is but a 'vehicle' on the journey through the history of humankind (p. 97). A provisional vehicle and only relatively necessary, it is destined to be eclipsed and to be gradually sublimated at an increasing pace into the pure religion of reason (p. 106). Wholeheartedly following Lessing, Kant constantly reiterates that, as far as he is concerned, the historical-factual has no authority of its own. The idea, the ideal content, is all-important. The historical fact of Jesus Christ remains excluded from the province of proper, ideal and eternal

---

[21] *Der Streit der Facultäten*, 64 (ET *The Conflict of the Faculties*, 79).

religion (p. 11); and this external fact is a man whose history, like all history, is but an episode.

Kant's intention consisted not least in giving a kind of pastoral aid to the numerous educated people who, like Kant himself, 'practised' the public Christian religion only with a bad conscience. He set about accomplishing this aim by interpreting for them as many revealed truths as possible as pure truths of reason in the sense of his philosophical ethics. He bestowed on them a new rational sense, seeking in this way to indicate a passable way between philosophical conviction and civic loyalty. Kant never denied that, as far as he was concerned, cultural and church-political goals were bound up with his scholarly and pastoral aims. These were the transformation of the faith of the Church into the faith of religion (the latter being dexterously adapted to ecclesiastical language and specialist theological terminology), the transformation of the Church into an ethical bourgeois society, and the transformation of Christianity into humanity. For this reason, notwithstanding his otherwise unconcealed rejection of Church and theology, he showed a notably conspicuous interest in theological education. This is proved by his concrete proposal in a remarkable passage from the preface to the first edition of *Religion within the Limits of Reason Alone,* 'upon completion of the academic instruction in biblical theology, always to add, by way of conclusion, as necessary to the complete equipment of the candidate, a special course of lectures on the purely *philosophical* theory of religion (which avails itself of everything, including the Bible), with such a book as this, perhaps, as the text (or any other, if a better one of the same kind can be found)' (p.10).

In accordance with what has been previously outlined, we can maintain that Kant's philosophy was intended in every way to be a kind of mediation. It was a rational mediation for the educated of his day, not merely between English empiricism and Franco-German rationalism, but also between free-thought and orthodoxy, reason and Bible, knowledge and faith, indeed even in a certain sense between sin and grace. Nor was he entirely mistaken when, *vis-à-vis* the earlier mediaeval mediation and hence to some extent also *vis-à-vis* Reformation philosophy, he was disposed in his own essay in mediation to lay more stress on the subject than on the object, on personality than on community, on the individual soul than on the visible Church, on the conscience than on institutions, on faith than on dogmas, and on practical than on theoretical reason. The danger inherent in his brand of autonomous mediation, however, consisted in its remaining in the end of the day but a *circulus humanus* and hence, with reference to genuine mediation, no more than a *circulus vitiosus.* Kant certainly had too deep an experience of man and the world to have been able to overlook the moral rift in reality. But he located the origin of this rift exclusively in an immanent inner strife on the side of man (in the radical evil of human nature), and not in man's having been torn away from God. In this a thoroughly modern man, he believed in creative personality, which he deemed capable of healing the rift through self-legislation and self-redemption, in an autonomy without theonomy.

We should be doing Kant an injustice, though, if we cast doubt on his robust faith in God. For him as for Rousseau this was a truth of the heart and of the conscience prior to and beyond all philosophical reflection and demonstration, as he confesses towards the end of the *Critique of Pure Reason*: 'In other words, belief in a God and in another world is so interwoven with my moral sentiment that as there is little danger of my losing the latter, there is equally little cause for fear that the former can ever be taken from me.'[22] In both his *Critiques,* mindful of the scepticism, atheism and materialism that were on the upsurge in western Europe, and in opposition to the loud attacks of reason, Kant had taken faith in God under his wing, seeking to hoist its foes in their own petard. For his *Religion within the Limits of Reason Alone* this and only this has the status of binding dogma: faith in God as creator (better, lawgiver), preserver and judge. To this threefold faith there corresponds the threefold separation of powers in constitutional law into legislative, executive and judicial (p. 131).

Kant has been praised for getting to grips with the transcendent and mysterious dimensions of the concept of God, for having cut loose the latter from the analogy of human relationships, and for having abandoned the image of the organiser and ruler of the world in favour both of an Absolute withdrawn from every kind of finite description and of a supra-temporal and eternal idea of the Godhead no longer accessible to human thought. Kant's significance here was truly epoch-making, not only with reference to the *aporias* of the proofs for the existence of God. There should, on the other hand, be no talk of naive psychologising in the description of divine judgment and activity, and least of all may one speak of an arbitrary God. But from our theological perspective we may not overlook the fact that, when measured in terms of the Old and New Testaments, Kant's God appears to be a remote God. He is not a present, living God of history, acting with power and committed to the world, but a postulate of the practical reason, intrinsically incapable of further description and only requiring peripheral consideration as a means of establishing harmony between resolute moral duty and human happiness (p. 230). This distant God's 'works of grace' 'we cannot adopt...into our maxims either for theoretical or for practical use' (p. 49). The binding authority of the moral law is not to be found in God, but in man himself, in the moral resolution of practical reason. This distant God is no longer competent

---

[22]*Critique of Pure Reason,* 650.

85

to establish morality; rather, morality establishes him (p. 4f). Is it to be wondered at, then, that Kant has been accused of naturalism and Pelagianism? Kant both overlooked and deepened the rift where it already existed. He deepened the remoteness of God from man and magnified the distance between man and God: the difference between the two was no longer a genuine distinction, but an absolute dissimilarity. The ultimate root of Kant's naturalism and Pelagianism is to be located in the end of the day in his deism.

After J. Bohatec established the significance of Reformed dogmatics, especially those of J. F. Stapfer, for Kant's philosophy of religion, H. Redmann has recently pointed out that Kant was, already in his pre-critical period, decisively influenced by a Calvinistic understanding of God and creation. Stapfer's thoughts and formulations about the sublimity of God and the limits of reason exercised a remarkable influence on Kant's dialogue with Newton and Leibniz; so he had theological motives in conferring independence on the material world. But it was just this concern for the self-reliance of the world and for the distinction between the world and God (e.g., against occasionalism) that finally led to God's withdrawal from the world and to the latter's being left to its own devices.

We can unfortunately apply a reliable test to demonstrate the remoteness of Kant's God: in his philosophy *prayer* dies. '*Praying,* thought of as an *inner formal* service of God and hence as a means of grace, is a superstitious illusion (a fetish-making)' (pp. 182f). It is true that Kant recommends the 'spirit of prayer without ceasing'; but this boils down to 'the disposition, accompanying all our actions, to perform these as though they were being executed in the service of God' (p. 183). 'Devotion' is nothing but the subjective 'operation of the moral idea' (p. 185). He appeals to the needfulness of everlasting 'adoration', as a spiritual mood (p. 185) in order to dispense with prayer as such. Since, in the opinion of the Enlightenment, religion must be preserved for 'the people', Kant demands the retention of public prayers. 'Hence it also comes about that the man who has already made great progress in the good ceases to pray, for honesty pertains to his first maxims.' Honest as he was, he did not even go to church services, and it was his custom on academic occasions to fall out of the festal processions in front of the Church and go home. 'Thus, in spite of all our veneration for Kant both as a personality and in respect of his life-work, it will have to remain the case that he had no understanding for prayer.'[23]

In terms of Kant's deistic theology and naturalist-moralistic anthropology it is all too understandable that he could have little comprehension for the Christ-event in its theanthropic structure. In his thought a genuine encounter marked by a genuine confrontation of God and man could not arise. He certainly endeavoured to unite God and man by means of the idea of an ethical mankind (the 'Son of God'), which proceeds, uncreated, from the Being of God, but which is 'incarnate' in that the idea of moral perfection 'has established itself in man' and thus 'has *come down* to us from heaven and has

---

[23]W. A. Schulze: *Kant und das Gebet*, 63.

assumed our humanity' (p. 54). The theologian, however, will scarcely find a convincing presentation of the transition from the Christology of the Idea (cf. the chapter heading on p. 54, 'The Personified Idea of the Good Principle') to the Christology of the historical person of Jesus. In our contemporary idiom, 'Jesus the proclaimer' (significant as a teacher of morality and as an example of a humanity well-pleasing to God) and the 'proclaimed Christ' (rationally transposed into the ideal and universal) are well-nigh unbridgeably sundered from one another in Kant's thought. The *disposition* basically takes the place which Jesus occupies in Christology; and it is the disposition which redeems, accomplishes atonement, and is the ground of grace and justification. Therefore faith in the 'Son of God' appears in the end of the day to be man's faith in himself, and redemption appears to be an event in which man behaves as his own representative (pp. 70-72). To this end Kant consistently reverses the way of grace proclaimed in the Gospel: good conduct does not proceed from grace, but grace proceeds from good conduct. Justification becomes self-improvement, justifying faith becomes a moral disposition and the ethic of love becomes the ethic of law (pp. 40-49).

If this presentation of Kant's position is correct, then it is incontestable that his reinterpretation distorts decisive characteristics of the biblical tradition. To put it sharply, what the Bible intends theologically, christologically and ecclesiologically Kant understands morally, anthropologically and subjectively. All of this only becomes possible for him in virtue of his peculiar hermeneutical approach, according to which the rationalist understanding is made the criterion of all scriptural interpretation. Should his prior understanding be measured against the biblical message itself, fundamentally different results would be achieved.

Even if we do follow Kant's hermeneutical approach, however, we still find ourselves confronted by open questions. Let us take note of just one of them with reference to Kant's ethic of obedience and law. In the first Foreword to *Religion within the Limits of Religion Alone,* Kant maintains that, in what reason authoritatively presents to man as end or final end, 'man seeks something that he can love' (p. 6). Now love is more than respect. Kant also characterises 'love of the law' as 'the goal of moral perfection of finite creatures' (p. 136), this goal being attained when the law is not merely observed out of respect (i.e. fear of God) but also out of childlike duty conceived as the 'love of God' (p. 170). Bearing these aspects of Kant's teaching in mind, H. Blumenberg poses a critical question which takes on a special significance in our christological context. 'Does the key lie here to those aspects of religion that remain a closed book as far as Kant is concerned? For love has an intense need of a face and loses heart before the "physiognomically" inconceivable, before what is too "pure" to be able to assume a shape or "become flesh". The strength of religion lies precisely in the "*anthropomorphism*" of God, which is the very substance of the Christian incarnation and the very thing that Kant's "pure faith of religion" was meant to resist. The reality which we might dub the "physiognomical" factor in religion is not perceived by Kant in its full significance, which is certainly offensive to "pure" reason, while being "humanly" irresistible. Religious phenomena are significant for him as mere "vehicles" which the pure faith of religion will discard in the course of its realisation. But what if God always needs vehicles to be able to be "real" for man? There is indeed more to being real than to be expected, in hope, out of the dimension of the *future*. What is at stake in all religion is the *presence* and *presentation* of the divine . . .'[24]

From this point of view the christological question is posed afresh and transmitted to Kant's successors: should it not be possible after all for something universal to be taking place in this individual, something eternal in this history, the ideal in this empirical reality, subjectivity in this objectivity, the idea in this fact and the Absolute in this relativity? And should this not be possible precisely because the limit set for man is no limit for God himself, and because for the believer God himself has entered the arena in this virtuous man Jesus?

M. Seckler gives an exquisite account of how the question transmitted to Kant's successors was one that had already been imposed on his predecessors. 'If for Thomas the last time (*ultima aetas*) is inaugurated in a definitive manner by the event of Christ, if therefore an historical individuality inaugurates a supraindividual time and state of being, this means that here *universal significance* is conferred on a *single fact*, that a supra-individual norm is given in an historical-individual existence, that a portion of history is elevated to the level of omni-historicity, because it is absolute, or, in other words, that there is given here the *universale concretum* (concrete universal). This solution of the problem of universals in the sphere of the historical question is not explicitly found in Thomas. This problem was not posed for him sufficiently acutely or urgently for that. It would seem, however, that this solution is a legitimate conclusion drawn from his own presuppositions. For him Christ is the definitive event which inaugurates a new and definitive time and state of being. He is the head (*caput*) and the universal principle (*universale principium*) not only of the Church, but also of all men (*caput omnium hominum*). As a matter of fact, he is to be understood in Thomas as the *universale concretum*. With reference to our enquiry about the medium of perception of the historical sense – about the *universale* of history – this means that this *universale* cannot be given *ante rem*, as a plan already given and known *before* the event, but only *in re*. The *universale* of history lies *in* the historical and once-for-all event of the incarnation; supra-time lies *in* time; universal value lies *in* a moment. Indeed, they lie in *this* event, in *this* time, in *this* moment of Christ. A section of recent Protestant theology is characterised by the twin tendencies of dissolving Jesus' "facticity" as a result of his universal significance, and of whittling him down to a mere fact as a result

---

[24]H. Blumenberg: *Kant und die Frage nach dem 'gnädigen Gott'*, 570.

of his historicity. Both trends stem from the rending asunder of the *universale* and the *concretum*, from the abyss that yawns between fact and meaning or, to express it in the Thomistic idiom, from the problem of universals in its historical aspect being thought of either in a nominalistic or in a Platonic manner.'[25]

As the very titles of his major works indicate, Kant was essentially a critical thinker on a grand scale. His prime concern was to question, to distinguish and to examine. For personal as well as technical reasons, he was unable to accomplish the systematic exposition of post-critical metaphysics that he planned. But just as a Plato and an Aristotle came in the wake of Socrates, so the systematicians Fichte, Schelling and Hegel followed the critic Kant. As the preceding fragments showed (for instance, with reference to the sharp separation of reason from sensuality), Hegel was already on the way to his goal, and by this time had already gone beyond Kant. There has been much discussion of the question how it came about that Hegel could write such a Kantian *Life of Jesus*. Specific differences between Kant and Hegel, such as those shown up by Haering,[26] carry little weight in this context. This thoroughly Kantian *Life of Jesus* remains a *crux interpretum* right up to the most recent publications. It occasions the more surprise in that Hegel was not so disposed to take over Kant's way of thinking, which bordered on the scrupulous and was marked by a continual urge for precise definition, nor his basic scholarly and moral attitudes, as he was to take over positive results of Kant's practical and religious philosophy. What had in fact taken place? It has been conjectured that we are dealing here with a relapse into Kantianism on Hegel's part; but this hypothesis explains nothing. Or was it a mere exercise in Kantianism? But the *Life of Jesus* was written with too much interest and sympathy for us to suppose that. Or was it, as Haering believes,[27] some sort of preliminary spade-work (in the sense of a historical analysis of Jesus' moral life and teaching), and perhaps an early attempt to answer the question, to what extent the person of Jesus is suited to Hegel's folk religion. We may pose the counter-question, however, whether the radiant power of Jesus as the great, noble and pure man proclaiming the triumph of truth over the lie, of liberty over servitude and of virtue over vice, is meant to be highlighted in a genuinely positive manner in the province of folk religion. We have already repeatedly learned from Hegel that Jesus' religion was conceived not as a folk, but as a private religion (*N, 360*). This might well prove to be our starting-point in solving the riddle: Jesus' life and teaching are not to be used for folk religion, but they are to be used for 'private religion', 'for the development of

---

[25]M. Seckler: *Das Heil in der Geschichte*, 209f.
[26]cf. *op. cit.* I, 185.
[27]*op. cit.* I, 186ff.

individual men' (*N,* 41). This holds good at all events so long as this teaching of Jesus is understood, in company with Hegel, in a Kantian, moral manner. According to Hegel the teaching of Jesus and the teaching of Kant have this in common, that they are usable not for folk, but only for private religion. Hence we are in a position to explain the context of Hegel's *Life of Jesus* with reference both to what had gone before and to what was to come. On the one hand, it becomes clear how at one and the same time he could be so Kantian in his description of the life of Jesus (in the sense of the *Religion within the Limits of Reason Alone*: his knowledge of the theoretical writings was inadequate at that time) *and* so post-Kantian in the requirements he would exact of a folk religion (as we saw in the preceding fragments). And it also becomes clear, on the other hand, how the Kantian *Life of Jesus* is inwardly bound up with the following fragment which, in its turn, bears a post-Kantian stamp. This connection is to be located in the fact that, with his *Life of Jesus,* Hegel had clarified the presupposition needful to answer the question which, for him, was the most important of all, namely how Christianity, originally a pure private religion, could become a positive religion, but not a genuine living folk religion. Had it been published, this *Life of Jesus* would certainly have created quite a stir as the most significant *Life of Jesus* composed on the basis of the new religion of reason. Even so, as far as Hegel himself was concerned, this manuscript was not ripe for publication.

4. From Proclaimer to Proclaimed

'How did the proclaimer become the proclaimed? As far as Hegel was concerned, the reply given to this question is identical with the solution to the problem how Christianity was able, indeed obliged to become an objective, positive religion.' Echoing R. Bultmann's way of putting the matter, G. Rohrmoser[28] thus paraphrases what was for Hegel the central hermeneutical issue. This was made plain especially in the final fragments from the Bern period, which Nohl collected under the title *The Positivity of the Christian Religion*[29] (=*K,* 67-145). Nohl's departure here from the chronological sequence by placing a revised Introduction from the year 1800, i.e. dating from Hegel's later sojourn in Frankfurt (*N,* 139-151; *K,* 167-181), *before* the bulk of the manuscript from the year 1795 (*N,* 152-213; *addenda* 214-239: *K,* 67-145; 145-167), has wrought confusion for many interpreters down to the present day, even for Rohrmoser.

---

[28] *Subjektivität und Verdinglichung,* 30f.
[29] Quotations from Nohl's *Hegels theologische Jugendschriften* (Tübingen, 1907) will be given, where possible, from the translation by T. M. Knox: *Early Theological Writings* (Chicago, 1948). References will be given as *K* followed by the appropriate page number.

Only when we start our reading with the original draft of the manuscript, the date of whose composition was very close to that of the *Life of Jesus,* does it become clear to how great an extent the substance of this fragment is bound up with the latter. The general wording of the revised draft scarcely permits us to recognise the Kantian stamp Hegel had placed on the proclamation of Jesus (cf. *K,* 179f); the Kantian flavour of the original version, however, cannot be overlooked (cf. *K,* 68f) and confirms our interpretation and classification of the *Life of Jesus.* In this fragment too Jesus is the Kantian teacher of virtue, who 'undertook to raise religion and virtue to morality and to restore to morality the freedom which is its essence' (*K,* 69). In this process only 'in obedience to the moral law ... not to descent from Abraham, did Jesus ascribe value in the eyes of God' (*K,* 70). He taught 'the value of a virtuous disposition and the worthlessness of a hypocritical exactitude confined to merely external religious exercises' (*K,* 70). But this 'simple doctrine, which required renunciation, sacrifice, and a struggle against inclinations', was not able to prevail against Jewish national pride, hypocrisy and sanctimoniousness. For 'Jesus had the pain of seeing the utter shipwreck of his plan for introducing morality into the religious life of his people', and he 'was sacrificed to the hatred of the priesthood and the mortified national vanity of the Jews' (*K,* 70).

This set the scene for the problem which Hegel sought to solve: How could a 'positive' religion, that is, one that rested on an external authority, of an historical and ecclesiastical nature, emerge from Jesus' purely moral religion of reason and virtue, consisting, as it did, in eternal truths (*K,* 71f)? With this essay the historical questions posed by neology, that is, by Semler, penetrated the province of post-Kantian philosophy. Lessing's distinction between the eternal and universal and the historical and positive had posed the problem in an acute form, as had the subsequent distinction drawn by Kant himself between the pure faith of reason and the statutory faith of the Church. In this fragment Hegel now attempts to arrive at a solution through an analysis of the historical element. The things that had already been stirring him in the *Life of Jesus* are here rendered explicit. In the context of the contemporary religious and political situation, he is concerned with critical reflection on the historical origin of Christianity. He does not intend to pursue a general historical enquiry 'how this or that positive doctrine has been introduced into Christianity, or what changes have gradually arisen along with any such doctrine' (*K,* 74), or an abstract-rational reflection 'whether this or that doctrine is wholly or partly positive, is knowable purely from reason or not' (*K,* 74). Rather he is concerned with the question of the historical origin of Christianity, which was for him by no means normative and unambiguous, i.e. with 'those features in the religion of Jesus which led to its becoming positive, i.e. to its becoming either such that it was postulated, but not by reason, and was even in conflict with reason, or else such that it required belief on authority alone, even if it did accord with reason' (*K*, 74).

Being as he was under the influence of Kant's vision, Hegel, in his *Life of Jesus*, had not yet clearly seen that Jesus himself had preached more than a pure doctrine of virtue, that 'Jesus was compelled for his own purposes to speak a great deal about himself, about his own personality' (*K*, 75). The reason for this lay in the fact that the concrete historical situation, that is, the legalistic historical consciousness of the Jews, forced him to do so. In the face of a people which attributed all its ritual, political and civil laws directly to divine authority, the desire to appeal to reason alone 'would have meant the same thing as preaching to fish' (*K*, 76). Jesus, unlike Kant, 'therefore demands attention for his teachings, not because they are adapted to the moral needs of our spirit, but because they are God's will' (*K*, 76). Furthermore, the Jewish expectation of the coming of the messiah (*K*, 77), along with the general interest in his person (*K*, 78) and, in particular, his miracles (*K*, 78-81)[30] conspired to bring about an emphasis on the person of Jesus. Even so, 'it was not Jesus himself who elevated his religious doctrine into a peculiar sect distinguished by practices of its own' (*K*, 80). On the contrary, the sectarian character of the Church and the cult of Jesus were the work of his zealous but intellectually limited disciples, who 'were distinguished neither as generals nor as profound statesmen' (*K*, 81). When the latter now proclaimed the doctrines of virtue as commandments of Jesus, the upshot was that 'though this is otherwise a contradictory conception, the religion of Jesus became a *positive* doctrine about *virtue*' (*K*, 86). Thereby the foundation was laid for that disastrous development of the succeeding era which Hegel, largely under the influence of Edward Gibbon's *Decline and Fall of the Roman Empire* (1737) and with reference to Moses Mendelssohn's *Jerusalem: A Treatise on Religious Power and Judaism* (1783), verbosely expounds and criticises with the utmost hostility (cf. *K*, 85-145). That is to say, the anti-legalistic private religion of Jesus is turned, against its nature, into a legalistic public religion. But Christianity does not remain the religion of a puny sect, for growth in numbers and other political influences conspire increasingly to pervert the religion of Jesus (even in Protestantism!) into a state religion with compulsory membership and into a disfigured folk Church, which permits itself to be guaranteed and sanctioned by the authority and power of the state right down to the level of cult and school. In short, there is a merger of Church and state. Hegel perceives that the process has come full circle and deems its upshot to be fourfold: the inconsistent re-Judaising of Christianity; theological rationali-

---

[30]On the lack of clarity in the question of miracles, cf. Haering: *op. cit.* I, 265-268.

sation of the religious and political enslavement wrought by an originally anti-legalistic religion; a perversion of virtue and morality into hypocrisy and legalism; and the historical success of Christendom on the basis of its objective failure.[31] A positivity fashioned in this way adds up finally to the 'externalisation' of man, who thereby ceases to be man (cf. *K*, 144). This calls forth a protest on Hegel's part, which appears in many respects to anticipate Feuerbach's and Marx's critique of religion. An example of this protest is given in the pages that got added on to the original fragment, in which Hegel once more, in utopian and critical vein, takes sides with the genius of a living Greek folk and fantasy religion against the sad and tiresome ecclesiastical Christianity (*K*, 145-167). 'Apart from some earlier attempts, it has been reserved in the main for our epoch to vindicate at least in theory the human ownership of the treasures formerly squandered on heaven; but what age will have the strength to validate this right in practice and make itself its possessor?' (*K*, 159). As far as Hegel is concerned, the upshot of this unprecedentedly pungent criticism levelled at historical Christianity is clear. It must not be restricted to a mere change of attitude, but must issue in the rejection of the orthodox, theological system and of the political, feudal system, in the disentanglement and separation of Church from state, and in the renewal, both religious and political, of a moral society. This is to take place for the sake of political liberty, and Marxist interpreters are right in detecting the influence of vigorous impulses from the French Revolution here. But what many Marxists overlook is that this is also to take place for the sake of religion. Indeed, this is demanded by the very concept of religion. 'If one may speak of political atheism in Hegel's case, then one may not do so in the sense of a root and branch denial of religion, but only in the sense of his calling into question the orthodox ecclesiastical political system and the theological presuppositions contained in it.'[32]

A distinct understanding of faith forms part of the theological presuppositions of this ecclesiastical system, a system which has purchased its ideological significance at the cost of a real loss of meaning. This understanding of faith is sharply rejected by Hegel in a manuscript to be found in *Nohl*, 233-239,[33] which stems from the winter of 1795-96 and is most fitly dealt with at this point. It is a 'positive faith', in the sense of an intellectually conceived *fides quae* ('a system of religious propositions or truths'; *N*, 233), which exacts of man a *sacrificium intellectus*. According to Hegel it is the characteristic of a

---

[31]cf. the acute, even if (anti-)theologically biassed, analyses in H.-J. Krüger: *Theologie und Aufklärung*, 62-80.

[32]G. Rohrmoser: *op. cit.*, 40.

[33]On the dating of this manuscript, see G. Schüler: *op. cit.*, 130 (No. 54), and cf. 143f. This is not included in *K*.

positive faith that man does not receive the truth in virtue of his own insight, but merely as a duty of faith on the strength of authority and command. Two further ideas are implied by this 'positive faith'. First, there is a well-defined concept of God as an independent Lord and governor, whom it behoves people in their creaturely capacity to obey and to thank. Secondly, and as a correlate of the first notion, there is the claim that human reason is marked by the attributes of incompetence, helplessness and bondage. 'Whoever recognises the superior authority of another Being, not only over the impulses of his life (bearing in mind that this must be acknowledged by everyone, be it under the name of nature, fate or providence), but even over his spirit, indeed over the whole range of his being, cannot avoid a positive faith. The ability to hold such a faith presupposes as a matter of necessity the forfeiture of the freedom and independence of reason, which is accordingly incompetent to offer resistance to any alien force. Here is to be found the point of origin of all belief or unbelief in a positive religion. At the same time it is the centre round which all controversies revolve; and even if it is not plainly and consciously perceived, it forms the reason for all submissiveness or obstinacy. It is precisely at this point that the orthodox have to hold fast and give nothing away . . .' (*N*, 234).

A momentous change in the concept of God, albeit one which first comes to systematic fruition in Hegel's Frankfurt period and to which we shall have to return at the start of the next chapter, is foreshadowed in this rejection of an intellectual isolation of God from man and an absolute opposition between them, and in the rejection of an absolute divine transcendence and a passive submission on the part of human reason. In every respect, Hegel's thought is on the move. This is apparent in his attitude to the 'positivity' of Christianity and in his breaking through from an almost total rejection of everything positive to a growing understanding of the phenomenon (even while still withstanding it), and at length to a clear acceptance of a good (alongside the bad) kind of positivity. The extent to which he underwent this development becomes clear when we glance at the section which Nohl placed at the beginning of this group of fragments. The revision of the Introduction, penned at the close of the sojourn in Frankfurt and dated 24 September 1800, makes it strikingly clear just how open everything basically was for Hegel during his time in Bern. The Bern Introduction bespoke a clear rejection of (a basically bad kind of) positivity, while the revision composed in Frankfurt testifies to a discriminating affirmation of (a legitimate kind of) positivity. Hegel continues uncompromisingly to reject the following sequence: a bad kind of positivity leading to religio-political enslavement and terror, superstition, servile submission to authority, legal compulsion, the spirit of subjectivity, isolated objectivity and absolutised contingency (cf. *K*,

170). The difference in Hegel's maturer position, however, resides in the fact that his polemics are now directed against the rejection by the Enlightenment (and by Kant) of any and every kind of positivity. As he shrewdly perceives, this rejection rests on a completely abstract, supposedly well-known and universally valid concept of human nature measured against which everything positive must seem anti- or supernatural, anti- or suprarational (cf. *K*, 167-170). He is now prepared to accept a positivity which is given along with the structure of every kind of religion and spiritual life, for '[r]eligion has to become positive at this stage, or there would be no religion at all' (*K*, 169). Let it be noted how the idea of positivity is now narrowed down to the bad variety, and how Hegel now comments on the subject with studied discrimination. This is, by the way, a formal example of how the dialectical method was developed by being applied to such concrete phenomena. In the quotation which follows a number of elucidations are inserted in brackets. 'Actions, passions, and associations may all count as sacrosanct in a religion. Reason proves their accidentality (formerly: positivity in the bad sense) and claims that everything sacrosanct is eternal and imperishable (formerly: that is to say, not positive). But that does not amount to a proof that these religious matters are positive (in the bad sense!), because imperishability and sacrosanctity may be linked with accidentality and must be linked with *something* accidental; in thinking of the eternal, we must link the eternal with the accidentality of our thinking (i.e. positivity in the good sense). It is another thing altogether if the accidental as such, i.e. as what it is for the understanding, makes claims to imperishability, sacrosanctity, and veneration; at that point reason's right to speak of (bad) positivity does come on the scene' (*K*, 171).

What is taking place here is that the positivity of religion is being recognised and differentiated – albeit without actually using the word – as historicity. There is a historicity to do with human nature: 'The living nature of man is always other than the concept of the same, and hence what for the concept is a bare modification, a pure accident, a superfluity, becomes a necessity, something living, perhaps the only thing which is natural and beautiful' (*K*, 169). Likewise there is a historicity proper to religion: 'An ideal of human nature, however, is quite different from general concepts of man's vocation or of man's relation to God. The ideal does permit of particularisation, of determination in detail, and therefore it demands appropriate religious actions, feelings, usages, demands an excess of these, a mass of excessiveness which in the lamplight of general concepts seems only ice and stone' (*K*, 170). Hegel now acknowledges the limitations of reason, which he had rejected in the earlier manuscript: 'The universality of this criterion must therefore be restricted, because understanding and reason can be judges only if appeal is made to them . . . Understanding and reason may claim to sit in judgment on everything; they readily pretend that everything should be intellectual and rational. Hence they descry positivity easily enough, and the screams about mental slavery, superstition, and suppression of conscience continue without end' (*K*, 171). Hegel now thinks than even the Christian view of man, which he had formerly loathed, 'cannot in itself exactly be called positive; it rests on the surely beautiful presupposition that everything high, noble, and good in man is divine, that it comes from God and is his spirit, issuing from himself' (*K*, 176).

The tide has indeed turned; for a new and no longer onesidedly rationalistic hermeneutic is in the making. Hegel no longer intends to join in the 'endless, vacuous, and wearisome frightful chatter, . . . whether there are positive commands and doctrines in the Christian religion' (*K*, 172). His present conviction is 'that what our time needs instead perhaps is to hear someone proving the very opposite of what results from this 'enlightening' application of universal concepts' (*K*, 172). Hegel instantly hastens to qualify this statement by adding that such a proof would – of course! – 'not proceed on the principles and the method . . . of the old dogmatics'. Instead it would take the form of a refurbishing of the old dogmatics that had been cast off by the Enlightenment, albeit in a new form and according to a new method: 'It would derive that now discarded theology from what these days we know as a need of human nature and would thus exhibit its naturalness and inevitability' (*K*, 172). Hence we can now clearly see just how far Hegel has distanced himself from the idea of 'denuding tradition of its power' and from the notion of a 'prejudice against prejudices', which we termed above, in the company of H.-G. Gadamer, as the prejudice of the Enlightenment. Hegel professes an historical fairmindedness with respect to the past: 'An attempt to do this presupposes the belief that the convictions of many centuries, regarded as sacrosanct, true, and obligatory by the millions who lived and died by them in those centuries, were not, at least on their subjective side, downright folly or plain immorality' (*K*, 172). On the subject of Jesus' life and teaching Hegel now simply wishes discreetly to ask whether misunderstanding might not have caused certain aspects of them later to become positive (in the bad sense): 'whether, in the form of his teaching, in his relationships with other men, both friends and enemies, such accidentals appeared which either of themselves or owing to circumstances came to have an importance not belonging to them originally' (*K*, 177).

5. Representations of Christ in the Modern Age

In his revision of the original manuscript Hegel did not progress beyond preliminaries, and we shall presently learn the reason for this. Even so, with an eye to what had gone before and to what was to transpire later, might we not ask whether his new hermeneutics had not already swung the door wide open to a completely new understanding of Christology which would go beyond the approval accorded to Jesus by the Enlightenment and Kant as a man embodying the ideal of virtue? We do not, of course, mean to imply by this that we should exclude the achievements of the Enlightenment from our consideration of Christology, nor that we should lightly esteem the modern understanding of the man Jesus, which had prevailed since the work of Semler, Reimarus, Lessing and Kant, and which was reflected in Hegel's *Life of Jesus* and in his *The Positivity of the Christian Religion.* On the contrary, let us once more make it quite plain, before we enter upon a new phase of Hegel's thought, that whoever (as still often happens) sees in the development of the modern conception of Christ since the Enlightenment mere apostasy not only undervalues the fertile new impulses that emerged here, but also fails to appreciate the many throwbacks that are made to representations of Christ of earlier ages.

We can illustrate this, though obviously only by highlighting certain instances, by pointing to the historical *interdependence* (which cannot be further discussed here) between the conception of Christ in *theology* and that in Christian piety, especially in Christian *art.* We may permit ourselves the following remarks on this.

The historico-critical exegesis that took shape in the Enlightenment is certainly to be regarded as dependent on the rational bibical criticism carried through by Spinoza, Grotius, Hobbes, Erasmus and Valla, and consequently as standing in the tradition of modern humanism. But within and beyond this movement, manifesting itself in the urge to lay hold of the historical and the empirical, another tradition was consciously being developed further. This was the mediaeval, and supremely the late mediaeval, tradition of piety and art focussed on Jesus Christ, which had made the transition from the supra-terrestial *Christus triumphans* to the earthly *Christus patiens.* It may be that the reaction to the abstract divine image of Christ espoused by scholastic theology – a reaction of which men were only partly concious at the time of the Enlightenment – provoked a swing to the opposite extreme. It was a long road, and full of surprises, that led from the empty cross, sumptuously studded with precious stones (the very reverse of the heathen cross with the donkey's head that emitted scorn and contempt!), and from the passion scenes *minus* the crucifixion, to the representations of a (for the time being) still unbroken Christ on the cross, which made isolated appearances in the post-Constantinian era from the fifth century onwards. The same may be said of the path that led from Christ the king and world judge, enthroned on the cross, who was portrayed on romanesque portals and apses, to the late Gothic *pie Jesu* passions (designed to provoke *compassio*), and to the gruesomely realistic *Man of Sorrows* (already bearing the mark of Protestant piety) depicted in Dürer's *Christ in Agony* and in the last crucifixion to come down to us from Grünewald. It may be that the naively free and easy instinct for the humanity of Christ, conditioned as it was by the Jesus piety of the age of the Crusades, tended to minimise the mystery of the incarnation in the spheres of piety and art: the path was long and laden with problems that led from the bridal mysticism of Bernard of Clairvaux's commentary on *Canticles,* and from the crib-mysticism of Francis of Assisi who bore the stigmata of the Crucified, to many all too human forms of devotion and to many all too sweet late mediaeval portrayals of the crib replete with the Madonna and the child Jesus. This path led at length to the classically beautiful paintings of the Italian Renaissance, which were, however, scarcely acquainted with the pains of the Crucified, and in which an idealised conception of man broke loose from the naturalised picture of Christ and came to stand on its own feet. But in spite of all this, the concern shown by late mediaeval mysticism, piety, painting and sculpture and then by Martin Luther for the concrete and human, remained a profoundly *Christian* preoccupation. Who would not fall silent before the unfathomable humanity of the suffering Son of God as it is portrayed in the Isenheim altar? Here, right in the middle of the turning point between the epochs (1516!), something is breaking through with elemental force which had not been forgotten, but which had certainly received a raw deal, in scholasticism's learned meditation on the subject of the *relatio relationis* of the impassible eternal Logos to the passible human nature and in the cerebral speculation concerning the possibility of Christ enjoying the *visio beata* even while on the cross.

The image of Christ inevitably carries with it a certain polarity in the idea of the *man* Jesus in whom *God* is revealed, and this remained a problem, for artists as well as for theologians. In seeking to grasp one of the two sides of the problem, they ran the danger of eluding the other. None of the conceptions of Christ entertained by the greatest masters of art (Giotto, Jan van Eyck, the French Gothic school, Fra Angelico, Michelangelo) and of theology (Origen, Augustine, Bernard, Thomas Aquinas, Luther, Calvin) was able to help faith out of its dilemma. Faith was continually seeking a solution to its state of dissatisfaction and continually wanting to look upon two incongruent conceptions as one. There was the *Beau-Dieu* of Chartres *and* the German saviour of mercy, the unsuffering beauty of Raphael's *Disputa and* Michelangelo's portrayal of the one who dies a human death, Velasquez' depiction of lofty suffering *and* Greco's of a death in writhing torment, William Blake's mystical-symbolic vision *and* Georges Rouault's comfortlessly comforting Christ crowned with thorns . . . Theology likewise had the Christ of the Alexandrines *and* that of the Antiochenes, the Christ of Latin scholasticism *and* that of mediaeval Jesus mysticism, the Christ of the Reformers *and* the Jesus of German critical exegesis . . .

But a harmonious marriage of enduring validity and beyond improvement did not come about in the case of this central theme of Christian art and Christian theology. As the *christologia caelestis* developed in the ancient Church, especially in its Greek part, the beardless, youthful and kind-hearted shepherd (or Orpheus) of the catacombs was eventually superseded, though this human youthfulness of Christ was temporarily recalled once more in the manuscript illustrations of the Carolingian-Ottonian period. This image was supplanted by the bearded, victorious *Imperator* and *Cosmocrator* who appeared in his incomparably glorious divinity in the visual representations of the imperial cult of late antiquity. The golden mosaics combined with the 'divine liturgy' and 'sacred theology' to form one *single* doxology to the 'holy, immortal God'. But under the weight of the courtly and inflexible untouchability of this awe-inspiring, eternal and majestically threatening Son of man who had been thus exalted to a golden heaven, at the deepest level people found it more and more difficult to get through to their high mediator. The upshot of this was that the people of the middle ages imagined and then painted an increasing number of other sacred figures in that central spot between heaven and earth where the *one* mediator between God and *all* men occupies his unshakable position. At the other end of the spectrum, the *christologia terrestris* characteristic of modern men (theologians, philosophers, artists), whose roots we have shown to lie in the middle ages, tugged with all the might of the force of gravity in a downward direction. The moderns were only seldom able to maintain the tension of paradox. It had been in these terms that, at the threshold of the modern period, Nicholas of Cusa (*Deus humanatus – copula universi – coincidentia oppositorum*), Luther (*Deus sub contrario*) and even Grünewald had sought to conceive of Christ. Grünewald, though, was not able to express his pictorial image of Christ in one, but only in two representations. This reflects the tension that obtained between the piteous and profound humanity of the highly exalted One, which found its ultimate expression in the clenched fingers and thorn-covered face of the Crucified, and the majestical and sublime divinity of the humiliated One, which radiated from the golden eternity of the risen Lord with pierced hands and feet.

To the extent that they have declined to pay homage to the mystical yet worldly pathos of the antithetical baroque, in turning to the man Jesus, people of the modern period have largely turned their back on the God who willed to reveal himself in him. We have already observed where this can lead in philosophy and theology under certain circumstances. In the province of art this is attested on the one hand by the sentimental representations of the Sacred Heart in late baroque Catholicism, and on the other by Rosalba Carriera's smooth saloon portraits executed in the style of the Enlightenment and by Fritzsch's delineations in the same *genre* of Jesus as an elegant popular philosopher. Then there were the pictures, current among Catholics and Protestants in the eighteenth century, of Jesus as a gardener or as an apothecary dispensing virtue powder; at a later date there was Thorwaldsen's classical saviour, who gave offence to Kierkegaard on account of the elimination of the scandal of the cross; and finally there was the mild and wishy-washy humanity of Jesus characteristic of the French and German Nazarenes and of the English Pre-Raphaelites. How one now once more harks back with nostalgia to the 'strong God' of Byzantium or to the *majestas Domini* of the middle ages! But we may no more regard the modern images of Jesus, especially those of philosophers and theologians, as a mere narrowing of perspective than we may pass the same judgment on late mediaeval Jesus piety. Apart from such purveyors of Christology in novel form as Bahrdt (who, as we have seen, was even attacked by Kant), these modern philosophers and theologians unmistakably engaged in a genuine and serious struggle to understand the humanity of Jesus in the context of a new age. This new age was no longer satisfied with a sterile scholastic Christology, nor did either Jesus mysticism and dramatic mystery plays or painting and sculpture fit the bill. Moreover, it had been largely deprived of the last-named aid by the removal of images from the churches at the Reformation, a loss which was made good neither by Bible illustrations and Lutheran-pietist hymns nor by Handel's incomparable *Messiah* and the grandiose *Passions* of Schütz and Bach. Something new was called for. The Enlightenment saw the emergence of an alienation of Christianity from art which took away the fertile ground out of which fresh images of Christ might grow; and it is only in the twentieth century, in particular since the 1920s, that eminent artists have once more been fashioning major representations of Christ (e.g. Beckmann, Corinth, Nolde, Masereel, Grosz, Rouault, Picasso, Barlach, Chagall, Matisse). It was otherwise in the case of theology, where significant results were achieved at an early date. These must not be played down in Church and dogmatics for reasons of apologetic concern.

The Enlightenment had unleashed an original vital impetus toward perception, understanding, reason and scholarship, and since its inception men had desired to speak rationally even of the man Jesus. Many things contributed to this development, not least pent-up resentments against dogma. But a hidden yearning for the genuine, true Jesus was also at work. Men would no longer rest content with uncontrollable legendary rumour, supra-temporal christological speculation foreign to real life, or edifying fantasy such as was to be found in Klopstock's *Messiah* of 1773 (on Hegel's aversion to this see *N,* 364). Instead – and we recall that Lessing had already flung the fire-brand of the *Wolfenbüttel Fragments* in 1778 – they were concerned with acquiring sober historical knowledge about this Jesus who, there and then in those towns and vilages, had lived, eaten, drunk and taught as man, Jew and rabbi. The problems bound up with such historical knowledge and the perils latent in such rational scholarship were clear to many from the beginning, and already at the time of the debate about Reimarus many had the impression that the whole substance of Christology was disintegrating in a blaze of critical fire. Even so, the desire to dispute the genuinely intellectual character of this critical scholarship would be tanta-mount to concurring in the Enlightenment prejudice that faith is not trusting perception but inhuman blindness and irrational violation of the intellect. The path from Semler, through Reimarus, Lessing and Kant to Hegel certainly has its limits and its pitfalls, but is not simply a wrong way nor is it merely the equivalent of unbelief. Secular attacks have rendered the orthodox Christian of today somewhat immune at least as far as this knot of problems is concerned, so that it is easy for him to summon into the world his faith, which is not of the sort to be troubled by reason. But who knows, at that time when reason was being aroused in humanity, perhaps even he would have swum along in the current of those days as a man of the Enlightenment, propelled by a harmless enthusiasm for the new rational exegesis? And his aim in so doing would have been to rescue the new exegesis. Or perhaps he would have declined any special commitment amid such stormy waves, preferring as a 'believer' full of anxiety before 'another gospel' to stay put in his secure ghetto on the dry but unfruitful sand of 'orthodoxy'? Whatever may have been the fate of our hypothetical believer, at that time it was not easy for thinking Christians of good will – and no one has a right to exempt Lessing, Kant and Hegel from this band of men – to find their way about a complex new set of problems thrown up by a new age. And we must lay it to the credit of Kant and Hegel that they dealt with the figure of Jesus in an intensive and fruitful manner, without having recourse to the critical fanaticism displayed by many a rationalistic polemicist. Thus they used their new spiritual experience to perform a work of translation, enabling the figure of those past times to speak in intelligible tones to the present day. Moreover we cannot overlook the fact that, for all his sober moralistic narration, in many places we can detect in Hegel a simple emotion and a subdued reverence. Much was distorted, in the violent and naive manner that characterises the opening stages of every revolution. But a decisive step was taken, cutting a path through all contemporary and traditional prejudice in order to advance both to the original biblical Jesus *and* to the discernment of a fresh significance for this Jesus as the Christ of today.

Chapter Three: The God-man

'The son of God is also son of man; the divine in a particular shape appears as a man. The connection of infinite and finite is of course as "holy mystery", because this connection is life itself.'(*K*, 262).

1. Forward to Unity

At the beginning of Hegel's sojourn in Bern, Hölderlin wrote to him as follows: 'I am certain that you have been thinking of me from time to time since we parted, with the watchword "kingdom of God". I believe that, after every metamorphosis, we should recognise ourselves by this watchword. Whatever may become of you, I am sure that time will never erode this feature in you; and I fancy that this shall also be the case with me' (XXVII, 9). This friendship had lasted and when Hölderlin, both in *Hyperion* and in *Empedocles,* dealt with the figure of the philosopher, he was inspired by the person of Hegel. Toward the end of his stay in Bern Hegel had himself dedicated his poem 'Eleusis' to Hölderlin. In this poem stand the phrases:

'I surrender myself to the Infinite,

I am in it, I am everything, I am it alone' (XXVII, 38).

Pantheism in its Spinozistic form had already at a very early date made a strong impression on both Hölderlin and Schelling. But what about their like-minded colleague Hegel? Even if he did not come to Bern as a pantheist, was it not the case that he left the city with such a persuasion? A movement from Enlightenment deism to a basically pantheist attitude was the trend of the times. Apart from the more subliminal influence exerted by the natural sciences and by mysticism, the responsibility for this shift lay on the shoulders of three figures who influenced the Tübingen friends: Kant, Lessing and Goethe.

However little the details of Kant's critique of the traditional proofs for the existence of God were actually understood, the educated thereafter deemed it to have been rigorously demonstrated that the existence of God is not patient of stringent proof and that the concept of God is not a matter of knowledge. While the idea of God was seldom totally denied, it had become the questionable furthest horizon of man's world-view and had assumed a vastly different form from what it had been hitherto. Instead of speaking of God as the thinking and acting creator and governor of the world, people were increasingly wont to talk of a 'Deity' which eluded all the limiting definitions of human thought. The 'Father, creator of heaven and earth' was turning into 'the Absolute'.

At the same time Lessing, who had died in the year in which the *Critique of Pure Reason* appeared, had posthumously introduced the ideas of Spinoza to the intellectual *avant-garde*. His enlightened friends in Berlin were deeply shocked when, four years after his death, Friedrich Heinrich Jacobi reported a private conversation he had had with Lessing shortly before his demise (*On the teaching of Spinoza in letters to Mr Moses Mendelssohn,* 1785). In 1780 he was supposed, according to his own words, to have abandoned the orthodox ideas of God; appealing to Spinoza, he had rejected the notion of God as personal cause of the world and come to conceive of him as a kind of soul of the universe embracing the world as one and all. Thus Jacobi accused Lessing not only of pantheism, but also of determinism, fatalism and atheism. Not even the exertions of Lessing's friend Moses Mendelssohn, who was a Wolffian and a fellow-worker of Nicolai, the leader of the Berlin enlighteners, were able to dispel the suspicion that he was a Spinozist and hence (relying at the same time on Leibniz) the founder of a specifically German form of dynamic pantheism.[1]

Goethe exercised his influence indirectly through his poetry, but it was rendered the more vigorous by his amiable, harmonious and almost self-evident worldliness. To begin with he was influenced by pietism and throughout his life was more than reserved *vis-à-vis* the radical French Enlightenment. The encounter with Herder's concept of nature and the debate with Lavater's Christ-piety enabled the Goethe of 'storm and stress' to win through to his own understanding of the divine. For him God was not the 'architect of the world' but the inscrutable 'ground of all things', a creative inventiveness and an active nature. He too would soon be accused of pantheism and atheism.

The Tübingen friends had made a precise study of the controversy over pantheism. Already in Tübingen and to a greater extent in the following years Hölderlin and Schelling had come under the spell of Spinozistic ideas, as had Herder, Fichte and Schiller before them. Indisputably the case with Hölderlin and Schelling, this is not so transparently true of Hegel. The reason for this consists chiefly in the fact that, apart from a few problematic formulations, Hegel's Bernese writings may certainly not be termed Spinozistic. As was made plain by the criticism levelled at Dilthey,[2] the Hegel who during his sojourn in Bern was not at all interested in theoretical speculation cannot be labelled as a 'mystical pantheist'. On the other hand, however, it is scarcely contestable that at an early date Hegel entertained sympathy for ideas tending toward pantheism and that, perhaps unbeknown to himself, a pantheistic

---

[1]For a very good treatment of Lessing's 'Spinozism', see R. Schwarz, who also offers a bibliography of the most important literature on this subject.
[2]H.-J. Krüger: *Theologie und Aufklärung,* 81f.

glimmer flickered over many of his religious expressions. So there was a starting-point for further development along these lines during Hegel's time in Frankfurt.

Dilthey's chief argument is supplied by the poem 'Eleusis' which Hegel sent to Hölderlin in August 1796, i.e. shortly before his departure from Bern. This poem was published by Rosenkranz in 1844,[3] but the original was long supposed to have disappeared until it was found again in the University Library at Tübingen and published by Haering as a facsimile in his first volume in 1929 (cf. also *H*, 380-383). In virtue of this discovery Haering was able to allege against Dilthey that Hegel, probably out of a feeling of having associated himself too closely with Hölderlin,[4] later crossed out the so-called pantheistic section 'I surrender myself to the Infinite &c'. And verses 70ff, which Asveld cited in support of his argument,[5] are by no means so clear-cut as the deleted verses 30ff. On the other hand, however, Niel has correctly observed against Haering that, while Hegel did indeed cross out that part of the poem, he had after all written the words in the first place! Niel remarked further that we may not sweepingly rule out any association of Hegel with 'mysticism', especially if we do not regard the latter – as did Haering – as an impersonal union, but rather as the consciousness of participation in an Absolute.[6] Hence we may not estimate Hegel's connection with Schelling and Hölderlin too lightly.

Much information can be gleaned from the correspondence Hegel carried on with Schelling from Bern. In a letter penned on the Eve of Epiphany 1795, Schelling was critical not only of the coalition between the Tübingen school theology and Kantianism, but also of the enlightened advocates of natural religion: 'I am firmly convinced that the old superstition not only of positive but also of so-called natural religion has already been combined in most heads with the letter of Kant's philosophy. It is amusing to watch them pulling in the moral proof as on a string. Before one knows what has happened, the *deus ex machina* leaps out – the personal, individual being that sits in heaven above! (XXVII, 14; Kaufmann, 301). Hegel was not just reserved in the face of these doubts about a 'personal individual being': 'One expression in your letter . . . I do not quite understand . . . Do you believe that we really cannot go that far?' (XXVII, 18; Kauffman, 303). This time Schelling was surprised by Hegel's words, and he made the following reply, quoting Lessing according to Jacobi's report: 'I confess that this question surprised me; I shouldn't have expected it from a friend of Lessing; but presumably you only asked to find out whether I had answered it *definitely for myself*; for you it has surely been decided long ago. For us, too, the orthodox concepts of God are no more. My answer is: We can go *beyond* a personal being. I have meanwhile become a Spinozist! Don't be amazed. You'll soon hear how. For Spinoza, the world (the object as opposed to the subject) was – *everything*; for me this is true of the *ego*.' (XXVII, 21f; Kaufmann, 304). In Hegel's next letter, from 16 April 1795, we read of his enthusiastic agreement with Schelling: 'I see in this the work of a man of whose friendship I can be proud, and who will make his great contribution

---

[3] *op. cit.*, 78-80
[4] *op. cit.* I, 291f.
[5] P. Asveld: *La pensée religieuse du jeune Hegel*, 144.
[6] H. Niel: *De la médiation dans la philosophie de Hegel*, 41f; cf. H. Glockner: *Entwicklung und Schicksal der Hegelschen Philosophie*, 84, and K. Schilling-Wollny: *Hegels Wissenschaft von der Wirklichkeit und ihren Quellen* I, 224f.

to the most important revolution in the system of ideas of the whole of Germany. It would be an insult to offer you any reassurance or to give a complete exposition of your system, since the activity of grasping such an object needs no such support. I expect Kant's philosophy, when fully developed, to bring about a revolution in Germany. It will proceed from principles that lie ready to hand and will, subject to general revision, only need to be applied to all previously existing knowledge. Certainly an esoteric philosophy will always remain, and the idea of God as the absolute ego will form part of it. In a recent study of the postulates of the practical reason I had a foretaste of the things you so clearly expounded to me in your last letter, things which I found in your writing and which will fully open up to me Fichte's *Foundation of the Theory of Knowledge*. The consequences that will flow from these things will fill many gentlemen with astonishment. Men's heads will swim at this highest peak of all philosophy, by which man is so greatly enhanced' (XXVII. 23f; cf. also 29-33; cf. Kaufmann, 305).

Kurt Wolf is going too far when, in connection with this letter and in opposition to Haering, he talks of an 'epochal climax' and of a 'change to the pantheistic system of identity'[7] and makes continual reference to Hegel's 'turning to metaphysics'.[8] On the other hand it will not do to play down this epistolary text as Haering does;[9] for the following factors all point patently in the same direction: Hegel's correspondence with Schelling and his contact with Hölderlin; the overall tenor of the poem 'Eleusis' and some individual statements in the Bernese fragments (e.g., *N*, 234); the peculiar extract (*N*, 367) from the end of his sojourn in Bern with a genuinely mystical passage culled from Meister Eckhart ('We have what we want there,' Hegel is later said to have remarked to F. von Baader about Eckhart[10]).

We can discern no epoch-making shift of direction towards speculative system of identity in the Hegel of the Bernese period, for in those days he exhibited no interest in any kind of speculative system. Yet we can discern the ripening of certain ideas and intuitions which, since the Tübingen days, had taken a back seat in the mind of this 'intimate of Lessing' and Spinoza, but which acquired more emphasis with the passage of time. Beneath all the Kantian formulas that he had used since the Tübingen period there shimmered a feeling for life which could not in the long run be harmonised with a purely moral 'thou shalt' ethic compounded of duties and commandments. Religion, being grounded in the depths of human subjectivity, was a matter of much more immediate concern for Hegel than it was for Kant, in whose thought it was belatedly attached to morality. 'Mystical pantheism' is not, however, the best way of describing the attitude which Hegel now came to adopt in his Frankfurt period, at least if 'pantheism' is taken to mean the indiscriminate identification of all things with God and 'mystical' to signify

[7] *Die Religionsphilosophie des jungen Hegel,* 28f.
[8] *op. cit.,* 39f, 95f, 128f.
[9] Haering: *op. cit.* I, 186-214; cf. 413-428.
[10] H. Glockner: *op. cit.* I, 158.

the private and direct religious experience of union with God. On the contrary, it may well be that Hegel's thought and piety – already in Bern, but soon much more decisively in Frankfurt – is in a state of transition away from the earlier separation of God and man towards the rational (not mystical) participation of man in the life of the Absolute (not unification). T. Steinbüchal has devoted a book to 'the basic problem of Hegel's philosophy', which he is disposed to see in the relation between the universal and particular or rather between the universal in the particular and the particular in the universal. He expresses the matter thus: 'In such an association there is a communal bond which does not negate particular being as such, but only *as* mere separated being, and which desires to incorporate it in its concreteness into that comprehensive being which binds together everything particular. Man and God, finite and infinite do not melt into indistinguishable oneness, but are bound together in an association of comprehensive unity.'[11]

Still lacking in Hegel's thought, however, is the clearly conceived and theoretically thought out principle of unity, namely, a monism of Spirit. Likewise still lacking is a recognition of the antithetical nature of all life, that is, of the dialectical structure of reality in general. Furthermore, there is as yet no sign of an impartial assessment of antithetical phenomena free from emotional bias, to wit, of a truly historical intellectual attitude. Our further task, however, will not be to describe the general philosophical development, but rather – against the background of this development – to give an account of Hegel's attitude to Christ. In Bern Christ had become intelligible to Hegel as the ideal of virtue, as virtue itself. In a letter of 30 August 1795, he had informed Schelling that it was also problematic for him 'what it might mean to draw near to God' (XXVII, 29; Kaufmann, 306). As Hegel now proceeds to take more seriously the unity of God and man, should not new and hopeful perspectives open up for Christology in this next period of his life?

But the Hegel who moves from Bern to Frankfurt[12] does not make a particularly hopeful impression on us. On an earlier occasion he had written to Schelling: 'I believe that, as for those theologians who are procuring critical building tools to reinforce their Gothic temple, it would be interesting to disturb them as much as possible in their ant-like zeal, to make everything difficult for them, and to whip them out of every corner of refuge till they can find no other and have to show their nakedness completely to the light of day'

---

[11] *Das Grundproblem der Hegelschen Philosophie* I, 204.
[12] On the Frankfurt period cf. the literature on Hegel's youth alluded to at the beginning of ch. 1; cf. also the recent specialist examination of the young Hegel's idea of God by E. de Guereñu in *Der Geist des Christentums und sein Schicksal*. J. Splett's monograph on Hegel's doctrine of the Trinity commences with the Frankfurt period.

(XXVII, 16f; Kaufmann, 302). Even so, in contrast to Schelling, Hegel had not as yet had the opportunity to shine. He had not yet published anything under his own name, nor did he have a teaching post. Notwithstanding these drawbacks he was glad to be able to move away from Bern in the autumn of 1796. He was immensely looking forward to seeing Hölderlin once more. The latter had decisively counselled him against becoming a 'coach' (*Repetent*) in Tübingen: 'If we are on the verge of chopping wood or handling boot wax and pomade, then . . .' (XXVII, 41). To this end Holderlin had procured Hegel a domestic tutorship near himself in Frankfurt, in the house of the merchant Gogel. Hegel replied to Hölderlin in November 1796, telling him '[h]ow great a part in my speedy decision is played by my longing for you – but nothing of that!', and assuring him that '[y]our unshakeable friendship toward me speaks out of every line of your letter' (XXVII, 44, 42). But when he stopped over for a few weeks in his home town of Stuttgart he was, in the words of his sister, 'turned in on himself . . . and cheerful only in the familiar circle' (*H*, 394). On his arrival in Frankfurt in January 1797 he felt more comfortable than in Bern, and he had more time to himself. His letters to a former girlfriend reveal something of his doings at this time. In addition to some well-meaning jokes aimed at the Catholic profession of his 'dear good-natured Nanette' (Endel), at St. Alexis and world-denying asceticism (XXVII, 49, 54), at Capuchins and confession (XXVII, 50) and at the rosary and the veneration of the saints (XXVII, 52, 54), he tells of his regular trips to the Comedy (XXVII, 52, 56), of the *Magic Flute* and *Don Juan* (XXVII, 52) and finally of balls: 'I am very Well disposed toward balls, for they are the most joyous feature of our sorrowful times' (XXVII, 58; Kaufmann, 312). Just so! 'Sorrowful times'! This did not only refer to world politics. In Frankfurt Hegel received the distressing news, transmitted by his sister Christiane in three curt sentences, of his father's death (XXVII, 58; Kaufmann, 313); and he later spoke retrospectively of 'that miserable Frankfurt' (XXVII, 333). Apparently, it just was not the place for him. By contrast, things were going smoothly for Schelling. Five years Hegel's junior, he was already called to join Fichte in Jena, now the centre of German philosophy, as *extraordinarius* professor in that discipline just one year after Hegel entered on his domestic tutorship in Frankfurt. And the final blow was supplied by Hegel's having to witness in Frankfurt the tragedy of his friend Hölderlin. The latter, a domestic tutor with the Gontard family, had greatly looked forward to Hegel's arrival, and he wrote afterwards that 'Hegel's company was very salutary' for him.[13] But his love for Frau Susette Gontard, his Diotima, was a dead end; after his employer reappeared

---

[13]Quoted in K. Fischer: *op. cit.* I, 42.

in September 1798, he made an abrupt departure, completely shattered, to wander hopelessly through Germany and France for years on end. Diotima died in 1802. Hölderlin, who had risen to the highest achievements in his *Hymns,* finally succumbed to the night of madness in 1806, and it was in this state that he was to live for another thirty-seven years in Tübingen on the Neckar (cf. the correspondence between Schelling and Hegel [XXVII, 71, 73; Kaufmann, 313, 314] which is ably reticent on this point).

The theological writings which Hegel penned in Frankfurt are also all unpublished personal notes, but the reader is immediately struck by the change in Hegel's use of language. In Bern he still had a youthfully straightforward, often somewhat passionately vehement style. The style is now becoming darker, the sentences cumbersome, and the thought exploratory. Admittedly a couple of somewhat awkward attempts at poetry come down to us from this period: 'To his poodle'; 'Moonshine bath'; 'Spring' (*H,* 383-385). Despite this, it is in the realm of scholarly prose that Hegel is striving after his own unmistakable style. Hegel's Frankfurt development in the fields of language and thought does not display a clean break with what went before, but it does demonstrate a strong change of direction, a fundamental crisis of growth. This occurred in the context of his not exactly brilliant personal circumstances and especially under the influence exercised on him by Hölderlin (and Schiller) and, as we shall show in greater detail, in the context of his preoccupation with the fate of Jesus.[14]

His friendship with Hölderlin, the *doctor seraphicus* of German Idealism, must have been of the greatest importance for Hegel during his time in Frankfurt. F. Rosenzweig already made it clear that 'his dealings with Hölderlin must be accounted of the highest significance' with respect to the new philosophical stance adopted by Hegel in Frankfurt, especially since, 'at least on Hegel's side, this friendship was the warmest, in personal terms, of his youth'.[15] J. Hoffmeister gives a detailed account[16] of how Hegel assisted his friend to a proper appreciation of *ratio* and insight; for a superabundance of poetic sensitivity and of a religious sense of lofty ideals had led Hölderlin to undervalue man's powers of cognition. Hoffmeister also shows how Hölderlin in turn aroused and intensified Hegel's own potentialities through his experience-filled concepts. Of particular importance were the multi-dimensional idea of fate and the concepts of life, love, beauty and nature, which are all modes of reconciliation.[17] According to this interpretation, Hegel took over central ideas from Hölderlin, while it would seem that Hölderlin borrowed from Hegel some significant aspects of his representation of Christ, above all with respect to the central figure of his unfinished tragedy *The Death of Empedocles.* 'Even though Hölderlin scarcely conceived his

[14]T. Haering: *op. cit.* I, 469-479.
[15]*Hegel und der Staat* I, 66.
[16]*Hölderlin und Hegel,* 15-19.
[17]*op. cit.,* 24-32.

Empedocles as Christ or consciously portrayed this character as an analogy to him, there is nevertheless a close connection between the fate and redemptive work of both. In a thoroughly unarbitrary way he bestowed on his saviour figure the characteristics of Christ, especially of Hegel's Christ. This is shown, not only in the parallels of person and situation, but also in the christianisation of the figure and fate of the ancient sage, a process which became more marked as the work matured.'[18]

E. de Guereñu has recently drawn attention to three basic ideas that run through Hölderlin's philosophical essays and that stand in parallel to Hegel's thought:[19] first, the characteristic importance of the scheme: original unity, separation, final unity; secondly, the importance of the word, of language, which, by bringing to fulfilment man's second, creative, power of reflection, has a similar function to that of knowledge in Hegel's thought – knowledge which is the consummation of love and thereby of reconciling unity; and, thirdly, the significance of Empedocles in Hölderlin's thought in comparison with Hegel's Christ. 'In the final version the necessity of his [Empedocles'] death is no longer, as in the first draft, bound up with any guilt of his own, for example, that of *hybris*. His going out of himself into the whole as he dies itself shoulders the whole; it occurs not for himself but for the many. This shows up the proximity to the mediator idea characteristic of Hegel's Christ and is thus further proof of the intellectual kinship that obtained between Hegel and Hölderlin notwithstanding all their dissimilarity.'[20]

Even so, it would be muddle-headed to twist Hölderlin's understanding of Christ into conformity with orthodox Christology. Hölderlin's own roots lay in pietism, but he was soon fascinated by the idealised notion of the religion, beauty and lifestyle of ancient Greece. As happened to many of his contemporaries, the world of Bible and Church had become alien to him. At an early date he came into contact with the thought of Kant and Spinoza, but after his time in Tübingen he switched his attention to Fichte in Jena. Subsequently turning away from Fichte, in Frankfurt he achieved a definitive breakthrough to a pantheistic feeling for life and exerted influence on both Schelling and Hegel. But the whole time – beginning with the early elegy 'Bread and Wine' and the almost programmatic hymn 'Reconciler, who wast ne'er believed' right through to the hymns 'The Solitary One' and 'Patmos' which stem from the period just before his mental breakdown – Hölderlin was wrestling with Jesus. His aim was to reconcile him with his other divine figures under the one Father, and to incorporate him on equal terms into his pantheon, his comprehensive vision of life and love. But in vain.

Emmanuel Hirsch's appraisal of Hölderlin's significance for the history of thought gives us food for reflection. 'Hölderlin belongs to those natures who would never at any time or under any intellectual or religious circumstances have fitted into the existing religious, intellectual or ecclesiastical scheme of things. In earlier centuries he would have ploughed his own furrow as a heretic, mystic or enthusiast. Around 1700 he would have been a radical pietist. Instead of the *Hyperion*, he would have written an autobiography; and instead of composing odes in the Greek style, he would have sounded forth heartfelt tunes of Christian piety. His now taking such a completely different path is a sign of the times. For as early as 1800 the crisis of transformation had

---

[18]*op. cit.*, 41.
[19]*Das Gottesbild des jungen Hegel*, 101-105.
[20]*op. cit.*, 104.

worn away a substantial part of the self-evident validity of Christianity. Even within pious Protestant Germany the inner power of the Christian faith was far weaker than was suspected in state, Church and theology'.[21]

Yet we can scarcely concur with Hirsch's view of Hölderlin as one who had advanced to an anti-Christian position and as a forerunner of Nietzsche. More correct is the judgment made by W. Michel (without reference to Hirsch) in his classical biography of Hölderlin. 'Theology has a word to say about the religion of these men, and we ought to heed it. But we should also listen to the voice of that wordless life which is not confession but longing. It is a voice that speaks with the tongues of those provisional times which God institutes so that something further should take place through the preparation of the abyss, that abyss which according to Hölderlin is plumbed by mortal rather than by celestial beings. It is certain that Hölderlin never lived out a brusque and systematic "No" to the Christian religion. Rather he did live out such a "Yes" to life in its entirety, a "Yes" which did not involve a closed mind even to Christianity.'[22]

Perhaps we ought to give Hölderlin himself the last word as we round off this brief excursus. In a letter to his mother dating from his time in Frankfurt (January 1799) and thoroughly in accord with what we have said above, he wrote as follows: 'I certainly do not wish to consider as witnesses of my inner and living faith the scribes and pharisees of our age, men who turn the dear holy Bible into a cold twaddle that destroys heart and soul. I know full well how they have come to this position, and because God forgives them for killing Christ more dreadfully than did the Jews, in that they turn his word into a letter and him, the living One, into an empty idol, because God forgives them for it, I forgive them for it too. Only I do not like to give myself and my heart where it is misunderstood; so I am wont to keep silence before those who are theologians *by profession* (that is, before those who are such not freely and with the heart, but with a coerced conscience and by reason of their office), just as much as before those who do not wish to know anything at all of the whole business because every kind of religion, which is after all the first and final need of man, has been marred for them from their earliest days by the dead letter and by the appalling command to believe. The present state of affairs generally – and of religion in particular – was bound to come about; indeed when Christ came into the world religion was in almost the same condition as it is today. But just as spring comes after winter, so new life always come after men's spiritual death, and the sacred remains for ever sacred even if men are heedless of it. And there is surely many a man who is more religious in his heart than he cares or is able to say; and perhaps many a preacher, simply unable to hit upon the right words, says more in his discourse than others suspect because the words that he uses are so conventional and subject to thousandfold misuse.'[23]

---

[21] *Geschichte der neueren evangelischen Theologie* IV, 455.

[22] *Des Leben Friedrich Hölderlins*, 72f. On the piety of the young Hölderlin, cf. 68-74; on his friendship with Hegel in Frankfurt, cf. 199-207; and on the late religious hymns, cf. 467-483. W. Binder's Zürich inaugural lecture on Hölderlin's poetry in the age of Idealism is important with reference to a possible overcoming of Idealism in Hölderlin's later works. On a general level cf. also H. A. Korff: *Geist der Goethezeit* III, 353-453, and M. Konrad: *Hölderlins Philosophie im Grundriss.*

[23] *Werke (Stuttgarter Ausgabe)* VI, 289. Hans Urs von Balthasar characteristically prefaced the third volume of his great work on theological aesthetics with this passage.

Although Hegel's theological thought in Frankfurt displays a special degree of concentration and mental effort, this did not occur simply in virtue of an interest in speculation nurtured by a more or less private inwardness. For in Frankfurt too all his philosophical and theological reflections grow out of socio-historical soil, and his abstract ideas of a philosophical and theological nature are shot through with sociological notions. This makes it impossible for us in this period as well to pick and choose in favour of either a purely theological or a purely sociological interpretation.

In these years of Germany's thoroughgoing political decadence, importance and disintegration Hegel worked out a political memorandum 'On the latest internal affairs of Württemberg' with special reference to the deficiencies of the municipal constitution, and he composed the first draft of a *Constitution of the German Reich* (*H*, 282-288). Also extant are some shorter political fragments dealing with Prussian law (e.g., the prison system) and with the relationship of Church and state. In addition to this Rosenkranz unfortunately only passes on to us some reports about Hegel's preoccupation with economic problems and especially with property (e.g., a precise examination of English parliamentary debates on taxes for poor relief), about his study of Kant's theory of law and metaphysics of ethics, and about a commentary on Stewart's book on the economics of the state (*H*, 278-282). Hegel's universal range of interests is attested not only by various undated little historical fragments (on the spirit of Orientals, Greeks and Romans; on memory, professional mourners, witchcraft and the public enforcement of the death penalty; on Schiller's history of the Thirty Years War; and on the voice of the Catholic priest: *H*, 257-277), but also by his studies in geometry (*H*, 288-300, 470-473) and by a short treatise *On Card Playing* (*H*, 277f). Hegel, who was far removed from the humourless severity of the social critics of today, was to cultivate this diversion until his old age. 'Inclination to card-playing is a principal feature in the character of our times. *Intellect* and *passion* are the spiritual attributes that are active in this pursuit.'

In our analysis of Hegel's Christology we must have recourse to the major work he produced in this period, a fragment to which Nohl gave the title *The Spirit of Christianity and its Fate* (*N*, 243-342[24]); indirectly we shall also take into consideration the preliminary essays and drafts which Hegel wrote at the same time (Nohl included these in his appendix; *N*, 368-402[25]).

'The son of God is also son of man; the divine in a particular shape appears as a man. The connection of infinite and finite is of course a "holy mystery", because this connection is life itself. Reflective thinking, which partitions life, can distinguish it into infinite and finite, and then it is only the restriction, the

---

[24]Knox: *op. cit.*, 182-301. Quotations in the following pages will be given from this translation unless otherwise stated, references being given by *K* followed by the relevant page number.
[25]According to Nohl the first of these were perhaps written while Hegel was still in Bern, while according to G. Schüler (*op. cit.*, 131f) they all stem from the Frankfurt period (only *N*, 378-382 are translated by Knox).

finite regarded by itself, which affords the concept of man as opposed to the divine. But outside reflective thinking, and in truth, there is no such restriction' (*K*, 262). There is a striking difference here from Hegel's earlier utterances in Bern. In place of the 'teacher and ideal of virtue', Hegel now speaks of the 'Son of God' and 'Son of man'; instead of the 'addition of the divine element', he now talks of the 'divine in a particular shape'; while 'reason' is succeeded by 'mystery' and 'morality' by 'life'. How are we to understand this? Our task is to undertake a precise examination of Hegel's *Spirit of Christianity* in the light of this question. This interpretation of Jesus and primitive Christianity was undoubtedly the most profound to be ventured by Idealist philosophy up to that time. Again unpublished by its author it is the most attractive item in Nohl's collection. The essay will demonstrate how, along with the influence of Hölderlin, it was precisely Hegel's reflection on Jesus' self-evident being in God that was determinative for his decisive advance beyond Kant toward a greater unity of life, indeed toward the profound unity of God and man.

2. Alien God and Alienated Man

Christ can be properly seen only in a socio-historical context, against the background of his people. The problem of the first fragment (*K*, 182-205; cf. the rough drafts in *N*, 368-374[26]) is *Judaism* as the setting for the figure of Jesus. In these pages Judaism is treated in the light of phenomenology, of the history of religions and of philosophy and theology. The Flood, Noah, Nimrod, Abraham, Moses in relation to the liberation from Egyptian servitude and to the giving of the Law, the Kings, the post-Babylonian periods – in all of this Hegel is concerned with the *one* spirit, which 'appears in different guise' (*K*,182). Earlier, in Bern, he had made a most intensive study of the gospels; now he set about conducting a dialogue with the Old Testament. Our present concern is not with the intricacies of detail, but rather with the broad pattern in terms of which Hegel sees Judaism. Notwithstanding certain positive promising hints,[27] this pattern is one of abstraction, for according to Hegel Judaism is something severed or rent asunder. Or it is in a condition of alienation, for the Jew is a 'stranger', a divided man; what is lacking is unifying love (cf. e.g., the portrayal of Abraham; *K*, 185-188).

The 'vertical' dimension of the problem of religion appears for the first time on terms of unambiguous equality alongside the 'horizontal'. In addition to their

---

[26]There is a total of nine of these, and *N* is slightly to be supplemented by the Hegel archives; cf. W.-D. Marsch: *Gegenwart Christi in der Gesellschaft*, 62-78.

[27]See J. Wahl: *Le malheur de la conscience dans la philosophie de Hegel*, 23f.

isolation from nature, which had smitten all people in the Flood (K, 182f), the Jews, following in the footsteps of Noah (K, 182f) and above all of Abraham, the great type of Judaism (K, 185), are also alienated from their people and from God. The God of the Jews is an 'alien God' (K, 187), a 'perfect Object on high' (K, 186), 'the infinite Object' (K, 191), 'the invisible Object' (K, 203), a 'thought-product' (K, 183), 'supreme separation' (N, 374). He is a projection and objectivisation of the things in which man is deficient. He is a God who as Lord confronts the people, his servant, in unsurpassable transcendence (K, 274). Hence springs the Jews' overbearing and exclusive universalism which foolishly and fanatically excludes all other national gods (K, 188). Hence comes also this people's egotistic individualism on the subject of salvation, in which attitude they lovelessly look to themselves alone (K, 185-189 etc.). Even the messiah|expected by the Jews is an alien (N, 386). All in all it is 'a religion out of misfortune for misfortune' (N, 373), the prototype for the unhappy consciousness. Its overall trend is toward 'antithesis' rather than 'synthesis'. It is worthy of note that these terms, which are much quoted with reference to Hegel's dialectic even though he himself rarely employs them elsewhere in a positive sense, along with others that will be important for him in the future, make their first appearance in this religious context (K, 191f)! If Judasim already made the effort to achieve unity, then this was only in the sense of an abstract, intellectually conceived unity or in the sense of succumbing to bondage (K,182-186). The dominant categories here are master and servant, object, confrontation and alienation (K, 182f). Thus we have here a radical externalisation, along with remoteness from God and corrupting alienation. What is lacking is love.

The interpreters are agreed that Hegel's criticism of Judaism is in fact meant for Kant. Hegel deemed the latter's legalistic morality a return to Judaism. Admittedly, Kant subjected reified objectivity to criticism; but he was not equally radical in his approach to isolated, critical, moral subjectivity. Thus, as in Jewish so also in Kant's ethics man is cut loose from God and torn within himself (between reason and sensuality, duty and inclination). On all sides there was a deep desire for reconciliation. And precisely because Kant summarised the essentials of the entire modern development, Hegel's criticism of Judaism is at the same time aimed at this recent development insofar as it had led to confrontation between God and man (and hence between man and man, people and people). J. Wahl has rightly observed that Hegel uses the categories 'master' and 'servant' in a universal sense and not simply with reference to the Jews.[28] The problems of Abraham and the Jews are universal

---

[28]*op. cit.*, 23f; cf. *N*, 390.

human problems. It was not in vain that just at this time Hegel's thought, not-withstanding and indeed in the midst of a manifestly growing personal participation in the problems, was increasingly taking on universal dimensions and moving in the direction of the universal philosophy that was now on the verge of taking shape. Abstraction, alienation, division and antithesis on the one hand, and the effort to achieve concretisation, unification and synthesis on the other: these themes will remain Hegel's abiding problem. A lively demonstration of this fact, covering various facets of Hegel's thought under the slogans 'misery' and 'happiness', has been given in Wahl's book. In the form of Judaism Hegel truly hit upon the old wound of the modern period, and it will presently become clear how he proposed to heal it.

Hegel's appraisal of Judaism, however, is still far removed from the greater degree of fairness which he was later to bestow upon it. Nor should we overlook the fact that we are dealing here with an example of modern Old Testament exegesis. Such exegesis had begun with a renewed study of the Hebrew language and people, with the controversy over rabbinic-masoretic pointing and with the origin and inter-connection of the individual books of the Bible. The modern historical consciousness reacted dispassionately to the often harmonising, idealising and allegorising exegesis that had characterised antiquity and the middle ages. The example in our text is Abraham, whom Hegel seeks to describe in his Jewish humanity and historicity, without turning him into a Christian saint whitewashed of all shady features. But under the influence of Enlightenment theology with its disdain for the Old Testament, Hegel succumbed in his exegesis to a simplifying attitude. This almost took on the form of a brand of neo-Marcionism, in which the *Deus terribilis* of the Old Testament is set in radical opposition to the *Deus amabilis* of the New. The heartless words with which he brings this fragment to a close show better than a multitude of separate examples how little Hegel sympathised with Judaism at this period: 'The great tragedy of the Jewish people is no Greek tragedy; it can rouse neither terror nor pity, for both of these arise only out of the fate which follows from the inevitable slip of a beautiful character; it can arouse horror alone. The fate of the Jewish people is the fate of Macbeth who stepped out of nature itself, clung to alien Beings, and so in their service had to trample and slay everything holy in human nature, had at last to be forsaken by his gods (since these were objects and he their slave) and be dashed to pieces on his faith itself' (*K*, 204f; cf. later *N*, 312).

Hegel's anti-Judaism is *no longer* the specifically 'Christian' antipathy toward Judaism that had marked such men as Chrysostom, Isidore of Seville, Innocent III and Clement IV, which had deployed theological motifs, such as the guilt of the Jews for Christ's death on the cross and God's cursing of Israel. The consequences of that brand of anti-Judaism were gruesome.

After some progress had been made by humanism (Reuchlin, Scaliger) and pietism (Zinzendorf), it was attacked by the Enlightenment with its advocacy of human rights. Conversely, Hegel's anti-Judaism is *not yet* bound up with the neo-pagan 'anti-Semitism' (the very name is wrong!) which in the wake of such racial theorists as Gobineau and Houston Stewart Chamberlain, deployed racialist arguments and witnessed a frankly demonic eruption in National Socialism. Hegel's antipathy to Judaism is of a 'philosophical' kind: in the spirit of Judaism he perceives the anti-ideal to the unity and wholeness of man and humanity for which he longed. In the division and alienation of the Jew (from nature, from his fellow man, from God), Hegel was increasingly wont to see the division and alienation of enlightened man in general: nature stripped of its mystery, domination and servitude in the political sphere, the objectivisation of God.

In his antipathy toward Judaism Hegel parts company with Moses Mendelssohn whom he otherwise so frequently utilises. But even if he interprets the fate of the Jews in universal human terms, his hostility to Judaism is not made any less dangerous thereby. The general question arises here whether, in all this, Hegel did not overlook the decisive factor in the Old Testament relationship to God. This decisive factor, which also connects the Old Testament with the New, is that the relationship between God and man is a relationship of *grace*. Yet this is precisely what Hegel did not overlook. On the contrary, he accords it full emphasis: the Jews had 'their possessions only on loan and not as property,' and even the soil 'was only conceded to [them] by grace' (*K*, 197f). Thus it is precisely what Hegel finds missing in the Jews that is, in the perspective of the biblical theology of the Old and New Testaments, the most problematic aspect of this fragment: '"There is one God" is an assertion which stands on the summit of the state's laws, and if something proffered in this form could be called a truth, then, of course, one might say: What deeper truth is there for slaves than that they have a master? But Mendelssohn is right not to call this a truth, since what we find as truth among the Jews did not appear to them under the form of truths and matters of faith. Truth is something free which we neither master nor are mastered by; hence the existence of God appears to the Jews not as a truth but as a command. On God the Jews are dependent throughout, and that on which a man depends cannot have the form of a truth. Truth is beauty intellectually represented; the negative character of truth is freedom' (*K*, 196).

The tendency of Hegel's thought is toward the overcoming of the disintegration, abstraction and alienation of man, toward a new wholeness and unity of man and nature, man and man, man and God. The *Greeks* continually appeared to him in the role of a model people; he was impressed by their natural directness, their city-state democracy, their self-confidence and their

115

activity, their life-enjoying piety. All this stood in stark contrast to the pessimism, passivity, dependence and perpetual need for help that character-ised the Jews. The Greeks' relationship with God was a carefree affair as opposed to the Jewish people's consciousness of servitude to its ruler-God. At this point in Hegel's thought we detect a genuine concern for Judaism *and* Christianity, both of which were widely misunderstood in his day. But did he reflect sufficiently on the Old Testament understanding of the significance of grace for man, on what election implies: namely, the experience of man's 'fate' as a 'claim of a personal nature, which is clear freedom with regard to itself, and which accordingly demands the freedom of man, man as person',[29] on grace which furthers man's independence, and on election which promotes his freedom? Was not Hegel's deepest concern itself bound to lead to the question whether perhaps the God of Israel in his glory as ruler is the God of love, whether the 'wholly alien' is the 'wholly near', whether it is not God's grace that gives man the most secure independence, and whether for this very reason the helplessness of the Jews is perhaps their hidden strength, their passivity a condition of activity, their obedience a form of joyous superiority; in a nutshell, whether being a servant cannot actually mean being a master?

The Greek way of living and the Greek state, Greek forms of aesthetic beauty and religiosity and especially Greek thought in terms of unity and wholeness will always remain important for Hegel. And if his discrimination against the Jews was conditioned by the theology of the Enlightenment and the disdain it showed toward the Old Testament, then his idealisation of the Greeks was likewise largely determined by the neo-humanism of his day. Thus both Jews *and* Greeks were misunderstood, albeit in very different ways, by Hegel and his age. We cannot then overlook the fact that Hegel had recourse to an unhistorical Greek world consciousness; but neither would we be justified in ignoring or undervaluing his genuinely Christian impulses and motives, as we shall demonstrate in the following chapters.[30]

---

[29]So runs O. Pöggeler's objection to Hegel in his *Hegel und die griechische Tragödie*, 302. My pupil J. Nolte has drawn my attention to the fact that the late Eduard Spranger, in his personal copy which was bequeathed to the Tübingen University Library, repeatedly asked about the place of grace and love in the *Early Theological Writings*, e.g. in marginal comments on pp. 237, 279, 283 (see the presentation copy of the 1907 Tübingen edition given by H. Nohl to E. Spranger, University Library class mark 3 A 14333).

[30]Against the background of the epochal change of consciousness toward the modern era wrought by the French Revolution, H. Schmidt's book achieves great merit in bringing out the young Hegel's idealisation of the Greeks (227-244) and discrimination against the Jews (244-249). Even so, its habit of schematising and generalising on the strength of a relatively slender textual basis calls for some corrections, especially with reference to the 'Hellenisation' of Christianity. Of interest in this connection is the distinction drawn by W.-D. Marsch who demonstrates that, insofar as Abraham's fate becomes 'a prototype of emancipated existence along with its specific dangers' (*Gegenwart Christi*, 62), Hegel's interpretation of Judaism does have a positive side to it.

3. Life Reconciled in Love

The problem of reconciliation is openly posed for Hegel with the God who is alien to man and with the opposition of God and man as subject and object. The reconciliation of heaven and earth and hence of divided man with himself is the theme of all the ensuing fragments. This holds good even with respect to those short and frequently enigmatic fragments (*N*, 374-383) which are to be placed before the major fragment on *The Spirit of Christianity* (*K*, 182-301). From different angles they all endeavour to press onward to reconciliation and are thus, with the exception of the last fragment, dominated by the idea of *love*, which was the great leitmotif of the Frankfurt period.

By way of sundry observations on positivity, morality and religion, the first draft (*N*, 374-377) draws attention to the fact that *love* alone, which presupposes a fundamental equality and wills neither to dominate nor to be dominated, can create true religion. For the gulf between subject and object can be closed neither by the syntheses of theoretical reason which confront the subject as object, nor by practical reason whose subjectivity dissolves the object. Only in the love which unites God and man is neither God nor man a mere object, nor do man and God oppose each other as subject and object. On the contrary, in love the trans-objective unity of both is now experienced (*N*, 376). The next two fragments (*N*, 377-382; cf *K*, 302-308) enlarge upon this idea, often in powerfully impressive language. 'Religion is one with love. The beloved is not contrasted with us, he is one with our being. In him we see only ourselves, and yet once again he is not identical with us. This is a wonder which we cannot grasp' (*N*, 377). Hegel lays particular emphasis on true love as a feeling for life, as a union of living persons, as something in process of development. He also lays stress on the distinction in unity of those who love, on the significance of the body and of shame in spiritual love, and on the role of private property.

The last of these drafts, to which Nohl gave the name *Faith and Being*, outlines the same problem under the general aspect of separation and unification, in which being itself is comprehended: 'unification and being are synonymous' (*N*, 383). But positive religion can only bestow a 'lower kind of unification': 'for what is united in the activity that arises out of a positive faith is itself in turn something antagonistic which determines what is opposed to it. There is here but an incomplete unification, for both elements remain opposed to each other, the one as determining and the other as determined' (*N*, 384). Hegel censures those things in positive religion to which he had already taken exception in Kant: 'Divinity holy will, man absolute negation; in the idea this antinomy is united, ideas are unified – idea is a thinking process, but the thing thought of is no existent being' (*N*, 385). What was already becoming perceptible in the fragments on love is here repeated in plainer terms. Hegel affirms the unification of God and man, yet this does not spring from grace but occurs – in love! – on a basis of mutual equality. He likewise affirms reconciliation, yet this is not thought of as a reconciliation of the sinner in virtue of God's pardon, but as a reconciliation – in love! – of a life which brings about its own renewal.

But these fragments are merely rough drafts.[31] Let us therefore examine what Hegel says on the subject of reconciliation in the principal fragment (*K*, 205-301; cf.also *N*, 385-402). *Jesus* now steps once more into our field of vision, as the direct opposite of disrupted Judaism (*K*, 205-224). Hegel vividly places Jesus in the current of Jewish history, but not without sharply emphasising the necessity of his coming on account of the politico-religious decadence of late Judaism. Hegel differs from Kant in that his Jesus stands in the continuity of Jewish history, albeit not as a continuator but as a revolutionary. He strives not to inject new life into divided Judaism, but to abolish it. And it was for this reason that he was defeated, at any rate within the bounds of Judaism. Little is said in this section about the person of Jesus. It is otherwise with respect to his moral teaching, although Hegel now employs a different idiom from before and his words announce the contrast between himself and Kant with sharp clarity. He discusses the various kinds of laws, cultic (*K*, 206-209), moral and civil (*K*, 209-212), against which Jesus set his face. By way of a thoroughly malicious quotation, the legalistic Kant is covertly criticised in the shape of legalistic Judaism: on the one hand, man divided between duty and inclination, reason and sensuality, concept and life, and, on the other hand, the universality of the ethical commandment. It could not be a matter of replacing an outward with an inward legalism. The only difference between the advocate of legal heteronomy and the advocate of Kant's moral antonomy is 'that the former [has his] lord outside [himself] while the latter carries his lord in himself, yet at the same time is his own slave' (*K*, 211). It is life that must be set against positivity, just as Jesus rose above any kind of legalism by dint of a morality which fulfilled the law – the fulfilment of the law that is far above all taint of legalism being love. In Jesus' commandment to love it is certainly not, as Kant thought, the commandment that is the essence of morality: rather it is only a form of expression. In not destroying inclination through law and duty, Jesus' ethic of love is distinct from Kant's rigorism; and it is distinct from his formalism, in not confronting man with abstract universality but setting him in the midst of concrete life. While Abraham was the founder of the spirit of division and alienation,

---

[31]T. Haering: *op. cit.* I, 307-430.

Jesus intended to be the bringer of the spirit of unification and living renewal. Hegel expounds this by way of a lengthy analysis of the Sermon on the Mount (*K*, 212-224), which is less concerned with an exegesis faithful to the text than with polemic against Kant, and which favours a natural religion of life and love. The goal of religion is reconciliation. With reference to religious practices Hegel writes that 'it is our endeavour to unify the discords necessitated by our development and our attempt to exhibit the unification in the *ideal* as fully *existent*, as no longer opposed to reality, and thus to express and confirm it in a deed' (*K*, 206). Thus Jesus is affirmed as 'one who wished to restore man's humanity in its entirety' (*K*, 212).

Almost as a matter of course Hegel has grown out of Kant's critically constricted subjectivity. Yet he did not accomplish this, as Fichte and Schelling did, by magnifying the subject into an absolute entity which posits itself and its world. Rather he achieved it, in his religious analysis, by subjecting the social legalism characteristic of Judaism and of Kant to a conceptual critique, in which he drew out the inadequacy of Kant's concepts. From the perspective of practical philosophy and its problems he overcame the limits which Kant had set to pure reason: can reason in theory be hindered from reaching that on which, according to Kant, it is utterly dependent in practice? What man needs is integration, wholeness and rational and moral unity; he needs to overcome the dualism of form and content, universality and particularity, necessity and contingency, subjectivity and positivity. Hölderlin's vision, set as it was upon the reattainment of unity, and later, to an increasing extent, the approaches mapped out by Fichte, Schelling and – with some reservations – Spinoza, were better able to assist Hegel in this work of reconciliation than was Kant. In this context we may not overlook the extent to which the intellectual situation had undergone a fundamental change in the few years that had elapsed since Hegel had studied in Tübingen. At that time it was still customary for men to declare themselves for the Enlightenment, even though Kant's *Critiques* had already laid bare the problems latent in it. Now, however, Germany's advanced intellectuals considered 'man of the Enlightenment' a term of abuse, and a 'pure Kantian' was already to some extent deemed disreputable. Between 1794 and 1798 Fichte had vigorously directed the learned public beyond Kant in his early outstanding essays ('*Theory of Science*' '*Natural Law*' '*Theory of Ethic*'). Hegel himself had progressed beyond Kant by another route: he had addressed himself in a new way to the religion of individual existence. According to Marxist dogma, this renewed interest in individual religion can only be understood as a compensatory escape from disappointment at the impossibility of political and social change. Yet according to Hegel himself (as is shown by his political essays from this very period) dedication to political and social change and reflection on individual religion are by no means mutually exclusive. He had always looked on the two as interdependent.

As far as the Frankfurt Hegel was concerned, it was plainly religion, mediated at a higher level along with the Enlightenment, which held out to man the promise of real and genuine reconciliation, of reconciliation in love, indeed even of the reconciliation of fate in love. Reconciliation only makes sense when it is genuine reconciliation. This is the subject-matter of the ensuing fragment (*K*, 224-253).

Reconciliation is *spurious* when it is understood as reconciliation with an external *law*. For to what end does the guilty man submit to the law and its penalty, thus vindicating justice, if he remains himself tied to his bad conscience and thus unreconciled (*K*, 226f)? Reconciliation is also spurious in the event of its being wrought by someone else, by a *stranger*. For what purpose could it serve if the guilty man 'flies to grace' and resorts to 'dishonest begging' in the hope that Another 'will close an eye and look on him as other than he is' (*K*, 227f)? Such an endeavour, even including vicarious penal suffering, is untrue and immoral.

Reconciliation is *genuine* when it is understood as reconciliation with *life*. The sin of the transgressor lies in the fact that he destroys life. The punishment of the transgressor, however, lies in the fact that immortal life struggles against him: 'The trespasser intended to have to do with another's life, but he has only destroyed his own, for life is not different from life, since life dwells in the single Godhead. In his arrogance he has destroyed indeed, but only the friendliness of life; he has perverted life into an enemy. It is the deed itself which has created a law whose domination now comes on the scene; this law is the unification, in the concept, of the equality between the injured, apparently alien life and the trespasser's own forfeited life. It is now for the first time that the injured life appears as a hostile power against the trespasser and maltreats him as he has maltreated the other. Hence punishment as fate is the equal reaction of the trespasser's own deed, of a power which he himself has armed, of an enemy made an enemy by himself' (*K*, 229f). For Hegel punishment is fate, not, as for Kant, an abstract-universal postulate for the future, but an individual, concrete-present, avenging answer of life rooted in natural necessity. And yet it is precisely along these lines that reconciliation can be the more easily achieved, for Hegel was not concerned, as is the law, with an insurmountable opposition, but with an antithesis internal to life: 'And life can heal its wounds again; the severed, hostile life can return into itself again and annul the bungling achievement of a trespass, can annul the law and punishment' (*K*, 230). This occurs in virtue of love, which is, according to Hegel, the emotion of life.

While Kant's morality simply confronts the reality of life with the law, thereby disrupting the unity of life and setting man in contradiction to himself and to others, love is capable of reconciling man himself with the harshness of life, indeed even with *fate*, and of re-establishing the menaced unity of life. Since love can waive its rights and achieve an inward renunciation of self, and because it can put up with the hostile and destructive side of life, it is competent to reconcile man even where he has wrought his own fate through genuine guilt or pigheaded strife: 'It is in the fact that even the enemy is felt as life that there lies the possibility of reconciling fate. This reconciliation is thus neither the destruction or subjugation of something alien, nor a contradiction between consciousness of one's self and the hoped-for difference in another's idea of one's self, nor a contradiction between desert in the eyes of the law and the actualisation of the same, or between man as concept and man as reality. This sensing of life, a sensing which finds itself again, is love, and in love fate is reconciled' (K, 232). Love also reconciles man with virtue, that is, it reconciles the individual virtues with each other and annuls their limitations by taking them up into unity (K, 244ff). Thus what the law does not accomplish is achieved by love, namely, the abolition of domination and the liberation of man. 'In contrast with the Jewish reversion to obedience, reconciliation in love is a liberation; in contrast with the re-recognition of lordship, it is the cancellation of lordship in the restoration of the living bond, of that spirit of love and mutual faith which, considered in relation to lordship, is the highest freedom. This situation is the most incomprehensible opposite of the Jewish spirit' (K,241).

But where is this reconciliation of fate through love, this apex of morality, this true spiritual beauty more clearly seen than in *Jesus*? It is not only Jesus' teaching which has something to say to us, but also his deeds and his entire life, in short, precisely his 'fate'. Jesus is truly the one who takes the correct attitude to fate, for he chose neither rebellious struggle nor powerless pain, but rather elected to conquer fate in love. Fate is not something alien to life, nor is it something that befalls man through an alien deed or force. Rather the way in which a man relates to it decides whether or not fate is meaningful. Jesus conquered fate by taking it freely upon himself. He is, as Hegel puts it with a catchword popular in the closing years of the eighteenth century, the 'beautiful soul' which unites valour without antagonism – with endurance without pain. His is a passive activity, a forgiveness without struggle, hatred and bitterness (K, 234). In company with Greek valour, Christian endurance, which had earlier been rejected as weak-kneed, appears in positive guise.

Yet we shall not overestimate Jesus in his role as reconciler, for the decisive part is played by life itself: '. . . in love, life has found life once more. Between sin and its forgiveness there is as little place for an alien thing as there is between sin and punishment. Life has severed itself from itself and united itself again' (K, 239). This is a fact fully recognised by Jesus himself: 'Jesus too found within nature [i.e. in "life"] the connection between sins and the forgiveness of sins, between estrangement from God and reconciliation with him, though this is something which can be fully shown only in the sequel . . . Here, however, this much may be adduced. He placed reconciliation in love and fulness of life and expressed himself to that effect on every occasion with little change of form. Where he found faith, he used the bold expression [Luke vii. 48]: "Thy sins are forgiven thee." This expression is no objective cancellation of punishment, no destruction of the still subsisting fate, but the confidence which recognized itself in the faith of the woman who touched him, recognized in her a heart like his own, read in her faith her heart's elevation above law and fate, and declared to her the forgiveness of her sins' (*K*, 239). When Jesus forgives sins, this simply means that he declares the forgiveness of sins by way of announcement and exhortation. As one who is stronger, he helps the weaker in a spirit of affectionate understanding. He is indeed the one who is joined to the 'fulness of life' and 'who bears in himself the whole of human nature'. Hegel writes of him that 'an integrated nature penetrates the feelings of another in a moment and senses the other's harmony or disharmony; hence the unhesitating, confident words of Jesus: "Thy sins are forgiven thee" (*K*, 240). The same may subsequently be said of Peter and the Apostles (*K*, 242f).

From this perspective we see how the outpouring of the blood of Christ is to be understood in the context of the eucharist, where Jesus' love is objectified in bread and wine. It is not that one does it *for* all, or *in the stead* of all but that one does what *all* do with him! 'The connection between the blood poured out and the friends of Jesus is not that it was shed for them as something objective to them for their well-being, for their use. The connection (cf. the saying "who eats my flesh and drinks my blood") is the tie between them and the wine which they all drink out of the same cup and which is for all and the same for all. All drink together; a like emotion is in them all; all are permeated by the like spirit of love' (*K*, 250). Thus reconciliation does not consist in a stranger's giving himself *for* men and women, but in an event which takes place within the context of life itself through the all-pervasive spirit of love. Forgiveness of sins is thought of as a forgiveness which itself imparts life.

4. God in Jesus

The most diverse dimensions of Hegel's thought in the Frankfurt period have now been marshalled before the reader; so that we may venture to state more precisely to what extent it is proper to speak of a *turning to Christology* in Hegel's thought during this period, a change of mental orientation closely bound up with the breakthrough there of a new understanding of God. It is our intention to capture this new significance ascribed to Christ in three moves, best understood on the analogy of a spiral moving inexorably inwards to the heart of the matter.

1. The problem of reconciliation has become more acute for Hegel during these years in Frankfurt. Reconciliation is not only necessary within the confines of human society but also (and at a much more fundamental

level) for the relationship between God and man. For the younger Hegel the problem of God had only been important as an issue which cropped up on the horizon of morality, but as he now attains the age of thirty this question is thrust into the very centre of his thoughts. The division between God and the world and between God and man must be overcome to ensure that man is not divided in himself. Using a variety of approaches Hegel continually alludes to 'the Jewish principle of opposing thought to reality, reason to sense; this principle involves the rending of life and a lifeless connection between God and the world, though the tie between these must be taken to be a living connection; and, where such a connection is in question, ties between the related terms can be expressed only in mystical phraseology' (*K*, 259). The antithesis is not meant to be overcome merely on the intrahuman level, nor is it meant to be simply a reconciliation of man with himself. It is not only a question of morality but also of religion. This is indeed the decisive point for Hegel as opposed to Kant: Jesus is of importance not only for morality but also for religion. This is demonstrated with especial clarity by the central fragment *K*, 253-281.

For Hegel religion is the fulfilment of love, just as love for its part is the fulfilment of morality and morality the fulfilment of positivity. Unity is established in religion, not only of man with man on the level of common humanity, but also of man with the ultimate ground of all that is real; so that God is not only an ethical postulate, but also a reality that can be experienced. In the province of religion we have, simultaneously with love, reflection, that is, the consciousness of the connection of all life in love. Love, which must not be a mere blurring, melting, unity, is strengthened by reflection: 'The task is to conceive of pure life . . . ' (cf. *K*, 254). And this means nothing other than that God must be conceived as *Spirit:* after 'life' and 'love' we encounter here a further, biblically inspired basic concept from the Frankfurt period. This 'pure sensing of life' (*K*, 255) consists in a personal-spiritual relationship which excludes both objectifying opposition and abstract, empty generalisation. Even with all the means at its disposal reflective thought cannot capture the Godhead. Yet spirit can discover itself in spirit and thus finite life can be elevated to the infinite level: for 'the activity of the divine is only a unification of spirits. Only spirit grasps and embraces spirit in itself' (*K*, 255). To overcome the opposition in the Jewish concept of God, Jesus taught the relationship of father and child: 'To the Jewish idea of God as their Lord and Governor, Jesus opposes a relationship of God to men like that of a father to his children' (*K*, 253). Even this, however, is to be understood spiritually, in terms of an 'inspiration' which rises above all objectifying opposition (*K*, 255). 'The connection of the infinite with the finite is of course a holy mystery, because it is life and thus the mystery of life' (*N*, 304).

2. That Jesus is significant not only for ethics but also for religion implies that he has a special relationship with God. This presupposes in turn that, as we explained at the beginning of this chapter with reference to the post-Kantian development, the understanding of God has itself undergone change. No longer is there, as in Judaism, 'service of and bondage to a stranger' (*N*, 386) under a 'positive religion', where 'on the one hand, man is determined and dominated, and, on the other, God is the ruler' (*N*, 390). Nor is there, as in Kant, a 'morality', in which man stands under an inner 'moral law' and hence 'still under an alien power' (*N*, 390f). Instead of this, Hegel advocates 'a lively dwelling of God in men' (*N*, 391).

No fragment demonstrates so plainly the great extent of the change in Hegel's understanding of God that accompanied his new understanding of Christ as does the one draft page *N*, 391, which belongs with the principal fragment *On The Spirit of Christianity*. On this one page J. Splett makes the just observation that it seems 'to contain in condensed form Hegel's whole understanding of the Christian spirit'.[32] 'There are not two independent wills or two substances; God and man must be one, but with man as Son and God as Father. Man is not independent, nor does he exist of his own resources; he only exists insofar as he is opposed to something else, only insofar as he is a modification, only insofar as the Father is in him. In this Son there exists also his disciples; they too are one with him; so that there is a real transubstantiation and a real indwelling of the Father in the Son and of the Son in his pupils. All of these are not simply separate substances which are only united in a universal concept; rather it is as with a vine and its branches: there is a lively indwelling of the Godhead in them' (*N*, 391).

This new understanding of God enabled Hegel to give a precise statement of Jesus' religious significance. As far as faith is concerned, what is of decisive importance about him is not his role as a human teacher but God's presence in him: 'To turn him into a mere teacher of men is tantamount to taking the Godhead away from the world, nature and man. Jesus called himself the messiah; he was a son of man and no other could fulfil this role. Only unbelief in nature could expect another, a supernatural being. The supernatural is only present with the sub-natural, for the totality must always exist, albeit in severed form. God is love, love is God, there is no Divinity other than love. Only something which is not divine and which does not love must have the Godhead in the idea, outside itself. Whoever cannot believe that God was in Jesus and that he dwells in men, despises man' (*N*, 391).

It is evident from this passage, however, that while Hegel is concerned with

---

[32] *Die Trinitätslehre G.W.F. Hegels*, 17.

Jesus, he is equally concerned with 'men'. Just as the living presence of God cannot be objectified into an ideal or a concept, a supernatural understanding cannot limit it to this one man Jesus.

3. The 'God in Jesus' requires further explanation, and Hegel gives it in the light of the Gospel of John. 'Matthew, Mark and Luke are more disposed to expound Christ in contrast to the Jews, in terms of morality. John, however, is more disposed to treat him in terms of himself; so that here there is more by way of religious content: his relation to God and to his Church; his unity with the Father; and how his followers are to be one with him among themselves' (N, 389). The principal fragment offers a brief but intensive interpretation of the Johannine Prologue. Even here, according to Hegel, it proves difficult to conceive of the divine. Consequently, the often objectifying (Jewish) reflective language of the Gospels must be understood with the aid of common sense. The Gospel statements are not to be accepted in a passive and spiritless manner, but should be interpreted spiritually, 'in terms of inspiration' (K, 256). This is the way in which we should understand the statements about the Logos: 'Of the two extreme methods of interpreting John's exordium, the most objective is to take the Logos as something actual, as individual; the most subjective is to take it as reason; in the former case as a particular, in the latter as universality; in the former, as the most single and exclusive reality, in the latter as a mere *ens rationis*' (K, 257). Hegel wants neither of these two alternatives or, rather, he wants them both in one. What the language of opposing reflection dissects into distinct entities must be seen in a living religious context: 'God and the Logos become distinct because Being must be taken from a double point of view by reflection, since reflection supposes that that to which it gives a reflected form is at the same time not reflected; i.e. it takes Being (i) to be the single in which there is no partition or opposition, and (ii) at the same time to be the single which is potentially separable and infinitely divisible into parts. God and the Logos are only different in that God is matter in the form of the Logos: the Logos itself is with God; both are one' (K, 257f). It is a question of the one infinite pure life which, as reflected life, is at the same time light and truth. In this one life God and the world are joined into a living whole: 'The multiplicity, the infinity, of the real is the infinite divisibility realised: by the Logos all things are made; the world is not an emanation of the Deity, or otherwise the real world would be through and through divine. Yet, as real, it *is* an emanation, a part of the infinite partitioning, though in the part (ἐν αὐτῷ is better taken with the immediately preceding οὐδὲ ἕν ὅ γέγονεν), or in the one who partitions *ad infinitum* (ἐν αὐτῷ is taken as referring to λόγος), there is life. The single entity, the restricted entity, as something opposed [to life], something dead, is yet a branch of the infinite tree of life. Each part, to which the whole is external, is

yet a whole, a life. And this life, once again as something reflected upon, as divided by reflection into the relation of subject and predicate, is life ($\zeta\omega\acute{\eta}$) and life understood ($\phi\tilde{\omega}\varsigma$ [light], truth)'(*K*, 258). John, the forerunner of Jesus, had, to be sure, a limited understanding of this light which is 'in every man' and even 'in the world itself', and of which every man simply needs to be made aware (*K*, 258).

J. Splett gives an excellent account of Hegel's view of the inter-relationship of God, Logos and world: 'The Logos is the divine consciousness, God over against himself, and as such the fundamental source of the possibility of further oppositions. These constitute the world, which is not simply divine, as even at a later date Hegel will always make clear in the face of accusations of pantheism. Even so, God is the "matter" (*K*, 258)|which is shared out here. The reality of the world is a realisation of a divine possibility, and at the same time it is real only in virtue of the sole reality of God, in which this possibility is contained (in the Logos). Individual things only exist *in* this life, but in it they can exist truly in and for themselves, thus once more reflecting the relationship of God and the Logos as that of life and light. In such a limitation life and light are no longer simply one and the differences between them are distinctly felt. Nevertheless, they are encompassed by the knowledge of unity – and this holds true even with reference to the world. Hegel defines the world or $\varkappa o\sigma\mu o\varsigma$ as "the whole of human relationships and human life, i.e. something more restricted than the $\pi\acute{\alpha}\nu\tau\alpha$ and $\ddot{o}$ $\gamma\acute{\epsilon}\gamma o\nu\epsilon\nu$ of verse 3" (*K*, 258). Thus he doubtless regards it as the ecclesiastical, social and political system whose animation and "illumination" is the proper concern of his intellectual endeavours.'[33]

What is the relationship of the Logos to the existence of Jesus? Hegel unequivocally relates the pivotal statement of the Prologue 'and the Word was made flesh' (Jn. 1:14) to an individual: 'Up to this point we have heard only of the truth itself and of man in general terms. In verse 14 the Logos appears modified as an individual, in which form also he has revealed himself to us ... John bore witness, not of the $\phi\tilde{\omega}\varsigma$ alone (verse 7), but also of the individual (verse 15)' (*K*, 259). The 'individual' referred to is undoubtedly Jesus, but Hegel's exegesis unfortunately breaks off abruptly at this point. The protest against a 'lifeless connection between God and the world' and in favour of a 'living connection' in which the ties between the related terms can be expressed only in mystical phraseology' (*K*, 259) forms the transition to a more detailed systematic description of Jesus' relationship to God, which Hegel most frequently and characteristically expresses by the term 'Son of God'. Hegel's testimony to 'God in Jesus' can now be described with greater precision. The most accurate way of defining his new christological development is to say that Hegel henceforth regards Jesus not simply as Son of man, but also as Son of God.

---

[33]*op. cit.*, 18f.

The expression 'Son of God' proves to be particularly apt to capture Hegel's new experience of the unity of life: 'The designation of this relation is one of the few natural expressions left by accident in the Jewish speech of that time, and therefore it is to be counted among their happy expressions' (*K*, 260). The reason for this is that the 'relation of a son to his father is not a conceptual unity (as, for instance, unity or harmony of disposition, similarity of principles etc.), a unity which is only a unity in thought and is abstracted from life. On the contrary, it is a living relation of living beings, a likeness of life. Father and son are simply modifications of the same life, not opposite essences, not a plurality of absolute substantialities. Thus the son of God is the same essence as the father, and yet for every act of reflective thinking, though only for such thinking, he is a separate essence'(*K*, 260). Hegel produces a striking analogy from the field of organic biology, which is typical of his new way of thinking about God: 'What is a contradiction in the realm of the dead is not one in the realm of life. A tree which has three branches makes up with them one tree; but every "son" of the tree, every branch (and also its other "children", leaves and blossoms) is itself a tree . . . And it is just as true to say that there is only one tree here as to say that there are three' (*K*, 261).

Thus divine Sonship signifies not merely logical unity or unity of disposition, but a living and immediately experienced unity. Son of God means 'the divine in a particular shape' and 'a modification of the divine' (*K*, 261). Now the son of God is at the same time a son of man, and the divine takes shape in the form of a human life: 'The son of God is also son of man; the divine in a particular shape appears as a man' (*K*, 262). Because, however, 'man' is not 'one nature, one essence, like the Godhead' (*K*, 262), but only a universal concept; and thus because, in contradistinction to 'Deity', 'man' is only an *ens rationis*, Son of man does not mean 'modification of man," but is simply something logically subsumed under the concept of 'man' (*K*, 262).

The unity of life in general, in which there is no separation between infinite and finite, divine and human, is fundamental to this unity of the God-man: 'The connection of infinite and finite is of course a "holy mystery", because this connection is life itself. Reflective thinking, which partitions life, can distinguish it into infinite and finite, and then it is only the restriction, the finite regarded by itself, which affords the concept of man as opposed to the divine. But outside reflective thinking, and in truth, there is no such restriction' (*K*, 262).

5. Christ and Faith

Hegel understands the reality of the one who is Son of God and Son of man, i.e. of the God-man, in terms of the unity of the totality of life. It is *for this reason*

127

that he is concerned with 'a holy mystery'. It is also *for this reason* that he is concerned with 'faith' (cf. *K*, 264) in contrast to the 'knowledge' of the reflective intellect. Intellectual knowledge of a reflective and therefore also of a disruptive and destructive kind cannot grasp this relationship between Jesus the Son of God and the Father. With an eye to the two natures doctrine of traditional Christology, which united two substances by way of reflective thought, Hegel states that '[k]nowledge posits, for its way of taking this relation, two natures of different kinds, a human nature and a divine one, a human essence and a divine one, each with personality and substantiality, and, whatever their relation, both remaining two because they are posited as absolutely different' (*K*, 264). This starting-point puts us on the horns of a dilemma between unity and difference from which there is no avenue of escape for the intellect: 'Those who posit this absolute difference and yet still require us to think of these absolutes as one in their inmost relationship do not dismiss the intellect on the ground that they are asserting a truth outside its scope. On the contrary, it is the intellect which they expect to grasp absolutely different substances which at the same time are an absolute unity. Thus they destroy the intellect in positing it' (*K*, 264). But whoever *denies* the unity of the natures thereby does away with Christ: 'Those who (i) accept the given difference of the substantialities but (ii) deny their unity are more logical. They are justified in (i), since it is required to think God and man, and therefore in (ii), since to cancel the cleavage between God and man would be contrary to the first admission they were required to make. In this way they save the intellect; but when they refuse to move beyond this absolute difference of essences, then they elevate the intellect, absolute division, destruction of life, to the pinnacle of spirit. It was from this intellectualistic point of view that the Jews took what Jesus said' (*K*, 264). Because they did not take unity as their starting-point they accused him of blasphemy: 'Spirit alone recognises spirit.' They saw in Jesus only the man, the Nazarene, the carpenter's son whose brothers and kinsfolk lived among them; so much he was, and more he could not be, for he was only one like themselves, and they felt themselves to be nothing. The Jewish multitude was bound to wreck his attempt to give them the consciousness of something divine, for faith in something divine, something great, cannot make its home in a dunghill' (*K*, 265). The reason for Jesus' fate lies in the Jews attitude of stony rejection, which eventually turned into outright hatred, toward his endeavour to achieve their inward liberation, to bring them back to the divine life, and to have them become children of God in truth.

We know Christ by faith alone (*sola fide*): 'The essence of Jesus, i.e. his relationship to God as son to father, can be truly grasped only by faith; and faith in himself is what Jesus demanded of his people. This faith is characterised by its object, the divine' (*K*, 266). This faith is only possible where disproportion and heterogeneity are overcome and where unity in the divine is presupposed: ' "God is spirit, and they that worship him must worship him in spirit and in truth." How could anything but a spirit know a spirit? . . . Faith in the divine is only possible if in the believer himself there is a divine element which rediscovers itself, its own nature, in that on which it believes, even if it be unconscious that what it has found *is* its own nature' (*K*, 266) Yet, notwithstanding this unity in the divine, faith is not already the ideal state of things: 'The middle state between darkness (remoteness from the divine, imprisonment in the mundane) and a wholly divine life of one's own, a trust in one's self, is faith in the divine. It is the inkling, the knowledge of the divine, the longing for union with God, the desire for a divine life. But it lacks the strength of [that state of mind which results when] divinity has pervaded all the threads of one's consciousness, directed all one's relations with the world, and now breathes throughout one's being. Hence faith in the divine grows out of the divinity of the believer's own nature; only a modification of the Godhead can know the Godhead' (*K*, 266).

Faith is thus 'only the first stage in the relationship with Jesus. In its culmination this relationship is conceived so intimately that his friends are one with him' (*K*, 267f). The culmination consists in the cancellation of the antithesis, given in faith, between Jesus and the disciples, and in the complete fulfilment by the Spirit of all who are united in love. What holds for Jesus must be said of all. It was no accident that in the phrase 'Jesus, the light individualised in a man', Hegel replaced the emphatic 'the' with 'a', a change whose effect is at once to restrict and to universalise the scope of the remark (*K*, 268). Jesus ought not to be separated from the many; on the contrary, the many ought to be raised to his level. Such believers would then become, on their own account, godmen who no longer stand in need of either faith or Christ: 'So long as he lived among them, they remained believers only, for they were not self-dependent. Jesus was their teacher and master, an individual centre on which they depended. They had not yet attained an independent life of their own. The spirit of Jesus ruled them, but after his removal even this objectivity, this partition between them and God, fell away, and the spirit of God could then animate their whole being' (*K*, 268). There was certainly a vast difference between Jesus and his disciples so long as he lived, for at that time the disciples only had faith in virtue of his mediation. Jesus was the first one to discern and experience the unity of man with God, that is, to discern and experience that he was in the Father and the Father in him. The same can happen to everyone who lets himself be liberated by him: such a man experiences in himself the unity of the divine and the human. In this respect faith in Christ is a transition phase. After the culmination of Jesus' fate in death and the necessity 'for his individual self to perish' (*K*, 272), the wall of partition fell away, the state of dependence was terminated, and all things became one: 'All thought of a difference in essence between Jesus and those in whom faith in him has become life, in whom the divine is present, must be eliminated. When Jesus speaks of himself so often as of a pre-eminent nature, this is to contrast himself with the Jews. From them he separates himself and thereby his divinity also acquires an individual form ... "I am the truth and the life; he who believes on me" – this uniform and constant emphasis on the "I" in St John's Gospel is a separation of his personality from the Jewish character, but however vigorously he makes himself an individual in contrast with the Jewish spirit, he equally vigorously annuls all divine personality, divine individuality, in talking to his friends; with them he will simply be one, and they in him are to be one' (*K*, 268f). There must be no false incomprehensibility: 'Just as for the intellect the most incomprehensible thing is the divine and unity with God, so for the noble heart it is alienation from God' (*K*, 269). The consummation is already given now where two or three are united with the divine and the Spirit is present in their midst: 'Thus specifically does Jesus declare himself against personality, against the view that his essence possessed an individuality opposed to that of those who had attained the culmination of friendship with him (against the thought of a personal God), for the ground of such an individuality would be an absolute particularity of his being in opposition to theirs' (*K*, 271).

Thus the goal of the whole historical development is unity in God, the unity of natures, which, though given from the very outset, is to be realised in the midst of all separations, just as it is symbolically realised in baptism (*K*, 274), which is a self-immersion into the unity of all life: 'The culmination of faith, the return to the Godhead whence man is born, closes the circle of man's development. Everything lives in the Godhead, every living thing is its child, but the child carries the unity, the connection, the concord with the entire harmony, undisturbed though undeveloped, in itself. It begins with faith in gods outside itself, with fear, until through its actions it has isolated and separated itself more and more; but then it returns through associations to the original unity which now is developed, self-produced, and sensed as a unity. The child now knows God, i.e. the spirit of God is present in the child, issues from its restrictions, annuls the modification, and restores the whole. God, the Son, the Holy Spirit!' (*K*, 273).

The consummation, which was not realised by the ancient Church, but which is now attainable through the Spirit, is unity: unity of the divine, unity of life, and unity of the Spirit. Nor has the old catchphrase of the Tübingen friends been forgotten: 'The idea of a *Kingdom of God* completes and comprises the whole of ... religion as Jesus founded it' (*K*, 278). The sphere in which God alone rules, which the Jewish language, with its partiality for heterogeneity, calls the *king*dom of God, is thus realised in the living, inspired unity of all people in God, not by faith, but by *love*: 'What Jesus calls the "Kingdom of God" is the living harmony of men, their fellowship in God; it is the development of the divine among men, the relationship with God which they enter through being filled with the Holy Spirit, i.e. that of becoming his sons and living in the harmony of their developed many-sidedness and their entire being and character. In this harmony their many-sided consciousness chimes in with one spirit and their many different lives with one life, but, more than this, by its means the partitions against other godlike beings are abolished, and the same living spirit animates the different beings, who therefore are no longer merely similar but one; they make up not a collection but a communion, since they are unified not in a universal, a concept (e.g., as believers), but through life and through love' (*K*, 277).

6. True to the New Testament?

Such, then, is the understanding of Christianity which Hegel developed during his time in Frankfurt. It took as its point of departure the contemporary socio-historical situation, but at the same time intensified its concentration on the religion of the individual. Many questions arise here which cannot be answered. What was said in the Preface must be reiterated at this point, namely that, within the limits of our *theological* discussion of Hegel, confined as that is, moreover, to Christology, we must refrain from analysing the various aspects of his thought that would deepen our understanding of his philosophical ideas. From a *philosophical* point of view such a procedure is absolutely essential, but it must be left to the philosophers. In this context it is more important that theologians pose their theological questions and confront Hegel directly with classical Christology and, ultimately, with the biblical message itself. These theological questions may not be regarded as *a priori* snares and traps; for Hegel himself continually confronted the biblical message. The limited scope of this study, to which allusion has been made, will sometimes oblige us in the following pages to make an abrupt transition from listening to the philosopher to putting the questions of the theologian. Yet we do not mean thereby to interrogate Hegel, using as our weapon a questionnaire which would put him in a straitjacket before he even opens his mouth. Our desire is to listen to him with the aim of learning for ourselves from the questions posed to him. In this sense every question directed at Hegel is one directed at ourselves; each such question is, moreover, a provisional question. Only in the course of the book will it become apparent what significance is to be accorded to Hegel's statements at the end of the day.

If, then, we shelve a number of possible philosophical reflections for the time being, the following theological question arises: with this unified theology of life, love and spirit, essentially inspired, as it was, by the New Testament, did not Hegel develop for his own day a theory of reconciliation which was at once up-to-date and truly Christian? Let us not immediately talk glibly of *pantheism*. Doubtless the question of pantheism can be more seriously posed with reference to Frankfurt than to Bern. Admittedly up to now we have not been able to establish that Hegel's thought underwent an epochal change in the direction of a speculative system of identity even in Frankfurt. Yet a change in his thought, which had been brewing since his early days, has now become plain for all to see. There was a shift away from the separation of God and man characteristic of the Enlightenment and of Kant toward the oneness of infinite and finite, divine and human in the oneness of life, of spirit, indeed of the divine. Hegel unequivocally turned his back on dualistic deism, which expelled God into a faraway transcendence and permitted him to exist as a mere contrasted opposite (*objectum*) without connection and fellowship with man and the world. Does not this fact alone signify a turning to monistic pantheism? Hegel certainly did not want a faraway God; on the contrary, he wanted a God of nearness, but in such a way that the finite should exist *in* the infinite. Yet the finite was not meant simply to be merged in the infinite. The Frankfurt Hegel definitely wanted nothing to do with pantheism in the sense that 'everything is God'. But he would have thought it right to affirm a *penentheism* in the sense of a vitally dynamic 'being in God' of man and the world, of a oneness-in-distinction of life, love and all-encompassing Spirit. It is appropriate to speak of a basically pantheising attitude to the extent that personal categories are avoided wherever possible, as they are in the understanding of God that had been outlined from the time of Kant, Lessing (Spinoza) and Goethe. God as the one over against us would appear to have been displaced by the all-encompassing divinity.

Haering (in company with various modern Hegel scholars) is undoubtedly not mistaken when he counters Dilthey's more grand scale and global presentation with his sober, detailed and chronologically ordered analyses.[34] He demonstrates that Hegel never denied the freedom and independence of the individual, that he did not fundamentally dispute either the distinctive personality of man or the individuality of God. There is a certain ambiguity in that God is sometimes – more dualistically – conceived as but the second term in a divine-human relationship elevated into the 'whole', while he is thought of at other times – more monistically – as, so to speak, the whole or oneness itself. What makes sense of this ambiguity is the fact that, for Hegel, God is

[34]cf. the analyses of *The Spirit of Christianity* in T. Haering: *op. cit.* 1, 307-535; W. Dilthey: *op. cit.*, 69-117; and on pantheism in particular. cf. Haering I, 463-465, 547-555; Dilthey, 138-157.

correctly understood neither as a mere individual personality nor even as purely and simply the whole (in the pantheistic sense), but only within that spiritual unity which embraces even the antithesis of God and man. Certainly, we cannot overemphasise the influence exerted on Hegel, occupied, as he was, with the philosophy of Spirit, indeed chiefly with the philosophy of religion, by the pantheists, by Hölderlin and above all by Schelling who was at that time engaged in natural philosophy. But pantheistic-sounding formulas, which Hegel might perhaps have taken over from Spinoza and others, are to be understood in terms of what we know of Hegel's own thought. That is to say, they are not to be taken to imply a rolling into one of God and man, but as a unity of both in a living whole. Let us think of the latter as a mysterious vital connection of a spiritual kind which is to be understood neither by pure rationality nor by an enthusiastic orgy of emotion.

Yet Haering does not attach sufficient weight to Dilthey's views that the root of this understanding of Christianity is a feeling for life and spirit which can be described at the very least as 'pantheising' – Hegel himself employs the word 'mystical' on one occasion (*K,* 259). This feeling seems more often to be natural than personal in character (cf. Hegel's biological analogies). We have here a total vision which, while certainly not intending to roll God and man into one, aims at the unity of all things and particularly of man *in* God, in a divinity which, even in its distinction from man, is rarely described as a living, active person in an I-Thou relationship, but rather as a creatively present universal life and Spirit.[35]

By emphasising this revolutionary rupture with legalistic piety as a characteristic of Jesus' proclamation and a cause of his death, Hegel, during the Frankfurt period, undoubtedly hit on a decisive feature of Jesus' proclamation and fate, notwithstanding the fact that – as he could have learned from Reimarus – Jesus' opposition to legalism can only be understood in terms of the proclamation of the eschatological kingdom of God. Yet Hegel is right to maintain that, however much the law demands man's 'heart', Jewish Torah-piety remains committed to the principle of an external heteronomy, that it entails a subjection to an alien will whereby God together with his instruction remains 'outside' as the 'other' – an other which approaches and challenges me, yet is impotent to reach and justify me completely in my inwardness. Over against the Torah-God of the godly, Jesus, the friends of the ungodly (sinners, taxgatherers, Samaritans) spoke of the Father's acceptance of precisely the lost son. He did indeed preach the same God, but one whose image has undergone a great change. Thus he appears as a God of proximity and love who reveals the real guilt of the godly and the possible justification of the ungodly.

In this proclamation of God's kingdom and will Jesus does not indeed set himself against the law, but he does set himself *de facto* above it. By appealing

---

[35]P. Asveld: *La Pensée religieuse du jeune Hegel,* 218f, 230. A similar point of view is also advanced in the recent study by E. de Guereñu: *Das Gottesbild des jungen Hegel,* 29f.

from the law to the will of God (as I personally perceive it), and by appealing to the good of men (for whose sake the law exists), Jesus teaches and lives a contagious new freedom and inwardness which stands in marked contrast to all kinds of external legalistic piety. As Hegel once more correctly emphasises against Kant, the novel element introduced by Jesus was not an inward legalism, but love. In the light of Jesus' fate the apostolic proclamation experienced and described this new union with God not only as a life in love, but also as life in the Spirit and as new existence. At every point here Hegel perceives genuinely biblical elements, even though we may not overlook the fact that the context in which he is thinking is that of panentheism.

Furthermore, especially bearing in mind the onesidedness of Enlightenment theology, we may not overlook just how much of the essence of classical Christology has been incorporated into Hegel's theory of reconciliation. For example, sin is thought of as a fact of life, or rather, of death – not merely a moralistic-juristic fact, but a discord truly tearing man apart. Hence reconciliation is correspondingly thought of as a living event wrought by God in the Spirit, an occurrence in which man united with God appears quite simply as ideal man. Has not Hegel impressively brought out the divine love over against any false understanding of a vindictive, punitive justice on God's part? Cannot many of the formulas used by Hegel, such as Son of God as modification of God etc., be just as properly understood as many Greek or Latin formulas of classical Christology? Are there not even in the New Testament some statements about a living solidarity between Christ and believing Christians and even about the identical destiny shared by Christ and Christians? Are not *all* believers meant to be reborn through him in baptism as the children and sons of God? Hence do not all believers form one body, that is, *one* community of life, love and Spirit, and not just a juridically conceived *societas* as the theology of the Enlightenment usually emphasised? Did not Hegel, on the other side, counter a shallow rationalism by presenting the whole event of reconciliation, the unity of God and man, as a holy mystery, indeed explicitly as a mystery of faith and not of scientific knowledge? Many a line of approach, only hinted at by Hegel, might be drawn out in this way; rudimentary notions might be extended and turned to good account; trains of thought might be interpreted *in optimam partem* and constructively carried further. This is to some extent what Hegel himself will do in the ensuing period. Limits are set, however, on the present study. Its theological starting-point requires at this juncture that we pose some critical theological questions from the point of view of the biblical message to which Hegel constantly appeals.

1. The question about *faith* must be repeated. Since his arrival in Frankfurt

Hegel has distanced himself even further from the rationalism of the Enlightenment. He counters the intellectual knowledge that tears things apart by laying the greatest emphasis on faith: faith alone recognises Christ, it alone discerns the true relationship of God and man. Even here, however, we must ask whether the faith so distinctly delineated by Hegel is in fact what the New Testament means by faith. We take this to be not a blind or irrational trust but a confidently daring and hence understanding reliance of the whole man on the Christian message and, contained in this, the obedient recognition which Jesus expected of man's utter dependence on the God who bestows on man what he does not deserve. Could *this* faith be understood as simply a knowledge of spirit by spirit, as a feeling of harmony (*K*, 266)? Or as the knowledge that one's own life is a participation in the life of divinity? Does this New Testament faith simply stem 'out of the divinity of the believer's own nature', so that what is 'found' through it is only 'his own nature' (cf. *K*, 266)? Are the serious urgency of the divine demand proclaimed by Jesus and the unprecedented openness toward religious outcasts which paradoxically accompanies this attitude an expression of Jewish heteronomy and disruption (*K*, 254ff, 262f, 277)? Is it in keeping with the New Testament that a universal life should so level down the relationship between God and man that it only allows for a being-in-God and not for a being-before-God, that is, for an upstaging of *coram Deo* by *in Deo*? It would appear, on such a view, that all sin and guilt are but a severance from the totality of life, and all reconciliation is but a reunification with this totality (in which man comes to himself). Does this not mean, in the end of the day, a re-establishment in a new form of that utter dependence of man on God stressed throughout the Old and New Testaments, and of that claim of human piety on God which Jesus had annulled? Can all Hegel's scriptural quotations, especially those concerning the Spirit, blind us to the fact that his technique is actually silently to bypass Scripture? At least this is the case insofar as Scripture bears witness not only to an all-pervasive Spirit and to fate, but also to a living God who intervenes and acts in history by issuing a challenge and an invitation to man. How could there otherwise be room for the only reality able to create faith in the New Testament sense, namely for the Word of God which makes itself known in the words of Scripture? Is there any way of understanding what the New Testament means by reconciliation, life, love and Spirit other than in terms of this creative Word of God?

Yet it would be to simplify the problem to suppose that Hegel himself consciously overlooked all these factors. As if they could be overlooked by any intelligent reader of Scripture! On the contrary, what we have laid bare is the logical outcome of the philosophical hermeneutic, customary since Kant, whereby the philosopher 'borrows something [from Scripture] in order to use it for his (!) purpose',[36] even if 'this interpretation may, in the light of the text . . . , appear forced – it may often really be forced';[37] one 'keeps on interpreting, until . . .'[38] Hegel too was fully conscious of subjecting the Bible to speculative reinterpretation and ideological use. The only difference is that his interpretative canon in Frankfurt was no longer Kant's moral religion of reason, but his own specific religion compounded of life, love and Spirit. For this, his motives were *in part* derived from Scripture. What we have here, then, is a hermeneutical circle *sui generis,* whose decisive constituent was not the biblical message itself, but Hegel's preconceived ideas. To this extent Hegel did *not* inadvertently overlook anything. On the contrary, he actually intended to overlook some things, or rather, to see them differently. This is true not only of faith, but also of the understanding of love and, finally, of the figure of Jesus himself.

2. By appealing from faith as the 'first stage in a relationship with Jesus' to *love,* Hegel hits on a central concern of the New Testament. For with a radicalism at once concentrated and comprehensive, Jesus emphasised love as the chief commandment on which hang all the law and the prophets. In the light of Jesus' word, behaviour and fate, the entire New Testament regards love as a summary expression of the will of God. For Paul it is greater than faith, which without love is nothing, while as far as the Johannine literature is concerned it is the universal directive which presupposes faith as a matter of course and almost totally takes the place of all particular admonitions. But is the love praised by Hegel the love of the New Testament? Does the New Testament conception of love ever allow the merging of parties to a relationship, whether between persons as loving subjects or between the latter and the God who is love? Could the New Testament statement quoted by Hegel, that God is love, ever be taken to mean that the independent worth of the 'other' might be elevated into an all-encompassing whole? Could this ever lead to the New Testament conception of love turning into a general 'sense of being one' (*K,* 252) or universal vital feeling, into a 'feeling of unity of life, a feeling in which all oppositions, as pure entities, and also rights, as unifications of still subsisting oppositions, are annulled' (*K,* 278)? Can being 'related to one another by love' mean 'belonging to a whole which as a whole, as one, is the spirit of God' (*K,* 278)? Is it permissible to reverse the biblical proposition 'God is love' into 'love is God' as Hegel did, even though he did not understand it in atheistic terms as later transpired with Feuerbach?

W. Kern proves in an important essay that Hegel had not always thought in

---

[36]I. Kant: *Religion Within the Limits of Reason Alone,* 9.
[37]*op. cit.,* 101.
[38]*ibid.*

this way.[39] In the Bern period love was regarded as an ethical principle and put on a par with reason. Probably as a fruit of his discussions with Hölderlin the Frankfurt Hegel recognised the central importance of love, now ranking it higher than both reason and morality. At the outset of the Frankfurt fragments Hegel laid proper emphasis on the individual value of the 'other' in love. Contrasting it with theoretical knowledge and practical activity, he wrote: 'Theoretical syntheses are thoroughly objective and entirely opposed to the subject. Practical activity annihilates the object and is completely subjective. We are one with the object in love alone; it does not dominate, nor is it dominated' (N, 376). And also with reference to religion: 'Religion is one with love. The beloved is not opposed to us, he is one with our being. In him we see only ourselves, and yet once again he is not identical with us. This is a wonder which we cannot grasp' (N, 377). In this genuine dialectic of love the self permits the other, who is one with him, to be himself. Yet W. Kern gives a correct interpretation of both the early and the later, contrary, currents of Hegel's thought when he writes: 'We thought to find in Hegel's *Early Writings* a valid dialectic of love, in which being oneself as an individual remains bound to the being of the other as such. Even the *Early Writings,* however, seemed to us to be increasingly bent on reducing the individual to a modification of a whole. This showed itself first as a whole made up of love and life and, ultimately, as a whole formed by spirit, by knowing spirit, in whose self-mediating motion in the other will, love and freedom become subordinate, "elevated" moments.'[40] It is obvious that here too everything depends on the hermeneutical starting-point, as could be demonstrated in connection with faith too and with respect to Kant's interpretative method.

3. The most important question, however, concerns the understanding of *Jesus.* We might perhaps join with Hegel on the basis of the New Testament to advocate the view that the doctrine of the unity of the two natures in one person 'destroys the intellect' (cf. *K,* 264), a consequence which can be appraised positively or negatively. We might, moreover, join Hegel in the opinion that the Chalcedonian solution to the christological question is no longer comprehensible in a changed era, with the result that it ought to be replaced by a new solution. But is not Hegel's affirmation of the Pauline 'God in Jesus' tantamount to the surrender of crucial elements of the New Testament message? To the extent that he was prepared to recognise God in Jesus, the Son of God in the Son of man – a position in which he has the whole New Testament witness behind him – Hegel, during his time in Frankfurt, led

---

[39]W. Kern: *Das Verhältnis von Erkenntnis und Liebe als philosophisches Grundproblem bei Hegel und Thomas von Aquin,* 394-427.
[40]*op. cit.,* 406.

the modern development in the philosophy of religion decisively beyond the Enlightenment and Kant. However this pivotal New Testament proposition is to be interpreted (and already in the New Testament itself there are some highly important differences on this score) the crucial question remains: Would the New Testament ever permit the reversal of 'God in Jesus' into 'Jesus in the Divinity' or – in Hegel's terms – into a 'Divinity in the world, nature and man' (cf. *N*, 391)? Can 'the light of men' (Jn. 1:9) be reinterpreted as a light 'in every man' (cf. *K*, 258)? Is 'the true light that lightens every man' identical with the ἄνθρωπος who is φῶς, . . . the man who is self-developing' (cf. *K*, 258)? Is it correct that up to v. 14 of the Johannine Prologue 'we have heard only of the truth itself and of man in general terms' and not of an 'individual' (cf. *K*, 259)? Is the relationship of Son and Father merely a question of 'modifications of the same life' (*K*, 260)? Do not the New Testament in general and John in particular, with his precise assertion that Jesus is *the* Word of God, *the* Truth, *the* Light and *the* Son of God, rule out the possibility of a simple conversion of the incarnation of God into a deification of man, and of God's kenosis into man's apotheosis?

That Hegel's reinterpretation was entirely deliberate is demonstrated not only by his thoroughgoing attack on Jesus' individuality and uniqueness (and on the synoptic messiah who spoke of guilt and punishment, repentance and forgiveness), but also by the last two fragments on *The Spirit of Christianity*. All our previous comments render a more detailed examination of these passages unnecessary. In the first, which deals with the 'Fate of Jesus' (*K*, 281-289), an historically illuminating treatment of the death of Jesus is given, in which Jesus consciously and freely reconciled himself with fate. Hegel presents Jesus' death as a consequence of the tragic entanglement with his Jewish environment imposed on him by necessity, but not as the wisdom of the cross, in which, according to Paul, the foolishness of God proved itself wiser than the wisdom of man. The second fragment discusses the 'Fate of the Christian Church' (*K*, 289-301). In its largely justified criticism of church religion and its Jesuolatry, this fragment explains how the myth of the god Jesus, his miraculous birth, his miracles and his resurrection was produced by the faith of the Church in a manner analogous to the creation of the Hercules myth. The upshot is that the place of the Divinity or the divine is now taken by God's being captured in visual form as a god. As a requirement of man, or rather of the secluded church, this religion stands in need of an objective concrete entity on top of the subjectivity of love. That is, it needs the deified Jesus, in its fantasy, as the particular, concrete ideal of love. This ideal springs, however, from an exclusive love which unites this god not with all people, but only with believing Christians, thus restricting him to the role of God of the Church. A man who, precisely in virtue of his human characteristics, is meant to be God even in the form of a servant! That 'prayers are also offered to the man who taught, who walked on earth and hung on the cross' is for Hegel a 'monstrous connection' (*K*, 293).

Long before David Friedrich Strauss and in brilliant anticipation of future developments, Hegel, who still lacked the philological critique and historical method that came later, was adducing congregational consciousness and myth to explain the religion of the Church. He also initiated the process whereby the biblical message was subjected to speculative demythologisation and at the same time to speculative ideologisation, the latter being beyond the power of Strauss to develop. Both these elements – the critical-destructive and the speculative-constructive in one – constitute Hegel's whole approach both to Christianity in general and to Christology in particular. He thereby carried into effect the anti-Enlightenment programme concerning Christian tradition and dogma which he had himself demanded in the Frankfurt revision of the Bern *Positivity of Christianity* already quoted: 'Hence what our time needs is perhaps to hear someone proving the very opposite of what results from this "enlightening" application of universal concepts . . . though of course such a proof would not proceed on the principle and the method proffered to the old dogmatic theologians by the culture of their day . . . On the contrary, it would derive that now discarded theology from what we now know as a need of human nature and would thus exhibit its naturalness and inevitability.' According to Hegel, '[a]n attempt to do this presupposes the belief that the convictions of many centuries, regarded as sacrosanct, true, and obligatory by the millions who lived and died by them in those centuries, were not, at least on their subjective side, downright folly or plain immorality' (*K*, 172). The issue is simply this: Is not the pristine biblical message upstaged and 'domesticated' in Hegel's project by Greek thought, operating in terms of unity and totality, and by a Greek understanding of the world and man, of faith, love and, finally, of Christ himself?

We come to the close of the Frankfurt period, at which time Hegel was occupied with another work, the so-called *Frankfurt Fragment of a System,* of which only a few pages are now extant (*K*, 309-319). Starting with his socio-political and religious intentions, Hegel moved increasingly toward the development of a uniform system. It is a matter of debate whether in this work he was really concerned to construct a comprehensive system, but the question cannot be resolved on the strength of these few pages.

Haering[41] emphasises against Dilthey[42] that the following formal and material

---

[41] *op. cit.* I, 536-579.
[42] *op. cit.,* 141-144.

ingredients of such a system are lacking: the uniform implementation of the dialectical method, then in its infancy, and the inclusion of the sphere of external nature, i.e. a philosophy of nature. The absence of these elements indicates that this fragment is completely taken up with the very religious and practical problems that have occupied Hegel until now. This is especially noticeable at the end of the fragment, which also forms the end of the entire essay. Even so, the perspective of the fragment is continually widening to encompass the universal, a feature illustrated most notably by the examination of spatiality. Notwithstanding his increased attention to theory, during the whole of the Frankfurt period Hegel was never concerned with merely theoretical knowledge. For him, knowledge – as the rendering conscious of infinite life – always stood in the service of the general development and enlivening of the individual and society.

The first of the two extant sheets is more concerned with the idea of an all-encompassing life characterised at once by division and unification, multiplicity and unity, incompleteness and wholeness, finitude and infinitude. Life is here conceived as a unity which begets unity, in which the self-assertive individual and the union of this individual with the life of the whole are contained from the outset, or, as Hegel says, as 'the union of union and nonunion' or even as 'the union of synthesis and antithesis' (*K*, 312). Along with reflection and philosophy, the intellect, whose function is to distinguish and hence also to divide, is impotent to achieve this one distinct whole: 'Philosophy therefore has to stop short of religion'(*K*, 312). Only in religion is enquiry into the finite – which could be continued infinitely – *aufgehoben*[43] into true infinitude: 'This partial character of the living being is transcended in religion; finite life rises to infinite life' (*K*, 313). We note that in this sentence the concept of *Aufhebung* achieves its double or rather triple sense.

The second extant sheet, which is dated 'fourteenth of September 1800', is actually the end of the fragment. Making brief allusion to the 'antinomy of time' (moment and time of life), a topic which was obviously treated in the pages that have not survived, this sheet speaks of the 'objective antinomy with respect to the thing confronting us', i.e. of the antonomy of space. In this context of the presence of God in spatial temples there follows, together with a quotation from a Christian hymn, a remarkable christological statement: 'The infinite being, filling the immeasurability of space, exists at the same time in a definite space, as is said, for instance, in the verse:

He whom all heavens' heaven ne'er contained
Lies now in Mary's womb'[44] (*K*, 315).

---

[43] Rendered here by Knox as 'transcended', the notoriously difficult *aufgehoben* has occasionally been translated in the foregoing pages as 'elevated'. In the following chapters it will usually be rendered as either 'sublated' or 'superseded'.
[44] From Luther's Christmas hymn: '*Gelobet seist du, Jesu Christ*'.

The last sentence of the fragment launches what appears to be a two-pronged attack on a religion 'sublime and awful, but . . . neither beautiful nor humane', in which 'an absolutely alien being which cannot become man . . . or if it did become man (namely, at a point in time) would, even in this union [between eternal and temporal, infinite and finite], remain something absolutely specialised, i.e. would remain just an absolute unit' (*K,* 319).

Hegel was certainly making plans and preparations for some kind of system at that time. Ten days after the completion of the *Fragment of a System* he began the already mentioned revision of *The Positivity of the Christian Religion* with the declared wish for a renovation of Christian dogmatics. It is significant that this revision ground to a halt in its preliminary stages. Another epoch was dawning! The second of November already saw the dispatch to Schelling in Jena of that humble yet self-confident letter which betokens the fateful change in Hegel's life: 'I think, dear Schelling, that a separation of several years cannot make me uneasy about appealing to your kindness on the subject of a particular wish. My entreaty concerns some addresses in Bamberg, where I wish to stay for some time. Since I am finally in a position to leave my present employment, I am resolved to spend a while in a state of independence, devoting this period to essays and studies which I have begun. Before I venture to entrust myself to the literary revels of Jena, I wish to be strengthened through a sojourn in a third place . . . The rest is of no great importance, although I would prefer a Catholic to a Protestant town; I wish to see that religion close up for once . . . I have witnessed your great public career with admiration and joy, but you will dispense me from the necessity of either speaking of it in humility or of showing off before you myself. I steer a middle path between these two extremes in the hope that we shall once more find ourselves as friends. In my scholarly training, which started from the subordinate needs of people, I had to be driven onwards to scholarhip; and the ideal which I had in my youth had to be changed into something which was at once a form of reflection and a system. Now, while I am still occupied with this change, I ask myself how I am to return to contact with the life of people' (XXVII, 58-60).

Perhaps the ecumenist will not give the impression of being unduly obtrusive if – especially in view of the fact that in the end Hegel did not move to Catholic Bamberg after all – he takes the liberty of posing a parenthetical question. Is Hegel's conspicuous interest in things Catholic, evident in Frankfurt and indeed already in Bern, simply due to his Catholic sweetheart Nanette? Or do we have here the first, albeit obscure, intimation of an issue which was shortly to find a visible resolution in the celebrated conversions of Stolberg, Schlegel, Werner, Brentano, Gallitzin, Haller, Overbeck and Philipps? Whether, in spite of his Protestant confession, the structure of

Hegel's thought does not go beyond a typically Protestant position, is a question of some importance, notwithstanding the fact that it has seldom been asked by the interpreters of the *Early Writings*.[45] The conversions we have just mentioned preclude our returning a simplistic answer to this question. In his *Magic Mountain* (ch. 6: *Operationes spirituales*) Thomas Mann has the future Jesuit Leo Naphta (in reality none other than Georg Lukács!) speak, though not without a hint of ambiguity, even of the '"Catholic" thinker' Hegel and of 'Hegel's Catholicity'. However this may be, let us permit ourselves the anarchronistic thought that, had he been born in another epoch, Hegel would perhaps have engaged in 'ecumenism' no less than did his esteemed Leibniz. And this surmise holds up quite apart from Nanette.

---

[45] An exception to this rule is found in the position of H. Schmidt, according to whom Hegel remained 'under the spell of the Greek "Catholic" principle' and became 'a post-Christian scholastic and therefore at the same time the consummator of Christian scholasticism' (*op. cit.*, 525), a state of affairs which can surely be appraised more positively than it is by Schmidt.

Chapter Four: Turning to Philosophy

'The content of religion is indeed *true,* but this being *true* is an affirmation without insight. This *insight* is philosophy the absolute *science*. It has the same content as religion, but in *conceptual* form' (XX, 272).

1. Changing, Yet the Same

'I cannot give you much news concerning my theological labours, which have been of only secondary importance to me for almost a year. The only thing which used to interest me was historical investigation of the Old and New Testaments and of the spirit of the first Christian centuries – it is here that most still remains to be done – but I discontinued even this work some time ago. Who wants to bury himself in the dust of antiquity, when in every moment the movement of *his* time is once more opening him up and carrying him along on the tide of its advance? These days I live and move in philosophy. Philosophy is not yet at an end. Kant gave the results, but the premises are still lacking. And who can understand results without premises? A Kant, to be sure, but what good is that to the great mass of men? . . . We must make further advances in philosophy!' (XXVII, 14; Kaufmann, 300). Such was the content of a letter from Schelling to Hegel, written as early as 1795, i.e. at a time when Schelling was still far from the Christian faith. We are now in the year 1801 and cannot help asking whether the thirty year-old Hegel had the same experience as did the precocious Schelling at twenty. That is, did he feel that nothing more was to be had from theology, at any rate as far as one interested in the present was concerned? What a difference there is between the Frankfurt and the Jena Hegel! Does not the latter live a whole storey higher than the former – i.e. at the level of philosophy – and has he not swiftly become acclimatised to the new metaphysical conditions, retaining only a weak recollection of the theological habitat in which he formerly 'lived and moved'? Only seldom does a fleeting glance light upon the recently quitted spaces, dominated by the image of Jesus. The great topics of yesterday – folk

143

religion and Christianity, the life of Jesus, the positivity of the Christian religion, the spirit of Judaism and of Christianity – seem to have been completely superseded by other, secular objects: logic, metaphysics, the philosophy of nature, the philosophy of Spirit and the problems that arise from these branches of study.

The shift of emphasis in Hegel's studies was certainly partly due to his change of address. The journey from Frankfurt to Jena is admittedly not in the category of round the world travel, but even so the move which Hegel made in the year 1801, having refrained from going to Bamberg, signified for him entrance into a new world. At last he stood on his own two feet; for after the death of his father he possessed a few thousand thalers, allowing him to lead for some time a life free of the cares of a domestic tutor. He could now devote himself completely to scholarship without needing to worry about a second source of income. And where better to do this than Jena? Here, in the capital of philosophical and literary life in the Germany of those days, he at last felt in congenial surroundings. How he had longed to be there already when, in Bern, he heard and read of Fichte, Jena's intellectual giant, as well as of Fichte's predecessor Reinhold (in Kiel since 1794) and Schiller. But after Fichte was dismissed in 1799 as a result of the ill-fated atheistic controversy and moved to Berlin, the 'literary revels of Jena' were on the decline. Tieck and Schlegel had left the city, Novalis had died and Schiller had moved to Weimar.

But the consciousness of the generation of young intellectuals was already emancipated. And under the care and protection of Goethe and of a prince of the stamp of Charles Augustus, Hegel's friend Schelling was affording adroit and agile leadership in the struggle over the modern philosophy. Schelling had reached the pinnacle of his early fame through his original writings on natural philosophy and above all through his essay on transcendental Idealism. Hegel, by contrast, was still a *lumen obscurum*. Yet this did not discourage him. He hung on in Jena until 1807 and participated in all facets of life in the town: in convivial evenings among hospitable Jena families, where he was well liked as a cheerful and agreeable guest, and in many activities of the university where, as one *Privatdozent*[1] among many, he delivered his first lectures – Jena having twelve lecturers in philosophy at that time. Due to his rather limited gifts as an orator and to a manner of verbal expression which appeared to be locked in combat with itself, these lectures were not a great success. Hegel lectured on logic and metaphysics, on natural law and the philosophy of Spirit and, finally, in 1805, on the history of philosophy. He had no influence on the bulk of the students, being held in rapturous esteem only by a small circle. He

---

[1] A non-salaried, freelance lecturer.

144

had previously won his scholarly spurs[2] through his doctoral thesis *De Orbitis Planetarum,* a work which affords proof not only of his perennial and lively interest in mathematics and natural science, but also of his struggle against the abstract, mechanistic atomism characteristic of a mathematical approach to the study of nature and in favour of a living, dialectical apprehension of nature (I, 347-401). Bound up with this was a public disputation with his friend Schelling on twelve theses which corresponded to the position advocated in Hegel's dissertation (I, 403-405).

The year 1802 saw Hegel join with Schelling to launch the *Critical Journal of Philosophy,* which, as Hegel informed a friend, 'has the tendency partly to increase the number of journals, partly to call a halt to unphilosophical excesses. The weapons which the journal will use are highly diverse. They'll be called clubs, whips and rods. It is all being done for the good cause and for the *gloria Dei*' (XXVII, 65). This mention of the *gloria Dei* recalls the old catchphrase of the Tübingen friends concerning the kingdom of God, so that the journal can also be regarded as a realisation of the original Tübingen intention to achieve a renewal of philosophy beyond the position attained by Kant. Schelling began by conducting lengthy negotiations with Fichte (and also with Schleiermacher, Reinhold and the brothers A. W. and F. Schlegel), but in the end of the day they could not agree to work together. Schelling parted company with Fichte. The public settlement of accounts was soon forthcoming in the shape of Hegel's first printed work from the year 1801: *The Difference between Fichte's and Schelling's Systems of Philosophy* (I, 1-113). Among Hegel's other critical writings from the Jena period which appeared in the *Critical Journal of Philosophy* and in the *Erlanger Literaturzeitung* (cf. I, 117-346), the following are important for our purposes: the articles on the essence of philosophical criticism; on philosophy and man's common sense; on faith and knowledge; and on the relationship of scepticism to philosophy. All these essays plainly come from Hegel.

The authorship of various of these essays is disputed because, in their dual role of author and editor, Schelling and Hegel appeared as a single unit in *The Critical Journal of Philosophy,* refraining from differentiating between their several contributions. In his essay on Hegal and *The Critical Journal,* H. Buchner gives precise information about the plans for, the negotiations about and the process of editing the magazine, as well as about the arrangement and content of the six instalments of the journal and about the date and authorship of the individual essays. In fact, the journal forms a unity. It is impossible to prove that either Hegel or Schelling was *solely* responsible for any of the individual essays and notes, though Hegel's philosophical participation in the journal was much more significant than Schelling's. H. Buchner and O. Pöggeler were accordingly right to incorporate the whole of *The Critical Journal of Philosophy* in

---

[2]Lit. 'he procured for himself the *venia legendi'.*

their superbly produced revised edition of the *Jena Critical Writings* (1968), which forms the first and thus far solitary volume of the long awaited new critical edition of Hegel's *Collected Works* (expected to run to about 40 volumes!). We shall confine our attention to those essays which, according to H. Buchner and O. Pöggeler, indisputably come from Hegel. These were already contained in the Lasson Edition of Hegel's first published writings, from which our quotations are taken (vol. I).

As a member of various learned societies, Hegel busied himself in Jena with a renewed study of mineralogy, botany, physiology and medicine. Here he also worked out, in connection with his lectures, his first outlines of an overall system, the so-called *Jena Systems* (published by Lasson-Hoffmeister, vols. XVIII-XX). Finally, it was also in Jena that Hegel wrote his first major work of genius, the *Phenomenology of Spirit* (1807).

In Frankfurt Hegel had gone through a highly independent development, working without stress under conditions of privacy and engaging in personal intellectual discussion about his deepest problems with hardly anyone except Hölderlin. Now in Jena, by way of contrast, he stepped into the dazzling light of his great contemporaries' (especially Schelling's) sphere of influence. Given the general tendency of the time, it should occasion no surprise that a comparable intellectual attitude was evident in the leading minds of Jena (and Weimar). Notwithstanding the pronounced dissimilarity of these great individualists, this cast of mind was shared not only by Fichte, Schelling and Hegel, but also by Goethe, Schiller and the Romantics. It was a unified phenomenon in the history of thought, developing logically from 'Storm and Stress' via classicism to early and high Romanticism. In his monumental work H. A. Korff sought to understand it as the 'Spirit of the Age of Goethe' (from 1770 to 1830). This intellectual affinity made it easier for Hegel to find his way from Frankfurt to Jena. However independent Hegel's previous development had been, he would not have become what he did in Jena without Fichte and Schelling.

If, then, we are obliged to establish the difference between the 'theologian' of Frankfurt and the 'philosopher' of Jena, our prime reason for doing so is furnished not by his geographical, but by his intellectual change of abode. Three factors in particular account for this: a) the open debate, now become necessary, with the intellectual movement of *Idealism*, which had been initiated by Kant's transcendental philosophy and was now being mediated through Fichte and Schelling. The chief feature of Idealism was its radical principle of taking the subject as starting-point: Kant's finite and human subject becomes the absolute subject in Fichte and the absolute identity of subject and object in Schelling, to be thought by Hegel at a later date (at any rate as he himself understood the distinction) no longer simply as undifferentiated, but as a dialectical concept and as spirit; b) the related debate with the neo-Spinozistic and pantheistic feeling for life, nature, world and God which had been heralded by Lessing, encouraged by Kant, and had broken through in 'storm and stress'. It achieved expression in Herder's, Goethe's and Hölderlin's re-divinisation of nature, after the Enlightenment had stripped nature of its divinity through natural science. It was Rousseau who first opposed the Enlightenment's solidarity with culture by a preponderant emphasis on solidarity with nature – and, above all, in the early works of Schelling. It amounted to a sense of the living, comprehensive totality of all that is, of living nature and the living God, that is, of nature understood as alive and of life understood as divine; c) following from these debates, the (to some extent) rather artificial cross-fertilisation of intentions which were genuinely Hegel's with philosophical lines of thought characteristic of Fichte and above all of Schelling.[3]

Hegel's first publication, one of the first things written during the Jena period, is typical of the change in his work: *The Difference between Fichte's and Schelling's Systems of Philosophy...by Georg Wilhelm Friedrich Hegel, Doctor of Philosophy* (Jena, 1801). It is obvious that Hegel is no longer teaching 'divinity' here, but 'philosophy'. The debate was carried on within the Idealist camp, Hegel lining up with Schelling against Fichte. The reason for Hegel's choice was not that Fichte was wrong (cf., e.g., I, 42), but that his starting-point was not adequate to bring about the unification of the great antitheses to which Hegel still attached great importance (I, 43). Hegel carries out a brusque, pitiless and sovereign exposure of Fichte's inability, despite his initial identity of subject and object ('I=I'), to see this unity (between the positing subject and the posited object) through to the end. All he was left with by way of a final synthesis was: 'I must equal I' (cf. I, 39-74). According to Hegel it was Schelling who united the I and the not-I, Spirit and nature, the I-philosophy and the philosophy of nature, and who thrust beyond the subjective identity of subject and object (which Fichte had deemed absolute) to a truly absolute identity, to the Absolute and its unity. Still almost unknown to the public, Hegel appeared as a completely subordinate comrade-

---

[3]On the relationship between Hegel's philosophy and contemporary philosophical tendencies, cf., in addition to the already mentioned standard work by H.A. Korff, the studies by R. Kroner, J. Schwarz, H. Glockner, K. Schilling-Wollny, N. Hartmann etc. On the religious problems, cf. esp E. Hirsch, T. Steinbüchel, H. U. von Balthasar, K. Barth. On the Jena period, cf., in addition to the bibliography on Hegel's youth listed at the beginning of ch.1 (esp. T. Haering): O. Pöggeler: *Hegels Jenaer Systemkonzeption*; H. Kimmerle: *Dokumente zu Hegels Jenaer Dozententätigkeit* (1801-1807); *idem*: *Zur Chronologie von Hegels Jenaer Schriften. (chart 135-145); idem*: Zur *Entwicklung Hegelschen Denkens in Jena*; F. Nicolin: *Unbekannte Aphorismen Hegels aus der Jenaer Periode*; H. Buchner: *Hegel und das Kritische Journal der Philosophie*. On specialist topics see M. Riedel (critique of natural law), N. Merker (origins of logic in Jena) and H. Girndt (Hegel's critique of Fichte in the *Difference*).

in-arms in Schelling's battle for transcendental Idealism, and he was in fact immensely impressed by Schelling's great achievements. Already, however, by laying stress on the variegated and intense profusion of all definite realities, he has secretly – unconsciously and perhaps even consciously – transcended the grey neutrality of Schelling's Absolute in the direction of what he understood as absolute Spirit (cf. I, 75-93; esp. 21, 76f). Nevertheless, in view of the daily companionship of the two friends at home and at work during these first years in Jena, we might be well advised to look with some reserve on the arguments adduced by the kind of Hegel-philology which would requisition this or that passage as 'typically Hegelian' or 'Schellingian'.[4] At this time they undoubtedly considered themselves united in an absolute alliance against Fichte.

We cannot here answer the question whether Hegel did justice to Fichte, since the latter's theology and Christology would require a study in their own right. But it would be an immense underestimation of this profound and passionate thinker to suppose that the idea of a greater unity and of a genuine identity never entered Fichte's head.

Nor should it be forgotten that Johann Gottlieb Fichte – eight years older than Hegel and, like him, initially occupied with his finals in theology and subsequently a domestic tutor, then, shortly after Hegel's departure from Tübingen, professor in Jena – had just moved away from a greater unity. Thinking along the lines of the last secret thoughts of Lessing and of the young Goethe, he had for a long time been fascinated by identity in the Spinozistic sense.[5] *God* was not understood as a personality endowed with a living free will, but as an eternally necessary being – a being which certainly 'is' not the universe in any simple sense (in Spinoza individual things are modifications of God), yet one who thinks the universe and thereby establishes it (in the early Fichte individual things are thoughts in the great thought of the universe entertained by God). Hence the *world* is understood as an interconnected whole in which man is fatally determined by the primal thought of the Deity (providence becomes fate and sin the necessary consequence of finitude). Finally, *Christ* is understood as a kind-hearted teacher of morality who has been deified and who therefore represents a gratifying humanisation of the concept of God, his atoning death signifying the cancellation of all false fear of God. These thoughts are expressed in Fichte's *Aphorisms on Religion and Deism* of 1790.

Kant's practical philosophy freed Fichte from this kind of identity and from this fatalistic view of God and the world, permitting him to see the dignity of the free and responsible moral personality. Thenceforward he held that there were two possibilities for a consistent philosophy: *either* fatalistic Spinozism *or* a philosophy of freedom rooted in the moral consciousness – namely, his own system of pure moralism. Spinozistic pantheism can only be refuted on the basis of the free moral personality, but with this sole weapon it can really be refuted. In this sense it is true for Fichte that

---

[4]cf. the apposite remarks of H Buchner: *Hegel und das Kritische Journal der Philosophie*, 131-133.
[5]On the history of J. G. Fichte's development cf., in addition to E. Coreth, the works of E. Hirsch. The latter treated Fichte with especial love both in his early essay on Fichte's philosophy of religion (1914) and in his comparison of idealistic philosophy with Christianity (1926) and, finally, in his *Geschichte der neueren evangelischen Theologie* (1st ed., 1949; IV, 337-407).

'the kind of philosophy one chooses depends on the sort of person one is'.[6]

We only do justice to Fichte when we clearly perceive this ethical starting-point of his philosophy. It is of vital importance for him that man is not merely a product of things or a part of a whole determined by iron necessity, even if this whole is not absolutely conceived in natural scientific and causal terms but in terms of religion and metaphysics, as in Spinoza's case. It is of vital importance for Fichte that man holds on to the belief in his own nature as something in the last resort unconditioned, as this is revealed in consciousness of duty - belief, that is, in man's nature as a free, autonomous, ethical personality. Only from the point of view of this starting-point can we judge the system which Fichte first drew up in his *Theory of Science* of 1794[7] (which Hegel had read in Bern) and which he set forth in a summary and more comprehensible form a year before the appearance of Hegel's *Difference* (Schleiermacher's *Monologues* appeared in the same year, 1800) in his *The Vocation of Man*.[8] It contains three major steps: a) 'doubt' (Spinozism as dogmatism); b) 'knowledge' (criticism as epistemological idealism); c) 'faith' (moralism as a religion of conscience consisting in duty).

Of interest in our context is the fact that Hegel's rupture with his own past is plain for all to see. The strong influence of Schelling is already apparent in the new topic of research itself and in the extension of the problems treated to embrace the philosophy of nature and aesthetics. However, Schelling's influence is much more decisively discernible in Hegel's underlying inner attitude. Hegel's thought had formerly revolved around religion; it now followed Schelling's in concentrating on speculative philosophy. Christianity had formerly conspired with the Greeks to dominate his thought, a role now filled by the great philosophers. The glory which had formerly belonged to the reconciler Jesus now belonged to Schelling. The dominance once exercised by faith and love was now exercised by transcendental knowledge and transcendental intuition. Hegel had formerly been concerned with the relationship between rational and positive religion; now, he was occupied with the relationship between philosophy and particular systems. The struggle against isolation which he had formerly waged through an analysis of Christian love he now carried out through a universal ontology. Knowledge was formerly content to be crowned by religion, but now, in a manner reminiscent of Napoleon, it has taken the crown into its own hands and performed its own coronation for its own self-sufficient role. The absolute knowledge of absolute reason is, along with its concomitant system, a totality which 'is measured and complete in itself, having no external cause, but rather being self-explanatory in its beginning, middle and end' (I, 34).

A consciousness of the universal philosophical problem is making its first

---

[6] J. G. Fichte: *Erste Einleitung in die Wissenschaftslehre 1797, Werke* III, 18.
[7] *Über den Begriff der Wissenschaftslehre* (*Werke* I, 155-215).
[8] *The Vocation of Man* (tr. Wm. Smith, London, 1848).

appearance here. The key which is to unlock all the mysteries of being and becoming is the idea of dialectical unity. The pithy entries in Hegel's Jena notebook testify to his unlimited philosophical self-consciousness, which – symptomatic as it was of so-called absolute Idealism – was here making itself felt: 'Do not be a sleepyhead, but be wide awake at all times! For if you are a sleepyhead, then you are blind and dumb. But if you are awake, then you see everything and you say what everything is. This, however, is reason and dominion over the world' (*H*, 357). 'The reply to the questions which philosophy does not answer is that they ought not to be put in such a way' (*H*, 360).

Thus the transformation of the theologian into the philosopher, which was brought about by Hegel's entry into a new intellectual world and by his association with Schelling, is simply a fact. However, the comparison of the Jena *Difference* with the Frankfurt writings demonstrates that it is equally a fact that Hegel remained the same amidst the change. At the deepest level the change which came about in Jena was no more than a coming to the surface of something which had been hiddenly present for a long time. A philosopher's heart beat in the 'theologian' of Frankfurt, just as a theologian remained hidden under the cloak of the 'philosopher' of Jena. This is why the early Hegel is reproached with 'underhand' philosophy and the later with 'underhand' theology. But do such remonstrances do justice to him? Neither in Frankfurt nor in Jena are either of the labels 'theologian' or 'philosopher' unequivocal when applied to Hegel. Hegel's intention was – and did he not have very great predecessors in this? – to be a philosopher and theologian rolled into one.

A deep *continuity* lies hidden beneath all the change between Frankfurt and Jena. The intrusion of Schelling (and Fichte) into his thought does not form the sole cause of Hegel's reorientation. On the contrary, the Jena development was embryonically prefigured in the 'theologian' of Frankfurt. All that was needed was the decisive impulse from outside in order to bring the hidden dimension into the bright light of day.

Prefigured was the *monism of Spirit*: already in Frankfurt Hegel gave expression to the living, spiritual unity of all things and the spirituality of *all* life, in contrast to the isolation of a solitary God from this world, by introducing the concept of Spirit along with the recognition of its dialectical structure and its identification with other fundamental concepts such as life and love.[9] Prefigured at the same time was the *dialectical scheme*: by not thinking in abstract terms, but rather by examining empirically all possible concrete, spiritual and psychological antitheses (sensuality – reason,

---

[9]cf. T. Haering: *op. cit.* I, 520-525.

150

God – man, man – man, man – people), Hegel had gained insight into the necessary and natural living unity of the antitheses and into their reconciliation in the whole, that is, into the justification of contradictions in reality, and into enduring life as it actually is.[10]

In Frankfurt, however, Hegel had not yet subjected these insights to a uniform and logical development. This would have entailed the emergence of the monism of Spirit as a universal, systematically implemented principle and of dialectic, not only as a structural scheme, but also as a way of thinking, as a form of systematic presentation and thus ultimately as a metaphysical and real process – namely, the being and eternal becoming of the whole of life itself. Along with Schelling, Hegel was chiefly indebted to Fichte for the breakthrough to this systematic and universal arrangement of thought.

It is very difficult, but also unnecessary for our present purposes, to define what Hegel had already learned in Frankfurt from Fichte (and from Schelling). What is certain is that his daily personal contact with Schelling in Jena brought him face to face with the challenge of Fichte in a new way. Hegel and Schelling alike were greatly in Fichte's debt both for the development of the monism of Spirit and for the development of dialectic.

In his early works Fichte, under the influence of Kant, had sought to confute Spinoza by grounding all necessary phenomena of human consciousness in man's primal moral certitude. In the call to duty I view myself with irrefutable certainty as 'I', as pure, living, automatically active reason, which is neither the Deity itself nor yet identical with the individual, but is the universal spiritual and rational foundation of the individual, empirical consciousness. This spontaneously active 'I' is for Fichte both the beginning and the end of philosophy, which is itself emphatically philosophy of the 'I'. The gulf between subject and object is overcome in this 'I' and its intellectual intuition, and the world is comprehended in the 'I' through the 'I', so that the concept of a free and objective thing in itself can be relinquished. This 'I' moves and propels the individual man in his cognition and activity to an absolute freedom in the accomplishment of his moral duty, yielding a strict ethic of disposition and conscience; and insofar as this ethic also includes the culture-producing activity of humankind, it is at the same time a comprehensive ethic of utility and culture. Thus there is an indissoluble intertwining of personal and general factors, of genius and morality. Fichte himself therefore did not wish to be understood in individualistic terms, although the Romantics did understand him in this way, mistaking his pure 'I', which is in fact the spiritual and rational foundation of the individual, for the individual himself.

In this way Fichte made the two 'discoveries' which were to remain fundamental for post-Kantian Idealism. These were subsequently taken over and remodelled by the two younger men, without showing too much gratitude to Fichte!

a) *The monism of Spirit.* By overcoming Kant's dualism of subject and object, form and content, Fichte developed a comprehensive basic unity in strict speculative consistency. This was the 'I' or the subjective reason, which proves to be a creative force and a productive power or, to use another name, *Spirit.*

---

[10]cf. T. Haering: *op. cit.* I, 467-469, 478f, 569-573.

151

b) *Dialectic*. Strictly speaking, the philosopher can only share in the unfolding of the pristine subjective reason in the role of an observer. This reason, meanwhile, exists in conflict with the contradiction which arises in the course of its development; that is, the 'I' exists in conflict with the 'not-I'. Thus the structures and forms of the world arise out of the creative reason. The latter posits itself, continually confronting and overcoming the antitheses afresh. Hence, the genesis of Spirit occurs in the threefold act of thesis, antithesis and synthesis, or, to use another word, in *dialectic*.

Schelling was undoubtedly responsible for the fact that Hegel's closer involvement with Fichte immediately took the form of sharp opposition. At the outset of Hegel's sojourn in Frankfurt Schelling was still thoroughly well-disposed towards Fichte. But he went on to display enormous versatility in devoting all his energy to developing a speculative philosophy of nature, under the impetus of Goethe's idea of nature, Goethe's research into nature and the new discoveries in the fields of chemistry and electro-physics. In this venture Schelling was able to give proof of his originality on completely new territory. He was taking further steps here towards working out a comprehensive, complete system, overstepping the limits of Fichte's 'I'-philosophy (subjective Idealism) in the direction of an Absolute. He thought of this as the immanent ground of the being and becoming of all creatures, in which all people too, including their independence and freedom, live and move. This is the system of transcendental (or absolute) Idealism. All of this made an extraordinary impression on Hegel. In Jena he made his own – albeit in his own way – both the speculative philosophy of nature and, in association with this, absolute Idealism.

As late as 1796, in his *Letters on Dogmatism and Criticism*,[11] Schelling had unequivocally made the Fichtean choice between the two philosophical systems which, according to Fichte, alone possessed the attribute of consistency. Both of these – each in his own way – wanted an absolute identity of subject and object. Thus Schelling decided against Spinozism (the 'dogmatic' philosophy), which elevates the human subject into the objectively conceived Absolute and bestows on man an absolute passivity over against the superior force of an objective Deity. He opted for the 'I'-philosophy (the 'critical' philosophy), which elevates the object into the absolutely posited subject, signifying absolute activity for man in such a way that he can elevate all objective oppositions into the absolute subject and realise thereby his unconditional freedom: 'My *definition* of critical philosophy is: *to strive after unalterable selfhood, unconditional freedom, unrestricted activity*. The supreme requirement of critical philosophy is: *be!*'[12]

In contrast to Fichte, though, Schelling is here already plainly rejecting the moral proof of the idea of God in Kant's sense, so that faith in God is threatening to disappear and the idea of God to sink to the level of a religiously glorified expression of human

---

[11]F.W.J. Schelling: *Werke* I, 205-265.
[12]*op. cit.* I, 259.

freedom. Schelling makes the pathetic statement: 'Here alone lies the final hope for the salvation of humankind, which, after it has long borne the shackles of superstition, is at last permitted to find *in itself* what it had been looking for in the objective world, so that it might thus return from its boundless excesses in a strange world to its own world, from selflessness to selfhood and from the enthusiasm of reason to the freedom of the will.'[13]

Yet Schelling pressed on further still. He boldly planned to deduce a systematic knowledge of nature from logical principles. This aim, while at odds with the now customary mechanical thought in the field of natural science, anticipated both the idea of development characteristic of research into nature at a later date and many a subsequent highlighting of the living and spiritual aspects of nature. Thus Schelling set about constructing what he delighted to call a 'speculative physics', which would attempt to explain nature as an organic whole in development towards Spirit as the highest form of life. Schelling advocated such a view above all in his *First Draft of a System of Natural Philosophy* of 1799.[14] To achieve such a speculative deduction of nature it seemed appropriate not to proceed from an absolute 'I' as an ultimate principle, but from the Absolute thought of as an independent unity of antitheses. Thus already here Schelling is on the way from 'I'-philosophy towards an Absolute in a more Spinozistic sense.

Schelling already took a new and large step in this direction in the following year in what was probably the most important work of his early period (he was now twenty-five years old) which bore the presumptuous title *System of Transcendental Idealism.*[15] What a dowry – together with Fichte's *The Vocation of Man* and Schleiermacher's *Monologues* – for the newly incipient nineteenth century! Schelling has now left Fichte far behind. He has resolutely extended his philosophy of nature into a universal system intent on encompassing 'all parts of philosophy in one continuity and the whole of philosophy as what it is, to wit, the continuing history of self-consciousness, for which the whole record of experience serves only as a memorial and a document'.[16] In a deduction of, first, theoretical and, then, practical philosophy in accordance with the principles of transcendental Idealism, the author analyses 'what for all knowledge are the unalterable and fixed factors in the history of selfconsciousness. In experience these are characterised by a continuous sequence of stages which can be exhibited and carried on from simple matter to organisation (through which unconsciously productive nature returns into itself) and from here via reason and wilfulness to the supreme union of freedom and necessity in art (through which consciously productive nature is concluded and consummated in itself)'.[17]

Thus Schelling constructs a unified philosophy of nature and history, striding beyond Fichte's notion of 'I' and freedom to a higher principle, which he describes as *'absolute identity'* which simultaneously furnishes the foundation of both the freedom and the regularity of history. This identity is 'as it were the eternal sun in the kingdom

---

[13]*op. cit.* I, 263.
[14]*op. cit.* II, 1-268; *Introduction to the Draft* II, 169-326; preliminary studies already 1797-8: cf, I, 413-723; for works on natural philosophy from the years 1800-01 cf. II, 635-737.
[15]*op. cit.* II, 327-634 (ET by P. Heath, Charlottesville, Virginia, 1978).
[16]*op. cit.* II, 331; ET, 2.
[17]*op. cit.* II, 634; ET, 236.

of spirits', whose light 'stamps its identity on all actions', being the 'invisible root' of all things, the 'subject of an eternal mediation'.[18] This Absolute is accordingly invisibly present in history, being successively revealed through history: 'History as a totality is a continuous and gradual revelation of the Absolute.'[19]

Schelling dissociates religion from fatalism (fixation on the object) and from atheism (fixation on the subject), viewing it as 'the system of providence' in which 'reflection is elevated to that Absolute which is the common basis of the harmony between freedom and the intelligent agent'.[20] Yet religion is not final, for it is circumscribed by art as the most complete synthesis of necessity and freedom.[21]

Readers of Hegel's *Phenomenology* easily forget his indebtedness not only to Fichte but also to Schelling. This debt ought to be recorded at this point, since the understandable partisanship of Hegel interpreters for their great author means that they are in danger from the very outset of emphasising most of all Hegel's independence at this decisive turning-point in his thought. But what would Hegel have been without Fichte and Schelling? And it is not in the least detrimental to Hegel's greatness if – in a good Hegelian and dialectical manner – we recognise in the midst of change the same Hegel, and that it really was the very same Hegel in the midst of change. We therefore note without prejudice the simply startling difference in terminology, tone and subject-matter which obtains between the author of the *Spirit of Christianity* and the man who wrote the *Difference*. The latter would often seem to have more affinity with Schelling's *System of Transcendental Idealism* than with Hegel's own *Spirit of Christianity*.

Only if we refrain from the long-standing customary habit – to which Hegel's subsequent system and especially his view of the history of philosophy have made an appreciable contribution – of unwarrantably devaluing Schelling and degrading him to the level of forerunner of the messiah, do we have the right (which we intend to exercise throughout this whole book) to show how Hegel always continued to plough his own furrow. This holds good even of Jena, where Hegel's thought was crossed with Schelling's. Yet in many respects, especially in the understanding of Spirit and nature, this blending was unclear and not altogether convincing, so that the alliance between the two did not hold fast in the long run. Hegel's distancing of himself from Schelling in the Foreword to the *Phenomenology,* whose uncordial tone must have hurt his friend very much in view of their long-standing and deep personal relationship, was consequently no overnight development but something which had been in preparation throughout the Jena period from

---

[18]*op. cit.* II, 600; ET, 209.
[19]*op. cit.* II, 603; ET, 211.
[20]*op. cit.* II, 601; ET, 209.
[21]On the philosophy of art, cf. *op. cit.* II, 612-629.

the writing of the *Difference* onwards. He and Schelling were one in the principal tendency of their thought, which was the vivification of the individual through his inclusion in the whole. The more brilliant Schelling, however, found his starting-point above all in nature, while the more prosaic Hegel found his in spiritual phenomena. Schelling was more interested in art, Hegel more interested in religion. Schelling lived more in the realm of purely intellectual developments, Hegel more in contact with political and social reality as a whole. Schelling's Absolute was an undefined, antithesis-negating, almost naturalistic unity, while Hegel's Absolute was – as is portended in the *Difference* – a reality-filled, antithesis-sublating, hard-won unity. Thus, with his emphasis on the role of reflection in intellectual intuition, Hegel had already in Jena advanced beyond Fichte's 'ethical separation' (which could never entirely subdue the activity of freedom) and beyond Schelling's indifferent 'absolute identity' to the truly dialectical unity of the absolute Spirit in his own sense.[22] Hence, notwithstanding all the influence exercised on him by Fichte and Schelling specifically during his first years in Jena, it is permissible to draw attention to Hegel's independent and steady course. Some things which will appear new in the sequel are old elements in new dress, and some things are even old elements in old dress.

Let it be noted that the continuity between the 'theologian' of Frankfurt and the 'philosopher' of Jena concerns not merely the general philosophical problems, but in equal measure the religious issues. Even the principle of awarding philosophy precedence over religion, which made its debut in the *Difference* and was then clearly formulated in the weighty treatise *Faith and Knowledge* (I, 221-346), was only relatively novel. There are two reasons for this. In the first place, what was earlier called 'philosophy' (i.e. bad philosophy, 'philosophy of reflection') remains, even in the new epoch, subordinate to religion. Secondly, what was earlier called 'religion' was even then, in its own way, a penultimate matter, a transition stage which had to be overcome. Thus traditional rational philosophy remains subordinate to both religion and true (speculative) philosophy. The novel element in all this – to which we must return – is that speculative philosophy is understood as the highest conceptual form of a religion elevated to the level of conceptual consciousness.

The most telling evidence of the inner continuity is perhaps the fact that in the great change which occurred in Jena Hegel's primary concern remained

---

[22]On these differences cf. Haering, *op. cit.* I, 684-692. Further, from Schelling's perspective, cf. W. Kasper: *Das Absolute in der Geschichte,* 98f (with reference to H. Fuhrmans). From Fichte's perspective H. Girndt endeavours to oppose the customary classification of Fichte's philosophy as subjective idealism on the strength of an isolated analysis of Hegel's *Difference*. Girndt's argument is unconvincing both with regard to method (in general and in detail) and on material grounds (with respect to Fichte and especially to Hegel).

'religion'. He was still intensely concerned with reconciliation in a living unity; indeed, he was more concerned than ever with reconciliation: 'But the task of philosophy consists in uniting these presuppositions and in positing the union of being with not-being – as becoming; the union of division with the Absolute – as its appearance; and the union of the finite with the infinite – as life' (*Difference* I, 16). 'Whether they are called 'I' and nature, pure and empirical self-consciousness, perception and being, positing and opposing oneself, or finitude and infinitude, these two contrasting realities are simultaneously posited in the Absolute. Common reflection sees nothing but contradiction in this antinomy and reason alone sees truth in this absolute contradiction, which both posits and annuls the contrasts, which are not two things and are yet two things at once' (I, 93). Hegel, then, is still concerned with reconciliation. Yet Frankfurt prompts us to ask: Where does this leave the reconciler?

2. Christ in Eclipse

There is at all events, notwithstanding all the continuity amidst change, one difference which cannot be overlooked between the erstwhile 'theologian' and the present 'philosopher'. That is, the meaning of Hegel's geographical and spiritual change of abode is that the figure of Christ appears to have vanished – one might almost say without trace. Jesus finds no mention in Hegel's first published work and just as little in the other articles and reviews written at the beginning of his time in Jena. Apart from an unimportant reference to 'Christ' in the essay on scepticism (I, 167), 'Jesus' only crops up in the article 'How man's commonsense takes philosophy', where he is put in a list of the 'greatest individual characters' in the company of Moses, Alexander and Cyrus (I, 149). Is it not thoroughly surprising that Hegel made no mention of the name of Jesus in Jena? As if all Hegel's thoughts in Frankfurt had not centred on this one figure! Such a silence cannot be accidental.

Why, then, does Hegel keep silent about Jesus? Clearly not out of slothful negligence. Perhaps Hegel had left him behind, perhaps he was simply no longer able to find him interesting and had advanced beyond him. As we have established, Hegel had certainly shown an increasing measure of understanding for Christianity in the course of the years, and with the passage of time his rejection of Jesus had turned into friendly tolerance and at length into deeper understanding. There were two main reasons for his interest in Jesus. First, there was the claim made on him by a whole world which persisted in calling itself Christian. Neither Christianity nor Christ nor their relation to one another could be a matter of indifference to the reformer intent on socio-political renewal. Secondly, and most importantly, he was increasingly wont to look on the Jesus whom he studied in the gospels as the ideal man. Indeed, he was disposed to go beyond the Enlightenment and Kant to see in him the man reconciled to God, who lives a true life beyond all dead and abstract separation in unity with the Godhead, and who – as Son of God and Son of man – reveals the true unity of God and man.

Yet Hegel himself had made it plain with all the clarity that one could desire that the unity of the totality of life in general (in which there is no divorce of infinite from finite or divine from human) is more fundamental than unity with God in Christ. The 'Godmanhood' of man in general is more important than the one 'God-man'. All movement in the process of Spirit, life, love and reconciliation as Hegel understands it is in principle movement on one and the same level. Jesus is the revelation of that Godmanhood which is the hidden, true nature of *every* person. In other words, man does not have any need of a permanent *unus mediator,* for according to the precedent of this one man *every* person becomes a mediator himself, just as Christ both could and had to be such within the all-vivifying Spirit. As early as Frankfurt Hegel's entire thought is reducible to the merging of the *one* divine-human reconciler through the Spirit into all. In this way biblical Christology can be speculatively demythologised and faith in Christ speculatively ideologised. According to Hegel, faith in Christ means to acquire a sense of Godmanhood in the Spirit through sympathetic feeling. In Christ is revealed an interconnection of sin, punishment and reconciliation which is, however, ultimately given in nature itself: the one universal life is destroyed through guilt and reacts as fate to this destruction; but reconciliation occurs in love as the feeling for life.

All this means that Christ must already have been overtaken by speculation before Hegel came to Jena. Yet it was only in Jena that he drew the radical consequences from this fact to the extent that – through his entry into a new spiritual world and his involvement with transcendental philosophy – the two considerations we have adduced for Hegel's special interest in Christology had both to recede into the background.

First, Hegel's tendency to combine practical-religious with socio-political interests retreated before *pure theory.* That this religious and socio-political tendency had certainly not completely disappeared is attested not only by the Jena *System of Ethics,* the work on the imperial constitution and the treatise on natural law, but also in its own way by the *Phenomenology.* But religious and socio-political concerns were no longer the universal leitmotif. This is attributable not only to the influence of Schelling, but also to that of world-political events, especially the collapse of the German Empire already portended in the Peace of Lunéville in 1801. Esoteric philosophy was increasingly replacing Germany's intellectual revolution as his prime interest. Not for nothing have scholars spoken from this point on of Hegel's 'contemplative' Idealism, of a struggling through which became a thinking through. Under external influence the practical reformer turned into what he was by disposition: a philosophical thinker. The main issue was no longer thinking about doing, but thinking about thinking! This development was reinforced by Hegel's theoretical breakthrough from resistance to antithesis to 'sublation' of antithesis. With this he was moving toward a basically anti-revolutionary but also highly qualified acceptance of the practical *status quo* of society. For all his faith in progress Hegel was more prepared than previously – when he had derided the laziness of those in authority, evident in their always taking everything as it is – to reconcile himself with existing reality (cf. in this context Hegel's second thesis for his Jena doctoral disputation: 'The beginning of moral science is respect for fact'[23]; I, 404). The consequence of this intense concentration on an esoteric philosophy was that Hegel's interest in the fact of the Christian religion in this society was bound to wane. Christianity, and therefore the figure of Christ himself, receded before a speculation which, despite its practical overtones, was primarily theoretical (on this subject cf. the remarks on philosophy as 'something esoteric' and 'incapable of popular presentation' in the essay of 1802 'On the essence of philosophical criticism'; I, 126f).

Secondly, occupation with concrete history receded before a *universal systematic way of thinking*. Hegel's philosophy admittedly remained stamped and shot through by history, and the historicity of all philosophy would remain his enduring concern. Yet in the Jena period Hegel followed Schelling in temporarily turning away from the concrete course of European history. He was obliged to concentrate his vigour on the development of his system. This meant in its turn that Hegel's interest in Old and New Testament history as a phase (however understood) of the concrete course of history was itself bound to diminish. Along with Judaism and primitive Christianity, the historical figure of Jesus receded before a universal historico-philosophical ontology. In this perspective, after he had adopted a critical attitude towards the contemporary philosophical scene during the Jena years, Hegel strove to renovate the heritage of the history of philosophy.[24]

Thus, Hegel was moving away from practical experience, and this caused him to disregard the practical 'world-view' of the surrounding 'Christian' world. He was moving away from the concrete course of history, and this caused him to disregard the historical ideal of the man joined to God in a living union. In short, Christ had been eclipsed. But we have already been able

---

[23]'*Principium scientiae moralis est reverentia facto habenda.*'
[24]On this subject see the report composed in 1840 by Hegel's pupil and successor in Berlin, G. A. Gabler: *Hegel in Jena i. J. 1805-6*; cf. H. Kimmerle: *Dokumente, 69f.*

to glean from the victorious tone of the Jena notebook and from the developed programme of the *Difference*, that a third factor lay hidden in this double development in the form of the *new status of reason*. This is an essential pre-condition for the possibility of the continuation of the old problem areas in a much more abstract and systematic way.

A high price is paid for the new status of reason and therefore of philosophy, namely, the displacement of love. Love has had to surrender its primacy: where love once stood, reason now stands. Hegel is fully aware of this momentous change, stating with a certain measure of regret that, '[f]or the concept of God as universal life the expression *love* is more intelligible, but *Spirit* is more profound'. Thus he writes at the outset of the work on the divine triangle (*H*, 304) which comes, not – as Rosenkranz thought[25] – from the early Frankfurt period, but – as Hoffmeister (cf. *H*, 474) correctly pigeonholes it – from his early days in Jena.

The changed order of precedence was rendered possible by the reinterpretation of love which had already taken place in Frankfurt. While there Hegel had given a fine account of how love allows the other to be himself without absorbing him. Love is placed above theoretical cognition, which does not overcome the antithesis to the object, and above practical activity, which annuls the object; for it alone can be one with the object without either dominating or letting itself be dominated (*N*, 376)! Already in our section on Frankfurt we had to join with W. Kern[26] in drawing attention to an opposite tendency in Hegel's writings. This was the tendency to identify love purely and simply with the whole, with the universal life, in whose movement of self-reconciliation the individual, with his freedom and his love, becomes a subordinate, 'sublated' element. All that is now needed to make possible the changed order is the identification of this whole of life and love with 'Spirit'. And we ascertained that this identification already took place in Frankfurt (cf. *K*, 278). Yet, as J. Splett aptly observes,[27] Hegel's Frankfurt understanding of Spirit was still in terms of the life-principle (soul), the rich, unifying force which lives through and holds together a community, a people or a culture. Only in the specialist philosophical atmosphere of Jena is 'Spirit' understood in terms of consciousness. Consciousness is then the fount and goal of the interpretation of all phenomena and cognitive Spirit is identical with reason. We can see in *K*, 265 an intimation of the modifying transition from the dialectic of love, life and Spirit (in general) to a dialectic of cognitive Spirit: '... one is to the other an other only in that one recognizes the other'.

---

[25] *op. cit.*, 101f.
[26] *Das Verhältnis von Erkenntnis und Liebe bei Hegel und Thomas von Aquin*, esp. 394-406.
[27] *Die Trinitätslehre Hegels*, 25.

At that time in Frankfurt *life* was defined as 'the union of union and nonunion' (*K*, 312), but now in Jena 'the absolute self' or even cognitive *Spirit* is described in quite analogous terms as 'the identity of identity and non-identity' (I, 77). Then it was *love* which annulled all oppositions and created unity (cf. *K*, 277), now it is 'reason' which, 'in the ceaseless activity of becoming and producing . . . unites what was separated and reduces absolute division to the level of a relative division conditioned by original identity' (I, 14). Praise was formerly heaped on *love*, which neither dominates nor lets itself be dominated (*N*, 376), but now it is given to all-perceiving and all-determining 'reason and to mastery of the world' (*H*, 357). In short, '[t]he dialectic of love and life has become the dialectic of cognitive Spirit. As an "absolute identity of subject and object" dialectic is the "autoproduction of reason", whose "activity" is "a pure presentation of itself" '.[28]

The consequence of the replacement of love by reason is the elevation of religion into philosophy. In Frankfurt religion was one with love and as such the fulfilment of morality, while in Jena philosophical knowledge is the agent of reconciliation: 'This conscious identity of the finite with infinitude and the union of the two worlds – sensual and intellectual, necessary and free – in consciousness is *knowledge*. Reflection (as the capacity of the finite) and its opposite, the infinite, are synthesised in reason, whose infinitude embraces the finite in itself' (I, 19; cf. *Faith and Knowledge* I, 223, 339f etc). Hegel formerly contended: 'Philosophy has to stop short of religion' (*K*, 313). Now, however, as we have already heard, he teaches: 'The reply to the questions which philosophy does not answer is that they ought not to be put in such a way' (*H*, 360).

Thus Hegel has extraordinarily high expectations of philosophy. If it needed to be pointed out with reference to the Jena period that Hegel's chief concern remained mediation and reconciliation, it must now be said plainly that it is *philosophy* which has to accomplish this mediation and reconciliation. A point to which we must presently return is that Hegel saw the problems inherent in the modern development against the stark background of that fundamental dualism of which Cartesianism is but a philosophical expression and ₍the political and religious revolutions but an outer manifestation: 'Cartesian philosophy was a philosophical expression of the all-pervasive cultural dualism characteristic of the recent history of our north-western world. The more silent changes in men's public life and the louder political and religious revolutions are merely variegated exterior manifestations of this dualism as they are of the decline of the whole old way of life. Every aspect of

---

[28]W. Kern: *op. cit.*, 402.

living nature and philosophy too was obliged to seek means of escape from this philosophy as from the general culture which it expressed' (I, 128). Thus Hegel's philosophy in its most various guises aimed to serve *reconciliation*: reconciliation between the one philosophy and the many systems (as in the essay just quoted 'On the essence of philosophical criticism'), between certitude and object (in 'The relationship of scepticism to philosophy'), between vulgar cognition and speculation (in 'How man's commonsense takes philosophy'), between faith and knowledge, religion and philosophy (in 'Faith and Knowledge'), or, as Hegel persistently put it in quite general terms, between subject and object.

Even though he unfortunately has no idea what to make of Hegel's early 'theological' writings, Ernst Bloch is undoubtedly correct in putting his 'Observations on Hegel' under the general heading 'Subject-Object': 'Thus Hegel always knew how to label the fundamental idea in which all the profundities and complexities of his thought are implicitly contained. We cannot miss here the essential and constantly-recurring ingredient of Hegel's philosophy: the dialectical subject-object mediation.'[29]

Even when he is silent about Christ, Hegel's teaching remains concerned with a redeemed world; it remains a 'doctrine of salvation'. He means to bestow depth, permanence, composure and unity on the superficial, cursory, dissipated and divided life of man and his world. The ultimate meaning of this is that the finite should find its own infinitude in the infinite and that man should find life and reconciliation in God as the Absolute.

Hegel's point of departure in this 'doctrine of salvation' of his was above all the Bible. But in the course of development the biblical and especially Johannine terms have taken on an increasingly universal meaning. 'Life', 'love' and 'Spirit' increasingly became expressive of dialectical reality in general. Study based on exegesis and biblical theology was transformed into universal-philosophical speculation, and the social and religious problem made way for the universal significance of every subject-object relation. But precisely because the problem of God turned into the more general problem of being, and precisely because the perceptions won from Christology and the religious relation of God and man were now being extended into a general consideration of ontology, for these very reasons Hegel's philosophy will bear the marks of its Christian past either openly or hiddenly as an indelible seal.

With reference to the two following chapters on the more 'philosophical' Hegel, confirmation is provided here of two methodological factors which are definitive for our own work: a) a purely philosophical interpretation of his philosophy, which leaves

---

[29] *Subjekt- Objekt,* 36.

its specifically Christian starting-point out of account, can only partly do justice to Hegel; b) a theological debate with Hegel's philosophy is enabled by this very same philosophy to put critical and discriminating questions to Hegel from the perspective of the original Christian message.

Nowhere is the continued presence of a Christian past in Hegel more plainly manifested than in the question of Christology. Even though Christ is obviously in eclipse in these Jena years, yet he is not simply absent. And if we look more closely at these texts, which are once more highly topical for present-day theology, then we ascertain with astonishment that Christology has not disappeared without trace. Hegel's silence on Christology could well be an eloquent silence. And if it was possible to show that the question of God was powerfully intensified for Hegel by the changes he underwent in Jena, then it will now become clear – in the face of modern atheism – that it was precisely Christology that wrought the ultimate intensification of the question of God for Hegel. With respect to our general topic, we come here to what was both then and now the heart of the matter.

3. The Death of God

Even though no mention is made of Jesus' life or work, Hegel does speak of a 'witness to the Word' and of an 'incarnation of God' (I, 90). And even though he nowhere speaks of Jesus' fate and death, he does make mention of a 'Good Friday' with its 'pain' and 'suffering', writing 'God himself is dead' (I, 345). There is nothing arbitrary or far-fetched about our choice of these two passages. They come from Hegel's two most significant publications prior to the *Phenomenology,* namely the *Difference* and the treatise on faith and knowledge, where they appear at the pinnacle of the argument.

The significance of these two passages is no more and no less than that christological statements are turning into statements about the Absolute itself. We might even say that Hegel sees theology itself as defined in terms of Christology, as christomorphic theology. Because he is concerned with God, with the Absolute itself, he speaks of an '*eternal* incarnation of God', of the 'witness of the Word from the *beginning*', of the '*speculative* Good Friday', of the '*infinite* pain' and of the '*absolute* suffering'.

The 'witness to the Word from the beginning' and the 'eternal incarnation of God' are predicated of the 'Absolute which becomes objective to itself in a perfect totality': 'The original identity, which diffused its unconscious contracted state – subjectively of feeling, objectively of matter – into an objective totality, i.e. the endlessly organised juxtaposition and succession of space and time, and then countered this diffusion by negating it through a subjective totality, i.e. a self-constituting contraction into the self-discerning point of

162

(subjective) reason, must unite both in the intuition of the Absolute becoming objective to itself in a perfect totality, namely in the intuition of the eternal incarnation of God and of the witness of the Word from the beginning' (I, 90). Schelling's influence is again discernible in the fact that this intuition of the Absolute occurs in art (to which religion is to be reckoned to belong as its living enactment) and in speculation: 'The essence of both art and speculation is divine service; for both are a living intuition of absolute life and consequently a union with it' (I, 91).

The 'speculative Good Friday', that is, 'absolute suffering', is predicated of the 'supreme Idea'. With reference to modern developments, we note that it is at this point that Hegel came out with the sensational expression 'the death of God'.

The following passage forms the end of the treatise on faith and knowledge and in the German original appears as a single sentence (!). We must pay attention to its exact wording in order to interpret it correctly with dual reference both to the historical situation and to Christology: 'Infinite pain – the feeling that God himself is dead – was previously experienced, historically speaking, only in the educated world. It is the feeling on which modern religion rests. It was enunciated only so to speak empirically in Pascal's words: *la nature est telle qu'elle* marque *partout un* Dieu perdu *et dans l'homme et hors de l'homme.* The pure concept – or infinity as the abyss of nothing, in which all being sinks – must characterise this infinite pain as simply a moment, and yet no more than a moment, of the supreme Idea. It must thus give philosophical existence to what was either a moral prescription to sacrifice empirical existence or else the concept of formal abstraction, thus providing philosophy with the idea of absolute freedom and hence absolute suffering or the speculative Good Friday – formerly thought of as historical – and restoring this very thing in the whole truth and severity of its godlessness. It is solely in virtue of this severity – just because the more cheerful, inscrutable and peculiar aspects of both the dogmatic philosophies and the natural religions must disappear – that the supreme totality both can and must rise again in its entire seriousness and from its profoundest depth, encompassing all things at once in the most serene freedom of its form' (I, 345f).

The complexity of the passage corresponds to the complexity of the problem. It would in fact be only too easy to break out of its dialectical structure to right or to left. In order to be clear about its meaning it is essential to bear in mind two factors:

1. Hegel has caught sight of modern atheism. Although, as he will later explicitly state, the sentence 'God is dead' is a quotation from a hymn of Luther's, as far as he is concerned it is not a pious way of speaking against an

orthodox theological background, but a harsh historical experience, an 'infinite pain'. Almost a century before Nietzsche's announcement that 'God is dead! God remains dead! And we have killed him!',[30] Hegel summed up recent history with the expression 'the death of God'. Clear-sighted and alert, he was fully alive to the precise historical context in which this basic religious feeling of the modern period is to be viewed. In the passage already quoted from the essay on the essence of criticism (I, 128) the following key phrases had been employed in interpretation of 'the recent history of our north-western world': the universal and all-pervasive cultural dualism and the decline of all old life – brought to philosophical expression in Cartesianism – whose external consequences were both the quieter changes in public life and the loud political and religious revolutions. What lies hidden behind these key phrases? In view of the collapse of the ancient world-picture brought about by the new mathematical natural science, the upshot of which had been to render the God in heaven homeless, Galileo's alert contemporary Descartes found himself faced with the difficult task of developing a new metaphysics to match the new physics (which was itself at that time still the target of vigorous persecution). Descartes' solution consisted in a sharp dualism between extension and thought (in man only apparently connected) and between the giant world machine and transcendent Spirit. This dualism precipitated not only the lasting strife between idealists and materialists, but also – later on, in the Enlightenment – that between faith and knowledge, theology and philosophy and positive and natural religion. The natural religion nurtured on the Cartesian soil of a Jean Bodin (forerunner of the French Enlightenment) and of a Lord Herbert of Cherbury (forerunner of English deism) was already overtaken in the emancipated France of the beginning of the eighteenth century by the advanced anti-religious scepticism of Pierre Bayle, who abstained on the question of the existence of God. Around the middle of the century open and aggressive atheism finally broke through.

Two factors were decisive for the breakthrough of atheism. In the first place there was the victory of mechanical natural science over an authoritarian Church which still largely identified its faith with a long superseded world-picture. In his *L'homme machine* of 1748 Lammettrie drew the radical consequence of a completely godless materialism from the mechanical world-picture, which – according to the statement of Pascal quoted by Hegel – bestowed on man a God who had 'gone missing' from both inside and outside man, but which d'Alembert and Voltaire still followed Newton in interpreting

---

[30] *The Joyful Wisdom*, no. 125 (Levy Edition X, 168).

deistically. The 'dogmatics' of this materialistic atheism, d'Holbach's *Système de la nature,* followed in the year of Hegel's birth.

Secondly there was the universal association of Church and religion with the political system of princely absolutism, which most severely discredited the Christian faith in the eyes of the aspiring classes and caused the French Revolution to turn into not only a political but also a religious revolution. In the same autumn of 1793 that Hegel moved to Bern, the Christian God was deposed in Nôtre Dame and atheistic reason proclaimed as a counter goddess.

Only in the ensuing years did belief in God start to become problematical in Germany too. Jean Paul Richter's horrific vision of a 'speech by the dead Christ from the cosmic system, saying that there is no God' (in the *Siebenkäs,* 1796-97) was admittedly intended as a purely hypothetical warning. Yet its influence was to make itself felt in all possible 'monks of atheism' (H. Heine) in the Romantic period up to Dostoyevsky's *Devils.* Atheism was now as it were in the air. Hegel was himself affected above all by the atheistic controversy which broke out two years later. In an essay of 1798, 'On the reasons for our belief in the divine government of the world', which was bound up with a likeminded and even more advanced essay by his pupil Forberg, Fichte had declared among other things that, '[t]he living and active moral order of things is itself God. We need no other God, nor can we conceive any other'.[31] He was accused of atheism. This was certainly an injustice, for in the depths of his heart Fichte was a believing, inwardly pious man. He meant by his statement to depict the divine as the All-One which conditions, bears and realises a world of freedom as its moral ground.[32] Yet neither was the charge entirely unjust, for his renunciation of fatalistic Spinozism under the influence of Kant and his turning to primal moral certitude seemed to obliterate any relationship to God from his thought. In the early period of the *Theory of Science* the idea of God is no more than a borderline concept; it is an Absolute which is neither personality nor self-consciousness and least of all is it creator of the world. Thus atheism was indicating to the whole world that the period of the Enlightenment's religious understanding of the world had expired. The question of the coordination of the various egos and of the synthesis of the world of spirits should actually have prompted Fichte to reflect more closely on the idea of God. Yet Fichte did not intend to propound any concept about God. Hence, initiating a trend which was subsequently to become exceedingly popular through Schleiermacher, he demonstrated that belief in God is an

---

[31]cf. the philosophical writings on the atheistic controversy edited by F. Medicus.
[32]cf. E. Hirsch: *op. cit.* IV, 351-364.

immediate and original certainty rooted in feeling. He defined the content of this religious faith in terms of Kant's idea of the highest good as the moral order of things, whereby – as a result of the performance of the good – the ideal state of things, the kingdom of God, is implicitly promoted.

Be that as it may, Fichte's impassioned *Appeal to the Public* ('A writing which we ask may first be read, before it is confiscated', 1799[33]) was impotent to prevent his dismissal from his Jena post after he himself had threatened resignation in a somewhat precipitate letter. His Excellency Johann Wolfgang von Goethe, whose Faustian credo – 'I have no name for it. Feeling is everything' – had brought the impugned essay to a close, voted for Fichte's dismissal. Even Schiller, whose 'words of faith' were quoted together with Goethe, acted ambiguously. Only in Berlin did the Consistory Councillors act to a man to prevent any steps against Fichte's writings, and Frederick William III finally granted refuge to the universally rebuffed philosopher: 'If it is true that he is engaged in hostilities with God, then let God sort it out with him; it has nothing to do with me.'[34] Fichte's final word in this rather unpleasant controversy was his work on *The Vocation of Man*.[35] It was this above all that Hegel considered in his essay penned two years later on 'Faith and Knowledge, or the subjective philosophy of reflection, as it found its completed forms in Kant's, Jacobi's and Fichte's philosophy' (1802; I, 223-346).

It goes without saying that for his part Hegel was by no means disposed to accuse Fichte of atheism. Nonetheless, he did establish an intellectual connection between Fichte's position and atheism. Hegel took as his starting-point the fact that the Enlightenment's victory over faith was a victory in which reason itself was taken in: 'The enlightening reason scored a glorious victory over faith, which, according to the slender measure of its religious comprehension, it regarded as its foe. On closer inspection, the outcome of this glorious victory is that the material with which reason made itself struggle, namely religion, did not remain religion. Nor did that which ostensibly triumphed remain reason. And the birth which triumphantly rises above these corpses as the child of peace (which, being common to both, unites both) is as little characterised by reason as by genuine faith' (I, 223). What was the achievement of Kant, Jacobi and Fichte, all of whom reacted against this Enlightenment? They all ultimately remained stuck in the Enlightenment's dualistic opposition between subjectivity and the Absolute: 'By understanding religion as something positive and not in idealistic terms,

---

[33] *Appellation an das Publikum, Werke* III, 151-198.
[34] Quoted by H. Knittermeyer in art. '*Atheismusstreit*', *RGG*[3] I, 678.
[35] *The Vocation of Man* (tr. Wm. Smith, London, 1848).

reason has been able to follow up its victory by nothing better than looking to its own interests, attaining self-knowledge and recognising its own nothing-ness in positing something better than itself (being itself no more than intellect) as a *transcendent reality* in a *faith which is beyond and above itself'* (I, 224). In particular, according to Fichte, 'God is something incomprehensi-ble and unthinkable. Knowledge knows nothing beyond the fact that it knows nothing, and must therefore seek refuge in faith' (I, 224).

In order that faith, which since the Enlightenment had been pushed severely on to the defensive, might resist the domination of the intellect, it withdrew into a 'pure' Protestant inwardness untarnished by any objectivity. It with-drew into the inwardness of the mind, of beautiful feeling, of self-sure subjectivity: 'The great form of the world-Spirit discernible in those philoso-phies is the principle of the North and – in a religious sense – of Protestantism. This is *subjectivity,* in which beauty and truth appear in feelings and sentiments, in love and intellect. Religion builds its temples and altars in the heart of the individual. Its sighs and prayers seek the God whose face it renounces because of the ever-present intellectual danger of mistaking what it sees for an object and confusing the wood with the woodsman' (I, 225). Precisely through this withdrawal into Protestant subjectivity (the pietistic alternative), faith has surrendered the objective reality of the world and man to atheism: 'Precisely because of its rigidity and flight from the finite, subjective faith finds that the beautiful turns into things in general, the wood into woodsmen and images into things which have eyes yet see not and ears yet hear not. And if ideals in fully intelligible reality cannot be taken as blocks and stones, subjective faith finds that they turn into fabrications, every reference to them appearing as an unreal game or as dependence on objects and as superstition' (I, 226). To this extent faith, which evaded the *aporia* of the Enlightenment by retreating into inwardness, bears a large share of the responsibility for the rise of atheism. Faith and reason alike were thus surrendered to the enlightened intellect, to the detriment of both faith and philosophical reason: of faith because it was thereby robbed of its content, or rather, its content was thereby put off into the hereafter, and of philosophical reason because it has thereby been reduced to the level of reflective intellect, being obliged to renounce any knowledge of the Absolute. In its realisation of subjectivity Fichte's philosophy does not get beyond the moral 'ought', since self-sure subjectivity will not surrender its usurped absoluteness and so cannot attain knowledge of the Absolute through reason. But if infinitude is opposed to finitude in such a way, then 'one is as good as the other' (I, 232). All the modern philosophies one might mention thus remain 'within this common basic principle, namely, the absoluteness of finitude and the consequent absolute antithesis of finitude and infinitude, reality and ideality, the sensible and the super-sensible, and the transcendent nature of the truly real and absolute' (I, 230). All this then stands behind the basic modern sense of the death of God and of that lack of God within and without man which Pascal had already bewailed.

2. Hegel understood modern atheism in post-atheistic terms. As far as he is concerned, there is no going back on the Enlightenment. Since justification by means of the concept became a necessity, the old naive immediacy of faith has been a thing of the past. The intellect has a right to engage in critical reflection so long as it refrains from absolutising things. It is by no means the case that Hegel simply rejected the philosophy of subjectivity. On the contrary, precisely Fichte's philosophy surpasses all previous philosophy to the extent that here, at any rate on the subjective level, the unity of thought and being is presupposed and accomplished against all separation of subject from object. But even if the union of finite and infinite in this way is only a subjective unity, nevertheless Fichte's 'philosophy of infinitude is closer to the philosophy of the Absolute than to that of the finite' (I, 345).

Hegel's concern, however, is precisely with this 'philosophy of the Absolute'. If the subjectivity which has been thrown back on itself, and which has been opposed to an empty infinitude, is not to succumb to nihilism, to the 'abyss of nothing, in which all being is submerged' (I, 345), then it must attain to a not merely subjective but actual unity of finite and infinite: a unity in the Absolute. This unity in the Absolute cannot be achieved by a compounding of finite and infinite, but rather by the continuous sublation of the finite in the infinite: 'If the Absolute were compounded of finite and infinite, then abstraction from the finite would certainly be a loss. But in the Idea, finite and infinite are one and finitude as such has therefore disappeared insofar as it was meant to have truth and reality in and for itself. Yet all that has happened is that the aspect of finitude which is negation has itself been negated and hence a true affirmative process has been posited' (I, 234).

The meaning of this is that the infinite pain at the lack or death of God has been sublated into God himself: 'as a moment of the supreme Idea' (I, 346). What was largely understood as a moral command, namely the 'sacrifice of empirical existence' (I, 346), must be understood in truly philosophical terms as a renunciation on the part of the Absolute itself. This is its 'absolute freedom' and hence also 'absolute suffering'. God empties himself into the world. By such a philosophical understanding of the Absolute in the unity of infinite and finite, philosophy will 'restore' not only the 'historical' (i.e. past) but also the truly 'speculative' (i.e. historic-eternal) 'Good Friday in the whole truth and severity of its godlessness' (I, 346). In a Jena aphorism which was unknown until recently, Hegel put the matter in this lapidary manner: '. . . God sacrifices himself, surrenders himself to destruction. God himself is dead: the supreme despair of complete abandonment by God.'[36] The basic atheistic feeling of the modern age must therefore be understood on the level of speculative philosophy. The historical Good Friday of Jesus' abandonment by God is to be understood on the speculative level, where faith and reason are found, as the Good Friday of the Absolute itself and hence as the Good Friday of the abandonment by God of all that is. All the superficial 'more cheerful aspects of both the dogmatic philosophies and the natural religions must disappear' (I, 346) before the universalisation of the historical Good Friday, before the 'severity' of this universal 'godlessness'. Only christological inter-pretation can manifest the 'entire seriousness' and the 'deepest depth' of godlessness.

Yet all this is not the end of the matter, for Hegel preaches no 'gospel of Christian atheism' but rather, if we wish to put it thus, a 'Christian sublation of atheism': not 'atheistically believing in God', but 'believing in God in a post-atheistic sense'. Precisely because it is the death of God, the resurrection follows upon Good Friday. Precisely because it is God's own Good Friday, infinite pain may be understood 'as a moment, and yet as no more than a moment, of the supreme Idea' (I, 346). Because it is the very Absolute, it 'can and must', as if surpassing itself, 'rise again' as 'the supreme totality in its entire seriousness and from its deepest depth, encompassing all things at once in the most serene freedom of its form' (I, 346). Thus the atheistic abandon-ment of the world by God is taken in and turned around from the perspective of Jesus' abandonment by God, which is understood as God's abandonment of himself.

Here for the first time there is posed with radical clarity the basic problem which has always constituted the one specifically theological aspect of the disputed sphere of classical Christology and which will from now on demand our constant and unremitting attention: in the event that God were to empty himself in such a way into this immanent reality, into history, into humanity, in the event that we can in fact talk of an incarnation of God and of a death and resurrection of God – how must this God himself be understood? What, on these presuppositions, do suffering and death mean for God or, to put it more generally – even if we do not yet express it explicitly even here – what does worldly 'becoming' mean for him? This will be Hegel's question concern-ing the living God.

The death of God is a topic of which Hegel will never again lose sight. The text which has just been analysed explains why Hegel, along with Nietzsche, was particularly

---

[36]Quoted in F. Nicolin: *Unbekannte Aphorismen Hegels,* 16.

influential on the 'death of God theologians'[37] who cropped up sporadically in America and Germany in the 1960s. According to Thomas J.J. Altizer, Hegel is 'the only thinker who made the kenotic movement of the Incarnation the core and foundation of all his thinking'.[38] And D. Sölle confesses that '[i]t is above all Hegel who attracts our attention . . . in the search for prototypes of and impulses towards such a theology'.[39] The author's call for 'a revision of our relationship to German Idealism' and for 'a fresh treatment of Hegel and his heirs' can of course only be welcomed in the light of the intentions of this essay on Hegel's Christology: 'At the present time the difficulties inherent in a Protestant systematic theology are more obvious than ever. They lie in its mistrustful and one-sided relationship to philosophy, as if there were none apart from Heidegger's. The influence which Kierkegaard has exercised for decades bears a good share of the blame for this awkward situation. For everything which German Idealism (between Fichte and Hegel) began to formulate by way of reply to the "death of God" was rejected in his name.'[40]

The death of God theology can count on Hegel's support when, with great honesty, genuine commitment and resolute solidarity with its secular contemporaries, it follows his example by a) taking with the utmost seriousness the secular world with its 'atheistic' self-understanding, along with the fact that God no longer plays any role in the modern experience of reality, so that we must live 'as though there were no God'[41]; b) attempting to understand this modern atheism christologically in terms of the death of God; and c) using its discourse about the death of God – whether intentionally or unintentionally – to provoke a lively discussion about a living God and to achieve what, in the wake of German Idealism and dialectical theology, would be a 'third concentration on the problem of *God*'.[42] Such an emphasis would draw attention to

---

[37]While they display considerable differences among themselves, the following works are to be counted among the products of the 'death of God theology': G. Vahanian: *The Death of God*; P. van Buren: *The Secular Meaning of the Gospel*; W. Hamilton: *The New Essence of Christianity*; Thomas J. J. Altizer: *The Gospel of Christian Atheism*; idem (with Hamilton): *Radical Theology and the Death of God*; D. Sölle: *Stellvertretung* (ET *Christ the Representative*, tr. D. Lewis, London, 1967); *idem: Atheistisch an Gott glauben*. Altizer offers 'readings' on the death of God theology in *Towards a New Christianity* (which contains a section on Hegel by J. N. Findlay).

On the discussion in America cf. J. Bishop: *Die Gott-ist-tot Theologie; cf.* also the two symposia *The Meaning of the Death of God* (ed. B. Murchland) and *Radical Theology Phase Two* (edd. C.W. Christian and G.R. Wittig).

On the discussion in Germany cf. J. Moltmann: *Theologie der Hoffnung,* 105-155 (*Theology of Hope,* 165-72), bristling with information on Hegel; G. Hasenhüttl: *Die Wandlung des Gottesbildes*; H. Fries: *Theologische Überlegungen zum Phänomen des Atheismus*; idem (with R. Stählin): *Gott ist tot?*; H. Mühlen: *Die abendländische Seinsfrage als der Tod Gottes und der Aufgang einer neuen Gotteserfahrung*; H. Thielicke: *Der evangelische Glaube* 1, 305-565 (ET by G. W. Bromiley, 219-385); M. Seckler: *Kommt der christliche Glaube ohne Gott aus?* The essays from the Marxist-Communist camp by R. Garaudy ('*Gott ist tot*') and V. Gardavsky ('God is not yet dead') are also important. W. Kern gives a discerning analysis of Hegel's view of the relationship of atheism, Christianity and the emancipated society in the context of a discussion with the recent literature.

[38]*The Gospel of Christian Atheism,* 24.

[39]*Atheistisch an Gott glauben,* 54.

[40]*op. cit.,* 70f.

[41]*etsi Deus non daretur.*

[42]S. Daecke: *Welcher Gott ist tot?,* 127.

170

the problems involved in a super-terrestrial, supernatural and theistic conception of God and enable us to look out for God as a this-worldly actuality.

Hegel's own thought prompts us to ask whether Helmut Thielicke is not guilty of oversimplifying the problem and hence of failing to do justice to the philosopher in his critique[43] when, in his gratifyingly detailed and thoroughly constructive discussion with the death of God theology ('Situation and Task of Theology in the Generation of the Supposed Death of God'[44]), he wishes to understand 'death of God' as a merely symbolic expression, posing the following dilemma: 'The slogan cannot be meant literally since it involves a logical contradiction. Either the God who is now dead never really was God, so that his death is in fact only the death of an earlier illusion, or the death of God means simply that he is dead for us, that a certain experience of God has gone, that a prior certainty has been extinguished, that a recognised concept of God has been weakened or revised, so that God himself is not really dead, but only a form of our faith or of our view of God. If God is dead, he cannot die, for there has never been a God and Feuerbach is right. Only belief in God can die, and it can do so only if there is no God. For if God is, he will constantly find recognition and kindle new faith.'[45]

This dilemma abstracts from the question which must be posed, even from a Christian perspective, concerning the significance of the incarnation for God himself. How are we to think christologically concerning the life, suffering and death of God? This is by no means to put a stamp of approval on the recent kind of death of God theology. On the contrary, Hegel's own thought compels us to make some critical distinctions with regard to this theology.

1. Hegel cannot be appropriated by any king of *atheism*. If this is true of the atheism of Feuerbach and Marx (except through a distortion of Hegel's own intentions), then it must be said against Altizer in particular that this is also true of 'Christian atheism' (if there is such a thing!). If Altizer differs from Vahanian in not protesting, in the name of the biblical revelation 'alone', against the 'death of God' in the immanence of modern civilisation and religiosity, and if he also differs from Hamilton and van Buren in regarding the death of God as an objective event of cosmic relevance which occurred in the death of Jesus, this is undoubtedly chiefly due to the influence of his first Crown witness, Hegel.[46] Apart from other contradictions entailed by what we can only call this mystically and mythologically understood death of God in the year 30, we need only draw attention here to the one basic contradiction to Hegel, requiring no further proof in the light of the above account: Altizer opposes Hegel by accepting the death of God in Christ as 'a final and irrevocable event, which cannot be reversed',[47] and by thinking it possible to merge God into the absolute immanence of the secular world. Quite apart from all counter-arguments, this represents an astonishingly frivolous misunderstanding of Hegel's 'negation of negation',[48] an absolutisation of the negative moment unsupported by any serious foundation and a blatant disregard for what can be gleaned from Hegel on the subject of the resurrection of the totality in the most

---

[43] *The Evangelical Faith* I, 259-264.

[44] *op. cit.* I, 219-385.

[45] *op. cit.* I, 312.

[46] *The Gospel of Christian Atheism,* esp. 62-69.

[47] *op. cit.,* 109.

[48] *op. cit.,* 102.

serene freedom. Hegel would count Altizer among the philosophers of reflection, who are wont to 'absolutise the individual dimensions of totality' (I, 344).

Against the background of Hegel's thought the death of God cannot be seen as anything other than a transitional stage, as the extreme nadir of the antithetical negation, in which, through the negation of negation, God does not remain in death, but comes to himself, giving a radical confirmation of his being as the living God. J. Moltmann is right to state that '[t]he romanticist nihilism of the "death of God", like the methodical atheism of science (*etsi Deus non daretur*), is an element that has been isolated from the dialectical process and is therefore no longer engaged in the movement of the process to which it belongs.'[49] H. Thielicke is likewise right to contend that 'Hegel certainly refers to utter hopelessness as the religious situation of the new age, but this is not at all the same as what death of God theologians have in view. It does not characterise a complete departure from transcendence and the definitive entry of modern man into autarchous immanence. The terror of a lost God is interpreted as a moment in God and the fear of the corresponding experience is seen as a moment in the process of finite consciousness . . . Nothing is further from Hegel than the conclusion of Nietzsche, who absolutises what is relative – a mere moment – in Hegel. There can be no question here of a proclamation of the autarchy of this world after the definitive death of God. This world is simply the finite which God has opposed to himself in order to be himself in the negation of the negation, to remain himself in it, to come forth from it'.[50] This interpretation finds endorsement from an unexpected quarter, namely the Marxist R. Garaudy: 'It is certainly impossible to consider Hegel himself as an atheist, for he conceives the reality of man in the language and categories of theology; and the objective Idealism of his system, which always leads him – despite the exigencies of his method – to posit Spirit not only at the end but also at the outset of the development of the totality, is a transposition of the fundamental themes of religious thought.'[51] In his essay on the proclamation of God's death in Nietzsche, E. Biser demonstrates that even authors like Nietzsche do not simply supply a string of proof texts[52] for the death of God theology, but that their individual statements severally stand in need of historico-critical interpretation.[53]

2. Hegel summons us to take pains with the Concept and to take God seriously. D. Sölle undoubtedly does not go along with Altizer in reducing reality to an absolute immanence tritely restricted to this world. With Hegel she is aware that our concern must be with mediation between death and resurrection[54] and between transcendence and immanence: 'such a theology will be obliged to engage with the godless world into which God has come as mediator'.[55] According to her we should bear in mind that '[t]he initial meaning of God's appearance in the relative and of his entry as mediator into the consciousness is simply that he is "put into relation" and that he is relevant to us who are conditioned by him. It would be short-sighted to believe that by conceiving God in terms of relation we thereby deprive him of his personality. On the contrary!

[49] *Theology of Hope*, 169.
[50] *The Evangelical Faith* I, 262.
[51] *Dieu est mort*, 428.
[52] *verba probantia*.
[53] '*Der totgesagte Gott*', *Lebendiges Zeugnis*, 53-66; cf. also *idem*: *Gott ist tot' – Nietzsche's Destruktion des christlichen Bewusstseins*.
[54] *Atheistisch an Gott glauben*, 54-58.
[55] *op. cit.*, 67.

There is no question – in the case of either God or man – of personal existence consisting in being in and for oneself'.[56]

At any rate Hegel's thought prompts us to make two important points:

a) Given that Hegel summons us to conceptual labour and effort, it is astonishing how carelessly and superficially the death of God theologians usually handle the central concepts 'God', 'death' and 'atheism' without bothering their heads with a precise conceptual analysis or with the plain use of the words, and without thinking through their presuppositions and conclusions. Altizer and Hamilton drew up a belated list of ten distinct meanings of the slogan 'death of God', themselves choosing number nine. Something similar might be stated with reference to the concepts 'death' and 'atheism'. 'Atheistic belief in God' is only possible if one departs from general usage by foisting on the word the meaning 'anti-theistic', in which case one can certainly create a sensation as an 'atheistic theologian'. The degree to which this phenomenon obscures the real problem corresponds to the degree to which it provokes a reaction of surprise on the part of the mass media. The latter, however, tends to be short-lived: 'In America even God dies rapidly.' Believers do not take the genuine and urgent concern of these theologians seriously, and unbelievers, who wish to see their atheism taken seriously and not mystified, feel more confirmed in their own, more thoroughgoing atheism than challenged to believe in God. A further question is whether it is wise if theologians, on the one hand and apparently out of ignorance, violently misrepresent the traditional theological idea of God, while, on the other hand, they court proximity to and dependence on contemporary intellectual trends. As far as the enlightened are concerned, this simply brings them into disrepute as mere appendages, devoid of originality.

b) Hegel summons us to take God seriously. While he himself also took atheism seriously, before all else he took God seriously. Just as any coquetry with atheism was far from him, so also was careless discourse about God, an especially irritating habit when indulged in by theologians. Many so-called Christian 'atheists' might learn from Hegel, and indeed from such genuine atheists as Nietzsche, not only to take atheism more seriously, but also to have an immense respect for God, of whom only small minds can speak belittlingly, whether in denial or in affirmation.

In view of the use by D. Sölle and others of the unbiblical and overworked idea of our common humanity to pinpoint God's place in the world – what a pity that divinity and humanity are not taken more seriously in all this! – we can only underline H. Zahrnt's critical question: 'Our decisive critical question to theology after the death of God is whether it does not seek to rescue man's faith in God from the implicit atheism of our age at the cost of God himself. Everything depends on what is understood by the expression "death of God". If "death of God" is not merely a figurative way of speaking, not merely a human experience capable of correction, but is rather an irrevocable historical reality, if God then is really dead, then no man can raise him to new life by any representative, however perfect. But in that case God was never alive in the first place!'[57]

---

[56]*op. cit.*, 71f.

[57]H. Zahrnt: *Es geht um die Existenz Gottes.* H.-W. Schütte protests sharply against using Hegel's expression 'death of God' in a sense contrary to that he intended (*Tod Gottes und Fülle der Zeit*, esp. 62-64). Likewise illuminating is S. Daecke: *Teilhard de Chardin und die evangelische Theologie*, 21-29.

The fact which for Hegel stretches the whole problem-area to the utmost is the fact that *God himself* is the ultimate issue in all the problems of man and the world. As he put it with elementary clarity in his essay on 'The intellect common to man' (I, 149), he wants nothing other than 'that which is the general concern of philosophy at the present moment, namely, the concern to put God once again absolutely at the very apex of philosophy as the sole ground of all things, as the sole source of being and knowledge. For long enough he had been put *alongside* or even after other finite realities as a postulate proceeding from an absolute finitude . . .'. Hence it is easy to understand Hegel's rather ironically sympathetic remarks about the static nature of a philosophy of reflection which reduces the problem of God to the level of the intra-human problem of humanity-in-relation, to what is naively called 'man'. He does not wish to commit himself to 'the aim of such philosophy, that is, to know not God, but what is called man. This man – and humankind in general – furnish its absolute standpoint, conceived as a static and insurmountable finitude of reason . . .' (I, 223).

At this point we can discern a clear continuity with the Frankfurt writings which goes far beyond any merely terminological and conceptual similarity. This does not, of course, signify the exclusion of the problem of man and humankind. On the contrary, it is only now that Hegel truly gets to grips with this problem. For it is only from the standpoint of the Absolute that a correct answer can be given to the question of the essence of man. Does this also hold good with respect to the question concerning the man Jesus? The pregnant final sentence of 'Faith and Knowledge' makes it inescapably obvious that, in both the Bern and Frankfurt periods, the man Jesus still remains in eclipse. Precisely where Hegel speaks of the incarnation and death of God he makes no mention of Jesus. Or was Jesus perhaps meant by the 'moral command to sacrifice empirical existence' (I, 346)? Hegel remains cryptic even in this passage. In his Jena diary we read the thought-provoking entry: 'In Swabia we say of something which happened long ago, "It occurred so long since that it will soon no longer be true". Christ likewise died for our sins so long ago that it will soon no longer be true' (*H*, 358).

We have no option but to leave our question unanswered, just as Hegel himself did – for whatever reason – at the end of his essay on 'Faith and Knowledge'. There now follows a period of silence. Apart from the treatise 'On scholarly treatments of natural law' of 1802, Hegel published nothing more until the significant year 1807. But during this period he was working with the greatest intensity.

4. The Drive Toward a System

Hegel's whole thought now contains an inner drive toward final maturity and fulfilment in a *system*: 'Because the relation of the limited to the Absolute is pluriform, and because limited things are themselves pluriform, our philosophising must aim at setting this pluriformity as such in relation. The need is bound to arise of producing a totality of knowledge, a scientific system. Only thus can the multiplicity of these relations be freed from contingency by retaining their place in the context of the objective totality of knowledge and by the accomplishment of their objective completeness' (*Difference* I, 34). Systematic thought is already to be found in the Hegel of the Frankfurt period, but it was only in Jena that Schelling's influence led to the awakening of the conscious desire to build a system.

Hegel's first incomplete and yet already rather grandiose efforts at system-building were heard during the following years in Jena as the substance of his lectures. According to the lecture list it is highly probable that one or two drafts preceded the first extant system of the year 1804 or 1804-5. For more than a century these notes remained unknown. After their first publication by Ehrenberg-Link in 1915, they were published as volume XVIII of the Lasson Edition in 1923 under the title *Jena Logic, Metaphysics and Natural Philosophy*.[58] The opening sections were lost, as was – probably by accident and not by design – an elaboration of organic natural philosophy and of the philosophy of Spirit. Beneath formulations and developments often themselves new (largely of Kantian, Fichtean-Schellingian and even of Aristotelian provenance) there lies concealed a systematic arrangement of old topics.[59]

The *Logic* (XVIII, 1-129) deals with abstractly isolated and concretely independent determinations: quality, quantity, quantum – with the relationships of being (substance/accident, cause/effect, interaction) and of thought (concept, judgment, conclusion) – and, finally, under the title 'Proportion', with definition, classification and systematic knowledge. The *Metaphysics* (XVIII, 130-186) opens with an account of the three basic principles of cognition (identity/contradiction, principle of the excluded middle, principle of ground and consequent); it goes on to treat of the soul, the world and the Supreme Being under the title 'Metaphysics of Objectivity', dealing finally with the theoretical ego, the practical ego and absolute Spirit as the 'Metaphysics of Subjectivity'. In last place, the *Natural Philosophy* (XVIII, 187-359) covers the topics: system of the sun (concept, appearance and reality of motion) and earthly system (mechanics, chemistry, physics).

---

[58]The first editors and Lasson date them in the year 1801-2. According to the most recent research by H. Kimmerle (*Zur Chronologie*, 164ff; cf. 126ff, 144, no. 72), the correct date can be taken to be 1804 or 1804-5. This dating shows that it was only an apparent problem how Hegel could have reverted from the allegedly earlier yet more independent draft to the more Schelling-like position of the *Philosophy of Nature and of Spirit* of 1803-4.

[59]T. Haering: *op. cit.* II, 12-21.

The system contains an inner drive toward the conception of all individual things as moments in the unified dialectical development of the whole, that is, of the 'absolute Spirit' thought of as a union of subject and object, being and thought, real and ideal. But at this stage the goal has only been very imperfectly realised. The individual partial disciplines confront one another as rather isolated speculative individual sciences, and there is no thorough working-out of either the dialectical method or the identity of the ideal and the real. Haering brought out in his analysis three distinct methods of classification with their different fields of application in the system: a merely general classification, a merely dialectical classification and a real-ideal-dialectical classification.[60]

Even so, admiration cannot be withheld from this system as a large-scale essay in reconciliation. Hegel is here conducting a battle on all fronts: *against* the splitting up of being, here termed 'isolation', 'abstraction', 'atom', 'point', and characterised as 'static', 'rigid', 'quantitative', 'indifferent', 'immediate'; *for* a living unity, hence for 'centre', 'indifference', 'purity', 'universality', 'concept', 'contemplation', 'form', 'idea', 'totality', 'infinity', 'absoluteness'! Hegel has the most varied names for this reconciliation: 'setting in motion', 'rendering fluid', 'reflection', 'deduction', 'construction', 'integration', 'realisation', 'totalisation', 'formation', 'justification', 'theodicy', 'reconciliation'. Time and place, quantity and quality, activity and passivity, universal and particular, analytic and synthetic knowledge, cause and effect, substance and accident, being and non-being, finite and infinite – all these things are meant to be seen in one. And not simply, as previously, under the mark of a more statically conceived good positivity or organic totality, but under the mark of a dynamic transition of the one into the other. In short, it is a question of the realisation of the all-reconciling absolute Spirit. 'The Spirit is the Absolute, and its Idea is only absolutely realised when the moments of the Spirit are themselves this Spirit. At that point, however, there is also no more going beyond itself' (XVIII, 186).

It would, moreover, be an error to suppose that Hegel's concentration on the philosophical system and on the esoteric problems of logic, metaphysics and natural philosophy had alienated him from the concrete problems of society. In his influential book,[61] which interprets Hegel as the theoretician of bourgeois society and hence of the modern consciousness, J. Ritter was able to make it transparently clear that Hegel sharply differed from formalist philosophies of reflection in being concerned with a hermeneutic of the historical world as it actually is and not simply with that world as it ought to be. It was because the Hegel of the Jena period wished to give a concrete

---

[60]*op. cit.* II, 67-157.
[61]*Hegel und die französische Revolution.*

demonstration of the already actually existent realisation of the Spirit that he was now thrown back on the historical and social reality that encompassed him. The religious intention, which he had expressed in 'Faith and Knowledge', would not permit him to surrender secular reality to objective godlessness through a retreat into pious subjectivity. The idea of an incarnation of God made it necessary for the problem of society to be posed with respect to the philosophy of Spirit as well. Whereas it was the separation of Church and state which stood more at the forefront of his early writings, this position is now occupied chiefly by the relationship of state and society.

G. Rohrmoser rightly reminds us 'that he detected in the negation of godless reality by pious subjectivity a form of denying the salvation wrought by God in the world through the incarnation of Christ. It was this which disposed him to use speculation to protect the vilified reality against the reproaches with which enlightened and devout reflection weighed and condemned it. But the solution to this problem was synonymous with the reply to the question of how the ethical and harmonious totality of a people might coexist with a society constituted by emancipation from it. For Hegel the problem of the relationship of state and society is posed both in the question concerning ethical identity, for him already realised and available in the totality of an historical people, and in the question concerning the needfulness and rightfulness of the difference which through the objective system of the satisfaction of men's sensuous and natural need breaks into this unity like an alien force, shaking its inmost foundations'.[62]

The essay of 1802 (fragments of which were already written during the previous year) on 'The German Constitution' (VII, 1-49; *PW*, 143-242[63]) affords impressive testimony to the fact that the thinker whose mind was concentrated on a scientific system did not limit himself to an abstract theory of society. This work ventures into all the details of the military, financial and juridical institutions of the German Empire, offering an acute analysis of both the historical past and the sorry present, ending with an anti-democratic appeal to rebuild a single, inwardly renewed and viable state with the aid of a strong man. Throughout his whole life Hegel was not to lose this interest in practical politics, as is attested by his report of 1817 on the proceedings of the Württemberg *Diet* and by his essay written in 1831, the year of his death, on the English Reform Bill.[64]

That Hegel's practical work was not only of a political but also of a systematic nature is shown by his attempt to develop his ontological system in the direction of ethics. His fragmentary *System of Ethics* (VII, 413-499: given its title by Rosenkranz) comes from the winter of 1802-3 or from early 1803. Hegel's desire in this work, in which he draws his central categories from Schelling, is to integrate the various phenomena of practical mentality in a unified fashion into the organic totality of folk

---

[62] *Subjektivität und Verdinglichung*, 86f. J. Splet (*Die Trinitätslehre Hegels*, 36-52) points out the hidden trinitarian references in the various Jena Systems.

[63] Selections from Hegel's *Schriften zur Politik and Rechtsphilosophie* are translated by T. M. Knox in *Political Writings* (Oxford, 1964; new edition, 1973) & are cited here as *PW* followed by the relevant page number.

[64] For a treatment of the relevant issues from the perspective of political science cf. R. K. Hočevar: *Stände und Repräsentation beim jungen Hegel*.

morality. While bourgeois morality tends to drop out of the organic totality of the folk, Hegel's intention is so to determine the meaning and principles of all practical activity in its various spheres as to discern in them the totality of life and 'the idea of absolute morality' (VII, 415). This occurs, often in a somewhat forced manner, through the 'subsumption' of 'intuition' under 'concept' and of 'concept' under 'intuition'. In accordance with this dialectical scheme of universal and particular, Hegel begins by discussing, in an often confusing sequence, the most diverse forms of natural morality: want, enjoyment, work, implement, machine, gesture, speech, property, money, price, exchange, contract, class, marriage, family, child . . . The second part speaks of those things which run counter to morality: 'the negative or freedom or crime' (crime, vengeance, justice, honour and life, domination and servitude, war and peace). Finally, the third and unfinished part deals with absolute morality in its pure form. In fact, however, this section only discusses the constitution of the state (social order and the government of the state). Hegel's description of 'absolute morality' shows how the fundamental problems of this practical philosophy are ultimately the same as those of his theoretical philosophy: 'It is the divine unveiled – absolute, real, existent, being – not in such a way as first to be elevated into the ideality of divinity and first to be drawn from appearance and from empirical intuition. On the contrary, it is immediate and absolute intuition' (VII, 465). Here too, then, Hegel's concern is with the union of the individual with the self-organising eternal Spirit.

The article of 1802 'On scholarly treatments of natural law' (VII, 325-411), primarily geared to a single problem (law) yet also oriented towards absolute morality, operates along the same lines as this 'system'. Already cutting loose from Schelling, Hegel criticises the 'empirical' theories of natural law of Hobbes and Rousseau along with the 'formal' theories of Kant and Fichte from the point of view of a traditional, teleological concept of nature. He defines the place of natural law in practical philosophy and its relationship to positive jurisprudence as a means toward integrating the state-corrosive tendencies of bourgeois society in the state. Religion here receives a new social function.

Hegel was not the man to be so easily imprisoned in the golden cage of a 'closed' system. There is continuous eruption and fluctuation as he works out his system. During these years he never tired of recasting his material, his way of looking at things, his terminology and his arrangement of the subject-matter.

The writings which, at their first publication, were labelled by Hoffmeister as *Realphilosophie I*, are not a separate statement of the philosophy of nature and Spirit, but manuscript fragments from the lecture course '*Philosophiae speculativae systema*', which was held in the winter semester of 1803-4.[65] It must be made plain from the outset that we do not possess the logic and the metaphysics here (Rosenkranz reports that the basic structure of these elements in Hegel's thought suffered the least change; cf. *H*, 344). Witness to Schelling's still vigorous influence on Hegel is afforded by the natural

---

[65] cf. Foreword p.v to the 1967 reprint of the *Jenenser Realphilosophie* of 1931, which now bears the appropriate title *Jenaer Realphilosophie*.

philosophy which has come down to us. It is in broad agreement with the first system of 1804 or 1804-5 (XIX, 1-191; summary 245-254). A new element here is an organic natural philosophy dealing with the 'vegetable' and 'animal' organism. The opening section of the manuscript, devoted to ether, time, place and astro-mechanics, has been lost.[66] There follows a second part, less comprehensive in scope but new as regards content, a 'Philosophy of Spirit' (XIX, 193-241). The spiritual forces operative in the world, in which the Spirit itself lives and moves, are interpreted here. This takes place in a new way: in terms of consciousness. It is Hegel's first theory of consciousness. Consciousness is the most basic form in which the life of the Spirit is successively expressed, maintained and realised. Hegel gives a phenomenological account of the structures of the Spirit as a sequence of self-unfolding forms of consciousness. Thus he describes as coming under the heading of consciousness not only the various spiritual faculties of memory and language (feeling, contemplation, memory, language and intellect), but also – this was subsequently to become a central topic for Marx – the power of work and of the implements of work and, finally, such total aspects of life as property, marriage and family. The one great process of the genesis of consciousness leads eventually – and this brings Frankfurt to mind – to the living folk Spirit, in which all previous categories are integrated. Having embarked on the way to absolute Spirit, we should like to learn more from Hegel; but the manuscript breaks off just at the point where it promises to become interesting for us.

Compensation for this loss is made by the lectures of 1805-6, which Hoffmeister was the first to publish as *Jenenser Realphilosophie II* (reprinted in 1967 as *Jenaer Realphilosophie*). Almost two thirds of these lectures consist of natural philosophy, which, despite a different external arrangement, is essentially at one with the fragments of 1803 (XX, 1-176). Together with this we possess here the first complete account of the philosophy of Spirit (XX, 179-273). Hegel has now found his form. As H. Schmitz[67] has shown, the earlier 'infinite judgment' is here superseded by the triply self-mediating syllogism of speculative reason. Schelling's concepts are in retreat. To a greater extent than in the previous philosophy of Spirit the accent lies on the work of reason and on Spirit as self-consciousness: Spirit as progressively self-revealing self. Hegel begins by considering the subjective forms of Spirit as intelligence (its self-realisation as intuition – language – memory – intellect – free intelligence) and as will (its self-procreation as impulse – sensual

---

[66] As an introduction to Hegel's natural philosophy during his time in Jena cf. J. Hoffmeister: *Goethe und der deutsche Idealismus*, esp. 12-82.
[67] *Hegel als Denker der Individualität.*

appetite – work – implement – artfulness – love – marriage – family – possession – struggle for recognition). Even so, will and intelligence must be seen in their supra-individual universality, apparent in mutual recognition, in exchange, property and contract, in the penalty which counters crime and in coercive law. In these spheres, according to Hegel, Spirit is active as 'real' Spirit. The world of laws exists concretely in the folk Spirit, which is considered in the various historical forms of political community (Machiavellianism, democracy, the ancient and the modern state) and of social classes as expressive of the self-consciousness of the political community (peasantry, bourgeoisie, civil service, government). Thus, in the process of attaining consciousness, Spirit bestows on itself its own 'constitution' (this being the title Hegel gave to the third part of his philosophy of Spirit).

Even so, it is only in the pure knowledge of itself, in the forms of absolute Spirit (art, religion and philosophy), that Spirit attains to its proper fulfilment, to the intuition of itself as itself. Hegel only deals with these three forms with great brevity at the close of this work as a subsection of the 'construction' of Spirit for the folk (XX, 263-273). Spirit is to be found immediately and intuitively but not yet with a clear knowledge of itself in *art*. The latter finds its fulfilment in *religion,* where the particular becomes universal: 'In religion Spirit becomes objective to itself as something absolutely universal, or as the essence of all nature, being and action, and in the *shape* of immediate selfhood' (XX, 266). Even though reconciliation takes place in religion, its truth is here only proposed, asserted, affirmed and believed. It must, however, also be discerned, conceptualised and known. Hence Hegel can give the following precise description of the relationship between religion and philosophy as he has learned to see it in Jena: 'The content of religion is indeed *true,* but this *being true* is an affirmation without insight. This *insight* is philosophy, which is absolute *science.* It has the same content as religion, but in *conceptual* form' (XX, 272).

This, then, is a bird's eye view of Hegel's first attempts at systematisation made during his time in Jena. Even the external structure of these essays is impressive. And whoever takes time to read through them carefully and ponder them from the inside will find them even more deserving of admiration. Admittedly, much has been imperfectly digested and the new edifice which is still under construction is characterised to some extent by a skeletal incompleteness and an unpolished provisionality. Yet this does not lessen our astonishment at Hegel's large-scale creative genius and at his minutely thought-through attention to detail. From a wealth of spiritual experience and specific observation he drew anything and everything into his great plan, creating a true microcosm in concrete universality.

But our task is not to carry out an exhaustive examination of all this. We are looking only for one particular figure in this rambling complex. The Frank-furt Jesus is not to be found in the preliminary writings of Jena. Apart from a single unimportant mention his name does not occur either in the *Difference* or in the supplementary essays. Even in the various draft systems we seek him in vain. Jesus is not seen, but he is provided for. He is present neither by name nor in person, but Hegel leaves open a place for him in his system.

5. The Career of God

Among the many hundred pages of the first Jena writings three pages at the end demonstrate that, despite this silence, the Frankfurt Jesus was not simply forgotten in Jena. In the short section on religion – in which, according to Hegel, Spirit becomes objective to itself as something absolutely universal and in the shape of immediate selfhood – a topic is taken up and given concrete form which had been announced only briefly and very vaguely at the close of 'Faith and Knowledge'. This topic was the incarnation of God, which is the content of absolute religion. 'All other religions are incomplete' in comparis-on with this 'absolute religion', which is 'profundity itself, come to light'(XX, 266f): 'Absolute religion is this knowledge, that God is the depth of self-conscious Spirit. He is thereby the self of all things. He is essence, pure thought; but even stripped of this abstraction, he is a real self. He is a man who has common spatial and temporal existence. And all individuals are this individual. The divine nature is not different from human nature . . . Thus in absolute religion Spirit is reconciled with its world' (XX, 266f).

It is indicative of Hegel's continuing basic interest in both religion and politics that he deals with the incarnation of God in a social context: the reconciliation of the Spirit with the world completes the self-elevation of the individual into the folk community. Yet the full attainment of this reconcilia-tion wrought by religion does not yet take place in the present, but only in a hereafter beyond this world. What, then, is the 'thought', the 'inward aspect', the 'idea of absolute religion'? 'That the self, the real, is thought, that essence and being are the same. This is posited in such a way that God, the transcendent absolute being, became man, this real man. But this reality too has been elevated and become a thing of the past, and this God – who is reality, who is elevated, i.e. universal, reality (the same as folk spirit) – only exists immediately as the Spirit of the community. The content of this religion and the object of this consciousness is that God is Spirit . . .' (XX, 268).

These brief but very dense christological remarks stand in a wide-ranging context which itself pinpoints the reason why, during his delivery of the *Realphilosophie* course in the summer of 1806, Hegel called 'the immanent dialectic of the Absolute *the career of God*' (according to Rosenkranz: *H,* 348f). The work under consideration should not cause us to prejudge Hegel's own published work in which he will say what he wishes to say and how he wishes to say it. The draft of these lectures was hastily jotted down in the form of catch-phrases and incomplete sentences, and its internal arrangement bears the marks of interruption and overlapping. The editor Hoffmeister was often obliged to supply words in order to make Hegel's ·shredded thoughts at all readable; likewise for the sake of readability these additions have not been designated as such in our quotations from the text. The literary nature of this text thus prompts us to ask whether we are offending against the restraint which is due to the author of these notes by holding him publicly responsible for everything he wrote for his own private use. A measure of caution in determining the mind of the author might well be more appropriate here than in the case of the Bern and Frankfurt manuscripts, which were to some extent worked out in detail. It is therefore fitting at this juncture that we give simply an account rather than an exposition of Hegel's thought. The reader may afterwards find it an interesting exercise to ascertain for himself to what extent this first private description of the 'career of God' (whose importance lies in its being a bridge for the understanding of what follows) was subsequently publicly confirmed, corrected, carried out and given concrete form by Hegel himself.

We begin with a marginal note of fundamental importance: 'α) *true* religion, to the extent that absolute being is spirit; β) *revealed* religion without mystery, for God is the Self, God is man' (XX, 268). There follows an embryonic doctrine of the Trinity as the 'essence of pure consciousness': 'The eternal being, Son and Spirit are here all the same being. We do not posit the difference but the parity of immediate being' (XX, 268).

The margin contains another remark: 'Philosophy of nature, *which goes into itself* and becomes evil' (XX, 268). This observation is further developed in the main text: 'God, the essence of pure consciousness, becomes an Other to himself, and this is the world. But this *existence* is Concept, being-in-itself, evil, and nature, the immediate, must be pictured as evil. Everyone must gain insight into his evil nature, that is, into the fact that nature reverses into Concept, becoming *evil*, a being-*for-itself* as opposed to a being-*in-itself*, while conversely likewise becoming a being-*in-itself*; that is, *God appears* in nature *as something actual*' (XX, 268f).

That 'this antithesis is itself empty' is manifested 'in the sacrifice of the divine man' (XX, 269), which is presented in three steps:

1. 'The sacrifice of the divinity, i.e. of the abstract and transcendent being, has already taken place in its becoming actual' (XX, 269). This statement is clarified in the margin: 'The externalisation and formation of abstract being is precisely that the divine, the *abstract* being, *sacrifices itself*. It is not this man who dies, but the divine. It becomes man in precisely this way' (XX, 268).

182

2. The 'elevation of the actuality' of the divine man takes place, along with 'the development of its universality, universal Spirit', defined as 'the Spirit of the congregation': '*immediate* self, *reconciled* nature, the self-projection of the divine into everything natural: the people, including the saints, stories about saints, appearances, everywhere *immediate presence,* new earth, natural sun extinguished – *pain*, of religion, the *pure feeling of externalisation* – but this is picture-thinking for the consciousness' (XX, 269).

3. 'The congregation must renounce its being-for-itself and its immediate nature': 'in the *cult*' the Self of the congregation must give 'itself the consciousness of unity with being'. It 'enjoys the body and blood which are daily *sacrificed* in the congregation and becomes this particular *Self* ' (XX, 269), living in '*devotion,* which knows itself in this Self ' (XX, 269).

At the end there follow some highly condensed remarks about the 'synthetic union of state and Church' (XX, 269). These read more like the beginning of a new section than a conclusion, and their importance for us resides in their relationship to the earlier remarks about Christianity as a folk religion. On the one hand, Hegel's persistent pungent criticism of the self-absolutising Church remains in force: 'The *fanaticism* of the Church is its *desire to introduce the eternal, the kingdom of heaven as such, on earth. Over against the reality of the state, this is tantamount to keeping fire in water. The actuality of the kingdom of heaven is the state,* reconciliation in thought, or the coexistence of both through the Church. If they are unreconciled, then both state and Church are incomplete' (XX, 270). On the other hand, we now see a contrast to Hegel's earlier position in his very clear affirmation of the Church in its relation to a living folk religion: 'The Church is the Spirit which knows itself as universal, the inner absolute security of the state. The individual counts as individual. Everything external is intrinsically insecure and unstable. It has its perfect guarantee in the Church. What man does on the basis of religion he does on the basis of his thought of himself, insofar as this is no observation. He is fulfilled by a universal thought which endures despite all the variegated multiplicity of the individual: this is duty, or I must surrender myself into this; it *is,* is justified in the absolute being, morality in the absolute being, insofar as it is my knowledge, there absolute being in general. God is everywhere, is pure thought; if man is secretly with himself, then his solitude and his thought are with him' (XX, 270f). This passage makes it clear at the same time that religion is not the ultimate reality: 'This insight is philosophy, which is absolute science. It has the same content as religion, but in conceptual form' (XX, 272). And now in an illuminating reduplication the same outline of religion is once again run through, this time on the level of pure philosophy (XX, 272): a) 'speculative philosophy: absolute being, which becomes another (relationship), life and cognition; and knowing awareness, Spirit, Spirit's knowledge of itself'; b) 'Natural philosophy: expression of the Idea in the structures of immediate being. It is a going-into-itself, evil, development into Spirit, into the concept which exists as concept'; c) 'But this pure intelligence is likewise the opposite, the universal, which sacrifices itself, thereby becoming the real and universal reality, which is a people, established nature, reconciled being, in which every man appropriates his being-for-himself by renouncing and sacrificing himself' (XX, 272).

The reconciliation which is developed on the level of philosophy culminates in '*world history*'. This marks the first appearance of a concept which, reaching far beyond the earlier master-concept 'folk-Spirit', was to be laden with significance for the whole future: 'The fact that only in itself is one being constituted out of nature and Spirit is realised in world history. Spirit becomes the knowledge of this very thing. Man does not become master of nature until he has become master of himself. World history is the development of Spirit-in-itself. Spirit must grasp for itself the fact that this in-itself *is really there*' (XX,273).

Analogous christological ideas from the Jena period are transmitted in papers by Rosenkranz and Haym, which Hoffmeister published as a 'Continuation of the *System of Ethics*' (*H*, 314-325; esp. 319-321). However, apart from the few passages in inverted commas, these papers possess 'no source value whatever' (*H*, 475).

Hegel's speculation on the divine triangle, which comes down to us through Rosenkranz, presumably hails from his first years in Jena. It is perhaps the concluding summary of a lengthy text about 'the sacred triangle of triangles' (*H*, 304), a theme which is open to the most widely differing interpretations.[68] While the first triangle treats 'only of the Deity with itself in mutual contemplation and cognition' (*H*, 304), the subject of the second is presumably the opposition in the Fall and the incarnation of the Son, and of the third the 'return of all things into God himself'.

Since we are free to choose between a wide range of possible interpretations here, and since the last part of the *Phenomenology* is pre-eminently a clarification of the problems that beset us here, it is well at this juncture simply to reproduce the text of the second triangle without commentary: 'In the *second* God's intuition has moved over to one side. He has come into relation with evil and the centre is the *bad aspect* of the mixture of the two. However, in virtue of the fact that pure Deity hovers over it, this triangle turns into a *square*. But its unhappy state does not permit it even to remain this triangle; rather, it must change into its opposite, the Son must go through the earth, overcome evil, and, when he steps on to one side as victor, the other side must awaken God's self-cognition as a new cognition at one with God, as the Spirit of God. In this way the centre becomes a beautiful, free, divine centre, *God's universe*. As something which exists in separation, this second triangle is itself a *twofold* triangle, or rather two of its sides are each a triangle, the one the opposite of the other, and in this movement of history the centre is the all-operating force of the absolute unity which hovers over

---

[68] cf. J. Splett: *Die Trinitätslehre Hegels*, 27-30.

the first triangle, taking up the latter into itself and there converting it into another. What is visible are the two triangles, but the centre is only the invisible force working within' (*H*, 305).

That the sources of these speculations are probably not the biblical writings alone is proved by those *Jena Aphorisms* in which Hegel – as, for example, in no. 45 (*H*, 363f) – either makes explicit reference to Jakob Böhme or else – as in no. 48 (*H*, 364-366) – gives a detailed account of his thought. Conversely, in his essay on the preparation of the *Phenomenology* in Hegel's *Jena Draft Systems*, J. Schwarz was certainly right to oppose an unhistorical, purely philosophical interpretation of the *Phenomenology* by pointing to the great importance of the figure of Christ – Christ as the individual self who is simultaneously a universal self (cf. XX, 266) – for the development of the *Phenomenology of Spirit*. And even if we do not sanction this alternative as such, we shall at least heed J. Schwarz's words as an expression of a contrary point of view: 'The change which lays hold of Hegel's metaphysics at this time and prepares the way for the *Phenomenology of Spirit* does not have its origin in the problem of that philosophical reason which strives for absolute self-cognition, even if the new experience now bestowed on Hegel is as it were demanded by the problematical nature of reason and can therefore retroactively illuminate the self-understanding of reason. On the contrary, the change begins with a new perception of the metaphysical character of human individuality, of which Hegel becomes aware through the *spiritual contemplation of Christ.*'[69]

Thus the 'career [*Lebenslauf*] of God' is consummated in world history. The reader ought now perhaps to be more aware of the significance of this word than was the case at the outset. About a hundred years previously this word had been borrowed as a German translation of Cicero's '*curriculum vitae*'. *Lebenslauf* conjures up a life which has been lived and which, because it has been lived, can be described. Was God to have a *Lebenslauf*, as it were a 'career'? (*Laufbahn* – a few years previously Jean Paul Richter had introduced this word, in the face of some resistance and in a new, spiritual, no longer bodily and local sense, as a German equivalent of the French '*carrière*' and the Italian '*carriera*'.) This would have momentous consequences for the understanding of God. Can it be said that God not only 'has' and 'is' life, but also that he himself both 'runs through' and 'lives through' a life? We should recall that this was the age in which people once more spoke of 'life' in a completely new way. This is true not only of the Frankfurt Hegel but also and preeminently of Goethe, who gave expression with his novel word formations and word combinations to the new 'feeling for life'. Hegel was the first to speak not only of *Lebensklugheit* and *Lebensweisheit* (life's worldly cleverness and wisdom), *Lebenskreis* and *Lebensraum* (sphere of life and living space), *Lebenszweck* and *Lebensvorteil* (purpose of life and advantage in life), *Lebensgabe, Lebensausdruck* and *Lebensfülle* (gift, expression and fullness of

---

[69]*Die Vorbereitung der Phänomenologie des Geistes in Hegels Jenenser Systementwürfen.*

life), but also – in a more dynamic sense with a view to life as an event – of *Lebensbewegung, Lebensinteresse* and *Lebensdrang* (movement of life, vital interest and the urge to live), of *Lebensgang* and *Lebensflug* (pace of life and flight from life), of *Lebensglück* and *Lebenshändel* (happiness in life and dispute about life), of *Lebensschicksal* and *Lebensüberdruss* (fate of life and weariness of life), and of *Lebenswonne* and *Lebensrausch* (delight in life and intoxication with life).

In short, is it the case that God not only has and is life, but also that he undergoes a life-event and a life history? The question might also be put in the form: To what extent is God a God? The following topics, to which we shall later return, are not to be dealt with in detail here: how ancient philosophy, excessively influenced by Parmenides, usually denied God the attribute of life just because it includes movement (life self-movement) and therefore change and hence imperfection; how Christian theology then ascribed life and vitality to God, especially in his role as creator and governor of the world, attributing at the same time a living, ordered becoming, in the sense of an unambiguous total history, to the world; and how, right up to the middle ages, this Christian theology at the same time upheld the old Platonic antithesis between construing the divine and perfect as what is unmoved (not just imperishable and without becoming)'and construing the worldly and imperfect as what is changeable and involved in becoming. Hegel was early aware of the fact that Eckhart brought about a fundamental change here with his understanding of the living God as the God who is simultaneously engaged in becoming and not-becoming, as a 'becoming without becoming', a life in power, fulness and love but without seeking any exterior aims. From Eckhart the torch was passed to the mystics of the following centuries: to Nicholas of Cusa, who had a new, scientific understanding of motion and who saw God as a living agent in absolute rest, as *coincidentia oppositorum*; to Giordano Bruno, who discerned in all world processes the pulse beat of the one divine universal life; to Jakob Böhme, for whom God was an eternal process of self-generation; and to Leibniz, who took up not only the impulses from Cusanus, Descartes and Malebranche, but also suggestions from the German natural philosophy stemming from Eckhart and Seuse (though without some of their more abstruse 'ideas), and who, while eschewing pantheism, permitted every substance and every monad to be its own principle of life and motion in a condition of change. We have already heard how the influence of mysticism subsequently conspired with that of the natural sciences to bring about a shift from the transcendent God of the Enlightenment to a new immanence of God, the 'Deity', in this world. The names of Kant, Lessing and Goethe were mentioned in this connection. Such thinkers learned from Spinoza with regard to the unity of the One and All, while decisively rejecting the

Parmenidian inflexibility of unmoved substantial being, which permitted only a geometrically constructed system.

Likewise bearing in mind Oetinger's *theologia ex idea vitae,* which anticipated many later developments, and Herder's and Hamann's understanding of nature and history, along with their notions about development and progress, we note that all these divergent motives and influences converged in German Idealism, first of all in Fichte and then in Schelling and Hegel. Hegel himself had gone on to forge fresh links between this philosophy of life and becoming and Heraclitus' much-contested idea of the living God. 'Life' had been his central concept in Frankfurt, and even if it was largely supplanted by 'Spirit' in Jena, Hegel still resolutely understood this Spirit as *living* Spirit. Thus it had now become possible for him in the *Realphilosophie* to describe the 'career [*Lebenslauf*] of God' as a self-renouncing path into and through worldly reality, culminating in the perfect coming-to-itself of the Spirit. The universal characteristics of 'life' had thereby also become the characteristics of this living world-Spirit: distinctiveness, extension in time, being bound up with an external form, complementarity with death.

Hence the immeasurable riches of the world had flowed into the concept of God, making possible a new consciousness of God and the world. This was undoubtedly a vigorous revaluation of the world and man, but was it also an enrichment of God? At all events it represented a danger: the danger of the concept of God's being overrun by ideas alien to it. Where did the boundaries lie? First the pantheistic controversy and then above all the atheistic controversy unleashed danger signals. And the chastened Fichte would have been the last to fail to understand them. He and Hegel certainly acknowledged the limits which Schelling, for example, proposed in his *System of Transcendental Idealism* of 1800 as a means of protecting the concept of the living God in a 'system of providence, i.e. of religion'. On the right, there is no question of *pantheistic fatalism,* according to which 'all free acts, hence even the whole of history' must be assumed to be 'simply predetermined', the upshot of which would be 'a completely blind predestination' by 'fate'. Nor, on the left, is there any question of *irreligious atheism,* according to which there is 'no law and no necessity in all action and activity', so that 'a system of absolute lawlessness' would be established. Schelling affirms instead the 'Absolute', which is the common 'basis of harmony between freedom and rational agents'.[70]

There were many possible views on the way in which this Absolute ought to be more precisely defined in its relationship to the world in general and to human freedom in particular, and Fichte, Schelling and Hegel presently fell out with each other on this score. Yet this dispute did nothing to lessen the fact

---

[70] F. W. J. Schelling: *Werke* II, 601 (ET *System,* 209).

that a consensus had come to prevail among the leading minds around 1800, despite all the differences that divided them, as a result of the intellectual development since the Enlightenment. This consensus has not been overtaken in the ensuing period, even though many are only now becoming fully alive to its radical implications.[71]

1. Despite divergent opinions on natural philosophy ('mechanistic' explanation of nature etc.), Fichte, Schelling and Hegel were at one in their avowal of the new *scientific explanation of the world,* at least to the extent that they no longer explained weather and victory in battle, sickness and healing and the fortune and misfortune of individuals, groups and peoples in terms of direct divine intervention, but in terms of natural causes. God's being thus pushed out of the world was in fact an opportunity, because it helped to explain what the living God is *not,* and that he cannot simply be equated with the processes of nature and history. Was this opportunity used? Was God's withdrawal from secondary causes recognised as the possible precondition of a more personal and inward encounter with God? Or, after the Enlightenment had stripped nature of her divinity, was it now resolved simply to redivinise her?

2. Despite their differing evaluation of the ego, of subjectivity and of consciousness, the German Idealists were at one in their profession of a new *understanding of authority* to the extent that they accepted no truth that went beyond the judgment of reason simply on the strength of the authority of Bible, tradition or Church. Rather they insisted on critical testing alone. The fact that belief in God had ceased to be simply something decreed by authority, a matter of tradition or confession and hence an ideological platitude, was in fact an opportunity. This was because man was once more challenged afresh, in a manner entirely in keeping with both his own dignity and the honour of God, to a genuine and personal appropriation of the faith of the Fathers. Was this opportunity used? Was the space which had become free for human autonomy used in such a way that people now trusted God with their heart as mature persons rather than appearing before him as slaves without a will of their own who believe things contrary to reason? Or, after the Enlightenment had demythologised authority, did people perhaps simply surrender to other mythical forces?

3. While their starting point could be more theoretical or more practical, more individual or more social, these thinkers were agreed on the need for *ideological criticism* of the kind which had been vigorously inaugurated in

---

[71] cf. among the excellently informative books by H. Zahrnt his textbook *Gespräch über Gott,* his *The Question of God* and his comprehensive article '*Es geht um die Existenz Gottes*', to which we shall refer in the following pages. At an earlier stage many were shaken by the well known book by J. A. T. Robinson, *Honest to God.*

Germany by Rousseauism and the French Revolution. This entailed uncovering the social misuse of religion by the state or even by the Church and rationally exposing personal or group interests which lay behind reliance on the Lord God as the mainstay of the whole range of temporal rulers and as the protector and guarantor of an existing order which was largely unjust. Even this extraction of God from involvement with political social power structures in fact meant an opportunity: that the man who could now stand upright before his earthly prince without degrading grovelling might also do the same before his God, acting not as his subject but as his partner. Was this opportunity used? Was this Enlightenment twilight of the gods understood in such a way that God no longer appeared as a product of selfish human needs but as the truly 'other'? Or did people now attempt in earnest to pigeonhole God ideologically into some world process or other?

4. Fichte, Schelling and Hegel were agreed on the rightfulness of the *shift of consciousness from the hereafter to the here-and-now*. This shift was part of the comprehensive modern process of secularisation which had achieved a decisive breakthrough in the Enlightenment. In this process man discovered that the independence of the orders of creation (science, industry, politics, state, society, law, culture) was no longer something of which he was only theoretically aware, but something which he could realise in practice. Yet this dismissal of empty promises of a hereafter and this intensified concentration on the here-and-now meant an opportunity: that life, which had perhaps lost depth, might now gain in density. Was the opportunity used? Was it perceived how, precisely in secularisation, God had as it were drawn closer to man in this life, challenging him in the very midst of his profanity? Or did secularisation degenerate to the level of a secular view of the world, so that God was lost from view as the immanently transcendent one who is always absolutely relevant to us precisely in this life?

Presumably no clear-cut answer can be given to these questions just at the stroke of a pen. Nor has any clear-cut answer in fact been given to them to this very day. At all events, despite everything that they continued to have in common, Fichte, Schelling and Hegel took very different paths in the post-Jena period. Hegel's own opinion was that he could best master the crises between atheism and pantheism by taking the life and vitality of God very seriously and by seeing God in his 'life-course' [*Lebenslauf*]. He sought to see God neither in terms of the absolute ego nor in terms of absolute indifference. but rather as the absolute Spirit, that is, as the God who passes through a *history* and reveals himself in this very history, as the one who is who he is in *becoming*.

Chapter Five: Speculative Christology

'Thus the life of God and divine cognition may well be spoken of as a disporting of Love with itself; but this idea sinks into mere edification, and even insipidity, if it lacks the seriousness, the suffering, the patience and the labour of the negative' (*PS*, 10).

1. Via Consciousness to Spirit

For a whole week in October 1806, Hegel carried some fateful pages for German philosophy in his coat pocket through a ransacked Jena. These pages formed the last part of the *Phenomenology of Spirit*,[1] which was finished with abnormal haste in a single restless night by a tormented author, hounded not only by the events of his time but also by a highly impatient publisher (XXVII, 112-124; see Kaufmann, 314-16). The day afterwards, with his customary lightning speed, Napoleon had given battle before Jena and won the victory, and Hegel then saw 'the Emperor, this world-soul, . . . ride out through the town to reconnoitre. It is indeed a wonderful sensation to see such an individual who, concentrated here in one point and sitting on a horse, overlaps and rules the whole world' (XXVII, 120; Kaufmann, 316). Hegel had himself been the victim of looting, so that he carried the pages on his person and was only able to send them to the publisher in Bamberg several days later (XXVII, 122-124; Kaufmann, 316f).

Schelling's departure for Würzburg in 1803 and the consequent cessation of writing for *The Critical Journal* meant that Hegel was now presented with more opportunity for deepening and developing his world of ideas. The fruit

---

[1] The author used the new edition of the *Phänomenologie des Geistes*, published by J. Hoffmeister in 1949 after a most minute study of the text of the original edition. This is in essence the fifth impression of the Lasson Edition of 1907, the fourth impression having been issued by Hoffmeister himself in 1937. Quotations from the *PG* will be given in the following pages, unless otherwise stated, from the English translation by A. V. Miller of the *Phenomenology of Spirit* (OUP, 1977). References will be given as *PS* followed by the relevant page number.

All the great Introductions to Hegel and in particular the historically oriented ones (esp. those

of this endeavour was the *Phenomenology of Spirit,* perhaps his most brilliant and yet at the same time most obscure work, a pioneering work in which the whole is already present. In a penetrating and assiduous summary, and as a first bold degisn, it gives a rich, concentrated and dynamic (if not unambiguous) expression to Hegel's previous development. Dangerously effervescent, to some extent (above all in the second half) gushing over, and yet in the last analysis held together in disciplined passion, it is, all things considered, a work of blossoming youth that already displays many signs of maturity. 'I am full of eager expectation concerning your work which is at last about to appear. What must be in the offing if your maturity is still taking time to ripen its fruits!' (XXVII, 134; Kaufmann, 317). So wrote Schelling to Hegel shortly before the manuscript went to press, blissfully unaware of the malicious criticism levelled at him in Hegel's Preface, which was to lead to a

---

by R. Rosenkranz and R. Haym) offer detailed comment on the *Phenomenology* (cf. the bibliographies at the end of our Introduction and on Hegel's youth at I, 1, esp. the works by T. Haering). The dissertations by J. C. Bruijn and W. Drescher can serve as commentaries. Then there is the commentary by C. Nink, which pays special attention to the basic sections of the *Phenomenology.* The two most important recent commentaries come from the pens of French authors. A Kojève, a pupil of Jaspers standing in the tradition of A. Koyre, aims in his Marxist-existentialist interpretation to give a 'contemporary statement of Hegel's thought', as the sub-title of I. Fetscher's German 'Selections' of this work puts it. Kojève's interpretation of the *Phenomenology* is intensive and brilliant, but it is tendentiously onesided in its contention that man becomes man in a history which is essentially determined by the social struggle of master and servant. By absolutising the second moment in the dialectic Kojève performs a conjuring trick with Hegel's Absolute for the benefit of an *a priori* atheistic interpretation. While Kojève's 'contemporary statement' of Hegel is in many ways a stimulating study, it has provoked criticism in its interpretation not only of Hegel but also of Marx. Thus we must prefer the commentary of the French translator of the *Phenomenology,* J. Hyppolite, the excellence of whose work has found universal recognition. For a comparison of these two interpreters cf. G. Fessard, who also repeatedly comments on the *Phenomenology* in his interesting dialectical interpretation of Ignatius of Loyola's *Spiritual Exercises,* esp. 164-177. M. Heidegger's commentary on the Introduction, which deals with the concept of experience, is also important. R. K. Maurer interprets the *Phenomenology* as philosophy of history. On the problem of language and linguistics in Hegel cf. H. Lauener, J. Simon, M. Zünfle and T. Bodammer.

Important essays on the theological problems which arise in connection with the *Phenomenology* have come from J. Möller and B. Welte (on questions to do with the philosophy of religion in general), from J. Wahl (on the unhappy consciousness) and J. A. Oosterbaan (on theological epistemology), from P. Henrici (who has compared the *Phenomenology* with Blondel's *Action*) and G. Rohrmoser (on the relationship of religious and historico-social problems). J. Splett once again offers a highly exact interpretation of the doctrine of the Trinity. R. Osculati attempts a comparison of the *Phenomenology* with the Catholic doctrine of grace. On the history of interpretation with especial reference to its well-known philological and historical difficulties, see – after T. Haering's address at the Hegel Congress held in Rome in 1933 on the genesis of the *Phenomenology* – the convincing expositions of O. Pöggeler (cf. also F. Nicolin). In this context the papers read at the Hegel colloquies of Royaumont in 1964 are informative. All of these were dedicated to the interpretation of the *Phenomenology* and are contained in *Hegel-Studien,* supplement 3, ed. by H.-G. Gadamer with essays by J. Hyppolite, J. Wahl, O. Pöggeler, H. F. Fulda, R. Wiehl, H.-G. Gadamer, J. Gauvin and A. Kaan).

speedy cooling of their cordial dealings with one another (cf. the correspondence: XXVII, 193f, 477; see Kaufmann, 321).

Notwithstanding the many fluctuations in its inner perspective and the great unevenness of its composition, the *Phenomenology* is a profound work of consummate language and consummate thought! On account of its lack of a clear-cut objective and especially in view of its obscure relationship to the *Logic, Encyclopaedia* and *Philosphy of History,* most systematic Hegelians have had no idea what to do with this work. Lively thinkers, by way of contrast, have found it all the more fascinating: D. F. Struass as much as Feuerbach and Marx, Dilthey as much as Jaspers, Heidegger as much as Bloch. With sober pathos the *Phenomenology* heralds a fascinating picture of the whole of reality suffused with Spirit. Hegel has now found his *language.* We may ridicule the awkwardness and obtuseness of his periods, but those subordinate clauses that sometimes agree with and sometimes contradict the principal clause afford us a glimpse into the thinker's weary struggle with the antithetical structure of real life. Here at any rate verbal complexity is *also* an expression of perpetually self-correcting patience in laying hold of living reality, an expression of the 'conceptual exertion' which Hegel both demanded and practised. Whoever suffers injury from these unyielding complex sentences without taking fright at equivocations is rewarded with the golden fruit of exquisite words, with the understanding of those speculative terms which, in their questionable ambiguity, say something different and yet the same ('*aufheben*': sublate; '*er-innern*': recall; '*ur-teilen*': judge; '*zu-grunde-gehen*': go to ruin). Hegel's language combines 'the anguish of the sentence with the artistry of the word'.[2]

After the sustained criticism made by Schopenhauer, Nietzsche and others, T. W. Adorno and E. Bloch have recently emerged as defenders of Hegel's language. Adorno takes Hegel under his wing when, in his exquisite analysis of the philosopher's language, he comes to speak of the equivocations: 'The objection most commonly voiced with respect to Hegel's alleged unclarity and still repeated in Überweg's *History* is that of the equivocations ... Where Hegel formally renders himself guilty of this failing, the reason is usually to be found in the subject-matter, in the explanation of the fact that two distinct moments are just as dissimilar as one ... Or the equivocations are in earnest as philosophical devices whereby the dialectic of thought intends to achieve its philosophical realisation. This is sometimes accompanied by a rather violent tendency, strongly suggestive of Heidegger, to confer independence on verbal as opposed to noetic realities. Even so, Hegel does this less emphatically than Heidegger and hence more innocently ... Such figures of speech are intended to be taken not literally but ironically, as mischievous stratagems. Without batting an eyelid Hegel uses language to convict language of empty arrogance when employed in a self-satisfied

---

[2] H. Glockner: *op. cit.* I, 38f.

sense. The function of language in such passages is not apologetic but critical. It disavows the finite judgment which postures as the possessor of absolute truth in its very particularity, objectivity and impotence. Equivocation is intended to demonstrate the inadequacy of static logic precisely by the application of logic to the object as it comes to be through its own sefl-mediation. Turning logic against itself is the dialectical salt of such equivocations.'[3]

In defiance of all critics and cynics, E. Bloch, himself a master of the German language, ventures to pronounce what is almost an encomium on Hegel's language: 'Many of his sentences stand like jars filled with a strong and heady potion but having little or nothing by way of a handle. Violations of civil grammar abound in his writings, and it is not only the grammatical purist who occasionally beats his head in despair. Yet the customary reproach that German philosophers, with the exception of Schopenhauer and Nietzsche, write badly is shown to be a nonsense by the very mention of Kant, and even more so of Hegel. The fact that so much attention has been devoted to this reproach leads us to suspect that it is but a device for keeping great thinkers at a distance. Hegel's manner of expression is admittedly often harsh and stilted, although he sometimes throws in some highly adventurous French and especially latin constructions (*'ex dissertatione proxime apparitura'*: 'from Mr. Hotho's soon to be expected dissertation I understand'). Yet it would be utterly absurd to let this fact deceive us as to the linguistic attributes of the great thinkers. There is an intoxicating precision about Kant's language, and the reader becomes aware of its worth as soon as he looks on it not as philosophy but as poetry. The same can be said of Kleist, whose prose is modelled on Kant's. At every point where the reader has managed to struggle through the highly individual terminology Hegel's language proves to be Luther's German set to music and endowed with the most startling vividness. This vividness is of the kind given by a shaft of lightning which emerges from a by no means cloudless sky, illuminating, specifying and embracing the whole landscape at one fell swoop. The only reason why Hegel's language breaks the customary rules of grammer is that it has something unprecedented to say for whose expression previous grammar was not equipped ... There is blood and marrow in Hegel's language, a body compsed of his South German heritage. And this gnarled creature blooms, often a Gothic enchanted garden, often a world figure, in a single sinuous detail. All this must be understood by the reader of these books. Hegel agitates by stirring things up and clarifying them; and, contrary to the widely held opinion about him, he thinks long in his soul. The good reader will feel as much at home with the uneven beauty of Hegel's German as in an old city with winding lanes and an obvious centre ... And if some effort fails to render every sentence clear to the reader, then let him reflect that there are also non-transparent precious stones. Our meaning is that an obscure matter expressed precisely as such is something completely different from a•perspicuous matter obscurely expressed. The first is like El Greco or light in a thunderstorm, the second is mere incompetence. The first constitutes precision appropriate to what must and may be said; it is an entirely relevant treasure such as we often find in Hegel; the second is merely dilettante and bombastic.'[4]

---

[3] *Drei Studien zu Hegel,* 127, 132f.
[4] *Subjekt-Objekt,* 18-21. Among the most recent articles on Hegel's understanding of language (H. Lauener, J. Simon, T. Bodammer) see esp. the highly detailed analysis undertaken by M. Züfle under a title coined by Hegel himself, *'Prosa der Welt'* ('The World's Prose').

The consummate language is an expression of consummate *thought*. It is a thought upheld by an immense courage to know and by a bold will to clarify, and hence – precisely in this work – a thought which pushes far beyond its original intention. Hegel is unlike many practitioners of hermeneutics in that he never gets bogged down in preliminaries, in methodological prolegomena and in formal opening remarks. He never simply introduces us to a problem; rather, he always conducts us through it. He always comes to the point, but not as a homespun enlightener intent on making anything and everything intelligible for the intelligent. Indeed, understanding is made easy for no one, and the *Phenomenology* belongs to the most difficult and uncomfortable works of philosophy. Hegel himself conceded that his readers would have difficulties in understanding his work (XXVII, 200; Kaufmann, 322). We shall have to return to the fact that external chaos was partly responsible for this state of affairs. The thought exhibited here can bring the reader's understanding to despair, but is excused by the fact that it is meant to bring him to despair. Already in the Introduction Hegel states that the road which the natural human understanding has to take here must 'be regarded as the pathway of *doubt*, or more precisely as the way of despair' (*PS*, 49). Our understanding of Hegel's path will entirely depend on whether we are able, without drowning in its depths, to project ourselves into his observant thought, to see, hear, experience and philosophise just as he himself saw, heard, experienced and philosophised, and, as it were, to adopt his way of looking at things without losing our own eyes. The *Phenomenology* is well placed to help us do this, for not only did he actually work out his philosophical thinking before writing the book, but he also provides us with a direct and indirect description of it. For at least according to its original plan the *Phenomenology* was supposed to be completely introductory, propaedeutic and pedagogic in character. The individual man, including the reader, is meant to be led to a genuinely scientific standpoint from that of the healthy and often so wrongheaded natural human understanding. He is intended to be led from the immediate sensual impression via all forms of consciousness to the self-cognisant Spirit: 'Science on its part requires that self-consciousness should have raised itself into this Aether in order to be able to live – and [actually] to live – with Science and in Science. Conversely, the individual has the right to demand that Science should at least provide him with the ladder of this standpoint, should show him this standpoint .within himself' (*PS*, 14f: the last clause comes from Hegel's revision of 1831).

If we start by understanding it retrospectively from its final form as the science of the *appearance of Spirit in its various guises*, then we find that the *Phenomenology of Spirit* is a patient step by step description of the process whereby natural consciousness achieves absolute consciousness or becomes aware of absolute knowledge: 'the way of the Soul which journeys through the series of its own configurations as though they were the stations appointed for it by its own nature, so that it may purify itself for the life of the Spirit, and achieve finally, through a completed experience of itself, the awareness of what it really is in itself' (*PS,* 49). But our understanding of this 'way of the soul' may not be simply psychological or pedagogical; it must at the same time be philosophical and historical. In the course of an intellectual development which drove him ever further on, Hegel made it clear that *this*educational path taken by the individual consciousness is at the same time the path on which the absolute Spirit manifests itself in its various guises. Hence this is not simply a case of 'fundamental philosophy' which, as a methodological introduction, has nothing to do with philosophy proper. On the contrary, notwithstanding the fact that Hegel's circular system is in principle without a beginning, the *Phenomenology* presupposes the end at the very outset. Thus Hegel analyses human cognition from the vantage-point of the absolute knowledge of the philosopher. The decisive factor underlying this *Phenomenology of Spirit* is that the Absolute and human cognition are not separated but hiddenly united. And the meaning of the empirical path taken in the *Phenomenology* is that human consciousness becomes aware of the Absolute and that the Absolute becomes aware of itself in human consciousness: 'It is this coming-to-be of *Science as such* or of *knowledge,* that is described in this *Phenomenology* of Spirit' (*PS,* 15). The philosopher's task in this is not to deduce reality but simply to give a spectator's description of it as it manifests itself to him in its history and as he experiences it from the wealth of ideas contained in his theoretical and practical, ethical, juridical, religious and philosophical consciousness. Consciousness is known in the world and the world in consciousness. This is a necessary historical experience, but it is also one which, as Descartes, Kant and Fichte held, takes its starting-point strictly from the subject, which, according to Descartes, is the only basically certain factor. That the world is experienced in virtue of consciousness and its recollection implies a far-reaching inward motion of the spirit, as M. Heidegger has made clear from his own point of view in his essay on Hegel's concept of experience.[5] Hence Hegel's starting from the individual subject does *not* mean that he is guilty of subjective individualism. In the *Phenomenology* we must once again take account of the relationship of his thought to society. The fact of his proceeding from the seemingly private immediate consciousness will only deceive one who has remained ignorant of the prehistory of the *Phenomenology* or of its later sections.

---

[5]*Hegels Begriff der Erfahrung* (ET *Hegel's Concept of Experience,* New York, 1970).

The view that any treatment of Hegel's thought must be simultaneously aware of both its social and religious dimensions has been a constantly reiterated premiss of this study. From this perspective we can say with T. W. Adorno: 'Society is the locus where dialectical contradiction is experienced. Hegel's own construction of a philosophy of identity demands that it be conceived just as much in terms of the object as of the subject; and in this very contradiction a concept of experience is crystallised which points beyond absolute Idealism. This is the concept of the antagonistic totality. The principle of universal mediation (as opposed to the immediacy of the mere subject) has its origin in the fact that the objectivity of the social process (right down to all categories of thought) has priority over the contingency of the individual subject. The metaphysical conception of the reconciled whole as the aggregate of all contradictions is likewise derived from the model of a society which is divided and yet nevertheless one. The importance of *society* in this context is to be stressed, for Hegel is not satisfied with the general concept of an antogonistic reality, for example with the notion of the primal polarities of being. On the contrary, proceeding from the neighbour, from the immediate consciousness of the individual man, in the *Phenomenology of Spirit* he accomplishes the mediation of this consciousness through the historical movement of being, a factor which carries him beyond any mere metaphysic of being.'[6]

The social dimension is partly responsible for the fact that the experience which reaches out in recollection is not exhausted in an initial 'methodological' doubt. Instead it lingers in a state of doubt (*Zweifel*) or rather of 'despair' (*Verzweiflung*) out of which there emerges a living and antithetical movement of dialectical 'sublation' (*Aufheben*). That is, what was considered absolute truth is *abandoned* while in this very abandonment – as a relative moment – being *reintegrated* and *elevated* into a higher unity: *tollere, conservare, elevare.* Through this affirmation, which is learned from concrete, individual and social experience, and which transcends itself as negation, thought falls into a living and dynamic fluidity. That is, consciousness shares in the dynamic of the Absolute, which is not an empty and rigid substance but a living subject propelling itself through all contradictions. It yields a history of the subject in which the subject constantly adjusts itself to its correlate object (and likewise the object to the subject) in perpetually changing contradictions and negations, on ever higher levels and in increasingly concrete configurations of consciousness and, finally, of the world. It becomes more plain in the process that this is not only a psychological but at the same time a logical, cosmical, socio-political, world-historical and indeed religious movement: religious in the dual sense of the self-revelation of infinite Spirit in finite spirit and of the contemplative immersion of finite spirit in infinite Spirit. In this way the dialectical process of self-knowledge takes place, consciousness becoming aware of itself in the Absolute and the Absolute becoming aware of

---

[6] *op. cit.*, **94**.

itself in conciousness: a permanent state of birth,[7] passing through all stages of knowledge and being, in continually new renunciations and intensifications, until it attains the perfection of absolute knowledge where certainty and truth, consciousness and world, subject and object, are brought into perfect harmony – in the Spirit which knows itself as Spirit. Hence Spirit essentially means the history of appearance, a painful and tragic – yet not entirely tragic but ultimately victorious – history of the self-denial and finding oneself again which are perpetually accomplished afresh in cognition: 'Appearance is the rising and passing away that does not itself arise and pass away, but is "in itself" [i.e. subsists intrinsically] and constitutes the actuality and the movement of the life of truth. The True is thus the Bacchanalian revel in which no member is not drunk; yet because each member collapses as soon as he drops out, the revel is just as much transparent and simple repose' (*PS*, 27).

Should we wish properly to understand and follow the dialectical mental act which Hegel meticulously rehearsed in the *Phenomenology,* and which he at least implicitly described in its pages (an explicit account is offered in the Preface), then it will be well to make a systematic distinction between *three stages of cognition* which have been impressively described by I. Iljin in terms redolent of Hegel:[8]

1. *Empirical-concrete* cognition which, despite all its variegated plurality, poetic consistency and inexhaustible richness, is marked by an unspeculatively naive and primitively deceptive immediacy, by a thoughtlessly confident and unconsciously engrossed contemplation and by a palpably sporadic and fleetingly random sensuality. To put it figuratively, one cannot see the wood for the trees.

2. The first stage of cognition must be surpassed and purified, yielding to a conceptually clear intellectuality and to a definite and pronounceable universality. Even this further stage of *formal and abstract intellectual thought* (along with the related phenomena of empirical philosophy and formal logic) merely constitutes an intermediate phase. Even though such thought is clear, definite, simple and stable, capable of being conceived and expressed and hence closely related to speculation, it does nevertheless have two negative characteristics. First, absolute abstraction leads to its becoming devoid of content and distinction: intellectual concepts are detached and divorced from individual and concrete reality, being monotone and unicoloured, deformed and devoid of reality; they aim to achieve the greatest possible scope and the least possible content. Secondly, unreconcilable opposition leads to its becoming isolated and unobtrusive: intellectual concepts are restricted and incomplete, identical, unchangeable, fixed, immovable, brittle, osseous, inflexible and dead; their order is an external, onsidedly dissected juxtaposition according to kind and species in which the merely individual concept clings to the individual content; it is not a connection sustained by inward vital motion. Hence such intellectual thought is ultimately devoid of reflection, conceptuality, ideas and spirit. It splinters and kills both reason and spirit, being unspeculative in its bad universality and formal identity. In spite of its

---

[7] *status nascendi.*
[8] *Die Philosophie Hegels als kontemplative Gotteslehre,* 17-74. J. Flügge: *Die sittlichen Grundlagen des Denkens* likewise offers a good account of Hegel's intellectual attitude.

value in lower spheres it is not good enough for philosophy. To put it figuratively once more, one cannot see the trees for the wood. What is required is to see the wood in the trees.

3. The philosopher must travel the road of self-denial to struggle through to *speculative, reasoning thought*, which has nothing to do with 'speculation' in the vulgar sense of the word: to a thought which merges with inner experience and especially with creative imagination to become genuinely visionary thought. It is imperative to cut loose from sense experience and external objectivity, to concentrate – aided by a thinking which is in keeping with the understanding – on the inner world, here to exercise speculative thought in conditions of incomparably more objective objectivity and in carefree disregard of any epistemological doubts. Just as in mystical and artistic experience, consciousness here stands in immediate relation to its object. What is happening at this point is abandonment, an immersion in the object, a forgetting of self which even goes so far as to forget that it forgets itself. As the object lives in the form of consciousness, so consciousness lives the content, the law of the object. The knowing subject gains entry into the objective essence of the universe through self-dissolution, which (as in mysticism) does not simply mean destruction. Hegel thus thinks visually and sees mentally, presenting us with a verbal picture and a pictorial logic. This is an intuitive intellectual vision, the inner experience of a rational mysticism. The individual-personal and sensual-empirical limitedness and contingency of consciousness are sublated in this objectivity of consciousness and consciousness of the object. Consciousness participates in the infinity, freedom, spirituality and divinity of the object. That which, when regarded empirically from below, is merely the life of the individual soul is, on the speculative level, nothing other than the life of the divine, the thinking self-determination of absolute Spirit. This is the liveliest of dynamics, in which unity is achieved through the constant mutual transformation of subject and object, thought and being. And this part human, part divine thought accomplishes the living union of the dead antitheses of the formal understanding in a tragic history of constantly renewed negation: the history of the knowing Absolute itself. 'The speculative Notion is accordingly a distinctively real ideality or else ideal being; the universal in the individual or else self-individuating universality; identity in process or else the process of the identical; self-concretising abstraction or else true concreteness in the element of the abstract. These definitions must not be taken as an exercise in word-play or paradox. On the contrary, a full measure of seriousness is in order here: the reader must suspect neither dreamed-up constructions nor philosophical abracadabra. No, we are dealing here with a mature and profound theory of the Notion, and anyone who declines to adjust his own thinking and seeing or to visualise this new field will understand scarcely anything of Hegel's thought.'[9]

The conscious ambiguity of Hegel's mental act goes some way towards explaining the ambiguity of the *Phenomenology* and its 'Spirit' to which allusion has already been made. Now since, unlike the Preface (*PS*, 1-45), it was actually written at the outset of the whole exercise, we may look to the Introduction (*PS*, 46-57) for a statement of Hegel's original educational-*cum*-

---

[9]I. Iljin: *op. cit.*, 67.

propaedeutic intention. And this Introduction makes it patently clear that the prime concern of the *Phenomenology* is with the elevation of the immediate empirical consciousness of the individual to the level of absolute knowledge. In accordance with this scheme and taking as his starting-point the unphilosophical consciousness, Hegel describes the dialectical phases which are necessary for the achievement of this elevation, phases through which consciousness (prompted by an indwelling logic in which it is itself unconscious) must pass in a process of externalisation and recollection.

The development of *Consciousness* (*PS*, 58-103) starts with what is simply given, with the naive consciousness which immediately confronts the object as the 'this' and the 'particular'. The development leads via the self-contradictory stages of the 'sensual consciousness' from the 'here-and-now' – including, first, 'perception' of the thing with its contradictory properties, a process entailing many deceptions, and, secondly, 'understanding' (which in its reflection knows as the content of appearances only the law and the ordering of the game of forces – to *self-consciousness*. The latter is no longer geared to the object, but to itself. It takes back into itself the duplications involved in the reflection of the understanding (inward and outward, form and content, essence and appearance) and coincides with its object in the certainty of itself: 'It is in self-consciousness, in the Notion of the Spirit, that consciousness first finds its turning-point, where it leaves behind it the colourful show of the sensuous here-and-now and the nightlike void of the supersensible beyond, and steps out into the spiritual daylight of the present' (*PS*, 110f). At this point, where there is an identity of truth and certainty, Notion and object, the analytical goal announced in the closing sentence of the Introduction seems to have been achieved: 'In pressing forward to its true existence, consciousness will arrive at a point at which it gets rid of its semblance of being burdened with something alien, with what is only for it, and some sort of "other", at a point where appearance becomes identical with essence, so that its exposition will coincide at just this point with the authentic Science of Spirit. And finally, when consciousness itself grasps this its own essence, it will signify the nature of absolute knowledge itself' (*PS*, 56f).

Surprisingly, perhaps, Hegel now interposes a further lengthy chapter on reason before the hoped-for absolute knowledge is finally reached in equally lengthy chapters on Spirit and religion. We must likewise break off here – at least briefly – to speak about the great controversy concerning the import, function and position of the *Phenomenology* within Hegel's system as a whole before we continue with our analysis.

We have already mentioned the fact that from the very beginning both Hegelians and anti-Hegelians have found it difficult to square the *Phenomenology* with Hegel's system as a whole. Now it may well be simply impossible to reduce the tensions and ruptures which we encounter along the path of Hegel's thought to a unitary system. Even so, the following factors prove that our difficulties with respect to the *Phenomenology* are not exclusively to do with our reconstruction of Hegel's thought:

1. While he never ambiguously distanced himself from the *Phenomenology*, Hegel afterwards proved unable to allocate it a clear-cut niche within his total system. Thus it did not form the basis of his lectures in Heidelberg and Berlin, and it amounted to only a very subordinate section of the *Encyclopaedia* (as the doctrine of consciousness it joined with anthropology and psychology to make up the second section of the philosophy of *subjective* Spirit).

2. After the early Hegel critics I. H. Fichte and R. Haym had already cast doubt on the clarity of the *Phenomenology* in terms of its content, T. Haering was able to demonstrate, in an address to the Hegel Congress held at Rome in 1933,[10] that Hegel himself had altered the conception of the work while he was still writing it, indeed even while Part One was being printed! This accounts for the conspicuous discrepancy between the Introduction, on the one hand, which was written at the beginning and obviously has only limited objectives, and the conclusion and Preface (likewise written at the end), on the other, which range much further afield. Hegel's original intention, recorded in the Introduction, had been to write nothing more than 'a science of the experience of consciousness'. What happened was that the fulfilment outstripped the plan. J. Hoffmeister and J. Hyppolite have indicated their basic agreement with Haering's explanation.

3. In the 1937 edition of the *Phenomenology* J. Hoffmeister stated that Hegel initially had the work printed under the title *Part One: Science of the Experience of Consciousness*, subsequently excising this title from the printed sheet and inserting *Phenomenology of Spirit* in its place. In some copies the first title remained intact, with or without its successor.

4. Finally, with his summary of previous research and correction of Haering's position, O. Pöggeler has convincingly explained how the originally intended *Science of the Experience of Consciousness* turned into the *Phenomenology of Spirit*.[11] For the aims of the *Science of the Experience of Consciousness* announced in the Introduction had actually been achieved after the first three chapters at the beginning of the fourth chapter on self-consciousness, that is, at the very point where we have just interrupted our analysis. It is questionable whether Hegel had originally planned to include in the *Science of the Experience of Consciousness*, as there now follows in the *Phenomenology*, a chapter on the realisation of reason. Even so, such a chapter can be deduced from the plan developed in the Introduction, according to which 'reason' in its turn must split up with the passage of time and manifest itself in historical forms. However, at any rate as far as observation of nature and self-consciousness is concerned, Hegel is here either frankly unable to develop any such forms or else – at a pinch – can do so only with respect to later periods. His original strict plan thus falls apart in these excessively lengthy chapters. Things begin to expand at an uncontrolled

---

[10]*Die Entstehungsgeschichte der Phänomenologie des Geistes*.

[11]*Zur Deutung der Phänomenologie des Geistes* (1961). Subsequently clarifying his own position in his article '*Die Komposition der Phänomenologie des Geistes*' (1966), Pöggeler made adjustments in his attitude to the question whether the *Phenomenology* tends in the direction of the *Philosophy of Mind* or in that of the *Logic*; cf. also F. Nicolin: '*Zum Titelproblem der Phänomenologie des Geistes*'.

pace: in the original edition the first chapter numbers 16 pages, the second 21, the third 42, the fourth 61, and the fifth 204. Hegel himself speaks of the 'great unwieldiness of the final parts' (XXVII, 161; Kaufmann, 319) and takes comfort, as he still sits at work, from a 'second edition to appear shortly', where everything is to be better and he intends to 'purge the ship of ballast here and there and set it afloat' (XXVII, 136; Kaufmann, 317). In the summer of 1806 Hegel must have lost all mastery of his work, as he now fell into dispute with the publisher, who had already started to print it in February. Even in purely quantitive terms, the work's centre of gravity is shifting towards the chapters on Spirit and religion. The name 'Phenomenology of Spirit' crops up for the first time in the lecture list of the winter semester of 1806-7. Hegel now hastily revised the arrangement of the work, bringing the three previous first chapters together into a single new chapter headed 'Consciousness' and adapting the titles of the following chapters accordingly. In his conclusion and Preface he reinterprets the whole thrust of the work, so that it is now concerned not so much with the experience of consciousness as with the experience of Spirit; moreover, the Notion of consciousness is overtaken by the Notion of Spirit, and the whole work is now called *Phenomenology of Spirit*.

The *Phenomenology* moves within the element of consciousness which is itself the sphere of the immediacy of Spirit. Furthermore, as a path towards science, it is itself already science: *System of Science. First Part*. As a matter of fact, it is more than this: it shows itself to be an anticipation of the mature system, and for this very reason it cannot be comfortably lodged within that system later on. On account of the many-levelled structure of the work, Hegel himself could not succeed in neatly classifying the *Phenomenology* on one side and the *Logic, Encyclopaedia* and *Philosophy of History* on the other. Nor is such a division feasible today. Even so, it is not as a part of a closed system but as the original *way* in which an original thinker thought that the *Phenomenology* has continually displayed an unhoped-for fruitfulness and a stimulating contemporary significance. We intend to pursue the layout of the *Phenomenology* further before we come to our specialist question.

Self-consciousness is thus also involved in dialectical movement (104-138). Since in real life it plays the part of covetousness, it carries on a struggle for mutual reconition in and with itself. This process of confrontation between dependent and independent consciousness, between master and servant, is, however, intensified in the progression from Stoic freedom via the freedom of the Sceptic of late antiquity to the unhappy (Christian) consciousness. This pious consciousness, split up in a mixture of pain and longing between an indigent here-and-now and a distant hereafter, is driven into self-alienation by speculative mediation with the unchangeable-eternal until, in the modern period, it arrives at the unity of self-consciousness with reality, of thought with being: self-consciousness arrives at 'reason'.

Reason, as self-consciousness become wide and universal, no longer loses itself in a far-off beyond, but rather cleaves to the real world. In its dialectical development (*PS,* 139-262) it appears initially as the observer's theoretical reason (classification of species, where organic and inorganic nature are concerned, the logical and psychological laws of human individuality, where psychology is concerned, and, finally, physiognomy and phrenology). Nevertheless, since it cannot find satisfaction in nature, reason changes course to become the reason which is practically at work in history: as the enjoyment of pleasure against the necessity of fate, as the heart which boils with indignation against the established order, as the virtue which revolts against the way of the world. Yet even in enjoying, improving and withstanding the world, reason cannot but be constantly falling afresh into contradiction until it finds its sublation as the rational self-consciousness which is the agent of its own self-realisation and as the individuality which is real in and for itself. But against the spiritual menagerie of satisfied individuals who, instead of struggling for *the* cause, struggle for their own cause, legislative reason takes the field, although it must in its turn dissolve of necessity into bringing test cases. This makes room for the next form of experience, that is, for 'Spirit' as objectively mediated reason.

As universal reason, *Spirit* is identical with the world. It is now a question of forms of the world instead of forms of consciousness: '. . . real Spirits, actualities in the strict meaning of the word, and instead of . . . shapes merely of consciousness, . . . shapes of a world' (*PS,* 265). The 'Spirit' or reason which the world itself is, albeit without being conscious of the fact, is now intensified in three stages, which coincide with certain phases of world history (*PS,* 266-409). Thus as realised universal reason, Spirit lives as (1) 'true Spirit', which does not yet have consciousness of itself and which exists in a condition of unaffected immediacy (Hellenism). However, this simple, beautiful and natural ethical order of society (family – people, husband – wife) dissolves into a world where persons exist in themselves in an abstract-*cum*-juridical fashion: a legally conceived state of affairs involving formal equality under a single lord of the world (Roman Empire). This process precipitates the break-up of the world, ushering the next phase of (2) 'self-alienated Spirit', which is divided into two abstract, self-reflecting worlds (the modern era): the world of education, which is enslaved by the here-and-now, and the world of faith, which is devoted to the pure beyond. These worlds for their part fall into a conflict (the Enlightenment), which is provisionally resolved in the French Revolution with its absolute, unbridled 'liberty' and the terror of the guillotine. From the miscarriage of the French Revolution there emerges, lastly, (3) 'Spirit that is certain of itself'. Having split up into the here-and-now and the beyond and having plunged headlong into the alienation of objectivity, the ethical world – notwithstanding all the dissimulation and contradictions of the moral world – is now reunited in the subjective conscience as the actuality of pure duty by the 'moral world-view' of German Idealism as represented by Kant and Fichte. Yet both the rigorism of universal, though non-actual, duty

202

(Kant) and the moral personality cult of the self-congratulating 'fair soul' prove impotent to resolve the fundamental contradiction of the moral self-consciousness. Only in the dialectic of the sinful and judging conscience does reconciliation with evil take place, only here does the Absolute take on the aspect of absolution in the forgiveness of sins, which is itself the gateway for a new phase where the Spirit appears in 'religion'.

While *religion (PS,* 410-478) is the self-consciousness of the Spirit, it is still tinged with imperfection in that the element in which it moves is not the perfect unity of knowledge but the imagination. Now religion is realised in three stages of externalisation and mediation, which do not follow 'Spirit' in a temporal sense, but rather have their own history: natural religion (the religion of nature); art religion (Hellenism); revealed religion (Christianity). The divergent strains within religion are at length overcome in *absolute knowing* (*PS,* 479-493), that is, in the science of the philosophy of the Spirit which knows itself in the form of Spirit.

As examined in speculative thought, consciousness is therefore one, or, rather, becomes one with the absolute subject and its history, which the individual consciousness must remember. The development from empirical to absolute consciousness is only possible when the former as individual ego becomes aware of the universal knowledge of humankind. That is, the individ-ego must unite with the ego of mankind, just as the ego of mankind must become conscious of itself in the individual ego. To be elevated into absolute knowing, reason must acquire the consciousness of its age, it must become world and this means world history. J. Hyppolite[12] therefore appropriately distinguishes between the two tasks which the *Phenomenology* has to fulfil (even though these do become identical in the end of the day): elevation of empirical consciousness into absolute knowing, and elevation of individual ego into human-universal ego, each being possible only by means of the other. The development of individual consciousness is thus tied to the development of world history and thence to the history of absolute Spirit. This is why Hegel sought to complete his doctrine of consciousness in the final chapters of the *Phenomenology* by sketching the historical development of objective Spirit and of religion, in which consciousness must participate before it may enter into absolute knowing. This fact also enables us to understand why, although the *Phenomenology* in itself does not purport to be a complete philosophy of world history, in its final chapters the forms of consciousness become forms of the world and world history is no longer – as in the first chapters – merely the source of illustrations, but seems instead almost to coincide with the develop-

[12]*Genèse et structure de la phénoménologie,* 44-48 (ET *Genesis and Structure of Hegel's Phenomenology of Spirit,* 39-45).

ment of Spirit (e.g. the Greco-Roman period, with the true Spirit of ethical order, the Enlightenment and French Revolution with the alienated Spirit, the world of Kant and Fichte with the Spirit that is conscious of itself; a similar account can be given of the three phases of religion). And it is also understandable from this perspective why the first three moments of the individual consciousness seem to repeat themselves in universal reason and other modes (consciousness in observant reason, self-consciousness in practical reason, reason in Spirit).

It is noteworthy that much material from the earlier *Jena Systems* has been incorporated into this system, albeit in a novel form which has involved intelligent recasting and comprehensive synthesis. And it is equally noteworthy that amidst all the welter of positions, negations, externalisations and intensifications this dialectical mediation between thought and being is geared from start to finish to a powerful, comprehensive process of reconciliation which represents a consistent continuation of the modern subjective approach initiated by Descartes and Kant in that it is carried out under the aegis of consciousness. Now while the 'unhappy consciousness' is a particular stage within the *Phenomenology,* consciousness is nevertheless at root an *unhappy* consciousness from the very beginning; it is simply unaware of the fact at the early stage of naive sensual certainty.[13] For consciousness is torn within itself in all directions, being obliged to suffer its infinite sorrow through a wide variety of phases, stages and forms. Only after it has struggled through the whole range of painful experiences and renunciations, thereby perfectly finding itself, does it find happiness in its unhappiness. This is the universal reconciliation which the entire *Phenomenology* seeks to realise: the reconciliation between Stoicism and Scepticism, Faith and the Enlightenment, Rationalism and Romanticism; between master and servant, Idea and feeling, desire and necessity, the law of the heart and the law of reality, virtue and the way of the world; between external and internal, in-oneself and for-oneself, object and subject, being and thought, the here-and-now and the beyond, the finite and the infinite. The *coup de grâce* is supplied by the *Aufhebung* of all things in absolute knowing, in the Spirit which knows itself as Spirit. Having now withstood all alienations and mediations, Spirit has now cast off all its externalisations, while at the same time conserving them in the Notion. And at the end of the *Phenomenology* Hegel is able to state in sober triumph: 'The *goal,* Absolute Knowing, or Spirit that knows itself as Spirit, has for its path the recollection of the Spirits as they are in themselves and as they accomplish the organization of their realm. Their preservation, regarded from the side of

___

[13]cf. J. Wahl: *Le malheur de la conscience dans la philosophie de Hegel.*

their free existence appearing in the form of contingency, is History; but regarded from the side of their philosophically comprehended organization, it is the Science of Knowing in the sphere of appearance: the two together, comprehended History, form alike the inwardizing and the Calvary of absolute Spirit, the actuality, truth and certainty of his throne, without which he would be lifeless and alone. Only

> from the chalice of this realm of spirits
> foams forth for Him his own infinitude' (*PS*, 493).

E. Bloch comments: 'This is one of the most celebrated conclusions in philosophical literature, dithyrambic *and* responsible, apotheosis *and* doctrinal statement. The slightly altered Schiller quotation (from the *Philosophical Letters*) has the effect of a prayer uttered at a pan-historical harvest festival: the grapes have been pressed and fermented, and the world forms are the chalices which capture the wine and in which its spirit is offered to the absolute Spirit. In its ascent to Spirit, the hierarchy of Ideas seems to be suffused with the exultation of bubbling champagne and likewise devoid of any earthly sediment. Thus the *Phenomenology* ends on a note of benefaction with the Idea, which is itself the quintessence of the world drink consecrated to it.'[14]

As we see: 'Having attained maturity, thought will now accomplish intentionally what it formerly performed only unconsciously; that is, it will write the history of Spirit and itself become the echo of the hour which has struck for it . . . It is this, rather than any superior volume of material, which prompts Hegel to load philosophy with content; this is what makes the climate of his thought so modern in comparison with Kant and even Fichte. Even so, when he drove philosophy to come to terms with its experience of the real in an intellectually consistent manner, he did not do so in unbroken burst of reckless thinking, whether of the naive-realistic variety or of what the vulgar turn of phrase would call unbridled speculation . . .'[15] 'Since in his thought philosophy turns into the observation and description of the movement of the Notion, the *Phenomenology of Spirit* virtually dictates the way in which its own history will be written. Hegel hastily attempts to model his exposition on the event itself, to philosophise as if he were writing history, as if this way of thinking necessitated the unity of the systematic and the historical conceived in dialectic. Seen along these lines, the butting in of the historical dimension is responsible for what Hegel's philosophy lacks in clarity.'[16]

---

[14]*Subjekt – Objekt*, 100.
[15]T. W. Adorno: *Drei Studien zu Hegel*, 80f.
[16]*op. cit.*, 141.

This is what Hegel in his old age would call his long 'voyage of discovery'[17] through the realm of Spirit, a journey which manifested itself as a veritable odyssey of Spirit. Restless as Faust and denied even a moment's fulfilment, consciousness has overtaken the finite in all directions, undergoing a multitude of adventures and struggles to attain at length that infinite by which it was surrounded from the very outset: a journey on which, in hard-won spiral and triangular movements, Spirit has actually been experienced. We must now speak of this journey in somewhat greater detail, mindful that failure to do so would mean that everything which now follows would not be seen in its true proportions. At the same time, this introduction into Hegel's now mature thought, undertaken with the help of the *Phenomenology*, will preserve us from getting lost in our forthcoming analysis of the boundless material contained in the major works which presently flowed from Hegel's pen.

2. The Religion of the Incarnation of God

The focus of our present concern is the phenomenology of religion, and, more particularly – remembering that religion, properly speaking, still includes art – *'revealed religion'* (*PS*, 453-478). Now while religion is Spirit's self-consciousness *qua* Spirit, this self-consciousness does not yet unfold smoothly in full unity, but rather as an object. Religion thinks in objective terms, re-presenting that which is one as far as the Notion is concerned. For this reason a further dialectical development is necessary. This is not only a development of the objective self-consciousness of Spirit to absolute knowledge, where that unity is known *as such* which in religion is known merely in hazy *non-conceptual* terms. For it is at the same time (precisely because self-consciousness is identical with the world *qua* Spirit) a development on the part of the World Spirit itself. This development, while it contains within itself all moments of the Spirit in timeless identity and repose, nevertheless bestows a temporal expression on its Being in a sequence of historical forms (natural religion – religion in the shape of art – revealed religion) within a variety of nations and communities, thereby realising its Being in history. Consequently – and this is the only factor which explains certain contradictions which many Hegel critics find incomprehensible – for Hegel religion possesses from the very outset a dual, as it were subjective-*cum*-objective, aspect. For the one reality of religion is *both* a movement of the self-consciousness of the individual (person or nation) *and* a movement of the absolute Spirit in the world, the corollary being that the history of religion consistently coincides with the history of World Spirit. Each national religion is but a form of the one religion, of the self-consciousness of Spirit, albeit only in a particular historical form. Each religion has its time and its hour.

---

[17]Rosenkranz: *op. cit.*, 204.

In primitive *natural religion*, chiefly that of the Orient, Spirit is initially depicted more formally than materially in the guise of natural immediacy: in the form of objective consciousness, in natural realities as god of light, as plant or animal spirit, as artificer (Egypt). In the *artistic religion* of the Greeks, which is embodied in sculpture and supremely in poètry, the Spirit acknowledges its opposition to nature: in the form of productive consciousness, which entails the abrogation of its naturalness, Spirit is shown as the observed Self. Not until the decline of the ancient world – which Hegel once again describes in a three-dimensional résumé (*PS*, 455) – do we encounter a coming together of Nature and Self. This is the hour of *revealed*, absolute *religion*, which – *qua* religion – is unsurpassable. Spirit is here revealed in the unity of Nature and Self, in the true form of being-in-and-for-itself where Spirit is pictured as it is in and for itself. The whole wealth of content is now present. But we must constantly refresh our memory concerning a fundamental reservation of Hegel's which is relevant precisely here: pictorial representation has not yet been transposed into the Notion, into conceptual knowledge (cf. *PS*, 409-418).

We shall search in vain in this chapter on *revealed*, absolute, unsurpassable religion (and, for that matter, in the whole of the *Phenomenology*) for the name of *Jesus Christ*. Is it an ambiguous phenomenon that his name is hushed up here too? While Hegel mentioned a variety of names in the *Phenomenology*, he also remained silent about as many as he did in fact specify, even where the allusion is obvious, as, for example, with Schelling, Napoleon and Louis XIV. In just this way Hegel dealt exhaustively with Jesus Christ too, albeit without naming either Jesus or Christ. Ideas which only became briefly audible at the end of the *Jena Systems* are here discussed at some length, and on several levels. Nor will anyone be able to deny that Christ has been awarded a central place: in the very inner sanctum of absolute Spirit. This is precisely what distinguishes revealed religion from the earlier stages of religion: *the incarnation of God has here become immediately actual!* What pre-Christian myth could only think, picture or produce is here immediate reality: 'The Self of existent Spirit has, as a result, the form of complete immediacy; it is posited neither as something thought or imagined, nor as something produced, as is the case with the immediate Self in natural religion, and also in the religion of Art; on the contrary, this God is sensuously and directly beheld as a Self, as an actual individual man; only so *is* this God self-consciousness' (*PS*, 459). Precisely this is the specific content of revealed, absolute religion: 'This incarnation of the divine Being, or the fact that it essentially and directly has the shape of self-consciousness, is the simple content of the absolute religion' (*PS*, 459; cf. 418).

The exposition of these pivotal sentences is not an entirely simple task, even though Hegel expatiated on this incarnation over many pages. These chapters, written in haste during a turbulent period, lack concision and precision. 'A deplorable state of confusion reigned over the whole business of printing and selling the book and even, to some extent, over the actual writing . . . I feel that my painstaking devotion to detail has worked to the detriment of the overall impression given by the whole. The latter, however, is, by its very nature, such a crisscrossing and zigzagging treatment of the material that any improvement of the arrangement would cost me a great deal of time before the book would emerge in a clearer, more finished form. I do not need to say that some individual points still require much effort to lick their presentation into shape. You will have only too much cause to make this discovery for yourself. With respect to the somewhat more marked lack of order in the final sections, pray be so forebearing as to make allowance for the fact that I put the final touches to the editing in the midnight before the battle near Jena.' So wrote Hegl to Schelling on 1 May 1807 (XXVII, 161; Kaufmann, 319). Despite these exceptional difficulties which face the interpreter, the two chief coordinates which determine this 'incarnation of the divine Being' ought at least to be clear.

1. The same development of absolute Spirit or consciousness is at stake in this incarnation as has concerned us hitherto. That we cannot simply read the customary Christian substance into this incarnation and into the various Christian formulations employed by Hegel ought to be clear from the sentence quoted above (from *PS*, 459), which unmistakably deals with 'Spirit' and 'self-consciousness'. And Hegel adds by way of clarification: 'In this absolute religion the divine Being is known as Spirit, or this religion is the consciousness of the divine Being that it is Spirit. For Spirit is the knowledge of oneself in the externalization of oneself' (*PS*, 459). The divine substance externalises itself, becomes human self-consciousness and thus enters into existence as a Self, just as, by the same token and at the same time, the self-consciousness externalises itself and becomes universality; only through the externalisation of both does 'their true union' come into being (*PS*, 457). We are conseuqently standing at the 'birthplace of Spirit as it becomes self-conscious' (*PS*, 456). In the case of this 'birth' – and we are dealing here with the speculative meaning of the virgin birth – we may speak figuratively of an 'implicit (*ansichseienden*) father' (i.e. the self-externalising implicit substance, the divine Being) and an 'actual mother' (i.e. the self-externalising actual self-consciousness of man): 'Of this Spirit, which has abandoned the form of Substance and enters existence in the shape of self-consciousness, it may therefore be said – if we wish to emply relationships derived from natural generation – that it has an *actual* mother but an *implicit* father. For *actuality* or self-consciousness, and the *in-itself* as substance, are its two moments

208

through whose reciprocal externalization, each becoming the other, Spirit comes into existence as their unity' (*PS,* 457). This then is how we are to understand the credal statements 'begotten of the Father before all worlds' and 'incarnate of the virgin Mary'!

2. At the same time, the truly historical existence of Jesus is at stake. That is, what is notionally necessary must appear and reveal itself in experience: 'That absolute Spirit has given itself *implicitly* the shape of self-consciousness, and therefore has also given it for its *consciousness* – this now appears as the *belief of the world* that Spirit is *immediately present* as a self-conscious Being, i.e. as an actual man, that the believer is immediately certain of Spirit, *sees, feels* and *hears* this divinity. Thus this self-consciousness is not imagination, but is *actual in the believer*' (*PS,* 458). In revealed religion God can truly be 'sensuously and directly beheld as a Self, as an actual individual man' (*PS,* 459), in which respect revealed religion differs from the myths of the natural and artistic religions, where this is simply 'imagination'. The theme of the man Jesus, which accompanied Hegel through all his early writings, is here resumed. Now, however, after his turning to Christology in Frankfurt, Hegel emphasises the man Jesus' unity with the divine.

As we shall soon see in greater detail, Hegel treats the historical existence of Jesus as one with the development of the Absolute, that is, he understands the incarnation of God in the sense of classical Christology in terms of the development of Spirit. In so doing Hegel is fully alive to the momentous *consequences of an incarnation of God understood along these lines for the understanding of the true nature of God*: 'Consequently, in this religion the divine Being is *revealed*' (*PS,* 459). And this revelation shows that dialectic is at home in God himself. Hence Hegel indulges in polemic against an abstract and static understanding of God: 'The Good, the Righteous, the Holy, Creator of Heaven and Earth, and so on, are *predicates* of a Subject – universal moments which have their support on this point and only *are* when consciousness withdraws into thought' (*PS,* 459f). The revealed God is the God who has visibly become man: 'Spirit is known as self-consciousness and to this self-consciousness it is immediately revealed, for Spirit is this self-consciousness itself. The divine nature is the same as the human, and it is this unity that is beheld' (*PS,* 460). This accounts for the transvaluation of all values, which is itself an event in virtue of the incarnation of God: 'The absolute Being which exists as an actual self-consciousness seems to have come down from its eternal simplicity, but by thus *coming down* it has in fact attained for the first time to its own highest essence ... Thus the lowest is at the same time the highest; the revealed which has come forth wholly on to the *surface* is precisely therein the most *profound*. That the supreme Being is seen, heard, etc. as an immediately present self-consciousness, this therefore is indeed the consummation of its Notion; and through this consummation that Being is immediately *present qua* supreme Being' (*PS*, 460). This matter is so important for Hegel that he comes to speak of this negative element in the Being of God once more in the famous Preface which he wrote at the end of the *Phenomenology:* 'Thus the life of God and divine cognition may well be spoken of as a disporting of Love with itself; but this idea sinks into mere edification, and even insipidity, if it lacks the seriousness, the suffering, the patience, and the labour of the negative. *In itself,* that life is indeed one of untroubled equality and unity with itself, for which otherness and alienation, and the overcoming of alienation, are not serious matters. But this *in-itself* is abstract universality, in which the nature of the divine life *to be for itself,* and so too the self-movement of the form, are altogether left out of account' (*PS*, 10). Hegel advocates the concrete God, and the concrete God is a living God, the God who externalises himself and becomes man, who passes through a 'life-history'.

Many a theologian will have his reservations concerning this Hegelian speculation. Even when – indeed, precisely when – he is supposed to be a right-wing Hegelian, he notices very keenly that the understanding of Christ taught here is not simply identical with the way Christ has been understood in the Christian tradition. Hegel, it goes without saying, likewise noticed this. And he proclaimed the fact with great clarity in twice broaching the subject of Christology in the *Phenomenology* (indeed, if we include the preliminary forms of revealed religion, then he raised the topic on several occasions). The second time he mentioned Christology here he did so on a significantly lower level, in the section on the alienated Spirit; we must expect to find the Christian tradition precisely on this less philosophical level. According to Hegel the point at issue here is not even 'religion', but merely 'faith'. In contrast to education and the Enlightenment, which are in bondage to this-worldly reality, faith is determined in purely transcendent terms (*PS*, 296f). Accordingly, in contrast to the pure insight of the Enlightenment, faith possesses the true content, but it enjoys this 'content' without 'insight' (*PS*, 323f). We are reminded of Hegel's remarks on the fruitless longing of the 'unhappy consciousness', which also thinks of God as the sole reality, seeks him and yet – the empty tomb! – fails to apprehend him (cf. *PS*, 131f). We must bear in mind that these remarks on faith and pure insight are obviously uttered against superstition and against the kind of theology that is too lazy to think (cf. *PS*, 329-429). Even so, we must not overlook the fact that the rubric 'superstition' can also encompass what previously, under Christ, went by the name of 'faith'. Hegel criticises traditional Christian faith to the extent that it is not understood and illumined by speculative thought. His reproach is 'that the *essence* of faith . . . is reduced to the level of something *imagined,* and becomes a supersensible world which is essentially an "*other*" in relation to self-consciousness' (*PS*, 324).

Thus this lower stage of the development of Spirit is already basically concerned with the content of the Christian religion. The content of faith is no different from the content of the Christian revelation, namely the Trinity, along with Christ as the self-offering second moment of the divine Spirit. '. . . so here, too, the first is the *Absolute Being*. Spirit that is in and for itself in so far as it is the simple eternal *substance*. But in the actualization of its Notion, in being Spirit, it passes over into *being-for-another*, its self-identity becomes an *actual*, self-*sacrificing* absolute Being; it becomes a *self*, but a mortal, perishable self. Consequently, the third moment is the return of this alienated self and of the humiliated substance into their original simplicity; only in this way is substance represented as Spirit' (*PS*, 325). Faith, however, only pictures this content and has no insight into it; it does not sense the necessity of this movement, which, as far as it is concerned, is a mere 'happening' (*PS*, 325). Here too it is a question of incarnation: the absolute Being externalises itself and sacrifices itself. Even so, this 'externalization of the eternal Being into the actual world' remains 'an incomprehended, sensuous reality' (*PS*, 326). Things therefore never come to a genuine reconciliation. God ultimately remains beyond man; the consciousness is alienated in faith; the here-and-now remains cut off from the beyond; 'the beyond has only received the further character of remoteness in space and time' (*PS*, 326). This stage – as earlier the stage of the unhappy consciousness, where a similar imperfect trinitarian and incarnational dialectic unfolds (*PS*, 128f) – must also be overcome by pure insight. The Enlightenment has thoroughly taken care of this (*PS*, 329f): 'This pure insight is thus the Spirit that calls to *every* consciousness: *be for yourselves* what you are *in yourselves* – reasonable' (*PS*, 328).

For his part, to be sure, Hegel presses beyond the onesidedly flat rationality of the Enlightenment, which was carried *ad absurdum* in the terror of the French Revolution, to the 'moral view of the world', which is to be speculatively superseded in its turn by religion and absolute knowledge respectively. The brief chapter on 'evil and its forgiveness', which forms the immediate prelude to 'religion', sheds further light on what is meant by the demand for 'insight' and, bound up with this, by the necessity for the movement of Spirit. The finite and the infinite emerge here as two concrete figures of conscience: as sinful conscience and as judging conscience, which move dialectically into each other, thereby ultimately finding their reconciliation in mutual exchange. Our attention is drawn here to two facts. First, 'evil' would seem to be nothing other than limited individuality in its relationship to universality: '*evil*, because of the disparity between its *inner being* and the universal' (*PS*,

401). Secondly, 'forgiveness' would seem to be nothing other than the self-healing of the Spirit: 'The wounds of the Spirit heal, and leave no scars behind. The deed is not imperishable; it is taken back by Spirit into itself . . .' (*PS*, 407). We see how radical is Hegel's struggle here for the concrete living God, for the unity of God and man. As will shortly be explicitly demonstrated, the dialectic of fall and redemption is, when speculatively understood, shifted into the Absolute.

J. Hyppolite: 'Like all romantics, Hegel wants to think through the immanence of the infinite in the finite. But this leads him to a tragic philosophy of history; infinite spirit should not be thought through beyond finite spirit, beyond man acting and sinning, and yet infinite spirit itself is eager to participate in the human drama. Its true infinity, its concrete infinity, does not exist without this fall. God cannot ignore human finitude and human suffering. Conversely, finite spirit is not a within-limits [*en-deçà*]; it surpasses itself, indefatigably drawn toward its own transcendence, and it is this transcending which is the possible healing of its finitude. Thus Hegelianism poses the problem of the unity of God and man, of their reconciliation which presupposes their opposition – what Hegel calls alienation.'[18]

3. Christology in the Context of the Community

The incarnation of God in this one man is only a beginning, it can only be a beginning. The dialectical process does not permit itself to be obstructed. What became actual in this one man must become universal actuality. Witness must be borne not simply to God's descent into the world, but also to the certainty of this fact here and now. The Christian religion is concerned not simply with the revelation of the transition of substance into self-consciousness (historical incarnation), but also with the transition of self-consciousness into substance, and this takes place in the self-consciousness of the *Church*. It is the Church, which, as the community of the Spirit, has access to the truth of the incarnation of God. We can go further by saying that the Church, as the community of the Spirit, is itself the result of the incarnation of God. There can and there must be a Church, because the one Christ died *and* rose again. It would be entirely possible for Hegel to say that the Church is the extended Christ. For as the individual man in whom the Absolute revealed itself, Christ is in the past tense, over and done with: 'This individual man, then, which absolute Being has revealed itself to be, accomplishes in himself as an individual the movement of *sensuous Being*. He is the *immediately* present God: consequently, his "*being*" passes over into "*having been*"' (*PS*, 462). Nevertheless, the very Christ who died must rise again in the Spirit: 'Con-

---

[18]*Genèse et structure de la phénoménologie*, 507f (ET *Genesis and Structure*, 525f).

sciousness, for which God is thus sensuously present, ceases to see and to hear Him; it *has* seen and heard Him; and it is because it only *has* seen and heard Him that it first becomes itself spiritual consciousness. Or, in other words, just as formerly He rose up for consciousness as a *sensuous existence*, now He has arisen *in the Spirit*' (*PS*, 462).

The immediacy of the present God thus demands mediation in the community, where sensuous faith is transformed into a faith and a life 'in the Spirit', and where a Christian sensuous present is transformed into a spiritual present. What is involved here is therefore not a return to the primitive Church or to the historical Jesus of the distant past – that would still be a form of imaginative alienation. 'This, therefore, is the movement which it accomplishes in its community, or this is the life of the community. Consequently, what this self-revealing Spirit is *in and for itself*, is not elicited by, as it were, unravelling the rich life of Spirit in the community and tracing it back to its original strands to the ideas, say, of the primitive imperfect community, or even to the utterances of the actual man himself' (*PS*, 463). Any such going back to the historical Jesus 'confuses the *origin* of the Notion as the *immediate existence* of its first manifestation with the *simplicity of the Notion*' (*PS*, 463) and therefore issues only in 'the the non-spiritual recollection of a supposed individual figure and of its past' (*PS*, 463). No, a reconciliation of this-worldly reality with the beyond is necessary here and now. And this takes place in the present of the community through an elevation of the imaginative self-consciousness into absolute knowledge, where the true content still preserves the supersensuous speculative form of the Notion appropriate to itself. Because true speculative knowledge is accordingly found in the Church, in the religious community, Hegel now gives a systematic description of the various moments of this consciousness by interpreting the community's religious knowledge – which is given only in pictorial language – from the lofty pinnacle of the philosopher's absolute knowledge. Spirit is thus described in three moments according to the communal consciousness of the community: in itself, externalised, reconciled.

1. *Spirit in itself.* Hegel attempts to give speculative and conceptual form to the community's knowledge of Christ by speaking first of all of Spirit in itself. What was already the content of the unhappy and the believing consciousness, albeit at this stage in the condition of remoteness and alienation, has 'the consciousness of the community . . . for its *substance*': the *Trinity* as 'pure thought' – 'picture-thinking' – 'self-consciousness' (*PS*, 464). These are the 'three moments' or 'elements' or 'determinations' of the divine Spirit, which thinks in living and dialectical terms, the modes whereby it 'unfolds its nature'.

This is what the Church pictures to itself as the *Father*: 'When Spirit is at first *conceived of* as substance *in the element of pure thought*, it is immediately simple and self-identical, eternal essence, which does not, however, have this abstract *meaning* of essence, but the meaning of absolute Spirit' (*PS*, 464). What the community pictures to itself as the generation of the *Son* is the dialectical movement of the eternal simple Being, which is Spirit and contains the negative as its own self-determination: 'But simple essence, because it is an abstraction, is, in fact, the negative in its own self and, moreover, the negativity of thought, or, negativity as it is in itself in essence; i.e. simple essence is absolute *difference* from itself, or its pure othering of itself. As essence it is only *in itself* or for us; but since this purity is just abstraction or negativity, it is *for itself*, or is the Self, the Notion. It is thus objective; and since picture-thinking interprets and expresses as a *happening* what has just been expressed as the *necessity* of the Notion, it is said that the eternal Being *begets* for itself an "other"' (*PS*, 465). But the very essence that has been differentiated by negation requires unity, which the community pictures to itself as an emergence of *Spirit*: 'But in this otherness it has at the same time immediately returned into itself: for the difference is the difference *in itself*, i.e. it is immediately distinguished only from itself and is thus the unity that has returned into itself' (*PS*, 465).

We can thus discern three trinitarian moments: a) the moment of '*essence*'; b) the moment of '*being-for-self* which is the otherness of essence and for which essence is'; and c) 'being-for-self, or the knowledge of itself *in the "other"*' (*PS*, 465). These moments are not to be understood as static relationships, but as a living movement of 'restless Notions' which are 'in themselves their own opposite' and find 'their rest' only 'in the whole' (*PS*, 465). 'Essence beholds only its own self in its being-for-self; in this externalization of itself it stays only with itself: the being-for-self that shuts itself out from essence is *essence's knowledge of its own self*. It is the word which, when uttered, leaves behind, externalized and emptied, him who uttered it, but which is as immediately heard, and only this hearing of its own self is the existence of the Word. Thus the distinctions made are immediately resolved as soon as they are made, and are made as soon as they are resolved, and what is true and actual is precisely this immanent circular movement' (*PS*, 465). Rooted wholly in the threefold structure of the dialectical method of absolute Spirit, Hegel's doctrine of the Trinity is formulated at the apex of speculation: 'But the picture-thinking of the religious community is not this speculative thinking; it has the content, but without its necessity, and instead of the form of the Notion it brings into the realm of pure consciousness the natural relationships of father and son' (*PS*, 465f). 'The object is revealed' to the consciousness 'by something alien, and it does not recognize itself in this thought of Spirit, does not recognize the nature of pure self-consciousness' (*PS*, 466).

2. *Spirit in externalisation.* We have to do here with the externalisation of Spirit itself: creation, fall and redemption are only correctly understood when they are seen as a process in Spirit. Even so, this does not mean that there is no fundamental distinction between the 'begetting of the Son' (objective divine thought: 'in the element of pure thought'; *PS, 464*) and the 'creation of the world' ('not merely in the element of pure thought', but as *'actual Spirit...*in the element proper to picture-thinking'; *PS, 467*). Indeed, it is precisely the first that forms the basis for the progress of Spirit to the second. Otherness must be posited as such, difference and opposition must become actual: 'In this *simple* beholding of itself in the "other", the otherness is therefore not posited as such; it is the difference which, in pure thought, is immediately *no difference*; a *loving* recognition in which the two sides, as regards their essence, do not stand in an antithetical relation to each other. Spirit that is expressed in the element of pure thought is itself essentially this, to be not merely in this element, but to be *actual* Spirit, for in its Notion lies *otherness* itself, i.e. the supersession of the pure Notion that is only thought' (*PS, 466f*).

How, then, is what the community pictures to itself as the *creation of the world* to be formulated in philosophical terms? In this higher idiom it must be said that 'Spirit becomes an other to itself' and 'enters into immediate existence': 'This *"creating"* is picture-thinking's word for the *Notion* itself in its absolute movement; or to express the fact that the simple which has been asserted as absolute, or pure thought, just because it is abstract, is rather the negative, and hence the self-opposed or *"other"* of itself' (*PS, 467*). Accordingly, Spirit's *'being-for-another* is at the same time a *world'* (*PS, 467*).

Only when it is consciously grasped as such does otherness, or actual antithesis, appear in its complete depth: in 'the *existent Spirit*, which is the individual Self which has consciousness and distinguishes itself as "other", or as world, from itself' (*PS, 467*). When existent Spirit (whose existence is, in itself, innocent) knows and consummates this otherness, it sets itself in antithesis to itself and becomes unequal to itself: 'it is not pure knowledge, but thought that is charged with otherness and is, therefore, the self-opposed thought of *Good* and *Evil'* (*PS, 468*). This is just what the community pictures to itself under the heading of the *fall into sin.* The community, however, here regards as contingent something which is in fact a necessary corollary of Spirit's becoming other: 'Man is pictorially thought of in this way: that it once *happened,* without any necessity, that he lost the form of being at one with himself through plucking the fruit of the tree of the knowledge of *Good* and *Evil,* and was expelled from the state of innocence, from Nature which yielded its fruits without toil, and from Paradise, from the garden with its creatures' (*PS, 468*).

The creation of the world achieves its immanent and necessary radicality in

215

the fall into sin of consciousness, which becomes contradictory on account of the opposition of Good and Evil. In this fall there is basically a repetition of the movement of the absolute, simple essence, which does not hold out in itself in a state of static transcendence, but determines the whole of reality as a living movement of Spirit. For this reason 'the becoming of Evil can be shifted further back out of the existent world even into the primary realm of Thought' (*PS*, 468), that is, into self-existent Spirit. This idea is expressed in the image of the fall of 'the very first-born Son of Light' (presumably an allusion to Böhme's doctrine) or of 'a multiplicity of other shapes' (traditional angelology; *PS*, 468). Even so, as far as Hegel is concerned, counting the moments – in terms of one-in-threeness, -fourness or -fiveness – is ultimately a useless exercise (*PS*, 469). Now Good and Evil are not powers which hover over man; rather, these opposites constitute man's very selfhood. The struggle therefore changes course so that 'just as Evil is nothing other than the self-centredness of the natural existence of Spirit, so, conversely, Good enters into actuality and appears as an existent self-consciousness' (*PS*, 469f). And this comes to pass in Christ, in whom the divine Being renounces its non-actuality: 'That which in the pure thought of Spirit is in general merely hinted at as the *othering* of the divine Being, here comes nearer to its realization for picture-thinking: this realization consists for picture-thinking in the self-abasement of the divine Being who renounces his abstract and non-actual nature' (*PS*, 470).

In order to resolve the antithesis and to achieve *reconciliation*, movement is necessary both in the divine Being and in the evil human Self. From the point of view of the second moment, this movement must begin with the immediate, implicit moment, that is, with the externalisation of the divine Being, which 'is depicted as a spontaneous act', while 'the necessity for its externalization lies in the Notion' (*PS*, 471): 'It is, therefore, that side which has not being-for-self but simple being as its essence that alienates itself from itself, yields to death, and thereby reconciles absolute essence with itself' (*PS*, 471). It is a question of an externalisation of the divine Being into natural human being, whereby alienation is superseded in death through Spirit's resurrection as actual Spirit in the universal self-consciousness of the community: 'For, in this movement, it manifests itself as Spirit; abstract essence is alienated from itself, it has natural existence and self-like actuality, this its otherness, or its sensuous presence, is taken back again by the second othering and posited as superseded, as *universal*. The [absolute] essence has thereby come to be its own Self in its sensuous presence; the immediate existence of actuality has ceased to be something alien and external for the absolute essence, since that existence is superseded, is universal. This death is, therefore, its resurrection as Spirit' (*PS*, 471).

And Hegel gives a more detailed description of this process of divine Spirit, which the community's picture-thinking sees unfurled in the incarnation, death and resurrection of Christ. The fact that the incarnation of God is involved here makes it clear that divine and human nature are not instrinsically separate and that evil existence is not alien to the divine Being: 'If we further consider the behaviour of picture-thinking in its progress, we find first of all the declaration that the divine Being takes on human nature. Here it is already *asserted* that *in themselves* the two are not separate; likewise in the declaration that the divine Being *from the beginning* externalizes itself, that its existence withdraws into itself and becomes self-centred and evil, implies, though it does not expressly assert, that this evil existence is not *in itself* something alien to the divine Being. Absolute Being would be but an empty name if in truth there were for it an "other", if there were a "fall" from it; on the contrary, the moment of *being-within-self* constitues the essential moment of the *Self* of Spirit. That this *being-within-self* and the actuality which follows from it belong to absolute Being itself, this which for us is *Notion,* and in so far as it is Notion, appears to the picture-thinking consciousness as an incomprehensible happening; the in-itself assumes for it the form of *indifferent being*. The thought that those moments of absolute Being and of the self-centred Self which seem to flee from each other are not separate, *also* appears in this picture-thinking – for it does possess the true content – but this picture-thought comes later, in the externalization of the divine Being who is made flesh' (*PS,* 471f). In that which the community pictures to itself as the sacrificial death of Christ, the incarnation is brought to an end and the reconciliation is consummated: 'The picture-thought is in this way still *immediate,* and therefore not spiritual, i.e. it knows the human form of the divine Being at first only as a particular, not yet as a universal, form; it becomes spiritual for this consciousness in the movement whereby this divine Being in human shape sacrifices his immediate existence again and returns to the divine Being: only when essence is reflected into itself is it Spirit. In this picture-thought there is depicted the reconciliation of the divine Being with its "other" in general, and specifically with the thought of it – Evil' (*PS,* 472).

To be sure, Hegel here already vehemently protests against the reconciliation of the divine Being with Evil being used as a pretext for making a simplistic equation of Good with Evil or of the divine Being with nature in its entirety. Only 'an unspiritual way of talking' (*PS,* 472) would make an undialectical identification of these statements. As if this were a question of static unity and not of dynamic, spiritual movement: 'The difficulty that is found in these Notions stems solely from clinging to the "is" and forgetting the thinking of the Notions in which the moments just as much *are* as they *are not* – are only the movement which is Spirit. It is this spiritual unity, or the unity in which the differences are present only as moments or as suspended, which has become explicit for the picture-thinking consciousness in that reconciliation spoken of above;

217

and since this unity is the universality of self-consciousness, self-consciousness has ceased to think in pictures: the movement has returned into self-consciousness' (*PS*, 473).

3. *Spirit reconciled.* The incarnation of God continues in the Church. Christ had to die, so that in this way the community would arise in the Spirit: 'This Notion of the transcended individual self that is absolute Being immediately expresses, therefore, the establishing of a community which, tarrying hitherto in the sphere of picture-thinking, now returns into itself as the Self; and in doing this, Spirit passes over from the second element constituting it, i.e. from picture-thinking, into the third element, self-consciousness as such' (*PS*, 471). Spirit is thereby posited in its universality and returns into itself: 'Spirit is thus posited in the third element, in *universal self-consciousness*: it is its *community.* The movement of the community as self-consciousness that has distinguished itself from its picture-thought is to *make explicit* what has been *implicitly* established. The dead divine Man or human God is *in himself* the universal self-consciousness; this he has to become explicitly *for this self-consciousness*' (*PS*, 473).

It is precisely the 'fall into sin' that leads to the 'swing of the pendulum'. Evil is sublated, insofar as self-consciousness, which had become evil by going-into-itself, becomes conscious of its own evil and thus radically goes into itself yet again. In Christ's incarnation and death this appears for the community in pictorial form. It is this that must be interiorised: 'The *death* of the divine Man, *as death*, is *abstract* negativity, the immediate result of the movement which ends only in *natural* universality. Death loses this natural meaning in spiritual self-consciousness, i.e. it comes to be its just stated Notion; death becomes transfigured from its immediate meaning, viz. the non-being of this *particular* individual, into the *universality* of the Spirit who dwells in His community, dies in it every day, and is daily resurrected' (*PS*, 475). Thus out of the chrysallis of the Christ-individual there proceeds the universal Christ: from the individual 'divine Man or human God' (*PS*, 473) there develops 'the universal divine Man, the community' (*PS*, 478). In this whole process we are concerned with the movement of consciousness, in which the element of picture-thinking (the Son) and that of pure thought (the Father) are taken back into the Notion of realised Spirit: 'The death of the Mediator as grasped by the Self is the supersession of his objective existence or his particular being-for-self: this *particular* being-for-self has become a universal self-consciousness. On the other side, the *universal* has become self-consciousness, just because of this, and the pure or non-actual Spirit of mere thinking has become *actual*' (*PS*, 476).

The realisation of the divine essence is thus consummated in self-knowing

218

Spirit, in which consciousness returns into the identity of pure thought, an identity, however, which contains all moments within itself. This is what is pictured by the hard saying about the death of God, which is now unfolded in greater detail: 'The death of the Mediator is the death not only of his *natural aspect* or of his particular being-for-self, not only of the already dead husk stripped of its essential Being, but also of the *abstraction* of the divine Being. For the Mediator, in so far as his death has not yet completed the reconciliation, is the one-sidedness which takes as *essential Being* the simple element of thought in contrast to actuality: this one-sided extreme of the Self does not as yet have equal worth with essential Being; this it first has as Spirit. The death of this picture-thought contains, therefore, at the same time the death of the *abstraction of the divine Being* which is not posited as Self. That death is the painful feeling of the Unhappy Consciousness that *God Himself is dead*. This hard saying is the expression of innermost simple self-knowledge, the return of consciousness into the depths of the night in which "I = I", a night which no longer distinguishes or knows anything outside of it . . . This Knowing is the *inbreathing of the Spirit*, whereby Substance becomes Subject, by which its abstraction and lifelessness have died, and Substance therefore has become *actual* and simple and universal Self-consciousness' (*PS*, 476).

The distance which forces a wedge between the community and reconciliation past and future (i.e. the one which once took place in Christ and the one which will take place for the community) must be sublated in the present. What appears as an act of satisfaction performed by an alien must be perceived as absolute Spirit's coming to itself through its own efforts. The kind of reconciliation which is merely an external appurtenance of the religious consciousness must become consciousness's very own work in 'the simple unity of the Notion' (*PS*, 483) and in 'the simple unity of knowing' (*PS*, 485). There must be a final uphill struggle in order to achieve that vitally moved figure where form and content become identical in knowledge, where substance and subject, individuality and universality, finite and universal become fully one in the 'identity of the Self with itself' (*PS*, 489), where, consequently, the absolute Self thinks itself and posits itself as Being, procuring its own reconciliation through its own efforts. 'This last shape of Spirit – the Spirit which at the same time gives its complete and true content the form of the Self and thereby realizes its Notion as remaining in its Notion in this realization – this is absolute knowing; it is Spirit that knows itself in the shape of Spirit, or a *comprehensive knowing*' (*PS*, 485).

It will therefore be conceded that 'the content of religion proclaims earlier in time than does Science, what *Spirit is*' (*PS*, 488). Even so, science, with its higher knowledge of Spirit, carries the day: 'only Science is its true knowledge of itself' (*PS*, 488). As Hegel had written to a friend while the last pages of the

Phenomenology were being printed, 'Science alone is theodicy' (XXVII, 137; Kaufmann, 318).

4. Christ Sublated in Knowledge

As the path along which the thinker thinks, the *Phenomenology* is at the same time the path along which the absolute Spirit lives. By faithfully writing the history of Spirit from the perspective of his own historical location, Hegel describes the 'career' of God. In this respect the *Phenomenology* is at once a philosophical and theological treatment of history. The modern age had achieved a deepening of man's understanding of God, and Hegel might justly claim that none of these insights had slipped through his fingers as he committed them to paper in the *Phenomenology*. He had described the new awareness of God's-being-in-the-world and of the world's-being-in-God, along with the new sense of the worldliness of God and of the divinity of the world, without falling victim to either pantheistic fatalism or irreligious atheism. On the contrary, the *Phenomenology* had clearly explained how God is and yet is not the world, how the world can be so horrifically non-divine and yet remain the external form of God.

A look back at the previous section prompts the question: How did Hegel actually achieve this mental feat? The answer is: through the idea of *development*. While the world is not identical with God in any simple sense, it is nevertheless *God in his development*. This God who is in development, *en route* and in history externalises himself towards the world *and* leads the world on an upwards course, first as nature and ultimately as Spirit, toward himself, toward his infinity and divinity. All of this takes place in a comprehensive and vigorous circular movement which had already been described by the Church Fathers and by mediaeval scholasticism: *exitus a Deo – reditus in Deum*.

There is, however, a significant difference between Hegel and his predecessors in that the dualistic scheme is here overcome in a throughly modern way. Hegel is not concerned just with the outward dualism of heaven and earth, which had been relativised by natural science, but also with the inward dualism of God and man. The Deity encompasses all of reality, without the difference of the Deity from all of reality being overlooked. Quite the opposite: this difference is perceived as already existing within God himself. The life of God consists in a struggle with antithesis; so that a debate takes place within God himself in the course of which the world proceeds from God and is reconciled in God. In this way dualism is resolved within God himself. As far as Hegel is concerned, the idea of the life and development of God 'sinks into mere edification, and even insipidity' if it is not understood as a *dialectic* internal to God himself (cf. *PS*, 10).

220

The fact that God himself is perceived in terms of such dialectical development has momentous consequences for the concept of God. It means that the concept of God includes the negative moment within God himself: the seriousness, the pain, the patience and the work of the negative. In order to give verbal expression to this deepening and purification of the traditional concept of God, Hegel prefers to speak of God as *Spirit*. The term 'Spirit' expresses the fact that God is involved in becoming and self-development, that he externalises himself along dialectical lines, that he comes to himself. Spirit denotes neither a purely inward subjectivity of consciousness nor an absorption into the substantial objectivity of a Deity. On the contrary, Spirit is the substance which is also the subject, which as the self is involved in movement, which externalises itself and goes into itself. As Hegel puts it at the end of the *Phenomenology*: 'Spirit, however, has shown itself to us to be neither merely the withdrawal of self-consciousness into its pure inwardness, nor the mere submergence of self-consciousness into substance, and the non-being of its [moment of] difference; but Spirit is *this movement* of the Self which empties itself of itself and sinks itself into its substance, and also, as Subject, has gone out of that substance into itself, making the substance into an object and a content at the same time as it cancels the difference between objectivity and content' (*PS*, 490). Or as he put it in the Preface, which is virtually a second closing chapter: 'That the True is actual only as system, or that Substance is essentially Subject, is expressed in the representation of the Absolute of *Spirit* – the most sublime Notion and the one which belongs to the modern age and its religion. The spiritual alone is the *actual*. . . But the life of Spirit is not the life that shrinks from death and keeps itself untouched by devastation, but rather the life that endures it and maintains itself in it. It wins its truth only when, in utter dismemberment, it finds itself' (*PS*, 14; 19).

Development – dialectic – Spirit. By conceiving God himself in these terms we can come to grips with all the antitheses of the world and society in their homogeneity and in their necessity. From the perspective of such an understanding of God, the tragic and unhappy splitting up of reality on its various levels can be sublated in a reconciliatory manner through the negation of negation. Hegel's consciousness suffered more from the unreconciled state of reality in general and of human society in particular than did any other philosophical consciousness before him. It had dawned on him with great clarity that all lower stages of alienation are but an anticipation and consequence of the supreme instance of alienation, so that genuine reconciliation is only possible in the event of its being achieved between the finite and the infinite, between the world and God.

The above account of Hegel's exploratory essays in Jena and the outline of the *Phenomenology* itself sketched in the immediately preceding section

221

afford ample proof that the latter work, like all of Hegel's earlier writings, can only be understood against the wider background of the whole problem of human society. As was already the case in the *Jena Draft Systems,* the *Phenomenology* too is simultaneously concerned with religious *and* social mediation. For this reason it can be examined (as has already been done by G. Lukács[19]) from the perspective of reflection on the fact that the genesis of the objective world and the internal difficulties of civil society are conditioned by economic factors. Already in the *Jena Draft Systems* work was characterised as an integral part of the self-mediation of Spirit. The *Phenomenology* can also be interpreted (as has been attempted by A. Kojève[20]) as a reflection on the historical process in terms of the changing countenance of political institutions. This line of approach is right to go beyond economic dialectic in highlighting the political factor of domination as a decisive condition of the historical process. Finally, the *Phenomenology* can also be interpreted as a history of the parousia of the divine, all-encompassing Being. This had been done by M. Heidegger,[21] who displayed a keen awareness of the theological significance of Hegel's discourse concerning the Absolute. Even so, as G. Rohrmoser clearly pointed out in the closing section of his book, all these interpretations become erroneous when taken in isolation. Hence Lukács's enquiry into the genesis and meaning of civil society and Kojève's enquiry into the function of modern legal principles must be seen together with Hegel's recourse to religion. Hegel was convinced that a reconciliation of man with the splintered reality of his world and with himself is made possible by religion alone.

G. Rohrmoser wholeheartedly recognises the positive concerns which inform the three scholarly treatments that have exercised the most influence on contemporary discussion of the *Phenomenology.* Even so, he has some reservations about all three positions which are undoubtedly justified by the text of the work. (For his own part, Rohrmoser scarcely takes sufficiently into account the Jena Hegel's sublimation of religion into philosophy.)

While G. Lukács does not dispute the fact of Hegel's recourse to religion, he regards it as a spurious solution of the real contradictions of civil society and as a religiously camouflaged flight into the subject-object identity of hypostatised Spirit. Rohrmoser is obliged to object that such an interpretation 'not only turns the intention which guided Hegel in his attempt at reconciliation into its opposite, but also prematurely distorts the root problem, which Lukács defines differently from Hegel. For Hegel's dialectic cannot be reduced to the dialectic of the social process of production. On the

---

[19]*Der junge Hegel,* 539-718 (ET *The Young Hegel,* 449-568).
[20]*Hegel, Versuch einer Vergegenwärtigung seines Denkens,* 172f (ET *Introduction to the Heading of Hegel,* 236f).
[21]*Hegels Begriff der Erfahrung,* esp. 186-189 (ET *Hegel's Concept of Experience*).

contrary, this kind of dialectic is itself the expression of a onesided false consciousness whose isolated abstraction into objective mediation negates the infinite self-being of the individual, thereby destroying the wealth of its historical becoming which has been stored in the memory of Spirit. In Lukács's declared aim (taken over from Marx) of sublating social objectification through society, the free ego would itself be sublated along with such objectification, so that history would not be consummated in the classless society, but would revert behind the immediate ethical reality of the polis into what would now be the frankly barbarous condition of the pre-historical beginning.'[22]

A. Kojève's view that the theme of the *Phenomenology* is the dialectic of domination and servitude results in an ideologisation of the Napoleonic epoch (political and legal recognition of the individual in his equality with all other individuals) and in atheism (Christianity as an ideologised need of the slave, while he was a slave). Against this interpretation Rohrmoser is moved to emphasise: 'Nor does the defamation – or glorification – of Hegel's philosophy as atheistic become any more convincing when one thinks oneself able to buttress this view by reading modern philosophical positions into it. Too high a price seems to be paid here for making Hegel's thought "contemporary"...One thing must be sufficiently plain from what has already been developed, namely that Hegel's view has been wrongly confused with the position of modern subjectivity, which holds aloof from its own externalisation and believes that it can serve its God best by keeping the world in quarantine from him.'[23]

In his interpretation of Hegel's concept of experience as the history of the parousia of Being, M. Heidegger overlooks the social and historical starting-point of Hegel's *Phenomenology*. It must be said that when a blind eye is turned to this factor 'the very quintessential and unmistakably distinctive element of Hegel's way of doing philosophy is lost from view. This is the element in which thinking moves itself to become a speculative understanding of what is, of what deserves the emphatic name of actuality. Heidegger's ontological difference, the exiling of Being from what exists, is precisely contrary to the sense and direction of Hegel's philosophy. Hegel was not concerned to restore the purity of Being from its degeneration into things, but intended to understand what Heidegger interprets as a degeneration of Being as its actualisation. The *Phenomenology* signifies the accomplished change of the hitherto self-centred transcendental consciousness into the Being of the things that lie outside itself. Hegel's philosophy is meta-physical in that it guards the definiteness of Being and of things against the purity of a thinking which is too impotent to meet them head on. But it shows itself to be theological and, in the strict sense of the word, Christian by obediently and unpretentiously corresponding to God's love for the world which was revealed in the death of Christ, to the will of the Absolute to exist "with us" and not without us.'[24]

Let E. Bloch have the last word in this little excursus: 'At all events, not every aspect of Hegel which does not yet stand in a direct and functioning relationship to Marxism can ... be ignored as a matter of principle ... Thus religious disputes *per se* cannot be eliminated from either the historical development or from the further implications of Hegel's philosophy without doing violence to them. Even so, the later master did not

---

[22]*Subjektivität und Verdinglichung*, 102.
[23]*op. cit.*, 104.
[24]*op. cit.*, 106.

drop down from heaven, least of all from the Church's heaven, with a ready-made system in his pocket.'[25]

Hegel treated no period of world history with such artistry and attention to detail as he devoted to the modern period, which according to him presents itself as a division between orthodoxy and Enlightenment, faith and pure insight, the beyond and the here-and-now. Hegel's most deeply cherished aims seemed on the brink of fulfilment. He could even assert of the French Revolution – admittedly only in a highly qualified sense, and indeed he was ultimately obliged to withdraw the remark: 'The two worlds are reconciled and heaven is transplanted to earth below' (*PS*, 355). Hegel did not follow the radical French Enlightenment and Revolution in seeking to procure this reconciliation apart from religion. On the contrary, he sought it through the agency of religion, in which self-conscious Spirit executes a complete return from total externalisation into social and objectifying Being.

What Hegel had in mind here was, of course, a religion in philosophical form. Nevertheless, despite being temporarily obliged to take a back seat as Hegel devoted a fresh burst of concentration to philosophy, Christ has ended up by keeping a firm place in this philosophical form of religion. In the full light of speculation he appears for this philosophical religion as the one in whom the grand reconciliation has been revealed: in him heaven and earth, supreme abstraction and absolute immediacy, have found each other; in him divine nature and human nature appear as one.

Judge Hegel's Christian credentials as you will, think what you will about the pneumatology and Christology of his *Phenomenology*, say what you will about the philosophical method and individual analyses of this work: the theologian of all people is under an obligation to begin with a truthful appraisal of what this work of reconciliation represents in the context of the history of modern thought (beyond a narrow understanding of the history of philosphy or theology). In brief, the *Phenomenology* attempts to present the doctrine of a comprehensive reconciliation of God and man which will be at one and the same time radically modern and radically Christian!

Hegel attempted to pursue an uncompromising middle way between the Christian scholastic dogmatics with which he had become acquainted in Tübingen and the unchristian kind of Enlightenment whose influence had reached Germany from France. Whatever they may think of the solutions which Hegel proposed, theologians may not ignore his earnest exertions. Some illustration of the effort involved in this middle way can be given by taking a look at the two extremes.

1. When considering the modern age it is right to defend the great and small post-

---

[25] *Subjekt – Objekt*, 52.

Tridentine scholastic theologians of both confessions, who, taking their stand on the tradition and the *doctrina communis,* worked diligently and cleverly (even borrowing from their enemies!) to construct and develop their tracts as impregnable bastions of truth. We can point to progress, to a more thorough statement of the prolegomena and a clearer arrangement of the material, to the provision of fresh safeguards and to concentration on endangered points. Yet it remains a fact that, notwithstanding the best of intentions, this work of construction (precisely in the 'area' of Christology, which, unfortunately, was only an 'area', a 'tract') all too often erected barriers to an overall perspective and to insight. Amidst the hundreds of *quaestiones* and *quaestiuncu-lae,* too little time was devoted to the one great question of the modern age. Amid all the countless scholastic controversies between Thomists and Molinists, fideists and rationalists, Protestants and Catholics, there was too little explicit consideration and study of the real controversy of the modern age, namely the alienation between God and the world. By way of contrast Hegel, who took as his point of departure the problem bound up with society *and* religion, noticed with great clarity just where the real split of the age was to be found, and he did at least try to heal it.

2. On the other hand, it is right to admire the bold discoverers and *conquistadores* of the modern period. Relying on their clear heads and on a providence which they often conceived in rather distant terms, they pioneered new paths for a new age in philosophy and enlightenment, in mathematics and mechanics, in natural science and technology, in economics and politics, and in biblical criticism and 'life of Jesus' research. We can point to the enormous advances made by liberty, tolerance, prosperity and clearsightedness against traditionalism, princely absolutism, superstition and ossified theology. Despite their overall perspective, however, modern people have often been wilfully blind to the real division. They have been more disposed to dissolve (the analytical age!) than to reconcile, and even the great architects of reconciliation (Bruno, Spinoza, Leibniz, Goethe, even the Kant of the three *Critiques,* the younger Fichte and Schelling) have by and large left Christ in the dark as far as their work was concerned. However, not only did Hegel intend to achieve reconciliation, but he also centred his whole philosophical work of reconciliation in Christ, as he felt obliged to understand him for the purposes of the new age.

Looked at in theological terms, Hegel's philosophical implementation of this Christian reconciliation is certainly in many respects a problematic undertaking. But for all that the *Phenomenology* remains a grand and highly fruitful attempt at achieving a comprehensive reconciliation between philosophy and theology, insight and revelation, enlightenment and dogma, modern humanity and a deeper form of Christianity. Was it not all in all a reconciliation in which Christianity seemed to have excelled itself? Very many educated Christians and theologians too were grateful to Hegel on this score at that time.

Some have responded to the *Phenomenology* with enthusiastic veneration (D. F. Strauss,[26] for example, extolled it as the 'alpha and omega' of Hegel's

---

[26] *Werke* X, 224.

philosophy, as his 'odyssey'), while others have reacted to it with an attitude of restrained admiration (for K. Marx[27] it is the true birthplace and the holy of holies of Hegel's philosophy). All, however, are obliged to acknowledge Hegel's brilliant achievement. The only theologian who may register his reservations concerning the pneumatology and Christology of this work is the one who can appreciate the *Phenomenology* for what it is – the triumphal prelude and emphatically not the final chord of Hegel's work of reconciliation. But he will be obliged to couch his reservations in careful terms: classical Christology itself will cause theologians to think twice about any objections they might raise, because undiscriminating criticism of Hegel could very well turn out to be tantamount to destruction of the classical christological dogma.

The theologian steeped in scholastic thought will accordingly here reconsider the reservations which may be adduced in the light of classical Christology. Hegel is said to use a novel, outright philosophical terminology (moment, consciousness, in-itself, for-itself . . .). But was not the now traditional christological terminology ($\phi\acute{v}\sigma\iota\varsigma$, $\acute{v}\pi\acute{o}\sigma\tau\alpha\sigma\iota\varsigma$, *natura, persona*) itself also novel once upon a time? Was not it also of philosophical rather than of biblical provenance, and was not it also rendered highly suspect in virtue of being used by orthodox and heretic alike? It is said to be Hegel's intention to have such expressions as 'Father', 'Son', 'generate' and 'give birth' understood in a speculative sense – but is not even traditional theology obliged to understand these words analogically (indeed, as more dissimilar than similar to the object of comparison) and therefore to sublate their meaning *per viam affirmationis, negationis et supereminentiae*? Hegel is said to make too little distinction between the act of generation and the act of creation, between the Logos and the world – but are we not obliged to see Logos and world as intimately bound up with one another, if the scriptural statement about a creation through the Logos, $\acute{\epsilon}\nu$ $X\rho\iota\sigma\tau\tilde{\omega}$. is to have any meaning? Hegel is said to identify sin with the Absolute – but does not Paul teach that the Son of God was made sin, and John that he became the Lamb that takes away the sin of the world? Hegel is said to teach the reconciliation of man as the self-reconciliaion of God – but is not the whole reality of reconciliation dependant on the fact that it did not take place in just any man, but was wrought of God in God's Son? Hegel is said to teach the replacement of the individual Christ by the universal Christ of humanity – but are not all believing men and women supposed, within the one *corpus Christi* and moved by his Spirit, to make up for what was lacking in Christ? Hegel is said to teach that there is a becoming on the part of God – but did not the eternal divine Logos *become* man? Hegel

[27] *Frühschriften*, 252 (ET *Early Writings*, 199).

is said to teach a necessary development – but does not Scripture know the salvation-historical necessity of the δεῖ? And, lastly, Hegel is said to teach a pantheism which puts God and the creature in the same category – but does not traditional Christology assert that in the one Jesus Christ, God is man and the creator a creature? Beneath the answers given by both Hegel and classical Christology there lurk certain fundamental problems which can be formulated in a variety of ways. Every theologian is keenly aware of these problems, and the fact that they are still unresolved afflicts us to this day.

One particular reservation demands more detailed treatment, since it has to do not with a partial problem which ought perhaps to be interpreted differently, but is directly concerned with the basic starting-point and overall structure of the *Phenomenology* and with the place of Christ within the whole. What has befallen Christology in this marvel, the *Phenomenology,* which unites within itself epistemology and ontology, psychology and anthropology, philosophy of history and a critique of the age? What has become of Christology in the crowning final phase of the *Phenomenology*? Hegel himself would say that Christ (and, along with him, Christianity as a whole) has been caught up in absolute knowing – caught up in an act of redemptive sublation over against all who abandoned Christ, either overtly (i.e. the purely rationalist men of the Enlightenment) or covertly (i.e. the intellectually lazy traditionalist theologians). Faith in Christ, he would say, is not only presupposed in his way of doing philosophy, but frankly given a new lease of life in his religious independence, that is, without any recourse to symbolic flights of fancy. This faith must only – and this is actually a self-evident procedure as far as modern educated people are concerned – be translated into contemporary language and interpreted in philosophical terms. This is why Christ must be caught up into absolute knowing.

It is entirely in order to ponder this reply further in a philosophical context, but a theological perspective requires us to delve behind it by posing yet another question. Has Christ – and, along with him, Christianity – really been merely caught up in this absolute knowing? Does not Christ much rather appear to have been incarcerated here in the dialectically woven hunter's net of an imposing speculative science? Is not this speculative mode of knowing, insofar as it interprets the 'pictorial' antithesis of religion on the basis of an absolute identity, an attempt to penetrate behind the mystery of Christ and lift the veil, an endeavour which perhaps only succeeds in discovering man's own face?

But it is easy for the theological critic to make things too simple for himself here. It would never have occurred to the Hegel of the *Phenomenology,* as it did to many an enterprising practitioner of Enlightenment thought, to incarcerate Christ within a system of *human* knowledge. Hegel's brilliant solution consists in Christ's being caught up into *divine*-human knowing. As far as Hegel is concerned, speculation is more than something merely rational and intellectual. Human reason is more than human reason. On the lofty heights of speculation man knows about himself because he knows about the Absolute, and *vice versa*. For this reason he basically – *in potentia* – knows about everything. Purified from all empirical knowledge acquired through the senses and from all abstract knowledge gained through the understanding, unshakably trusting in what is his best and most his own, that is, in his reason, in which thought and being are one, man shares in absolute knowing, and not only in the sense of a *participatio*. On the contrary, in his knowing he has, by externalising himself, put himself at one with divine knowing: with the divine knowing which is itself the divine universal method, the method through which all that exists in heaven and on earth, in the heart of men and in the heart of world history, is encompassed and understood. Ought it not thus to be both possible and necessary for man's philosophy to be the true and highest kind of theology, where man speaks of God by letting God speak through man about man? Man's speech becomes God's speech, and the science of God becomes the science of man. Ought not Christ to be sublated in the best possible sense in this divine-human knowing? It has by now become abundantly clear that Hegel had no intention of denying the Christ-event. On the contrary, in an act of unprecedented boldness he established himself in the mystery itself in order to make the Christ-event unassailable by unbelieving denial. From this position, which is truly the centre of rational reality, the philosopher knowingly examines God, man and the God-man. From this position he assumes Christ and, with him, humankind as a whole into his science. Is it not the case that the one who gives himself over to divine knowing with the utmost confidence in God both can, may and must, with the utmost self-cofidence, speak *knowingly* of Christ?[28]

We shall not do justice to Hegel if we forget that he is essentially arguing in terms of a different, transformed and deepened modern concept of God. And we shall scarcely make any headway against him by simplistically invoking the God of the Bible, at any rate so long as we neglect to take into account the great indebtedness of the Bible's picture of God to a particular world-picture. Hegel was disposed to treat the Copernican Revolution (in physics that of Copernicus, in thought that of Kant) with radical seriousness. He was a thoroughly modern thinker insofar as he had finally parted company with a picture of God belonging to a bygone age. He left behind the naive and anthropomorphic picture of a God who in a literal or spatial sense dwells

---

[28]cf. K. Barth: *Protestant Theology in the Nineteenth Century*, 417-421.

'above' the world, but with whom we nevertheless have permanent contact. And he also decisively rejected the enlightened and deistic picture of a God who in a spiritual or metaphysical sense exists 'outside' the world in an extra-terrestrial beyond (architect of the world, clockmaker God), a God without whom practical day-to-day life runs perfectly smoothly. As opposed to these two pictures of God, Hegel's exclusive concern – coming, as he did, after Spinoza, Lessing and Goethe – was with the God who exists *in* the world. We have already seen that this had nothing to do with atheism. Nor did it, despite his overwhelming concentration on the one world, have anything to do with naturalism. Like so many poets and thinkers at that time, Hegel certainly felt himself to have been freed from the earlier sense of anxiety in the world and from the ancient horror of the world, so that he could actually trust the world, making it the object of his piety and even of his passion. The earlier feeling of mistrust toward nature had been displaced by a feeling of confidence in nature. Moreover, folk did not simply focus their attention on living crea-tures, but rather understood nature in its totality as something living, inter-connected and inter-related, even spiritual. Indeed, the religious instinct was not assuaged until the depths of the earthly world had received a divine character.

Nevertheless, something much more decisive was at stake for Hegel in all this, namely that God himself should be taken for what he is, that he should not be limited as in the earlier pictures of a supra-terrestrial or extra-terrestrial God. This is why he wished to term God 'the Absolute' or 'absolute Spirit', expressions which indicate that God holds aloof from all limiting definitions. This is why he did not wish to have God understood as a 'Supreme Being': even though conceived as above, outside and beyond this world, a 'Supreme Being' would still exist alongside and over against this world, so that God would ultimately remain merely a part of reality as a whole, a finite thing alongside finite things. This is why he wished to understand God as the Infinite *in* the finite, as the ultimate reality in the heart of things, in world history. Hegel's specific cognitive attitude and cognitive piety must therefore, as J. Flügge has well established in his book,[29] be seen precisely in this struggle against the self-assertion of the finite. The finite ought not to be clung to, nor ought it to cling to itself; rather, it ought to be sublated in the Infinite. He had only recently expressed these thoughts in Jena: 'the concern to put God once again absolutely at the very apex of philosopy as the sole ground of all things, as the sole *principium essendi* and *cognoscendi*. For long enough he has been put alongside or even after other finite realities as a postulate proceeding from

---

[29] *Die sittlichen Grundlagen des Denkens.*

229

an absolute finitude' (I, 149). God is accordingly thought of as the inexhaustible 'ground of all being', as the one who exists both in the here-and-now and in
the beyond, as transcendence in immanence!

In the face of such earnestness and intellectual exertion as this,
theologians should refrain from invoking the Bible in order to reiterate their
reservations on the basis of a pre-Copernican conception of a supra-terrestrial
or exta-terrestrial God. The task that faces us with respect to the concept of
God (and perhaps we can do no more than sketch its contours within the
compass of this book) is much more complex. We must both act as modern
men and women, accompanying Hegel and thinking along with him, and at
the same time reflect the biblical picture of God – just as it has always been
reflected in the history of the Church – in order to translate it without loss
from the world-picture of yesteryear into the world-picture of today. Or
should the God of Abraham, Isaac and Jacob, the God of Jesus Christ, finally
be beaten into silence by the God of the philosophers? We wish to attempt
further clarification of the problems involved here.

Hegel was right to progress beyond the alternatives of atheism and theism
(the latter being understood here in the specific sense of advocating a
supra- or extra-terrestrial God), and hence also beyond the alternative
between a dualistic supranaturalism and a monistic naturalism. He was
chiefly concerned no longer to make God into a specific object as a being
above or outside the world – that is, no longer to define him in terms of the
subject-object scheme of the world of time and space. God as the union of
union and non-union, as the union of synthesis and antithesis, as the identity
of identity and non-identity, as a combination of in-itself, for-itself and in-
and-for-itself – all of this is anything but an affected speculative jargon for
initiates. On the contrary, it represents the utmost conceptual exertion to
make clear just what is this identity of subject and object within absolute
Spirit, which has been perfected through an immanent outward movement.

Hegel could also use the single word 'Spirit' to denote this modern
rewording of the concept of God and the victory over the spatial and spiritual
subject-object scheme. As a result of a change which he had observed in Jena,
he understood this Spirit as reason enganged in cognition. In reason's act of
cognition it is crystal-clear that the subject-object scheme has been overcome:
in the one who knows subject and object *are* really one. In this respect
'Spirit' – 'the most sublime Notion' – in fact proved a more profound description for God than 'Love'. And in this respect the *Phenomenology* of 'Spirit'
did actually become a grand dialectic of cognition, to which love is completely
subordinated and attuned. The very name 'philosophy' (*love* of wisdom) is no
longer to Hegel's taste, and he openly explains in the Preface to the *Phenomenology* that '[t]o help bring philosophy closer to the form of Science, to the

goal where it can lay aside the title "*love* of knowing" and be *actual* knowing – that is what I have set myself to do' (*PS*, 3).

By taking this path Hegel brought his though to a condition of unparalleled differentiated unification – still more, a unity of reality itself, of the finite and the infinite, of God and the world, of the subject and the object. For a long time Hegel fascinated and blinded his contemporaries with this differentiated identity that had been forged in the matrix of the identity-producing dialectic of knowledge. In this novel experience of reality he had himself already been fascinated and blinded by the dazzling light of this knowledge. To criticise Hegel while at the same time to do justice to him has always been a notoriously difficult task. After all, to do justice to him would necessarily involve adopting his own speculative standpoint, and would it still be possible to subject him to a thoroughgoing critique from this perspective? Critics fancy that they can hear Hegel's counter-questioning reply to each objection: Have I not already said and considered this myself? The root difficulty of every critique of Hegel stems from the fact that we can find much that we wish to find in his system – along with its very opposite. This state of affairs is a direct result of the all-encompassing sublation of all manner of antitheses in Hegel's absolute Spirit. It is therefore more appropriate to charge Hegel with onesidedness than with negation in his account of certain sides of reality.

Notwithstanding these factors, however, contemporary Hegel critics (whether philosophers or theologians, Marxists or Christians) display a certain negative agreement among themselves on the subject of Hegel's speculative identity of finite and infinite. For many today that proclamation of identity seems to have been a beautiful idealistic dream, which has been shown to be mere froth in the face of Kierkegaard's counter-dialectic of the human existence of the individual on the one hand, and of Marx's confrontation with the unchanged and unreconciled reality of society on the other.

E. Bloch observes on absolute knowing and on the idealist sublation of the object: 'Already here it becomes clear that all of this appears only in the contemplative mind, for which reason it need detain us no further. Unmitigated disaster may be piling up outside, but the Spirit that is sure of itself is not longer affected. A new world may be coming on the scene outside, but the memory of absolute knowing already has everything behind and in itself . . . And it was this insubstantial ending of the *Phenomenology* which caused the theme of its subject-object relationship – i.e. self-knowledge for the purpose of self-control, hence objectification of the essential element – to dissolve Narcissus-like in the vapour of Spirit.'[30] And Bloch quotes K. Marx: 'Hence any reappropriation of the alienated objective essence appears as an incorporation into the self-consciousness; the man who takes possession of his essence

---

[30]*Subjekt – Objekt*, 99, 101.

231

is only the self-consciousness that takes possession of objective essence; hence that objects' return into the self is the reappropriation of the object.'[31] Thus the sublation of alienation (i.e. of the process, characteristic of the capitalist world, whereby man and his work become a commodity) takes place purely in philosophical theory and not in practice.

But these objections do not, after all, deal a death blow to Hegel's dialectic, as Marx thought, or to his grand idea of a unity between the finite and the infinite. For all its brilliant fresh insight, Marx's analysis was too short-circuited and above all too superficial to have this effect. Hegel himself would not have hesitated to regard Marx as a lapse to a stage of knowledge which he had already overcome. He would have found Marx's uncritical and matter-of-fact adoption of Feuerbach's atheism particularly objectionable (the limitations of collective work are shown up in the characteristic division of labour). As opposed to Marx's one-dimensionality, which conspicuously fails to do justice to man, Hegel's many-levelled dialectic of the finite and the infinite has so much to be said for it that neither the whole range of socio-economic change nor the illuminating news that it is but the opium of the consciousness has been able in reality to abolish or extirpate it. We have the impression now more than ever that Marxism's 'God is dead'[32] is turning out to be a 'God is not entirely dead',[33] because the 'new' man himself seems to be less alive than ever, notwithstanding all Marxist prophecies to the contrary.

But whatever may be the case with respect to Marxism, there is no getting away from the charge brought by Christian critics that Hegel was guilty of one-sidedly over-emphasising the identity of subject and object and of finite and infinite. And it is significant that even Hegel's skilfull interpreter and apologist, R. Kroner, joins such critics as Przywara, Litt, Iljin, Niel, Möller, Coreth, Ogiermann, Henrici and others in making this point: 'Philosophy misunderstands itself when it ranks its own reflective work of reconciliation above that achieved by religion, when it fancies that it has finally reconciled consciousness by its own efforts. As reflection, philosophy grasps something quite different, namely the impossibility, indeed the absurdity, of a state of absolute reconciliation. Philosophy misunderstands itself when it fancies itself to have accomplished absolute reconciliation by thinking the total *self-realisation* of Spirit as its step-by-step, progressive *self-comprehension...*'[34]

In the end of the day criticism of this sort will always in some way boil down

---

[31] *op. cit.*, 101
[32] cf. R. Garaudy: *Dieu est mort.*
[33] cf. V. Gardavsky: *Gott ist nicht ganz tot* (ET *God is Not Yet Dead*).
[34] *Die Selbstverwirklichung des Geistes*, 224; cf. 222. And cf. the critical remarks in K. Nadler: *Der dialektische Widerspruch in Hegels Philosophie*, 130-143, a work which quotes Kroner.

to the position which J. Möller has formulated with great clarity: 'Thus, in spite of everything, sublation in absolute Spirit remains but a demand and an assertion. As a matter of fact, in Hegel's system all-encompassing reconciliation is always merely intended, never actually achieved and accomplished; for we human persons remain finite. The determinative questions of Hegel's philosophy were finitude and infinity, faith and knowledge, God and man. His solution to them has proved unable to hold its ground, but the questions remain. To have opened up the latter in their enormous depth is Hegel's abiding merit.'[35]

In the same book J. Möller has clearly delineated the valid element in Hegel's basic solution.[36] According to Möller, Hegel was right when he took as his starting-point – as, in the last analysis, every philosophy does – an 'unproven' but not arbitrary presupposition. He was right to suppose that the individual entity, as it encounters us in finitude, can neither endure nor be understood in terms of itself alone, and to suppose that even the summation of these individual entities would offer no further metaphysical explanation, but that only absolute Spirit can give an absolute explanation. The finite must therefore be understood in terms of the infinite, and in the process it must not be simply placed alongside the infinite. The infinite absolute Spirit must rather somehow manage to include the finite within itself, so that the finite does not, in its own 'ab-soluteness', impose a limit on the single Absolute. The relation of absolute Spirit to the finite consequently involves identity as well as difference. It does not, however, follow from this that absolute Spirit is the identity of identity and non-identity in the sense of the fatefully necessary self-differentiation and self-sublation that takes place in and through the finite. An identity which incorporated the finite in *this* way would remain a pure demand and would ultimately come to grief against the indestructable facticity of the finite and against the logical corollary of this fact, namely the irreducible difference between finite and infinite being. In the fulness of its infinitude, absolute Spirit is the simple and immediate unity of being. It comprehends, envelops and shelters all that exists 'sublatingly' within itself, but it does so in such a way that, as the primal ground of being which is equal to itself and knows itself, it carries all that is within itself, recognising it as a possibility which is identical with its simple essence and explaining and preserving it in its whole being out of divine perfection and creative freedom.

In a sensitive critique of Hegel's *Philosophy of Religion* B. Welte speaks in like manner of a 'participative identity'[37] of finite with absolute Spirit. Welte proceeds from a metaphysic of knowledge and begins by demonstrating both the meaning and the limitations of the statement (which is *decisive* for Hegel's conception of absolute Spirit) that *thinking is identical with being*.

a) The good *meaning* of Hegel's equation consists in the *ontological* identity of thinking and being which is given in thinking. This identity sets forth the universal

---

[35] *Der Geist und das Absolute*, 155f.

[36] *op. cit.*, 189-204; cf. *idem: 'Thomistische Analogie und Hegelsche Dialektik', ThQ* 137, esp. 148-159.

[37] '*Hegels Begriff der Religion – sein Sinn und seine Grenze*', *Scholastik* 27, 221.

Spirit-relatedness and spiritual nature (*intelligibilitas*) of being and elevates being into the realm of truth: 'I become . . . the other *quodammodo* thinking (but also: willing, loving etc.), this other is the substance and reality of my thought, which in its turn is the reality of my being.'[38] In onto-logical identity, therefore, what is agrees with its Logos in thinking.

b)The *limitation* is supplied by a factor which Hegel did not omit, but which he did not sufficiently develop, namely the *ontic* identity – which cannot be destroyed by thinking – of both the thinker and the object with itself. While ontic is included in ontological identity, it must at the same time be simply accepted and presupposed as something posited. Now in its *first* origin being is Spirit, but as far as *our* spirit is concerned, being (albeit Spirit-related being) takes precedence over its thinking Hence the plane of thinking must again and again be traced back to the prior plane which explains and supports it, namely the plane of being (of both the thinker and what is thought): 'I *never* become the other *in the same way,* in the same ontological mode, just as I do not *become* but rather *am* myself. And yet the object, which I think and which is my thought in virtue of the fact that I think it, is not identical with my thought *in the same way* as it is identical *with itself.*'[39] Now Hegel was not simply wrong to develop his whole philosophy from the ontological plane; but, since he did not adequately carry through the difference between ontological and ontic identity, he remains profoundly ambiguous: 'Hegel leaves open the possibility of his development being understood not only in ontological but also in ontic terms, and where the latter occurs his grand view of things becomes, to speak with Kierkegaard, warped and wretched and pathetic. For it is warped and wretched and pathetic if I, as this individual existent being who I happen to be, should say that I am ontically the other, the object, the We, the state, the epoch. All of this can, however, be correct, if it is understood ontologically in the appropriate way. At the same time it remains possible to misunderstand Hegel as teaching that, on account of the principle of the identity of thinking and being, everything should be understood as existing *solely* in the consciousness, as *mere* thought, so that the posited ontic reality of what is would be simply obliterated.'[40]

Armed with these thoughts, Welte maintains that we can mark out philosophically the meaning and limitations of Hegel's *concept of religion*:

a) Its good *meaning* consists in a factor which Hegel was right to emphasise, namely the *ontological infinity* of man as a spiritual being. As a thinking and willing spiritual being, man cannot be satisfied by any of his finite objects; in his thinking and in his willing he constantly exceeds any limit by holding himself open to further possibilities, so that he is himself an infinite striving which reaches beyond everything finite. In this infinite striving man is one with the absolute and divine ground of all that is true and good, which dwells within him: 'What on such a view of things appears as an infinite element, also appears at the same time as an *absolute* and *eternal* element in the inmost essence of man. For in his *thinking* man only attains himself, his own essence as a thinking agent, when he attains the *absolute* ground of truth, in which *all* possible questions come to maturity and which is itself beyond the range of the problematical. And in its *willing* human spirituality is never congruent with itself, except in that which

---

[38]*art.cit.*, 214.
[39]*art.cit.*, 214f.
[40]*art.cit.*, 215.

is *eternal* and *absolute* and in every respect good. Under all other circumstances human willing finds itself separated and split off from the reality of the truth of its essence and is in *this* sense not identical with itself. The plane of identity which emerges here shows itself as a modification of the ontological plane, and to the extent that it is the identity of a striving agent with that for which it strives it may be called intentional identity. But to the extent that it signifies the reflective accomplishment of the reality characteristic of self-possessing and self-enacting Spirit, it may be called reflective or existential identity.'[41] In this sense, therefore, religion always involves relation to oneself and the unification of the spiritual consciousness, the 'restless heart'. It must thus be urged against any deistic interpretation of religion that the 'spiritual nature of human spirit is attributable to the fact that the divine mystery is an inner element of its vital reality. For this reason religion must never be defined as a merely external and accidental relation, in which man would be related to a mere other'.[42] We can speak here of a participative identity.

b) The *limitations* of Hegel's concept of religion, of which he himself was not sufficiently mindful, stem from the *ontic finitude* of man even as a spiritual being. As one who thinks and wills, man always remains this finite individual in the indestructible reality of the ontic. The concomitant ontic identity of the individual ego with itself exists in indestructible difference over against all higher modes of identity. In ontic terms the ego never becomes anything different for this finite being, however much it is ontologically one with the infinite. Again Hegel did not adequately discuss this range of issues: '. . . however much it expresses an essential truth, we are obliged to observe in Hegel's definition of religion an intensified form of that ambiguity which was already discernible in his basic starting-point. Since Hegel does not distinguish in a wholly appropriate manner between the various spheres of identity and therefore does not precisely define their relationship to each other, so that this relationship remains indeterminate, it is possible to give completely different interpretations of his formula of identity, in which he expresses the essence of religion. On the one hand, it can be misunderstood as a *pure ontic identity,* according to which divine and human Spirit in religion would be simply the same. Or else the formula can be taken for the expression of a *mere logical identity,* according to which religion would only be in relationship of man to a mere human thought, which would not need to lead beyond the thinking being of man.'[43]

These critical comments are highly relevant to the question of God, for they make it clear that the most effective way of pondering more deeply on the issues raised by Hegel will involve extending rather than jettisoning his dialectic of knowledge. W. Kern's approach[44] (which, while substantially related ·to the comments cited above, is nevertheless slanted differently) might prove particularly fruitful in a theological perspective. Now Kern

---

[41]*art.cit.,* 220.
[42]*art.cit.,* 221.
[43]*art.cit.,* 222f.
[44]*Das Verhältnis von Erkenntnis und Liebe als philsophisches Grundproblem bei Hegel und Thomas von Aquin', Scholastik* 34. On the central significance of love for the genesis of Hegel's philosophy cf. also V. Rüfner.

demands that Hegel's dialectic of knowledge be extended by a dialectic of love, and it is important to note that he issues this demand in the name of Hegel himself, that is to say, of the young Hegel who, as we have seen, manifested an original spiritual experience of love: of the love which unites without dominating or being dominated, which permits the self-assertion of the other, willing and affirming the other in his otherness. There is a danger that this dialectic of love might be upstaged by an identification of love with life as a whole, in which the individual would be increasingly reduced to a modification of a whole made up to begin with of life and love and then of Spirit as knowing reason. This is precisely what befell the thought of the Jena Hegel, which had been prepared in Frankfurt. Now if this danger is averted, that is, if the dialectic of love is tenaciously upheld, then a genuine identity of subject and object might be achieved. We must concede to Hegel that everything undoubtedly *can* be sublated in thinking, to the extent that everything can be known. But insofar as Hegel himself can occupy a higher level of reflection to reflect and speak *about* thinking and *about* absolute knowing, then the speculative standpoint is in fact even for him no longer the unsurpassable perfect circle. And we must also concede that in his dialectic of knowledge Hegel achieves the identity of subject and object insofar as the object is realised in the subject, the other in the self. Even so – and here an extension is necessary – such an identification remains one-sided, for it must also be executed in the other direction. And since, even according to Hegel, this identification cannot be accomplished half-way in a non-existent in-between, the subject must simultaneously be realised in the object, the self in the other. And this is precisely what takes place in love (in willing, in freedom), which, as Hegel was taught by his Frankfurt experience, represents, along with knowledge, a basic mode of the subject-object identity of Spirit. Since *The Difference between Fichte's and Schelling's Systems of Philosophy* Hegel had understood and expressed this experience of the unity of the self with the other as an identity of subject and object, and this identity of subject and object dominates and pervades his entire system. Now to demand from the standpoint of the young Hegel that the dialectic of knowledge be extended by the dialectic of love is not to subject Hegel's thought to extrinsic criticism. On the conrary, it would be tantamount to joining in the subject-object consummation of Spirit as such, while at the same time freeing it from its cognitive one-sidedness and inner curtailment. By issuing this demand we should help to emphasise love and freedom, to bring into play the existential and volitional moment along with the intellectual and cognitive moment.

W. Kern explains this as follows: 'A dialectic of *mere knowledge* cannot *recognise aright* the being of the other, nor can it even acknowledge the actuality and value of its own self-being. On account of its onesidedly cognitive basic structure Hegel's dialectic is restricted to a merely formal knowledge of essence . . . But there is in fact no *merely* cognitive, conceptually couched, object-like relation to such "objects" as being, actuality. person. will, love and freedom . . . Those who do not consummate love within themselves do not know what love is . . . If the You of the other person were not (also) consummated in itself, but (only) in something other, for example, in the I-subject, then the other person would become a means, a utility; at all events its *proprium* would elude me. Precisely all knowledge of being – which is the very source of all philosophising – presupposes in the knowing agent a fundamental and radical openness and readiness for the letting-be of what is and, from first to last, of being in general. This attitude is basically one of intentional surrender to the being-itself which receives, supports and anticipates the subject, and, so long as the freedom of the knowing agent does not turn into guilt, it ripens into free loving devotion . . . To affirm in oneself the other thing and, supremely, the other person is exclusively a work of the will and of the purest and fullest form of the will, namely love.'[45]

Irrespective of whether it is achieved in this or in some other way, an enhanced version of Hegel's dialectic would have spectacular consequences for the concept of God. While it would take too long to draw out all the implications of such a development, it is fitting to point briefly to just one result: in the best sense of the word, a *post-Hegelian concept of God* would appear on the horizon. Such a concept of God, which would be decisively important for a more solidly based Christology, would be post-Hegelian in a twofold sense. First, there would be no going back behind Hegel to a naive anthropomorphic or even enlightened deistic picture of God on the basis of a supra- or extra-terrestrial God deemed to exist alongside and over against this world and man. Against *biblicism's* appeal to the God of the Bible and against *traditionalism's* appeal to the God of the Christian tradition, we must stand by the post-Copernican modern insight: God in the *world,* transcendence in *immanence,* the beyond in the *here-and-now.* Secondly, we should have to go beyond Hegel to achieve a new conception of the *living* God. The dialectic of love creates fresh space for God's Godness, freedom and love and for all those factors which are onesidedly curtailed by a stunted dialectic of knowledge. Against *modernism's* appeal to the God of the (modern) philosophers it would thus be possible to express afresh the insight: *God* in the world, *transcendence* in immanence, the *beyond* in the here-and-now.

'So waiting, I have won from you the end: God's presence in each element'. These lines from Goethe form the motto of Martin Buber's significant book *I and Thou.* Buber formulates the dialectic of exclusiveness and inclusiveness in man's relation with God as follows: 'In the relation of God, unconditional exclusiveness and unconditional

---

[45] *art.cit.,* 423f, 427.

inclusiveness are one. For those who enter into the absolute relationship, nothing particular retains any importance – neither things nor beings, neither earth nor heaven – but everything is included in the relationship. For entering into the pure relationship does not involve ignoring everything but seeing everything in the You, not renouncing the world but placing it upon its proper ground. Looking away from the world is no help toward God; staring at the world is no help either; but whoever beholds the world in him stands in his presence. "World here, God there" – that is It-talk; and "God in the world" – that, too, is It-talk; but leaving out nothing, leaving nothing behind, to comprehend all – all the world – in comprehending the You, giving the world its due and truth, to have nothing besides God but to grasp everything in him, that is the perfect relationship. – One does not find God if one remains in the world; one does not find God if one leaves the world. Whoever goes forth to his You with his whole being and carries to it all the being of the world, finds him whom one cannot seek. Of course, God is "the wholly other"; but he is also the wholly same: the wholly present. Of course, he is the *mysterium tremendum* that appears and over-whelms; but he is also the mystery of the obvious that is closer to me than my own I. When you fathom the life of things and of conditionality, you reach the indissoluble; when you dispute the life of things and of conditionality, you wind up before the nothing; when you consecrate life you encounter the living God.'[46]

For those of us who no longer wish to fly in the face of the dominant world picture of modern physics by pressing the claims of a supranaturalist apologetic, a post-Hegelian concept of God would make possible a fresh statement of the meaning of the *Word* of God in the radically altered intellectual conditions of today. We are concerned here with the Word of God that speaks in the heart of our actual life, and we take the Word of God to be a proper characteristic of the *biblical* God. This approach would mean that the God of Abraham, Isaac and Jacob, who spoke through the prophets and with ultimate binding force through Jesus Christ, would not be brought to silence by the God of the philosophers. Nor would he be brought to speech by the God of the philosophers either. But in such an approach philosophy would help the believer to achieve a fresh *understanding* of the God of the Fathers commensurate with the conditions of a new age, to understand him as the one who he is, that is to say, as the God who is alive even today. This God would no longer be the God of the gaps whose aid is invoked where our human science can take us no further or where we can no longer cope with life, and who is becoming more and more intellectually dispensable, superfluous and unbelievable as man progresses. And this God would no longer be the Being which dispossesses man of what is most intimately his and makes him lazy (Feuerbach), no longer the opium which causes him to run away from reality and which prevents him from perceiving his social responsibility to change existing conditions (Marx), no longer the reflection of our bodily and mental

---

[46] *I and Thou*, tr. W. Kaufmann (Edinburgh, 1970), 127f.

fears and longings (Freud); that is, God would no longer be all of those things which make him seem not only emotionally and existentially dispensable but even harmful and pernicious to the human consciousness which has now attained maturity. On the contrary, God would be the one who in and through the conditioned reality of our life and of our common humanity proves himself to be the Unconditioned One, who is absolutely relevant to us as the depth and ultimate meaning of our life, who is infinitely removed from us and our superficial life, and yet who is closer to us than we are to ourselves; who sustains, supports and encompasses us as the origin, ground and goal of our being, and at the same time encounters us with a claim and a commission, demanding of us answer, responsibility and action.

Through the dialectic of love space would be created *within* the one reality not only for God to be himself but also for *man* to be himself, indeed for all those things to which Hegel's dialectic easily fails to do justice: for the importance of human willing, for freedom's power of decision, for the reality of sacrifice. That is, the dialectic of love would have this effect *if* man did not culpably fail in his task. This very real possibility is not fully taken into account in Hegel's dialectic. Moreover, the dialectic of love could clarify the nature of love in relation to God. What we are dealing with here is a love which, like all love, can only be genuinely perceived by one who himself loves; a love which cannot simply be known, but which wants to be dared; a love which presupposes that someone is trusted. And in relation to the one who is not seen, who is not tangibly present or immediately accessible in the world, a quite different confidence is expected from that which is placed in one who is seen. Although he is present, it is impossible to pin down the God who is both near and faraway. both immanent and transcendent, both in the here-and-now and in the beyond. A radical kind of confidence is called for here. We recall that 'trust' is the literal translation of the New Testament πιστεύειν, which, like its Hebrew and Latin equivalents, has to do with 'faithfulness' and is customarily translated as 'faith'. I can only love God when I rely on him, trust him, *believe* in him. The πίστις of God is matched by the πίστις of man: only those who trust God are assured of the faithfulness of God. To this extent love presupposes faith. And it is not simply a matter of verbal form but of underlying content when the German 'believing' (*glauben*) is found to be etymologically related to 'loving' (*lieben*) and to 'praising' (*loben*); as the factitive of the word *lieb* (fond), *glauben* has the root meaning of 'becoming fond of, familiar with something'. Hence ultimate unity with God can never simply be a question of pure knowledge, of reason, of knowing, of a branch of study which absorbs all else. The whole man in his unreduced totality is here challenged in his freedom – which is man's primordial risk – to let himself be given everything which is not simply at his disposal.

The above remarks do not, of course, imply that Hegel, with his brilliant combination of ancient intellectualism and modern evolutionism, was not striving resolutely and with exceptional intensity not only to amass items of knowledge, but attain knowledge itself, the *knowledge* of God. It is inappropriate to harbour a theological aversion to reason and rationality, knowledge, enlightenment and speculation. And Hegel was right to oppose theologians to his right and left with the decided opinion that Christianity is not a matter either of mechanically transmitted doctrines, dogmas and formulae or of irrational feelings and sentiments, but rather of a strict, full, divine *truth* which is to be grasped by laborious dialectic. As the historical self-penetration of Spirit, the *Phenomenology* does not intend (as does, for example, Schleiermacher's theory of hermeneutics) to overcome alienation toward tradition by reconstructing or restoring the pristine understanding of Christianity. Rather, clearly conscious of the impotence of all purely historical restoration, it aims to overcome this alienation by integration, by re-appropriating externalised Spirit, and thus by a mediation, in the sphere of thought, between the past and the life of the present. In this respect the *Phenomenology* represents a peerless discharge of the hermeneutical task as a question about *truth*.[47]

The New Testament itself is decisively concerned with truth, and in its pages Christ, to the extent that he stands for God, counts as 'the truth' (Jn. 14:6). Even for the New Testament there is such a thing as speculative knowledge. However, this 'seeing face to face' (*speculatio facie ad faciem*) is to be understood as a *videbimus,* and is thus reserved for the future. Only the *eschaton*, indeed only the God of the future himself, will cause me to understand God 'fully, even as I have been fully understood'. Only the God of the future – 'when the perfect comes' and 'the imperfect will pass away' – will, according to the New Testament, produce that 'identity' between finite and infinite which will not upstage love, but consummate it: a unity which could not be greater, because at that time God will not just be in all, but rather 'God will be *all* in all' (cf. I Cor. 13: 8-13; 15: 28).

Yet the way of this *eschaton* is not the observer's knowledge of speculative reason, but knowing faith and believing knowledge. Hegel has the New Testament behind him when he sets his face against the view that faith and knowledge are simply unreconcilable, although he overlooks in the process the decisive New Testament contrast between faith and unbelief. Paul frequently speaks of the believer's knowledge, and John largely equates faith and knowing: there is no difference between the two as far as their object is concerned. Faith can be understood as the precondition of knowing, in that

---

[47]H.-G. Gadamer: *Truth and Method,* 146-150.

knowledge grows out of faith as the first act involved in turning to Jesus. Conversely, knowing can also be understood as the precondition of faith, in that faith as an ongoing attitude grows out of knowing.

Precisely on account of this hermeneutical weaving together of faith and acquaintance, of believing and knowing, it is according to the New Testament incorrect to distinguish between faith and knowledge (acquaintance) as, so to say, the first and last stages of early Christian experience. Hegel was not the first to do this, for it was already attempted by the early Christian Gnostics, who derived from this distinction the notion that there are two classes of Christians, the simple believers (pistics) and those who believe and know in a philosophical way (gnostics). In contrast to *gnosis* old and new the New Testament holds that knowledge cannot soar beyond faith, that it cannot dialectically supersede faith. Now faith does, admittedly, come to itself in the act of knowing; and let it be reiterated that in this insight Hegel has the New Testament, especially John, behind him. At the same time, however, as far as early Christianity was concerned knowing remains an inalienable part of believing. The New Testament is not acquainted with any 'gnostic self-redemption of finitude', as Gadamer terms Hegel's sublation into absolute knowing.[48]

We return to the christological question with which this critical reflection began: Can Christ be sublated in speculative knowing, which is what Hegel did with him? This is hardly possible on the basis of the New Testament. Nor can the speculative Good Friday shed any light on the historical Good Friday. And there is no need to quote Nietzsche in order to remind oneself that knowledge of a speculative Good Friday can completely collapse before the reality of the historical Good Friday: without the resurrection we remain in unbelief. That God has acted in this Christ theology is wont to call a 'mystery': not because it is unclear and incomprehensible (precisely Hegel's interpretation reveals a deep meaning), but because it must be *spoken* (and constantly reiterated) to people. Apart from this medium of communication it is impossible to grasp how people could arrive at or remain committed to the heart of the Christian faith, which is not (like the faith of the Old Testament) simply a matter of interpreting the history of a people as God's saving act, but of tying salvation, ultimate and unsurpassable salvation, to this one man, who was judged by a secular court and ended as a complete failure by dying the death of a criminal. Faith in this one man is and remains, according to Paul, 'a stumbling block to Jews and folly to Gentiles' (I Cor. 1: 23). This faith cannot be speculatively transcended – after all, Paul is not concerned with the acceptance of a theoretical Christology – although it certainly can be practically realised: by our renouncing any pious claim on God, by undergoing the radical experience of receiving all that we are or have as his gift, by letting him make us fit to serve other people. In this respect the New Testament does not teach merely that those who *think* but rather that those who *do* the truth will know that is the truth (cf. Jn. 3: 21; 7: 17).

Hegel's intention was that the Christ who, according to the New Testament, is '*the* truth' (i.e. of God), should be sublated – positively, negatively and eminently – in absolute knowing. In the light of all that has been said above, there can be no doubt about this intention. Even so, it may be that all of this can be viewed from a quite different angle. Given that the truth revealed by the dying Christ both is *and* remains such a 'stumbling block' and such 'folly', and given Hegel's resolute intention to cleave to this truth, it is just possible that – although he programatically proclaimed the very opposite – in the sweat of his brow and in the last existential analysis he did, after all, practise his philosophy more on the basis of faith than on that of speculative knowing. Indeed, it is possible that he could proclaim his speculative knowledge so boldly only because (and here we should not forget Hegel's development) it was firmly sublated in a faith whose roots went deep into his existence. Hegel would not be the first to believe more than he knew.

At the close of this chapter on the *Phenomenology* and its speculative Christology we venture to express the hope that the reader has not been exhausted by the long and tortuous route. Let him be comforted with the thought that he already has a great deal under his belt. This remark refers not just to what lies behind the reader, but also to what lies before him. Thus the thirsty stretch may well be at an end. Moreover, in now going on to unfold Hegel's thought as it climbs, beyond the *Phenomenology,* to its systematic summit, we shall often be able to leave the detail of the texts to the reader's own interpretation without surrounding it with such a copious commentary as was called for by the *Phenomenology* itself.

Chapter Six: The System

'To raise doubts on the basis of formalities or details about whether this is an external reality is foolish and pitiable. What matters to faith is not what occurs *physically*, but what occurs *eternally. God's* history! (XXI, 293).

1. God Before the World

In the meantime Hegel had already moved to Bamberg, which at the beginning of the nineteenth century was an important publishing centre. He had striven without success to secure regular professorships in Heidelberg (XXVII, 83), Erlangen (XXVII, 89) and Berlin (XXVII, 107). His letter to Voss had likewise been in vain: 'Luther taught the Bible to speak German, and you have done the same for Homer ... should you wish to forget these two examples, then I wish to say concerning my efforts that it is my intention to teach philosophy to speak German. Having got thus far, it is infinitely more difficult to give platitudes the semblance of profound discourse' (XXVII, 99f; draft: Kaufmann, 314). Having in 1804 besought Goethe's assistance as 'the oldest of the unsalaried philosophy lecturers[1] here' (XXVII, 84f), Hegel earned in 1805 the distinction of being appointed extraordinary professor (XXVII, 93, 108f, 111, 113, 125, 141). Even so, conditions in Jena and at the university had become unpleasant in the extreme after the battle, as Hegel graphically related in his letters to his friend Niethammer (XXVII, 119 – 127; see Kaufmann, 316-7).

Hegel was therefore immensely relieved when Niethammer, who had now become head of the provincial administration in Bamberg, suggested that he take over the editorship of the *Bamberger Zeitung,* which had just fallen vacant (XXVII, 143f). 'The duties involved will interest me, since, as you yourself know, I follow world events with curiosity,' wrote Hegel in his reply to Niethammer (XXVII, 145). In this unforeseen way his socio-political bent had found a practical sphere of operation. He had never been either willing or able to disown the *homo politicus* who was lurking within the philosopher's

---

[1] *Privatdozent.*

breast, and he had always displayed a zealous concern for spreading his philosophy by journalistic means (by founding periodicals etc). Hegel was thus now in a position to put his theory to the test of practice. W. R. Beyer has drawn attention, albeit in excessively Marxist tones, to the political Hegel of the Bamberg years. And he may have been right to point to a secondary motive behind Hegel's departure from Jena which the philosopher's biographers have often concealed. For it is possible that Hegel feared unpleasant consequences for his continuing academic career in Jena on account of the birth of an illegitimate son, Ludwig, borne him by his housekeeper (who was later to bear a grudge against him on this score).[2] Not that Hegel intended to remain in Bamberg on a permanent basis: he was still thinking in terms of a chair at Heidelberg or at the new Protestant University which was just about to open its doors in Bavaria: 'I grow daily more convinced that theoretical work accomplishes more in the world than practical. If the realm of imagination is once revolutionised, reality cannot hold out for long' (XXVII, 253; Kaufmann, 323). Yet for all that, he now had a respectable salary: 'Experience has convinced me of the truth of the biblical saying and made it into my guiding star: Seek ye first food and clothing, and the kingdom of God shall be added unto you . . .', wrote Hegel to Knebel from Bamberg on 30 August 1807, evidencing a mixture of pleasure and dissatisfaction (XXVII, 186). From March of this year he accordingly styled himself 'editor', overseeing his newspaper in keeping with the prescribed allegiance to the government and party line. Any other editorial policy would have been frankly unthinkable in those days of the French Empire and the *Confederation of the Rhine* (1806 – 1813), nor was it such a great burden for Hegel given his enthusiasm for Napoleon, 'this extraordinary man . . . , whom it is impossible not to admire' (XXVII, 120). He toiled solidly and at the cost of some self-denial– after all, he had always had 'a proclivity for politics' (XXVII, 186). Even so his enthusiasm displayed an increasing tendency to wane. Not only censorship, but also journalistic superficiality and the speed involved in producing a daily newspaper were not to his taste. Hence he soon longed to be 'delivered from the yoke', from the 'penal servitude' of newspapers (XXVII, 239, 240): 'For every minute spent at my newspaper job is a loss and waste of life, for which God and yourself are obliged to render account to me and give me compensation,' he wrote to Niethammer (XXVII, 245). And when the latter was called to Munich as grammar school inspector, Hegel's plea was issued to him as it had been previously in Jena (XXVII, 113): Lord, remember me when thou comest into thy kingdom (XXVII, 204).

---

[2]W. R. Beyer: *Zwischen Phänomenologie und Logik*, 18; cf. the material collected by Hoffmeister and Flechsig in the volumes of correspondence XXIX, 433 – 435; XXX, 121 – 136, 213.

At last, in October 1808, he received the news from Niethammer, who was now engaged in reforming the Bavarian educational system, that he had been appointed headmaster of the Nuremberg Grammar School (XXVII, 249f; cf. 225). Hegel left Bamberg with great joy already in November, thenceforth to bear the joys and sorrows of a school master with resignation. The adolescents of those days were once again worse than their fathers had ever been, which could scarcely occasion any surprise in such unruly times. Headmaster Hegel won respect, however, both on account of his universal learning and because it was known that he had been a university professor.

Hegel taught the four upper forms mathematics, religious instruction and philosophy. Each year he had to give a speech when the school broke up for the holidays. Two of these addresses have been handed down to us, the last from the eventful year 1815. They deal with the meaning of a classical education, with the training of citizens for the state, with the grammar school curriculum, with the school and moral education and with the reform of the school system (cf. XXI, |297 – 373). He was able to acquire much pedagogical experience, not only in the sphere of practical education but also by way of reflection on the school reform then in progress. Especially informative on this score is his Nuremberg correspondence with Niethammer, who was the inspiration behind the Bavarian reform of studies (cf. XXVII, 269 – 430; XXVIII, 1 – 42). In addition to various reports to the Nuremberg and Munich school authorities (XXI, 377 – 414), these years saw Hegel draw up professional opinions on a variety of subjects: in 1810, on the position of places of learning which offered a modern as opposed to a classical education (*Realinstitute*); and in 1812 and 1816, on the mode of teaching philosophy at grammar schools and universities respectively (cf. XXI, 417 – 457)

'Humanism as profane religion'. With this catchphrase G. Schmidt describes the notion of humanism entertained by a Hegel who had to teach religion and philosophy at the same time.[3] As far as a genuine Protestant is concerned, universities and schools are just as important as churches: 'You yourself know best how highly Protestants esteem learned educational establishments; how the latter are as dear to them as churches and certainly of as much value. Protestantism does not so much consist in a particular confession as in a mentality propitious to reflection and higher, rational education; its mentality is not directed to utilitarian training with a view to this or that worthwhile goal' (to Niethammer; XXVII, 337). To assert that Hegel's was a 'profane' religion would nevertheless be misleading if we were to disregard the fact that as far as he was concerned religion in its perfect form is essentially Christian religion.

As a teacher of philosophy, Hegel had the opportunity of deepening his system afresh from an increasingly pedagogic point of view. It was certainly

---

[3] *Hegel in Nürnberg,* 44 – 46.

not entirely easy to initiate fifteen year-olds into the rudiments of 'science'. Hegel's instruction was decisively stamped by the need to offer something concise, distinct and easily understandable on the popular level (XXVII, 332, 390). Hegel dictated the important conceptual definitions and then explained them. His manuscripts were edited by Rosenkranz and Hoffmeister as the *Nürnberger Propädeutik* (hereafter referred to as the *Nuremberg Propaedeutics*). They represent a transitional work, falling between the *Jena Systems* and the *Phenomenology* on the one hand, and the *Logic* and *Encyclopaedia* on the other.[4]

In the lower form Hegel dealt with logic and practical philosophy (XXI, 51 – 62, 127 – 198); in the middle form likewise with logic, then with the theory of consciousness, of the Notion, and of religion (XXI, 11 – 50, 63 – 101, 103 – 119, 199 – 210, 211 – 233); and in the upper form with the theory of the Notion, with the theory of religion and with philosophical encyclopaedia (XXI, 103 – 119, 211 – 233, 235 – 294; on the syllabus cf. 3 – 10). Because Hegel could not expect his pupils to grasp the speculative logic which he had worked out during his time in Jena, he was forced to compromise by reviving the old formal logic in speculative terms (cf. XXVII, 389f, 397f, 428). The theory of consciousness, on the other hand, consists of a much amputated *Phenomenology of Spirit,* now reduced to the level of a subordinate partial system. All that remains of the *Phenomenology* are the stages consciousness – self-consciousness – reason, the sections on Spirit, religion and absolute knowledge having been left out. The theory of law and duty is seen in connection with the philosophy of the state.

The theory of religion contained in the *Nuremberg Propaedeutics* is to be understood as philosophical theory about religion. The most significant elements lurking within these pages are a discussion of the proofs of God's existence and a description of God as Being in everything, as absolute substance and as Notion and Spirit. Hegel presently comes to speak of Christianity here, above all in the course on philosophical encyclopaedia designed for the upper form (XXI, 291 – 294; cf. the more vague allusions 133, 197f).

The course for the lower form already contains a terse *Outline of the Theory of*

---

[4]The philosophical portions of the *Propaedeutics* were first published from Hegel's literary remains by K. Rosenkranz, the transcripts of his pupils being worked into this text alongside Hegel's own notes. We have made use of the textually improved and partially enlarged critical edition by J. Hoffmeister: *Nürnberger Schriften* (1938 = XXI). With reference to Hegel's sojourn in Nuremberg, cf. G. Schmidt: *Hegel in Nürnberg. Untersuchungen zum Problem der philosophischen Propädeutik;* F. Nicolin: '*Hegels propädeutische Logik für die Unterklasse des Gymnasiums',* in *Hegel-Studien* III, 9-38; cf. further secondary material of a pedagogical bent in the study edition of Hegel's *Works* ed. by K. Löwith and M. Riedel, vol. III, 361. A. Reble deals with about fifty titles in his bibliographical report on Hegel and educational science.

Religion (XXI, 196 – 198). After some remarks on the presence of absolute Being in our pure consciousness, on faith which must ripen into knowledge (the latter by no means thought of as superior to reason), and on the Notion of religion, *God* is described as '*the absolute Spirit*', who 'in his becoming other simply returns into himself and is identical with himself': 'According to the moments of his being, God is (1) absolutely *holy,* in that he is purely and simply intrinsically universal Being. He is (2) absolute *power,* in that he realises the universal and preserves the particular in the universal or is the eternal *creator of the universe.* He is (3) *wisdom,* in that his power is exclusively holy power, (4) *goodness,* in that he accords full scope to the reality of the individual and (5) *justice,* in that he eternally returns it to the universal' (XXI, 197).

Evil is 'alienation from God', namely the self-assertion of the individual and to this extent 'the nature of finite free being'. Even so, precisely as such it is at the same time 'intrinsically divine by nature'. This is the foundation of *grace* and *reconciliation*: 'This perception that human nature is not truly alien to divine nature assures man of divine *grace* and causes him to grasp the same. In this way the *reconciliation* of God with the world or the disappearance of its alienation from God takes place' (XXI, 197f).

Hegel's definition of 'worship' (*Gottesdienst*) is revealing: it is a 'certain preoccupation of mind and sentiment with God, whereby the individual strives to effect his unity with God and to give himself the consciousness and assurance of this unity. The agreement between his will and the divine will is meant to be proved by his disposition and behaviour in his real life' (XXI, 198).

The chief definition of religion is that it engenders man's unity with God and assures him of it. It consists essentially in love, and this religious love is not simply a natural loyalty, moralistic goodwill or hazy sentiment: it 'proves its mettle in the individual by absolute sacrifice. "Love one another, even as I have loved you"' (XXI, 292). Religious love is 'infinite power': 'Divine love *forgives sin,* and it makes *what has happened not to have happened* as far as Spirit is concerned . . . Love even goes beyond *ethical considerations*' (XXI, 292). It is therefore true to say that '[t]he substantial relationship of man to God is the forgiveness of sins. The basis of love is *the consciousness that God and his Being are love* and thus at the same time supreme humility' (XXI, 292).

The tenor of these utterances is extraordinarily reminiscent of Frankfurt, and the same holds good of the brief summary of Christology which now follows: 'The substantial relationship of man to God *seems* in its truth to lie in the *beyond,* but the love of God for man and of man for God sublates the separation of this world from what is conceived as a beyond and *constitutes eternal life.* This identity is *perceived in Christ.* As Son of man, he is Son of God. As far as the God-man is concerned, there is no beyond. His importance consists not in being this *individual* man, but in being universal man, the true man. The external must be distinguished from the religious aspect of his history. He went through reality, lowliness and ignominy; he died. His pain was the depth of unity of the divine and human natures in life and suffering. The *blessed gods* of the pagans were conceived as existing in a beyond; through Christ common reality, this *lowliness,* which is not contemptible, *is*

247

itself sanctified. His *resurrection* and *ascension* exist for faith alone: it was *in a vision* that Stephen saw him at the right hand of God. God's eternal life is this, return into himself' (XXI, 292f).

This quotation again makes it distinctly clear that Hegel was not concerned with the empirical historicity of Jesus as such, but with the history of God himself which took place in him and which is espied by faith: 'To raise doubts on the basis of formalities or details about whether this is an external reality is foolish and pitiable. What matters to faith is not what occurs *physically,* but what occurs *eternally. God's* history! (XXI, 293).

The Church is the locus where God's history is known, a history which is by no means contingent or arbitrary but rather rooted in the necessity of his being: 'The *reconciliation* of God with man – as *something which has taken place in and for itself,* not as a contingent reality or as an arbitrary action on God's part – is known in the *Church.* To know this is the *Holy Spirit* of the Church' (XXI, 293).

These Christian words certainly do not defuse the difficulties of the *Phenomenology,* nor are we at liberty to play down the momentous paragraph which immediately follows them. Hegel speaks here of the 'science' which embraces religion, which is 'the inclusive knowledge of absolute Spirit', where 'all alien being is sublated in knowledge' and the Notion 'has itself as its content and understands itself' (XXI, 294). At the same time it is also true that, though this work was not intended for publication, here in this theory of religion the *name* of Christ was once again explicitly mentioned after a long period of silence. And may we not suppose that many hearts were sincerely moved by the simple and profound words with which Hegel endeavoured to set the greatness and the depth of the Christ-event before his grammar school boys? During the school year 1815–6 Hegel took the upper form 'through the doctrine of the Christian faith according to the Athanasian Creed' (XXI, 9). What a pity that only this brief record of these lessons remains extant!

In the meantime Hegel was eager to leave Nuremberg, and not only because he was overburdened with administrative tasks, had a scanty salary and was forced to work in deficient classrooms (cf. the sustained and vehement complaints in the correspondence with Niethammer, XXVII, 269-430; XXVIII, 1-142, esp. 377, 382, 384, 392). Everything was drawing him to the university. Casting side-glances in the direction of Heidelberg (correspondence with Paulus, XXVII, 373–381) and even of Holland (correspondence with van Ghert, XXVII, 290-292, 297, 298-300), he was particularly hopeful of procuring a post in Erlangen (correspondence with Niethammer, e.g. XXVII, 337f etc.). So certain was he of a call thither that he got engaged in April 1811 to the high-ranking Nuremberg lady, Maria von Tucher: Herr von Tucher had made the marriage conditional on Hegel's being called to a university (XVII,

356-367). Already over forty and having almost fallen prey to confirmed bachelorhood, Hegel had finally fallen in love with a charming girl of twenty. This was a love which conferred on him a childlike happiness, so that he took to writing poetry again: 'To Marie' (XXVII, 352f, 355f; Kaufmann, 331f). At the same time, the letters between the betrothed couple (XXVII, 367-370; Kaufmann, 332–35) also show that this was a love which did not shun stirring discussions of the deeper problems of life. They also shed light on an otherwise usually hidden aspect of Hegel's life, namely a serious piety, a feature which likewise shines through his theory of religion. Marriage was for him more than just a question of happiness and peace, as he sought to explain to his young fiancée after a not entirely harmonious discussion on this subject: 'But what I have been saying to you for a long time is that the result which has become clear to me is that marriage is an essentially religious bond; that for its completion love needs something higher than what it is in and for itself alone. What it means to have perfect contentment and to be entirely happy, this can only be consummated by religion and the feeling of duty . . .' (XXVII, 367; Kaufmann, 333). Even so, this is a piety *sui generis* and bound up with an unconcealed aversion to certain forms of contemporary Christianity. Not only was Hegel's extreme fury unleashed by the 'no salvation outside . . .' attitude or, as he angrily put it, by the old Bavarian – reactionary – Catholic 'no salvation outside Munich bestiality' which none too fastidiously made things impossible for Protestants like Jacobi, Niethammer, Thiersch, Jacobs and Schelling (XXVII, 302-306, 495f; in this context he uttered the pious ejaculations 'God direct everything for the best', 'God grant . . .'; XXVII, 327). For he could not abide the official Protestant Church either. Rather that brand of Protestantism which 'does not so much consist in a particular confession as in a mentality propitious to reflection and higher, rational education; [whose] mentality is not directed to utilitarian training with a view to this or that worthwhile goal' (XXVII, 337; cf. XXVIII, 141). When it had been expected of him to give the customary traditional Protestant religious instruction on top of his philosophy course, he had already replied in Bamberg that he did not wish 'to be at once a whitewasher and a chimney-sweep, to take Viennese drinks and then drink Burgundy into the bargain. I, who for many years have nested on the free rock with the eagle and been accustomed to breathe the free mountain air, am now supposed to learn to gnaw from the corpses of dead or (of modern) stillborn ideas and to vegetate in the leaden air of empty chatter! For I would willingly lecture in theology at a university, and I should probably have done so after continuing to give philosophy lectures for a few years. But α) *enlightened* religious instruction, β) for schools γ) in Bamberg, δ) with the prospect of the claims which the Protestant Christian Church hereabouts would thus be in a position to make of me – all this is a contingency the very thought of which sends a shiver through all my nerves, as if the Christian Church were a charged galvanic battery, ϵ, ζ, η etc.! Lord, grant that this cup may pass away from me!' (XXVII, 196). What a remarkable statement about theology in this letter to Niethammer, who in Nuremberg became godfather to Hegel's son, Thomas Immanuel Christian. In a letter to his father on his baptism, Thomas Immanuel *Christian's* godfather expressed the hope that he would be 'a Christian not of weak but of strong spirit, as befits one who begins as Thomas! May he in his whole life share his godfather's heart-felt abhorrence for the weak-minded breed which makes an unholy racket about Christianity with cross, blood death, mortification and vicarious self-debasement' (XXVIII, 46; cf. Hegel himself, 45).

Hegel had thus departed from the custom of most modern philosophers from Bruno to Kant, with the exception of Fichte and Schelling, by getting married. And in contrast to Schelling he was very happy with his wife for the rest of his life. Two further sons, Karl and Immanuel, were born to him in Nuremberg (XXVIII, 9, 39), after his firt-born daughter had died aged only a few weeks old to his and his wife's great grief (XXVII, 414f, 424f). In the meantime Hegel was waiting for his chair with mounting impatience: 'Hope does not disappoint us, it says in the Bible. But I venture to add that it often lets us wait a long time. Easter is here yet again, and I am still in the same rut as previously .. !' (XXVII, 396). This was written in 1812, when the political situation was more unsettled than ever. Hegel had tied the marital knot before Napoleon marched into an empty Russia. And now Europe's lord and emperor had been toppled and sent into exile: 'Great things have happened around us. It is a dreadful spectacle to see an enormous genius destroy himself' (XXVIII, 28). Two months before Napoleon's abdication Fichte had died (27 January 1814), and Hegel was still a grammar school master in Nuremberg, now forty-five years old.

Yet absence from a university environment meant that he had time for a work which was to become the ripe fruit of those long years in Nuremberg: the *Science of Logic.*[5] Many a harassed scholar might find a crumb of comfort in the fact that this work too was published with undue haste. Hegel would rather have 'brought it before the public more complete in every respect' (cf.

---

[5]The text of the *Wissenschaft der Logik* used for this study was the unaltered 1951 reprint of G. Lasson's edition of 1934. Quotations from the *Logik* will be given in these pages, unless otherwise stated, from the ET by A. V. Miller, *Hegel's Science of Logic,* London, 1969. References will be given as *SL* followed by the relevant page number.

There is no large-scale, detailed commentary on the *Logic;* so cf. in addition to the general presentations of Hegel's philosophy (esp. those by K. Fischer, R. Kroner, N. Hartmann, E. Bloch and I. Iljin) and the works on the problems to do with the philosophy of religion mentioned at the

XXVII, 426): 'But, the injustices of the times![6] I am no academic. I would have needed another year to get it into proper shape, but I need money to live' (XXVII, 393). Thus the first volume was already published in two parts in 1812-13, while the second volume did not follow until 1816.

Where the *Phenomenology* stops, the *Logic* begins. Hegel himself explained the often discussed mutual relationship between the two in the Foreword and Introduction to the *Logic* (as he had already done in the Foreword to the *Phenomenology*). It may be that Pöggeler's definition of this relationship hits the nail on the head: '*Phenomenology* and *Logic* [represent] something like a tree with two trunks growing from one root.'[7] At the same time, however, we can emphasise the difference between the two writings by saying that while the path of the *Phenomenology* is experience's strenous uphill climb to the level of absolute knowledge, the *Logic* is the mountain path of absolute knowledge *qua* truth itself. The *Phenomenology* is a dialectical mastery of the strife between consciousness and object, between the act and the substance of thought, and between certainty and truth; the *Logic* is the dialectical development of the pure Notion, which leaves this strife behind. The *Phenomenology* considers conceptual definitions in the order in which they appear in the individual subject or in the universal Spirit, while the *Logic* considers them in their own right as pure essences in their relationship to pure knowledge. Even so, the *Phenomenology* and the *Logic* are not mere parts but rather moments of the one system; each in its own way contains the whole: the same content, first as forms of consciousness and secondly as forms of the Notion. The circle has no beginning.

Just like a mathematician who in forgetfulness of self plods on with the application of immanent rules from one operation to another, in this 'exposition of truth as it is without veil' (*SL*, 50) Hegel almost automatically

---

end of the Introduction (esp. those by J. Möller, E. Schmidt and J. Splett, the works of M. Clark, E. Coreth, J.N. Findlay, J. Hyppolite, H. Marcuse, J. van der Meulen, J. McTaggart, G.R.G. Mure, G. Noël and J. Wahl, R.E. Schult is highly informative on the various interpretations. T. Koch bases on the *Logic* an interpretation of Hegel's theology as difference and reconciliation. On more specialist questions cf. the works J. Kruithof and D. Henrich (on the starting-point of the *Logic*), G. Günther and P. Lorenzen (on the problem of formalisation), W. Schulz (absolute reflection), W. Bröker (formal, transcendental and speculative logic), U. Guzzoni (becoming of self as self-foundation and self-explanation of the Absolute), W. Albrecht (proof of God), J. Fleischmann (Objective and subjective logic) and W. Flach (negation, otherness, ultimate implications). The relationship of Hegel's *Logic* to other philosophies is dealt with by E. Coreth, J. Fleischmann, K. Hartmann, A. Redlich and R. Wiehl. Especially in Part One of his *Logique et religion chrétienne dans la philosophie de Hegel*, C. Bruaire offers not an historical but rather a freely speculative theological interpretation of Hegel's *Logic* in the light of his philosophy of religion.
[6]*iniuria temporum.*
[7]*Zur Deutung der Phänomenologie des Geistes*, 290-294; *idem: Die Komposition der Phänomenologie des Geistes*, 52.

follows the inner consequence of pure, veilless thought; so that what we have here is a trek in the thin, clear air of immaterial Notions, in which one's hearing and sight can, and is perhaps meant to, disappear. It is not entirely surprising that people like Schopenhauer, who had never managed to feel their way properly into Hegel's mental process, should feel unwell on this logical trek. Abusive remarks about 'besotted verbiage' and the like in no way undo the fact that this *Logic,* by way of contrast to customary essays in logic, is neither a matter of mere 'stuff' (i.e. divisions, definitions, cataloguings and juxtapositions; cf. *SL,* 54f, 58f) nor of mere 'words'(i.e. empty words, abstract 'Notions' and subjective 'categories'; e.g., *SL,* 38f. Hegel's concern is therefore not with 'these dead bones' of formal logic (*SL,* 53), but rather with a creatively real *onto-logic:* 'As science, truth is pure self-consciousness in its self-development and has the shape of the self, so that the absolute truth of being is the known Notion and the Notion as such is the absolute truth of being' (*SL,* 49). In his letter to Niethammer Hegel himself speaks of an 'ontological logic' (XXVII, 393). Hegel, the great empiricist, here joins not only Descartes and Leibniz (whose method was oriented toward mathematics) but also, Kant, Fichte and Schelling in thinking along strictly *a priori* lines. In doing so he develops not a shoestring logic of static classifications, but a logic centred on the *movement* of the Notion: in a gigantic effort he leads every category, starting with being and nothingness, into its antithesis, only to lead it back again into the antithesis of the antithesis, making the reader dizzy as he relativises all antitheses by constantly elevating them to richer precision and fulness. In the *Logic* the highly knowledgeable Hegel is concerned less than ever with the content of knowledge; rather, his interest focuses on the act of knowing, on apodictic cognition of coldly advancing logical necessity, which reason can peruse, examine and ponder without its needing to take on material form and which reason can even develop out of itself: self-movement of the rational 'content'. Even though we have to do with *universalia ante rem* here, we are not confronted (as is the case in the thought of Plato, Plotinus and Augustine) with a multitude of Ideas reposing in a state of immutable heavenly transcendence. On the contrary, we have here one and the same Idea which, amalgamating being and becoming, moves itself as Logos and forms itself into the Notion.

Hegel's *Logic* is therefore more than a general ontology, it is 'speculative theology'.[8] Its content is not a subjectively limited Logos existing as one or many, but rather the ideal-real Notion, which develops into concrete fulness

---

[8] K. Rosenkranz: *op. cit.,* 286; cf. T. Koch: *op. cit.,* 17: 'As "metaphysical theology" Hegel's *Logic* simply bristles with power for the hermeneutical task of disclosing what exists in nature and finite Spirit.'

through dialectical suffering, and which is not only universal substance but also creatively active subject and all-animating Spirit. The subject of this *Logic* is none other than the *divine* Logos, the absolute divine essence: 'and the logical process in question would in fact be the immediate exposition of God's self-determination to being' (*SL*, 707). Or, as Hegel proudly announces in the Introduction, in words reminiscent of the style of a manifesto: 'Accordingly, logic is to be understood as the system of pure reason, as the realm of pure thought. This realm is truth as it is without veil and in its own absolute nature. It can therefore be said that this content is the exposition of God as he is in his absolute essence before the creation of nature and a finite mind' (*SL*, 50). In this sense logic enjoys a logical – but not a temporal! – precedence over other branches of study (e.g., natural philosophy and the philosophy of mind) when it comes to describing what God is. It describes the first stage of God's one, infinite and timeless path in terms of the pure Notion and within the 'realm of pure thought' (*SL*, 50). It describes the path trodden by the divine Logos in an act of dialectically creative self-determination, increasingly improving itself as it passes through every organically related form of being, until it reaches its peak as the quintessence of all perfections and the absolute Idea. God infinitely perfect in the process of reason, in movement, in event; God unleashing all the contradictions of being in the acts of distinction, division and sublation, in thesis, antithesis and conclusion. On this basis the *Logic* appears as a real analytic and synthetic development of categories, with the one pure essence developing out of the others with organic necessity in an unbroken dialectical sequence: supplanting, preserving, enriching and concretising the other essences, starting from the emptiest form of pure being and going through all the intermediate stages of being to the full being of the absolute Idea. 'Hegel's *Logic* is onto-logy, just as the latter is at the same time theo-logy: onto-theo-logic . . .'[9]

The *Logic,* which is the most meticulously structured of all Hegel's works, cannot be summarised, and for our purposes a commentary is neither possible nor necessary. Even so, this 'unified, imposing and long-winded act', this 'unified, mysterious event', which according to Hegel is realised in the three phases of *Being* (*SL*, 67-385: determinateness – magnitude – measure), *Essence* (*SL*, 389-571: within itself – appearance – reality) and *Notion* (*SL*, 575-844: subjectivity – objectivity – idea), has been precisely described by I. Iljin: 'The *Logic* depicts the path of "Being", whose "quality" has found its "measure" in "quantity"; the "essence" of this "measured and determined Being" asserts its "reality" in its "appearance"; the "Notion" of this "essence of measured and determined Being as it appears in reality" has in its further self-determination as indefinite "universality" worked through to identity with "parti-

[9] K. Löwith: *Hegels Aufhebung der christlichen Religion,* 194.

253

cularity", subsequently struggling through the pain of judgments (*Ur-teile:* splitting into parts) to speculative "conclusion" and victoriously asserting its "organic-teleological" nature, in which "ideality" and "reality" are one. In this way the "Idea" has emerged as an identity of the "ideal" with the "real", for the "Idea" is real "life", which coincides with ideal "cognition", i.e. it is the living, all-embracing system of logical contents or the "Idea of the True". The living, real "truth", however, is nothing other than precisely the highest "Good" or the "Idea of the Good"; and the identity of these two Ideas merges into the crown of the entire process, the "absolute Idea".'[10] 'Hence the *Logic* is the first and the true self-revelation of God in the element of pure thought.'[11]

Should this whole process of the *Logic* strike us as terribly abstract – and Hegel did, after all, mean to it to remain on the level of pure thought – then let us recall that Lenin prescribed the study of the *Logic* as obligatory reading for every serious Marxist. In company with Lenin, both Marx and Engels had made a thorough study of the *Logic*. These men were captivated not only by dialectic in general, but also by the development of a whole series of serviceable categories which proved their great efficiency by giving a theoretical basis to revolutionary practice. One need only think of Hegel's explanations of the abrupt mutation of quantity into quality, of the tension between essence and appearance (and the accompanying critique of all façades), and of contingency and necessity in development. This work can obviously not be dismissed as a passé collection of the categories of capitalist society. For the *Logic* has proved itself as a key to practice, in this way manifesting its immense and enduring socio-political significance for subsequent generations.

2. Christ Sublated in Being

According to Hegel's divine logic, God lives in a progressive self-determination to being, in a development from seminal to fully real perfection. Even so, in the *Logic* as the world of shadows, this is visible only 'in pure thought', as '*truth as it is without veil and in its own absolute nature*', and in the lonely eternity '*before the creation of nature and a finite mind*' (*SL*, 50).

Our interest focusses on the *theological* aspect of the *Logic* and, in connection with this, on its *christological* aspect also. But the problem we have to face is formed by this very connection, for Hegel executed the whole development of the eternal divine modes of being from pure Being to the speculative concreteness of the absolute Idea without explicit or implicit mention of the name Jesus Christ in any of the intermediate stages. His

---

[10]*Die Philosophie Hegels als kontemplative Gotteslehre*, 206f.
[11]*op. cit.*, 209.

254

concern here would seem to be exclusively with *pure divinity*, with God as he is in himself. And what importance is Jesus meant to have with respect to this God? He will in fact be accorded his place in the dialectical development which follows in the train of the *Logic*. Hegel accordingly emphatically observes: 'Hence logic exhibits the self-movement of the absolute Idea only as the original *word*, which is an *outwardizing* or *utterance* [*Äusserung*], but an utterance that in being has immediately vanished again as something outer [*Äusseres*]: the Idea is, therefore, only in this self-determination of *apprehending itself*; it is in *pure thought,* in which difference is not yet *otherness,* but is and remains perfectly transparent to itself' (*SL,* 825). This statement calls for clarification:

1. It is clear from this important text on the 'absolute Idea' taken from the final chapter of the *Logic* that Hegel is here resorting to the classical distinction between the inward and the outward Logos (ἐνδιαθετος-προφορι-κός) which was used by the Greek Fathers to describe the incarnation of the divine Logos. As in the case of the Johannine Prologue and Greek patristic thought, so also in Hegel there is a confluence of two extremely ancient currents of tradition, a fact which proves that there is indeed a relationship between the Logos of Hegel's *Logic* and the Logos of the Bible. E. Bloch invokes many analogies in his comment on Hegel's definition of logic as an exposition of the divine essence as it was prior to the creation: 'There is a remarkable similarity between this statement and Goethe's remark on Bach's music, namely that it lets us hear how things looked in the bosom of God before the creation of the world. Thus in Goethe as in Hegel we are reminded of the maternal realm, that is, of the realm of the pre-worldly mobile-immobile thoughts of God or primordial Ideas in the sense of the Plotinian theory of categories *ante rem.* In the Christian world this was linked with the late biblical hypostasis of the "Wisdom of God" (Prov. 8:22), that *sophia* which existed before God created anything and which he is said to have had at the very beginning of his ways. Thus in Hegel's *Logic* there is a harmony between the Christian and the neo-Platonic Logos.'[12] The same author adds a critical observation from the perspective of his own thought: 'in the beginning was the Word and not the Deed, and the doctrine of the Word is purely and simply pre-existent ontology. All Platonists are tempted by this gigantic somersault from abstract *posterius* to abstract *prius,* and looked at in this light the logician Hegel is the last neo-Platonist of the theory of categories. Even so, notwithstanding these predecessors his *Logic* presents the most colossal and also the most monstrous theologisation which the *a priori* has

---

[12]*Subjekt – Objekt,* 161.

ever found: *in the dialectic of the pure Notions of reason man thinks the flowing thoughts of God before the creation of the world.*'[13]

We must rest content with a brief allusion to the various ways in which Hegel's '*divina logica*' is related to Plato (in that truth consists in the Logos's dialogue with himself), to Aristotle (in that truth is ultimately νόησις νοήσεως that is, self-thinking thought), to Kant (in that the definition of the transcendental subject is the chief condition of truth), and also to the Old Testament wisdom speculation (which, despite certain weighty differences, already stands under Greek-Hellenistic influence). Even so, Bloch's charge of neo-Platonism prompts an immediate riposte, for in fact Hegel's *Logic* displays no tendency toward the Platonic and neo-Platonic depreciation and devaluation of historical reality in favour of the eternal reality of the Ideas. On the contrary, no Notion (not even the very highest) is so solid as to be incapable of being melted; no abyss is so deep as to be insurmountable in a reversal; and no night is so black that bright day could not emerge from it. Precisely in the *Logic,* where Hegel's original intention is not yet obscured by the concessions involved in putting it into effect, this truth is better expressed than in any of his subsequent writings. In this eternal process of realisation, in which the divine Logos develops from the 'abstract universality' (*SL,* 827) and 'indeterminate immediacy' (*SL,* 81) of pure being via all the determinations and concretisations of being to 'fulfilled being', to 'the Notion that comprehends itself' (*SL,* 842), Hegel laid the foundation for a comprehensive reconciliation of all antitheses. Beyond every fissure and through every kind of alienation, Hegel upheld the primacy of the totality and of the whole over its finite, deficient and contradictory parts and moments: the primacy of synthesis as opposed to strife and devaluation. In this being, whence the movement of thought proceeds and whither it returns, *all* antitheses – even nothing, the antithesis of being itself – are actually sublated in both a negative and a positive sense. The one and the good are interchanged,[14] even to the extent of embracing nothing.[15] On this basis, everything eventually turns out for the best for the one who gets involved in movement. This idea undoubtedly picks up a highly Christian motif.

According to this view, which flies in the face of Platonic mistrust, in the deepest depths of being absolutely everything is good: day *and* night, heaven *and* earth, joy *and* pain, soul *and* body, man *and* woman, the humanities *and* the natural sciences . . . As far as such an all-embracing confidence in being is concerned, the *Logic* is the place

---

[13]*ibid.*
[14]*ens et bonum convertuntur.*
[15]*nihil.*

where the methodological and objective foundation was forged, even though Hegel's achievement here may well have stemmed more from unavowed faith than from proclaimed knowledge. With a high degree of probability we can detect in this achievement an after-effect of the Christian idea that God is the creator and Lord of *all* things, that he created both day *and* night, that he lets rain fall on both the good *and* the bad, and that he holds in his grasp history *in its entirety:* peace *and* war, good harvest *and* crop failure, health *and* sickness, plenty *and* hunger, life *and* death. There is deeper significance in Hegel's having been called the last of the scholastics than might be gleamed simply from the externally scholastic appearance of his system. F. Heer has provocatively drawn attention to the fact that, with his 'archaic confidence', Hegel as the last great thinker of old Europe stands in a great European tradition.[16] This archaic primordial confidence and consciousness of identity is manifested in popular proverbs, such as '*Deus impar gaudet*', '*Tutte le cose son buone*', 'Whatever is is right', '*Beeten scheev hot Got leev*', and 'God writes precisely on curved lines' (German). Having been silently lived, borne and endured by succeeding races and generations, Heer contends that this folk wisdom was elevated into philosophical consciousness by Aristotle against Plato, by Thomas against Augustine, and by Leibniz and Hegel (whose mediaeval predecessors were Eckhart, Anselm von Havelberg and Nicholas of Cusa) against Luther, Calvin, Jansen, Pascal, Kant (and, later, Kierkegaard). We thus have a struggle against the world-hostile dualism of Platonism, Gnosticism, Manichaeism, Protestantism and Jansenism. Yet this struggle is also directed against ascetic haters of self and pious inquisitors, against denouncers and fearmongers in the spheres of learning, politics and the Church, and against all liquidation of others (nation, group, party, confession, people, life). We therefore have an anti-Platonic defence of the lower and neglected element: of the 'evil' world and its wisdom, of 'hostile' nature, of 'bad' matter, finally also of motherhood (woman as the incomplete male,[17] the supposedly inferior estate of matrimony, sensual love), of the masses (the lower orders, chaotic democracy, the stupid layman), and of material things (the body derided as prison of the soul, the less decent parts,[18] eros and sex, manual labour).

All of this is obviously a schematisation and simplification of the material, for the various lines cross in a thousand places and precisely those thinkers to whom we have alluded by name are not simply opposite poles, but at the same time in their turn themselves meeting places for the diverse currents, alignments and attitudes. And, as we shall see, this is true of Hegel also. Now Hegel was by no means able unambiguously to see through to the end the trust in being whose rationale he had set forth in the *Logic*. In the course of his philosophical development, notwithstanding his great respect for Aristotle (indeed, just like the Stagirite himself!), he made ever more momentous concessions to the aristocrat Plato by devaluing the empirical-concrete, the material, the individual and the various forms of refuse deposited by the World Spirit. Even so, it ought never to be forgotten that the aim of Hegel's original intention, which was purely speculative, was not the disqualification and elimination of *aporiae* and antinomies, contradictions and oppositions, but the *encouragement* of multiplicity and of a fulness which transcends pluralism. Hegel stood here in a great tradition

---

[16] *Hegel,* 11.
[17] *mas occasionatus.*
[18] *partes minus decentes.*

essentially stamped by Christianity: acceptance of one, whole, untorn reality (*ens ut unum*), of its rationality and intelligibility (*ens ut verum*), and of its goodness and benevolence (*ens ut bonum*).

2. As an exposition of the divine Logos before the creation of the world, the *Logic* not only does not signify a Platonic devaluation of historical reality as opposed to the eternal reality of the immutable Ideas; rather, it frankly represents the historicisation of the eternal Logos himself. All that has been said hitherto has already made it clear that this Logos is unacquainted with a static existence: its essence is dynamism, evolution and dialectic.

H.-G. Gadamer's construction of a philosophical hermeneutic reaches its climax in a significant chapter on the ontological use of hermeneutics against the backcloth of language. He traces the minting of the concept of 'language' through the history of western thought with a view to contemplating afresh the unity of word and thing (*verbum* and *res*). Gadamer ascribes the fact that 'western thought's forgetfulness of language could not become complete' to 'the Christian idea of incarnation', which 'is no Greek idea'.[19] After the Greek Fathers had employed the Stoic conceptual antithesis of inner and outer Logos to interpret the incarnation, Augustine and scholasticism sought to acquire the conceptual means to elucidate the mystery of the Trinity by concentrating on the inner Word, on the word of the heart and its relationship to *intelligentia*. It was above all Thomas who systematically reconciled the Logos doctrine developed from the Johannine Prologue with Aristotelian thought. Using the neo-Platonic concept of *emanatio intellectualis,* Thomas was able to describe both the process character of the inner Word and the process inherent in the Trinity itself: 'It can thus be understood that the generation of the Word was understood as a genuine image of the Trinity. This is a matter of real *generatio* and birth, although there is of course no conceiving parent here alongside the one who begets. Precisely this intellectual character of the generation of the Word is, however, decisive for its function as a theological model. The process of the divine persons and the process of thought really have something in common.'[20]

Even so, Gadamer insistently draws attention not only to the correspondences but also to the differences that exist between divine Word and human word. The divine Word is endowed with such pure and perfect actuality that we cannot describe it as a genuine progressive process in the sense which is appropriate to the human word. The human word alone is a) 'potential before it is actualised'; b) 'imperfect by its very nature'; and c) 'a mere accident of the

---

[19] *Wahrheit und Methode,* 395 (ET *Truth and Method,* 378).
[20] *op. cit.,* 401; ET, 383f.

Spirit', so that it is characterised by 'imperfectability' and 'infinitude' in the progress of the spiritual process.[21]

There is no more cogent proof of the historicisation of the divine Logos in Hegel's *Logic* than the fact that the three characteristics highlighted by Gadamer apply here not only to the human word, but also to the divine Logos (some minor qualifications must, however, be made to this judgement, especially with regard to the third characteristic). After all, it is this *divine* Logos which undergoes a genuine process from potentiality to actuality, which is constantly in transition from incompleteness to greater completeness, and which, while not characterised by accidentality, is certainly marked by incompletability and infinite progression.

U. Guzzoni interprets the *Logic* as the Absolute's becoming itself in a unity of 'self-foundation' (*Sich-Gründen*) and 'self-explanation' (*Sich-Begründen*). The following paage, which involves a subtle word play on the nuances of *gründen* (found, establish), *begründen* (explain) and *Grund* (cause, reason), goes to the heart of the matter: 'Thinking has always been ascribed to God, but this thinking has invariably been conceived as infinitely remote from the finite human desire to know. Is not the self-thinking of Hegel's Absolute more closely related to Aristotle's θεός than to the vain thinking of men? Yet the truth of the matter is quite different . . . The self-thinking of the Absolute is (nevertheless) a thinking of itself *qua* cause [*ein sich als Grund denken*], and this means an act of explanation [*ein Begründen*]. As an act of explanation [*Begründen*] it retains the "finite" character of the desire to know, even though this finitude has the ring of infinity about it, given that the reality which here wills to know itself is none other than absolute knowledge . . . Now what stands at the beginning for the self-thinking of the Absolute is not only something unexplained [*ein Unbegründetes*], but this unexplained reality [*dieses Unbegründete*] is moreover uncaused [*ein Grundloses*], insofar as the cause [*Grund*] only establishes [*gründen*] itself as what it is meant to be by movement. Thus the thinking of the Absolute is still a path from not-knowing to knowing – all the more so, since the act of foundation [*Gründen*] which we are to picture to ourselves did not occur beforehand, but is only accomplished in the same act as that of explanation [*Begründen*]. Because the being of the Absolute is a self-foundation [*Sich-Gründen*], the thinking of the Absolute must be a self-explanation [*Sich-Begründen*]. The unexplainedness [*Unbegründetheit*] of its beginning – and this means its "finitude" – is now no longer the result of the limitations of human thinking, which has direct access only to what has been founded [*das Gegründete*], but it follows from the distinctive nature of the act of self-foundation [*Sich-Gründen*] itself, or, in other words, from the fact that the Absolute exists as movement, as becoming's movement to itself.'[22]

3. Is this divine Logos of Hegel's *Logic* the same as the Logos of St John's Gospel? Much of the foregoing might well point in this direction. As the original Word prior to the creation of the world the divine Logos of the *Logic* moves in an infinite circle which leads from being to being. Does not the *Logic*

---

[21] *ibid.* 401; ET, 384f.
[22] *Werden zu sich,* 10f.

THE INCARNATION OF GOD

richly and patiently unfold all the presuppositions which make a Logos in the flesh a possibility? Does not the latter – like everything that is – presuppose as a condition of its possibility that 'pure being' (*SL*, 82), which may not, however, be identified with God himself? How could any existent reality be conceived other than as a modification of this pure being, which stands at the beginningless beginning of the eternal Godhead? Consequently, does not the Logos become flesh presuppose, as a temporal-historical being, the entire eternal process of realisation in which the divine Logos develops from the 'abstract universality' (*SL*, 827) and 'indeterminate immediacy' (*SL*, 81) of pure being through all the determinations and concretisations of being to 'fulfilled being . . . , the Notion that comprehends itself' (*SL*, 842), to the Logos which has come to itself? Accordingly, is not the eternal Word in first place 'life' and true 'light' (Jn. 1) for itself, before it is these things for men and women: 'the absolute Idea alone is *being, imperishable life, self-knowing truth,* and is all truth' (*SL*, 824)? Is not the stage set with perfect timing for the *entrée* of the Logos become flesh – a prospect held out by Hegel at the end of the *Logic* – precisely when the absolute Idea or eternal Logos sets forth its being (*Dasein*) in nature, Spirit, art and religion and then gains its final self-understanding and confers on itself an appropriate mode of being (*Dasein*) in philosophy (*SL*, 824)?

At issue, then, is the problem of the *beginning.* 'In the beginning was the Logos', according to the first verse of St John's Gospel. In the beginning was the deed, according to other writers, in deliberate contrast. In the beginning was *Being,* according to Hegel's Logic.

It is striking that the *Great Logic* in its entirety has found no great commentator, and that no alternatives to Hegel's interpretation have been worked out in the case of the many difficult sections of the text. The opening section of the *Logic,* however, forms the significant exception to this rule.[23] A controversy began already in Hegel's lifetime and has endured to this day concerning the fact that the *Logic* opens with *being*: being which as indeterminate immediacy passes abruptly into nothing, so that as both being and nothing pass into each other they have their truth in becoming: as transition from being to nothing, decay; as transition from nothing to being, generation; as unity of being and nothing, existence (*Dasein*).

We can obviously not aim to settle the philosophical dispute between those who, like the Hegel critics A. Trendelenburg and E. von Hartmann, maintain that a progress of Notion from being into nothing or from nothing into being is impossible, and those who, on the other hand, like well-nigh all of Hegel's pupils and successors, surrendered

---

[23]On the problem of the opening section of the *Logic* cf. esp. the works of D. Henrich (here also the older literature), J. Kruithof (with a review of the most important recent Hegel interpretations), U. Guzzoni (*op. cit.*, 30-39, 52-66, 76-85), E. Coreth (*op. cit.*, 71-89, 118-135), K. H. Haag (*op. cit.*, 43-48), and T. Koch (*op. cit.*, 78-106). On the general problem of the starting-point of Hegel's philosophy see the recent work by K. Schrader-Klebert, and on the analogous problem of Schelling's starting-point cf. W. Kasper: *Das Absolute in der Geschichte,* 97-105.

the dialectic with which the *Logic* opens for the sake of the consistency of the system. Among the latter Rosenkranz, Ulrici and other Hegelians admittedly took being as their starting-point, but they denied that the *Logic* is properly speaking a science of the Absolute. Yet this is precisely what Hegel wished to preserve at all costs. And it is significant that when he reissued the first volume of the *Logic* almost twenty years later immediately before his death, taking the trouble to rewrite almost all the important sections of the book, the logic of pure being was the only part which he incorporated completely unaltered into the revised edition, even though he was well aware of the objections which it had encountered. We must therefore seek 'its "proper" centre and the driving force of its process' here rather than in any later chapter of the *Logic*; here lies 'one of the bases of any possible certitude concerning the absoluteness of Spirit'; 'the immediacy of the beginning remains present at each stage of the unfolding of the system.'[24]

We may concede that it is improper, as E. Coreth has plainly demonstrated,[25] to contrast Hegel's *Logic* as a metaphysic of being with a metaphysic of Spirit; we may also concede that, as Adorno has observed against Heidegger's wrong-headed theologising of being,[26] the pure being with which the *Logic* opens is at root a negatively reflected, highly abstract and meagre kind of being; and we may concede that Hegel himself did not shrink from subjecting even this primary logical Notion to critical scrutiny. Nevertheless, it cannot be gainsaid that the opening chapter of the *Logic* presents the whole book in a nutshell: '*Omnia ubique* is the rule here too, for the initial dialectical triad in the book on being, i.e. being – nothing – becoming, already contains the whole of Hegel's logic *in nuce*. The absolute Idea with which the *Logic* ends is likewise only the perfected self-reference of the simple being with which it begins; for after the unleashing of the abstracted productive forces, the absolute Idea fulfils and restores this simple being.'[27]

'The transition from being to nothing forms the model of all dialectical processes of differentiation and generation. What takes place in them is always basically nothing but variation of the dialectic of being and nothing. The upshot of this is that even the final result of Hegel's dialectic, the absolute Idea, is still marked by the substantial poverty of its first result: the synthesis of being and nothing.'[28]

'In the *Logic* external history is swallowed up by the inner historicity of the theory of categories. This development, which is in keeping with the subject-matter of the book, is probably also attributable to the fact that Hegel became more rigid as he grew older.'[29] A reproach which is brought against Hegel's *Logic* in a variety of ways is that this absorption of history involves abstrac-

[24]D. Henrich: *Anfang und Methode der Logik*, 34.
[25]*Das dialektische Sein in Hegels Logik*, 157-162.
[26]*Drei Studeien zu Hegel*, 45f.
[27]E. Bloch: *Subjekt – Objekt*, 165.
[28]K. H. Haag: *Philosophischer Idealismus*, 43.
[29]T. W. Adorno: *Drei Studien zu Hegel*, 160.

tion from history. If it were simply a matter of formal logic, this reproach could easily be fended off; but since what is at stake is onto-theo-logic, a quite different kind of speculative concreteness is called for. This particular issue presents itself for the philosopher too, provided, at least, he does not share the opposite tendency toward a formalisation of logic.

The *Logic* obviously continues to pose many other questions for the philosopher. While we may disregard such detailed questions as the relationship between subjective and objective logic or the analysis of individual categories, we must mention the problem of the formalisation of Hegel's logic, its translation into the language of formal calculus and the re-emergence of the problems with which it deals in the territory of modern mathematical logic. G. Günther[30] tries to open up this area, whereas P. Lorenzen[31] registers the critical question whether a 'polyvalent' logic can already be read into Hegel and whether polyvalent logics in general are of any use for reflection on our thought. It is also possible to establish many historical connections, both backwards (Plato, Spinoza, Kant) and forwards (Heidegger, Sartre) in time. This has been done by J. Wahl[32] in his commentary on large portions of the first book of the *Logic* (and on the corresponding sections of the *Little Logic* of the *Encyclopaedia*), in which following Husserl rather than Hegel, his intention is to disregard the dialectical becoming of the categories in favour of their phenomenological development.[33]

According to I. Iljin,[34] the following are a sample of the questions which might be registered concerning the speculative concreteness of the *Logic:* Does this essay in logic involve the disintegration of the speculative-dialectical conception, in that, while the *Logic qua* speculative universality vitally and really penetrates the lower spheres, it nevertheless fails to incorporate these spheres in either its scope or its content? Does an unspeculative, formal-logical or temporal-genetic interpretation hover clandestinely on the margin of Hegel's thought, keeping pace with his strong emphasis on a speculative interpretation? Now it may be conceded that the absolute Idea is an omnipresent and all-pervasive essence [*Wesen*] and that the categories and patterns of existence with which the *Logic* works are also the categories and patterns of existence which fully and completely indwell every existent thing, so that the whole content of the absolute Idea is preserved in each individual and particular entity. Yet should not Hegel's understanding of the speculative-concrete likewise demand that the content of the individual and particular be incorporated in the absolute Idea and that the entire content of the philosophy of nature and Spirit be subsumed in the *Logic?* Would not logic itself, according to this reading, be the only all-embracing science? Would this fact not put a question mark against the impossibility of subsuming material alien to the sphere of pure intellectuality, thus abrogating the pure divinity of pre-mundane logic? Would this not wreak wholesale chaos with respect to the whole order of divine

[30]*'Das Problem einer Formalisierung der tranzendentaldialektischen Logik'.*
[31]*'Das Problem einer Formalisierung der Hegelschen Logik'.*
[32]*La logique de Hegel comme phénoménologie.*
[33]On the historical associations of the *Logic* cf. the works of E. Coreth (on Aristotle), R. Wiehl (on Plato)), A. Redlich (on Eckhart, Böhme and the Idealists), J. Fleischmann and W. Brocker (on Kant), and K. Hartmann (on Sartre).
[34]*Die Philosophie Hegels als kontemplative Gottslehre*, 212 – 230.

development? Conversely, however, if this full inclusion of Spirit and nature into pure Notion does not occur, how can this Notion still be genuinely concrete-speculative? Hegel brings the world into God insofar as he permits the development of the divine logic to be at the same time the plan for the world and history which God drew up prior to creation, a plan which in its ideal way anticipates, prepares and predetermines world history, so that the immanent development of the divine Logos necessarily has a sublime sequel in the development of the world. Even so, how are we to explain the fact that in this speculative process of concretisation the lowest levels of the world by no means unite *all* the preceding levels in speculative consistency, but rather only require the lowest levels as a stepping-stone to their own existence? Is not a way out provided here through a hidden transition to the formal-logical interpretation of the *a priori* of the science of logic (i.e. logic thought of as containing the philosophy of nature and Spirit as mere 'sub-sections', without subsuming their specific content into itself), in which these three basic sciences are bound as a matter of course to sink to the level of specialised branches of study without any mutual and inner speculative interpenetration? Or is the way out through a hidden transition to the temporal-genetic interpretation of the science of logic (i.e. logic thought of as an ideal order which precedes the historical development in nature and Spirit), in which the speculative process must be dissolved in empirical reality and ultimately rehabilitated in a second logic of consummation (through and in the human spirit)?

Viewed in theological terms the question of abstractness becomes particularly acute when posed with regard to the *beginning*. H.-G. Gadamer observes of Hegel's *Logic*, that '[w]herever it is posed, the problem of the beginning is in truth the problem of the end. For from the perspective of the end the beginning is defined as the beginning of the end. Should we presuppose absolute knowledge, which is the precondition of speculative dialectic, this may lead to the problem of where to begin, which is insoluble in principle. All beginning is end and all end is beginning. At all events, with a circular consummation of this kind the fundamental question concerning the starting-point of philosophical science is formulated in terms of its consummation.'[35] The question becomes more urgent when we consider that according to Hegel's speculative presuppositions we are here concerned not merely with the logical starting-point of science, but with the ontological, 'absolute' beginning – in an eternal rather than temporal sense – of God himself before the creation of the world (*SL*, 70).

Hegel too is undoubtedly convinced that the God of the beginning is the same as the God of the end, that there are not two gods who alternate with one another, but rather one God – the Absolute as such. But even though, according to Gadamer, the beginning is defined in terms of the end as the beginning of the end, the reverse is equally true: the end is defined in terms of the beginning as the end of the beginning. Hegel would have been the last to

---

[35] *Wahrheit und Method*, 448; ET *Truth and Method*, 429.

THE INCARNATION OF GOD

underestimate the significance of the beginning. Although one may choose a starting-point in a circular system at random, since a circle may be taken to begin anywhere, even so – after acute reflection on the question: 'With what must the Science begin?' (*SL*, 67-78) – Hegel remained convinced that the *logical* starting-point must be located not at some arbitrary point but rather where he determined that it must be: in pure *being*. From this perspective alone will it be disclosed what is to be understood by 'the absolute, or eternal, or God' (*SL*, 78). The primordial dialectic of being and nothing therefore forms the beginning and the continuation: '[It] must be said . . . *that nowhere in heaven or on earth is there anything which does not contain within itself both being and nothing*' (*SL*, 84f). In terms of this beginning as the alpha, everything, including the plan of the world and its entire course, is determined right up to the omega. In view of this alpha we must expect an endless flow of new reality. Even so, in the end of the day none of this will be absolutely new.

E. Bloch interprets Hegel accurately when he says that in 'Hegel's *Logic* the omega or end is nothing but the informed alpha, and it returns to this beginning. "Hence it can be said that in teleological activity the end is the beginning, the sequel the basis and the effect the cause; and that it is a becoming on the part of what has become." This statement holds good with respect to all the categorical functions and determinative activities of Hegel's *Logic* as a whole. Everywhere and yet nowhere it teaches the power of the leap and of the mediated *novum,* for the form of movement appropriate to the leap is the circle. The latter leads from the in-itself [*Ansich*] of the beginning to the in-and-for-itself [*An- und Fürsich*] of the end, which is the beginning. The first is only past in that the last is again the first, this being already nothing but logical material. When the chips are down there is no leap, no surprise, no inclusion of the matter of logic into something wholly other, namely into the enquiring and intensive dimension of each "beginning". Rather, as far as Hegel is concerned logic is an unceasing process: "Thus in the absolute Idea even logic returns to this simple unity, which is its beginning; and the pure immediacy of being, in which all determination initially seems either extinguished or else left behind by abstraction, is the Idea which has come to its corresponding equality with itself through mediation, that is, through the sublation of mediation." In this way the in-itself [*Ansich*] of the Idea, which is the prime feature of Hegel's *Logic,* has ended the cosmic plan, described its course and set it aside. The categories collected during the historical development of human reason therefore date back to the immemorial antiquity of a cosmic alpha, where they have their undisturbed place in an *a priori* pre-cosmos.'[36]

Pure being is thus established and explained as the absolute beginning, while the beginning is the basis of all advance and all advance is nothing but a return to the primal basis (*SL*, 70f). Now does this dialectic of being pre-determine God himself in such a way as to rule out his being placed, as Hegel

---

[36]*Subjekt – Objekt*, 178.

himself had once demanded, 'absolutely from the very outset at the apex of philosophy as the sole cause of all things, as the sole source of being and knowing'[37] (1, 149)? Two further factors likewise prompt us to ask whether Hegel has already settled his attitude to the incarnation in advance, so that Christ is to be viewed as having been sublated into this dialectic of being from the word go. First, he urges that the dialectic of being develops immanently from its own absolute beginning and 'contains . . . within itself the beginning of the advance and development' (*SL*, 830). And, secondly, he contends that the dialectic of being should be acknowledged 'as the unrestrictedly universal, internal and external mode; and as the absolutely infinite force, to which no object, presenting itself as something external, remote from and independant of reason, could offer resistance or be of a particular nature in opposition to it, or could not be penetrated by it' (*SL*, 826).

A decisive interest in the God of the beginning is also taken by the the Old and New Testaments, which insists that the God of the end is to be none other than the God of the beginning. The Bible supposes everything to have taken place in a meaningful way from the very beginning. Already before the creation of the world there was only one God and thus neither, as in many mythologies, two gods in succession, nor, as in the dualistic world views with their good and evil principles, two gods alongside each other. 'For us there is one God, the Father, from whom are all things and for whom we exist, and one Lord, Jesus Christ, through whom are all things and through whom we exist' (I Cor. 8:6). The first half of this verse distinguishes the Christian conception of the beginning from pagan mythology, while the second distinguishes it from a purely Jewish belief in creation. Paul has just as little intention of making a cosmological statement with this remark, whose inspiration is drawn from the Jewish wisdom literature, as he has with the christological hymn in Col. 1:15-20, which deals with Christ's mediatorship in creation. The substance of his concern has to do with the soteriological significance of this beginning for man. Paul undoubtedly does not mean us to think of any mythological being made or begotten in time prior to the whole creation when he speaks of the eternal Son (Rom. 1:3f), the Wisdom of God (I Cor. 1:24-30), and the first-born of all creation, in whom, through whom and for whom all things are created (Col. 1:15-20). Even so, he is insistent that the God who stands at the beginning should be none other than the God who stands at the end: not a dark, evil or even simply an unknown God, but rather the God who has revealed his nature in Jesus. Paul is not preocuppied with the universal Greek question of the beginning, but it is nevertheless important for

---

[37]*principium essendi et cognoscendi.*

him that the beginning has a name. Paul's method is to infer the God of the beginning from the God of the end, thus seeing him in terms of Christ and ruling out the possibility that there is a different, dark, hidden God lurking behind the present and future God, that there is a secret, unrevealed world plan based on a graceless ἀνάγκη or τύχη apart from the one world plan, or that there is a different, uncanny beginning endued with its own gruesome dialectic above the gracious beginning which we know.

The New Testament Logos is therefore not nameless, and while the author of the Johannine Prologue may have used as his model a hymn of either late Jewish (J. Rendell Harris), Mandaean (R. Reitzenstein, R. Bultmann) or Christian (R. Schnackenburg, H. Conzelmann) provenance, and while the root of his Logos concept may ultimately lie in syncretistic Hellenism or in Hellenistic Judaism or in the Old Testament (the relationship of the $d^e bar$ Yahweh to the creation of the world), the decisive factor is that this concept, which was part of the mental furniture of the New Testament period, is already precisely defined at the beginning in terms of the end. This Logos of the beginning, who as the revelation of God is himself God, light and life, is not a different, higher or purer Logos than the one who became flesh. His essence and nature do not stand under the immanent constraint of a dialectic, but are revealed in this incarnation prompted by grace. That Jesus is the Logos precisely as the one who has become man is to be understood not ontologically, but soteriologically.

Perhaps it is now clear why the entire New Testament is so concerned that the beginning be defined in unequivocally christological terms from the perspective of the end. The whole New Testament constantly reiterates its insistence of the christological beginning: in the beginning, from the beginning, before all things, before all time, before the foundation of the world, from the beginning of the world, since the creation of the world, since the beginning of the ages and generations, before Abraham was . . . : all in all 'the revelation of the mystery which was kept secret for long ages but is now disclosed' (Rom. 16:25; cf. esp. Jn. 1, Col. 1, Eph. 1-2, Heb. 1). Should we pose the question of the 'exposition of God as he is in his eternal essence before the creation of nature and a finite mind' (*SL*, 50) in biblical perspective, the New Testament will point us to the divine Logos and, more especially, to the incarnate Logos. From the vantage-point of the end we can see standing at the very beginning the indestructible figure of one who cannot be upstaged by any dialectic of being, one who in one of the last writings of the New Testament is tersely dubbed 'the beginning', 'the alpha' (Rev. 1:8; 21:6; 22:13). It is solely on the basis of this beginning that all confidence in being may no longer be ultimately questionable, that being may ultimately be one, true and good, incorporating all that is warped and crooked, and that this world may be the best of all possible worlds. It is exclusively on the basis of this beginning that we may guarantee a good end.

The purpose of these remarks is by no means simplistically to rule out of court the philosophical problems raised by Hegel's *Logic*. Nor ought it to be assumed that everything boils down to the exclusive solution attempted by early dialectical theology: 'either God or Jesus'.[38] And least of all do we advocate a synthesis between the Christian God and the God of the philosophers in the manner of a natural theology. We should think rather on the lines of a critically conservative, negative-*cum*-positive 'sublation' of the God of the philosophers by the God of Jesus Christ. One thing ought at all events to have become crystal clear, namely, what it is that is of decisive importance. For when we are confronted with the alternative between *either* an abstract logic's dialectic of being *or* Jesus as the concrete Logos of God there can scarcely be any doubt about the answer which would be given by the New Testament.

3. God in the World

At long last Hegel received the call for which he had been waiting for so many long years: to Heidelberg. And he was glad to get away from Nuremberg. Waterloo had not remained without influence on university politics. In Munich there was a resurgence of those Catholic forces which were ill-disposed toward Protestant Nuremberg (XXVIII, 59 etc.), so that Niethammer lost influence, and Hegel's attention turned northwards. Through the good offices of, among others, the Prussian government official Raumer, to whom he had sent the professional opinion on the teaching of philosophy in universities mentioned above (XXVIII, 96-102; see Kaufmann, 344ff), he had already taken soundings in Berlin. There was, moreover, a prospect of his getting a professorship in languages at Erlangen. Even so, Heidelberg proved marginally preferable to Berlin and Erlangen (cf. Hegel's correspondence with Paulus, Boisserée and Daub; XXVIII, 74-144). On the basis of conversations in Nuremberg Boisserée reported to Heidelberg that 'Thibaut is said not to have spoken well of him in Jena, since his delivery was bad and he had to read everything from a script. But Hegel has given up this habit here. On the whole I only hear good things about him, and conversations with him prove him to be a first-class thinker with a thorough mind. I freely grant that he does have some Swabian rough edges, but plead in mitigation that his individual merits would not exist without them' (XXVIII, 396f). At length Pro-Rector Daub wrote to Hegel: 'But if you accepted this call, Heidelberg would have in you a philosopher, for the first time since the university was founded (Spinoza once was called here, but in vain, as you presumably know). Industry the philoso-

---

[38]On this subject cf. the recent work by H. Benckert: *Sive Deus sive Jesus*.

pher brings along, and the philosopher whose name is Hegel brings along many other things as well, of which, to be sure, very few people here and everywhere have the slightest intimation so far, things that cannot be gained by mere industry. (XXVIII, 95; Kaufmann, 343f). Glad 'to be delivered from that hangover of school, studies and organisation' (XXVIII, 111), he began to lecture in Heidelberg in October 1816, dealing with logic, law, anthropology, psychology, aesthetics, the history of philosophy and encyclopaedia. To begin with very few came to hear him – 'for *one* lecture I had an audience of only four' (XXVIII, 148) – but the ranks of his students presently swelled to one hundred and fifty-four. And he wrote almost daily to his sick wife, who remained behind in Nuremberg, longing to have her join him soon with the children. At the age of forty-six Hegel now taught for the first time as a regular professor; well-equipped in all respects, he was now competent to set forth his ideas in a comprehensive and precisely formulated system.

The two years spent in Heidelberg saw him write the already mentioned paper on the Estates of Württemberg, which is symptomatic of his enduring interest in politics. And he produced two further reviews of Jacobi's philosophy (vol. X), which, while highly conciliatory in tone, were nevertheless strongly insistent on conceptual discipline. However, the chief fruit of his labours during these years, was the *Encyclopaedia of the Philosophical Sciences in Outline. Taken from his Lectures* (1817).[39]

---

[39]The author's quotations from the *Encyclopaedia* are taken from J. Hoffmeister's 1949 revision of the Lasson edition of 1905. Lasson had omitted the supplementary passages which come from student notes of the lectures, while Hoffmeister included the numerous additons made by Hegel himself in the second and third editons of 1827 and 1830 respectively. No substantial changes were made in those passages which are of importance for Christology, apart from a detailed footnote appended to para. 537 of the second edition which deals with the relationship between philosophy and religion and the charge of pantheism. Polemic against agnosticism is a recurrent feature of the important prefaces which Hegel wrote for each of the three editions. English versions of the several parts of the *Encyclopaedia* have been used in this translation. In the following pages quotations are given, wherever possible, from the second edition (1892; repr. OUP, 1975) of William Wallace's translation, *Hegel's Logic Being Part One of the Encyclopaedia of the Philosophical Sciences* (i.e. the *Little Logic*). References are given as *Wallace* followed by the relevant page number.

As secondary literature one might use all those previously listed works which deal with Hegel's system as such, especially those by K. Rosenkranz, F. Staudenmaier, K. Fischer, R. Kroner, N. Hartmann, E. Bloch and I. Iljin. On issues to do with the philosophy of religion, cf. the contributions of J. Möller, E. Schmidt and J. Splett (and the bibliography given at the end of our Introduction). On the understanding of Hegel's dialectic, cf. especially the works of E. von Hartman, J. van der Meulen, R. Heiss, W. Flach, C. Fabro, J. Barion, F.G. Jünger, I. Landgrebe, H. Ogiermann, R. Franchini, J.B. Lotz and K.H. Haag; on the genesis of the dialectical method in the Jena period cf., in addition to the works by T. Haering and J. Schwarz, H. Schmitz: *Hegel als Denker der Individualität* (Part Two: The Infinite Judgement and the Syllogism as Principles of Dialectic); and on ontology in the *Encyclopaedia*, cf. the article by C. Brunet.

Anyone who has followed the development of Hegel's philosophy up to this point is aware that the first impression created by this system is false: by no means is it something which has been 'constructed' or 'deduced' with a minimum of effort. To be sure, Hegel here paints with broad strokes – indeed, encyclopaedically! – but this was only possible because it had been preceded by the vast amount of unremitting detailed work which he had carried out as an empiricist: penetrating observation of natural and spiritual reality, diligent preoccupation with the empirical sciences spanning decades, untiring remodelling of categories and terminology, vital restructuring of the system itself both as a whole and in its several parts. 'You know that I have been too involved, not only with ancient literature, but also with mathematics, and of late with higher analysis, differential calculus, physics, natural history and chemistry for me to be deluded by the fraud of natural philosophy, namely to philosophise by imagination without hard facts or to take the empty fantasies of folly itself for genuine ideas. This could have only a negative value for me.' Hegel had written these words to Paulus while he was still in Nuremberg, unmistakably alluding to Schelling (XXVIII, 31). He was convinced that the true scope and the true content of a Notion are related, not in inverse ratio, but in direct proportion to each other.

Only when we are aware of the vast amount of preparatory work done by this indefatigable scholar – his portrait shows us large open eyes – shall we assess Hegel aright as the most significant system-builder of modern times. Let the topic under consideration be stones or plants, Kepler's laws or Newton's theory of light, let discussion range from electricity through the association of ideas to police and property – while his knowledge was not such that he could meet every specialist on his own ground, he was well able to hold his own with every all-round scholar. What distinguished him from such men as Varro in the ancient world and Vincent of Beauvais in the middle ages, and what placed him on the same level as Aristotle and Leibniz, was the depth of insight which he combined with breadth of vision and which caused him to become not a mere collector, but a thinker. Indeed, this marriage of aptitudes led him to surpass Leibniz by being a coherently encyclopaedic thinker and to surpass Aristotle by being a theological thinker. It is accordingly appropriate to ask with Karl Barth why Hegel did not 'become for the Protestant world something similar to what Thomas Aquinas was for Roman Catholicism.'[40] Why was it that Hegel (whose place in the history of thought comes immediately after early Idealism as embodied in Kantian criticism and hard upon the heels of a variety of attractive and brilliant advances and prototypes

---

[40] *Protestant Theology in the Nineteenth Century*, 384.

associated with such men as Fichte, S. Maimon, the young Schelling and Jacobi) failed to become what Thomas Aquinas (who for his part came after early scholasticism and contrived to learn from both Christians and pagans, Jews and Arabs) was for the middle ages, and what Christian Wolff (though to a lesser extent since he had very little originality as compared with Hegel) was for the Enlightenment: namely the *doctor communis* who manages to scan the material piled up by history *intra* and above all *extra muros,* giving it a fresh conceptual arrangement and achieving the new, comprehensive synthesis which had become necessary for the age in question by a feat of creative scholarship? After all, Hegel had a sure instinct for what was in the air. And what the modest Thomas demonstrated quietly Hegel professed in programmatic form: a new age has dawned, the old syntheses are no longer adequate and the time has come for a fresh résumé of the *status quaestionis.* This view is expressed especially clearly in Hegel's various inaugural lectures and prefaces. Thus it only remained to light the powder. There was an urgent need for someone to have the courage to use a new key to open up to fuller truth doors which had either been prematurely slammed or else never even opened. But someone needed to possess the right key in the first place! Through the good offices of the Arabs and Albert the Great the theologian Thomas had found such a key in Aristotle, and it seemed to him that he had thoroughly purged it of any residual heathen taint. Now Hegel's modern master-key was a gift from his idealist brethren: the dialectical method. Although this method, which simultaneously combines the qualities of rigidity and flexibility, is not easy to handle, it struck Hegel as the Spirit's generous gift to a new age for opening not just one but all closed doors. We have already seen in the *Phenomenology* that the dialectical method, which Hegel appropriated from Fichte and projected on to the Absolute, is more than just a piece of intellectual equipment; rather, it *is* the life, life-principle and self-movement of Spirit and contains the *passer par tout* within itself. It is, moreover, the force which drives toward totality, toward a universal system (for the *Logic* see *SL,* 838-843; for the *Encyclopaedia* see *Wallace,* 19f, 292). 'Unless it is a system, a philosophy is not a scientific production' (*Wallace,* 20). Hegel now explains much more clearly than in the *Jena Draft Systems* or even in the 'voyage of discovery' of the *Phenomenology* that the truth can only be liberated from contingency and incoherence, and the strict necessity of the development be demonstrated, in a system which *is* the self-comprehending, organised Spirit.

In comparison with a high mediaeval *summa* the *Encyclopaedia* is a relatively short book, though there is an affinity between the two forms in that neither was designed exclusively for teaching purposes. Even so, Hegel's express intention was simply to offer an 'outline' or 'survey' (V, 3) for classroom use, while the lectures themselves would form a colourful wealth of substantial tissue, equally rich as regards both content and artistic skill. 'In the form of an Encyclopaedia, the science has no room for a detailed exposition of particulars, and must be limited to setting forth the commencement of the special sciences and the notions of cardinal importance in them' (*Wallace*, 20). Even in its almost excessive brevity, however, this remains one of the proudest works in the history of philosophy. A sure hand here sketches a truly impressive synopsis of the problems of time and eternity, outlining the cosmic work of reconciliation achieved by a creative reason thinking and contemplating in dynamic dialectic: 'Similarly it may be held the highest and final aim of philosophic science to bring about, through the ascertainment of this harmony, a reconciliation of the self-conscious reason with the reason which *is* in the world – in other words, with actuality' (*Wallace*, 8). Hegel had had much practice before he ventured to create this universal synthesis, so that he was now able to draw on his earlier achievements. Thus the whole first part (perhaps it would be better to say 'moment') of the *Encyclopaedia*, namely the *Little Logic* (*Wallace*, 25–122), is but a shorter, improved (but also significantly more arid) version of the great Nuremberg *Logic*, adhering to the same basic division of contents according to Being, Essence and Notion, and culminating once again in the 'absolute Idea'.[41]

From the pinnacle attained by the Idea when it reaches the highest stage of development of the logical process, there now occurs the remarkable leap from pure form into content: the 'externalisation' (V, 50; cf. *Wallace*, 24) of the Idea in *nature*. We shall be disappointed if we expect Hegel to furnish detailed explanations at this decisive juncture of the development of the Absolute. Even so, he does go on to award thorough treatment to the whole area of the *philosophy of nature*[42] according to a scheme with which we are already familiar: mechanics (space and time, matter and motion, absolute mechanics); physics (physics of the universal, particular and total individuality respectively); and organic physics (terrestrial and plant nature, the animal organism) (*PN*, 4–443). In the company of Fichte – but not of Schelling – Hegel had always been more interested in the philosophy of Spirit than in the development of the philosophy of nature, so he now simply lifted the philosophy of nature worked out in Jena and incorporated it basically unchanged into the *Encyclopaedia*.

---

[41]On the differences cf. J. McTaggart: *A Commentary on Hegel's Logic*, 150f.

[42]Quotations from the *Naturphilosophie* will here be given from *Hegel's Philosophy of Nature. Being Part Two of the Encyclopaedia of the Philosophical Sciences*, tr. A. V. Miller (OUP, 1970). References will be given as *PN* followed by the relevant page number.

271

Even so, Hegel still puts forward plenty of fantastic analogies in the manner of Romantic philosophy of nature: 'Air is *in itself* fire (as is shown by compressing it) and fire is air *posited* as a *negative* universality or a self-relating negativity. It is materialized time or selfhood (light identical with heat), the absolutely restless and consuming Element; just as this Element destroys a body when attacking it from without, so too, conversely, does the self-consumption of body, e.g. in friction, burst into flame. In consuming an other it also consumes itself and thus passes over into neutrality' (*PN*, 110). Such is the view taken of the elements in the physics of universal individuality. Even so, we may not overlook the fact that Hegel's reaction to the purely quantitative-mechanistic understanding of nature characteristic of Democritus, Galileo or Newton was not entirely devoid of justification. Building on the view of Aristotle and Thomas Aquinas that the universe was constructed in stages, he anticipated Darwin by many years in understanding nature as a dialectical history of phased development directed toward man. All of this is dealt with within a relatively broad frame of reference.

Nevertheless, like the *Logic* before it, the *Encyclopaedia* offers, in the shape of some very pithy and thoroughly enigmatic remarks, only a few crumbs of enlightenment concerning the starting-point of this historical development and the transition from pure thought into a real other-being: 'This is true in still greater measure of absolute spirit which reveals itself as the concrete and final supreme truth of all being, and which at the *end* of the development is known as freely externalizing itself, abandoning itself to the shape of an *immediate being* – opening or unfolding itself [*sich entschliessend*] into the creation of a world which contains all that fell into the development which preceded that result' (*SL*, 71; cf. *SL*, 842f). 'Enjoying however an absolute liberty, the Idea does not merely pass over into life, or as finite cognition allow life to show in it: in its own absolute truth it resolves to let the "moment" of its particularity, or of the first characterization and other-being, the immediate idea, as its reflected image, go forth freely as Nature' (*Wallace*, 296). What room is there, however, within a system of inner necessity, for the Idea freely to decide in favour of its own externalisation? Is 'de-cision' (*Ent-schluss*) here, rather like 're-collection' (*Er-innerung*), more than just a metaphor?

It is understandable that scarcely a single critic has been satisfied with Hegel's answer: 'Now from the realm of the mute logic a state of affairs is said to spring where stones fall, stomachs digest and people kill themselves. Oddly enough Hegel was unaware of the colossal question of what sparked off all of this. How can specific tangible reality such as matter, how, in the end of the day, can things which have been wildly and so to say badly brought up (which is precisely how Hegel regards most natural things) originate from such a spiritual source? . . . Thus it only goes into external existence through the self-destruction of the pre-worldly Notion. There is no other alternative, but each body now stands as a foreign body. The divide is plain for all to see; force and matter cannot be deduced from a spiritual source.'[43]

Hegel's riposte would presumably have been to enquire whether the derivation of spirit from matter and force, which Bloch has in mind, is any less obscure and arbitrary! Beneath Bloch's mocking allegation that Hegel employs a 'kind of court language' to tell how the absolute Idea majestically 'resolves' in 'absolute freedom' to 'eject' abruptly and without transition into nature,[44] there lurks the significant question whether Hegel was not in fact more aware than Bloch of 'the colossal question of what sparked off' all things, here showing himself once again to be more theological and more Christian than may appear at first glance. Bloch himself remarks with a frown that the statement about the absolute Idea's ejecting itself into its becoming-other is in fact a translation of the catechetical proposition that God created the earth.[45] The freedom of the Idea thus turns out to be reminiscent not so much of the freedom of the absolute prince, nor simply of Schelling's falling away of the Ideas from God, but much rather of the freedom of God the creator.

Now Hegel believed that the only way of maintaining the unity of his system – and hence of living and spirit-filled reality as a whole – lay in regarding creation from nothing as a religious image, but not as a philosophical Notion in the strict sense. Instead, he would understand the becoming of the world as an externalisation of God, the absolute Idea. He therefore sought to implement his speculative scheme in the *Philosophy of Nature* too, demonstrating how the various realities of nature are (unconscious) modifications of the rational, speculative, divine Notion. At the very outset of his work he describes nature as 'the Idea in the form of *otherness*' (*PN*, 13). Is this tantamount to an identity of God and the world? Or to pantheism? It certainly does not involve the divinity of the finite, but rather the finitude of the finite, and precisely in this way the sublation of the finite in God, who alone truly exists, and who produces everything else from himself, distinguishing it from himself and yet at the same time being one with it.

As we return yet again to a question which often cropped up in connection with the young Hegel, it is scarcely necessary to list the authors who have declared themselves

---

[43]E. Bloch: *Subjekt – Objekt*, 203. For an exposition and critique of this decisive seam of Hegel's system, cf. B.Wigersma: *Wordende waarheid*, 54-62; K.H. Volkmann-Schluck: *Die Entäusserung der Idee zur Natur*'; and J. van der Meulen: *Hegel. Die gebrochene Mitte* (145-237: Idea and spatio-temporality).
[44]*op. cit.*, 203f.
[45]*op. cit.*, 204f.

either for or against the mature Hegel's pantheism (panlogism, panepistemism).[46] In any case, the reply given to the question is itself dependent on our understanding of these dazzling concepts. Moreover, there are many Hegel interpreters who are in substantial agreement even though they choose to express themselves differently. The standard authors of today are probably fundamentally agreed among themselves about two points: on the one hand the mature Hegel held no brief for trivial popular pantheism; on the other – as we have constantly been at pains to point out – an intimate unity of God and man was a distinctive part of his teaching. The fact is that Hegel's major works are at one with his early development in continually emphasising that God and the world must on no account be concieved in an abstract unity, which is how the unspeculative understanding tends to see them. On the contrary, as speculative reason alone can discern without neglecting the factor of variety, they must be understood in correct unity (cf., e.g., *PS*, 22 [Preface]; *SL*, 84f, 834f).

Well aware of the gravity of the problem, at the very end of the second edition of the *Encyclopaedia*,[47] Hegel devoted a special section to a detailed consideration of the charge of pantheism. He sharply rejects any pantheism which involves a divinisation of the empirical world. Should anyone say: '*Everything is* (empirical things, without distinction, whether higher or lower on the scale, *are*) – all possess universality; and so... each and every secular thing is God', then Hegel feels it 'is only his own stupidity, and the falsification due to such misconception, which generate the imagination and the allegation of such pantheism' (*PM*, 305, cf. 76, 482). At the same time, he no less sharply rejects a dualistic juxtaposition according to which 'the infinite is parted from the finite' (V, 585; cf. *PM*, 310), rendering possible at most a 'quite abstract indeterminate unit' (*PM*, 311). On the contrary, Hegel professes a 'concrete unity' (*PM*, 311) which is rooted in the spiritual nature of God and allows the things of the world no 'fixed undisturbed substantiality' (*PM*, 305; cf. 308). Understood along these lines, 'concrete unity' involves 'monotheism' and ce-cosmism' (V,484; cf. *PM*, 310), the 'unity of absolute mind' (*PM*, 311), and the 'assertion of the ubiquity of God': the 'absolute universality (*an und für sich seiende Allgemeinheit*) which philosophy asserts concerning God, and in which the being of external things has no truth' (V, 479; cf. *PM*, 305; this statement invites comparison with the Preface to the second edition of 1827: V, 7-13).

Hegel had not always spoken with such prompt clarity, and it was undoubtedly the harsh attacks made on him by his opponents which compelled him over the years to state his case more and more precisely. His later works and the additions made to the *Encyclopaedia* in the editions of 1827 and 1830, while not representing a turning-point in this process, do bear witness to an increasing lucidity of expression. T. Litt has characterised Hegel's viewpoint as follows: 'Can an infinite still honestly be called an infinite when it has a finite outside itself, a finite which confronts it as something distinct and separate? For if and insofar as the infinite does not include the finite, it finds in it as something which exists in and from itself a barrier against which it must

---

[46]For a survey of the range of opinion, cf. H. Niel: *De la médiation dans la philosophie de Hegel*, 229f. and I. Iljin: *Die Philosophie Hegels als kontemplative Gotteslehre*, 402-404. *Noteworth statements of recent attitudes are give in F. Grégoire: Études hégéliennes. Les points capitaux de système, 140-220, and R.C. Whittemore: Studies in Hegel, 134-164.*
[47]Quotations from Part Three of the *Encyclopaedia*, the *Philosophie des Geistes*, are here taken from *Hegel's Philosophy of Mind*, tr. William Wallace and A. V. Miller (OUP, 1971). References are given as *PM* followed by the relevant page number.

come to a halt and therefore inescapably ceases to be an infinite. Since it is necessarily restricted by the finite as the other, the infinite itself becomes finite, thus contradicting its own Notion. The infinite can only exist as such when the allegedly complete finite refrains from asserting itself against it, surrendering the posture of an unassailable reality externally confronting it, and letting itself be embraced and incorporated by it. At the same time, however, we may not understand this incorporation as a means whereby the finite disappears and vanishes in the finite. An infinite which could only assert itself as such by causing the finite to disappear within it would simply deprive Being of what was annexed in this way and would thus once again cease to be truly infinite. It is important so to define the relationship that, while the external contrast between the two is surrendered and the finite renounces its independence in favour of the infinite, at the same time the infinite integrates the finite in itself in such a way that it preserves the selfhood of the finite, albeit in the modified form which results from the integration.'[48]

Even though this may not be tantamount to pantheism in the vulgar sense or everything being identical to God, it nevertheless entails a *panentheism* in which God remains fundamentally superior to all things, although – and here this scheme differs from theism – he is necessarily related to all things. We are thus faced with an inner unity of all things in God and with a sublatedness of all being in the divine Notion. This basic approach laid the foundation for the 'panlogism' which formed part of Hegel's programme, at any rate in his early days, and, since the all-embracing divine Notion is speculatively unfolded in universal science, for his 'panepistemism'.

On the basis of Hegel's introduction of the irrational into self-negating thought by means of dialectic, Kroner strongly emphasised the philosopher's irrationalism.[49] This dimension of Hegel's thinking is not necessarily ruled out of court by the ambiguous terms 'panlogism' and 'panepistemism', which are to be understood according to the definitions given above.[50] Moreover, insofar as he had advanced beyond Kant's critical Idealism, Fichte's ethical Idealism and Schelling's aesthetic Idealism, Hegel was able to understand the philosophy of nature as a simple concretisation of his speculative scheme.

Even so, there is veritable conglomeration here of the difficulties deffered in the *Logic*. At the outset of the *Philosophy of Nature* Hegel points out that '[i]n *itself,* in the Idea, Nature is divine: but as it *is,* the being of Nature does not accord with its Notion; rather is Nature the *unresolved contradiction*' (*PN,* 17). Moreover, 'Nature exhibits no freedom in its existence, but only *necessity* and *contingency*', it is 'at the mercy of the unreason of externality' and 'each

---

[48]*Hegel,* 80f; cf. also H. Ogiermann: *Hegels Gottesbeweise,* 186-192, and the accounts of Hegel's acceptance of the personality of God in T. Dieter: *Die Frage der Persönlichkeit Gottes in Hegels Philosophie,* and K. Domke: *Das Problem des metaphysischen Gottesbeweises in der Philosophie Hegels,* 85-89.
[49]R. Kroner: *Von Kant bis Hegel* II, 271f.
[50]I. Iljin: *Die Philosophie Hegels als kontemplative Gotteslehre,* 181-202.

separate entity is without the Notion of itself' (*PN*, 17). What is at stake in nature is no less than the '*self-degradation* of the Idea' (*PN*, 17). This has the most grievous consequences for philosophy: 'This impotence of Nature sets limits to philosophy and it is quite improper to expect the Notion to comprehend . . . these contingent products of Nature' (*PN*, 23).

Hegel met the difficulty by pooh-poohing it: the empirical-concrete nature of the world has nothing to do with true science, with the speculative order or with the divine Notion. He here abstracts from what is intrinsically negative in the world, from what constitutes man's misfortune and distress, from the whole volume of the well-nigh unbearable problems of this world. Now does this not involve an incomprehensible capitulation of the all-reconciling speculative science before this worldly sphere? Is it not tantamount to the shipwreck of the perpetually self-perfecting divine Idea, which is unable to absorb the concrete individual thing and the lower orders of being, which loses itself in an unconscious, thoughtless and wordless nature, and which is overwhelmed in its speculative impotence by the autonomy of the '*immediately* concrete thing' (*PN*, 23)? Does it not in the end of the day add up to the dissolution of an Absolute which has been brought to the very limits of endurance? In all probability no one will ever quite get to the bottom of the mystery of how and to what extent Hegel personally believed himself to have mastered these fundamental difficulties. Even so, it seems that the Hegel of the *Encyclopaedia* believed that, notwithstanding the immense difficulties which he pessimistically diagnosed in this sphere, he had in essentials carried through his all-reconciling, maximal speculative scheme. In the light of the date of publication of the third edition, we may conclude that he held this opinion to the end of his days.

The reader will once again concur with I. Iljin's superbly substantiated account of how Hegel, constantly granting new and singular concessions and aided by a series of different solutions, managed to cling to his speculative scheme: 'Hegel does not end his philosophy where he began it, nor does he bring it to full self-consciousness. Even so, this affords him the possibility of intertwining solutions to the problem in a quite remarkable way, causing them to be glimpsed at random, while almost simultaneously – as in a single breath – giving voice to his romantic-religious dream, its collapse and the compromise solution. *One* solution emerges for him out of all of this, but it contains so to say several answers; and there are moments when this unified solution can be deciphered and formulated only with the greatest difficulty.'[51] Engrossed in the concrete sciences, Hegel had increasingly dissociated himself from the attempt to deny true being to the empirical-concrete or speculatively to eliminate it, and had won through to a cautious epistemological symbiosis of philosophy and empirical observation (cf. the earlier remarks in the *Logic* on the blending of speculative, formal-logical

---

[51]*op. cit.*, 250.

and temporal-genetic method). In the light of this combination of solutions we can understand why it is so difficult to give a clear-cut judgment on Hegel's 'pantheism', 'panlogism' and 'panepistemism'.

Notwithstanding all the difficulties which lay in his path, in the *Encyclopaedia* Hegel guided the development of the divine Idea through the whole range of the philosophy of nature to the *Philosophy in Mind*. We are already acquainted with this grand process from the *Phenomenology* and from the Jena writings: having lived in complete external objectivity in Nature, the Notion has sublated its externalisation [*hat seine Entäusserung aufgehoben*] and became identical to itself. And in three vigorous strides Spirit freely returns from nature into itself: 1. It does so with reference to itself, in the self-knowledge of the concrete Spirit. We have to do here with the 'subjective Spirit' in the fields of anthropology (the natural, the sentient and the real soul), phenomenology (here organised within the narrowest of frameworks as a doctrine of consciousness), and psychology (theoretical, practical and free Spirit): 2. It does so with reference to the world which is to be and in fact is produced by Spirit. Here we encounter the 'objective Spirit' in the fields of law (property, contract, right *versus* wrong), morality (intention, well-being, good and evil), and customary behaviour (family, bourgeois society, state). 3. It does so with reference to the union of subjective and objective in an identity which eternally is, returns and is returned into itself, and in the universal, spiritual and self-knowing substance. Our concern here is with the 'absolute Spirit' in the fields of art, revealed religion and philosophy.

After all that was said or not said on the subject of Christology in the *Jena Systems,* the *Phenomenology* and the *Logic,* the reader will not expect anything essentially new from the summing-up at the end of the *Encyclopaedia.* Hegel here defines the general relationship between religion and philosophy (*PM,* 292, 302) much as he had done previously, and in the whole of the *Encyclopaedia* there is not a single mention of the name Jesus or Christ. In one respect, however, progress was made in that those things which were formerly presented in rather disorderly fashion (particularly in the hastily cobbled-together final sections of the *Phenomenology*) are here formulated in encyclopaedic brevity and precision and distinguished according to three spheres, namely universality, particularity and individuality.

Let us begin with the *inner-trinitarian* relationships of this God, who is not just a rigid substance, but much rather a living Spirit in thinking counter-position, existing as the Absolute itself (Father), its being-other (Son), and its unity with itself (Spirit). The Trinity, then, is the true home of all dialectic! We have here the 'absolute Spirit', which is the '*creator* of heaven and earth: but yet in this eternal sphere rather only begetting himself as his *son,* with whom, though different, he still remains in original identity – just as, again, this differentiation of him from the universal essence eternally supersedes itself, and, through this mediating of a self-superseding mediation, the first substance is essentially as *concrete individuality* and subjectivity – is the *Spirit*' (*PM*, 299).

Then consider the *creation of the world* in the movement of absolute Spirit: 'Under the moment of *particularity,* or of judgement, it is the concrete eternal being which is presupposed: its movement is the creation of the phenomenal world. The eternal "moment" of mediation – of the only Son – divides itself to become the antithesis of two separate worlds. On one hand is heaven and earth, the elemental and the concrete nature – on the other hand, standing in action and reaction with such nature, the spirit, which therefore is finite. That spirit, as the extreme of inherent negativity, completes its independence till it becomes wickedness, and it is that extreme through its connection with a confronting nature and through its own naturalness thereby investing it. Yet, amid that naturalness, it is, when it thinks, directed towards the Eternal, though, for that reason, only standing to it in an external connection' (*PM*, 300).

Lastly, let us turn to the *reconciliation* in Christ: 'the place of presupposition is taken by the *universal* substance' (God!) 'as actualized out of its abstraction into an *individual* self-consciousness' (in Christ!). 'This individual, who as such is identified with the essence – in the Eternal sphere he is called the Son – is transplanted into the world of time, and in him wickedness is implicitly overcome. Further, this immediate, and thus sensuous, existence of the absolutely concrete is represented as putting himself in judgement and' (on the cross) 'expiring in the pain of *negativity,* in which he, as infinite subjectivity, keeps himself unchanged, and thus, as absolute return from that negativity and' (in the Church) 'as universal unity of universal and individual essentiality, has realized his being as the Idea of the spirit, eternal, but alive and present in the world' (*PM*, 300). What occurred in this one Christ must become universal as the 'movement to throw off his immediacy, his natural man and self-will, to close himself in unity with that example (who is his implicit life) in the pain of negativity, and thus to know himself made one with the essential Being. Thus the Being of Beings through this meditation brings about its own indwelling in self-consciousness, and is the actual presence of the essential and self-subsisting spirit who is all in all' (*PM*, 301).

The climax of the *Encyclopaedia* is accordingly the revelation of absolute Spirit. While this revelation is complete with respect to its content, it must be elevated from the form of imagination into that of thought; and this is the task of philosophy (apart from the numerous footnotes, this is dealt with with great brevity, *PM*, 302-315).

4. Christ Sublated in the System

At the climax of the development of Spirit, then, Christ appears in the very holy of holies of this powerful system. One cannot but admire the wealth of material, all-embracing range and well structured uniformity of this system, the like of which had never been tendered to Christendom before. 'His system is no more a scientific umbrella organisation than a conglomerate of genial observations. It will sometimes seem to the student of his work as if any progress which the mind, equipped with a clear-cut methodology and a watertight empiricism, fancies itself to have made against Hegel since his death is in fact an unparalleled regression. On the other hand those philosophers who believe that they adhere to something of his heritage usually find that the concrete content which proves the value of his thought tends to elude their grasp.'[52]

Hegel learned an enormous amount from others, as is demonstrated by the countless names we have encountered on his previous path. Perhaps someone might even come up with the idea of asking what would remain as quintessentially Hegelian if we were to subtract from his thought everything that he received from others. The answer must be: all of it. Both the whole of his thought and the process whereby each single element was incorporated and moulded into this whole unmistakably constitute the essential Hegel. The whole shows him to have been a genius of synthesis, dialectical synthesis. Let it be recalled that some of the most stirring decades in the history of thought had provoked a keen awareness of the issues, that an excess of material had been prepared in all fields, and that a variety of methods had been tested out in rapid succession. Had not the time then come for a new comprehensive synthesis, the rare historical *kairos* for a great system which would gather from the past, interpret the present and determine the future? In this *Encyclopaedia of the Philosophical Sciences in Outline* Hegel had produced a *summa universalis* and hence by this very act a *summa summe theologicae*. In comparison with much that was produced in theology at that time this was in every respect a modern work throughout at the very apex of the age. Here we neither stand with both feet in the middle ages, nor, as was the case with so many contemporary theologians in both the Catholic and Protestant camps, do we stand with one foot in the old and the other in the new era. Hegel here stands firmly and securely with both feet in the modern period, while at the same time resolutely professing a *philosophia perennis* which had lost none of its perennial validity in either the thirteenth, the seventeenth or the eighteenth

---

[52]T. W. Adorno: *Drei Studien zu Hegel,* 15.

century: his technique was to test everything and keep what is good. The present writer's impression of the *Encyclopaedia* was shared by many theologians at the time: what a wonder in the context of the philosophy of the day, faithless and hostile to revelation as it was! In the system proposed here Christianity was neither malevolently eliminated nor indifferently cold-shouldered; rather, it was adopted in a well-meaning rescue attempt, indeed, sublated in the best sense of the word. This system not only followed its predecessors by amalgamating antiquity and Christianity, but also combined the Renaissance with the Reformation, the Enlightenment with Romanticism, and, finally, the middle ages with modernity. It was a system which united analytics with synthetics, subjectivism with objectivism, thought with being, reflection with contemplation, understanding with heart, rationalism with irrationalism, spirit with nature, physics with metaphysics, Logos with ethos, theory with practice, philosophy with life, conscience with law, and ego with society. Dogma and insight, science and faith, this world and the world to come, finite and infinite, in short, *all* conceivable antitheses are here reconciled in the absolute Spirit. Moreover, amidst this vast range of subject-matter Hegel's system aims to be nothing but religion, self-thinking and self-knowing Christianity. Was it not appropriate that, locked as it was in the controversy between the men of the Enlightenment and the theologians of pure feeling and affected by the onslaught of modernity in general, Christendom should fervently clutch at the deliverance offered by this Christian system? Was it not just that, while it would, admittedly, have to make many corrections in detail (and Hegel would be sufficiently generous to concede this point), Christendom should nevertheless be grateful that, in a manner which was at once traditional and modern, the Christian faith was here in the storms of the times offered not a straw, but a minutely construed new vehicle characterised by systematic reliability and compelling necessity?

But is it in fact self-evident that Christianity – or, rather, the Christian *message* – presents itself as a *system*? To gain an awareness of the problems inherent in an all-inclusive science we do not need to emulate F. Heer's impressive achievement[53] of examining Hegel's gigantic systematic edifice in its historical relationship to those other modern disciplines which hold the key to the universe (e.g. to the earlier alchemical, theosophical and at the same time mechanical-physical science of the baroque thinkers, as well as to the universal science of the gnostics of the French Revolution, and also to the Marxist scholarship, the positivistic scientism, and the increasingly ambitious planners, programmers and cosmic engineers of the future). For a glance at

---

[53] *Hegel*, 21-23.

the history of theology suffices to establish five basic points. a) The earliest form of Christian theology was not the 'system'. Quite apart from the fact that the original meaning of the Greek θεολογία was bound up with fiction concerning the gods, so that 'theology' only gradually acquired its philosophical sense and then came in the context of Christianity to denote a doctrinal statement concerning God, the earliest model of Christian theology was the *tract*. More precisely, it was the apologetic tract, which, while never being oriented exclusively to a single subject, at the same time made no attempt to grasp the whole. b) Throughout the whole history of theology there have been other no less important forms of Christian theology: treatises directly related to catechesis, on the one hand, and exegetical commentaries proper, on the other. c) Even the theological *summae* or 'compendia' of the middle ages – which also produced *summae* in medicine, law and other fields – can be termed 'systems' only in a qualified sense: they were not derived in an *a priori* fashion from a single concept or principle; they stood under certain given authorities (especially the Bible); and they grew out of the tendency to penetrate the tradition of the Fathers in depth, to harmonise it and to present it as a whole. Very much the same can be said of the great systematic works of the Reformation. d) It is only since the seventeenth century that people have spoken of a theological 'system'. The view that theology itself forms a 'system', a whole which is internally structured according to certain principles and which ought to be presented in a rounded, complete and concise form and in intellectual and logical perfection, soon coalesced with the tendency to understand 'system' as simply a technical term for dogmatics and ethics. e) Since they tend to alienate, impoverish and distort, the comprehensive programmes of systematic theology have very often represented a threat to the message and faith of primitive Christianity.

The five claims made in the preceding paragraph will now be backed up in greater detail:

a) It follows that the first Christian theologians were the 'apologists'. It is self-evident that the more significant apologists, such as Justin Martyr and Irenaeus (whose great work against the gnostic heresies led to his being dubbed the first Christian dogmatician), did not wear themselves out with a purely negative defence of the faith. Even in later periods the tract remained an important genus of theological literature, especially at the great turning points of theological history: for example, in the cases of Augustine, Thomas (*Summa contra gentiles*), Bonaventura (writings against Averroism), Luther (reformational manifestos and sermons), Kierkegaard, the Anglican Tractarians (J. H. Newman), and in the opening stages of dialectical theology (tracts now appearing in the guise of 'essays' and 'papers'), to say nothing of the lower species of anti-heretical polemical literature.

b) The towering figures of ancient Christian theology merit mention here. Gregory of Nyssa's work on 'dogmatics', the *Great Catechism*, has the form of a λόγος καταχητικός. Moreover, the only two comprehensive blueprints to come from the pen of Augustine, namely the *Enchiridion ad Laurentium* and the *De doctrina christiana,* are catechetical and hermeneutical in character. The same can be said of the significant works produced at the time of the Reformation, for example, of the catechisms of Luther and Calvin. Turning to the exegetical form of theology, it can be said that both the theology of Origen and the more historically oriented theology of the Antiochene school (Theodore of Mopsuestia and Theodoret of Cyrus) are to be found chiefly in exegetical works. Among the Latin Fathers as typified by Augustine, in the middle ages as represented by Rupert of Deutz and Thomas Aquinas, and in the Reformation as exemplified by Luther and Calvin, commentaries on Scripture carried at least as much weight in the whole enterprise of theology as did writings of a more systematic nature. This is to say nothing of the later biblicistic currents against the excessive systematisation practised by Protestant orthodoxy (i.e. pietism as represented by J.A. Bengel and his school, by Menken and by J.C.K. Hofmann).

c) Having been painstakingly collected by Isidore of Seville, the numerous 'sentences' of the Fathers (especially of Augustine and Gregory the Great) were then put to general use for the purposes of instruction. The real or putative discrepancies between these authorities made it imperative for them to be reconciled, minutely analysed and systematically mastered. This task was begun by Peter Abelard and Hugh St. Victor and comprehensively achieved for the first time in the *Libri quattuor sententiarum* of Peter Lombard. The labours of the latter were to set the pattern for many theologians of the ensuing period, as can be seen from the *summae quaestionum* and commentaries on the *Sentences* which proliferated in the twelfth and thirteenth centuries. Sterling service was performed by the 'dialectical method' in the sense of Aristotle's logic, so that after Lombard's *Sententiae* had been accepted as a textbook in the high scholasticism of the thirteenth century the path was cleared for such men as Alexander of Hales, Albert the Great and Ulrich and Hugh of Strassburg to produce independent *summae* proper, whose concern to be concisely exhaustive underscored their impressive credentials. Most notable of all was the achievement of Thomas Aquinas, who set forth the totality of revealed truth within the grand cycle of a *descensus a Deo* and an *ascensus ad Deum.* Why he never completed his *Summa* remains an unsolved mystery to this day. And the first editions of Calvin's *Institutio* (this, the most significant and influential systematic work of the Reformation period, was initially patterned on Luther's catechism) and Melanchthon's *Loci Communes* were similarly not designed as comprehensive statements of Christian truth. Not until the later editions did their systematic character come strongly to the fore.

d) The technical term *systema* presupposes the idea of the body as an organic unity of its members and was used in the middle ages to denote either the Church made up of believers or else doctrine articulated into dogmas. In 1614 the Reformed dogmatician B. Keckermann published a *Systema SS. theologiae* which no longer followed the synthetic method of the *Loci* by loosely juxtaposing one set of statements alongside others. Instead, it proceeded analytically from a single *principium* or *finis* to exhibit an ordered doctrinal structure. As a result the qualities of orderliness, completeness, correctness and certainty pertain to a system where principles and conclusions are deduced from correct definitions. System and science became indentical in the Enlightenment, and especially in the thought of Christian Wolff. As far as Kant was concerned, 'system' has the further sense of the unity of multiple items of knowledge under the aegis of a single Idea, while for Hegel's immediate predecessor Fichte, it denotes the deductive derivation of the several sciences from a first and supreme principle.

· e) This is true even with respect to the first two large-scale essays in theological system building, namely Clement's reflection on ethics, the Παιδαγωγός, and – *par excellence* – the young Origen's cosmologically orientated Περὶ ἀρχῶν. It is also true, though in a different sense of the great mediaeval *summae*, where the casting vote on important questions was all too often given not by biblical message, but by philosophy. Something similar must be said of the systematic presentations of Lutheran orthodoxy, which, while invoking the Protestant *sola Scriptura,* were in fact largely attuned to Aristotle. Great theologians have often tended to distort the original Christian message not so much by teaching positive errors as by forcing the material into a systematic straitjacket (e.g., the treatment of the doctrine of pre-destination by Augustine and Calvin).

Hegel might well reply – and later on he will explicity do so – that the very theologians who intend simply to reproduce the content of the Bible already bring a particular understanding to the sacred text (as examples of this tendency we might mention both Cocceius' biblical covenant theology and Karl Barth's *Epistle to the Romans*). If this were not so so, then why should one man read something different from another out of the same Bible? For it is a fact that everyone approaches the Bible moved by his own prejudices, questions and concerns. And what can he do to remedy this state of affairs? He can honestly admit his commitment to himself, enter into the hermeneutical circle and let his prejudices, preconceptions and former beliefs constantly be corrected anew by the text.

But is this what Hegel wanted? For a critical and self-critical hermeneutic of this kind can be hampered by a system which develops its own autonomous constraint in blithe disregard of the reality which is to be interpreted. Understanding is thus not hampered by systematic thought as such, which is after all an unavoidable tool of scholarship, but by the autonomous constraint of a system. Is not Hegel's *Encyclopaedia,* not only in its philosophy of nature but also in its treatment of 'revealed religion', constrained by the exigencies of a system, which demands both a specific kind of necessity and the sacrifice of true historicity? He constantly stressed that the truths of faith must be liberated from their historical contingency and elevated into true speculative necessity: 'This cognition is thus the *recognition* of this content (viz., religion) and its form; it is the *liberation* from the one-sidedness of the forms, elevation of them into the absolute form, which determines itself to content, remains identical with it, and is in that the cognition of that essential and actual necessity. This movement, which philosophy is, finds itself already accomplished, when at the close it seizes its own notion – i.e. only *looks back* on its knowledge' (*PM,* 302). Now Hegel's concern was with science, and science involves a system, and a system involves necessity. Is not Hegel perfectly right, however, and is not the critic once again making things too easy for himself? Should we not appraise Hegel's insistence on this necessary connection as first and foremost a resolute repudiation on his part of all brands of positivism and agnosticism?

Hegel was convinced that the natural science which had forced its way into the traditional precincts of scholastic learning necessitated a new order of scholarship, a reconciliation of old and new, indeed a new system of thought. Even so, he was little disposed to rest content with additions and inductions of facts, with recording what is and what happens, in short, with a positivism which pays no heed to the understanding and grasp of the wider context. Such worship of the 'facts' works with uncritically accepted vague general concepts; with its credulous healthy commonsense it succumbs to the very 'principles' which it pretends not to have; and in the end of the day it is nothing more than a declaration of bankruptcy on the part of thought. As he made clear in the Preface to the first edition of the *Encyclopaedia,* Hegel had no use for a philosophical speculation which affected an air of 'forced eccentricity, aping the hollow style of a studied, methodical and cheap pun forged out of baroque combinations' (V, 4). Nor did he have any time for the opposite failing, that is, for 'the superficiality' of those who 'parade the dearth of ideas as if it were the acme of cleverness and indicative of a kind of criticism remarkable for its intellectual modesty, their conceit and vanity increasing the while to match their emptiness of ideas' (V, 4). In opposition to these things Hegel strove 'impartially and unconceitedly for the philosophical interest and for the earnest love of *higher knowledge*' (V, 5). For this reason he dedicated the *Encyclopaedia* 'to this concern for *knowing the truth*' (V, 5).

While Hegel was convinced that the unreflected presuppositions and fateful consequence of the traditional conception of a supra- or extra-worldly God merited radical rational criticism, he was correspondingly disinclined to profess the kind of agnosticism which pretended to be able to know nothing of God. 'The voluntary diffidence of agnosticism, i.e. the belief that the cognition of all really important things is denied us, can learn from Hegel (as from Aristotle, Thomas Aquinas and Leibniz) what a strong man and world power are Notion and reason respectively.'[54] And (at least as far as Hegel is concerned!) God takes pride of place in this cognition of the 'really important things'. Thus he added a section in the third edition of the *Encyclopaedia* in which he took issue with the 'novel protestations . . . — and these assertions are no more than protestations — . . . that man cannot know God': this viewpoint turns Christians into 'heathen, . . . who know not God' (V, 472; cf. *PM,* 298).

Philosophy must accordingly be concerned with the knowledge of God, with the knowledge of the necessary being of the Absolute. And for this very

---

[54]E. Bloch: *Subjekt – Objekt,* 110.

reason, Hegel would say, the objection about the constraint of the system fails to strike home. (As he is reported to have said to a lady admirer who stared at him as a genius: 'Those things in my books which come from me are false, Madame.') Philosophy must focus on the absolute system, on the system of the Absolute itself: God as he is in himself, as he divests himself into externality and returns into himself, the system of this God in the world! This 'circular teaching' (*en-cyclo-paideia*), in which each component part of philosophy is a 'circle rounded and complete in itself' and the whole 'resembles a circle of circles' (*Wallace*, 20) is, when understood in genuinely philosophical terms, nothing other than history of the Absolute itself, which the philosopher faithfully and pertinently accompanies and ponders, a system whose necessity in detail illuminates the freedom of the whole: 'The thought, which is genuine and self-supporting, must be intrinsically concrete; it must be an Idea; and when it is viewed in the whole of its universality, it is the Idea, or the Absolute. The science of this Idea must form a system. For the truth is concrete; that is, while it gives a bond and principle of unity, it also possesses an internal source of development. Truth, then, is only possible as a universe or totality of thought; and the freedom of the whole, as well as the necessity of the several sub-divisions, which it implies, are only possible when these are descriminated and defined' (*Wallace*, 19f). According to Hegel the elevation of the Christian faith to the heights of a scientific system means man's becoming conscious of the true divine essence. For the Absolute – and absolute science in its train – simply follows its own spontaneous impulse, its own immanent law, its own inner divine necessity: that is to say, since the Absolute is identical with necessity, it simply follows itself. Sovereign self-determination by inherent laws and an ab-solute autonomy detached from all else: this necessity is supreme freedom. Hegel's system does not rule out freedom, but presupposes it in its necessity.

Even so, we cannot stifle the question whether the God of this system is not in fact his own prisoner. Classical Christian theology will assuredly not wish to doubt for a moment that God in his being is absolutely necessary. For it has constantly emphasised that there is nothing contingent in God insofar as all thought, intention and action are identical with the necessary essence of God himself. God is thus pure necessity, and precisely *qua* pure necessity he is absolutely independant of everything outside himself and consequently free. His absolute freedom is expressed in the fact that he is a law unto himself (*sibimetipsi lex*). Nevertheless, he is emphatically not his own prisoner! Or is this God *compelled,* if not by another then at any rate by himself, to develop thus rather than otherwise? Does his essence *oblige* him to function according to an excyclopaedic scheme which can be fathomed by man and to differentiate himself into finitude? Is he accordingly *obliged* in an inexorably stringent dialectic to create the world and reveal himself in man? Classical Christian theology would make precise distinctions here: while the *de facto* existence of the world and man is based on God's essence, which is at once absolutely necessary and absolutely free, nevertheless, since its source lies in God's free and necessary essence, this *de facto* existence was not created *of necessity*. God's gracious willing and acting in creation and incarnation is in keeping with his free and necessary essence, indeed, identical with it; but that this gracious willing and acting is identical with God's necessary and free essence is precisely not necessary. In other words, *when* God creates and *when* he reveals himself in a man, this creating and revealing is necessarily identical with his necessary essence. *That* he creates, however, and *that* he decisively reveals himself in a man is, in virtue of God's absolute sovereignty over and plenitude of being and on account of his self-sufficiency and freedom, precisely not necessary. The necessity of God's creation and revelation is accordingly a *factual* necessity (i.e. based on a free decision and to this extent not ontologically necessary) and consequently absolute freedom.

All of this may appear to be abstract and at all events extremely difficult. Even so, a great volume of historical experience prompted classical theology to wish to ward off primitive misunderstandings and to make clear just what is essential for the biblical God (to whom Hegel also appealed) in this context. After all, is there a single page in the Bible where the freedom of God is not directly or indirectly involved? How is this God of the Bible meant to create, act, save and fulfil other than in freedom? For God enjoys freedom from everything which might be before him, alongside him or against him, freedom in the face of all chaos and darkness, and freedom over against men's evil deeds, which are powerless to hinder him, and their good deeds, which are impotent to force his hand. Now man has been given no more exalted pattern than himself in terms of which he may speak of God in image and symbol. Accordingly the greatest variety of anthropomorphisms is used to express this freedom of his, which, notwithstanding the whole emphasis on his freedom of wrath, is, according to the Bible, first and last a freedom of *grace* as revealed in what faith sees as the decisive salvific event which took place in Jesus. Not for nothing does the New Testament call him '*the* grace of God' (Titus 2:11).

In a mental effort which bears comparison with that of Anselm and Thomas, Hegel endeavoured to exhibit the speculative necessity of the *cur Deus homo*.[55] But it is possible to overlook an aspect of Anselm's thought which already earned the mild censure of Thomas, namely that when man

---

[55]On this theme cf. R. Haubst's recent historic-systematic investigation *Vom Sinn der Menschwerdung.*.

thinks that he knows all the ins and outs of necessity this confidence is purchased at the expense of God's freedom. The biblical message prompts us to ask a similar question with respect to Hegel's thought: Is not the Christ who appears at the climax of the dialectical development in revealed religion enclosed in a quite different but no less stringent way in the necessity of a system of science? Is he not thus encapsulated in a closed system, which, while intended not as a rigid construction but as a fullness made up of living movement, nevertheless, as the necessary self-movement of the divine-human Notion and as the applied absolute method, moves irresistibly forward in a cast-iron threefold act – a dialectical act which can be impeded by no abyss for the very reason that it tumbles headlong into each one that crosses its path and is hoisted far beyond it precisely through the affirmation of negation – a dialectical act which boldly surrenders to antithetical contradiction in order in this very way, through the negative power of error and evil, to achieve promotion into the full synthetic truth which leaves nothing out of account? Is not this cast-iron threefold act of the system positively bristling with problems? We ask this question not because there is something intrinsically objectionable about a triad, nor because triads should be superseded by tetrads, nor yet because the individual triads ought to be subjected to pedantic criticism, but because the grandiose three-part rhythm of this system attempts to incorporate even the salvific event in Christ, so that those things which according to the Bible are to be understood exclusively in the light of man's guilt and God's free grace might be reinterpreted as a dialectical consistency and necessity of the divine Notion and human consciousness, and as an immanently necessary *bouleversement* into, first, evil and, in due course, into an even better good. Christ, who according to the New Testament is purely and simply God's act and gift of grace, appears to have been 'sublated', intercepted and captured anew in the golden texture of a system whose cogency is seen in its movement.

Once again, therefore, Hegel's concern is vindicated in that while the Christian God of grace may not be a God of systematic compulsion, neither may he, on the other hand, be a God of unsystematic arbitrariness. In his essay on 'Kant and the question of the gracious God' H. Blumenberg was right to venture a severe philosophical criticism of the idea of God cherished by late mediaeval nominalism, which 'pushed the traits of absolute sovereignty and autocratic arbitrariness to the extreme', of Luther's '*mutabilissimus Deus*' and of Jansen's God as '*ipsissima libertas*'.[56] Such a God, who can 'send' good or evil at whim, can become morally insupportable. Inaugurating a tradition

---

[56]'*Kant und die Frage nach dem "gnädigen Gott"*', 555.

whose progress can be followed to Nietzsche, Sartre and Camus in modern times, the philosophers of the ancient world had already striven to whittle away the power of the gods by invoking the aid of morality. Whether expressed by Ivan in Dostoyevsky's *The Brothers Karamazov* or by Orestes in Sartres's *Flies*, the protest against a despotic and unreliable arbitrary God has right on its side.

It is accordingly inappropriate to understand the criticism of the element of constraint in Hegel's system as being tantamount to partisanship for a God of freedom as opposed to a God of reason. Nor is anything to be gained by isolating either the divine *will* as an authority alien and indifferent to reason (as did nominalist and oftentimes also Reformation theology) or the divine *reason* as a schematic principle of cosmic order (as did Descartes, Wolff and many thinkers of the Enlightenment). What has already been demonstrated with respect to the *Phenomenology* holds good here too: there can be no going back on Hegel. To speak of a God of grace does not necessarily involve the naive, biblicistic conception of an almighty, absolutist ruler who deals with the world and man in a capricious exercise of unlimited power. Nor does it imply enlightened deism's conception of God as, so to say, a constitutional monarch, who, while committed to a constitution based on natural and moral law, has largely withdrawn from the concrete life of the world and man. What is entailed by a God of grace is a God who lives *in* the world itself, present but not caged within it, immanent within it yet also transcending it, concerned with this world without neglecting the next, close to and yet at the same time also other than the world. He is a God who, precisely as the one who sustains, upholds and embraces us, is constantly ahead of us in all our life, movement, progress and regress; a God who, precisely in that which *must* not be but really *is,* who, precisely in his non-self-evident promise, in his unmerited forgiveness, in his uncoercible fulfilment, indeed, according to Scripture, precisely in his free grace, is not an irrational, but much rather a reliable, constant and faithful God.

This is the reliability, constancy and fidelity of a grace which does not destroy, but rather renders possible the freedom, independence, spontaneity and self-responsibility of the human subject. We may not speculate with this grace, for it is not cheap, nor may we speculate about it, for it is not calculable. Even though God's grace is not arbitrariness, it is nevertheless a mystery; and while it does not license calculation, it does encourage hope. Even so, we should not construct an exclusive contrast between the 'gracious God' and God as 'rational Being'. It is simply that God's reason can cause grace to rule even where as far as human reason is concerned justice is the sole remaining option. It is God's reliable, constant and faithful grace, which, as a 'higher righteousness', excludes all arbitrariness and chance from first to last.

The magnitude of the gift seems to have blinded Hegel to the benevolence of the giver. Perhaps, though, there was more gratitude lurking in his thought than his system permits us to discern.

5. God Through the World

Hegel in Fichte's chair! The year 1817 had already seen the publication of the *Encyclopaedia* against a background of seething unrest in university fraternities and sporting clubs intoxicated with the notion of liberty. It was also to witness his call to the up and coming militaristic and educationally orientated Prussia by that state's first '*Cultusminister*' Altenstein (XXVIII, 170-200). Since this move to the University of Berlin, which had been founded in 1810 in the wake of W. von Humboldt's educational reforms and already boasted a number of first-rate scholars (among them Schleiermacher, Niebuhr, F.A. Wolf, Savigny, Fichte!), would afford deliverance from a Heidelberg which had already become too parochial for him, Hegel accepted the call. And the reader who has been mindful from the outset of the socio-political dimension of his thought and work will not be surprised when, among the reasons adduced by the philosopher in his application for discharge to Baden's Ministry of the Interior, he mentions his wish 'with advancing years to be transferred from the precarious function of teaching philosophy at a university and put to use in some other activity' (XXVIII, 182). What Hegel had in mind was administrative and governmental activity, perhaps even at the Academy.

Having arrived after a long and tortuous path at the summit, Hegel now had all the opportunity in the world peacefully to consolidate every aspect of his system. The foundation had been laid and the master plan worked out. Immediately after taking up his post in the winter semester of 1818-19 Hegel lectured, quite inconspicuously and without creating a stir, on the philosophy of law (*Recht*), and in 1821 the *Elements of the Philosophy of Right* appeared in print.[57] Again, this work too was conceived primarily as a concise 'guiding thread' for the use of those who had attended the lectures, although at the

---

[57]In the German original the author quoted the *Rechtsphilosophie* from the fourth impression of the Hoffmeister edition, which is based on the original edition published by Hegel himself in 1821 and supplemented with the marginal comments written in Hegel's own hand in his author's copy. The translation by T. M. Knox, *Hegel's Philosophy of Right* (Oxford, 1942), has been used here. Quotations will be given as *PR* followed by the relevant page number. It is appropriate to draw the reader's attention here to Knox's remarks in his Foreward concerning the problems of finding a suitable English equivalent for the German *Recht*: 'The difficulties of translating the *Philosophy of Right* begin with the title. *Recht* is the German equivalent of *jus, droit,* and *diritto* as distinct from *lex, loi,* and *legge.* There is no corresponding distinction in English. "Right" has been selected almost everywhere as perhaps the least confusing rendering of Hegel's meaning, although

same time, in what may be seen as a further indication of Hegel's socio-political commitment, the *Remarks*, which supplemented the main text, had been somewhat expanded with an eye to the 'general public': 'This text-book is an enlarged and especially a more systematic exposition of the same fundamental concepts which in relation to this part of philosophy are already contained in a book of mine designed previously for my lectures – the *Encyclopaedia of Philosophical Sciences*' (*PR*, 1; Preface).

'*What is rational is actual and what is actual is rational*" (*PR*, 10)! This sentence, which was directed against those philosophers who concentrated on the heart and the feelings, was later to become the object of frequent and disdainful quotation. In the printed version Hegel caused it to be spaced out for emphasis, thereby indicating his intention to retain and execute the basic speculative scheme of his system. Let no one indulge in cheap criticism of this statement, which has frequently been misunderstood as it has been properly understood. For Hegel does not assert the rationality of the entire world or of human society as it is. Indeed, the irrational and the unreal also exist! Even so, 'the infinite variety of circumstance, . . . this endless material . . . this is not the subject-matter of philosophy' (*PR*, 11). Nor did he set his seal of approval on conformist accomodation to the *status quo* or servile subjection to the establishment. On the contrary, 'the great thing is to apprehend in the show of the temporal and transient the substance which is immanent and the eternal which is present. For since rationality (which is synonymous with the Idea) enters upon external existence simultaneously with its actualization, it emerges with an infinite wealth of forms, shapes, and appearances. Around its heart it throws a motley covering with which consciousness is at home to begin with, a covering which the concept has first to penetrate before it can find the inward pulse and feel it still beating in the outward appearances' (*PR*, 10f).

---

this leads at times to phrases unnatural in English' (*PR*, vi). In Dr. Küng's own text, however, *Recht* is sometimes translated as 'law' where appropriate.

In addition to the general introductions and works on the philosophy of religion mentioned at the end of the Introduction, the reader may find the following suggestions regarding further bibliography of value. On the *Philosophy of Right* in general (presentations and criticism), see the works or articles by E. Gans, K. Marx, F. Bülow, H.A. Reyburn, J. Binder – M. Busse – K. Larenz, M.B. Foster, T. Haering, H. Marcuse, E. Fleischmann, E. Topitsch and M. Riedel. On Hegel's idea of the state see especially F. Rosenzweig, G. Giese, J. Löwenstein, A. von Trott zu Solz, K.R. Popper, E. Weil, F. Grégoire, M. Rossi, G. Rohrmoser and J. Barion. On Hegel's concept of freedom see especially J. Hommes, V. Fazio-Allmayer, W. Seeberger and H. Schmidt. On his assessment of the French Revolution see J. Ritter and J. Habermas; on the relationship between theory and practice see M. Riedel and on that between Christ and society see W. D. Marsch. And there is a variety of essays on problems to do with the *Philosophy of Right* in the *Hegel-Jahrbuch* vol. V (1967). Further bibliography on Hegel's political theory for the years 1905-1956 has been compiled by K. Gründer in the appendix to Ritter's *Hegel und die Französische Revolution*.

While sovereignly disregarding the irrational as unreal, and yet at the same time constantly being compelled to reintegrate it, Hegel here examines the rational reality produced by the rational operation of reason. And one of the forms of the absolute divine Idea which has externalised itself into the world is – after the philosophy of nature and within the philosophy of Spirit – the philosophy of right, embracing the formation of law and the state as the sphere of the objective Spirit. Constantly mindful of empirical experience and its juridical categories, Hegel deals in three stages with the voluntary order and with the varieties of ethical phenomena. To a much greater extent than anthropology, phenomenology and psychology (i.e. than the doctrine of 'subjective Spirit'), the *Philosophy of Right* sets forth a process of liberation; and the freedom involved here is no longer restricted to the individual sphere of the subjective Spirit, but takes shape in the social sphere of the objective Spirit. 'The basis of right is, in general, mind; its precise place and point of origin is the will. The will is free, so that freedom is both the substance of right and its goal, while the system of right is the realm of freedom made actual, the world of mind brought forth out of itself like a second nature' (*PR*, 20).

Hegel accordingly regards the activities of the human world in the spheres of law and morality, family and society, and state and history as a rational, dynamic system of voluntary formations and ethical phenomena, which in their true reality are nothing other than speculative units of the divine Notion itself in this human world. And he causes the threefold process in which the Idea of freedom is realised to stem from the sphere of formal or abstract individual law (*PR*, 37-74): the immediate will of the person (private law). Man realises himself as man in relationship to external reality (i.e. the natural and the human world) in the forms of property, contract and wrong. The dialectical process leads thence into the sphere of morality (*PR*, 75-104): the will of the subject as it is for itself. Here man realises himself as man in relationship to inward reality in the modes of purpose and responsibility, intention and welfare, good and conscience. Inward and outward reality are eventually united in the sphere of ethical life (*PR*, 105-223), where law and morality, outwardness and inwardness, objectivity and subjectivity, freedom and necessity find their synthesis. This takes place in the formations of the family as natural Spirit (individuality), of civic society as divided Spirit (particularity), and, lastly, of the state (universality). It is in the state that the objective Spirit sets about achieving its own completion in the absolute freedom of the now universal will: as folk spirit it plunges into world history through the inter-relationship of particular folk spirits to become real as the universal World Spirit.

This, then, is how the individual integrates himself into the various social spheres with their various laws and norms, realising himself and his freedom by passing through all the concrete formations of ethical reality. It finds its fullness solely in that highest and most perfect speculative-political order of life, the rational state, where there is a spiritual unity between the individual, as an abstract being-for-itself, and the people, as an abstract being-in-itself, where, in short, 'freedom comes into its supreme right' (*PR*, 156). The individual's 'supreme duty is to be a member of the state' (*PR*, 156). Now the state must not be confused with the conflicting and contradictory phenomenon of civil society, concerned only with the defence of property and personal liberty. As far as Hegel is concerned, the 'state is the actuality of the ethical Idea' (*PR*, 155), 'the absolutely rational element' (*PR*, 157), 'the actuality of concrete freedom' (*PR*, 160). Indeed, as a ripe form of ethical life the state is an appearance of God himself in the world, a divine state: 'The state is the divine will, in the sense that it is mind present on earth, unfolding itself to be the actual shape and organization of a world' (*PR*, 166). What has happened is 'that the true reconciliation which discloses the state as the image and actuality of reason has become objective' (*PR*, 222).

The true essence of freedom thus consists in community. Now Hegel had no wish for a collectivism which would dissolve the individual and his freedom in the universal, and he had equally little desire for an individualism which would simply derive community from individuals. The individual person must not be regarded as an abstraction in himself, but must be seen from the very outset only in his essential relationship to 'the other', that is, in his fellow humanity, where the individual exists as a member of the social whole and 'I' exist as 'We'. True freedom and the whole meaning of ethics consist in accepting the other, giving oneself to the other, finding one's own will in the other and hence in the universal divine will: 'The state is the actuality of concrete freedom. But concrete freedom consists in this, that personal individuality and its particular interests not only achieve their complete development and gain explicit recognition for their right (as they do in the sphere of the family and civil society) but, for one thing, they also pass over of their own accord into the interest of the universal, and, for another thing, they know and will the universal; they even recognise it as their own substantive mind; they take it as their end and aim and are active in its pursuit. The result is that the universal does not prevail or achieve completion except along with particular interests and through the co-operation of particular knowing or willing; and individuals likewise do not live as private persons for their own ends alone, but in the very act of willing these they will the universal in the light of the universal, and their activity is consciously aimed at none but the universal end. The principle of modern states has prodigious strength and depth because it allows the principle of subjectivity to progress to its culmination in the extreme of self-subsistent personal particularity, and yet at the same time brings it back to the substantive unity and so maintains this unity in the principle of subjectivity itself' (*PR,* 160f).

Chiefly on account of the theory of the state which it propounds, the *Philosophy of Right* is regarded as Hegel's most conservative work. The Tübingen enthusiasm for the French Revolution and the social criticism lèvelled at the aristocratic oligarchy of Bern seem to lie far back in the past. In his first great work, the *Phenomenology of Spirit,* he had been far in advance of his age. Now, however, even the genial generosity of his imagery can do nothing to mitigate the fact that in this late philosophical work he allocates to philosophy a quasi-posthumous task: 'One word more about giving instruction as to what the world ought to be. Philosophy in any case always comes on the scene too late to give it. As the thought of the world, it appears only when actuality is already there cut and dried after its process of formation has been completed . . . When philosophy paints its grey in grey, then has a shape of life grown old. By philosophy's grey in grey it cannot be rejuvenated but only understood. The owl of Minerva spreads its wings only with the falling of the dusk' (*PR,* 12f). Even so, does not Hegel's own philosophy itself refute such a theoretical-passive view of philosophy, and cannot the same be said for the history of philosophy which came from his pen, with its repeated flair for pointing to the history-forming function of philosophy?

In the same Preface (*PR,* 11) Hegel had declared that the philosopher ought not to meddle in the petty details of practical life, as Plato had done with his advice to nurses about rocking babies, and Fichte with his efforts to perfect passport regulations. In the *Remarks,* however, Hegel had ventured – and surely he was obliged to venture – some vigorous forays into the province of practical politics, with the result that he very soon came to hear severe and often unjustified rebukes against his *Philosophy of Right.* Some have castigated Hegel as a reactionary, without giving simultaneous consideration to his modern liberalism. His *Philosophy of Right* has been decried as a canonisation of the absolutist Prussian system (kingship and nobility), without due heed being paid to his far-reaching differences from it. After all, he demanded the equality of citizens before the law, popular participation in legislation and the granting of taxes, the public administration of justice and trial by jury, and the emancipation of the Jews. His rejection of the July Revolution has been censured, without his enduring veneration for Rousseau and the ideas of 1789 provoking an equal measure of praise. His beatification of the state, his justification of war and his glorification of power have been proclaimed as the forerunners of every possible 'ism', without honourable mention being made of his advocacy of 'right' in the state and of the freedom of the individual. It is appropriate in this context to recollect his courageous intervention with the police authorities for the harassed students 'Carove

(XXVIII, 242-244, 455-471) and Asverus (XXVIII, 216f, 432-442; XXIX, 14f), and for the Parisian philosopher Cousin (XXIX, 75-78).

While the lower boundary of Hegel's state is formed by the family and by civil society (which is in fact distinct from the state), as 'objective Spirit' it is itself subordinate to the configurations of 'absolute Spirit', i.e. art, religion and philosophy. Hegel's political ideal was not the Prussian absolutism of 1820, but rather – notwithstanding his rejection of the theory of divine right – a rationally based constitutional monarchy on the English model. This attitude led to his own rejection by F. K. von Savigny, the founder of the historical school of jurisprudence, whose own background in anti-rational Romanticism caused him to take offence at Hegel's 'rationalistic' substantiation of 'right', and by F. J. Stahl, the initiator of the Prussian Conservative Party, who frankly preferred the English Tory Edmund Burke to Hegel. Having during his lifetime vigorously attacked total authority as advocated by, say, the Bernese aristocrat Haller in his *Restoration of Political Science,* Hegel was posthumously accused of high treason against the Prussian state by a Silesian conservative, and was later to become, appropriately enough, the object of Nazi hatred. No damage would be done if the now somewhat jaded labelling of Hegel as the 'Prussian state philosopher' were to disappear from even Anglo-Saxon literature, for, after all, '[i]n the end of the day Hegel's state purported to be the "polis" of Pericles as seen through the prism of a greatly molycoddled and highly idealised but not absolutised Prussia.'[58] While E. Weil's liberal interpretation of Hegel's thinking about the state may well be too positive, Sir Karl Popper's totalitarian interpretation may also be too negative in many respects.

In the *Philosophy of Right* Hegel was much more realistic and critical than one might suspect on the basis of a superficial reading, and the obvious reason for his wholehearted espousal of the cause of the state is that in an age of political ferment and revolutionary unrest the contradictions of civil society seemed to him to be so great that their only hope of resolution lay in their dialectical sublation in the state as rationally understood. And if the second part of the sentence quoted above, according to which all that is actual is rational, might boil down to the apologetic justification and conservation of the political *status quo,* the second and fundamental part of the same sentence, according to which all that is rational is actual, is capable of a thoroughly revolutionary interpretation. That is to say, it could be understood as a rallying cry against the bad 'phenomenon', which ought not to be as it is, in favour of a true, rational reality, against the irrational state of the

---

[58]E. Bloch: *Subjekt – Objekt,* 255.

ancien régime for the rational modern State, for the rational in the state which had been visibly embodied in the great French Revolution. It was precisely on account of such sentiments as these that Hegel could be equally disinclined to advocate either permanent revolution or reactionary restoration. He opted instead for the path of decisive institutional reform. And when even the revolutionary Marx came out against abstract utopianism, Jacobinical anarchy and pseudo-revolutionary *putsches*, it was not least from his master Hegel that he learned to take this line.

While we shall endeavour to do justice to Hegel's *Philosophy of Right* in terms of its own age, it will nevertheless be impossible to ignore the presence here also of the discordant notes which have already been noticed in the *Logic* and in the *Philosophy of Nature*. Now Hegel certainly praised the state as the speculative form of the objective Spirit, but was the power of the Spirit able to take up the resistant sphere of the concrete-empirical fully into itself according to the law of speculative con-creteness? According to his basic speculative scheme Hegel's state is obliged to present the face of an ethical reality which is at once perfect, harmonious and free; but is it not in fact a thoroughly ordinary state notwithstanding all of his speculative panegyrics? Was it not really built on power, the exercise of coercive authority and highly un-virtuous citizens, few of whom consciously participated in the life of the state? (Hegel himself, we recall, set a highly unedifying example with his appeal to the authority of the state against a critic of his *Philosophy of Right*!) Did not the harsh necessity of realistic compromise cause the speculative-perfect state asserted by Hegel to come down to the level of an empirical-historical state in a nineteenth-century form, a state which would jealously guard its unspeculative exclusiveness over against other states? All in all, this real state was to prove a severe handicap for the perfect culture in art, religion and philosophy that was meant to be built on this 'perfect' ethical reality.[59]

6. Christ Sublated in 'Right'

Given its speculative backround, Hegel's *Philosophy of Right* could be understood as a 'political theology', if we may use a term which has recently become fashionable again.[60] On account of the basic tendency of his thought, which was religious *and* social and which we have noticed from his Tübingen days onwards, Hegel did not for one moment hesitate to relate his now ripe

---

[59]I. Iljin: *Die Philosophie Hegels als kontemplative Gotteslehre,* 305-322.
[60]The most prominent advocate of *'political theology'* in the most recent period has been J.B. Metz, who has developed his own position in dialogue with E. Bloch, A. Gehlen, J. Habermas, W. Benjamin, H. Lübbe, H. Schelsky, T.W. Adorno, H.Marcuse, H.Albert and others. Metz has

speculative system programmatically and *in extenso* to social reality. From the beginning there had been for him no wordless thought of an isolated subjectivity, for which only an inter-personal I-Thou relationship can be of significance. From the beginning he had acknowledged no barrier of the private and a-political: the world and society were included in his thought. Hegel's *Philosophy of Right* presents the consistent and explicit unfolding of the social and political implications of his philosophy of Spirit, in which political practice appears as an expression of speculative theory. And insofar as this philosophy of the objective Spirit represents a form of the externalised divine Idea itself, it would indeed be possible to speak in a certain way of a 'political *theology*' with respect to this account of 'right' and the state, which, as a ripe form of ethical reality is an appearance of the divine will in the world.

Even so, we cannot ignore the fact that earlier theology had already in its own way made great efforts to relate to social and political reality and to assert its own socio-political dimension and relevance. As is well known, the separation of dogmatics and ethics into distinct spheres of work came about only gradually, and even then it was very much a matter of making a virtue of necessity. Not only the classic systematic works of the Reformation period (Melanchthon's *Loci communes* and Calvin's *Institutio*), but also the mediaeval *summae* (especially that of Aquinas, which was of fundamental importance in the systematisation of ethics) treat dogmatics and ethics in one. In historical perspective, therefore the *Philosophy of Right* represents the taking up and speculative reorganisation of two disciplines of practical philosophy. Now this is clearly illustrated by the sub-title which Hegel appended to his *Elements of the Philosophy of Right,* namely *Natural Law and Political Science in Outline.*

M. Riedel comments·as follows: 'The concepts of the last-mentioned title designate two disciplines of practical philosophy, one of which, belonging as it does to recent Europe, was developed largely in the eighteenth and nineteenth centuries, while the other had been handed down from classical Greek philosophy, being discussed in scholastic philosophy under the heading of *politics* right up to the time of Christian Wolff. Now the essence of classical political science consists in the fact that it

---

advocated his views in various publications, e.g. ın his book *Zur Theologie der Welt* (ET *Theology of the World*) and in a number of articles: '*Das Problem einer politischen Theologie und die* ſ*Bestimmumg der Kirche als Institution gesellschaftskritischer Freiheit*' (*Concilium* 4, 1968, 403-411; ET 'The Church's Social Function in the Light of Political Theology', *Concilium* 4, 1968, vol 6, 3-11), 'Polistische Theologie' (*Sacramentum Mundi*¹ III, 1968, 1232-1240; ET 'Political Theology' vol 5, 34-8); *Die Zukunft des Menschen und der Kommende Gott' (Wer ist das eigentlich Got?* ed. H.J. Schultz, 1969, 260-275); and '"*Politische Theologie" in der Diskussion' (Stimmen der Zeit 184, 1969, 289-308). For a critical treatment of Metz's own position see* H. Maier: '*Politische Theologie? Einwände eines Laisen*' (*Stimmen der Zeit* 94, 1969, 73-91); *see also Metz's reply: '"Politische Theologie" in der Diskussion'*.

acknowledged no separation of natural law from political science; its idea of the best constitution is to be understood as a setting forth of natural law and a ('civil') society conceived in legal terms (*societas civilis*), which is identical with the state (*civitas, res publica*) . . . The antithesis between natural law on the one hand and political science on the other thus ushered in the modern revolution and has accompanied its subsequent progress. Now Hegel's *Philosophy of Right* not only presupposes this antithesis, but is also a philosophical-political attempt to overcome it. Mention of natural law and political science is preceded by the title which gave the work its actual name: *Elements of the Philosophy of Right*. Hegel's political philosophy is to be understood in a highly specific sense as a "philosophy of 'right'", since it seeks to sublate the antithesis between a natural law which existed prior to the state and the positive law of the state by basing both on the "Notion" of "right", to wit, on the freedom of man *as* man. As far as Hegel is concerned, this Notion has an historical content, which consists – since the entrance of Christianity into world history – in the equality of souls before God, and – since the end of the eighteenth century – in the equality and liberty of individuals before the revolutionary state.'[61]

We are wont today to reproach traditional theology for taking too little care to develop its social and political implications directly from its central concepts and images, but this point of view should be balanced by observing that there is some evidence that this method has been employed with all too much success in the history of theology and the Church. The first great blueprint of a Christian 'political theology', that of the Constantinian court bishop Eusebius of Caesarea, already developed a partly religious, partly political imperial theology which became the pattern for many with its programme of 'one God, one Logos, one Emperor, one Empire'. Today we are glad to make the critical observation that what took place here was an uncritical and uncontrolled surrender of theology (and, indeed, of the Christian message itself) to a socio-political ideology which was thoroughly 'modern' in its day. Now it follows from the above outline of Hegel's partly affirmative, partly critical attitude to the Prussian state that this very reproach cannot be brought without further ado against the *Philosophy of Right*. Against the background of the recent demand for a 'political theology' which is meant to be neither simply an exercise in applied theology, political ethics or social theory, nor even a new theological discipline in its own right, but rather a distinctive feature in the construction of the critical-theological conscious-ness as a whole, misunderstanding can perhaps be averted by insisting that, notwithstanding his endorsement of the social relevance undoubtedly pertain-ing to every aspect of his thought, Hegel nevertheless remained on his guard against deducing his philosophy of right directly from his philosophy of religion or *vice versa*. This caution evidences, on the one hand, his respect for

---

[61]*Einleitung zu Hegel, Studienausgabe II*, 9-28; cf. *idem: Hegels Kritik des Naturrechs.*

the modern secularity of law, society and state, all of which are included in the secularisation of the world and need no neo-integralist theologisation, and, on the other, his respect for religion, in comparison with which political reality, which is a form only of the 'objective' and not of the 'absolute' Spirit, cannot itself be the absolute but only something of penultimate importance. In this way Hegel managed to avoid the pitfalls which lie in the path of a political theology, which – albeit against its will – would as it were retrospectively saddle the Christian message with a particular political ideology and pronounce certain political thought-forms of contemporary society to be categories of the Christian revelation. At the same time, however, Hegel demonstrated his ability, while avoiding pseudo-political 'theological' lines of argument and cheap abstract sociological clichés, to get to grips as a thinker with concrete political issues, that is, with right, law, constitution, institutions, and with the whole range of difficult details involved in social common life, things which the 'political theology' of today deems itself sovereignly entitled to ignore.

Now an important corrective is undoubtedly supplied when, in order to fend off these and similar objections, some scholars become 'post-critical' in a leftist sense, invoking Hegel's concept of 'negative mediation' and a 'second reflection' to advocate a 'political theology' whose relationship to the social present is not one of identity but rather critical-dialectical in kind, a 'political theology' which exercises a critical-liberating function toward society. Nevertheless, we cannot overlook the possibility that a reactionary (neo-) politicisation of faith from the right will be matched by an equally perilous revolutionary (neo-)politicisation of faith from the left. To counter-balance the example of the establishment theology of Eusebius and his numerous successors right up to the present century, it is sufficient to mention the Anabaptist revolutionaries of Münster, who are representative of much of the 'fanaticism' (*Schwärmertum*) which results from mixing religion with politics. In Münster, be it recalled, the absolute will for justice, freedom and peace – hence for the realisation of the kingdom of God (or Zion) in this specific society – led, in a particular, critical negation, to the use of revolutionary violence in order to establish the revoltingly cruel communist reign of terror by a leftist Christian integralism. In the light of this cautionary example we may ask whether it was simply due to a lack of intellectual consistency or of insight into the relationship between theory and practice when the post-revolutionary Hegel showed himself to be more than reserved toward the spectre of revolutionary protest and towards a reflection which turns into revolution, and when he displayed as little inclination to fall under the spell of permanent revolution as he did to succumb to the charms of romantic restoration.

Both J. Ritter *and* J. Habermas are correct in their account of the mature Hegel's attitude to revolution. J. Ritter: 'No other philosophy is in its inmost impulses so much a philosophy of revolution as is Hegel's.'[62] J. Habermas defends the complementary thesis 'that Hegel elevated revolution as the principle of his philosophy for the sake of a philosophy which overcomes revolution as such'.[63] 'Hegel made revolution the core of his philosophy in order to preserve philosophy from becoming the pimp of revolution.'[64] Thus, while the older Hegel by no means 'joined the counter-revolution',[65] the enlightenment which came with Robespierre's reign of terror caused him to warn against revolutionary violence, thereby earning Habermas's censure. According to Hegel 'the complete abolition of tottering structures can only be calmly and honourably achieved by way of prudent reform.'[66]

Hegel's avoidance of the concept of a 'political theology', notwithstanding the obvious relatedness of his theological thought to society, should therefore not prompt a sudden fit of depression. For in its historical context this concept of $\theta\epsilon o\lambda o\gamma\acute{\iota}\alpha\ \pi o\lambda\iota\tau\iota\kappa\acute{\eta}$ (or *theologia civilis*, which in the thought of the Stoa was distinct from mythical and natural theology) meant the direct theologisation of the existing forms of state and society in the sense of that mixture of state and religion which had provoked the vigorous and justified criticism of Augustine. Christian 'political theology' thereby proved itself to be the direct successor of the religious state. ideology of ancient Rome, whose theological sanctioning of the primacy of politics and legitimisation of the absolute claim of the state continued to wield influence not only in the Renaissance, in Machiavelli and in Hobbes, but also in the political Romanticism of Hegel's day. Given that it is encumbered with the two thousand year-old tradition of an integralist view of state and society geared to the restoration of the old order, it would be no easy task at the present time dictatorially to recast the concept of 'political theology' into a critical-revolutionary construct. The difficulties inherent in such an enterprise are underlined by the dubious notoriety acquired by the concept of 'political theology' in the recent past through its use by the Catholic constitutional lawyer and unwilling precursor of National Socialism, Carl Schmitt,[67] against whom the theologian E. Peterson directed his detailed study on 'monotheism as a political problem'.[68]

---

[62] *Hegel und die Französische Revolution*, 15.
[63] *Theorie und Praxis*, 103 (98-107: ch. 3 – Hegel's Critique of the French Revolution); ET *Theory and Practice*, 136.
[64] *op. cit.*, 106; ET, 139.
[65] *op. cit.*, 101; ET, 134.
[66] *op. cit.*, 97; ET, 129.
[67] *Politische Theologie. Vier Kapitel zur Lehre von der Souverantität* (1922, reissued 1934!), esp. 47-66. Something similar holds good also with respect to the term 'political Christ'.
[68] *Theologische Traktate*, 45-147.

Building on an understanding of the Trinity which is no longer without problems of its own, E. Peterson endeavoured to refute C. Schmitt by 'proving, through one concrete example, the theological impossibility of a "political theology"'.[69] His conclusion runs as follows: 'Only on the soil of Judaism or paganism can there be such a thing as a "political theology". While the Christian proclamation of the triune God stands beyond Judaism and paganism, the mystery of triunity exists only within the Godhead itself and not within the creature. Just as the peace sought by the Christian is granted by no emperor, but is the exclusive gift of the One who "passes all understanding".[70] The constitutional lawyer H. Maier recently made this remark on these words: 'Even today there is nothing to be added to these words apart from a reference to their enduring relevance. For even the new political theology is but a secularised, "dialectical" variant of the old.'[71]

It may thus be conceded that the glittering *concept* of 'political theology', burdened down with historical baggage and currently prone to misunderstanding as it is, constantly displays an immanent tendency towards 'politicised theology' to right and left. Yet this admission is not sufficient to write off the numerous *concerns* of 'politcal theology' which have been advocated by J. B. Metz. The latter has attacked the tendency of a transcendental or existential hermeneutic to confine its attention to the sphere of the private and has engaged in a critical-constructive debate with leftist Hegelianism's critique of ideology and religion, which seeks to unmask religion as a function derived from certain social conditions and as the false consciousness of a society which is not yet properly conscious of itself. Metz thus opposes a onesided stress on the inward, the spiritual and the individual by emphasising the Gospel's validity for social ethics and its social relevance, the primary rather than merely retrospective public character of the Christian message, and the socio-critical function and practical reference of theology and the Church! The conceptual pairs 'private – public', 'theory – practice' and 'eschatological – political' do indeed need to be thought through afresh.

Even so, precisely when theology is meant, from a specific perspective and within specific limits, to realise a critical function in society, then it must be in a position not only to know but also to justify the *basis on which* it criticises. If in its negative or positive criticism it only says what society itself has been saying all along, then its criticism is superfluous. It is thus scarcely sufficient to join everyone else in calling for justice, freedom and peace, even if this is done under the label 'kingdom of God'. Nor is it sufficient to place this divine kingdom of righteousness, freedom and peace under an 'eschatological proviso', especially if the latter can under certain circumstances be misunder-

[69]*op. cit.*, 147.
[70]*op. cit.*, 105.
[71]*'Politische Theologie?'*, 91.

300

stood as simply an inner-historical 'Not Yet' or – at least in principle – be harvested in the near or distant future by the revolutionary removal of injustice, servitude and conflict which will ideally result in the 'new man' and other 'socialist achievements'. The decisive factor for the entire Christian message of the New Testament is, on the contrary, that this coming kingdom of the absolute future has already dawned for the believer in the Christ-event. Should anyone wish within the context of a 'political theology' to characterise the relationship between faith and socially related practice as the fundamental 'hermeneutical' problem of theology – an enterprise liable to misunderstanding – then this cannot be done without a serious theological effort to determine the content of Christian faith and the Christian message. Ought one, for example, to speak of the Christian message without speaking very clearly of Christ? And ought one to be able to speak very clearly of Christ without speaking of him as the Crucified One to whom Christian faith, love and hope are and remain bound?

The archaeologist on his dig would often seem to be better aware than the political theologian that the cross is the *signum* of what is specifically Christian. Would not a discriminating Christian critique of society be bound to speak in terms of this discriminatingly Christian *signum*? As W. Schultz ascertained in the course of going through Hegel's philosophical work,[72] the philosopher had not, in his output up to this point, suppressed the cross nor had he emphasised only secondary aspects of it, such as its public character. The entire seriousness of the cross was displayed in that monstrous slogan, the 'death of God'. The question nevertheless remains whether Hegel took up the original Christian message of the cross in an appropriate way.

Since for its own part it is nothing other than 'its own time apprehended in thoughts' (*PR*, 11), the *Philosophy of Right* is, as Hegel programmatically spells out in the Preface, principally concerned with the *cross of the present*. That is to say, it focusses on the whole gamut of existent unreconciled modern social reality, which is at the mercy of arbitrariness and chance unless people succeed in discerning rational meaning, indeed reason itself, as the *rose* in the cross of the present: 'To recognize as the rose in the cross of the present and thereby to enjoy the present, this is the rational insight which reconciles us to the actual, the reconciliation which philosophy affords to those in whom there has once arisen an inner voice bidding them to comprehend, not only to dwell in what is substantive while still retaining subjective freedom, but also to possess subjective freedom while standing not in anything particular and accidental but in what exists absolutely' (*PR*, 12).

---

[72] *Die Transformierung der Theologia crucis bei Hegel und Schleiermacher*, 290-308.

This is accordingly man's historic task here and now in modern society. Hegel sets his face against pure utopians who build for themselves in their imagination 'a world, *as it ought to be*', but not such a world as exists in reality; and he transforms the '*Hic Rhodus, hic salta*' addressed to the boastful pentathlete who is said to have performed a mighty jump in Rhodes into '*Here* is the rose, dance thou *here*' (*PR*, 11). To achieve the concrete-historical reconciliation of socio-political reality (as opposed to its merely utopian or abstract-*cum*-supratemporal reconciliation), one must first of all succeed in understanding this reality in rational terms, and as far as Hegel is concerned this involves connecting it with a sense of reality, with reason, with the Absolute, with God.

Ideas which will subsequently be expressed with an altogether different kind of clarity on the level of the philosophy of religion – 'one must take the cross upon oneself in order to pluck the rose in the cross of the present' (XIII:I, 37) – already come into their own here at the level of 'right'. The significance of the negative dialectic, namely that the rose can be found solely in the cross – and in Hegel's view this by no means rules out the possibility of social change – is that liberty can be found solely in limitation. 'If we hear it said that the definition of freedom is ability to do what we please, such an idea can only be taken to reveal an utter immaturity of thought . . .' (*PR*, 27). This kind of liberty is anything but true liberty, indeed it is 'arbitrariness', 'the will as contradiction' (*PR*, 27; cf. 21, 23–31). True liberty is self-determination in self-*limitation* and precisely thus in self-*unfolding*: 'It is the *self*-determination of the ego, which means that at one and the same time the ego posits itself as its own negative, i.e. as restricted and determinate, and yet remains by itself, i.e. in its self-identity and universality. It determines itself and yet at the same time binds itself together with itself. The ego determines itself, in so far as it is the relating of negativity to itself' (*PR*, 23; cf. 29-31). But it is precisely the negative dialectic which releases the positive: duty, which seems to be 'a restriction on . . . indeterminate subjectivity or abstract freedom, and on the impulses either of the natural will or of the moral will which determines its indeterminate good arbitrarily', is in truth 'liberation' (*PR*, 107). There is gain in loss. By submitting to integration into the universal divine reason and its forms of ethical order, the individual is ultimately obeying himself and finding freedom in necessity. True ethical reality comes about in freedom, that is, in the ethical World Spirit, 'the self-will of the individual has vanished together with his private conscience which had claimed independence and opposed itself to the ethical substance. For, when his character is ethical, he recognizes as the end which moves him to act the universal which is itself unmoved but is disclosed in its specific determinations as rationality actualized. He knows that his own dignity and the whole stability of his particular ends are

302

grounded in this same universal, and it is therein that he actually attains these' (*PR*, 109). Subjectivity and objectivity, freedom and necessity, right and duty are one.

In all of this Hegel has not overlooked the social dialectic of mastery and servitude, wealth and poverty; on the contrary, he has discovered these things, and that for the benefit of none other than Karl Marx! Hegel was the first to subject to philosophical analysis the contradictions of civil society, in which the human person appears as subject and object of a system of need which is dialectically determined by the arbitrary self-interest of individuals on the one hand, and by their all-round and thoroughgoing dependence on the other. For it is precisely *particular* interests whose multiplication and refinement compel people with their inner logic – since, after all, the multiple and refined needs of modern society can only be satisfied by the division of labour – to acknowledge and show consideration for other people, or, to put it in a nutshell, to serve the *general* interest. Nevertheless, the dialectic of the system of needs does not disintegrate. It is not clear why this should be so, but reality itself actively takes the lead here: 'In these contrasts and their complexity, civil society affords a spectacle of extravagance and want as well as of the physical and ethical degeneration common to them both' (*PR*, 123) It goes without saying that Hegel never held the naive view that these contradictions ought to be sublated only in thought and not in reality: it is well known that he considered 'speculation' to mean something completely different from mere 'thought'! According to him such a sublation could not be achieved through the agency of the formal civil constitutional state with its *de facto* injustice and material inequality. At the same time, though, neither did he think that it could be accomplished – as was subsequently believed – through the establishment of a classless society. On the contrary, he held that the sublation should be executed through the realisation of the ethical state, which would balance out the arbitrary contradictions of social class and thus defend the revolutionary principle of liberty against, on the one hand, the restoration of the pre-constitutional *status quo ante,* and on the other, also against the revolution itself, namely against its capsizing into the terror which would dispense with any notion of civil liberty. According to Hegel this ethical state can only be realised when, as has already been described, the individual realises his liberty in restriction, when he determines himself by restricting himself.

Hegel was the first to make the distinction between civil society and the state and his speculative mediation between the two could not long be maintained after he was gone. Marx analysed the state in terms of political economy as a *phenomenon* of civil society, which would in due course die off with the latter. Even though the great majority were not prepared to go as far

303

as this, after Hegel's death the state was no longer understood speculatively as the reality of the ethical Idea, but was rather interpreted sociologically as a product of social movement. If they agreed about nothing else, Marx, Saint-Simon, Auguste Comte, John Stuart Mill and Herbert Spencer were at least of one heart and mind about this. Even so, quite apart from this *consensus omnium,* Hegel's idea of freedom through restriction remains of the greatest significance. But how did Hegel actually come to think up this freedom in restriction, this development through self-renunciation, this affirmation through negation?

The whole foregoing account of Hegel's thought has adequately explained just how decisive a role his christological understanding of God played at this very point. Such restriction, renunciation and negation are demanded of man because they are precisely what the Absolute demands of itself. Consequently, man simply accompanies and re-lives what the absolute Spirit itself achieves in the common history of the world and society. Already in Jena Hegel had spoken of the 'speculative Good Friday', of the 'infinite pain' and of the 'absolute suffering' of the Godhead (I, 345; *Faith and Knowledge*). And the closing words of the *Phenomenology* proclaimed that 'to know one's limit is to know how to sacrifice oneself. This sacrifice is the externalization in which Spirit displays the process of its becoming Spirit in the form of free contingent *happening*' (*PS,* 492). The history of Spirit is not simply a matter of conserving and self-preserving remembrance, an inward flight to self, but rather at the same time a sacrificing and self-surrendering 'Golgotha', a renunciation of itself (*PS,* 493). Hence we now read in the *Philosophy of Right:* 'The history of mind is its own act. Mind is only what it does, and its act is to make itself the object of its own consciousness. In history its act is to gain consciousness of itself as mind, to apprehend itself in its interpretation of itself to itself. This apprehension is its being and its principle, and the completion of apprehension at one stage is at the same time the rejection of that stage and its transition to a higher. To use abstract phraseology, the mind apprehending this apprehension anew, or in other words returning to itself again out of its rejection of this lower stage of apprehension, is the mind of the stage higher than that on which it stood in its earlier apprehension' (*PR,* 216). God himself is indeed the repose within motion, the peace within struggle and the reconciliation within conflict. The intensification and exaltation of man accordingly takes place simultaneously with the externalisation and humiliation of God: 'The ethical life is the divine spirit as indwelling in self-consciousness, as it is actually present in a nation and its individual members' (*PM,* 283).

It is once again conspicuous that in the whole of the *Philosophy of Right* Hegel breathes not a word of Jesus, with the single exception of a quotation from him in a context of only secondary importance (*PR,* 94). Even though the background of his thought is manifestly Christian and christological, the concrete Christ is frankly missing. Hegel takes no account of the concrete Christ whose challenging demand and pragmatic commitment, as evidenced not only by his word and teaching but also by his life and death, show people a concrete way, or, rather, show him to be *the* concrete way. His system had no room for the concrete Christ who shows how true freedom, genuine self-preservation and positive affirmation can be found only in constraint, self-renunciation and negation respectively, how life can be won only by being lost, in short, how the rose can be found solely in the cross.

As we have examined Hegel's thought from many angles in the course of this study, we have realised why it is that he could ignore the concrete Christ while at the same thinking in christological terms. He could explain such a way of thinking speculatively on the basis of the immanent path of the Notion. As far as he was concerned, after all due respects have been paid to the divine 'freedom', God's essence is self-humiliation and self-limitation, so that man's essence is likewise self-humiliation and self-limitation. This is simply 'logical', just as it is true in general terms that the Notion contains its opposite from the very outset and is obliged to externalise itself into its opposite. This dialectical process consequently occurs in a completely automatic and natural way in true ethical reality also, that is, in the 'right' whose freedom is necessity and whose necessity is freedom. God's acting in this way is no more than simply . . . '*right*'. Embracing both natural and positive law, this 'right' *qua* 'Idea' (*PR,* 33) 'is a purely immanent progress, the engendering of its determinations' (*PR,* 34): 'It is only because right is the embodiment of the absolute concept or of self-conscious freedom that it is something sacrosanct' (*PR,* 33; cf. 107f). All things automatically discern their true path in this 'right': God and man in one, through limitation to development, through humiliation to exaltation.

The only question is whether a fundamental christological scheme can be convincing apart from the concrete Christ. For his teaching, life and death show us the way not *in abstracto* but entirely *in concreto,* not just theoretically but in a highly practical form, not in passing but as the very heart and core of his mission, not simply as the way things turned out but as the result of his conscious intention. Indeed, Jesus is the personal embodiment of '*the* way' (Jn. 14:6). In the concrete programme of the Bible this way is neither Socrates, Epictetus, Buddha, Confucius, Mohammed, Moses, Spinoza, Kant, Bentham, Spencer, Nietzsche, Schopenhauer, Feuerbach, Marx nor Freud: on the contrary, the way is Jesus alone.

What is the point of a *theologia crucis* without the Crucified? In the absence of the latter it must remain abstract, devoid of challenge and inpotent to

305

summon man to practical discipleship. Now it is patently obvious that, in Hegel's comprehensive system, what the whole history of thought has understood by 'ethics' gets something of a raw deal. Again, it is striking that, notwithstanding its general coverage of such topics as conscience, the Good and the forms of evil, the section on morality in the *Philosophy of Right* does not appear to be particularly concerned to give an answer to specifically ethical questions. Is this deficiency wholly accidental, or should we put it down to nothing more than Hegel's aversion to mere inwardness and armchair moralising, and to his concern for the fusion of personal and public existence?

E. Bloch: 'No matter how emphatically he speaks of man and subordinates everything else to man's concerns, he still prefers to speak of man as of something external to himself from which he likes to keep his distance. The *agora*, the market, the *res publica*, public affairs are what bring Hegel's – not deficient but as it were simple – ethics to life. We catch a glimpse here of a characteristically Hegelian recapitulation brought about by a variety of inter-related causes: just as Hegel's logic is devoid of epistemological sting, so his work on "objective Spirit" lacks specifically moral bite.'[73]

The concrete Christ has been both incorporated and counterbalanced in this *Philosophy of Right,* and – as Hegel would doubtless put it – 'sublated' in the best sense of the word. For his sixtieth birthday he had received from his pupils a specially minted medallion on whose obverse was depicted his own image and whose reverse showed a genius sitting between a scholar stationed before an owl and a female figure with the cross. This was a course meant to represent Hegel himself mediating between philosophy and theology, between a philosophy of reason and a theology of the cross.[74] The delighted Hegel caused one of these to be sent to Goethe, but the poet was thoroughly revolted by this combination (*contignatio*) of the cross and philosophical reason: 'I have no idea what it is supposed to mean. In my stanzas I have given proof of my ability as a man and as a poet to honour and embellish the cross, but I take no pleasure in the fact that a philosopher should lead his pupils to this arid contignation along a detour through the primordial and nugatory grounds of essence and non-essence. This idea can be had at a lower price, and it can be more becomingly expressed.'

Even so, Goethe agreed with Hegel that the severity and nakedness of the cross should be spiritualised and humanised in such a way that it would be rendered acceptable: 'a light honorary cross is always something merry in life,

---

[73]*Subjekt – Objekt,* 257.
[74]K. Löwith: *Von Hegel zu Nietzsche,* 28.

but no rational man should trouble to dig up and erect the wretched gallows of the cross, which is the most repulsive object under the sun.' Thus Hegel and Goethe both use the image of rose and cross, in order to 'sublate' the cross of the concrete into either reason or humanity.

K. Löwith: 'However, there are the following differences in the use made of the same symbol. For Goethe the emblem of the cross remains a mystery which cannot be grasped in words; for Hegel it is simply the sensual representation of a relationship which can be grasped conceptually. Goethe sublates Christianity in humanity and the mysteries reveal what is the "purely human"; Hegel sublates Christianity in reason which – *qua* Christian Logos – is the "Absolute". Goethe causes the cross to be liberally swathed with the rose of humanity and he keeps philosophy distinct from theology, while Hegel sets the rose of reason in the midst of the cross and philosophical thought is meant to annex the dogmatic conceptions of theology. In Goethe's explanation of his poem the event is admittedly placed in Holy Week, but he takes the celebration of the death on the cross and the resurrection of Christ to mean simply the "setting of a seal" on exalted states of the human psyche. In the meantime, Hegel's philosophy aims at "breaking the seal" of the historical events of Holy Week by turning the latter into "speculative Good Friday" and Christian dogmatics into a philosophy of religion where Christian suffering and Christian theology become identical with the Idea of supreme freedom and philosophy respectively.'[75]

The origin of the connection between the rose and the cross lies neither with Hegel nor with Goethe. Hegel must have become acquainted with it in two contexts during his time as a theologian in Tübingen. For the rose and the cross made up the coat of arms of the Rosicrucian sect, which developed in various places on the basis of a legend concerning its foundation invented, so it is supposed, by the Tübingen theology student J. V. Andreä at the beginning of the seventeenth century. At the same time, Martin Luther's coat of arms consisted of a black cross set inside a red heart surrounded by a white rose. The Reformer's motto ran: 'The Christian heart treads on roses when it stands under the cross'. And Luther interpreted this as a 'hallmark' of his theology: 'For the righteous man is to live by faith, but by faith in the Crucified One.'[76]

The cross of Christ as the cross of Jesus of Nazareth was never a timeless myth or a profound religious symbol. On the contrary, it was a harsh and cruel historical fact. At the time of Jesus and in the environment of early Christianity no one, whether Jew or pagan, would have stumbled on the idea of associating the profane and shameful death of slaves and political rebels with

---

[75]*op. cit.*, 32.
[76]From Luther's letter to Lazarus Spengler in Nuremberg 8.7.1530, *W A Breife* 5, 445 (*LW* 49, 356-359); cf. also J. Moltmann: *'Die "Rose im Kreuz der Gegenwart". Sum Verständnis der kirche in der modernen Gessellschaft'*, in his volume of collected essays *Perspektiven*, 212-231, esp. 230f.

a religious idea. Following in the steps of the early Christian Church and especially of Paul, Luther never attempted to 'sublate' the paradox of the cross, which was a stumbling-block for Jews and folly for Gentiles, and only for believers the power of God and the wisdom of God (cf. I Cor: 18-25). He stoutly refrained from 'sublating' the cross either by interpreting it with the rose of reason or by toning it down with the aid of the rose of humanity. Faith is and remains faced with a challenge here to enter into the real dialectic of lived-out discipleship of Christ. The Christian's heart finds itself cushioned on a bed of roses precisely when he takes his own cross on himself in believing trust in the Crucified. He is empowered to live hoping in the life of the Crucified One precisely when he says the 'Yes' of faith to the cross of the Crucified and accordingly to the cross of the present. In this case the light of meaning can shine where pure reason is obliged to capitulate into meaningless distress and guilt.

The essence of Christianity is therefore the cross or, rather, the Crucified as the one who confers meaning and makes life possible, the Crucified as the living Christ whom God has accepted and exalted. It goes without saying that neither Paul nor Luther believed that the message of the cross is competent to solve the innumerable great and small questions posed by the order of human law, society and state. They took due account of the secularity of the world which must solve secular questions with the secular means which stand at its disposal. Faith in the Crucified is not a cheap way of discounting the problems and hopes of society, nor is itn opium of empty promises. On the contrary, such faith directs us to the here-and-now and aims to bring about change where rulers threaten to smother the ruled, institutions threaten to smother persons, order threatens to smother liberty, and power threatens to smother right. At the same time, however, this faith takes the problems and hopes of society more seriously than society itself can do according to its lights.

Faith in the living Crucified One neither can nor will render law superfluous; it neither can nor will abolish power in society. Even so, faith in the Crucified One embraces the spheres of law and power, radically relativising them and thus making man truly free. It causes man to become so free within the order of law that he becomes capable of disclaiming a right without receiving anything in return, even to the extent of going two miles with one who has demanded only one mile of him. This faith causes man to become so free amidst the struggle for power within society that he becomes capable of using power at his own expense in favour of the other, even to the extent of giving up his cloak as well as his coat. The words of the Sermon on the Mount, which were backed up by Jesus' life and death, are not intended to establish a new law or to create a new legal system. Indeed, they intend to free people from the law. They aim to make possible the very things which cannot be expected of man in civil society, built entirely on self-interest and mutual dependance, but which are nevertheless infinitely important for the whole common life of humankind: the possibility of limitless forgiveness instead of the calculation of debt, the possibility of unconditional reconciliation instead of adamant insistence on set positions, the higher righteousness of love instead of continuous legal strife, the peace which passes all understanding instead of the merciless struggle for power.

In this radical way faith in the Crucified One permits the realisation of the good concerns of a 'political theology', while avoiding the peril of a naive politicisation of the Christian message according to the passing fashions of contemporary society.[77] As an 'earnest' of the Spirit of Christ this faith is the sole instrument through which the unconditional yearning for justice, freedom and peace can be achieved without injury to man, and it alone permits the dawning already in the here-and-now of the kingdom of full justice, unsurpassable freedom, unbroken love, universal reconciliation and eternal peace. And while human co-operation is of course needful here, in the end of the day this state of affairs cannot be procured by any human effort – and it matters little whether this takes the form of the progress of bourgeois society or of the socialist achievements of a postulated classless society – but must be given to man as a gift of the perfert God. Thus this faith prompts man to be fully and effectively active in this society in the spheres of learning, commerce, politics, the state, society, law and culture, and at the same time it enables man to withstand disappointment where no progress is being made, where neither social evolution nor socialist revolution are capable of overcoming the tensions and contradictions, the fissures and absurdities of human society. And it preserves man from despairing of justice, freedom and peace even in the midst of abysmal injustice amongst conditions marked by an utter lack of liberty and peace. The same faith produces hope where there is no longer any ground for hope, it engenders a love which includes even one's enemies, and it furthers the humanisation of society where people disseminate nothing but inhumanity. In terms of the concrete Christ alone can we explain the meaning of the rose in the cross, not merely *in abstracto,* but concretely, programmatically, convincingly and challengingly.

As we now reach the end of the last work which Hegel personally saw through the press, we must cast a brief backward glance. This thinking is immeasurably rich and at the same time astonishingly Christian. It has become inescapably clear that, formally at any rate, it has been deeply

---

[77]For the most up-to-date information, cf. the important theological details given in J. Moltmann: *'Politische Theologie'*.

influenced by the Christian message. Not that we may suppress the other side of the coin: while the oft-reiterated charge that Hegel philosophised away the concrete Christ is certainly without foundation, he has nevertheless philosophised him into his own wider philosophical scheme, and he has done this in such a way that the concrete Christ can no longer be himself. Precisely on account of the christologically determined basic conception of Hegel's philosophy, the disappearance and suppression of the name of Jesus Christ should alert our suspicion, As we were constantly obliged to state afresh in connection with the *Phenomenology*, the *Logic*, the *Encyclopaedia* and the *Philosophy of Right*, the concrete Christ has been interwoven into and 'sublated' by this philosophy: 'the truth' – sublated in knowledge (*Phenomenology*); 'the beginning' – sublated in being (*Logic*); 'grace' – sublated in the system (*Encyclopaedia*); 'the way' – sublated in right (*Philosophy of Right*)! And precisely because the *Phenomenology*, the *Logic*, the *Encyclopaedia* and the *Philosophy of Right* are moments of one and the same philosophy, precisely because Reason, Idea, Spirit and Freedom are names of one and the same Godhead, and precisely because, when regarded from another angle, 'the truth' is also 'the way' and the true way is also 'grace' and the true way of grace is also 'the beginning' – for these very reasons it is clear that there can be nothing accidental about either the prison or the prisoner in the case of this particular 'sublation', that if the concrete Christ is a prisoner anywhere in this system he is a prisoner all along the line. Hegel's system has no centre, so that it is universally of a piece. The same misgivings which have been voiced under the heading of 'sublation' could also have been raised under any other rubric; and the same misgivings which have been expressed at this point could also have been voiced at any other juncture. Even the misgivings are ultimately congruous and interchangeable.

Nevertheless, these misgivings cannot be our last word on the subject, even if only because the *Philosophy of Right* was not the last word for Hegel himself. In this work – obviously on account of a certain wariness of the historical-empirical element which militates against any form of system-building – Hegel had resisted his deepest intentions by opting once again for the customary separation of the historical from the systematic. However, even this decision could not prevent the *Philosophy of Right* from drawing to a close by pouring forth like a wide river into the terrain of world history. Notwithstanding its lofty attributes, even the state is for Hegel not an immovable ultimate or even the supreme reality. For over the state there stands, as a new authority, *history*. In history even the state is exposed to the game of contingency, in which 'the universal mind, the mind of the world exercises its right – and its right is the highest of all – . . . in the "history of the world which is the world's court of judgment"' (*PR*, 216). Will the concrete

Christ of history come into his own afresh and by name in the concrete history of the world, the four chief phases of which Hegel has briefly sketched at the end of the *Philosophy of Right* and to which he now hopes to devote a course of weighty lectures in Berlin?

Chapter Seven: Jesus Christ in History

'God is known as spirit when known as the Triune. This new
principle is the axis about which world history revolves. World
history proceeds from and moves toward this point' (VIII, 722).

1. Old Age as Return

'I am permitted to wish and hope that I shall succeed in winning and
deserving your confidence on the path which we shall tread. To start with,
however, I may claim no more of you than confidence in this branch of study,
faith in *reason, confidence and faith in yourselves.* The prime precondition for
the *study of philosophy* is *courage for truth* and *faith in the power of the
Spirit.* Man is meant to honour himself *and to deem himself worthy of the
very highest'.* Such was Hegel's proclamation in his inaugural lecture held at
Berlin on 22 October 1818 (XXII, 8). In the meantime his wishes and hopes
had been richly fulfilled.[1]

He had begun his work in Berlin with the minimum of fuss, but he was soon
not only a professor but also the greatly admired and adored head of a
philosophical school. We can learn what forms this adoration could take from
his own account of his birthday celebrations in the year 1826 (XXIX,
134-137). He soon became a dominating figure in the university as a whole.
Thus his pupils took to holding revision classes, *conservatoire* sessions and
then even lectures of their own on the master's philosophy. People flocked in

---

[1]Our basic sources for this period in Hegel's life are his letters (XXVIII-XXX) and the freshly,
impeccably and comprehensively edited documents from the Berlin period published by
J. Hoffmeister under the title *Berliner Schriften.* This volume includes speeches, reviews, articles,
references, opinions, excerpts, remarks and records of the Faculty of Philosophy. We shall
conform to the original numbering of the critical edition by quoting the *Berliner Schriften* as vol.
XXII. The Faculty records are highly informative on the subject of Hegel's personal honesty,
putting him in a good light over the Beneke 'case' (XXII, 612-626) and over the 'cases' of Heinrich
Ritter and Friedrich Schopenhauer. The latter behaved extremely presumptuously from the
outset, even though his work met with no success. After Hegel's death Schopenhauer defamed
him in the most repulsive manner, although Hegel had made no difficulties for him either with
his *'Habilitation'* or subsequently (cf. XXII, 587-592).

droves to hear him from the whole of Germany and abroad, and his listeners included even his colleagues – for example the theologian Marheineke, who ater became the leader of the right-wing Hegelians. Nor did a whole troupe of up-and-coming professors disdain to sit at his feet: the lawyer Gans, the philosophers Henning, Michelet, Hotho and Rosenkranz, all of them well known as editors of Hegel's works. But it was his theological adherents who caused the greatest stir later on: David Friedrich Strauss, a pupil of the Tübingen scholar Ferdinand Christian Baur and Marheineke's antipode on the left wing; Bruno Bauer, who made a dialectical somersault from the radical right to the equally radical left; and Ludwig Feuerbach, from whom Marx was to take over his critique of religion. Immediately after his death we find nine of Hegel's direct pupils at the University of Berlin alone, and in the last decade of his life Hegelian philosophy was taught in Belgium, Holland, Denmark and Finland. Thus, in Hegel's lifetime the newly established Hegelian school seemed to be here to stay, the impression of robust durability being the more easily achieved in virtue of Hegel's close relations with Minister Altenstein and his correspondingly great influence on appointments to state positions. Hegel had himself been appointed a member of the State Commission for Academic Examinations (XXVIII, 232). As might be expected, however, passionate opposition to him mounted in proportion to the enormous growth of his power (cf., e.g., XXIX, 289). Nevertheless, neither anonymous writers nor such public opponents as Beneke, Fries, Herbart and Schopenhauer were able to make headway in their campaign against him. Even the ploy of denouncing him to the king failed to achieve the desired result. On the contrary, along with Schleiermacher, he received the Order of the Red Eagle (XXIX, 330f, 464).

Moreover, with the foundation in 1827 of the *Year Book for Scholarly Criticism* (*Jahrbuch für wissenschaftliche Kritik*) Hegel now had at his disposal a domestic mouthpiece through which he was able, whether directly or indirectly, to express his opinions and give vent to his criticisms. However, the opponents of this publication – who were especially incensed at the exclusion of Schleiermacher from thanks of the contributors (he retaliated by blackballing Hegel's admission to the Academy) – soon dubbed it the '*Hegel Magazine*' (XXIX, 118, 390-399). Hegel was accordingly pushed increasingly onto the defensive, being obliged to defend himself against the embittered accusations that he was un-Christian and set on self-deification. In these pages appeared the celebrated article on Hamann, with whom Hegel was most profoundly in agreement concerning the *coincidentia oppositorum* in the essence of God, even though he was put off by his unsystematic obscurity. And the *Year Book* also featured the reviews on Wilhelm von Humboldt, Solger, Göschel, Ohlert and Görres, along with Hegel's vigorous essays in self-defence against the anonymous *On Hegel's Teaching, or Absolute Knowledge and Modern Pantheism* and against Schubarth's and Carganico's *On Philosophy in General and Hegel's Encyclopaedia in Particular* (XXII, 83-447). Hegel's domination of the *Year Book* was a major factor in his increasing transformation from 'state philosopher' into 'philosopher of fashion' as well.[2]

The year 1829-30 saw Hegel at the pinnacle of the University of Berlin (XXIX, 285). In his inaugural lecture as *rector magnificus* he spoke about the proper use of academic freedom, and in the jubilee lecture which he delivered – in the face of some opposition[3] – on the Confession of Augsburg, he dwelt on the Christian freedom mediated through the Reformation (XXII, 30-55). Leaving out of account all the academic backbiting, from which he was not spared, it is hard to see how he could have risen any higher. His good Swabian bonhommie and his straightforward bourgeois simplicity, which his machinations for power did not wholly efface, conspired to make the philosopher a popular figure in elegant Berlin society, although he could also on occasion display a tyrannical and angry side of his character. Away from the bustle of Berlin Hegel took care to recuperate from the strenuous life of the head of a school by indulging in travel – and here too he received vigorous ministerial support (XXVIII, 310-312, 315f, 494-496). His journeys took him to Rügen and Dresden, right across Germany to Belgium, the Netherlands, Vienna, Austria and Paris (to the philosopher Cousin), and finally in 1829 via Weimar and Jena to Karlsbad and Prague (cf. the travel accounts in the numerous letters to his wife, XXVIII and XXIX, and especially the interesting reunions with Goethe, XXIX, 203-206, and Schelling, XXIX, 270, 445). In truth, Hegel had been abundantly compensated for the long wait for his professorship.

In company with others before him, Hegel too rediscovered his youth in his old age. To begin with, this is shown by the fact that, just as he published no works as a young man, even so he published no great works in his old age. As has been stated above, the *Philosophy of Right* which was issued in Berlin in 1821 was the last great work which Hegel himself earmarked for publication. Thereafter only a very few articles from his hand appeared in the *Year Book*. (In addition to these his Preface to Hinrich's *Philosophy of Religion* also merits mention; XXII, 59-82. It was here that he made the wounding remark about Schleiermacher's understanding of religion as a feeling of dependence: in that case, says Hegel, any dog can be religious; XXII, 74f, 80f). The great historical lectures which round off his system – on the philosophy of art,

[2]K. Rosenkranz: *op. cit.*, 394.
[3]E. Hirsch: *Fichtes, Schleiermachers und Hegels Verhältnis zur Reformation*, II.

religion, world history and the history of philosophy – were published in the years following 1832 by the 'Association of Pupils and Friends of the Deceased' (to be republished unchanged as the Jubilee Edition by H. Glockner).

It is well known that the editions of the these lectures abound in deficiencies. After all, the work was accomplished at great speed at a time when Hegel's philosophy stood at the centre of philosophical discussion. Moreover, the editors lacked the financial backing for long-drawn-out editorial work (the profits of the edition were intended for the Hegel family in token of gratitude). Thus a hard and fast, quasi-dogmatic system was put together entirely in the spirit of the Old Hegelians: texts from various periods (many even coming from the Jena lectures), along with hand-written notes by Hegel himself and the lecture notes and even independent compositions of his pupils – these were the materials which the editors patched together, forming their own chapters and oftentimes indulging in arbitrary triadic structures as they went along. Much was omitted, transposed and revised in order to bring out the 'one mould'. On the whole this editorial recasting 'normalised' and 'standardised' Hegel in such a way as to make it significantly more difficult to ascertain just what were his thoughts in this final period of his life.

Even so, such an enterprise is perfectly possible to the extent required for our present purposes. For one thing, the *Encyclopaedia,* which was revised and reissued in 1827 and 1830, furnishes us with the authentic 'guiding principles' with which to interpret the lectures of Hegel's last decade. For another, through the critical works of Lasson and Hoffmeister, we have access to Hegel's own papers from this period also. In particular, we have the 'Introductions', which enable us to determine with certainty the general import and content of the majority of the lectures, and whence the christological passages can be seen in the correct perspective. Even though we do not have autograph copies of the majority of texts from this period, they currently exist in editions some of which are adequate, and some of which are very good. (Hoffmeister's arrangement of the Introduction to the *History of Philosophy* is exemplary. With a clear overall view of the sources and receiving some help from new source material, he worked out the text according to the principle of the juxtaposition and chronological arrangement of the various sources as they appeared year by year. In the intervening period at least a further five manuscripts have been discovered). Finally, as we shall presently see, the task of interpretation is rendered easier by the fact that the clearly recognisable christological texts are in basic agreement with each other. With respect to this period it is no longer at all possible to talk of 'development' in the sense of the earlier works, since the lectures took shape not in chronological sequence but side by side in a way which produced a variety of repetitions. It is appropriate here to allude to Ernst Bloch's remark that, '[i]f *repetitio* is the *mater studiorum*, then this is especially true in hegel's case'.[4]

Notwithstanding the special difficulties, an unambiguous interpretation of these lectures is entirely feasible. Even so, we shall have to undertake this work with caution. To ascetain the general sense of the individual lectures we shall

---

[4]*Subjekt – Objekt,* 84.

rely chiefly on the statements of basic attitude which can almost always be gleaned from Hegel's hand-written Introductions (or, failing that, at any rate from the *Encyclopaedia*). To achieve a definitive interpretation of Hegel's Christology in this period, we shall weigh his harmoniously expressed basic ideas rather than any specific propositions. By now the foregoing analyses and explanations should have equipped the reader to assess Hegel's lectures and especially their christological passages as directly as possible without any protracted commentary. For the same reason the theological discussion is postponed to the end of this chapter.

The second way in which Hegel rediscovered his youth in his old age was by rediscovering *history*. When Hegel in his Berlin period develops the philosophy of history in the broadest meaning of the word in the greatest variety of directions, this is not a matter of the systematic philosopher taking steps toward the 'application' of his system. Now it was certainly the trend of his system that led him to the philosophy of world history. However, we have been able to observe that Hegel differed sharply from many of his philosophical contemporaries in that an intellectual preoccupation with history already marked the beginning of his career. In those early days in Tübingen, Bern and Frankfurt he was concerned less with nature (the chief interest of Schelling and many romantics) than with history – with the concrete history of Hellenism and of Christianity, with the history of Christ and of the community, with that of the state and of the Church. Here Hegel had found his philosophical problems, here he had formed his categories and his terminology, here he had also prepared his speculative solutions and his system as a whole. Nor did he subsequently forget history in Jena, Bamberg and Nuremberg (he not only wrote the *Phenemonology of Spirit,* but also lectured on the history of philosophy!); indeed, his entire system was meant to be and in fact is essentially an historical system. It was nevertheless obvious that from Jena onwards the dominant factor was no longer history but the system: the centre of his thought was to be found here in the sphere of the systematic. And we have seen that in the *Philosophy of Right* Hegel had even surrendered the unity of systematic and historical perspective, which he had earlier demanded on principle, in favour of purely systematic thought. Having in 1822-23 lectured for the first time on the philosophy of world history, in his later years in Berlin Hegel once more became intensively involved with concrete history, awarding it a quite different centrality in his last lectures from that which it had enjoyed in the preceding epoch. In pursuing this course he returned to his old habitat, albeit as a different man from the one who had quitted it so long before – as a mature man whose rich fund of philosophical and historical experience told him how he had to contemplate and judge the world and its course – as the course of the World Spirit.

In a third and final respect Hegel rediscovered his youth by displaying a renewed interest in *religion*. Now it is incontestable that he had always taken a certain kind of interest in religion. Even so, we cannot ignore the fact that, in Jena and in the period when he was engaged in constructing systems, the vital religious concerns of his early years were concealed and supplanted by a new philosophical impetus and systematic drive, making way for some highly dubious and questionable transformations. A change now came about in this respect. Hegel's *Philosophy of Religion,* on which he started to lecture in 1821, attests a highly intense preoccupation with religious problems (antedating, therefore, the *Philosophy of World History,* which by rights is prior to the *Philosophy of Religion* on the systematic scale!). Furthermore, while Hegel had formerly by and large kept quiet about the name of God (cf. the remark in the *Phenomenology; PS,* 40), he now mentions it with astonishing frequency. Over and over again he emphatically stresses that the whole of philosophy is concerned with knowing the essence of God (*Philosophy of Right: PR,* 8; *Philosophy of World History:* VIII, 40-49; *Aesthetics: A* I, 19, 80; *Philosophy of Religion:* XII, 1ff; *History of Philosophy:* XV, 12, 21). Hegel constantly discovers a fresh pretext for speaking about the relationship between philosophy and religion. Of interest in this context are the various Prefaces which he wrote to the *Encyclopaedia:* while nothing is said about religion in the first edition of 1817, the Prefaces of 1827 and 1830 are almost exclusively devoted to the relationship between philosophy and religion (V, 6-27). And detailed accounts of this relationship are also contained in the Prefaces or introductory chapters to the *Philosophy of Right* (*PR,* 2-7; 12f.), to the *Aesthetics* (*A* I, 110, 117-120), and – to say nothing of the *Lectures on the Philosophy of Religion* – to the *History of Philosophy* (XV, 16f, 40-59). And while Hegel always has hard things to say against the 'triviality and shallowness' of the philosophers of emotion and heart, he speaks with the utmost goodwill of religion itself and of Christianity.

A certain new trend of the times may not have been without influence on this change of heart, a tendency which went by the name of 'restoration' (for, after all, 'the recent period has directed attention once more to a pure subject, higher ideas and religion'; letter to Raumer, XXVIII, 101). At every juncture of his career Hegel displayed a striking adeptness (attributed to opportunism by some, to his basically speculative way of thinking by others) for obedience to the new historical hour of the World Spirit and for accomodating himself to the changed situation. And this adaptability was not adversely affected even by a cast of mind which remained in all essentials the same, and not only where things political were concerned. At all events, it is clearly noticeable in the passages referred to in the foregoing paragraph that Hegel is here on the defensive. He was increasingly obliged to justify himself, urging that his kind of 'rationality' and 'science' sublates Christianity not negatively but positively (the 'Halle controversy' against the theologians Wegscheider and Gesenius showed Hegel how dangerous the catchword 'atheism' in particular could become; XXIX, 321f, 460f; but cf. already XXVIII, 268, 272).

Yet Hegel's renewed intensive preoccupation with concrete history must have been an even more important factor than external events in awakening his increasing interest in religion. It was pointed out above how the depreciation of concrete history in favour of a philosophical system in the Jena period was a major reason why the historical Christ could have only a very limited effect on those *Draft Systems*. It cannot therefore be accidental, nor can it be a mere 'symptom of senility' (even though the psychological phenomenon of the 'religiosity of old age' may well be a contributory factor here) that in his last years, which were devoted once again to the intensive study of concrete history, Hegel increasingly directed his gaze toward Christianity and toward the concrete historical Christ.

2. Christ in World History

The *Encyclopaedia* and the Introductions to Hegel's various lectures prompt us to deal with the material in the following order: philosophy of world history; philosophy of art; pilosophy of religion; philosophy of philosophy (history of philosophy).

There is a danger that the flow of our account of these lectures might give the false impression of a cut and dried system. A quotation from H. G. Hotho's description of Hegel the teacher in the Berlin period will go a long way toward averting this peril. Hotho splendidly captured the gradual, unfinished and dialectical nature of Hegel's thought as this was reflected in the literary form of the public lecture:
'He would sit weary and fatigued, crumpled up in himself with head bowed, turning over the pages as he searched back and forth, up and down in the long folio volumes, talking away the while; the unremitting throat-clearing and coughing disturbed all flow of speech, so that every sentence stood in isolation and came out with great effort in a state of total dismemberment and disarray; only with reluctance did each word and syllable break loose for that metallic voice to give them a wondrously thorough emphasis in broad Swabian dialect, as though each word was the most important of all. Even so, the whole phenomenon compelled such profound respect and such an awareness of the speaker's dignity – indeed, the very naïveté of such overwhelming earnestness was itself attractive – that, even though I was ill at ease and could have understood little enough of what was said, I was riveted, nay cemented to the performance. Hardly had my zeal and persistence caused me to become rapidly acclimatised to the outer form of Hegel's delivery, when its inner excellencies dawned on me with increasing clarity. The inner excellencies merged with the outer deficiencies to become a single whole which carried the criterion of its consummation within itself alone.
'Smoothly flowing eloquence presupposes that the speaker knows his subject-matter

inside out, and formal adroitness can glide forward with the most charming garrulousness in a mixture of half-truth and commonplace. But Hegel's task was to extract the most vigorous ideas from the deepest depths of things; and if these were to have a vital influence, then they were obliged to reproduce themselves in contemporary form in his own person, even though this entailed the painful business of their being unremittingly hammered out afresh for years on end. The sheer difficulty of the task and the severe effort which it involved cannot be more vividly illustrated than by Hegel's mode of delivery. The ancient prophets afford a useful parallel here: the more intensely they grappled with language itself, the more they were able to master and conquer, inch by inch, the fundamental issues which raged within their breasts. Just so Hegel struggled to victory through the medium of his heavy-handed, terse style. Exclusively and utterly immersed in his subject-matter, he seemed to develop it from and for itself alone, scarcely to be using his own mind to unfold it for the benefit of his audience. And yet it did in fact derive from himself alone, and an almost fatherly concern for clarity would moderate the rigid seriousness which might well have deterred the listeners from taking in such difficult ideas. He would begin falteringly, try to go on, start up again, then stop once more. Thus he would alternately speak and reflect. One moment the *mot juste* seemed lost for ever, the next it erupted onto the scene like a flash of lightning; it seemed the most natural thing in the world, and yet it was matchlessly appropriate; it was obsolete, and yet it was the only word that fitted. Thereupon it always seemed that the heart and core of the matter were about to follow, and yet it had already been expressed as fully as possible without our noticing it. Having now grasped the clear meaning of a sentence, we ardently hoped to move forward. In vain. Instead of moving forward, Hegel's thought would now settle down to revolve about the same point with similar words to the ones he had just been using. If one's wearied attention strayed for just a moment, to return with a sudden start to the lecture only minutes later, its punishment was to be wrenched from the whole context of his thought. For, advancing quietly and reflectively forward through a set of seemingly meaningless middle terms, some fully rounded thought had been whittled down to onesidedness, chopped up into various component elements and enmeshed in contradictions. Only the reunion of this thought with its opposite number could enforce a victorious solution of the contradictions. He thus kept on solicitously hammering away at his earlier points, so that, after he had recast them into something more profound, he might develop thence his later points, which would themselves be more intense, both in discordance and concordance, than their predecessors. After this fashion the most wondrous flow of ideas would intertwine, surge and wrestle with one another. Even so, irrespective of whether his discourse took the form of isolated snippets or interconnected résumés, of sporadic hesitant statements or enthusiastic torrents of erudition, it surged inexorably onwards. Yet anyone who could follow his mental act in full possession of his intellectual faculties, looking aside to neither right nor left, would see himself thrust into the strangest tension and anxiety. He conducted one's thought down to such abysses and tore it apart into such infinite contradictions, that one deemed all previous gains to have been lost and all the foregoing effort to have been in vain, for even the very highest powers of cognition seemed compelled to stand in dumb silence before the limits of their competence. But in the very depths of the seemingly indecipherable, Hegel's powerful mind was rumaging and weaving in sublimely self-assured ease and tranquillity. Only then would he raise his voice and flash his eyes attentively over the assembled students, illuminating them in the silently blazing fire of that radiance of his, so replete with conviction, while he penetrated all the heights and depths of our souls with a never-

319

failing flow of words. What he expressed in these moments was so clear and exhaustive and of such simple truthfulness that everyone who was able to grasp its substance deemed himself responsible for its very discovery. Moreover, so complete was the disappearance of all earlier ways of imagining things that no memory remained of those dreamy days when the same thoughts had not yet awoken the same knowledge.'[5]

The *Philosophy of World History*[6] developed directly from the last work discussed above. As we have seen, the *Philosophy of Right* culminates in the chapter on world history (*PR*, 216-223; as was already the case in the *Encyclopaedia; PM*, 277-291). The basic outlines of the development of the *Philosophy of World History* are already prefigured here, as Hegel himself points out in his Introduction (*PWH*, 11). Hegel gave a new set of lectures on the philosophy of world history in a biennial cycle from the winter semester of 1822-23 onwards, thus lecturing on this subject five times in all (until the winter semester of 1830-31). World history was in fact bound to become a favourite topic of his, given that he had from the beginning been a teacher of lively 'becoming' as opposed to dead 'being', and that history had more and more ceased to be an embarrassment for him and had become the proper medium of philosophy.

In his *Philosophy of World History,* Hegel does not intend to offer just any old treatment of this topic, but rather a decidedly *philosophical* study of world

---

[5]*Vorstudien für Leben und Kunst,* 384-388.
[6]The lectures on the *Philosophy of World History* were first published by Gans in 1837, and then by Karl Hegel in 1840. These editors based their text on student notes, although they were able to use the autograph copy for the opening chapters. Their work was thoroughly revised and supplemented by Lasson (in 1917, 1919 and 1920), in whose editions those portions which come from Hegel's pen were printed in large type to distinguish them from the rest of the text. The first volume was revised yet again by Hoffmeister (in 1955). The author has used this volume along with the Lasson edition, but in order to avoid undue confusion we shall continue to refer to the *Philosophy of World History* under the volume number customary in the old edition, i.e. as vol. VIII instead of XVIIIa. The reader's attention will be drawn to texts from Hegel's autograph copy by an asterisk. H. B. Nisbet's translation of the opening chapters (*Lectures on the Philosophy of World History,* CUP, 1975) has been used wherever possible, and will be quoted in the following pages as *PWH* followed by the relevant page number. The older translation by J. Sibree (*The Philosophy of History,* London, 1894) is too widely at variance with the text of Lasson-Hoffmeister to be serviceable in the present context.
  In addition to the frequently mentioned general works, the works of the following authors are specially relevant to the *Philosophy of World History*: P. Barth, F. Brunstäd, G. Lasson, K. Leese, M.B. Foster, J. Plenge, H. Marcuse, J. Hyppolite, J. Ortega y Gasset, G. Fessard, K. Löwith. And the works of the following are recommended on more specialist topics: on the 'cunning of reason', R. F. Beerling and G. Schmitz; on the Idea of liberty, J. Hommes, V. Fazio-Allmayer, G. Lunati, W. Seeberger, H. Schmidt; on the rise of the Christian religion, H. Reese; on the relationship between atheism, Christianity and an emancipated society, W. Kern; on the world-historical understanding of the Orient, E.Schulin; on the *PS* as philosophy of history, R.K. Maurer. There are also various articles on Hegel's philosophy of history in the *Hegel-Jahrbuch,* vol. 1 (1961).

history (cf. here the distinction between original, reflective and philosophical history; *PWH*, 12-24): 'But the philosophy of history is nothing more than the application of thought to history' (*PWH*, 25*). Given the fundamentally speculative nature of Hegel's conception of things, this can have only one meaning: 'the simple idea of *reason* – the idea that reason governs the world, and that world history is therefore a rational process' (*PWH*, 27). Hegel presupposes this in the present work, and at the same time he proves it in a study of concrete world history which proceeds not from some '*a priori* fictions' (*PWH*, 29*), but from what is, as a matter of fact, given, from the history which – in its temporal sequence and empirical juxtaposition – is, at first glance, so arbitrarily chaotic. Even so, to the seeing eye of the thinking philosopher this history shows itself as 'the record of the spirit's efforts to attain *knowledge* of what it is in itself' (*PWH*, 54). It is the history whose 'ultimate end ... [is] the spirit's consciousness of its freedom (which is the precondition of the reality of this *freedom*)' (*PWH*, 55*; cf. 65f). World history is accordingly nothing but 'the rational and necessary evolution of the world spirit. The spirit [is] the substance of history; its nature is always one and the same; and it discloses this nature in the history of the world' (*PWH*, 29).

The World Spirit is roused to consciousness in world-historical peoples and individuals. Ultimately untouched and unassailed, in its '*cunning*' it proceeds on its course through all the unreason, sufferings and struggles of world history: 'For it is not the universal Idea which enters into opposition, conflict, and danger; it keeps itself in the background, untouched and unharmed, and sends forth the particular interests of passion to fight and wear themselves out in its stead. It is what we may call the *cunning of reason* that it sets the passions to work in its service, so that the agents by which it gives itself existence must pay the penalty and suffer the loss' (*PWH*, 89). However resolutely they pursue their own aims, even the great individuals of world history ultimately serve to pull the World Spirit's chestnuts out of the fire.

'Whoever looks at the world rationally will find that it in turn assumes a rational aspect; the two exist in a reciprocal relationship' (*PWH*, 29*). World history accordingly demonstrates to the philosopher 'that the world is *governed by providence*, ... that the world's events are controlled by a providence, indeed by a divine providence' (*PWH*, 35*). World history takes place for the '*glorification of God*, ... to do honour to God' (*PWH*, 150). World history is a realisation of the kingdom of God on earth! The philosopher's observant eye discerns the unhindered march of the free and good World Spirit throughout all catastrophes, wars and revolutions. Forms, configurations, peoples and individuals must disappear, yes *must* disappear, in order to make fresh room for something else. Spirit marches onward, although everything which it formerly discarded is in the best possible way preserved in the new. Even though it assumes a variety of forms, the Spirit is present in each age with the whole fullness of eternity, so that each age is itself the perfect end of time. Each age has its good points when it is viewed as the *kairos* of the all-inclusive World Spirit. Even the worst catastrophes have a good meaning. Genuine pessimism is sublated in the optimism of Spirit. For *God himself is in history*! Eternally perfect in himself, he unfolds his entire opulence in time in the midst of the whole misery of the world. Because God takes all misery on himself in his course through history, the evil element in world history is encompassed by the Good from the very outset. As was said already at the end of the *Phenomenology*, world history is the 'Golgotha of the Absolute Spirit' (II, 564; cf. *PS*, 493). 'From this point of view, our investigation can be seen as a theodicy, a justification of the ways of God (such as Leibniz attempted in his own metaphysical manner, but by using categories which were as yet abstract and indeterminate). It should enable us to comprehend the ills of the world, including the existence of evil, so that the thinking spirit may be reconciled with the negative aspects of existence; and it is in world history that we encounter the sum total of concrete evil. (Indeed, there is no department of knowledge in which such a reconciliation is more urgently required than in world history . . .)' (*PWH*, 42f).

The function of the philosophy of history must be viewed from this perspective: 'Philosophy, therefore, is not really a means of consolation. It is more than that, for it transfigures reality with all its apparent injustices and reconciles it with the rational; it shows that it is based upon the Idea itself, and that reason is fulfilled in it' (*PWH*, 67). This theodicy is therefore no longer carried out in accordance with the unhistorically abstract categories of Leibniz; rather, it is put into practice in the concrete history of the world, being applied organically to the great epochs of world history. It is implemented in a mighty east-west movement of growing liberty from the oriental world as the age of childhood (VIII, 267-514: China, India, Persia, Western Asia, Egypt) to the Greek as the age of adolescence (VIII, 527-658) and to the Roman as the age of adulthood (VIII, 661-748) and from thence in last place to the German world as the ripe old age of humankind (VIII, 757-938: early period – middle ages – modern times). In this whole eschatological process everything is set irreversibly toward the final goal of history, which is nothing more nor less than the reality of liberty. Shod with the seven-league boots of his speculative Notion, the philosopher accompanies this way and movement of the World Spirit in a series of vigorous marches.

His technique at once analytic and synthetic, Hegel unites political history (which enjoys a clear primacy here) with cultural and religious history, and he combines his grandiose spiritual vision, at once intuitive and unitary, with a wealth of all-round detailed knowledge. In this way Hegel sets forth the history of humankind in its spiritual context as a unique unconscious-*cum*-conscious, mysterious development toward an ever deepening consciousness and an ever increasing perfection and liberty. Moreover, this world history is not – as has frequently been charged (following Schopenhauer) – an anodyne, harmonious development. As one who was never a naive believer in progress, Hegel lived from the experience of an antagonistic society. World history, which might rather be termed an abattoir, is a step by step process of production and sublation wrought within the context of dialectical struggle. Each step within this process has its particular, characteristic principle in the spirit of a people, in which are sublated the activities of the instruments, namely specific individuals, including even the great individuals of world history. It is thus within the spirit of a people that this process takes place, returning again and again, throughout its ascent, culmination and descent, to the universal World Spirit: world history is the world's judgement! And it is the philosopher who ascertains the court verdicts which have been delivered on nations and states, their victories and defeats, their rise and fall (on this subject cf. especially Hegel's Introduction).

Hegel could learn much from his predecessors. G. B. Vico's *Scienza Nuova,* which he seems not to have known, had been the first step toward a philosophy of history. On account of its emphasis on reason the Enlightenment has been mistakenly censured time and time again for abstract-rational-ist, unhistorical thinking, even though it was responsible for getting modern historical scholarship under way: Montesquieu, Gibbon, Voltaire, Condorcet. And the anti-rationalist and anti-Enlightenment interpretation of history as an anthropomorphis of God, as stated by J. G. Hamann, was highly influential on the whole following period, in Germany in particular. There followed the unified, organic-living synopsis of all things in Goethe, Schiller, Schelling, and – with regard to history – especially in Herder, and, finally, the new instinct for the course of reason and for the significance of ethical community in Kant and Fichte. But it was Hegel who, with his original conception of the World Spirit and its world-historical development, managed to forge a more refined idiom than had been achieved by Vico, Hamann and Herder, thereby gathering all their ideas into a comprehensive-systematic synthesis which must be regarded as the crown of the modern philosophy of history. It may well be that none of his works has attained such great popularity, even among his opponents, as have these 'lectures'. The fact that it was sketched on the broad canvas of the history of thought did not prevent Hegel's account of the development of world history from being precise as well, and its genial phenomenological grasp of the historical characteristics of particular nations, despite its rigid structure and its archaism, makes it in certain respects the parent of our own modern study of the 'world picture'. Quite apart from its immediate outward influence, Hegel's philosophy of history was to have an incalculable effect on the historicisation of thinking in general.[7] The purely historical scholarship of the historical school is enormously indebted to Hegel at this point, even though the renunciation of Hegel's speculative '*a priori* construction' of world history was, so to say, its birth certificate.

We can obviously not overlook the element of systematic constraint which lurks in the *Philosophy of History* also, where Hegel is obliged not only to indicate the factual sequence of world history, but also to bring out its underlying necessity. There is no need to labour the point that historical scholarship was obliged to take quite different paths here. E. Schulin has extolled Hegel's 'completely relaxed and open, broad preparedness to think and to comprehend everything that can be thought'[8] and his 'immediate interest in all that is factually at hand, his delight in empirical material'.[9] That this frame of mind was partly responsible for opening up new vistas, even in purely historical terms, is proved by a comparison of Hegel's attitude toward the East – which is all the more remarkable in view of the world-historical perspective of today – with that of the later great historians Leopold von Ranke and Jakob Burckhardt: 'Hegel devoted himself to the Orient with the utmost intensity, while Ranke's thought was already centred almost wholly on Europe, and later on Burckhardt was to exclude the Orient from the mainline historical tradition.'[10] As far as Schulin is concerned, Hegel is the philosopher of history 'who has plunged deepest into empirical history'.[11]

Much can be gleaned from a comparison – such as has in fact been executed by G. Mehlis – between Hegel's *speculative* and Auguste Comte's *positivistic* philosophy of history. To begin with, there are the things which they hold in common, probably because they were both influenced by the general ethos of the Age of Restoration: emphasis on the principle of order as opposed to the concept of development, on community as opposed to the individual, and on the universal as opposed to the personal; furthermore, the threefold development of Spirit, the parallel between the development of humankind as a whole and the development of the individual, and the significance of the moral word for the constitution of state and society; and, finally, the expectation that humankind would attain a rational-moral state of maturity, reaching a provisional conclusion in the development of European man.

The differences between the two are no less significant: 1. In their basic attitude: 'For Hegel this was the certainty of the absolute, and for Comte it was the certainty of the relative . . . While the relative is for Hegel a necessary form of the absolute, for Comte

---

[7] cf. the conclusions in the final chapter of E. Schulin: *Die weltgeschichtliche Erfassung des Orients bei Hegel und Ranke.* Using the single example of the world-historical understanding of the Orient in the thought of Hegel and Ranke respectively, Schulin gives an impressive demonstration of Hegel's achievements in the disciplines of history and the philosophy of history; cf. esp. 125-143.
[8] *op. cit.*, 125.
[9] *op. cit.*, 126.
[10] *op. cit.*, 2f.
[11] *op. cit.*, 274.

324

the absolute is a fiction, since all things possess the same character of relativity as do the cognitive powers of the human mind.'[12] 2. In their relationship to past and future: 'Hegel has the view that the world in truth "is" rational, and that it is necessary merely to reveal the true countenance of life in order to convince all people of the fact. Conversely, Comte believes that the life of men and women is *en route* to a goal in keeping with reason and attainable within a short period of time, and he feels himself to be the prophet and proclaimer of this new age.'[13] 3. With respect to the relationship between theory and practice: 'Even though the theoretical element is overwhelmingly preponderant, in the last analysis Comte's lectures on positive philosophy serve the reforming purposes of positive politics, the construction of a positive order of society, while for Hegel the theory, the philosophical system, is everything and the order of life necessarily arises in keeping with theory; for knowledge and cognition are the inmost essence of the Spirit which shapes life.'[14] 4. In the definition of the object of a philosophy of history: 'For Hegel it is the absolute Spirit or the pure reason which is unfolded in the life of the world and, more specifically, in historical events, and which attains to ever higher forms of self-understanding and self-knowledge, while for Auguste Comte it is humankind, the great universal essence, which increases and enriches its knowledge at every stage of the dynamic process. For both thinkers the dominant factor in their "dynamic" approach is the theoretical or intellectual moment of the Spirit.'[15]

It is obvious that we glimpse afresh the inner difficulties of Hegel's basic scheme precisely in his *Philosophy of World History*. How could he have brushed aside so easily the blood and tears, hunger and misery, crises and catastrophes, injustice and insipidity which have marred the visage of world history? After all, every man starts here with his 'Why?', and a philosophy of history must start here also. When we get down to detail, there is such an infinite volume of things that are accidental, capricious and unjust. And in a frankly dramatic sketch Hegel points 'with profound pity' to the 'most terrifying picture', where 'we look upon history as an altar on which the happiness of nations, the wisdom of states, and the virtue of individuals are slaughtered . . .' (*PWH*, 69*). And what is Hegel's reaction? He has no wish to confront this horrid empirical reality directly: 'From the very outset, we rejected the path of reflection as a means of ascending from the spectacle of historical detail to the universal principle behind it' (*PWH*, 69*). And he appeals to the *cunning* of the rational World Spirit, which manages to maintain and preserve itself amidst this whole fearful commotion of unreason. It can be asked whether an outright tragic view of life is in fact the basis of Hegel's optimism regarding the philosophy of history.[16] Given that he was

---

[12]G. Mehlis: *Die Geschichtsphilosophie Hegels und Comtes*, 91.
[13]*op. cit.*, 92.
[14]*ibid.*
[15]*op. cit.*, 94.
[16]R. F. Beerling: *De List der Rede in de Geschiednisfilosofie van Hegel.*

unable simply to deny the existence of the irrational, what option was left to him but to patch together a *de facto* compromise between the lofty speculative course of the World Spirit and the inferior, empirical and irrational stuff of which world history is made?[17]

Hegel's powerful scheme deserves to be exempted from the indignity of cheap objections. While he was of course dependent on the state of knowledge of his day, he certainly took great pains to achieve historical precision and to give an unadulterated account of the facts in their proper context. Many of the usual objections also overlook the fact that Hegel was not concerned with just any kind of history, but quite specifically with world history. This was why he selected particular peoples who were of world significance, at any rate in a restricted or qualified sense. And this factor also accounts for his strong stress on political history, an emphasis which had already been a marked feature of antiquity from Thucydides to Polybius and Livy (later on, of course, Hegel would deal in detail with the history of art, religion and philosophy). Lastly, we see here the reason for the division of world history into such and such periods.[18] Nevertheless, we remain saddled with the critical question of how we can go on regarding world history as the speculative history of the rational World Spirit when this process of the Spirit's self-enhancement toward greater freedom is marked by such an infinite volume of waste and debris in terms of individuals, whole peoples and eras, and when not a single one of Hegel's speculative basic laws is successfully enacted.

How do things stand, then, with the law of speculative universality? *'Hegel's philosophy of history does not prove the rationality of world history, but merely the rationality of what is rational in world history.* This means that Hegel concedes without further ado the *abundance of irrational reality* in existence.'[19] And how do things stand with the law of dialectic? 'By and large *dialectic tends to disappear in the current of empirical events.* Nor can we discern any longer the strict homogeneity of the dialectical line. On the contrary, we espy an *empirical splintered multiplicity of processes.*'[20] And, lastly, how do things stand with the law of speculative concreteness? '... *the peoples remain lumbered with their claims and presumptions and know nothing of self-abnegation and humility.* They accordingly do *not* become concrete organs of the divine totality; and everything remains at the stage of the *separateness of pretentious and quarrelsome rivalry...'*[21] Are we not thus obliged to speak of an empirical distortion of the Spirit's speculative passage through world history when Hegel sketches before our eyes 'an empirically correct, but speculatively disappointing drama of world disruption'?[22]

---

[17]I. Iljin: *Die Philosophie Hegels als kontemplative Gotteslehre,* 330-339.
[18]cf. G. Lasson: *Hegel als Geschichtsphilosoph.*
[19]I. Iljin: *op. cit.,* 331f.
[20]*op. cit.,* 334.
[21]*op. cit.,* 335.
[22]*op. cit.,* 337.

Although the 'cunning of reason' is perhaps the most remarkable example of Hegel's dialectical artistry – and, moreover, a parallel to Leibniz's attempt to solve the problem of evil – the question nevertheless arises whether the 'cunning of reason' is not the Achilles' heel of Hegel's philosophy of history, and whether he is not advocating precisely here more of a dualistic than of a speculative conception: namely, the ultimately irrational conception of a self-outwitting of the absolute subject insofar as it is simultaneously the object of its own cunning.[23]

Following the history of the Roman state, in which the absolutisation of the finite subject (the Roman emperor) calls for the infinitude of the East, Hegel offers a detailed treatment of *Christianity* (VIII, 720-748).

Depending on how the God of a people or the people itself is defined, this people itself becomes Spirit and becomes free. 'It is in terms of religion that a nation defines what it considers to be true' (*PWH*, 105). In India and in Judaism there was a presentiment of the unity of finite and infinite, even though in both of these milieux the idea remained abstract, albeit in different ways. For the Greeks the notion was still superficial and in Rome's isolation of the single individual it was merely an object of longing. It was therefore in Christianity, where there is a meeting of Judaism and Rome, that the unity of finite and infinite became a reality: 'Under Augustus himself, under this completely simple ruler of particular subjectivity, there appeared the very opposite, namely infinity, but in such a way that it included in itself the principle of absolute finitude' (VIII, 720). Hence the root of the characteristic world-historical significance of Christianity is to be found in the incarnation of God: 'The Christian religion came on the scene, this decisive concern of world history' (VIII, 720). Or, as Hegel already alleged in his Introduction: 'Within the divine Idea, the unity and universality of spirit and of consciousness in its true existence have their being; in other words, the finite and the infinite are united. Where the two are separate, the infinity of the understanding is dominant. But in the Christian religion, the divine Idea is revealed as the unity of divine and human nature. This is the true Idea of religion' (*PWH*, 106).

Likewise in the prolegomena to this work, Hegel had already given a brief description of the triune nature of God, in which he manifests himself as the 'movement of mediation' or precisely as Spirit (cf. *PWH*, 41f). Within this framework the world-historical significance of Christianity can also be formulated in trinitarian terms: 'God is only known as Spirit when known as the Triune. This new principle is the axis about which world history revolves. World history proceeds from and moves toward this point. In this religion all

---

[23]R. F. Beerling: *op. cit.*, 80-152.

riddles are solved and all mysteries have become manifest; Christians know what God is inasmuch as they know that he is triune. The first way to know this is by faith, and the second is by thought, which knows the truth and thus is reason. Between these two ways there is the understanding, which holds fast to the differences' (VIII, 722).

Now when 'the time for the appearance of the Spirit was fulfilled, God sent his Son': 'The meaning of this is that the consciousness of the spiritual world has raised itself to the moments which pertain to the Notion of spiritual self-consciousness. These are moments of worldly consciousness, and it is needful that these moments be united and interpreted in truth' (VIII, 723). Looked at in world-historical terms, what is at stake here is a series of reconciliations which have been rendered necessary by the exigencies of the dialectical process: between Judaism and the Roman world; between the eastern and the western principle; between belief in infinity and faith in finitude; between abstract subjectivity (the insipid personality of the emperor) and abstract objectivity (the universal one God of the Jews). But the outer conflict is bound to bring to consciousness the inner conflict which lurks within the breast of man himself, namely the knowledge 'that he is in himself a disunited and divided being' (VIII, 727). This reality is 'mythically represented . . . in the story of the fall into sin', 'the eternal myth of man, whereby he becomes human' (VIII, 728): sin consists in knowledge of good and evil; it is through knowledge alone that man acquires guilt: evil is located in the consciousness. Being-for-oneself and consciousness inescapably involve separation from the universal divine Spirit. But precisely because we are faced here with discord in the act of knowing, it is in the very act of knowing that the reconciliation of the Spirit is contained; for the act of knowing is simultaneously tantamount to a return from separation to the self. 'What is now posited in the self-consciousness of the world is the reconciliation of the world' (VIII, 730).

In what, then, does the reconciliation of the world consist? 'The peace of this reconciliation consists in the unification of the infinite with the finite. The need for this unification is the consciousness of the unity of the two extremes. To this pertains the absolute possibility of this reconciliation or the unity of divine and human nature' (VIII, 733). This unity is given in the inner life of God: just as the Son of God appears as the second divine moment in the pure *Idea,* even so the world (nature and man) appears as the second divine moment in the form of the *particular.* The unity of God and man is thus given in God himself, though not in any superficial sense, 'as if God is merely man and man is likewise God. On the contrary, man is only God inasmuch as he sublates the naturalness and finitude of his spirit and raises himself to God' (VIII, 734): hence 'for the thinking, speculative consciousness' (VIII, 735).

But this intrinsic (*ansichseiende*) unity must proceed to 'sensual certainty' and appear 'in time': 'This intrinsic reality [*Ansich*] must therefore . . . become an object for the world, it must appear, and that in the sensuous form of Spirit, i.e. in human form. Certainty of the unity of God and man is the Notion of Christ, the God-man . . . God was therefore obliged to reveal himself in human form. The world longed for man, who conceived himself merely onesidedly as an end and knew his infinitude within himself, to be understood as a moment of the divine essence. By the same token, the world also longed for God to come out of his abstract form to be contemplated in human appearance. This is reconciliation with God, who is thus pictured as the unity of divine and human nature. Christ appeared as a man who is God and as God who is man; in this event the world's peace and reconciliation took shape' (VIII, 735; cf. *PWH*, 106f).

It is accordingly imperative to take seriously both the divinity and the humanity of Christ! If we wish to regard the humanity of God as a virtue, then we cannot play off Hellenism against Christianity: 'For the Christian God is in truth immensely more human than the gods of the Greeks. In the Christian religion it is said that God appeared in the flesh, and Christianity is about worshipping Christ as God and God as Christ. In terms of earthly presence, natural circumstances, suffering and ignominious death, the God-man Christ had an entirely different humanity from that of the beautiful Greek gods, he was man in a much more definite sense than they were' (VIII, 579; cf. 597).

At the same time, we must not regard Christ as simply an historical figure of the past; in this case we should be putting him 'on the same level as Socrates and others': 'If Christ is meant to be merely a superlative, even sinless, individual and only this, then this involves a denial of the image of the speculative Idea and of absolute truth. These things, however, are the heart of the matter and must be our starting-point. Make what you will of Christ in exegetical, critical and historical terms. Likewise demonstrate, as you desire, that the doctrines of the Church at the Councils took shape because of this or that interest or passion of the bishops, or flowed from here or there – all these particulars may be as they will; the only question is what the Idea or the truth is in and for itself' (VIII, 737).

The appearance of the *one* God is itself *unique*: thus, 'to begin with, the unity is available in a single individual; the possibility for every individual to achieve this unity already exists, but not yet the reality. For this reason the unity must be elevated from the immediacy of appearance in this individual to the universality of Spirit. Sensual existence, in which the Spirit is, is therefore but a transitory moment. Christ died, and it is only as one who has died that he was raised [*aufgehoben*] to heaven and sits on the right hand of God, and only in this way is he Spirit. He himself says, "When I am no longer with you, the Spirit will lead you into all truth." It was only at the Feast of Pentecost that the

329

apostles were filled with the Holy Spirit. For the apostles, Christ during his earthly life was not yet what he later meant for them as Spirit of the Church, in which form he first became the focus of their truly spiritual consciousness' (VIII, 736f; cf. 580f).

Reconciliation only becomes *universal* for the single individual when the external event itself becomes internal, that is, when it becomes certain in faith: 'this means that man must regard it as absolutely true that God is the unity of the individual and the divine. The second pertinent factor here is love' (VIII, 738). In this way reconciliation becomes universal through the Christ, who, as the Spirit, 'dwells in his Church and enters into the hearts of all people' (VIII, 738). 'In this respect he is the Spirit, the Holy Spirit' (VIII, 738).

The history of Christ is thus continued in the history of the Church (VIII, 741-748). Christianity emerges as an historical force to play a decisive role in the final world period of the Germanic peoples. The three epochs into which this period is divided can be understood in trinitarian terms: as the kingdom of the Father (from the emergence of the Germanic peoples within the Roman Empire to Charlemagne), the kingdom of the Son (the rupture between Church and state until Charles V), and the kingdom of the Spirit, which began with the Reformation (VIII, 763-767; cf. 768-932). Hegel ends the *Philosophy of World History* with a glance at the present, and ends with the words: 'That world history is this process of development and the genuine becoming of the Spirit amidst the changing scenes of its unfolding record – this is the true theodicy, the justification of God in history. It has been my endeavour to develop for you this process of the World Spirit. The Spirit is only what it makes of itself, and to this end it is necessary that it presupposes itself. Only insight can reconcile the Spirit with world history and with the reality that what has happened and what happens every day not only comes from God and is unthinkable apart from him, but is essentially the work of God himself' (VIII, 938). World history as the justification of God and therefore as the judgment of the world!

In his *Philosophy of World History,* Hegel intended to give not only a highly concise and impressively profound interpretation of world history, but also an essentially *Christian* one. We are obliged to acknowledge this fact, whatever we may make of the concrete realisation of Hegel's intentions. To buttress his contention 'that the modern philosophy of history corresponds to the biblical faith in a fulfilment and that it ends with the secularisation of its exemplar',[24] K. Löwith was moved to chart a line of development which led backwards as follows: Burckhardt – Marx – Hegel – Proudhon, Comte, Tur-

---

[24]*Weltgeschichte und Heilsgeschehen,* IIf (ET *Meaning in History*).

got, Condorcet – Voltaire – Vico – Bossuet – Joachim of Fiore – Augustine – Orosius. The same author has alleged: 'In other words, the history of the world is to Hegel a history B.C. and A.D. not incidentally or conventionally but essentially. Only on this presupposition of the Christian religion as the absolute truth could Hegel construct universal history systematically, from China up to the French revolution. He is the last philosopher of history because he is the last philosopher whose whose immense historical sense was still restrained and disciplined by the Christian tradition. In our modern universal historics and historical maps, the Christian time-reckoning has become an empty frame of reference, accepted conventionally like other means of measurement and applied to a material multitude of cultures and religions that has no center of meaning from which these cultures and religions could be organized, as they were from Augustine to Hegel. What distinguishes Hegel from Augustine in principle is that Hegel interprets the Christian religion in terms of speculative reason, and providence as "cunning reason".'[25] We must delve far back into the past in order to discover some forerunners in this enterprise. Indeed, we must go right back to the twelfth and thirteenth centuries to such theologians and historians as Otto of Freising, Anselm of Havelberg and Rupert of Deutz.[26] Around this time we encounter a chiliast such as Joachim of Fiore[27] on the one hand, and the great works of such as Thomas and Bonaventura on the other. The unsuspected 'historical formulae' and historico-theological insights of these great scholastics have been unearthed of late by M. Seckler[28] and J. Ratzinger.[29]

F. Heer has pointed out in his inimitable way just how deeply rooted in the European tradition is Hegel's vision of history: 'It is, as far as both ethos and content are concerned, German Romanesque of the twelfth century in its most austere form. Thus Rupert of Deutz had looked on the epochs of world history as "the victory of the divine Word", of incarnate God. Many features of Rupert's thought are strikingly redolent of Hegel, for example, his theory of four ages, his conception of the course of world history from East to West, and his matter-of-fact conviction that Europe with Western Christendom forms the summit and consummation of world history ("Europe is quite simply the end of world history . . ."). Again, in addition to the Carolingian-Hohenstauffen imperial theology and understanding of world history, this period

[25]op. cit., 59f; ET, 59.
[26]cf. A. Funkenstein: *Heilsplan und natürliche Entwicklung. Formen der Gregenwartsbestimmung im Geschichtsdenken des hohen Mittelalters.*
[27]cf. E. Benz: *Ecclesia spiritualis. Kirchenidee und Geschichtstheologie der franziskanischen Reformation.*
[28]cf. M. Seckler: *Das Heil in der Geschichte. Geschichtstheologisches Denken bei Thomas von Aquin.*
[29]cf. J. Ratzinger: *Die Geschichtestheologie des heilegen Bonaventura* (ET *The Theology of History in St. Bonaventura*).

also boasted some forerunners of Leibniz, who – and not only in his *Annals* – delight-ed to draw upon the historical thinkers of the German high middle ages. And something of the inexorable force of Hildegaard of Bingen, with her visions of the history and judgment of the world, enjoyed a new lease of life in Hegel. Hildegaard had a predilection for conceiving God as steel; his judgments are as hard as steel on a world history which at the same time and according to its very essence is the history of the cosmos. Hegel was very close to her on this point also, for he too conceived of world history as a cosmic process. Even so, he went far further than Hildegaard of Bingen when he expanded this process into a theogonic process – into a process which discharges an infinite volume of debris: worn out peoples, worn out ages, worn out individuals, who have shown themselves to be weak, unserviceable and irrelevant in world-historical terms. "Injustice can also befall the individual; but this has nothing to do with world history, whose onward march is served by individuals as by means".'[30]

Nevertheless, it is hardly possible to speak of a philosophy of history proper or of a philosophical theology of history with respect to this period. It was something entirely new when in the Renaissance (Laurentius Valla and critical philology) and then, much more decisively, in the Enlightenment, people became keenly aware of history, motivated by a polemical concern to criticise the conditions and abuses which prevailed in Church and state. However, the criticism of the present in terms of the past had tended increasingly to turn into an interpretation of the present in terms of the past. The scope of knowledge had increased enormously, both in terms of time, especially with regard to the ancient world, and of space, the discovery of new continents and of the importance of Asia. And people were learning to sort out the causal connection between world-historical events, developing in this way the specifically modern approach to history. Even though they confronted Christianity with the danger of its absolute relativisation, these developments nevertheless made it possible for Christianity to be taken seriously once again as a historical religion, and at the same time for a fresh Christian interpretation of history to be carried out. With all his mental energy, Hegel took up this specifically Christian concern in the context of his philosophy, giving a brilliant presentation of it.

At the close of this section it is perhaps appropriate to elucidate what follows by reiterating our intention to reserve our theological discussion with Hegel, which has hitherto followed hard on the heels of our account of his thoughts, to the end of the whole chapter, where it will take the form of a résumé of the individual facets of the thought of his final phase (*Philosophy of World History, Aesthetics, Philosophy of Religion* and *History of Philosophy*).

---

[30] *Hegel. Auswahl und Einleitung,* 42.

3. Christ in Art

The *Philosophy of World History* can be viewed as having laid the foundation for Hegel's subsequent historical accounts of art, religion and philosophy. For culture – in other words, the world forms of art, religion and philosophy (*PWH*, 103*, 104-115) – emerges from the folk Spirits in which world history concretely occurs. Just as perfect will took shape in the absolute state, so now perfect vision assumes outward form in absolute art, perfect sensitivity and feeling in absolute religion, and perfect thought in philosophy. These three world forms constitute distinct spheres of the one historical development of God in the world: a process of Spirit's gaining consciousness, which is recorded in the three disciplines of the philosophy of art, the philosophy of religion, and the history or philosophy of philosophy. In these disciplines, as far as Hegel is concerned, historical development and systematic presentation are the same thing. In his system, therefore, they represent both a further development of the *Philosophy of World History* and, at the same time, an implementation of the system which was depicted in the *Encyclopaedia*. While the *Philosophy of Right* and, as its culmination, the *Philosophy of World History,* describe the *objective* Spirit in systematic-*cum*-historical terms (after the *Encyclopaedia* Hegel never dealt in greater detail again with the *subjective* Spirit in anthropology, phenomenology and psychology), the same methodology will now be employed as the three moments of the *absolute* Spirit are now described in the *Philosophy of Art*, the *Philosophy of Religion* and the *History of Philosophy*.

Already in Heidelberg, Hegel had lectured in *Aesthetics* (which is the title usually given to his *Philosophy of Art*[31]), and he repeated the performance in

---

[31] Hegel's handwritten lecture-notes on the *Philosophy of Art*, which were still available to the first editor, H. G. Hotho, are no longer extant. Hotho's version of the *Aesthetics* has always been looked on as the best edition of any of Hegel's lectures, and in its combination of the qualities of precision and consistency it certainly deserves to be dubbed a magisterial piece of work. This makes it somewhat easier to live with the fact that we possess a critically improved text only for the general first part of the work ('The Idea and the Ideal', vol. X; in 1931 this became vol. Xa at the hands of Lasson, who drew chiefly on the well preserved lectures of 1823 and 1826). For the other two parts the author has used Glockner's Jubilee Edition, vols. XII, XIII and XIV, from which quotations are given in the German original, as from *G* XII, *G* XIII and *G* XIV. For the purposes of this translation use has been made, wherever possible, of T. M. Knox's translation of *Hegel's Aesthetics* (2 vols., Oxford, 1975). References will be given in the following pages as *A* followed by the relevant volume and page numbers. Friedrich Bassenge has recently (1965) produced a superbly revised edition of Hotho's version of the lectures. (This is in fact a licensed issue of the edition which appeared in East Germany in 1955. The beneficial changes made include updated spelling and the addition of relevant section headings and a detailed index.) On the general interpretation of the *Aesthetics*, cf. also the pertinent section in the *Encyclopaedia; PM*, 293-297. Additional aid is also supplied by the index to Hegel's *Lectures on Aesthetics* prepared and recently reissued by H. Bartsch.

Berlin in 1820, 1823, 1826 and 1828. The intervening periods were, as we have already observed, filled not least with long journeys on which Hegel devoted his attention to culture and art. A remark of Ernst Bloch will serve as a fitting introduction to the *Aesthetics:* 'Being is here vividly starting to become absolute. Life beyond work is called leisure. There dwell the Muses, the first comforters of the absoluteness of Spirit which is now beginning in Hegel's thought. The homecomer first reaches the gateway to "absolute Spirit", and he finds that it bears the heading: Beauty. The beautiful is the Idea at the level of vision, the appearance of the Idea through a sensual medium (stone, colour, tone, word), in the form of limited appearance.'[32]

Historians have an unfailing tendency (and it is obviously not always misplaced) to level against Hegel an undiscriminating charge of '*a priori* constructions'. It is therefore imperative to point out that the *Aesthetics* is based not only on an intensive study of the history of art, but also on a rich and varied experience of art itself. Here too it might be helpful to take a look at the man behind the philosophy. Once again we call on the brilliant editor of the lectures on aesthetics to describe Hegel as he knew him from their first meeting: 'I was still pretty much a freshman when one morning I stepped diffidently and yet confidently into Hegel's room for the first time in order to introduce myself to him. He was sitting at a wide desk, impatiently rumaging among a chaotic pile of books and papers. The prematurely aged figure was bent and yet radiated a pristine stamina and vigour. Although he was already fully dressed, he was wearing a yellow-grey dressing gown which looked slightly scruffy but comfortable as it reached from his shoulders to the floor. He displayed no outward trace of either awe-inspiring grandeur or captivating charm, and the first thing that I noticed about his manner was a goodly sense of civic uprightness. I shall never forget the first impression that his face made on me. The sallow and flabby features of his drooping, corpse-like

In addition to the general works on Hegel which have found frequent mention in these pages, some further bibliographical recommendations can be made with respect to the *Aesthetics*. Apart from the Hegelians K. Rosenkranz and F. T. Vischer, cf. the early works of W. Danzel and C. Benard. Important from the first half of this century are B. Croce: *Ultimi saggi*, 147-160, and the works of H. Kuhn. Among the most recent works, those by the following authors merit mention G. Lukács, F. Puglisi, G. Vecchi, B. Teyssedre, I. Knox, C. Dulckeit-von Arnim, C. Antoni, J. Kaminsky, W. Bröcker (*Auseinandersetzungen*, 33-57), G. E Müller (*Origins*, Part IV, esp. 429-557), and E. Heller. Among more specialist studies, cf. J. Taminiaux on the aesthetics of the young Hegel, H. Lauener on aesthetics and language, J. Patocka on the pastness of art (with a brief sketch of the provenance and development of Hegel's teaching), and W. Oelmüller on Hegel's thesis concerning the end of art. Further essays on the *Aesthetics*, especially from the Marxist camp, can be found in the *Hegel-Jahrbuch*, vols. II (1964), III (1965) and IV (1966). It is fitting to point out that it was in the context of the *Aesthetics* (and, admittedly, also of the *Encyclopaedia* and *Phenomenology*) that H. Lauener demonstrated that, while Hegel offers no coherent philosophy of language, language is nevertheless completely interwoven with the immanent movement of mediation which constitutes the system of the whole: 'Hegel's philosophy is the philosophy of the Absolute, which – *qua* Logos – consists *solely* in language' (p. 10). The *Aesthetics* explains how language 'loosens the tongue' of art. On Hegel's theory of language, cf. also the works of J. Simon, M. Züfle and T. Bodammer.
[32]*Subjekt – Objekt*, 274.

face were the mirror not of any destructive passion, but of a whole lifetime spent in silent, unremitting thought. These forty years of reflection, search and discovery seemed unharassed and untroubled by the torment of doubt or the turmoil of unappeased intellectual storms. The furrows on his forehead, cheeks and mouth were attributable solely to the indefatigable impulse to cultivate the embryo of truth which he had happily discovered early in his career, to develop it more and more richly, deeply and strictly, and to establish it more and more irrefutably. When this insight was in abeyance his features seemed old and shrivelled, but when it was roused to life it must of necessity cause his face to express the utter earnestness "of an intrinsically momentous subject matter which can be satisfied only by the hard work involved in a complete development, an earnestness which sinks into this subject matter for a long period in silent study". How dignified was the shape of his head, how noble that of his nose, of his high though somewhat concave forehead, and of his calm chin. The nobility of faithfulness and thoroughgoing uprightness in things both great and small, of the clear consciousness of having sought ultimate contentment to the best of one's ability in the truth alone – this quality had been most tellingly and individually etched onto his face. I had expected either an exploratory chat or a pep-talk, with the subject being in some way academic, and was hugely surprised at being presented with the very opposite. This exceptional man had just got back from a journey to the Netherlands, and he could only give a long report on the cleanliness of the towns, the charm and artistic fruitfulness of the country, the wide green meadows, the herds, the canals, the artistic treasures and the prim yet comfortable way of life of the occupants. The upshot of all this was that, after just half an hour, I felt completely at home, both in Holland and in his company.'[33]

Reasons of space forbid us to enter in any detail into Hegel's innumerable fascinating aesthetic analyses, but we shall at least venture to quote one short section on the colours in Dutch painting. This will give us an opportunity to verify Hotho's biographical observations, and to supply a little evidence from the *Aesthetics* itself for Hegel's precise observation, for his concrete experience of and highly developed instinct (even in a formal sense) for art: 'While here it is just the pure appearance of the things depicted that provides the true subject of the picture, art goes still further by making the fugitive appearance stationary. In other words, apart from the things depicted, the means of the portrayal also becomes an end in itself, so that the artist's subjective skill and his application of the means of artistic production are raised to the status of an objective matter in works of art. The older Dutch painters made a most thorough study of the physical effects of colour; van Eyck, Hemling, and Scorel could imitate in a most deceptive way the sheen of gold and silver, the lustre of jewels, silk, velvet, furs, etc. This mastery in the production of the most striking effects through the magic of colour and the secrets of its spell has now an independent justification. While the spirit reproduces itself in thinking, in comprehending the world in ideas and thoughts, the chief thing now – independently of the topic itself – is the subjective re-creation of the external world in the visible element of colours and lighting. This is as it were an objective music, a peal in colour. In other words, just as in music the single note is nothing by itself but produces its effect only in its relation to another, in its counterpoint, concord, modulation, and harmony, so here it is just the same with colour. If we look closely at the play of colour, which glints like gold and glitters like braid under the light, we see perhaps only white or yellow strokes, points of colour,

---

[33]H. G. Hotho: *Vorstudien für Leben und Kunst*, 383f.

coloured surfaces; the single colour as such does not have this gleam which it produces; it is the juxtaposition *alone* which makes this glistening and gleaming. If we take, e.g., Terburg's satin, each spot of colour by itself is a subdued grey, more or less whitish, bluish, yellowish, but when it is looked at from a certain distance there comes out through its position beside another colour the beautiful soft sheen proper to actual satin. And so it is with velvet, the play of light, cloud vapour, and, in general, with everything depicted. It is not the reflex of the heart which wishes to display itself in subjects such as these, as it often does in the case of a landscape, for example; on the contrary, it is the entire subjective skill of the artist which, as skill in using the means of production vividly and effectively in this objective way, displays its ability by its own efforts to generate an objective world' (*A*, 599f).

'These lectures are devoted to aesthetics, that is, to the philosophy and science of the beautiful, namely, of the artistically beautiful' (X, 1). Thus even aesthetics is philosophy: art is not considered as an imitation of nature or as a stimulation of emotion or as a consolidation of morality (cf. X, 28-51), but as 'a particular form of the appearance of Spirit' (X, 8). As a form of knowledge and a way of worshipping God, art is therefore intimately related to religion and philosophy, together with which it is 'a method and manner of expressing the divine' (X, 26; cf. X, 104; we are reminded of the *Phenomenology* and its 'religion of art'). It is a method of reconciling the here-and-now with the beyond, the concept with nature, the inward with the outward (X, 26; cf. also X, 82 and *PM,* 293). At the beginning of his lectures, Hegel discusses the way in which art was conceived by Kant, Schiller, Winckelmann, Schelling and Friedrich Schlegel. He has obviously learned much from these authors, although he differs from Kant and goes further than Schiller in professing a view of art which is determined not only by form but also by content.

But what is the distinctive feature of art? 'The characteristic quality of art is that it presents the higher itself in a sensuous manner, thereby bringing it closer to the perceptive nature' (X, 26). The artist both fetters and unveils spirit in matter, and works of art are *sensuous* appearances of spirit, *embodiments, incarnations* of the Idea, of the Absolute. '*The stuff of art is both spiritualised matter and materialised spirit*' (X, 66). Art, religion and philosophy therefore have the same content: 'the absolute Spirit' (X, 142f), 'God' (X, 150). As regards form, however, they are distinct: philosophy is a thinking and religion is a picturing of absolute Spirit, while art is merely a '*contemplation,* the immediate knowledge of the Absolute, and hence sensuous or immediate consciousness of absolute Spirit' (X, 150). A work of art is 'only a *sign* of the Idea' (*PM,* 293). For this reason art is subordinate to religion and philosophy. Indeed, we must even say that the 'deeper Idea, which at its highest level is the Christian Idea, cannot be pictured by art in sensuous terms' (X, 27). Does this mean that we shall hear nothing of Christianity and Jesus Christ in the philosophy of art? We must wait and see.

Art 'is the concrete *contemplation* and mental picture of implicitly absolute spirit as the Ideal', in the 'shape or form of *beauty*' (*PM*, 293). The means whereby art represents the absolute, the divine, the Idea is 'the beautiful' (X, 104). By this is meant not the naturally beautiful but the artistically beautiful, the beautiful which is born from and in spirit, which proceeds from creative freedom and is at the same time true and good. Here the Idea becomes the 'shaped Idea', the 'Ideal' (X, 112). The artistically beautiful or the Ideal is thus nothing other than '*the Idea pictured as existing*' (X, 214), 'the Idea defined more precisely as essentially individual reality, and an individual configuration of reality, with the proviso that it let the Idea appear essentially within it' (X, 111f), 'the genuine appearance' (X, 114), 'the union of content with the way in which this content exists, reality's being and becoming accomodated to the concept' (X, 114). In the highest and perfect kind of art, the form, the shape, the image and the presentation are in complete accord with the Idea; the shape has a genuine existence for itself. But just any kind of art is not the highest kind. The transition to the full Ideal, to full beauty, to artistic freedom consists in the increasingly intimate union of content with form, of the spiritual and universal with the sensuous and individual. In this way there takes place the increasingly pure and concrete revelation of the divine Spirit. The creative artist who joins in this work of revelation can on this account be called 'master of the God' (*PM*, 295).

Absolute Spirit comes to full self-realisation by getting involved, *qua* creative Spirit, in a living and dialectical process of self-development. This is a step-by-step process made up of inter-connected configurations which reflect the general state of the world, a process which expresses the situation of Spirit and hence of the essence of God at any given time. These configurations of Spirit are revealed in the styles proper to the works of art of the various epochs. Since even 'the spirit of art is a limited folk spirit' (V, 467; cf. *PM*, 294), the whole development keeps pace with the development of the various nations, thereby furnishing a parallel to the development of world history in general. By observing how the Idea relates to its successive shapes, we can ascertain various forms of artistic expression. Amidst the interplay of history these forms mount to increasing degrees of freedom and spirituality, and within themselves they are once again involved in rise, climax and fall.

In the first general part (vol. X), Hegel deals with the Idea of the beautiful as such, with what is naturally beautiful and with the proper subject-matter of aesthetics, namely, the artistically beautiful or the Ideal (and he treats of the artist here as well). In the second part, he goes on to unfold his basic systematic concepts in an historical development of the Ideal into the particular forms of artistic beauty. His starting-point is the *symbolic* or oriental form of art (*A*, 299-426), where the wholly indeterminate Idea seeks to take on pictorial form in appearance. At this stage content and form lie abstractly and incongruously on top of one another. From this basis there develops the *classical* or Greek form of art (*A*, 427-516), where the determinate Idea emerges into appearance. At this stage form and content find themselves in human shape, still incomplete and lacking absolute depth. Everything is ultimately consummated in the *romantic* or *Christian* form of art (*A*, 517-611), where the absolute Idea takes on spiritual form in the inner aspects of man and where form and content become a concrete spiritual unity. Each of these forms of art expresses itself characteristically in a particular type of art. The characteristic expression of oriental-symbolic art is to be found in architecture, that of Greek art in sculpture, and that of romantic art in painting, music and poetry. By exploiting these distinctions, Hegel manages in part three to set forth – not abstractly, but in the manner of a dialectical and historical development – a system, or, rather, a hierarchy of the individual arts, which he understands as objectifications of Spirit (*A*, 613-791; 792-1237). He climbs from the most outward form of art (architecture) to the most inward (poetry), passing through sculpture, painting and music (to the last of which he never acquired a close relationship, and which he discusses with great brevity). Each of these arts in its turn undergoes its own dialectic of internalisation (e.g. architecture, which develops from the edifices of the Orient to the classical-harmonious Greek temple to the internalised Gothic cathedral).

Notwithstanding his great empathy for poetry, Hegel never wished to be a 'poet-philosopher' or in some other remarkable way a man of varied talents. Even so, E. Bloch extols his aptitude for richly vivid description: 'The same philosopher who as a logician would doggedly and pallidly keep peace with the shadowy life of concepts, parades in his *Aesthetics* as one who has had the most concrete experience of art and is blissfully wedded to this subject-matter. The thinker who speaks here does not have a merely ancillary or incidental sensitivity for pictures, statues and plays; he does not speak from this seat in the stalls or from that sofa *about* art. On the contrary, it is almost a latent painter, sculptor and dramatist who here appears among his peers, present and alive *in the very midst of art*. He speaks the language of art, he speaks art in the medium of the concept, but be it noted that art itself is understood as *appearance*, not as concept. As far as Hegel is concerned, the fact that the work of art is sensuous appearance is just as important as the specific Idea that appears within it. Any separation of these two moments turns both of them into a mere externality.'[34]

The basic definition of *romantic* art is that Spirit here comes to itself. Its truth therefore does not, like classical art, consist in immersing itself into corporeality, but in returning from the external into its inwardness. This takes place in the shape of *spiritual* beauty, in which there is a perfect marriage of

---

[34]*Subjekt – Objekt*, 279f.

content and form. For this to be achieved it is necessary for Spirit to elevate itself from finite personality to the Absolute and, conversely, for the Absolute not to be understood as something which simply transcends man. Even so, a pure internalised infinitude of this kind implies the absolute negation of all external reality apart from the Absolute: 'In this Pantheon all the gods are dethroned, the flame of subjectivity has destroyed them, and instead of plastic polytheism art knows now only *one* God, one spirit, one absolute independence which, as the absolute knowing and willing of itself, remains in free unity with itself and no longer falls apart into those particular characters and functions whose one and only cohesion was due to the compulsion of a dark necessity' (*A,* 519). Nevertheless, at the same time this absolute inwardness must come to appearance in reality, so that art can grasp and depict it: 'Yet absolute subjectivity as such would elude art and be accessible to thinking alone if, in order to be *actual* subjectivity in correspondence with its essence, it did not also proceed into external existence and then withdraw out of this reality into itself again. This moment of actuality is inherent in the Absolute, because the Absolute, as infinite negativity, has for the result of its activity *itself,* as the simple unity of knowing with itself and therefore as *immediacy.* On account of this immediate existence which is grounded in the Absolute itself, the Absolute does not turn out to be the one jealous God who merely cancels nature and finite human existence without shaping himself there in appearance as actual divine subjectivity; on the contrary, the true Absolute reveals itself and thereby gains an aspect in virtue of which it can be apprehended and represented by art' (*A,* 519f).

Romantic or *Christian* art is therefore the supreme form of art, because the 'unity of divine and human nature' is here 'apprehended' not 'merely sensuously', but 'in spirit and in truth' (X, 119). There is a 'withdrawal from the sensuousness of picture-thinking into spiritual inwardness', and 'the unity of human and divine nature is a known unity which can be realised only through spiritual knowledge and in the Spirit' (X, 121).

Thus the God of romantic art appears in his inwardness. But the real existence of this inwardness expresses itself in a human mode of appearance, so that a new and wide Spirit-related multiplicity opens up over the context of the human. Hence while the content of this art seems constricted in relation to the divine, it has nevertheless been infinitely expanded with reference to all that has been opened up by inwardness (*A,* 524f). Religion thus forms the first but not the only sphere of romantic art. In addition to religion there is the formation of Spirit into worldly reality (chivalry, whose themes are honour, love, faithfulness and bravery; *A,* 552-572) and the formation of the formal independence of individual characteristics (in which we press forward beyond quixotry to the dissolution of the romantic form of art; *A,* 573-611).

In his postscript on the *Aesthetics,* G. Lukács shows himself to be imprisoned in ideological polemics and too ready to indulge in unworthy tactics when he dismisses Hegel's interpretation and evaluation of Christian art as follows: 'It is perhaps not superfluous for the contemporary reader to observe that Hegel's treatment of art as part of religious development is bound up with the backwardness of German philosophy at that time.'[35]

Lukács was correct but onesided to see in Hegel a résumé of the foregoing ideas and currents of thought on aesthetics from Kant through Schiller and Goethe to Schelling and Solger. This view has been complemented by J. Taminiaux, who has demonstrated the continuity in Hegel's conception of art from his early writings to the *Aesthetics,* written in his maturity.[36] While art and religion initially belonged together in Hegel's mind, it became clear to him from Frankfurt onwards that art is not wholly adequate to capture the Absolute, but is only the sensuous appearance of the Absolute. It is certain that, while Hegel adopted a great deal from his predecessors, he at the same time criticised and overcame them.

According to Hegel *the superiority of Christian art* over classical art consists in the fact that, despite all interiorisation, 'there cannot be any question in Christianity... of celebrating a solitary god,... his pure separation and detachment from the world emptied of gods' (*A,* 508). 'Looked at from this point of view, Schiller's famous saying: "Since the gods were then more human, men were more godlike" is altogether false' (*A,* 508). With its plurality of gods, the art of classical Greece has often been charged with being too anthropomorphic, but in Hegel's view it was not anthropomorphic enough: 'Christianity has pushed anthropomorphism much further; for, according to Christian doctrine, God is not an individual merely humanly shaped, but an actual single individual, wholly God and wholly an actual man, drawn into all the conditions of existence, and no merely humanly shaped ideal of beauty and art. If our idea of the Absolute were only an idea of an abstract innerly undifferentiated being, then it is true that every sort of configuration vanishes; but for God to be spirit he must appear as man, as an individual subject – not as ideal humanity, but as actual progress into the temporal and complete externality of immediate and natural existence. The Christian view, that is to say, implies an endless movement and drives into an extreme opposition and into an inner reversion to absolute unity only by cancelling this separation' (*A,* 435).

Thus what gives Christian art its depth is the real *incarnation of God,* its pain and its negativity in God himself: 'This moment of separation is that in which God becomes man, because, as an actual individual subject, he enters difference as opposed to both unity and substance as such; in this ordinary

---

[35] *Hegels Ästhetik,* 595.
[36] *La pensée esthétique du jeune Hegel.*

spatial and temporal existence he experiences the feeling, consciousness, and grief of disunion in order to come, through this opposition and likewise its dissolution, to infinite reconciliation. According to Christian ideas, this transition lies in the nature of God himself. In fact, through this process, God is to be apprehended as absolute free spirituality, in which the factor of nature and immediate individuality is present indeed but must equally be transcended' (*A*, 435f). This is why no satisfaction can be given by classical art with its untroubled harmony and its only superficial reconciliation: 'Whereas in classical art while the sensuous is not killed and dead, it is also not resurrected from death to absolute spirit. Therefore classical art and its religion of beauty does not satisfy the depths of the spirit; however concrete it is in itself, it still remains abstract for spirit because it has as its element not that movement and that reconciliation of infinite subjectivity which has been achieved out of opposition, but instead only the untroubled harmony of determinate free individuality in its adequate existence, this peace in that real existence, this happiness, this satisfaction and greatness in itself, this eternal serenity and bliss which even in misfortune and grief do not lose their assured self-repose. The opposition, grounded in the Absolute, classical art has not probed to its depths and reconciled' (*A*, 436).

In the interiorisation and spiritualisation of this art there takes place the transition from the self-satisfied purely human to the depth and sorrow of the Absolute. This occurs not in abstract, but in concrete terms: the Absolute is not outside the human, but within the human itself. Remembering that on the whole Hegel is now no longer – as he was previously – speaking of the religion of art, it is important to note that this unity is not produced by art but by religion itself; art makes this unity vivid and clear (*A*, 527). God in human shape! It is therefore understandable why religion is the first and inmost sphere of romantic, perfect art, and why 'its centre' in its turn 'is supplied by the history of redemption, by the life of Christ, his death and Resurrection' (*A*, 528): 'The man [Jesus] appears not as man in a purely human character with restricted passions, finite ends and achievements, or as merely conscious *of* God, but as the self-knowing sole and universal God himself in whose life and suffering, birth, death and resurrection there is now revealed even to man's finite consciousness what spirit, what the eternal and infinite, is in its truth. Romantic art presents this content in the story of Christ, his mother, his Disciples, and also of all others in whom the Holy Spirit is effective and the entire Godhead is present. For because it is God who appears in human existence, for all that he is universal in himself too, this reality is not restricted to individual immediate existence in the shape of Christ; it is unfolded into the whole of mankind in which the spirit of God makes itself present, and in this reality remains in unity with itself' (*A*, 521; cf. 533f).

In Christ it is assured that 'an individual man is God, and God an individual man' (*A*, 534)! Insofar as man is spirit, this unity of God and man is a simple matter of fact, albeit only implicitly, conceptually. Man has to realise this fundamental unity for himself in the face of all separation. Spirit's reconciliation with itself – absolute history, the process of truth – is to be made visible and certain in Christ through God's appearance in the world: 'this goal is at the same time the absolute beginning, the presupposition of the romantic religious consciousness that God himself is man, flesh, that he has become this individual person in whom therefore the reconciliation does not remain something implicit (in which case it would be known only in its *Concept*) but stands forth *objectively* existent for human senses and conscious contemplation as this individual actually existing man. It is on account of this moment of individuality that in Christ every individual has a vision of his own reconciliation with God which in its essence is no mere possibility; it is actual and therefore has to appear in this one man as really achieved. But, secondly, since this unity, as the spiritual reconciliation of opposed moments, is no mere *immediate* coalescence into one, it follows that in this *one* man the process of spirit too, through which alone consciousness is truly spirit, must attain existence as the history of this man. This history of the spirit, consummated in one individual, contains nothing except what we have already touched on above, namely that the individual man casts aside his individuality of body and spirit, i.e. that he suffers and dies, but conversely through the grief of death rises out of death, and ascends as God in his glory, as the actual spirit which now has indeed entered existence as an individual, as this subject, yet even so is essentially truly God only as Spirit in his Church' (*A*, 534f).

As has already been said, it is impossible for art to express the deepest and divine element of Christianity, whose basis lies in the inwardness of faith. From this point of view we might label the artistic representation of the history of Jesus Christ as 'something superfluous' (*A*, 535). And yet this is not ultimately the case, given that the externalisation of God in the incarnation is unsurpassably set before our eyes precisely in the sensuous and concrete isolation and outwardness of artistic representation. And insofar as in the incarnation of God in Christ 'the accent is laid on the fact that God is essentially an individual person, exclusive of others, and displays the unity of divine and human subjectivity not simply in general but as *this* man, there enter here again, in art, on account of the subject-matter itself, all the aspects of the contingency and particularity of external finite existence from which beauty at the height of the classical Ideal had been purified. What the free Concept of the beautiful had discarded as inappropriate, i.e. the non-Ideal, is here necessarily adopted and brought before our vision as a factor emerging from the subject-matter itself' (*A*, 536). The best artist, then, is not the one who depicts Christ according to the ideal and universal beauty of classical art, but the one who manages to combine the characteristics of this art with a flair for capturing the individual and the natural.

It goes without saying that in the artistic representation of Jesus Christ special significance will be accorded to the story of his suffering and resurrection. For it is here that the universal history of absolute Spirit, which first became actual in this single individual, reaches its climax: 'The real turning-point in this life of God is the termination of his individual existence as *this* man, the story of the Passion, suffering on the Cross, the Golgotha of the Spirit, the pain of death. This sphere of portrayal is separated *toto caelo* from the classical plastic ideal because here the subject-matter itself implies that the external bodily appearance, immediate existence as an individual, is revealed in the grief of his negativity as the negative, and that therefore it is by sacrificing subjective individuality and the sensuous sphere that the Spirit attains its truth and its Heaven. On the one hand, in other words, the earthly body and the frailty of human nature is raised and honoured by the fact that it is God himself who appears in human nature, but on the other hand it is precisely this human and bodily existent which is negatived and comes into appearance in its grief, while in the classical ideal it does not lose undisturbed harmony with what is spiritual and substantial. Christ scourged, with the crown of thorns, carrying his cross to the place of execution, nailed to the cross, passing away in the agony of a torturing and slow death – this cannot be portrayed in the forms of Greek beauty; but the higher aspect in these situations is their inherent sanctity, the depth of the inner life, the infinity of grief, present as an eternal moment in the Spirit as sufferance and divine peace' (*A*, 537f; cf. 823f).

Yet death is not an end, but a beginning of new life: resurrection! 'But the process of death is to be treated in the divine nature only as a point of transition whereby the reconciliation of the Spirit with itself is brought about, and the divine and human sides, the sheerly universal and the subjective appearance, whose mediation is in question, close together affirmatively. This affirmation is in general the basis and the original foundation [of the divine history] and must therefore also be made evident in this positive way. For this purpose the most favourable events in the history of Christ are supplied especially by the Resurrection and the Ascension, apart from the scattered moments at which Christ appears as teacher. But here there arises, especially for the visual arts, a supreme difficulty. For (a) it is the spiritual as such which is to be portrayed in its inwardness, (b) it is the absolute Spirit which in its infinity and universality must be put affirmatively in unity with subjectivity [i.e. in Christ] and yet, raised above immediate existence, must in the bodily and external shape bring before contemplation and feeling the entire expression of its infinity and inwardness' (*A*, 538f; cf. 541f, 543f, 820-822: esp. on the child Jesus).

Spirit *qua* Spirit cannot be the immediate subject-matter of art but only to the extent that it becomes the object of perception and vision. This happens in love, which becomes a leading motif of romantic art: 'The true essence of love consists in giving up the consciousness of oneself, forgetting oneself in another self, yet in this surrender and oblivion having and possessing oneself alone' (*A*, 539f). 'Love as the *Ideal* of romantic art in its religious sphere' is depicted in Christ as divine love, in Mary as maternal love, and in the love of the disciples, the friends of Christ, both male and female (*A*, 540-543).

Now what took place in the one Christ is meant to become universal in the Spirit in the shape of reconciliation for humankind, which exists as many individuals. The consequence of this fact for the subject-matter of romantic art, i.e. the Spirit of the *community* and the cancellation of individual finitude, is the emergence of further forms for Christian art: the re-enactment of the passion (the martyrs), inner repentance and conversion and the appearance of the divine in miracles and legends (*A*, 543-551).

Within the religious sphere of romantic or Christian art, then, these are the chief moments of the subject-matter which is both God's nature for himself, and a process through and in which he is Spirit: 'This is the absolute theme which art does not create and reveal from its own resources, but which it has received from religion and which it approaches, with the consciousness that it is the absolute truth, in order to express and display it. This is the content of the believing and yearning heart which in and for itself is the infinite totality, so that now the external sphere remains more or less external and contingent without coming into complete harmony with the inner sphere and therefore it often becomes a repellent material not thoroughly conquerable by art' (*A*, 550f).

With this last sentence Hegel casually alludes to something which had become only too plain in the *Philosophy of World History* and in the great systematic works: the actual historical material resists its integration into the grand comprehensive process of Spirit, and when we get down to concrete detail we find that the lofty speculative development of art cannot be upheld unimpaired. Hegel has everywhere been obliged to ignore certain elements, tolerate deviations, make concessions and strike compromises. Every art historian could here come up with countless examples. But how does this observation square with the claims Hegel made in the epilogue to his lectures on aesthetics? We read that 'right to the end' he has 'arranged every essential category of the beautiful and every essential form of art into a philosophical garland', and that in the process his concern has been with 'the liberation of the spirit from the content and forms of finitude, with the presence and

344

reconciliation of the Absolute in what is apparent and visible, with an unfolding of the truth which is not exhausted in natural history but revealed in world history'. His actual accomplishment, we are told, has been 'to seize in thought and to prove the fundamental nature of the beautiful and art, and to follow it through all the stages it has gone through in the course of its realization' (*A*, 1236f). Should we rigorously test the claims made in this triumphal conclusion, then we might be tempted to apply to the *Aesthetics* I. Iljin's observation on the *Philosophy of World History:* 'All the concessions in the world do nothing to dispel the philosopher's impression that *the conception is treated as though it had been successfully carried through and the final product as if it were in keeping with the original idea.* The formulations of the *problem* are expressed as if the problem itself had been *solved,* and the realised speculative minimum is surreptitiously equated with the demanded and intended maximum.'[37]

With respect to the philosophy of art also a critical question may be posed both generally and in detail. To what extent have Hegel's basic laws of speculation here achieved a breakthrough? We think of the law of speculative universality, the law of dialectic, and the law of speculative concreteness.

But a general appraisal of the *Aesthetics* cannot be our concern. Notwithstanding all the criticism which must be levelled at it, it remains itself a work of art, based as it is on the personal experience of art and on the study of the history and philosophy of art. Amazement and admiration are constantly wrested from us afresh by its enormous spatial and temporal expanses and the profound, detailed knowledge it displays of all epochs and subjects, by its highly refined layout and the great intelligence manifested in its being carried through from a simultaneously absolute and historical standpoint. Certain fundamental questions broached by Hegel – such as the conditionedness by time and history of art *and* the arts (generic theory), and the pastness and distinctive contemporaneousness of art – are still on the agenda and can scarcely be resolved solely by recourse to phenomenological stocktaking and theories of structure. The criticism we have expressed ought not therefore to detract in any way from the praise which is fitly bestowed. What Hegel says of art can be said of large parts of his philosophy of art: 'art makes every one of its productions into a thousand-eyed Argus, whereby the inner soul and spirit is seen at every point. And it is not only the bodily form, the look of the eyes, the countenance and posture, but also actions and events, speech and tones of voice, and the series of their course through all conditions of appearance that

---

[37] *Die Philosophie Hegels als kontemplative Gotteslehre,* 330.

art has everywhere to make into an eye, in which the free soul is revealed in its inner infinity' (*A*, 153f).

C. Dulckeit-von Arnim has pointed out that Hegel's *Aesthetics* must be seen as a riposte to the Enlightenment's secularisation of art: 'Hegel's philosophy of art must be understood as a reaction against the secularisation of art which took place in the formalist aesthetic of the eighteenth-century Enlightenment. German Idealism turned away from the non-objective theory which focussed on the subject of the aesthetic experience, with his creativity and enjoyment, feelings and reactions. But it was no more satisfied by the kind of comparative study of art that was oriented exclusively to the object, and that would limit itself to ascertaining and arranging among themselves the constitutive forms and regularities of the individual works.'[38]

With these words, however, this author glimpses only one of the fronts on which Hegel was fighting. The other was German classicism and Romanticism, with their deification of art into a religion of art.[39] The 'age of Goethe' was indeed 'the time when art was most intensely valued and venerated, the time when art became a veritable religion', when art 'achieved not only man's redemption *from* reality, but also *his reconciliation with* reality' (the poet as the true man, as genius and sage).[40] The most telling proof of Hegel's sceptical attitude toward the romantic absolutisation of art is supplied by his astonishing statements about the 'dissolution of art altogether' (*A*, 1236). These remarks, which immediately precede the brief personal epilogue just quoted, and which follow on Hegel's discussion of comedy, bring him to 'the real end of our philosophical enquiry': 'All art aims at the identity, produced by the spirit, in which eternal things, God, and absolute truth are revealed in real appearance and shape to our contemplation, to our hearts and minds. But if comedy presents this unity only as its self-destruction because the Absolute, which wants to realize itself, sees its self-actualization destroyed by interests that have now become explicitly free in the real world and are directed only on what is accidental and subjective, then the presence and agency of the Absolute no longer appears positively unified with the characters and aims of the real world but asserts itself only in the negative form of cancelling everything not correspondent with it, and subjective personality alone shows itself self-confident and self-assured at the same time in this dissolution' (*A*, 1236; on 'the decay and dissolution of art itself', cf. above all *A*, 575f, 593–611).

With his thesis concerning the dissolution or end of art, Hegel has brought

---

[38] *Hegels Kunstphilosophie*, 286.
[39] cf. G. Vecchi: *L'estetica di Hegel.*
[40] H. A. Korff: *Geist der Goethezeit* I, 24, 25.

down on himself much criticism, both direct and indirect, from Hegelians and non-Hegelians alike. The direct criticism has centred on charges that his system involves arbitrary compulsion, that he displayed a lack of historical and aesthetic awareness, and that he suffered from conservative, classicistic prejudice. The indirect criticsm meanwhile has been apparent in the critical attempts to work out a new rationale for aesthetics (although it must be said that these endeavours have themselves proved unable to dispel the unease at the continuing presence of art in the contemporary world): in Kierkegaard, who surpassed Hegel's critique of Romanticism; in Schopenhauer, Wagner and Nietzsche, who developed further the romantic theory of genius; in the liberal Hegelians and 'Young Germans', who put aesthetics on a new footing by recourse to nationalist and revolutionary ideas; and in the new twentieth-century attempts to work out a rationale as evidenced by phenomenology, existentialist philosophy and functionalism on the one hand, and by the neo-Marxist theories of Bloch and Lukács on the other.[41] The chapter headings chosen by Croce ('*Morte dell'arte*'[42]) and Vecchi ('*Morte e resurrezione dell'arte*'[43]) express in manifesto form the nature of the controversy about art which Hegel unleashed, but it cannot be expected that we shall settle this dispute here. Our concern, however, is not simply with the question whether we can give the word 'dissolution' a positive meaning with respect to art (which, after all, is what Hegel himself manages to do now and then in other places), so that this death can at the same time mean the resurrection, or rather the rebirth, of art. The decisive question is much rather whether we can cogently demonstrate that Hegel did in fact possess a flair for art, a basic theoretical openness not only for post-classical but also for post-romantic art, and an artistic awareness that had been renewed in the spirit of his philosophy. This question is bound up with the problem of the post-Hegelian future in general, to which we must return in a more general context. At this juncture we are more concerned with an indubitable corollary of the texts we have quoted concerning the end of art, namely with the fact that it is impossible for art itself to be the ultimate and supreme reality. This fact is bound up not least with the situation brought about by Christianity: 'The deep rupture and reconciliation of subjectivity revealed by Christianity cannot therefore be adequately depicted by art. This is another reason why, as far as Hegel is concerned, art has irrevocably lost its supreme vocation.'[44]

---

[41] cf. W. Oelmüller: '*Hegels Satz vom Ende der Kunst*', 75-77.

[42] *Ultimi saggi,* 147-160.

[43] *L'estetica di Hegel,* 177-196.

[44] W. Oelmüller: *op. cit.,* 86.

W. Oelmüller takes the view that Hegel spoke 'solely of the end of its supreme vocation, of exceeding its highest possibility . . . but nowhere of the end of art in general'(?).[45] He invokes three experiences of Hegel to show why art has irrevocably lost its vocation to be the supreme organon of truth:[46]

1. In modern society and in the modern state it is, according to Hegel, no longer possible for art to achieve an adequate representation of man and his contemporary world as a totality.

2. 'Art's claim to be able adequately to express supreme truth is, for Hegel, more decisively refuted by Christianity than by modern society and the modern state, which as far as he is concerned are just moments of the contemporary world . . . Hegel discerns what is new and distinctive in the Christian religion and in the incarnation of God as lying in the fact that the truth there revealed is no longer – as was the case with the truth of the "Indian incarnations" and of Greek art – expressed solely in picture-thinking and the power of imagination on the territory of art. The truth is now "not imagination, but hard and fast reality".'

3. While there is still a kind of art and of artistic theory which attempt in the world of today to preserve, or rather to renew, the absolute claims of art, their failure is demonstrable. Hegel demonstrated this failure with respect to the artistic theories of Schlegel, Schelling and Solger and with respect to the art of Hölderlin, Novalis, Tieck, E.T.A. Hoffmann, Jean Paul, Kleist and Carl Maria von Weber.

What has already become clear from the Hegel texts quoted above is at all events confirmed by the dispute on the end of art: according to the mature Hegel it is not art but only religion that can bestow the true revelation of Spirit. The 'philosophy of art' therefore almost automatically leads to its own sublation in the 'philosophy of religion'.

4. Christ in Religion

'Beautiful Art, like the religion peculiar to it, has its future in true religion. The restricted value of the Idea passes utterly and naturally into the universality identical with the infinite form; – the vision in which consciousness has to depend upon the senses passes into a self-mediating knowledge, into an existence which is itself knowledge – into *revelation*. Thus the principle which gives the Idea its content is that it embody free intelligence, and as "absolute" *spirit it is for the spirit*' (*PM*, 297).

From our point of view we have now arrived at the *terminus ad quem*. It is likely, however, that many studies of Hegel's Christology have taken this point as their *terminus a quo,* and it would indeed be perfectly legitimate for them to do so. We refer to the work in which one would most naturally look for Hegel's Christology, to his *summa theologicae*: his *Lectures on the*

---

[45]*op. cit.*, 87.
[46]*op. cit.*, 78-87.

Philosophy of Religion.[47] But precisely because this *summa theologicae* is the holy of holies of a *summa universalis* which, as we have shown, is itself in its entirety and in a comprehensive sense a *summa summe theologicae,* we have let ourselves be advised to undertake a thorough inspection of the outer precincts before presuming to step through the main gateway. Now Hegel's *Philosophy of Religion* must be viewed against the background of the *aporia* between Christianity, as it has taken doctrinal and institutional shape, and modernity, as it has left its mark on science and society. It has accordingly been our intention to ascertain how Hegel – who, standing as he did in the footsteps of Lessing, Hamann, Kant, Fichte and Schelling, was placed between orthodoxy and Enlightenment and then between Enlightenment and Romanticism – set about overcoming the alternatives that came on the scene with the Enlightenment between faith and knowledge, tradition and progress, heteronomy and autonomy, objectivity and subjectivity, and immanence and transcendence, before presenting and unfolding them in systematic form in his *Philosophy of Religion.* The route hither has been long and, we hope, not too tiring, but in our view it has been necessary. With our gaze fixed on religion

---

[47]Not until he came to Berlin did Hegel start to lecture on the philosophy of religion. He gave lectures on this subject in the summers of 1821, 1824, 1827 and 1831 (in the summer semester of 1829 he dealt with the proofs for the existence of God), each time restructuring the introduction and the fundamental part. These lectures already appeared in print in 1832, edited by Marheineke, and Bruno Bauer superintended the second edition in 1840, which still appeared under the name of Marheineke. Both of these editions are highly unsatisfactory, and the ET by Spears and Sanderson is based on the Marheineke/Baur edition of 1840 and is therefore not suitable for rendering quotations in this text. The author has used the critical edition published by G. Lasson from 1925 to 1929 (reprinted 1966), in which the extant script from which Hegel lectured (denoted here by an asterisk) is clearly distinguished from the notes taken down by his hearers by the use of a different print. According to the original numbering we are dealing here with vols. XII-XIV.

In addition to the general works on Hegel alluded to all along, cf. the general works on his *philosophy of Religion* by the following authors: C.A. Eschenmayer, R. Schmitt, F.A. Staudenmaier, L. Noack, E. Ott, G. Lasson, H. Groos, K. Nadler, J. Möller, E. Schmidt, B. Welte, M. Benvenuto, I. Iljin, G. Dulckeit, A. Chapelle, C. Bruaire, K. Löwith, R. Vancourt, E. L. Fackenheim, W. C. Shepherd, W. Oelmüller, M. Régnier.

We recommend the following authors on specialist problems to do with the philosophy of religion: J. Werner, G. E. Müller and M. Theunissen on the concept of revelation; H. Hadlich on the relationship between religion and philosophy; M. Riedel on the relationship between faith and knowledge; K. Domke, H. A. Ogiermann, W. Albrecht and Q. Huonder on the proofs for the existence of God; E. Coreth, J. Möller, B. Lakebrink, E. Heintel and J. B. Lotz on dialectic and analogy; O. Kühler on the exposition of Holy Scripture; T. Dieter, W. Steininger and C. Hötschl on the personality of God; J. Hessen and J. Splett on the Trinity; W. Schulz on the *theologia crucis;* J. H. Walgrave on the philosophy of worship; H. Reese and H. J. Schoeps on religion in world history. W. Schultz has compared Hegel with Schleiermacher, and H. Reuter, H. Gerdes, H. Schweppenhäuser and E. von Hagen have compared him with Kierkegaard. Further bibliographical tips on the *Philosophy of Religion* taken from the Hegel Archives in Bonn can be found in the appendix to the 1966 reprint of the Lasson Edition (XIV, 245-256). On the question of Hegel and atheism, cf. ch. IV, 3.

and society we have patiently pursued all the implications and complications of Hegel's thought through its various stages, and, instead of leaping straight from Stuttgart and Tübingen to Berlin, we have not been afraid to take the great hike which Hegel took through Switzerland, Frankfurt, Jena, Nuremberg and Heidelberg. Having gone to these pains, as we now catch sight of the wide religious and social horizon we can spare ourselves and the reader from a long-winded commentary on this *summa theologicae,* which already, without commentary, fills three goodly volumes on the concept of religion, the various religions and absolute religion. After all the foregoing, what is called for here is not expansion but condensation. The *Lectures on Religion* speak for themselves. Quite apart from detailed commentary, they are themselves the best commentary on everything which, whether overtly or covertly, expectedly or unexpectedly, is of relevance to theology and Christology in the other works of both the young and the mature Hegel. And now, after these connecting remarks, let Hegel himself take the floor with the least possible interruption from the author or any other dialogue-partner.

'Gentlemen, I have deemed it necessary to devote a separate part of philosophy to the consideration of religion. The subject-matter of these lectures is the philosophy of religion, and the subject-matter of religion itself is the highest there is, the absolute; it is also the subject-matter of the philosophy of religion, whose content is the absolute content itself... [Our subject-matter is] what is purely and simply true, what is truth itself, religion, in which are solved all the world's riddles, all the contradictions of more deeply reflective thinking, all the sorrows of feeling, the religion of eternal truth and eternal rest, the absolute truth itself, [absolute] satisfaction' (XII, 1*). With these words Hegel opened his lectures on the philosophy of religion. 'This is the position of the philosophy of religion with respect to philosophy in general and to the other parts of philosophy. God is the result of the other parts; here the end is made the beginning' (XII, 33).

1. *The task of a Christian philosophy of religion.* Hegel's *Philosophy of Religion* wages war on all fronts and assuredly has no intention of being an orthodox dogmatics which, in unfruitful polemic against the historico-critical sciences and against the reform of ecclesiastical institutions, would set the Christian faith at odds with all reason and make it into a merely positive system of propositions to be accepted only on the basis of 'authority'. But it is equally far removed from every kind of unenlightened Enlightenment which, armed with the abstract, commonplace intellect, would deem itself competent to construct a religion of reason valid for everyone and detachable from the Christian tradition. Hegel's *Philosophy of Religion* emphatically intends to be a *Christian* philosophy of religion. Over against not only French atheism but also Kantian agnosticism and every kind of romantic religion of feeling, it

350

is concerned with nothing less than man's highest and truly Christian task, the *knowledge of God*: 'He (God) is the starting-point before all and the end of all; everything takes its beginning from him, and everything returns into him' (XII, 1f*). It must therefore be the knowledge of God that is at stake notwithstanding all the false critical prejudices of the age. 'For the doctrine *that we can know nothing of God,* that we cannot discern him, has in our times become a universally acknowledged truth, an established fact. It is a kind of prejudice . . . The sphere of our knowledge of God has diminished in exact proportion to the increase in our knowledge of finite things – and the range of science has extended to become well nigh boundless, so that we cannot keep stock of all the fields of knowledge. There was a time when all science was science of God; our time, by contrast, is distinguished by knowing about anything and everything, by knowing an infinite amount on particular subjects, but nothing about God . . . How can we still heed and find meaning in the commandment: "You shall be perfect, even as your Father in heaven is perfect", given that we know nothing of him and his perfection?' (XII, 4f*). 'I declare this standpoint . . . to be diametrically opposed to the whole nature of the Christian religion' (XII, 6*).

In the *Philosophy of Religion* Hegel intends to pursue a *concrete* Christian philosophy. It will not consider God simply 'in an abstract, reasonable way, i.e. treat God as an essence', as did 'the metaphysical science of former days, . . . which was called *theologia naturalis*' (the enlightened philosophy of Wolff); 'we are not concerned here merely with God as such, as an object, but at the same time with God as he is in his community' (XII, 7*, 8). The *Philosophy of Religion* certainly does not aim to generate religion, to found a new religion. It has 'for its aim *to know and to understand religion as it actually exists*' (XII, 10*). The wretchedness of the modern age consists in the separation of believing from secular reflection, of piety from science, of Christianity from modernity. On the one hand, faithless philosophers and the *sciences exactes* strive for a self-contained 'system of the universe' (XII, 20*). On the other, mindless theologians indulge, if not in sterile defensive dogmatics, then in highly superficial 'erudition' about the history of doctrine or critical philology, in the 'erudition of historical chitter-chatter' (XII, 36). 'Those theologians are absolutely unconcerned with the true content, with the knowledge of God. They know only how a particular dogma was fixed by this or that council, what reasons moved the Fathers of such a council, how this or that point of view came to dominance' (XII, 27f). If this is no longer a positivism of dogma, it is nevertheless a historicism of dogma. Here the present age has its great intellectual mission of 'adjustment, [of demonstrating] the infinite in the finite and the finite in the infinite, of reconciling the heart with the head, and religion, absolutely pure feeling, with intelligence.

351

This [is] what is demanded by the philosophy of religion, [just as] it is required by philosophy in general' (XII, 22*).

The superiority of Christianity over all other religions stems from the fact that it does not, like 'pagan religion', contain a 'jolly awareness of reconciliation from the word go', but rather 'starts from sorrow', from 'original sin', from the man who is 'intrinsically evil' (XII, 23*). Now the Christian religion likewise already contains 'reconciliation', albeit to begin with only 'in unaffected faith'. From this matrix there grows the 'need to know [for the] purpose of unification, of the reconciliation of both [forms]', that is, of revelation and the knowing reason (XII, 23*). 'The mediaeval Church already . . . consistently and correctly . . . refused to permit' the un-Christian separation of faith from reason and philosophy from theology' (XII, 55); 'scholastic philosophy is one and the same as theology; the latter is philosophy, and philosophy is theology' (XII, 45). Instead of being severed and even set against each other, 'religion and philosophy perfectly coincide. As a matter of fact, philosophy itself is a form of worship. But while both religion and philosophy are forms of worship, this is true of each in its own characteristic way' (XII, 29). Each is a distinctive form of worship, for '[r]eligion [exists] as unaffected faith, feeling, contemplation, in the element of immediate knowledge and consciousness . . . [conversely,] the philosophy of religion is a thinking, *understanding knowledge* of religion; [in the philosophy of religion] absolute substantial content is identical with absolute form (knowledge)' (XII, 62*). Religion does not cease to be religion – and Hegel says this against despisers and defenders of religion alike – through being expressed in conceptual form.

The philosophy of religion is accordingly a truly speculative science: knowledge of absolute Spirit. It is knowledge of the Absolute, even if it is not yet absolute knowledge. While it is *thinking* reason, it is nevertheless not yet reason which thinks in the form of thinking as such, but in the form of picture-thinking. Hence it is not yet absolute philosophy, but philosophy of religion (cf. XII, 67). For absolute truth is still being thought of in terms of sensuous-*cum*-spatial juxtaposition and temporal sequence (example: 'the Son's being begotten of the Father'), and the norm of thinking is an authority located outside the thinking subject (cf. XII, 295-298). As speculative philosophy of *religion* it is, to be more specific – and *all* philosophy is knowledge of God! – the knowledge of absolute Spirit not only in the pure Concept (logic), but in its 'existence', in its 'appearance' (philosophy of Spirit), and indeed not only in its finite appearance (art), but 'in its infinite appearance' (XII, 32f). True speculative religion is not simply a human affair, but is at the same time the supreme vocation of the absolute Idea itself, 'a brain-child of the divine Spirit' (XII, 44). It must be understood neither along abstract subjective lines – only 'as a feeling, speaking and supplication towards him [God]' (XII,

160) – nor along abstract objective lines – '*theologia naturalis* as the study of the mere Idea of God' (XII, 159). A concretely thought philosophy of religion is, in the inter-relation of subjectivity and objectivity, a unifying, quintessentially divine-human philosophy: a philosophy which takes the unity of God and man utterly seriously from the very outset. Consequently, we have here a philosophy which transcends the antitheses of intellect and feeling, reason and faith, philosophy and theology, rationalism and irrationalism, natural and positive religion, and heteronomy and autonomy. It is thus a philosophy at the very summit of its age, a philosophy which has irrevocably surpassed both enlightened rationalism, which would dissolve everything historical in reason, and irrational romanticism, which would reduce the whole of religion to immediate feeling, at the same time taking care to incorporate whatever is genuinely valuable in these movements. According to Hegel the world-historical task of the present is just such a philosophy, which is Christian in the best – namely, speculative – sense, for it perceives the whole depth and true essence of Christianity. Hegel intends modern man to be able to give a consent to the Christian religion, which, precisely because it stems from critical reflection, is free and well-founded.

Finally, Hegel's *Philosophy of Religion* intends to be a specifically Christian philosophy by resolving to think in terms of Christ, of the God-man, of the incarnation of God: 'The human shape, the *incarnation of God* must emerge as an essential factor in the definition of the subject-matter of religion' (XII, 161). We must talk of this in some detail after we have pondered the basic understanding of religion in these lectures.

2. *The Concept and ideal moments of religion.* Hegel begins the general section of the *Philosophy of Religion* ('Concept of Religion': XII, 77-311; cf. 66-69) with an empirical observation. He would think through, as his point of departure, something given, namely the religious consciousness. This manifests itself as faith's immediate certainty of God, which is displayed in the feeling of the heart in the mode of picture-thinking. But what rules in this empirical sphere is the subjective, contingent, irrational. It is full of contradictions which must be overcome in thinking, in a dialectic which produces an organic synthesis out of both reason and the non-rational element, a dialectic which must elevate itself from the finite to the infinite. Finite and infinite are united in the speculative concept of religion, in knowledge of God. 'Speculative' (though not in the abstract thinking of the understanding!) means: 'Just as God is also the finite, even so I am the infinite; God returns into himself in the ego as in that which cancels its own finitude, and it is only as this return that he is God. *Without the world God is not God*' (XII, 148). It is no longer contingency that rules here, but true necessity! For religion is thus 'the relation of Spirit to absolute Spirit' (XII, 150): since 'Spirit as knowing agent

is the object of knowledge or absolute Spirit itself', religion is 'the idea of Spirit which is related to itself, the *self-consciousness of absolute Spirit*' (XII, 150). Religion, then, must not only be viewed 'from below' as a human affair, but man must be seen in his unity with the Absolute, so that religion must at the same time be viewed 'from above', as the 'self-knowledge of divine Spirit through the mediation of finite Spirit' (XII, 151). The essence of religion is, therefore, relation, counter-relation and inter-relation.

Three *ideal moments* result from Hegel's demonstration of the necessity and necessary development of religion as the divine-human knowledge of God. First, there is *absolute substance*: God as full universality and thus 'the source and starting-point, but at the same time quite simply the abiding unity, not just the soil from which the differences grow' (XII, 194). Hegel renews his resolute rejection of pantheism as the deification of all things, as identity 'in the abstract sense of the understanding' (XII, 195-199; cf. 254-257). Secondly, there is *absolute distinction*: we are dealing here with the 'judgment' of God concretely uttered in the 'creation of the world' (XII, 200). God is living Spirit and as such he is, in a necessary development, revelation: God is 'not jealous, so that he would not impart himself. The Athenians prescribed the death penalty for a man who would not let his neighbour light up from his torch, for he would lose nothing in the process. Just so God loses nothing when he imparts himself' (XII, 201). After all, in the shape of a human existence God is also the recipient of his own revelation. He thus reveals himself through the creation of the world in nature and Spirit, he exists for man in the element of consciousness of knowing. It is only with this duality and picture-thinking that religion as such begins, God as being and appearing for and in the consciousness. This entails God's presence in man and, conversely, man's life in God. 'God is God only insofar as he knows himself; his self-knowledge is, moreover, his self-consciousness in man and man's knowledge *about* God, which progresses to man's self-knowledge *in* God' (*Encyclopaedia*: V, 472). Finally, the third moment of religion is *absolute mediation*. We are here dealing with the knowledge of God as 'elevation to God' (XII, 206). Initially, this is carried out theoretically in picture-thinking, as expressed in the *proofs of the existence of God*. Subsequently, it takes place in the active sublation of disunion, in *worship* – and philosophy as knowing spirituality, whose first form is *faith*, is not the least important constituent of worship.

Fifty years after Kant's *Critique of Pure Reason* the proofs of the existence of God were utterly discredited. But as far as Hegel was concerned, Kant's say-so was by no means sufficient to consign them to the scrap-heap. He discusses both the *a posteriori* and the ontological arguments in detail (XII, 207-224; cf. XIII:1, 8, 40-58; XII:2, 20-48; XIV, 37-53). Hegel vindicates these proofs against Kant, though he departs from the traditional understanding by regarding them not as a series of logical inferences produced by the intellect, but as a form of religious meditation, as a dialectical-*cum*-speculative raising of finite consciousness to absolute Spirit, which realises itself in the medium of human spirit. Hegel discusses the three proofs (in principle there is a plurality of these) in an ascending order of importance: to begin with, the proofs that proceed from the finite, i.e. the cosmological and then the teleological or physico-theological proofs; and then the proof that proceeds from the infinite, i.e. the ontological proof, which was thought through by 'one of the great scholastic philosophers, Anselm of Canterbury, that great speculative thinker' (XII, 219). The cosmological proof is particularly appropriate to the religions of nature, the teleological to the religions of spiritual individuality, and the ontological to the Christian religion. A special lecture that Hegel gave on the proofs for the existence of God is still extant. In it he intended to give an overall account of the knowledge of God, but it remained unfinished (XIV: 2, 1-177[48]).

Worship involves a reciprocal divine-human event, namely the movement of God to men and of man to God. With reference to man the function of worship is 'for me to unite myself to God *in myself*, to know myself in God and God in me, this concrete unity' (XII, 227f), and this is to be achieved both in the inward conversion of heart and mind and in the outward deed. 'It is presupposed that reconciliation is either accomplished or else absolutely present, available from the word go' (XII, 235). In this respect, as an expression of unity 'the incarnation of God is an essential moment of religion and must feature in the determination of its subject-matter. This determination is perfectly developed in the Christian religion, but it also features in the lower religions, even if only to the extent that the infinite appears as in unity with the finite by appearing in stars or animals as *this* being, as this immediate existence' (XII, 232). Worship shares in the reconciliation accomplished against evil through devotion, sacraments and sacrifice, through contrition, repentance and ethical conduct, and pre-eminently through philosophy, which is 'a form of continuous worship' (XII, 236). For what is at stake in the whole of worship is nothing other than 'knowing spirituality' (XII, 238). And 'the first form' of this knowledge is 'faith' (XII, 248).

Faith ought not to be understood along either sentimental or rationalistic lines. It is neither a mere feeling, nor is it founded on scientific arguments. On the contrary, understood in Christian terms, it is 'Spirit's testimony to itself' (XII, 249). It is a question of an intimate unity between finite and infinite Spirit: 'Its [the knowing ego's] knowledge of the absolute content is the testimony which it gives to it, a testimony which at the same time is the very product of absolute Spirit itself, which only in this testimony produces itself as absolute Spirit' (XII, 252). God is not something above, outside or beyond, and faith is concerned with assurance of God's presence within us. This has nothing to do with pantheism, but is a genuinely Christian doctrine, for 'the Church likewise teaches about the grace of God which works within man, about the Holy Spirit who leads the members of the Church into the truth, about the justification of man' (XII, 256). Mediaeval theologians like Meister Eckhart perceived this better than do many contemporary Protestants (XII, 257). The practical realisation of faith in worship involves an act of God: God wills to dwell in man by grace! And at the same

---

[48]On Hegel's proofs for the existence of God cf. the detailed accounts by H. Domke, H. Ogiermann, and W. Albrecht; also J. Möller: *der Geist und das Absolute*, 132-140, 204-208; J. Flügge: *Die sittlichen Grundlagen des Denkens*, 120-131; Q. Huonder: *Die Gottesbeweise*, 90-104.

time it involves an act on man's part also: man wills by sacrifice to surrender his particularity into God! It is therefore 'a two-sided act: God's *grace* and man's *sacrifice*...This double activity is worship, and its purpose is God's existence in man. This reconciliation is absolute, hence *accomplished* in God himself. I am to pattern myself on God; this work is mine, and it is human. Looked at from his side, the same work is God's; he moves towards man and exists through the sublation of man; what appears as my act is in fact God's act and, conversely, God appears only through my activity. The two in one is absolute reconciliation' (XII, 258; on the various kinds of sacrifice: national, pagan and spiritual worship, cf. XII, 259-278).

3. *Preliminary historical forms and the supreme form of religion.* Hegel intends his *Philosophy of Religion* to be a Christian philosophy also when he considers the *concrete historical religions.* A philosophy of religion would remain abstract if it examined only the necessity and the ideal moments of the concept of religion. Rather, we ought to examine the concept in terms of its historical development by looking into the distinctive features of the particular religions. Part Two of the *Philosophy of Religion* accordingly discusses 'determinate or finite religion'. Religion is described as it actually is, in a living consciousness of the necessary development of Spirit: a description of the religious consciousness which draws at once from the consciousness of the individual man and from that of the great historical religions. Thus the individual and the universal consciousness, along with the idea of God and the idea of man, are depicted on a single canvas which captures the various stages of their development in an upwardly self-perfecting hierarchy, proceeding from immediate naturalness through an increasingly intense inwardness, spirituality and freedom to an increasingly perfect immanence of the finite in the infinite.

Hegel's conception of an ascending development moves him to reject the notion of a paradisical primal state or of a golden age at the beginning of history (XIII:1, 22-38). Instead, he looks to a vigorous history of religious development, which he is prepared to explicate with the aid of mysterious, profound names, with an extensive phenomenological description and with a dialectical-*cum*-speculative interpretation. The first phase in this development is formed by the religions of nature (XIII:1, 38-234). The Deity appears initially as a force of nature and as substance, and the following stages are formed in the process: from the religion of magic (unequivocally in the case of the Eskimos and Africans, indirectly in Chinese Tao-religion) through the religion of substantiality (of being-in-oneself: in Buddhism and Lamaism; of fantasy: in Indian religion) to the religion of abstract subjectivity (religion of the Good or of Light: Parsees; mystery religion: Egyptians and Syrians). The second phase is formed by the *religions of spiritual individuality* (XIII:2, 3-242). The Deity now appears as spiritual individuality, and the stages of this development are: from the religion of loftiness (Judaism) through the religion of necessity or beauty (Hellenism) to the religion of expediency (Roman religion). God is pictured as power and wisdom or as plastic beauty or as ruling expediency.

It would be easy to condemn the lower stages out of hand as error and superstition. Hegel's more profound concern is to see each stage in its (albeit limited) truth, in its self-developing truth. Each stage is religion, containing all the essential elements of religion, but not consciously containing them in their totality, not knowing the fulness of religion. It is the absolute, the Christian religion that first knows all these elements in their totality, only in this religion is form perfectly wedded to content, the historical shape commensurate with the concept. But it is precisely in the light of Christianity that the profound meaning of these lower religions becomes evident: they are preliminary stages of Christianity. Now in terms of the development of Spirit and of consciousness they are thoroughly *necessary* and for this very reason historically *real* preliminary stages of Christianity. In their truth they unfold the elements that are best preserved and transcended in Christianity. 'The idea of incarnation ... pervades all religions' (XIII:1, 6)! They represent Christian truth in embryo. And they prefigure – *in figura et umbra* (and often in a very dark shadow) – the mysteries of Christianity: the Trinity, the incarnation of God and hence the unity of God and man (XII, 161-232), the redemptive death and the resurrection of the God (XIII:1, 212-216). Thus even pre-Christian history is a hiddenly Christian history.

But precisely because the pre- and extra-Christian religions are preliminary stages, and because they are taken up and integrated into the perfect Christian religion, they are now also utterly superfluous: 'The earlier religions – in which the concept is less definite, more abstract, deficient – are determinate religions, which constitute the transitional stages of the concept of religion on its way to perfection. The Christian religion will show itself to us as the *absolute* religion. We shall therefore be dealing with its content.' Hegel already speaks along these lines in the Introduction (XII, 75*), and he presently goes on to devote the whole of the final part of the *Philosophy of Religion* to Christianity, the religion in which the philosophy of religion feels at home (XIV, 1-232).

Hegel gave a particularly elaborate exposition to the sublation of the Jewish, Greek and Roman religions into Christianity. Since Hegel tends to confuse the sequence of Jewish and Greek religion (XIII:2, 250f), we cannot deduce any fundamental subordination of Yahweh to Zeus and Jupiter. Hegel accentuates the pivotal importance of the idea of creation and preservation for Judaism, the religion of sublimity (XIII:2, 59-67). This idea confers on the world being, but not independence, issuing in the de-divinisation of the world of the religions of nature into a prosaic world (XIII:2, 67-69), in incoherent divine intervention through sporadic miracles (XIII:2, 69-71), and in the

357

setting apart of an elect people (XIII:2, 80-84). We note a restrained echo of the young Hegel's accusations against Judaism when we learn that the notion of God's arbitrary power and dominion, to which people have to subordinate themselves in full awareness of their sinfulness and servitude, remains characteristic of the religion of sublimity (XIII:2, 55-59, 71-80, 84-110). 'In all religion, Jewish and Mohammedan, where the God is conceived solely in the abstract determination of the One, this unfreedom of man is the real basis, his relationship to him a harsh service. In Christianity, [in the] Triunity, lies genuine liberation' (XIII:2, 91*).

At the same time the Greek religion of moulded beauty and of God's appearance in determinate sensuous individuality is itself sublated and liberated by the Christian religion as the incarnation of God: 'The god thus appears in stone, and the sensuous is still regarded as appropriate for the expression of the god as God. Only when the god himself appears as this individual and reveals that Spirit, the subjective knowledge of Spirit as Spirit, is there the true appearance of God, only then does sensuousness become free; i.e. it is no longer united to the god, but shows itself as inappropriate to his form: sensuousness, immediate individuality, is nailed to the cross. But in this reversal it is also demonstrated that this externalisation of God into a human shape is only one side of the divine life; for this externalisation and manifestation is taken back in the One, who thus first exists as Spirit for the idea and for the Church: this individual, existing, actual man is set aside and placed in God as a moment, as one of the divine persons. Thus man first exists truly in God as this man, thus the appearance of the divine is absolute and its element is Spirit itself. In this process of the divine life the Jewish and the Greek heritages are both contained and, as having been sublated, liberated from their limitedness – i.e. the Jewish notion that God exists essentially, albeit only for the idea, and the Greek stress on the sensuousness of the beautiful shape' (XIII:2, 146).

Finally, Rome's abstract religion of utility and expediency, whose whole earnestness is devoted to the state and which therefore culminates, as a political religion, in the cult of the emperor as an arbitrary lord of the world, is made redundant by its own dialectic: 'The aim served by this coolly calculating religion was none other than the Roman state itself, so that the latter is the abstract power over the other national spirits. The gods of all peoples are assembled in the Roman pantheon, and they wreak mutual destruction on each other by being united. The Roman spirit as this fate destroyed the happiness and serenity of the beautiful life and consciousness of the preceding religions, and it pressed down all configurations into oneness and sameness. It was this abstract power which produced enormous unhappiness and a universal sorrow, a sorrow which was to be the birthpangs of the religion of truth. The world's repentance, the doing away of finitude, and the despair of finding satisfaction in the temporal and finite order which now came to dominate the mind of the world – all of this served to prepare the ground for the true spiritual religion, a preparation which had to be accomplished on the part of man so that "the time might be fulfilled". These deep longings were answered in the Christian religion' (XIII:2, 241).

Concept and reality, finite and infinite Spirit have become fully one in Christianity on the level of picture-thinking. Religion has come to self-knowledge and to self-consciousness in supreme truth and in utmost freedom. 'Here for the first time Spirit as such is the object and subject-matter of religion, and Spirit is only for Spirit' (XIV, 4). But Spirit necessarily involves life, conscious life: thus Spirit must be involved in self-distinction, in making itself objective, in manifesting itself, in being for an other: in a nutshell, in revelation. 'A Spirit which is not public is not Spirit' (XIV, 35). Hence Christianity is the 'religion of *revelation*' (XIV, 32*), it is 'public religion' (XIV, 35), 'revealed religion . . . revealed by God' (XIV, 19). And because its content is God, it is 'the religion of truth' (XIV, 34*). And because this revelation of truth involves the fetching home of a world that has apostasised from God, it is 'the religion of *reconciliation* – of the world with God . . . the unity of divine and human nature' (XIV, 34*) and precisely as such 'the religion of freedom' (XIV, 35*).

Hegel deliberately intends to pursue a Christian philosophy of religion. For this reason he does not shrink from contradicting the whole thrust of Enlightenment thought by resolutely advocating '*historical* religion' (XII, 72), '*positive* religion . . . in the sense that it has come to man from outside, has been given to him' (XIV, 19; cf. XII, 54*). It is, in the end of the day, 'necessary' for '*everything to come to us externally*' (XIV, 19). The pairs Idea and history, positivity and rationality are by no means antitheses. The positive elements in Christianity are not to be denied, but at the same time they are also meant 'not to abide' (XIV, 21). Rather, they are meant to become rational, to be understood from inside! In that event those things that are inwardly necessary, eternal, spiritual and absolute will be perceived in the things that are external, contingent and historical.

Miracles have a foremost place among the external, positive proofs of Christianity. They can, admittedly, 'produce proof for the carnal man . . . This, however, is only the beginning of the process of proof, an unspiritual kind of proof, through which precisely the spiritual cannot be proved' (XIV, 21; cf. XIV, 191-194). 'Proof through miracle, like attacks on miracle, is a lower sphere which does not concern us' (XIV, 22). Obvious proof is spiritless proof. Even Christ had reservations about faith in miracles, and he said: 'The Spirit will lead you into all truth' (Jn. 16:13; XII, 249). The sole proof of spiritual things is the testimony of the Spirit, and this can take on a variety of forms: 'it is not to be demanded that the truth be produced in everyone along the path of philosophy' (XIV, 23). People can believe on the basis of authority, and they can also believe on the strength of miracles. Even so, 'the testimony of the Spirit in its highest mode is the mode of philosophy, bearing witness to the fact that the Spirit – purely as such, of itself and without any presuppositions – develops the truth, knows it by developing it and grasps the necessity of the truth in and through this development' (XIV, 22). This, then, is not only 'formal faith, but rather "true faith"' (XII, 249). The true proof of the truth of the Christian religion occurs in knowing the truth of what is believed, as this is mediated by philosophy.

Another reason why the Christian religion and philosophy of religion must be called 'positive' is that they are based on *Holy Scripture*: 'In that the doctrines of the Christian religion are available in the Bible, they are given in a positive mode. When they become subjective and the Spirit bears testimony to them, this can happen in a wholly immediate mode, so that man's inmost self, his spirit, his thinking and his reason, are touched by the Christian doctrines and consent to them. Thus for the Christian the *Bible* is this foundation, the chief foundation, which has this result on him, takes effect in him, and gives this steadfastness to his convictions' (XIV, 23f). It is, however, obviously impossible for man simply to accept the words of the Bible in a passive and mechanical fashion. How could he act other than precisely as a man, i.e. as a knowing, observing, thinking being! The basic problem of hermeneutics is posed here: if this acceptance of the Word is not to be a matter of simple reading and repetition (which can be left to simple pious souls), but is to be a real understanding, then man must explain and interpret the words of the Bible. This is true whether or not man intends it to be so. Theologians naively assert that they merely intend to remain faithful to the Word, to unleash the Word alone and nothing else: 'If, however, interpretation is not a mere exposition of single words, but rather an explanation of the sense, then it is easy to see that it must bring its own ideas into the foundational Word' (XII, 38). What matters is the inward meaning, the living spirit of the dead letter, and just such an exposition is impossible apart from one's own spirit. Man necessarily brings his own presuppositions, prejudices, ideas and thinking into his exegesis. These things do not hail from the Bible, but are brought to the Bible, and they have their own conditions and intrinsic forms before they come into contact with the Bible. And for interpretation, for exegesis, and, finally, for the theology of the reader of Scripture himself, everything hinges on 'whether his thinking is correct or not' (XIV, 24). And who but the philosopher, with his fundamental and universal science, is in a position to sit in judgment on the *a priori* correctness of thinking! Religious thinking should and must stick to the Bible, certainly, but it must already be intrinsically true, necessary and filled with Spirit, it must itself move on the loftiest speculative heights! Only when thinking is itself spiritual and itself brings along the correct spirit will it correctly understand the testimony of the Spirit in the Bible: 'The Bible is this form of the positive. Even so, one of its own saying is, "the letter kills, but the spirit makes alive". What matters, then, is which spirit one brings to the task, which spirit vivifies this positive religion . . . It should be the true, proper Holy Spirit which understands and knows the divine and its content as divine' (XIV, 26).

Because theologians have all too often approached the Bible with an unspeculative, purely intellect-related and contingent thinking, they have ceased to understand the most profound doctrines of Christianity and have emptied Scripture and dogma. Hence 'it has come about that the fundamental doctrines of Christianity have, for the most part, disappeared from dogmatics. Essential orthodoxy is nowadays – not exclusively, but preponderantly – the preserve of philosophy, for it is philosophy that preserves the propositions which have always been in force, the basic truths of Christianity' (XIV, 26f)! In terms of conceptual, speculative thinking it will be possible not only to preserve Scripture and dogma in the traditionalist sense, but even to realise its full potential in all its profundity and beauty for the new age. It is primitive rationalism to devalue the historical component of Christianity and distil from it a pure Christianity of reason. The serious and right-minded thinker gratefully accepts the Bible and the historical development of Christianity in its entirety, indeed he reflects speculatively on the whole historical development, demonstrating how it is a necessary development of Spirit. In this way the original historical bedrock of Christianity is elevated to conceptual purity, and the Bible and dogma are transfigured into supreme spirituality! For this reason – and here lies the core of his hermeneutic – Hegel can 'demand that, in the study of religion, we start from religion itself and not from the letter, and . . . invoke the right that religion be faithfully and openly developed from reason, so that the nature of God and religion may be examined without taking the determinate Word as one's starting-point' (XII, 39). His starting-point is the absolute standpoint, the standpoint of the Absolute itself. Only this standpoint is absolutely appropriate for the purposes of scriptural interpretation.

It is thus possible to know the general structure of Spirit 'empirically . . . from the perspective of ourselves': 'We know from our own Spirit, that, firstly, we think without this antithesis, this discord within us; that, secondly, we are finite Spirit, Spirit in its discord, severance; and, thirdly, that we are Spirit in feeling, subjectivity, in return to self, reconciliation, inmost feeling' (XIV, 29). But precisely because our Spirit is not simply extraneous to the divine Spirit, this distinction is to be perceived as a distinction of the absolute eternal Idea. The absolute eternal Idea, however, is (cf. XIV, 28-31): a) in and for itself, God in his eternity, on the ground of thinking: kingdom of the Father; b) in the severence and creation of the world, in the sphere of picture-- thinking: kingdom of the Son; c) in the sublation of severence, in the process of reconciliation: kingdom of the Spirit. This differentiation, in which we recognise those ideal elements to religion in general, distinguished in the first main part of this book, enables us to divide the discussion into the following sections.

4. *The Trinity*. How are we to describe God in and for himself, in his eternity prior to the creation of the world? We should certainly avoid the method customarily employed by natural theology of describing God through rigid abstract attributes, such as good, almighty, all-just, all-wise, omniscient. This approach would satisfy only the intellect (XIV, 13f, 54f, 64f, 75-77). 'Various predicates of God are demonstrated in this way . . . and afterwards, as it were apart from these predicates, the *history of God,* God's effectiveness and his

361

works' (XIV, 54*). The polarity-producing intellect pushes the predicates into insoluble contradictions, which it endeavours to solve in a purely abstract manner by 'having the attributes tone each other down through mutual interaction or by abstracting from their distinctiveness' (XIV, 13). But in adopting this approach the intellect does not take the antitheses sufficiently seriously: it sees them as located in its own act of knowledge and not in God himself, and it fails to take into account God's vitality and historicality. 'The vitality of God means that his specific characteristics and their resolution are not just an external matter, not something that is to be understood from our side alone' (XIV, 14). The various aspects in God are rooted not merely in our human ways of picturing things, but in God himself. God himself contains antithesis within himself, and he himself reconciles this antithesis. He is the dialectic. This is the God, proceding through polarity toward reconciliation, whom Hegel intends to describe – not in abstract propositions, but in a living process, focussing not on an abstract, dead divine essence, but on the concrete, living act that God himself is. Hegel is therefore concerned with the *living* God, which for him, in concrete terms, means the *trinitarian* God.

The Christian God is the trinitarian God. 'It is this trinity that makes the Christian religion stand higher than the other religions' (*Philosophy of History*: VIII, 59). 'The mystery of God is called the triunity; the content is mystical, i.e. speculative' (XIV, 69; cf. 57*). This is a mystery for both sense and intellect, but not for speculative reason: 'The speculative Idea contrasts not only with the sensuous, but also with the intellect, and is therefore a mystery for both of them. It is a μυστήριον both for the sensuous mode of enquiry and for the intellect. A μυστήριον is that which is rational and in the neo-Platonists this expression already means nothing more than speculative philosophy. The nature of God is not a mystery in the customary sense, least of all in the Christian religion, in which God has given himself to be known as what he is. Here he is revealed' (XIV, 77). Obscure intimations of this mystery are found also in the earlier religions, with the Indians and Pythagoreans, with Plato and Philo, and in the modern period Jacob Böhme and Kant have restored the triple scheme to its place of honour (XIV, 81-84). Thinking is meant to develop speculatively what religion possesses in the form of picture-thinking.

God is the Concept, the absolute Idea, the universal Spirit in eternal life, in eternal development: this is 'the history of God' (XIV, 54*). As feeling expresses it, God is 'eternal love' (XIV, 57*). As eternal love God loves Another, who is identical with him and loves him in return, in a Third. All of God is realised in each of these three forms: 'a game of love with itself' (XIV, 93). 'God is Spirit, and we may define him abstractly as self-separating universal Spirit. This is the truth, and the religion that has this content is the true religion. This is what in the Christian religion is called *triunity*' (XIV, 69).

God must be seen as a triune God apart from the world and its time, in an eternal being in and with himself. He must be seen in the sphere of universality and of thought, where Spirit differentiates itself while yet remaining with itself in the other and returning to itself. God must be viewed as *actus purus,* absolute activity, process, movement, life.

Hegel describes the triune life of God as it can be ascertained from the structure of Spirit in general: 'This life of God involves self-differentiation and self-determination on his part, and the first differentiation is that God exists as this universal Idea itself. Now this universal contains the whole *Idea* [of God], but it merely *contains* this Idea, is only *implicitly* this Idea. In this primordial division, the Other – i.e. the particular, that which stands over against the universal – is God as that which is distinct from God. Even though distinct [from God, this Other] is the whole Idea [of God] in and for itself, so that, even for each other, these two determinations [of God] are the same, this identity, the One. Hence this differentiation [in God] is not just implicitly transcended, nor are we the only ones to know this fact, but rather it is posited that these two distinct [moments within God] are the same and that these distinctions transcend themselves insofar as a) this differentiation is tantamount to positing the distinction as nugatory, and b) the first [moment in God] is at home in the second. This fact is the Spirit itself or, to express it according to the mode of feeling, it is eternal love: the Holy Spirit is eternal love' (XIV, 74f; cf. 56f*, 68f, 72). God is therefore conceived as triune 'in that he makes himself his own object, the Son, that he then remains in this object, and, moreover, that in this distinction of himself from himself he at the same time transcends the distinction and loves himself in himself, i.e. is identical with himself, and unites with himself in this love of himself. Only this is God as Spirit' (XII, 41f). It pertains to the in-comprehensibility of this mystery that it cannot be adequately expressed either by the numbers one, two and three, or by the label of 'person' (as a 'rigid, inflexible, independent being for itself'), or by such expressions as 'Father' and 'Son' (XIV, 80).

5. *Creation and evil.* God as Spirit is essentially a going out of himself, a revealing and manifesting of himself. This very fact implies his relationship to another, analogous, Spirit. Viewed only in this first, eternal sphere, in the kingdom of the Father, God is an abstract God. Indeed, God only is by being creator of the world. God's being Spirit therefore involves entrance into the sphere of appearance and picture-thinking, where God treads the path of difference and separation in world and time and becomes God for the other. This is the kingdom of the Son, God's becoming world. 'The second sphere for picture-thinking is the *creation* and *preservation* of the world as nature, finite world, spiritual, physical nature, the opening up of a wholly different territory, of the world of finitude' (XIV, 85*; cf. 56*, 65f). The world is the appearance of the Idea itself, 'the wisdom of God in nature' (XIV, 88*) and,

finally, in finite Spirit. Although the world is not simply God, the divine Idea nevertheless lives in the world. The creation of the world involves God's own externalisation, for it is a 'separation' and 'falling-off' of the Idea (XIV, 94), 'a going out, an appearance of God in finitude' (XIV, 92). As Spirit, God reveals or manifests himself through his primordial division and communication of himself, which ensures that another participates in him. The self-differentiation of Spirit must indeed go further. The abstract and universal inner-divine distinction must be determined, posited in actuality toward external reality, and separated in independent otherness. The inner-divine distinction appears in this way in the real world. This should not be taken to mean that the world is simply identical with the Son of God. Rather, what takes place immanently in the generation of the Son, within the pure divine Idea, is now carried forward, on a wholly different plane, into the world (XIV, 86). The first distinction is the presupposition of the second: 'The first element in the Idea is only the relationship of the Father to the Son, but that other also sustains the determination of things. It is in the Son, in the determination of difference, that the further determination of differences is carried on; it is here that the difference receives its right, its right to be different' (XIV, 94).

The world declines into the world of nature which has no immediate relationship to the spiritual God, and into the world of finite Spirit, for which nature represents the veil through which it must pass in order to arrive at truth. Spirit must move from discord, through interiorisation into unity. 'The third sphere is therefore objectivity as finite Spirit, the appearance of the Idea at and in finite Spirit, redemption and reconciliation as themselves divine history and at the same time as a transcending of external objectivity in general and hence as a real consummation of Spirit' (XIV, 95*). For 'the natural Spirit is essentially that which it is not meant to be and to remain' (XIV, 96*).

Accordingly man is not, as Rousseau believed, good by nature, but rather *both good and evil*! Note that he is not 'good and evil in equal measure' (that would be 'superficial': XIV, 116). On the contrary, he is good inasmuch as, *qua* Spirit, he surmounts the natural, and evil inasmuch as, in this very act, he falls away from himself: 'It is essential to say that man is good, for in himself he is Spirit, rationality, created with and according to the image of God. God is the Good and man, as Spirit, is the mirror of God; hence he is good in himself. This proposition is the sole basis for the possibility of man's reconciliation. The difficulty and ambiguity of this proposition, however, lie in the definition of "in himself". It is thought that we have said everything when we say, "Man is good in himself", but this "in himself" is an utterly onesided statement that does not say everything by a long chalk. That man is good in himself means that he is good only inwardly, according to his concept and therefore not according to his actuality. Inasmuch as he is Spirit man must be what he truly is, actual, i.e. for himself. To be good by nature, i.e. immediately good (and this is what Spirit is), is precisely not something natural and immediate. On the contrary, man as Spirit emerges from nature, and passes over into the separation between his concept and his immediate existence . . . but this is not to be taken to imply that evil comes on the scene only with the emergence from nature: on the contrary, this emergence is already contained in naturalness itself. The in-itself is the immediate, but because man's in-itself is Spirit, man in his immediacy is therefore already the emergence from immediacy, a falling-away from the latter, from its being-in-itself. This fact is the basis of the second proposition, namely that man is evil by nature, that his being-in-itself, his being natural is evil. His deficiency is present simultaneously with man's being natural; because he is Spirit, he is distinct from his being-in-itself, he is discord. Onesidedness is immediately present in naturalness. If man is only according to nature, then he is evil' (XIV, 113-115; cf. 102-105*).

Man is thus essentially *man in contradiction.* And man must become conscious of this contradiction, he must come to experience sorrow over it. He must be conscious not only of having trespassed against this or that commandment, but of being evil in himself: he must be conscious that the contradiction is absolute. 'There is within man a need for universal reconciliation (including divine, absolute reconciliation). Bound up with this is the fact that the antithesis has acquired this infinitude, that this universality encompasses the most intimate aspects of things, that there is nothing that lies outside this antithesis, hence that the antithesis is nothing special. This is the deepest depth' (XIV, 117). This absolute antithesis is displayed under two forms: on the one side in infinite sorrow as it finds historical expression especially in the Jewish people, i.e. as an 'antithesis against God'; and on the other side in the absolute unhappiness of dissatisfaction as revealed especially in the Roman people, i.e. as an 'antithesis against the world' (XIV, 117).

This and nothing else is what is related in the Genesis account of the fall into sin associated with the tree of knowledge (XIV, 121-129). It is not merely a contingent event that lurks behind the childlike, contradictory images present in this story. A deep speculative truth is hidden here, a truth at once historical and eternal: 'It is the eternal history of man, and the most profound element of this account is that it contains man's eternal history, his being consciousness' (XIV, 123f*). 'The first man' is precisely 'man as man' (XIV, 127), and sin comes about through the separation-provoking consciousness, through the knowing, disuniting and distinguishing of good and evil. In knowing, man emerges from the primitive innocence of an immediate association with nature, in which the child is akin to the animal. He falls within the differentiation of the intellect, and hence into the world of contradictions and especially of *the* contradiction: between the finite and the infinite, which the finite intellect is incapable of conceiving in infinite terms. The evil quality of knowing is this fall into contradiction, this severance of the intellect, this coming to a standstill and staying put at the stage of severance. In this way, at the tree of knowledge, man becomes aware of being evil.

The knowing consciousness, however, is not only the mainspring of discord and evil, but also provides the springboard of advancing beyond this stage (not, be it noted, for a return to the primordial state), for conversion to freedom and reconciliation as this was heralded in the promise of the new Adam and as, in the course of the development of Spirit, it became a world-historical reality in the period when the Jewish and Roman ways of life were so glaringly at odds with one another. The world had been seized by a tremendous sense of the need for redemption. 'The concept of the preceding religions purified itself into this antithesis, and when this antithesis showed and presented itself as an existing need, it was expressed thus: "*When the time was fulfilled,* God sent his Son" (Gal. 4:4). This means: the Spirit, the need for the Spirit, is present, indicating reconciliation' (XIV, 121).

6. *The death and life of the God-man.* How, then, is the antithesis overcome? How does reconciliation come about? How can finite and infinite, God and man be reunited? These things cannot be achieved by the power of man, but only through God's own intervention. 'Reconciliation neither is nor can be brought about by his [man's] subjective conduct' (XIV, 139). All of man's 'activity, devotion and piety' (XIV, 135) can achieve nothing under its own power. The decisive factor is that this unity of God and man is already the *presupposition* for all of man's activity. *Finitum capax infiniti*! An original relatedness of man to God! We must recognise 'that those antitheses are not intrinsic, but rather the truth, the inner reality, lies in the antithesis being sublated ... That the antithesis in itself is transcended constitutes the condition, presupposition and possibility for the subject also to transcend the antithesis for itself' (XIV, 139; cf. 136, 130f*). Reconciliation as a whole is conditional on its having happened implicitly from *eternity* for humankind as a whole, on God and man having been implicitly reconciled and made one from eternity in the living absolute Spirit. It is dependent then on 'the eternal emergence of antithesis, the equally eternal transcendence of antithesis, and on there being an eternal reconciliation' (XIV, 139). This is also expressed in human nature's being in the image of God and in the subjectivity of the human spirit. God and man are not intrinsically alien, nor are they intrinsically opposed to one another. The antithesis of the two is not the appropriate, but the most inappropriate state of affairs. Not that the disproportion between God and man should simply disappear: after all, the essence of Spirit involves

366

life, and that means antithesis, that means disproportion. What matters, however, is 'that there should be an identity of God and man notwithstanding the disproportion, and that the otherness, finitude, weakness and fragility of human nature should not prejudice this identity, which is the substantial element of reconciliation' (XIV, 140; cf. 134f). We have seen in the doctrine of the Trinity, where the Son is distinct from the Father and yet remains perfectly identical with him as God, how otherness does not preclude identity. And inasmuch as evil still contains affirmation even in the utmost negation, we recognise here too a hidden identity of man with God. But the man who lives in contradiction is meant to become conscious of this original unity. He is meant in a reconciliatory and conscious manner to fulfil his intrinsic nature. And he cannot do this without the historical incarnation of the Son of God, Jesus Christ. In order that 'the substantiality of the unity of divine and human nature may enter the consciousness of man' it is necessary in religion 'for man to appear to him as God and for God to appear to him as man' (XIV, 141): 'God as the concrete God' (XIV, 137). Only in this way does man become certain of the unity between himself and God in immediate tangible terms: 'God was obliged to appear in the world in the flesh in order that man might be assured of this. The necessity for God to appear in the world in the flesh is an essential provision. In the light of the foregoing it can be deduced as necessary' (XIV, 141). In Christ the implicit unity of man with God is assured, it can be seen and experienced.

At this juncture Hegel's *Philosophy of Religion* reaches its climax. Both the divine and the human here reach their apex. This is 'the momentous element', 'the most weighty moment in religion': 'God appears in human shape' (XIV, 137)! God and man are not different, but one! God and finite matter are not mutually exclusive – this is said against Platonism of every hue. God and finite matter are one: not only accidentally as in the burning bush or in the Indian incarnations, but substantially (XIV, 138): 'in this man, who should at the same time be known as a divine Idea, not as a teacher, nor simply as a higher being in general, but as the supreme [Idea], as God's Son' (XIV, 131*). The world-historical significance of Christianity consists in the fact that man is brought into immediate relation to the Absolute, while at the same time this Absolute is made man. The cosmo-theology of the Greeks seems to have been displaced by the anthropo-theology of Christianity.

God is in Christ in the shape 'of an *individual man*' (XIV, 137). This means, in the first place, that God is in the shape of the *one* man! 'Man in himself is the universal, the idea of man. Here, however, on this standpoint, we are not concerned with the idea of man, but with tangible certainty; consequently it is *one* man in whom this unity is contemplated' (XIV, 141). 'This is precisely why [the universal] had to appear as a single exclusive man for the others, this is why neither these others nor all individuals are [the universal], but only one man from whom they are excluded' (XIV, 142; cf. XIV, 133f*). This one man is the precondition for the actualisation of the incarnation, as a consequence of Christ's death and resurrection, in all men and women.

God is in the shape 'of an individual man' (XIV, 137). This means, then, that he is in the shape of one *man*! 'In the Church Christ has been called the God-man, and this astonishing compound is utterly at variance with picture-thinking and with intellect. Even so, through this formula people have been made conscious and certain of the unity of human and divine nature. Moreover, it has also persuaded them that this unity is not jeopardised by the otherness, or (as it is also expressed) by the finitude, weakness and fragility of human nature, just as the otherness in the eternal Idea does not jeopardise the unity that is God. It is the appearance of a man in a material mode of presence, for God in a material mode of presence can have no other shape than the shape of a man. In the material and worldly sphere man alone represents what is spiritual; thus, if the spiritual is to exist in material shape, then it must exist in human shape' (XIV, 142).

Contrary to many preconceptions about him, Hegel by no means bypassed the 'historical Jesus' in his philosophy. The spade work that he had accomplished in Bern for his *Life of Jesus* here comes into its own. An exhaustive chapter deals with the *teaching of Christ,* which, according to Hegel cannot be simply identical with 'what is later on the teaching of the Church, the community': 'Christ's teaching is not a Christian dogmatics, not the doctrine of the Church. Christ did not, then, present those things that the Church later made into doctrine' (XIV, 149f). The principal subject-matter of the teaching of Christ is 'the *heavenly kingdom,* the kingdom of God, [a] substantial intelligible world stamped by a rejection of all those values that are sought in earthly, worldly things. [His teaching] is not God alone, the One, but rather a kingdom of God, the eternal as a homeland for Spirit, the eternal with this element of what is native to subjectivity' (XIV, 143*). This kingdom of God is the goal of the Sermon on the Mount, whose beatitudes 'are among the greatest [sentiments] that have ever been expressed, they are an ultimate focus which abolishes all superstition and servitude of man' (for this reason Hegel demands the distribution of Luther's translation of the Bible as a book for the people: XIV, 144). As against the Mosaic Law, Jesus insists on a true disposition, which is the sole source from which true action can spring (XIV, 145). Jesus' concrete concerns were threefold: a) love – not the 'lame *abstractum*' and 'empty posturing' of a universal love of humanity, but the specific love of the neighbour (XIV, 145); b) cutting loose from the *status quo* – Jewish law, the worries of daily life, the family (XIV, 146–148); and c) Jesus' relationship with God, and that of people with him and with God, as it finds supreme expression in his authoritative forgiveness of sin – 'the reconciled-ness of men and women with God' (XIV, 155).

'The important thing' about his titles, such as Son of man, 'is not whether exegesis can flatten down these expressions'. What matters here is rather 'the truth of the Idea, what he was for his community, and the higher Idea of truth which was in him in his community' (XIV, 148). Christ is therefore not only to be viewed 'as man according to his outward condition', but much rather 'with the Spirit, which drives towards his truth' (XIV, 154). While Christ certainly had a human side, this was not the only side to his nature. An old Bern motif is reawakened here, but it is now employed in an unequivocally Christian sense: 'When we view Christ as we would view Socrates, then we view him as we would an ordinary man, just as the Mohammedans view him, as an ambas sador of God in the same way as all great men are amb-assadors and messengers of God in a general sense. If we say no more about Christ than that he was a teacher of humanity and a martyr for the truth, then we are not adopting a religious standpoint. This human side of Christ, his appearance as a living man, is but one side . . .' (XIV, 154; cf. XII, 263f). The Church's meditation on Christ in the Spirit presupposes Christ's human side. This means above all 'that he is immediately human as far as all external and contingent factors are concerned, in all temporal relationships and condi-tions. For example, he was born and as man he experienced the same needs as other people, only that he did not enter into the corruptions, passions and evil inclinations of other people, not even into particular worldly concerns in which uprightness and sound teaching can be exemplified. On the contrary, he lived only for the truth, only for its proclamation. His influence consisted solely in giving fulfilment to the higher consciousness of men and women' (XIV, 154).

There was, however, another side to Christ, and for religion this was the decisive side: 'The appearance of the God-man is . . . immediately to be considered in two ways . . . The second of these, however, is a meditation in the Spirit, a meditation with the Spirit, which drives toward his truth because he has within himself this infinite discord, this sorrow, because he wants truth, because he wants and is obliged to have a need for truth and a certainty of truth. Only this second side is the religious side' (XIV, 154). The teaching of Christ was accordingly more than mere teaching. It was backed up by his life and death: '. . . the main point is that this subject-matter was imparted not by teaching, but by sensuous contemplation. This subject-matter is nothing other than the life, suffering and death of Christ' (XIV, 153).

The seal on Jesus' teaching was his death (cf. XIV, 155). But this observa-tion is not the end of the matter, for Christ's life and death were the actualisation of his programme. The kingdom of God, which began as a universal Idea, 'enters through this individual into actuality' (XIV, 156*):

'Since it is the divine Idea which passed through this history, the latter is not to be regarded as just the history of a single individual. Rather it is to be taken in itself, as the history of an actual man who made himself the existence of Spirit' (XIV, 156*). In this way 'the kingdom of God has . . . its representative' (XIV, 157*). The divine Idea itself is revealed in the life and death of Christ. And this revelation is an externalisation of God not only into the temporal sphere, but into the sorrow of death, which is 'utmost negation', 'the utmost extreme of limitation and finitude' (XIV, 157*): 'It is thus this process of the nature of Spirit, God in human shape, that presents this life of Christ to the imagination – and, indeed, for the empirical, universal and immediate consciousness. This process is in its development the advance of the divine Idea to supreme discord, to the opposite of the sorrow of death, which is itself an absolute reversal, supreme love, in itself the negative of the negative, absolute reconciliation, the cancellation of man's antithesis against God. The end is present here as a *dénouement* into glory, as the honoured assumption of the human into the divine Idea. That first element, God in human shape, is what Christ really is in this process, which displays the severance of the divine Idea and its reunification, and whose consummation is the first intimation of truth. This is the whole of history' (XIV, 163f*).

Hegel constantly reiterates that the life of Jesus Christ is the history of God himself. If the life and death of Christ involved merely the life and death of an individual man, there would be no need to pay it any special attention. But the aweful mystery of this death (in contrast to the death of Socrates and of other great men) is that it affected God himself. Hegel now develops an idea which he had earlier (at the latest, in Jena) thought through and formulated – the death of Christ as the death of God: It is 'a monstrous, frightful idea' (XIV, 158*) that a 'divine history' (XIV, 164) is at stake. 'The first meaning of this death is that Christ was the God-man, the God who at the same time had a human nature, who indeed [had this nature] until death. It falls to the lot of human finitude to die, so that death is the supreme proof of humanity' (XIV, 165). Now this utterly ignominious and shameful death on the gallows of the cross is the 'externalisation of the divine' (XIV, 157*), 'and the meaning of this history is that it is the history of God' (XIV, 166). As Hegel says, not without an element of pathos: 'As a Lutheran hymn has it, "God himself is dead". This statement expresses the consciousness that the human, the finite, the fragile, the weak and the negative are themselves a divine moment, that these things are in God himself, that finitude, the negative and otherness are not outside God and that, as otherness, they do not preclude unity with God. This is otherness, the negative known as a moment of the divine nature itself. The highest Idea of Spirit is contained in this thought. In this way what is external and negative is transformed into the inward. This death means, on the one hand, the casting off of the human and the re-emergence of divine glory – it is a casting off of the human, of the negative. But at the same time this death itself is also the negative, the very zenith of that to which human persons as natural existents are exposed. Accordingly, this death is God himself' (XIV, 172; cf. 157f*).

As God's greatest act of love, the death of Christ is thus the reconciliation of the world with God and therefore of God with himself: 'This death is love itself, and in it we contemplate absolute love. It is the identity of divine and human, that God is at home in the human and finite, and that this finite is itself in this death a determination of God. Through this death God reconciled the world and eternally reconciles himself with himself' (XIV, 166). If it is appropriate to say of this death 'that Christ was delivered up *for us* [and that his death] may, as a sacrificial death, be pictured as the act of absolute satisfaction' (XIV, 158*; cf. 172f), we should nevertheless bear in mind that this formulation means to imply more than mere legal or formal imputation,. according to which God would be 'a sacrifice-demanding tyrant' (XIV, 166). This reconciliation is much rather to be understood as an absolute, eternal reconciliation, which occurs eternally in the bosom of the divine Idea: 'This death therefore makes satisfaction for us, since it presents the absolute history of the divine Idea, that which has occurred in itself and eternally occurs' (XIV, 159*). God himself sacrifices himself: 'This is not the history of an individual, but rather it is God that carries it out' (XIV, 160).

This death gains a special quality in virtue of the fact that Christ publicly died the degrading death of a criminal. With this emphasis there reappears the social horizon of the death of God, which Hegel had already unequivocally worked out in Jena. While the tyranny of the Roman emperor caused the Most High to become the most despised, the very reverse process took place in a frankly revolutionary way in the death of Christ: the most despised is made the Most High, so that the imperial state was deprived of its inner basis. This was an unpolitical revolution with political consequences: 'In a natural death finitude is at the same time transfigured as something merely natural, but here civic degradation – the cross – is itself transfigured, the meanest object that the mind can imagine, the instrument employed by the state for the purpose of degradation – this has been converted into the most sublime thing of all. Thus what was regarded as the lowest has been made the highest. What we have here is a direct expression of complete revolution against the *status quo*, against what is held in esteem by the public mind. By turning the degradation of existence into the highest honour, all the bands of human communal life have been assaulted, shaken and disintegrated at their very root. The cross corresponds to our gallows. When this symbol of dishonour was elevated into a banner and turned into a cockade, indeed when it was made into a banner

371

whose positive content is the kingdom of God, then the inner disposition at its deepest depths was withdrawn from the life of the state and from civic existence, and the substantial foundation of both was taken away' (XIV, 161f*).

7. *Spirit and Church.* Unless we realise that Hegel's exclamation 'God is dead' is only a provisional truth, we should fail to understand it aright. Its purpose is to afford a sensational and paradoxical proof of the proposition that the death of God is the death of death, in short, that God lives. This death is therefore not an end, but rather a fresh beginning. The stigma of the cross turns into a trophy of victory. For death is overcome by being taken into God himself, by becoming a divine moment. Out of death itself there follows resurrection: 'God has died, God is dead – this is the most appalling thought, that everything eternal and true is not, and that negation itself is in God; bound up with this is the supreme sorrow, the feeling of the utter absence of deliverance, the surrender of all that is higher. Yet the course of events does not grind to a halt here; rather a reversal now comes about, namely, God maintains himself in this process. The latter is but the death of death. God arises again to life: consequently, the process turns into its opposite. The resurrection pertains equally essentially to the faith . . . Hard on the heels of the resurrection follows the glorification of Christ, and the triumph of his exaltation to the right hand of God concludes this history, which in this consciousness is the explication of the divine nature itself' (XIV, 167; cf. 162-164).

From the negation of negation there here begins the process of return and consummation as the third sphere of Spirit (XIV, 164): 'The individuality of the divine Idea, the divine Idea as *one* man, is first consummated in actuality through having as its counterpart the many individuals and through bringing them back to the unity of the Spirit, to the community, and through existing there as actual, universal self-consciousness' (XIV, 164*). The second coming of Christ must be understood in spiritual terms, the 'future' being taken as a 'moment' of the 'present': 'Thus sensuous pictorial thinking has the *second coming,* which is essentially absolute return, but which presently shifts from the outward to the inward sphere: a comforter, who can only come when sensuous history as something immediate is a thing of the past. This is, then, the point at which the community is formed or it is the third point: it is the Spirit' (XIV, 168f). Inwardly understood, the second coming is the coming of the Spirit in the becoming of the community.

The *Church* emerged in the Spirit from the death and resurrection of Christ: in the Church his death and his resurrection are believed, known and attested. The appearance of the incarnate life in the world of sense was a transitory phenomenon, but it has been spiritually preserved in the community: 'The

372

formation of the community has this content, that the sensible form' of the appearance of God in the flesh 'passes over into a spiritual element' (XIV, 168). The incarnation advances forward into the Church for the benefit of everyone: having been accomplished *implicitly,* redemption now becomes actual *for* the individual. This is made possible by the outpouring of the Holy Spirit, which is the means whereby Christ remains spiritually present in the community. 'He is in them and they are and constitute the universal Christian Church, the communion of saints. The Spirit is eternal return into himself, infinite subjectivity. He is not a mere product of picture-thinking, nor is he the substantial in-itself of the Father or the Son (Christ), but rather actual, present divinity, the true in this form, objectivity. [Even though he is objectivity,] he is the subjectively present and actual, and it is only through this mediation that he is subjectively present precisely as externalisation into this objective contemplation of love and its infinite sorrow. This is the Spirit of God, or God as present, actual Spirit, God as dwelling in his community. Christ said, "Where two or three are gathered together in my name, there am I in the midst of them", and "I am with you always, even to the end of the world". Christ died, but in saying "with, in . . . you" he is the Holy Spirit. This is the absolute meaning of Spirit, this is the supreme and pure consciousness of the absolute Idea and of absolute truth, this is the absolute Idea and absolute truth as self-consciousness of themselves' (XIV, 180*; cf. 182). In this Church believers share through the Holy Spirit in the life of the God present in the community, whereby they are also a unity among themselves. The last great period of development of the absolute Spirit is thus the kingdom and age of the Holy Spirit and hence of the Church, an epoch whose final stage boasts the 'community of philosophy' (XIV, 175-232).

This might seem a fitting juncture to go on to discuss Hegel's ecclesiology, his vision of the development of the Church and its faith, their existence, endurance and full realisation. Although this topic must appeal to the Catholic systematician and ecumenist, not least in view of Hegel's demonstration of the differences between the confessions, we must, in order to keep this section to a reasonable length, resist the temptation of digressing here. Hegel himself has provided us with the perfect excuse: '[To examine the Church] in its concrete shape, taking account of its history and empirical existence, would take us too far afield, however tempting such a study might be' (XIV, 175*).

But let us not suppress Hegel's final remarks on the subject of the Church. He asks himself whether, like all historical formations, even the Christian religion stands under the law of emergence, preservation and decay. Hegel refutes this notion by appealing to Mt. 16:18, which speaks of the gates of hell which shall not prevail against the Church: 'To speak of decay would mean ending on a discordant note' (XIV, 231*). In the world, though, the cause of religion looked distinctly sickly. This accounts for Hegel's closing statement and recommendation: '[As a matter of fact] religion [must] take refuge in philosophy' (XIV, 231).

5. Christ in Philosophy

The deepest and ultimate purpose of the *philosophy of religion* is that it points not to, but beyond itself. Not that this discipline does not contain the ultimate and entire truth, but simply that it does not contain it in its definitive and unsurpassable form. In fact, the *philosophy of religion* points to the definitive form of truth, that is, to philosophy. And concrete philosophy is philosophy in its development, from its beginnings to its contemporary climax. Hegel depicts this development for us in his *History of Philosophy*.[49] *'The history of philosophy presents us with the gallery of noble minds which, through the boldness of their reason, penetrated into the nature of things and of man and into the nature of God. They have uncovered for us the depths of these things, and they have acquired for us the treasure of supreme knowledge.* This treasure, in which we ourselves intend to share, is constituted by philosophy in general. It is the development [of this corpus] that we shall get to know and learn to understand in these lectures' (XV, 6*; *HP* 1,1). With these words Hegel had, already in the Heidelberg Introduction, described the task of the history of philosophy, and he subsequently repeated them almost word for word in the Berlin Introduction (XIV, 21).

---

[49]The two highly important Introductions to the *History of Philosophy* are happily available to us in Hegel's own handwritten lecture notes (*). For the rest of the work we are dependent on his students' lecture notes and on the revision of further manuscripts from Hegel's own pen in K. Michelet's rather unsatisfactory first edition of the *History of Philosophy* (1833–36). The ET by Haldane and Simson is based on Michelet's 1840 edition and therefore corresponds to the Jubilee Edition but not to Hoffmeister. For the whole Introduction (including postscripts) and for the sections on Chinese and Indian philosophy we possess an exemplary edition by Hoffmeister (XV). This edition must now be supplemented by five newly discovered manuscripts. According to a new numbering of the volumes it now bears the number XX. The other parts of the work will be quoted here from the Jubilee Edition (*G* XVII-XIX), the ET by Haldane and Simson (3 vols), referred to here as *HP*1, 2 or 3.

We lack a fully up-to-date account of Hegel's *History of Philosophy,* and only with reservations can we refer the reader to the various introductory works on Hegel's philosophy, since they either totally fail to mention the *History of Philosophy* or else only award it perfunctory treatment. It is discussed in greater detail by K. Fischer, B. Croce, N. Hartmann and E. Bloch. In addition one should take into account the older works of A. L. Kym, C. Monrad, W. Windelband and M. B. Foster. The following authors are significant in our particular context: J. Stenzel (Greek philosophy), B. Lakebrink (Anselm of Canterbury), T. Steinbüchel (Meister Eckhardt), E. Metzke (Nicholas of Cusa) and G. A. Wyneken (Kant). R. O. Gropp discusses Hegel's *History of Philosophy* from the standpoint of dialectical materialism.

Philosophy is, as *history* of philosophy, the philosophy of philosophy. As such it is the absolute pinnacle of wisdom. Nevertheless, we should totally misunderstand Hegel if we took him to mean that the task of the history of philosophy is simply to supplant or to absorb the philosophy of religion (cf. XV, 166-221). Quite apart from the fact that religion offers revelation to everyone while the philosophical penetration of revelation can only be grasped by a small élite, Hegel insists that religion continue to be regarded as an absolute stage of knowledge. Religion too is an absolute knowledge of God and, indirectly, of nature and Spirit. Religion too possesses not only rationality, but also universal, infinite rationality. Religion too is already *'the sanctuary of truth itself, the sanctuary in which has dissolved all the other delusion wrought by the world of sense, by finite views and aims, by this field of opinion and arbitrariness'* (XV, 43*; *HP* 1, 62).

Note that religion is not deficient in content, in absolute truth. 'It is only the *form* in which this content is present in religion that differs from the way in which it is present in philosophy, and this is why a history of philosophy is necessarily different from a history of religion' (XV, 45*; *HP* 1, 63). What does Hegel understand by this 'form'? 'This form, however, in virtue of which the intrinsically universal content first belongs to philosophy, is the form of thinking, the form of the universal itself. But in religion this content is depicted by art for immediate, external contemplation and, furthermore, for picture-thinking, feeling' (XV, 46*). Philosophy, then, does not create a new truth or a new revelation, but rather aims to reflect on and to deepen actual religion. In absolute philosophy, though, thinking is now thoroughly at home. Here it is no longer a thinking that pictures reality through fantasy in the heart, mind and intellect, but a thinking that operates through pure thinking. It no longer thinks the Absolute as an object confronting it, but as self-knowing Spirit. Nevertheless, religion is by no means merely the *veil beneath* which one should seek the truth (were this the case, then it would involve a disparagement of myth in favour of philosophy). The veil of picture-thinking is in fact not a disguise but a laying bare, it is a genuine expression of truth. Why should one wish to separate the light from its shining! All that religion 'requires' is 'an *explanation*' (XV, 57). It simply needs to be '*translated* into spiritual and intellectual proportions' (XV, 58*) in order to be 'made *intelligible*' (XV, 59*).

This programme is carried through on this highest stage of knowledge by pursuing the development of philosophy. This involves the intellectual pursuit of pure thinking's own self-knowledge, that is, of the self-thinking of absolute Spirit as made visible in history. It involves selfless immersion in the spiritual river of tradition that has been swelling up through the centuries, in that river in which philosophy does not merely swim passively along but in which the

375

absolute science of absolute Spirit takes form. 'Γνῶθι σεαυτόν, *know thyself* – this inscription over the temple of the knowing God at Delphi is the absolute commandment that expresses the nature of Spirit' (XV, 36f*; *HP* 1, 32)!

If the history of philosophy had previously consisted in collecting anecdotes, biographies and isolated doctrinal propositions, Hegel now intends it to become a genuine historical science. The history of philosophy is something different from 'relating a *store of philosophical opinions*' (the malicious say '*Gallery* of follies . . . or at least of *errors*') or from boring 'learning . . . knowing a wealth of *useless facts*' (XV, 25*; *HP* 1, 12). Should we examine the various warring and successive systems in purely historical terms, there would be no alternative to ascertaining a chaos of opinions and succumbing to scepticism. Hegel's primordial confidence in reason voices itself when he opposes such a view, insisting that there is but *one* truth: 'Hence only *one* philosophy can be the true one' (XV, 27*; *HP* 1, 16). We should not conclude from this that the other philosophies are false; rather, we should see the wood in the trees, the one body in the many members! In the speculative vision it can be made clear that all of these philosophies are philosophy: various forms of appearance of the *single* truth. This truth may be multi-coloured, it may be prone in its necessary stages and moments to contradict itself or to get entangled in itself, but in its increasingly wonderful blossoming it is nevertheless *one* truth.

'Philosophy, then, is a system in development. Accordingly it is also the history of philosophy' (XV, 33*; *HP* 1, 29). This development can take place in two ways: either, as in logic, in the consciousness of its necessity, or, as in the philosophy of history, empirically, without this explicit consciousness. But both approaches belong together and Hegel regards it of decisive importance 'that the succession of philosophical systems in history is the same as the succession in the logical deduction of the conceptual determinations of the Idea. I maintain that if we [discuss] the fundamental concepts of the systems that have appeared in the history of philosophy on their own, divested of all that pertains to their external formation or to their application to the particular and such like, then we shall obtain the various stages of the determination of the Idea itself in its logical Concept. If, conversely, we take the logical progression on its own, [we shall come up with] the progression of historical appearances [arranged] according to their chief moments'(XV, 34*; *HP* 1, 30). There is an identity, then, of ontogenesis and phylogenesis!

Notwithstanding all the contradictions which constantly emerge and then resolve themselves, the history of philosophy is consequently unqualifiedly logical. We may go further to say that the history of philosophy is nothing other than the concrete development of supra-temporal, eternal logic in time.

The whole development is dominated by the strict coherence of the subject matter in movement: the necessity of the Concept, the divine Logos, the absolute Spirit. No element in this history is purely and simply false: even the Sophists receive their due. But every element is onesided, though to a diminishing degree and therefore, increasingly, intelligible. If we do not come to a standstill at the stage of onesidedness – and history does not come to a standstill – then everything will be rectified *en passant*, in contradiction and change, so that the history of philosophy is certainly not a disavowal of philosophy, but rather portrays its lofty ratification and verification.

At this elevated speculative altitude 'the study of the history of philosophy is a study of philosophy itself' (XV, 35*; *HP* 1, 30), and only a truly speculative history of philosophy deserves 'to be called a science' (XV, 36*; *HP* 1, 31). Only such an approach can discern the necessary philosophical succession implicit in the growing actualisation, concretisation and intensification produced by an unremitting series of fresh developments. It alone can esteem the unbudgeable knots that litter the predecessor's system as the true foothold for the successor's often only hiddenly meaningful attempts to climb further. It alone can portray the 'universal Spirit' which, with well-founded leisureliness and strenuous effort, takes fruitful detours 'in order to reveal itself in world history' (XV, 37; *HP* 1, 33) in that 'supreme form' (XV, 38) where 'the Spirit of the age is present' in the various nations 'as self-thinking Spirit' (XV, 39). Only a thinking that reconciles systems which succeed one another in meaningful antagonism is in a position to do justice to the historical development and essence of absolute Spirit.

Notwithstanding the contrary efforts of the god Chronos, Hegel threw himself wholeheartedly into ordering the initially confusing historical 'gallery of noble minds' according to the systematic (and, for Hegel, dynamic and fluid) categories of logic. His aim was to prove the congruence of systematic philosophy with the history of philosophy and to show how every philosopher and every philosophy enjoys just as much relative justification as does every logical category. At root every philosopher represents a corresponding category, and in the case of the earliest philosophers at any rate this hypothesis even fits the actual chronological sequence: Parmenides can be coupled with being, Heraclitus with becoming and the Atomists with being-for-self. The development leads unstoppably upwards, from the poorest and most insipid systems to the richest and most colourful, as Spirit is enriched by becoming conscious of the wealth which, already implicitly possessed, becomes visible in time in the 'gallery of noble minds' (XV, 6*; *HP* 1, 1)

A succession of great names appears here listing those who, exerting a dialectical counter-influence on each other, took part in this wonderful single history that

377

oscillates between problem and system. We must hear their names in order yet again (not neglecting to take note of the number of pages Hegel devotes to each), so that we may rightly appreciate the significance of Hegel's treatment of them. To begin with, Chinese and Indian philosophy are regarded as the first steps on the path to philosophy proper, which began with the Greeks. The first stage of *Greek philosophy* reached from Thales to Anaxagoras: the Ionians Thales, Anaximander and Anaximenes, the Pythagoreans, the Eleatics Xenophanes, Parmenides and Zeno, then Heraclitus and, finally, Empedocles, Leucippus, Democritus and Anaxagoras (*G* XVII, 204-434; *HP* 1, 166-349). The next stage takes us from the Sophists (Protagoras and Gorgias) to the Socratics (Socrates, Megarics, Cyrenaics and Cynics: *G* XVIII, 1-169; *HP* 1, 350-487) and, finally, to Plato and Aristotle (*G* XVIII, 169-423; *HP* 2, 1-231). This first period of Greek philosophy is followed by a second dominated by dogmatism and scepticism (Stoics and Epicureans, neo-Academics and Sceptics: *G* XVIII, 423-586; *HP* 2, 232-373) and by a third consisting in neo-Platonism (Philo, the Cabbala and Gnosticism, the Alexandrines Saccas, Plotinus, Porphry and Proclus: *G* XIX, 1-96; *HP* 2, 374-453). *Mediaeval philosophy* comprises three phases, the first of which was taken up with Arabian philosophy in the Medabberim (*G* XIX, 121-132; *HP* 3, 26-36), with the commentators on Aristotle and with the Jew, Moses Maimonides. The second phase was dominated by scholasticism (*G* XIX, 132-212; *HP* 3, 37-107): Anselm and Abelard build the doctrine of the faith on metaphysical foundations, Peter Lombard, Thomas and Duns Scotus present the concept of ecclesiastical doctrine, and Alexander of Hales and Albert the Great display an acquaintance with the Aristotelian writings. The contrary current of nominalism *versus* realism makes itself felt in Roscelin, Occam and Buridan, making its mark on formal dialectic with Julian of Toledo and Radbertus and, finally, in mysticism with Gerson, Raimundus of Sabunde and Raimundus Lullus. The third phase of mediaeval philosophy constituted a revival of learning and of the various branches of study (*G* XIX, 212-262; *HP* 3, 108-156). Three factors produced this revival: the study of the ancients (Pomponatius, Ficino, Gassendi, Lipsius, Reuchlin), the efforts at philosophical development (Campanella, Bruno and Vanini), and the Reformation. *Modern philosophy* begins with Bacon and Böhme (*G* XIX, 278-327; *HP* 3, 170-216), leading to the period of the thinking intellect (*G* XIX, 328-354; *HP* 3, 217-359) with its metaphysic of the intellect (Descartes, Spinoza, Malebranche; then Locke, Grotius, Hobbes, Pufendorf and Newton; and finally Leibniz, Wolff and popular philosophy), and then to a period of transition (Berkeley and Hume, the Scottish philosophers and the Frenchmen Holbach, Robinet, La Mettrie, Helvetius, Rousseau). This period is superseded by the most modern German philosophy (*G* XIX, 534-692; *HP* 3, 409-554) as represented by Jacobi, Kant, Fichte, the Romantics and Schelling.

And now, following all these great names, at once surpassing and expressing them all, we have 'the result', 'the present standpoint' (*G* XIX, 684; *HP* 3, 545). Situated on this awesome pinnacle, with the three thousand year-old upward process of Spirit behind and beneath him, we have – Hegel! 'Now the World Spirit has come this far. The final philosophy is the result of all previous philosophies; nothing is lost, and all principles have been preserved' (*G* XIX, 685; *HP* 3, 546). Hegel receives the whole inheritance. With respect to the millenia of '*the exertions of Spirit*' and of '*its most solemn labour*' he

378

pronounces that '[i]t took an enormous effort for Mind to know itself – *tantae molis erat, se ipsam cognoscere mentem*' (*G* XIX, 685; *HP* 3, 546)! And he proclaims the world-historical victory: 'A new epoch has arisen in the world. It seems that the World Spirit has now succeeded in divesting itself of all alien objective essence, in finally comprehending itself as absolute Spirit, in generating from itself that which becomes objective to itself, thus ensuring that [this objective reality] remain within the power [of absolute Spirit]. The struggle of finite self-consciousness with absolute self-consciousness (the latter having seemed to the former as existing outside itself) ceases . . . The whole of previous world history in general and the history of philosophy in particular depict only this struggle, and they appear to have reached their goal where this absolute self-consciousness, which they picture to themselves, has ceased to be something alien, where Spirit is actual as Spirit. For Spirit is only actual Spirit through knowing itself as absolute Spirit, and it knows this in science . . . This is now the standpoint of the present age, and it concludes for now the sequence of spiritual configurations. This fact *terminates* this history of philosophy' (*G* XIX, 689f; *HP*3, 551f).

An observation of Nietzsche's cannot be suppressed here: 'This Hegelianly understood history has been termed "God walking on earth", but it is well to remember that this God was for his own part only brought into being through history. This God became transparent and comprehensible to himself within Hegel's skull, where he already soared through all the dialectically possible stages of his becoming right up to his self-revelation. The result was that for Hegel the high-point and end-point of the world process coincided with his existence in Berlin. Indeed, he would have been obliged to say that all things which came after him are properly to be appraised as a musical code for the world-historical rondo, or, to put it yet more forcibly, as flatly superfluous. He did not say this outright: instead, he planted in the generations whose thought he leavened that admiration before the "power of history" which in practical terms is apt to topple over into naked admiration of success and to lead to the idolising of the status quo . . .'[50]

This climax brings us to the end of the philosophy of philosophy and accordingly also to the end of Hegel's circular system. And once again we seek *Christ* here in the history of philosophy which 'is the inner sanctum of world history' (*G* XIX, 685; *HP* 3, 547) and thus 'the *unveiling of God,* as he knows himself' (*G* XIX, 686; *HP* 3, 547). Surely he can be found here in this *sanctum sanctorum,* and precisely here. And we do in fact find him here. On this pinnacle – and Hegel clearly stated as much – religion is neither denied nor pronounced superfluous, but 'explained'. Those things that were expressed

---

[50]*Unzeitgemässe Betrachtungen* II, 8 (*Werke* I, 263); ET *Thoughts Out of Season; Complete Works*, vol. 2, 71f).

concerning Christ in the *Philosophy of Religion* are not taken back, but rather (let it be summarily mentioned here[51]) repeated and confirmed: the divinity and humanity of Christ (cf., e.g., XV, 174, 176, 179-181, 245f; cp. *HP* 1, 71-74, 105f; *G* XVIII, 119; *HP* 1, 446). Hegel robustly declares the following to be heresies, a distortion of Christian truth: Gnosticism, whose advocates 'evaporate the form of existence and actuality, which is an essential moment in Christ, . . . into a universal idea' (*G* XIX, 65; *HP* 3, 17); Docetism, with its doctrine of the 'illusory body' and the 'merely apparent', 'allegorical crucifixion' (*G* XIX, 66f; *HP* 3, 17, 19); and Arianism, whose adherents 'took Christ to be a mere man, inflated into a higher nature' (*G* XIX, 113, cf. 137; *HP* 3, 20). In his introduction to the philosophy of the middle ages, about which he obviously knows little and which 'we would suffer almost any inconvenience to get behind us' (*G* XIX, 99), Hegel engages in a fresh discussion of Christianity, in which 'what God is has come into men's consciousness and been revealed. More precisely, the unity of human and divine nature has entered men's consciousness' (*G* XIX, 99; *HP* 3, 2f). While discussing the philosophy of the Church Fathers, he speaks of Christ as follows: '. . . this Other in God is thus the Son, a moment in the divine . . . Yet it is not sufficient for the concrete moment in God to be known; rather, it is also necessary for it to be known in connection with man and for Christ to have been a real man. The connection with man is with man as *this* man. This man is the overwhelming moment in Christianity, the joining together of the most stupendous antitheses' (*G* XIX, 112, cf. 113-116; *HP* 3, 15, cf. 16-21). Hegel has the following to say *à propos* of scholastic philosophy: 'It is only by being elevated beyond the natural that man becomes spiritual and attains to the truth. The way in which man reaches the truth is for his certainty of it to take the form of contemplating the presence in Christ of the unity of divine and human nature, of contemplating the fact that in him the λόγος became flesh. We have here, first, the man who comes to spirituality through this process and, secondly, man as Christ, in whom this identity of the two natures is known. This is faith in Christ, and it is by means of this knowledge of this identity in Christ, by means of the knowledge of this original unity, that man then comes to the truth. Now since man in general is this process of being the negation of the immediate and of coming out of this negation to himself, to his unity, he ought therefore to renounce his natural willing, knowing and being. This relinquishing of his naturalness is contemplated in Christ's suffering and death, and in his resurrection and exaltation to the right hand of the Father.

---

[51]On the trinitarian (or it might be more appropriate to say 'triadic') texts from the ancient Indians and Greeks (especially Plato) to Böhme, Spinoza and Kant, cf. J. Splett: *Die Trinitätslehre G.W.F. Hegels*, 107-115.

Christ was a perfect man, and he endured the fate of all people, namely death. This man suffered, sacrificed himself, negated his natural essence and exalted himself in doing so. In him we contemplate this very process, this conversion of his otherness to Spirit, along with the necessity of sorrow in the renunciation of naturalness; but this sorrow, that God himself is dead, is the birthplace of sanctification and elevation to God. Hence those things that must take place in the subject, this process, this conversion of the finite, are known as having been implicitly accomplished in Christ' (*G* XIX, 133f, cf. 132, 134f, 137f, 145, 151; cp. *HP*3, 4ff, 15f, 54, 57f).

Christ can therefore be found even here in the 'inner sanctum of world history', in the 'unveiling of God, as he knows himself'. Philosophy does not abolish Christianity, but rather preserves it. Even so, the *Philosophy of History* is more insistent than any other of Hegel's writings in expressing the view that Christ, although necessary, was a transitory and only qualifiedly binding event in world history. The christological passages are located either in the introductory chapters on religion and its distinction from philosophy – in which case they belong not to the *History of Philosophy,* but to the *Philosophy of Religion* – or else in the section on mediaeval (including patristic and gnostic) philosophy – in which case their imbeddedness in a past epoch is evident.

It is only too obvious that the philosophy of philosophy ascribes no constitutive significance to Christ. Having appeared in the fullness of time, he was already left behind in the middle ages (or even already in the patristic period and basically already in the first Christian century). He had his place there in the realm of the objective, external and contingent. True subjectivity and inwardness, however, were still lacking: 'It was Church doctrine, itself admittedly speculative, but yet in the manner of external objects' (*G* XIX, 155; *HP* 3, 57). 'Reconciliation was formal, not in and for itself, reconciliation was to be had only in another world' (*G* XIX, 200; *HP* 3, 95f). Also lacking was true insight: 'The thinking intellect gets down to the mysteries of religion; they are wholly speculative in content, content only for the rational Concept. But the mystery, the Spirit, this rational element has not yet penetrated thinking' (*G* XIX, 202; *HP* 3, 97). The final missing element was true necessity: 'If this object [of the intellect] is God – as, for example, in the statement "God became man" – then the relationship between God and man is not drawn from their nature. What appears is God in general, any old how. We might hear the facile interjection: "With God nothing is impossible", or be faced with the red herring: "It is a matter of indifference in what determination the universal is posited"' (*G* XIX, 206; *HP* 3, 101). In brief, mediaeval religious thinking lacks that lofty speculative altitude on which the incarnation of God is understood and interpreted in terms of the essence of the universal Spirit.

Even the Reformation, which was implicitly a turning toward inwardness and spiritualisation, failed to interpret the incarnation in terms of its own starting-point: 'the philosophical development of the doctrines of the Church was put on one side' (*G* XIX, 259; *HP* 3, 151). This work was first accomplished by modern philosophy, which for its part took some anti-Christian detours in the process. Philosophy builds on Christianity: 'Philosophy has to be restored on the basis of Christianity' (*G* XIX, 157). Yet this task must also be accomplished in a new spirit: 'Philosophy properly emerges by freely grasping itself and nature in thinking, and – in this very act – by thinking and understanding the presence of rationality, the essence, the universal law itself. For the chief characteristic of us men is subjectivity, which, as involved in thinking, is infinitely free, independent and not minded to acknowledge any authority' (*G* XIX, 269; cp. *HP* 3, 161). 'The universal concern of science is to generate in *thinking* this reconciliation which is already *believed*' (*G* XIX, 274; *HP* 3, 165). Modern people have accordingly been increasingly successful at laying their finger on the pulse not only of contemporary religion, but even of historic Christianity and of the historical Christ himself. The modern discovery is that the core of religion is not something external, contingent or historical, but the absolute universal Spirit, the identity of subject and object, finite and infinite, God and man. Are not the concern of Christ and he himself preserved here in the best possible sense? It is not so much a question of the once for all event, of the individual historical concrete Christ (although he is not denied!), but rather of the absolute content and of the *Idea* of Christianity (which for their part are only intelligible in terms of Christ). The essence of religion, then, is the Idea of Godmanhood, the reconciliation of God and man in the absolute Spirit as an eternal process (cf. *G* XIX, 99-120; *HP* 3, 1-10).

It is therefore understandable why the historical Christ no longer has any role to play in the history of modern philosophy (even though the latter simply intends to be a higher stage of ancient philosophy!). Hegel scarcely mentions Christ once in this whole section (*G* XIX, 466; *HP* 3, 341: indirectly through a quotation from Leibniz who for his part was quoting the Bible). And it is understandable why the historical Christ cannot be found at the conclusion of the whole development in the eschatological result of the history of philosophy: the last word is spoken not by Christ, but by 'the Spirit *qua* Spirit' which 'knows itself as absolute Spirit' (*G* XIX, 690; *HP* 3, 553).

6. God of the Future?

We cannot here offer an appraisal commensurate with Hegel's powerful overall conception of the philosophy of history. Nevertheless, what we already established in connection with the *Philosophy of World History* has now been vividly confirmed by the *Philosophy of Art,* the *Philosophy of Religion* and the *History of Philosophy* (all of which branches of study were entwined in a differentiated unity from the very outset). That is, in mediating in the centuries' old conflict between Idea and history, Hegel produced not only an astonishingly concise and inexhaustibly profound, but also an intentionally and essentially *Christian vision of history.* Hegel intended his entire thought to be historical thought, his historical thought to be religious thought, and his religious thought to be interpreted in the light of the – albeit philosophically conceived – incarnation of God. What he intended to achieve was not a timelessly static metaphysic of Ideas, but a comprehensive and dynamic Christian philosophy of history. Hegel's onto-theo-logic manifested itself as a powerful theodicy, which, along its whole course and in all its strata, aimed to be at the same time a comprehensive justification of history.

And he did this at a time when a world picture that was over two thousand years old had been irrevocably smashed, bringing the previous picture of God and man tumbling down in its wake to become museum exhibits belonging to an irrecoverable historical past. Human history seemed to have been demystified and secularised. New economic and social conditions had taken shape, producing a revolutionary new 'bourgeois' society. Scarcely a single political, ethical or religious institution had been left unshaken by the French Revolution. The Enlightenment, and the conflict which it formulated between faith and reason, had passed far beyond educated circles to penetrate the people as a whole. Not only state and society, but even Christendom and the Churches, had suffered a grievous diminution of their unifying force, nor could this quality be restored to these institutions by a subjectivist Romanticism hostile to the Enlightenment. Many people at this time genuinely desired to be simultaneously critical *and* Christian, enlightened *and* believing, rooted in tradition *and* progressive; and such persons as these were overwhelmingly impressed by the fact that a thoroughly modern philosopher was here endeavouring to transcend both criticism of and apology for religion by furnishing a grandiosely systematic and concise up-to-date version of Christian truth which would enable critical modern man to give it his well-founded and thoroughly thought-through consent, dispensing him from having to give a naive consent to a heteronomous authority. In this great enterprise the modern schizophrenia between faith and Enlightenment was replaced by a differentiated unity of philosophy and theology, the alternative between rationalism and a religion of feeling by the union of intellect and feeling in reason, and the alternative between the biblicism of orthodoxy and a philosophical religion of nature by the systematic striving for a biblical hermeneutic appropriate to the age in question.

The texts of the lectures have themselves made it clear that, precisely in his

Philosophy of Religion, Hegel was more concerned than ever with the detailed study of Scripture; and that he had significantly clarified his thinking on various difficult issues which had been obscurely presented in the *Early Theological Writings* and in the major printed works. Among these topics feature the doctrine of the Trinity, the presence of good and evil in man, the distinction between the inner-trinitarian generation of the Son and the creation of the world, the uniqueness of Christ, the account of his message and his fate, and, finally, the meaning of the Spirit and the Church. While the *Philosophy of Religion* is assuredly not an example of orthodox dogmatics, it is anything but a product of shallow Enlightenment-style thinking.

In comparison with classical theology, this is conspicuously not a philosophical-*cum*-theological vision of history that shies clear of the 'exertion of the Concept'. Hegel's God is not a Spirit beyond the stars, who operates on the world from the outside, but rather the Spirit who is at work in the spirits, in the depths of human subjectivity. His doctrine of the Trinity is not a brand of conceptual mathematics remote from reality, but a trinitarian '*oikonomia*' brought into relationship with history. The creation of the world is not treated as an abstract *ex improviso* decision of the divine will, but is explained in terms of the essence of God. The governing image here is not emanation (from the perfect to the imperfect, with a paradisiacal golden age at the beginning), but evolution (from the imperfect to the perfect). Divine providence is not asserted in terms of an arbitrary God, nor is it proved along abstractly historical lines; instead, it is glimpsed in the concrete course of history. World history is not channelled into a constricted sacral *Heilsgeschichte* surrounded by profane history; on the contrary, the entirety of world history is seen as a single universal *Heilsgeschichte,* which, when looked at in religious terms, is centred on the event of incarnation. The non-Christian religions are appraised not as purely negative or as neutral and therefore unimportant phenomena, but as pre-Christian religions which *in umbra et figura* have to do with the one God, and which, as provisional forms, already herald the perfect. The incarnation of God is not simply whittled down in a pietistic manner to become an event for private piety, nor is it pocketed as the special theological property of the Church; rather, there is a demonstration of its significance as a global event for the whole of humanity. Sin and suffering are not belittled by a supra-temporal and abstract theodicy, but are rather presented as having been painfully and victoriously conquered by God himself in history in terms of a theology of the death of God whose essence is the concrete justification of both God and man. For this reason the observer of history will, according to Hegel, neither deny as an illusion the antitheses, contradictions and catastrophes of human and world history, nor will he stand clueless before them. He will neither resignedly renounce insight into the tragedy of the world, nor rebel in irrational anger against superficial senselessness. Instead, moved by reason's insight into the ultimate rationality of history which is hidden from the understanding, he will calmly accept actual history as it is. Might not this be a middle way between the shallow reasoning of the Enlightenment and the pious irrationalism of feeling, both of which are simply not competent in a technical sense? Ought faith to have anything to fear in all of this, if it is conceived in rational terms?

Even so, we may now fittingly register yet again all those reservations which the preceding two chapters have developed in detail concerning Hegel's major printed works. In the last analysis, the same factors have pressed themselves on our attention regarding the paths of the World Spirit in world history and of the Absolute Spirit in art, religion and philosophy that we were already able to observe and indeed obliged to call into question in the *Phenomenology, Logic, Encyclopaedia* and *Philosophy of Right:* the element of 'being sublated' in a graceless necessity and dialectic of being, in an insight of reason and science of history which upstage any proper role of faith. All of these factors have been apparent in this chapter too; indeed, they have found expression in the cited texts themselves. These reservations have not been dispelled.

The following comment is made by K. Löwith, with whose essay on 'Hegel's Sublation of the Christian Religion' we are, in the main, obliged to agree over against the counter-theses of C. G. Schweitzer: 'Hegel's relationship to Christian religion and theology is from the outset essentially ambiguous. It consists in a philosophical *justification* of religion through a *critique* of the pictorial form proper to religion, or, to express it in terms of the ambiguous root concept of Hegel's philosophy, in the "sublation" of religion into philosophy. Philosophy sublates religion in the sense of both preservation and destruction, and it does this through the intellectual elevation of religious pictures to the level of the Concept.'[52] This does not exclude our going beyond Löwith in giving a more positive account, both on the whole and with reference to particular detail, to what he himself holds characteristic of Hegel's later *Lectures on the Philosophy of Religion,* namely, a 'withdrawal of the critique of Christianity in favour of its justification in conceptualising thought'.[53]

All reservations aside, however, something else is now of greater importance for us. The significance of Hegel's thinking on the philosophy of history far transcends that of the branch of study that has gone by this name since Voltaire's day. As was already established in connection with the *Philosophy of World History,* Hegel represents the crown of a tradition developed by the Enlightenment, by Hamann, and by Herder. Indeed, so impressive was his

---

[52]'*Hegels Aufhebung der christlichen Religion*', 194f.
[53]*art.cit.*, 213; on this discussion, cf. P. Henrici's critical report '*Hegel und die Theologie*', 706-710.

achievement that it left its enduring stamp even on the largely anti-Hegelian understanding of history of a Marx, Kierkegaard or Dilthey. We might say that history is *the* grand theme of Hegel's philosophy as a whole. The things that were slowly germinating in the *Early Theological Writings* and then decisively broke through in Jena, that were unfolded in a first brilliant attempt in the *Phenomenology* in terms of consciousness and then afforded a most exact foundation in the pure thinking of the *Logic,* that were presented in the *Encyclopaedia* as a universal system and then applied to social reality in the *Philosophy of Right* – these things were rendered distinctively concrete in the great historical-philosophical lectures on world history, art, religion, and the history of philosophy: history as dialectical process, as accomplishment, self-presentation and self-revelation of the Absolute. By transposing history into the Absolute, and by having the Absolute itself become history, Hegel managed to overtake all previous forms of the 'philosophy of history' in an exciting way, assisting what would later be called 'historicality' (*Geschichtlichkeit*), and, in particular, the historicality of truth, to impinge on the scholarly consciousness. The contents of Hegel's thinking flatly forbid us to associate this development with the notion of relativism, of the rejection of any abiding truth, of the general cutting loose of thought from any objective basis.

The *matter* of 'historicality' was thought of long before the word *Geschichtlichkeit* itself was actually introduced. Moreover, that which the word denotes is much more important than the word itself: 'Scarcely a single element was later to emerge in the rich and disparate concept of "historicality" which could not in some way or another be traced back to Hegel, to which he had not at the very least alluded or on which he had not indeed reflected in some detail.'[54] Even so, it is not without interest that the word itself, which, in the wake of Dilthey, York and Heidegger, has become a fashionable term of the twentieth century, was first used – if Michelet's text does not deceive us – by Hegel. And it is significant in our present context that he first employed it in a christological setting.

Since no original text of Hegel is available here, we are obliged to rely on Michelet's edition, which is not without its faults. In two places, this edition produces the newly coined word 'historicality' (*Geschichtlichkeit*).[55] In a detailed analysis,[56] L. von Renthe-Fink has demonstrated that, in the passages mentioned, which at all events

---

[54]G. Bauer: '*Geschichtlichkeit*', 15f.
[55]Michelet's first edition of the *Philosophy of World History, Werke XIII,* 173f and XV, 137 (in the second edition produced by Michelet, XV, 107).
[56]*Geschichtlichkeit*, 20-46.

provide the earliest instance of the occurrence of the concept, the coining of the new word is 'most probably Hegel's own doing'.[57] Michelet's text finds indirect corroboration in attested formulations which come from Hegel's hand, and even apart from these we have abundant evidence of his linguistic predilection for abstract philosophical terms ending in -*heit* and – *keit* (e.g., '*Heimatlichkeit*', '*Besorglichkeit*', '*Offenbarkeit*', '*Menschlichkeit*', '*Sinnigkeit*' etc.). While in the first passage, where it is employed in the context of Hellenism, the word strikes us today as carrying an archaic sense, when it crops up in a christological context the word 'is used in a speculative sense proper to the philosophy of religion, a sense which closely approximates to the current understanding of the word. . . .'[58] In Michelet's first edition, the passage reads as follows: 'A further aspect of the essential teaching of the orthodox Church Fathers, who set their face against these gnostic speculators of whom Hegel has previously given an account, is that they held fast to the objectivity and reality of Christ, but in such a way that at the same time the basis of history is the Idea, that is, the inner union of Idea and historical form. *The true Idea of Spirit therefore exists at the same time in the determinate form of historicality.* The Idea as such, however, was not yet distinct from history, with the result that the Church's loyalty to the historical form of the Idea determined its doctrine concerning the Idea.'[59]

Historicality is here defined as the 'inner union of Idea and historical form', a union which Hegel detected in the 'reality of Christ', and which he emphasised as the speculative content of Christianity: 'This passage is supplemented in its turn by the countless passages in Hegel's works where he constantly returns to the christological-trinitarian problem, to the riddle of Jesus Christ. These passages make it clear that the speculative problem of the Godmanhood of Jesus Christ is fraught with existential significance for Hegel's basic systematic conception of philosophy, being (so to say) a primordial experience for him. As a matter of fact, a distinct and central aspect of Hegel's philosophy is nothing other than an exegesis of the Johannine text, "And the Word was made flesh".'[60]

Hegel employed the word 'historicality' neither to encapsulate the 'essence' of history itself as involved in becoming (the structure of occurrence), nor to denote the chief feature of human existence (in contrast to natural being) as a form of existence that attains to historical self-knowledge. Nevertheless, already in the *Phenomenology* he reflected on the various implications of the concept, such as temporality, secularity, corporeality, and alienation; and in the *Logic* he pondered such other implications as becoming, finitude, actuality, existence, and determinateness. Moreover, throughout his career he had highlighted dialectic, with its inherent antitheses and contradictions, as

---

[57]*op. cit.*, 29.
[58]*op. cit.*, 26.
[59]quoted from Renthe-Fink: *op. cit.*, 21.
[60]*op. cit.*, 24f.

the mode in which history moves and as the structure of human consciousness. Hegel already regarded history, which, when conceptualised, is the
process of Spirit coming to itself, from the vantage-point of the present, and
he already experienced man in his recollective self-knowledge, as conditioned
by history. Notwithstanding his disdain for 'mere' history, he stated in the
Preface to the *History of Philosophy,* in a quotation which we can cite from
the original manuscript: 'As a matter of fact, however, whatever *we* are, we are
at the same time historically' (XV, 12*).

Even though we are indebted to Hegel for coining the word 'historicality' in
its German form, and notwithstanding the fact that the problem of historicality occupied him most persistently throughout his life, we must at the same
time recognise that he did not elevate this concept into a technical term in
philosophy. On the contrary, according to R. Haym – who, in his discussion
of Hegel's philosophy of history, was the first to employ the word 'historicality' in the modern philosophical and conceptually precise sense – this did not
occur until Dilthey (who was connected with Haym) and York (the initial
instance of a technical usage came in a letter from York to Dilthey in 1886: 'A
Hegelian of this sort has a more intimate relationship to historicality.'[61]) At
any rate according to Renthe-Fink,[62] the reason for Hegel's declining to
employ the term as a systematic category stems from the fact that his
relationship to history remained ultimately divided against itself. A further
factor to consider is the tendency of the word 'historicality' to imply a
historical relativity which does not sufficiently attest Hegel's understanding of
history as the temporal process of the eternal self-becoming and self-unfolding of Spirit (and hence also of truth). Hegel did indeed, in principle, offer the
most intensive justification of history, which was for him a movement of
absolute Spirit itself in its various phases and forms. But he was obliged to
concede that, on the practical level, empirical history in its sheer facticity,
contingency and gloom cannot be fully subsumed in this process of Spirit:
'This is the state of affairs which Hegel himself termed the "inner conflict",
"*the doubled aspect*" in all history, the mingling of "merely outward" with
"divine history", of "history with not-history", which according to Dilthey
stemmed from the basic antinomy that characterised Hegel's philosophy as a
metaphysic, which Marcuse analysed as Hegel's "curious discord", and which
we have called the ambivalence of history in Hegel.'[63]

Whether or not we have here put our finger on the reason for Hegel's
avoiding 'historicality" as a technical term, his understanding of history *is*

---

[61]quoted *op. cit.,* 84.
[62]cf. *op. cit.,* 36-46.
[63]*op. cit.,* 42.

made up of contradictory elements. Moreover, his grandiose final lectures constantly bring to our attention just how great a gap there is between Hegel's original speculative conception and its concrete implementation. Notwithstanding the release of a frankly prodigal wealth of deep philosophical and historical insights in these lectures, they represent an intensification of the immanent philosophical difficulties of Hegel's system, which we have found throughout this study, and latterly in connection with the *Philosophy of World History*. Admittedly, Hegel did display stupendous knowledge of almost all areas of life, and chiefly of political and philosophical history, and of the history of culture, art and religion. And his brilliant synthesis was of a hitherto unattained scope, being marked by supreme formal art and thought-through detail. But for all that, Hegel was after all unable to demonstrate the ultimate speculative rationality of the entire reality of history. In this way, only with considerable effort fending off all the difficulties that arose, Hegel covertly transformed the original dialectical Spirit-monism of his philosophy of history into a disguised dualism. At the same time, though, he continued to proclaim the triumph of the original conception and to behave as if nothing had changed.

As I. Iljin demonstrated in his sparkling final chapter, things which could still be carried out relatively uncompromisingly in pure logic proved impossible to execute in the further development of Spirit in nature and history. A deep rift opened up between the philosophy of nature and Spirit on the one side, and between nature and human spiritual life on the other: 'The system of scientific categories consolidates into a complete system, but the river of world events, as a living, empirical development, continues on its course to accomplish its unknown and undetermined destiny in the yoke of bad necessity and in the game of evil contingency.'[64] 'The speculative Concept struggles with its double. The "empirical-concrete" is its burdensome "alter ego", which it can neither accept nor reject; and this "alter ego" transforms the religiously believed monism and panlogism of being into a philosophically insoluble task.'[65] Hegel constantly delighted in denying the empirical-concrete with a mere speculative wave of the hand, but, since he was after all also an empiricist and a realist, the longer he tried the less he succeeded. This being so, his original conception would leave him with no other alternative than to include the empirical-concrete in the majestic process of the Absolute. But Hegel could never fully resolve to include chaos in God and hence to deify everything. 'And look, Hegel's philosophy oscillates unflinchingly between a disguised dualism on the one hand, and the endeavour to "obliterate" the empirical-concrete by its own power on the other.'[66] From being a philosophical *fait accompli*, Spirit-monism becomes a creative assignment for the slow divine being and becoming, which philosophy has to follow at a leisurely pace. The originally rationalistic

---

[64] *Die Philosophie Hegels als kontemplative Gotteslehre*, 360.
[65] *op. cit.*, 353.
[66] *op. cit.*, 358.

389

panlogism becomes a rational-*cum*-irrational panteleologism. One cannot prove that everything is logical; it is easier to demonstrate that everything is teleological. While everything is not Concept, it is certainly organic-*cum*-functional. The dialectical-*cum*-organic self-thinking of reason becomes the organic-*cum*-creative reason of God: God creates even at those junctures where reason, in nature and history, falls away from itself and does not think itself. Pantheism as a form of God's being becomes a task for God's creative working. The Logos theodicy becomes a *telos* theodicy. In this way, Hegel's maximum programme attains to a minimum execution: 'While he [Hegel] did achieve this transition from rationalism to teleologism, he did not do so in the Schellingian manner of thinking everything out afresh but rather by way of persistent struggle with the object: he followed as it were the "divine process" and reported on the difficulties met with by the Idea in the world, where the "Logos" breaks down and "reason" must beat a retreat to "telos". This produced the curious and even confusing state of affairs where the Concept ceases to be Concept while yet remaining Concept and celebrating its putative triumph. In other words, Hegel's philosophy behaves like a pretentious, militant and successful rationalism, in which the actual, profound and final triumph belongs to the irrational element. The object has not accepted panlogism; it has in fact rejected it and clamoured for different criteria. Rationalism has been obliged to renounce its former claims and accept a much more modest programme. Even so, the rationalistic insolence remained: Hegel considered his philosophy to be panlogism, and the history of philosophy took his claim at face value.'[67]

The generation which succeeded Hegel (and this is true not only of Marx, but also of such skilled historians as Ranke, Droysen and Burckhardt) were no longer able to discern that everything proceeds reasonably in world history, or that the whole of history is the step-by-step dialectical self-unfolding of Spirit.[68] Nor did the twentieth century think any differently here – a point which holds not merely for Dilthey and phenomenology. Is Hegel's philosophy of religion therefore a dead duck, on account of its faulty starting-point? Or, to put the question in theological terms, does nothing ultimately remain of his blending of God and history, between eternal truth and historical contemplation, other than a mere passage of time bereft of meaning, the historicity of the individual which does nothing more than simply occur? Nevertheless, the problem of historicality does display other facets.

Keirkegaard had already countered Hegel's 'sublation' of everything in the history of Spirit by stressing historicality as a temporal 'moment': reality's unprecedented effect on each individual cannot be sublated into any historical process of absolute Spirit, but must be realised ever afresh only as Christian existence in faith. Motivated by a philosophical version of Kierkegaard's

---

[67] *op. cit.*, 371.
[68] On the breakthrough of historical thinking in the nineteenth century in Droysen, Dilthey and York von Wartenburg, cf. the study by P. Hünerman.

protest (and also by the 'dialectical theology' of the young Karl Barth, which had even earlier registered Kierkegaard's influence) and with reference to the concept of 'historicality' in explicit connection with Dilthey and York, Martin Heidegger sought, in the closing chapters of his *Being and Time*[69] in the setting of his analysis of *Dasein,* to answer the question to what extent and on the basis of what ontological conditions historicality pertains to *Dasein* as an essential constituent. As 'the hidden basis of *Dasein's* historicality', Heidegger designates 'authentic Being-towards-Death – that is to say, the finitude of temporality'.[70] Heidegger draws a sharp distinction between this existential-*cum*-temporal analysis of *Dasein* and Hegel's concept of time along with its relation to Spirit, which he describes as 'the most radical way in which the ordinary understanding of time has been given form conceptually'.[71]

But Heidegger's so-called 'turn' from merely human Being to Being in general demonstrates that his analysis of the historicality of *Dasein* by no means represents a definitive settlement of accounts with either the theme of historicality or the problem of Hegel's understanding of history. This turn was already indicated in the starting-point of *Being and Time* (cf. especially the initial chapter on the priority of the question of Being and the closing section on the question of the meaning of Being in general), but, given that the heralded Part Two of *Being and Time* never appeared, it was only fully reflected in Heidegger's later writings: from the allusions in *Vom Wesen der Wahrheit* (published in 1943, actually written in 1930–31; ET *On the Essence of Truth* in *Existence and Being*, ed. Brock) and in the letter on Humanism (1947) to *Identität und Differenz* (1957; ET *Identity and Difference*, 1974) the book on Neitzsche (lectures and essays of 1936-1946, published in 1961), and the lecture given in Freiburg on 30 January 1962 under the significantly reversed title 'Time and Being'. Heidegger no longer sought, as in his earlier work, to think, in fundamental ontology, of Being only by thinking *Dasein* through. On the contrary, he endeavoured to think Being itself in a language which, as it were, speaks from within Being and thinks Being (truth) and historicality together: the understanding of Being as 'history of Being', which is at the same time 'world history' (even though ontological history is to be sharply distinguished from innerworldly ontic history). Being becomes the driving force of history, consigning to man the stuff of his historical existence,

---

[69] 1st. German edition, 1927.
[70] *Being and Time* (tr. John Macquarrie and Edward Robinson, SCM, 1962), 424-455.
[71] *op. cit.*, 480-486. A clarification of Heidegger's starting-point in confrontation with Hegel's concept of Being in the *Logic* (and with the concept of the Being of life above all in the *Phenomenology*) is supplied by H. Marcuse: *Hegels Ontologie und die Grundlegung einer Theorie der Geschichtlichkeit.* Following A. Kojève, A. B. Brinkley shows, in the symposium volume *Studies in Hegel,* 3-15, that time is a key concept.

and existing as that which is there for man. Thus Being is no longer isolated from time; it acquires the character of event. It is neither inflexibility, abstraction nor empty formula, but a wealth and vitality which both contains and releases, which ordains without itself submitting, which occurs, establishes and prevails.

Yet we should thoroughly misunderstand Heidegger's combination of a radicalised treatment of the problem of historicality along with the original question of Being if we took it for a return to Hegel. This is not simply because Heidegger leaves the question of God out of consideration. Only in the context of the bringing of Being into thought, which for Heidegger is primary, can the holy be considered. Hence only at this stage may one pose the question of the divine and of God. Nor is it simply because Being is posited as connected with *Dasein*. Admittedly, *Dasein* is (understood in terms of existentialism and transcendental philosophy) made possible by Being, but the latter does not (on a metaphysical understanding) turn into the Absolute in the sense of Hegel's absolute Spirit (or, for that matter, of the scholastic *ipsum esse*). Rather, the connection is supremely attributable to the fact that, in his reflection on Being, Heidegger was mainly concerned to overcome the traditional metaphysic which found its last great representative in Hegel (and which, according to Heidegger, was not overcome even by Nietzsche). Through the centuries this metaphysic had upheld Plato's separation between the physical-sensuous and the metaphysical-supersensuous world, and in so doing it had not encompassed Being itself in thought, but merely that which is with regard to Being. As Heidegger endeavoured to demonstrate in a fundamental destruction (which is at the same time a transforming integration) of western ontology, the foregoing history of Being presents itself as a history of the oblivion of Being. And, according to Heidegger, metaphysics is itself responsible for the rise of nihilism.

In the Neitzsche essay of the *Holzwege* (i.e. 'The Word of Nietzsche: "God is Dead"' in *The Question concerning Technology*, which was published in 1950, but which was actually written after the Nietzsche book, which is itself, while unpublished until 1961, composed of lectures and essays from 1936 to 1946), Heidegger examines this problem in the context of an old Hegelian theme, which has already come to our attention, that is, in a penetrating and highly independent interpretation of the slogan 'God is dead'.[72] 'Hegel's prouncement carries a thought different from that contained in the word of Nietzsche. Still, there exists between the two an essential connection that cancels itself in the essence of all metaphysics.'[73] As far as Neitzsche was concerned,

---

[72]*Holzwege*, 193–247; (cf. esp. *Nietzsche* II, 335-490); ET *The Question Concerning Technology*, 53- 114.
[73]*op. cit.*, 197; ET, 59.

'death of God' referred to a historical process: the entire supersensuous world of Idea and ideals, goals and reasons – this world, which, since Plato and late Hellenistic Christian Platonism, had been regarded as the true and only authentic and real world, over against which the sensuous world seemed to be this-wordly, changeable, apparent, and unreal – this whole meta-physical world was losing its power to affect people's minds. Nihilism was on the rise: a devaluation and at the same time revaluation, a transvaluation of all values, of all the conditions for preserving and enhancing life, a transvaluation on the basis of a new principle, a new appraisal of life in general. Nietzsche considered this transvaluation of all values to entail a reversal and subjugation of all metaphysics. What Heidegger espies here is only a new (and, as he suspects, final) brand of metaphysics, a metaphysic of the 'will to power' and of the 'eternal return of the same'. For this metaphysic also, 'the respect in which the essence of man is determined from out of the essence of Being' remains hidden:[74] 'Unmindful of Being and its own truth, Western thinking has since its beginning continually been thinking what is in being as such.'[75] Thus the history of Being began with the forgetting of Being. And, because it does not contemplate Being itself, but merely the truth of that which is, metaphysics is essentially nihilism. This state of affairs does not proceed from mere omission or error, but stems from Being's evading and hiding from its own truth. The question of God, which the mad, deranged man 'seeks', remains open.[76]

Hegel's metaphysic, whose relationship to the history of philosophy is 'speculative and only in this way historical',[77] can, as Heidegger establishes in his *Identität und Differenz* on the basis of Hegel's *Logic,* be labelled 'onto-theo-logic'.[78] But because the onto-theo-logical character of metaphysics has become incredible as far as thinking is concerned, Heidegger prefers 'to keep silent concerning God in the realm of thinking'.[79] As onto-theo-logic, metaphysics thinks 'that which is as such in its universal and primary form *in one*

---

[74]*op. cit.*, 233; ET, 97.

[75]*op. cit.*, 238; ET, 104.

[76]Critical comments on Hegel's 'metaphysic of subjectivity' from a Heideggerian perspective and with reference to the question of God can be found in W. Strolz: *Menschsein als Gottesfrage,* 132-137, 217-225. After the philosophers had already discussed Heidegger's shift of emphasis (e.g., K. Löwith: *Heidegger. Denker in dürftiger Zeit,* 1953; and W. Schulz: 'Über den philoso-phiegeschichtlichen Ort M. Heideggers', 1953-54), the distinction of being the first to harvest its programmatic and systematic fruit for theology fell to H. Ott: *Denken und Sein. Der Weg Martin Heideggers und der Weg der Theologie* (1959). The thesis that the philosophy of the late Heidegger is much more in keeping with the theology of Barth than with that of Bultmann (which, in philosophical terms, is largely dependent on the early Heidegger) had the effect of provoking the Bultmann school. On the discussion, cf. the contributions by H. Braun, H. Ott, W. Anz, H. Franz and G. Ebeling in *Zeitschrift für Theologie und Kirche,* supplementary volume 2 (1961). The discussion is carried further in the first volume of the series *New Frontiers in Theology* (ed. J. M. Robinson and J.B. Cobb, Jr.) with the title *The Later Heidegger and Theology.* Alongside the contributions by the two editors and the reply by H. Ott, there are important essays by the Americans A. B. Come, C. Michalson, and Schubert M. Ogden.

[77]*Identität und Differenz,* 39; ET *Identity and Difference,* 44.

[78]*op. cit.*, 56; ET, 59.

[79]*op. cit.*, 51; ET, 55.

with that which is as such in its supreme and final form'.[80] Heidegger's intention, though, in 'essential thinking' is to ponder Being itself. For him 'the matter of thinking' is not, as for Hegel, Being 'with reference to its being thought in absolute thinking', but rather 'with reference to its difference from that which is'.[81] And we think Being 'correctly only when we think it in its difference from that which is, and that which is only when we think it in its difference from Being'.[82]

Thus man and Being belong together in the mode of mutual challenge. In the history of Being, releasing yet elusive Being opens and discloses itself to man as primordial truth, but this process of being affected by Being does not, as in metaphysics, provoke the manifestation of an absolute horizon or point of reference. Being itself, which conveys itself to us in language, approaches us as authentic historicality. Notwithstanding all this, however, we must here begin to ask whether this at once communicative and uncommunicative history of Being bracketed by human *Dasein* already represents a sufficient reply to the problem assigned to us by Hegel. Criticism of Hegel is unanimous in maintaining as certain that a sublation of the whole reality of history into a process of absolute Spirit is impossible. At the same time, though, it is thoroughly possible for Being – even when, along Hegelian lines, a necessary link between Being and *Dasein* is not presupposed – to be understood as something engaged in occurrence, as history of Being. It is by no means necessary for metaphysics to be a metaphysics of the static, of that which is, and Hegel is not the only one in whose thought metaphysics did not take this form. As a matter of fact, Being is currently understood as history and as a self-eventuating opening-up in constantly fresh modes and situations of primordial truth in the individual person, and in this way the primordial connection between Being, truth and historicality is recognised. Is it possible under these precise circumstances when considering the history of Being to dismiss the question of an absolute Being so lightly as Heidegger did with reference to Hegel? Is it possible, precisely when history of Being is handed to us and we are affected by it, to suppress the question concerning a Power which establishes this history? And precisely when, as in the metaphysical tradition (and in all brands of *theologia negativa*), there is an unremitting emphasis on the fact that it is utterly impossible for the Absolute to be represented adequately, can we overlook the fact that Being as historicality points beyond itself to a 'whither' of historicality and to a primordial 'whence' of historicality that renders happening possible in the first place?

---

[80]*op. cit.*, 58; ET, 61.
[81]*op. cit.*, 42f; ET, 47.
[82]*op. cit.*, 59; ET, 62.

Such questions are raised by J. Möller in his critical examination of the problem of the historicality and unhistoricality of truth. He correctly views our thinking as 'placed between Hegel and Heidegger',[83] and for this reason he sets his face against every historically undifferentiated, schematising interpretation of the history of philosophical problems. Such an interpretation would reduce the actual event of thinking (which is constantly engaged ever anew in by no means simply disparate attempts at expounding the basic event of truth) to certain lines which flow from the basic philosophical vision (whether Hegelian, Heideggerian or even Thomistic) of the interpreter. According to Möller, precisely when one presupposes Heidegger's historical understanding of Being, it can be demonstrated with reference to the question of truth and historicality that the historicality of human Being demands certain universally binding structures. These include universally binding structures in numan Being and supra-individual structures and continuity in the history of humankind. Nor could these factors be denied even by Dilthey and Troeltsch. 'Even if the historicality of human Being demands universally binding structures, recourse to Being as historicality is still unable to disclose the origin of historicality. Truth as self-opening Being points back to a final openness, which as far as we are concerned is at the same time hiddenness. The about-turn of thinking is only preserved in its radicality when it concedes this demand, while at the same time refusing to determine objectively the content of this demand.'[84] What is involved here is not purely and simply an overstepping of the bounds of the historicality of our thinking, but rather a fresh thinking through of its very possibility: 'In the historicality of self-opening Being is manifested to us the displaying and concealment of absolute truth, which encounters us historically.'[85]

The question can now be posed more precisely: Does this ultimate whence (and whither) of historicality belong in a 'supra-historical' realm? Does this not entail man's banishment to an eternity, which implies for him not unhistoricality, since it can be humanly understood only in a historical way, but certainly 'supra-historicality': 'a supra-historical Being, which, as absolute reason, is authentic truth'?[86] The question arises whether in this way we are not after all thrown back once again on the very Platonistic separation of the two worlds which Heidegger, at any rate for much of the time with justice, criticised as metaphysics? And does this not involve at the same time the surrender of a fundamental insight of Hegel, which ought perhaps not to be surrendered even when we reject his Spirit monism, namely that the *Absolute itself* has history, is *historical*?

In the theological perspective we might seek to reply along the following lines: Heidegger's criticism of Hegel as a representative of a Platonistic two-worlds metaphysics is unjust at any rate insofar as Hegel did programmatical-

---

[83]*Geschichtlichkeit und Ungeschichtlichkeit der Wahrheit*, 30.
[84]*op. cit.*, 33.
[85]*op. cit.*, 35f.
[86]*op. cit.*, 35, 39.

ly sublate a supra-historicality of God (postulating unhistoricality for God himself, though not for man and his knowing) into a radical historicality. He was of course unable to carry his programme through, because he united the historicality of God with a Spirit monism which failed to take into account the difference between God and the world and was therefore bound to come to grief against the power of hard fact. But can Hegel's conception of the historicality of the Absolute be discounted in the same breath as his Spirit monism? Could it not be thought that one might take seriously the inalienable difference between man and God while at the same time holding fast to a genuine historicality of God? That this appears impossible so long as we presuppose a platonising metaphysics stamped by the separation between a changeable 'physical' world and an unchangeable-*cum*-eternal 'metaphysical' world, requires no further explanation. But, even as we hold fast to the inalienable difference between God and man, are we not obliged to reflect on this corrective in historical terms and to take seriously its consequences, as Hegel worked them out for Platonistic metaphysics and its Parmenidean understanding of God? Might not, in this event, the historicality of Being prove less of a hindrance, not, admittedly, for the question of an 'unmoved mover' or of an immutable Idea of the Good, but for the question of an historical primordial source of Being? Should not, if perhaps not the traditional metaphysician, then at all events the Christian theologian think further along these lines if he were to designate the 'basic historicality to which our *Dasein* is related' the 'incarnation of God'?[87] Can we speak at all seriously of a 'basic historicality of Christianity' if we establish merely a 'supra-historicality' and not rather a *'basic historicality of God'* as the condition of the possibility of God's incarnation?

This brings us back to our central topic, namely Christology. A christological perspective could prompt reflection and provide some not insignificant materials[88] which might assist us at any rate to subject to critical reflection certain inhibitions, primarily of Platonistic provenance, militating against a positive understanding of the historicality of God. It was Hegel who demonstrated that such a conception has significant and complex philosophical and theological implications which reasons of space forbid us to explore fully here. Classical metaphysics and theology certainly demonstrated their ability to avoid some of Hegel's difficulties over the concept of God when they 'defined' God in terms of the concept of Being as the *'ipsum esse'* which excludes each and every kind of *'fieri'*. We can only ask whether the price of

---

[87]*op. cit.*, 40.
[88]cf. Excursuses I – V.

this ploy was not to take on board another set of difficulties whose effects are to be discerned not least in classical Christology. Thinking, first, along the lines of traditional metaphysics, we pose the following anticipatory question: Why should one brusquely rule out the possibility – which admittedly has wide-ranging consequences – of considering a refined version of the concept of historicality to be just as compatible and convertible with the concept of Being as are the similarly boundless ('indefinable') concepts of unity, truth, goodness and even beauty? All of these are concepts which surpass, transcend and encompass the limits of all the generic orders of existence, even the highest ones (i.e. the categories). Why may not historicality therefore also be understood as a supra-categorial, in the scholastic sense 'transcendental', concept (alongside *unum, verum, bonum,* also *res* as 'whatness', *aliquid* as 'otherness'), which can be applied to everything, but to everything in a different way? This would involve not the meaningless and completely equivocal, but the analogous application of the concept. Indeed, it would be employed in a different way not only with respect to God and man, but also with respect to man and nature. Historicality would then be actually (and, in fact, only so) a root disposition and characteristic of Being, from which absolutely nothing would be excluded. Might we not thus speak of an *analogia historiae,* according to which historicality is to be predicated of the finite and of the Infinite, of each existent thing in its ontological difference, and also of that existent thing that is being itself and in whose case the ontological difference falls away?

Thinking now along the lines of the biblical message, we pose a further anticipatory question: Why should one brusquely rule out the possibility of taking seriously the livingness of God, which confronts us on every page of the books of the Old and New Testaments, in another way than was possible within the framework of a theology which was bound to Greek metaphysics? May we respond to this biblical livingness of God simply by invoking the transcendence of God in the sense of Parmenides, Plato, Aristotle and Plotinus? Should not theology perhaps give more serious consideration to the other possibility for thinking, which, in the European history of thought, goes back to Heraclitus? And might not theology perhaps understand the historicality of God in a new sense if it made the biblical conception of the transcendence of God into the starting-point of its observations? 'In the Bible the transcendence of God is conceived not as the transcendence of mind over against the material and sensual world, as timelessness over against the course of history, but as absolute authority.'[89]

---

[89] R. Bultmann: *History and Eschatology,* 96.

In the German translation of Bultmann's Gifford Lectures, the biblical concept of the transcendence of God is further defined as the 'constant futurity of God'.[90] With the catchphrase of transcendence as *futurity*, we address a theme which is decisive for the contemporary understanding of God. According to the earlier understanding of time, God was mostly thought of as the timeless Eternal behind the one uniform stream of becoming and passing away of past, present and future. In the Bible he is perceived anew as the eschatologically future One, the 'coming One' (Rev. 1:8). He is the 'God of hope' (Rom. 15:13), as he was made known through the history and the future promises of Israel, not in such a way that we can 'have' him, but as we may actively expect him in hope. In this way theology turns into eschatology. Various factors have contributed to giving a new emphasis to the future dimension, to making it indeed the dominant aspect, the 'soul' of historical time.

By way of contrast to the idea of the kingdom of God of 'culture Protestantism' (i.e. Jesus as a merely human ethical teacher and the kingdom of God as an innerworldly, ethical kingdom, ideal, or good[91]) at the turn of the century Johannes Weiss[92] and Albert Schweitzer[93] sensationally established as the fundamental theme of the proclamation and existence of Jesus the very thing that Reimarus – albeit with political instead of apocalyptic accents – rediscovered, and that had similarly been emphasised by the young D. F. Strauss: its eschatological character, the breaking in of the kingdom of God through the very act of God himself in the near future. But while neither Weiss nor Schweitzer had any empathy for eschatology, Karl Barth, in the second edition of his *Epistle to the Romans,* programmatically set out to interpret Christianity for today as 'wholly and completely and utterly eschatology'.[94] Now the young Barth understood the *eschaton* in transcendental terms, as the eternal, unhistorical or supra-historical which breaks into every human history in judgment. And Bultmann – under the influece of Heidegger's analysis of existence (in *Being and Time* futurity had been displayed as an essential structure of the temporality and historicality of *Dasein*)[95] – sought to understand the *eschaton* in existential terms as the *kairos* of being affected by the word of proclamation, as the illumination and fulfilment of existence here and now.[96] Admittedly, the Barth of the *Church Dogmatics* subsequently revised his transcendental eschatology, bringing teleology into sharp focus. Even so, with his christological concentration, the accent remained very strongly on the present.

---

[90]*Geschichte und Eschatologie,* 107.
[91]cf. A. Ritschl: *Rechtfertigung und Versöhnung* (1870-74; ET *Justification and Reconciliation,* 1900); *idem: Geschichte des Pietismus* (1880-86).
[92]*Die Predigt Jesu vom Reiche Gottes* (1892; ET *Jesus' Proclamation of the Kingdom of God,* tr. R. H. Hiers and D. L. Holland, 1971).
[93]*Von Reimarus zu Wrede. Eine Geschichte der Leben-Jesu-Forschung* (1906; ET *The Quest of the Historical Jesus,* tr. W. Montgomery, 1910).
[94]*Der Römerbrief* (2nd ed., 1922), 298 (on 8:25); ET *The Epistle to the Romans,* 314.
[95]*Being and Time,* 436-439.
[96]*passim,* esp. *History and Eschatology,* 151f.

This is attributable not least to the fact that Barth did not live to develop fully the final part of his monumental work of dogmatics, namely, the doctrine of redemption. However after the Second World War (notwithstanding salvation-historical blue-prints such as those by O. Cullmann[97] and others) present eschatology in the sense of Bultmann's existential interpretation has largely dominated the field. Not until the 1960s, which for many reasons produced a tremendous upward evaluation of the 'future' in the most varied fields in the shape of future thinking, prognoses, planning, and futurology, was J. Moltmann[98] (under the impulse not so much of Teilhard de Chardin[99] as of E. Bloch[100]) able to achieve a prodigious theological breakthrough in the direction of a futuristic eschatology.[101] In the context of Moltmann's work, see, on the Protestant side, the most recent publications not only of W.-D. Marsch,[102] but also of W. Pannenberg,[103] E. Jüngel,[104] G. Koch,[105] and, in America, H. Cox,[106] and, in the Catholic sphere, of J. B. Metz,[107] K. Rahner,[108] and E. Schillebeeckx.[109]

In the most recent theological discussion, future is not understood merely as the future tense, i.e. as what can be construed from past or present history, but decisively as an advent which cannot be extrapolated from history, yet

---

[97] *Christus und die Zeit* (ET *Christ and Time*, tr. Floyd V. Filson, 1951); cf. *idem*: *Die Christologie des Neuen Testaments* (ET *The Christology of the New Testament*, tr. Shirley C. Guthrie and Charles A. M. Hall, 1959); and *idem*: *Heil als Geschichte* (ET *Salvation in History*, tr. Sidney G. Sowers, 1967).

[98] *Theologie der Hoffnung* (ET *Theology of Hope*, tr. J. W. Leitch, 1967); see also various essays in his omnibus volume *Perspectiven der Theologie*.

[99] *L'avenir de l'homme* (ET *The Future of Man*, tr. N. Denny, 1964); cf. S. Daeckes's interpretation of Teilhard.

[100] *Das Prinzip Hoffnung;* see in *On Karl Marx*, tr. J. Maxwell, 1971.

[101] cf. the volume in discussion of *Theology of Hope* edited by W.-D. Marsch. At the same time as Moltmann's book there appeared a volume tackling the philosophical-*cum*-theological problem of the future, G. Sauter: *Zukunft und Verheissung;* cf. also the felicitous formulations in the Foreword of the book by H. J. Schultz with the significant title *Auch Gott ist nicht fertig* ('Nor is God finished'; likewise the chapter on the 'Mobility of God', 25–32). The Catholic work of F. Kerstiens: *Die Hoffmungsstruktur des Glaubens* debates the Protestant blueprints of P. Schütz, W. Pannenberg, J. Moltmann and G. Sauter.

[102] *Zukunft.*

[103] See the essays 'The Question of God' and 'The God of Hope' in his volume of collected essays *Basic Questions in Theology* II (tr. G. H. Kehm, 1971), 201-233, 234-249; cf. also Pannenberg's *'Dogmatische Erwägungen zur Auferstehung Jesu'.*

[104] See his articles *'Vom Tod des lebendigan Gottes', 'Gott – als Wort unserer Sprache', 'Das dunkle Wort vom "Tode Gottes"'.*

[105] *Die Zukunft des toten Gottes.*

[106] *On Not Leaving it to the Snake.*

[107] *Theology of the World* (tr. W. Glen-Doepel, 1969); cf. also Metz' article *'Die Zukunft des Menschen und der kommende Gott'.*

[108] See 'A fragmentary aspect of a theological evaluation of the concept of the future', 'On the theology of hope', 'The theological problems entailed in the idea of the "new earth"', and 'Immanent and transcendent consummation of the world', *Theological Investigations* X, 235-289.

[109] *God the Future of Man* (tr. N. D. Smith, 1968). cf. also L. Boros: *Wir sind Zukunft.* (ET *We Are Future*, tr. W.J. O'Hara, 1970).

which rather announces its coming as something different and new (the category '*novum*') in the anticipation of the future. We no longer have a God above us or even in us, but rather a God *before* us, one whose deity is to be understood as the power of the future, a power which precisely in its futurity determines and alters the present. History is thus understood in terms of the promised *eschaton* of perfection, which as pure and entire present is the goal of the future, with the upshot that the *eschaton* is also understood in terms of history. And even though there is not – as chiliasm wrongly avers – an innerworldly end of history, there is nevertheless – as apocalyptic correctly alleges – an innerhistorical end of the world. History as recollection is encircled by history as hope, so that faith comes to its goal in hope, while hope has its abiding basis in faith. Such a hope demands not only an interpretation of world history or an illumination of history, but rather it demands, in contradiction to the present, the alteration of the world and existence.

On the basis of these and similar ideas J. Moltmann has developed a new concept of transcendence.[110] In this scheme even the borderline experience of immanence and transcendence is subjected to the march of history, in which process 'transformations of God' match 'transformations of history', yet in such a way as to entail the death of neither God nor faith. In the modern unitary world, transcendence can no longer be understood in spatial, but rather in temporal terms. From this perspective various models of transcendence can be seen to be no longer adequate in today's world.

a) Physics and metaphysics: the divine as the transcendence of the divinely ruled cosmos. The cosmos as the immanence of the invisible divine. Transcendence therefore in the shape of the infinite, immutable, ordering, and one.

b) Existence and transcendence: the boundary between transcendence and immanence no longer runs between God and cosmos, but rather through man himself. Transcendence is therefore experienced in existence, in one's own infinite subjectivity which transcends the objective world.

c) Alienated transcendence in the leisure-space cleared by modern society: the immanence of artifical-necessary scientific-technological civilisation and society releases abstract domains of transcendence. In anticipation of the realms of freedom, play and cheerfulness, a new experience of transcendence becomes possible. But because this experience is an escape from and not a conquest of the realm of necessity, it aims only at an alienated transcendence.

Given that, like the first, the two further models of transcendence are increasingly demonstrating their inherent weaknesses, another model, according to Moltmann, is now more than ever pressing itself upon us: history

---

[110]'*Die Zukunft als neues Paradigma der Transzendenz*' (ET *The Future as a New Paradigm of Transcendence*).

and eschatological future. History is being experienced as immanence: the impotence of the individual and the overweening power of autonomously operating industrial, technological and social conditions are the new 'boundary' at which contemporary man is posing the question of transcendence. Against the present situation and system, transcendence points to the future. Even so, the future only becomes a new paradigm of transcendence when it is not identified, as in one-dimensional technological thinking, with the automatic technological and cultural progress of society, or, as in the existentialist interpretation, with the existential potential of the individual and the futurity of his personal decision. The future only appears as genuine transcendence when it brings something qualitatively new, which at the same time prompts fundamental change in the present situation and system. The upshot of all this is that history itself, which in the existentialist interpretation (of both Heidegger and Bultmann) had tended to fade behind the historicality of *Dasein,* once more steps into the field of vision in its whole reality.

The most recent model of transcendence as future is also the most ancient, for it already determined the general Old Testament and more especially prophetic faith in the promise. And, supremely, in the context of apocalyptic, it determined the message and history of Jesus and the early Church. Viewed in terms of this history, the expected future is not just any empty future, but rather a future which starts from and is determined, disclosed and fulfilled by reality: the future of Christ and of the coming kingdom of God. Christian faith stretches itself out as hope from the experienced new life of the Crucified with God according to the promise of a still outstanding universal future of Christ which has nevertheless already dawned, a future brought about by the 'God of hope' (Rom. 15:13), who 'gives life to the dead and calls into being the things that are not' (Rom. 4:17). 'For in this hope we were saved' (Rom. 8:24). But this hope implies knowledge of what is not (yet) known, a knowledge in hope that reaches forward while at the same time being bound to the past, and which is geared towards a realm of absolute righteousness and unbroken peace, of full freedom, enduring love, eternal life and definitive reconciliation of God with the world: a realm which is still in the offing but which has nevertheless already dawned in Christ.

We may not here overlook the questionable features of such a theology of the future. From an exegetical perspective these have been registered by W. Schmithals[111] and E. Grässer,[112] whose writing contains vigorous polemic partly against J. Moltmann and

---

[111]*'Jesus und die Weltlichkeit des Reiches Gottes.'*
[112]*'Die falsch programmierte Theologie.'* In the *Diskussion über die Theologie der Zukunft,* cf. *the objections of W. Andersen, H. Berkhof and H. E. Tödt among others, and also the reply by J. Moltmann.*

above all against certain more superficial representatives of the 'theology of revolution' (which is related to the 'theology of the future'). Even though the constricted theology and exegesis of existentialism, with its abolition of a real future of the world and humanity (which is reduced to the constantly new futurity of human existence), bears a heavy share of responsibility for the sharp swing of the pendulum to the left (this ought to be calmly conceded in self-criticism), nevertheless no theology of the future may overlook or neglect the following factors:

1. that even for a Christian theology and proclamation that is geared to society, so long as it intends to remain Christian, the original Christian message in the Old and New Testaments must remain text and norm, and not the momentary historical and social conditions and movements, in which it is alleged that God's activity can be discerned directly and without recourse to any critical norm ('theology of the politics of God', 'proclamation as a horizontal-dialogical exchange of information'; as the kingdom of God was previously identified with the contemporary realm of morality, with the perfect bourgeois culture, and then with the Nazi thousand-year Reich, so now it is identified with the future socialist classless society).

2. that the kingdom of God is brought about neither by human evolution nor by human revolution, but by God's action, which does not exclude but rather includes man's action in the here-and-now both on the individual and social level (just as there was previously a false 'internalisation', so there is now a false 'secularisation' of the kingdom of God).

3. that, notwithstanding the whole dimension of future promise, the prolepsis of salvation is given in Christ, and that the function of the Gospel may not be changed into láw and morality (Easter is not merely a promise, but also a fulfilment, albeit one geared to consummation).

4. that commitment to the world and to changing the world is Christianly meaningful only in terms of the cross of Christ and of the faith and conversion of the individual (there is no Christian secularity apart from critically distancing oneself in 'de-secularisation').

5. that, even though under certain circumstances the political necessity of a political revolution may be granted for Christians, we are still faced with the 'revolutionary' Christian message of love (even of the enemy!), which may not be identified either with an ideology of conservation or with a 'theology' of revolution (just as there is no fundamental theological basis for preserving the *status quo* under all circumstances, even so there is no fundamental theological basis for change and social upheaval at any cost)

6. that the specifically Christian quality of all our worldly dealings (which Schmithals and Grässer have scarcely convincingly defined) may not be replaced or watered down by the ideal human, and that what is specifically theological may not be replaced or watered down by sociology, politology and psychology.

E. Schillebeeckx offers this balanced judgment: 'The new concept of God – that is, faith in the One who is to come, in the "wholly New One" who provides *us* here and now with the possibility of making human events into a history of salvation through an inward re-creation which makes us "new creatures" dead to sin, thus radically transforms our commitment to make a world more worthy of man, but at the same time it reduces to only relative value every result which has so far been achieved. The believer, who knows of the eschatological fulfillment promised to mankind and to man's history, will be unable to recognize in anything that has already been accomplished "a new heaven and a new earth". Unlike the Marxist, for example, he will not even venture to give a positive name to the ultimate fulfillment that is to come. The Christian leaves the future much more open than the Marxist: in his view, the Marxist tends to close the possibilities prematurely. For the Christian, it is an ideological misconception to call one concrete stage in the development of human history the ultimate point.'[113]

However one interprets the future theologically in detail, one thing is clear, being conceded on all hands today, and requiring no detailed explanation: for Hegel, the future is eliminated as a decisive dimension of historicality, indeed even of history. Even though the various characteristics of historicality (finitude, temporality, secularity etc.) are found already early on in Hegel's works, there is from the very outset a marked dearth of documentary evidence for the notion of futurity, which seems to be repressed and at length to be banished from the system.

This holds good already for the history of the human individual. Admittedly, we can find in Hegel a tension between time and eternity, along with a sort of 'immortality' of the individual in the guise of the finite's being sublated in the Absolute.[114] Even so 'the formal characteristic of Hegel's eschatology . . . is the abolition of teleological directedness towards an end in favour of a vertical relation to eternity'.[115] where absolute Spirit stands, everything finite *has* already been 'sublated' and become a moment of the Absolute: in *this* sense it is elevated beyond finitude and mortality, it is immortal.

And it holds good supremely of the history of humankind. With Lessing's *On the Education of the Human Race,* Herder's *Ideas on the Philosophy of the History of Mankind,* Kant's *Ideas on Universal History in Cosmopolitan Perspective*, and Schiller's *What Is and to What End Do We Study Universal History?*, Hegel's philosophy of history shares a missionary consciousness, a faith in the great task of humankind and in a meaning-filled history. And with many of them he shares the conviction of a third age of (scientific) Spirit. And yet Hegel never answered – indeed, he never even posed – the question of a post-historical future for man and mankind. Why was this? 'Lessing looked *forward to* the perfect stage, and Herder, where he applied the biological image, looked *back to* the ideal age. Hegel looks *back from* the perfect stage.'[116]

Hegel is not of course so naive as to be ignorant of the fact that the river cannot be suddenly halted and that life goes on. For him, history is not simply

---

[113]*God the Future of Man,* 186.
[114]cf. H. U. von Balthasar: *Apokalypse der deutschen Seele* I, 603-611, 618.
[115]*op. cit.,* 602.
[116]H. Groos: *Der deutsche Idealismus und das Christentum,* 271.

at an end, but it is at its goal: it has reached its *telos*. Hegel is convinced that he has achieved the mediation of all antitheses, and that he has definitively solved the problem. World history may admittedly not yet have reached its term, but there can no longer be any such thing as something genuinely new, something which is not already in existence, or any fundamental change in philosophy and history as they understand themselves at the present juncture. It would be superfluous to repeat the relevant texts here. We have already shown the *Phenomenology* and the *Encyclopaedia* to be not only a self-contained system but also, with respect to the future, a closed system. We now venture the following summary of the *Lectures on the Philosophy of History:*

World history has quite simply attained its final goal, the reality of freedom: humankind's condition of rational maturity has been brought about in principle; world history has turned out to be world judgment, and theodicy to be the justification of history. *Art* has come to itself in the romantic art of spiritual beauty and internalised infinitude: there is a perfect marriage of form and content; every essential determination of the beautiful and of art's formation has been arranged into a garland, and in this way there comes about the dissolution of art in general, its sublation in religion, which is alone competent to bestow the genuine revelation of Spirit. But *religion* for its part has in principle consummated its history in the realm of Spirit, which is infinite return into itself. What we have here is God as present reality, as the one who dwells within his community, which, in its final stage (and the manner in which the concrete Christian religion takes shape in the world can cheerfully be left to itself to determine) is the community of philosophy: religion sublated in philosophy, where its truth receives the finally valid form, the form of thinking, of the universal. And, finally, the *history of philosophy* has attained its conclusion in the latest philosophy, that is to say, in Hegel's philosophy, which is the outcome of all previous philosophies and contains all their principles. Through its labour and struggles, Spirit has finally succeeded – 'so much effort was involved in mind's knowing itself'[117] – in divesting itself of everything alien and accidental and in comprehending itself as absolute Spirit. The whole previous history of the world, its art, religion, and philosophy, is at its goal: Spirit is actual as Spirit.

E. Bloch: 'Hegel's philosophy culminates in a fixed quantity: the "revealed" without remainder and without fermentation in the womb of future ages gives it the unauthentic appearance of being contemporary and concise. The solution worked out for the problem of the world is related to a basic component concerning which – since it is involved in such tumultuous history and throws up such a welter of novel items – it is

---

[117] *tantae molis erat seipsam congnoscere mentem.*

by no means assured whether it is already worked out and cut and dried even with respect to itself.'[118]

A strictly guided teleology thus causes history to reach its climax in Hegel's present. Clearly, therefore, this high-point and end-point of the world process of Spirit is not accidental. All of this could not be otherwise in Hegel's thinking, it could not possibly be corrected at the end. No, this is the inner necessary goal toward which the system, this most comprehensive philosophy of history that there has ever been, is geared from the very outset. To have gained this final solution is not merely an ultimate claim, but is implicit in the very method. Hegel was able from the outset to think the whole in this way, because he had from the outset thought it in terms of this end. The conclusion is in principle given with the starting-point, the finish with the start. Only from the absolute standpoint, to which Hegel had raised himself through speculative thinking, could the history of absolute Spirit be known in this way from the beginning. 'This is now the standpoint of the present time, and this brings the series of spiritual configurations to a close for now' (*G* XIX, 690). The circle of circles has engulfed itself within itself. Total reconciliation is achieved. The 'kingdom of God' is present. For his part, Hegel has made good the watchword with which he long ago took leave of his Tübingen friends.

Does not this factor account for the lack of any element of eschatological expectation? Any still outstanding and unknowable future which can only be hoped for, is sublated into the known 'now'. And if all hope for definitive redemption is dropped, then it will occasion no surprise that in the end that name is dropped, with which for the Christian definitive redemption has always been associated. Just as there is no absolute future in general, so there is likewise no universal future of Christ. The history of Christ had closed with the glorification of the Risen One and his sublation into absolute Spirit (cf., e.g., *A*, 535; XIV, 171f, *Philosophy of Religion*). A *consummatio saeculorum*, a consummation of the world, a 'new heaven and a new earth' – these things lie completely outside Hegel's horizon. He only speaks of a 'second coming' of Christ by way of exception; often, when discussion of the topic seems to be just around the corner, he remains silent about it. At all events, it must be spiritually understood: the future is conceived as a moment of the present, the 'sensory picture of the *second coming*' as a 'figure of speech from outwardness to inwardness' (e.g. XIV, 168f, *Philosophy of Religion*). This means nothing but the coming of the Spirit in the becoming of the community: the sensory appearance is but transitory and is spiritually preserved in the community. Christ has shed his finite existence, and has entered into the

---

[118]*Subjekt – Objekt,* 363.

universality of Spirit. On the level of philosophy, the incarnation of God (which, on the level of religion, still appears external and contingent) is conceived in terms of the inner necessity of absolute Spirit, and in terms of the unity of God and man, subject and object, in absolute Spirit, which for speculative thinking is given from the very outset. Consequently, it is known as necessary and universal. Accordingly, no constitutive and abiding significance is ascribed to Christ on this pinnacle of the history of Spirit (in the unveiling of God, as he knows himself), in the philosophy of philosophy. For all his fundamental religious significance, he seems ultimately to have been but an 'instrument of the World Spirit', a 'world-historical individual', the 'manager of a purpose'. After the history of the middle ages and the Reformation he no longer plays any role, and he receives scarcely a single mention in the history of recent philosophy. Neither he nor even the future has the last word, but 'the Spirit as Spirit', which 'knows itself as absolute Spirit' (G XIX, 690). Plucked from both the past and the future, the once for all event, the concrete Christ of history, is sublated into the contemporary 'Idea' of Christianity, which coincides with what philosophy in the end of the day inwardly and necessarily knows from its own resources. The incarnation of God is eternalised and universalised for humankind.

In view of this sublation of the concrete Christ of history, we can now retrospectively obtain a better understanding and appreciation of much else in this grandiose theory of history. Apart from this sublation of Christ, would it have been so easy to shape the doctrine of the Trinity in such impersonal and abstract terms (Father, Son and Spirit as personal symbols for the immanent movement of the divine Concept in its abstraction, which strides forward in a threefold dialectic); to posit creation as eternally necessary ('creation' as a metaphor for the dialectical transition of God himself to otherness within the self-movement of Spirit); and to rationalise, by the logic of immanence, the fall into sin (given with the finitude of consciousness) and hence also redemption (as a life process, requiring no forgiveness)? An incarnation of God in accordance with the coercive scheme of absolute Spirit: identity – not-identity – identity of identity with not-identity? Apart from this ultimate abstraction of Christ, would it have been so easy to proclaim a more ideal than real sublation of the antitheses and liberation of man, an interpretation of reality without any change in reality, a freedom and a salvation which, since it largely abandons the ethical element to objective Spirit (the state), moves in the realm of the purely intellectual and speculative? A Church, which in its own consciousness sovereignly encroaches on its head and its Lord, and which is in the end of the day upstaged by that secular sanatorium, the state? A belief in progress which, when we take into account the constantly sinful world and the deeply unjust world judgment of world history, boils down to a justification of the *status quo* which we might well call reactionary? An outward revelation which, as a provisional pedagogical measure, is to be sublated in the authentic divine worship of philosophy?

What remains here of 'Jesus Christ, the same yesterday, today and for ever' (Heb. 13:8), of this Christ who through his death became 'historical', who through his new life with God became in eschatological terms the 'Coming One', and who precisely in this capacity opens up new history to us from the vantage-point of the future? Where abides the one who speaks, 'Behold, I make all things new' (Rev. 21:5)? Everything is here bound up with everything else: consistency demands that the one who cannot be 'alpha' cannot be 'omega' either! 'Hegel's circle adds to the alpha of the in-itself and the offence nothing but the omega of the mediated return; it brings to it nothing new by way of content. But a genuine identification – which can be acquired only through the new events of history, through a maximum of fresh content – is related to the alpha of the in-itself and the offence not as return, but as pure and simple increase, fulfilment.'[119]

Just as Hegel's circle of closed circles converged into one, even so it follows from the internal coherence of Hegel's thought that our circle of emerging reservations will likewise come together into a single whole. Those things which burst open all down the line in the *Phenomenology,* whose foundations were laid in the *Logic,* being accorded a systematic plan in the *Encyclopaedia,* and applied to social reality in the *Philosophy of Right* – these things were harvested, rounded off and brought to completion in the *Philosophy of World History,* the *Aesthetics,* the *Philosophy of Religion* and the *Philosophy of Philosophy.* And just as the One who according to the original Christian message is 'the truth' was sublated in the knowledge of the *Phenomenology,* and just as 'the beginning' was sublated in the Being of the *Logic,* 'grace' in the system of the *Encyclopaedia,* and 'the way' in the right of the *Philosophy of Right,* even so the One who according to the same message is 'the beginning *and* the end', 'the first *and* the last', and 'the alpha *and* the omega' (cf. Rev. 1:17; 21:6; 22:13), was ultimately sublated in *history,* in this known universal history of world politics, art, religion and philosophy.

The same holds good of the end as already held good of the beginning and the middle. Remembering that in the whole of our material we are concerned with moments of one and the same philosophy and at the same time with aspects of one and the same Christ, we may say that the historical lectures confirm the findings which we already registered after the chapter on Hegel's major printed works. That is, in this process of sublation there is nothing

---

[119]*op. cit.,* 364.

accidental about the agent of sublation or about the One who is sublated. As at the beginning, so also at the end, the concrete Christ of history must be ensnared. Just as the names for the Deity (Reason, Idea, Freedom, Spirit, the Absolute) are everywhere interchangeable, so also are the reservations.

After all this thought and all these reservations – and in the various chapters we have sought to distinguish between these reservations – is it surprising that Hegel's philosophy leaves behind at least *one* eternal doubt? That is, is Christianity here encapsulated by Hellenism, or is Hellenism encapsulated by Christianity? Is metaphysics christianised here. or is Christianity rendered metaphysical? Does philosophy, as Hegel alleged, furnish the Christ-event with a humble verification, or does it, as was held even before Feuerbach, represent the Titanic dissolution of Christianity? Do we have here a divinely blessed homage to Christianity, or a post-Christian evaporation of Christianity? Do not all these questions supply the reason why one's unequivocal final impression of this Hegelian form of Christianity is marked by an unfathomable *ambiguity*?

Right to the very end Hegel did not wish to commit himself; he intended to do justice to both forces, to both Christianity and his metaphysics, to both the Gospel and speculative reason. Two years before Hegel's death, Göschel suggested that his philosophy 'might, in *its departure*, . . . be more resolutely *linked to the Word of God* from which it developed, and might more definitely, *more explicitly* (i.e. by naming the very name) take sin as its starting-point . . .' (XXII, 318). Hegel replied with mild ambiguity that, while he could 'not dismiss' this suggestion, he would urge that one is not always under obligation to pass 'from picture language to the Concept' but might also pass 'from the Concept to picture language'. Yet 'with a view to offering an excuse for the deficiencies of his works in this respect' he emphasises 'that the starting-point . . . was chiefly responsible for his cleaving to the Concept, wrested as it was from picture language through an often severe struggle, and to the Concept's process of development. It was also responsible for his adhering more strictly to the path of the Concept in order that he might become sure of it' (XXII, 319).

It goes without saying that the reservations expressed here imply no disparagement of Hegel's personal religiosity. This was a highly specific *speculative religiosity,* which no one has a right to deny. It will hardly ever be possible to determine with certainty what Hegel felt when he wrote sentences such as this to his friend the theologian Paulus: 'Include us in your prayer' (XXVIII, 144), or when he urged his sister: 'Direct your soul to think on God and to receive strength and comfort in your heart from the higher Love' (XXVIII, 284). Was this mere convention, or was it more? Who will here set himself up as a knower and judge of the heart! Certainly, we have often had cause to point out that one cannot detect any sign of Hegel's having been existentially affected, in the New Testament sense, by Christ, either in his youth or in his university days or at any later stage. But who or what could have mediated such an experience to him at such a time and in such an environment – the joyless piety of his home, bogged down as it was in tradition? The humanistic grammar school? The enlightened atmosphere of the Tübingen seminary? Or the school theology of a Storr, with its rational proofs and its apologetics for Christ? Or Schelling and Hölderlin, the Bern aristocracy, his philosophical predecessors and teachers, his professorial colleagues in Jena, Heidelberg and Berlin, or the Minister for Religious Affairs, Altenstein? The lack of an existentially Christian factor in Hegel's beliefs accounts for not a little in his system and in his Christianity, even though it would be an idle question to reflect on how this philosophy might have taken shape if its author had, like Augustine, Luther, Pascal or Kierkegaard, gone through a *conversio* which put his whole existence in question.

What Hegel extolled to Göschel, he certainly also characterised as his own ideal: 'a first-rate union of deep Christian piety with the most thorough-going speculative thinking' (XXIX, 255); 'that the author shows himself to be in a pious sense both saturated in, and a practised spokesman for, both the truth of the ancient, i.e. authentic, Christian doctrines and the requirements of thinking reason' (XXII, 295). Hegel simply would not admit the validity of the 'distinction' which many of his interpreters wish to maintain, that is, the distinction 'which is wont to be trumpeted as an infinite distance and an unbridgeable chasm between Christianity and philosophical thought' (XXII, 295f). Was not Hegel (if we look, not at his system, but at himself as a man) marked by a pathos to know the real God? On his long toilsome way from Stuttgart and Tübingen to Bern, Frankfurt and Jena, and from there via Bamberg, Nuremberg and Heidelberg to Berlin, did he not wage an impressively truthful struggle through an orthodoxy gone rigid on the one side and the Enlightenment and Kantian moralism on the other, pressing forward to a deeper understanding of Christianity, going from an Enlightenment-style to a speculative religiosity, and hence from a rejection of Jesus via a more detached indifference to a thinking affirmation of Jesus Christ? Situated as he was in the midst of an increasingly non-Christian learned world, had he not made an energetic attempt to secure for this Christ a place – indeed, as he was convinced, the best place – in his system, being minded thereby to overcome the alienation between the historical Jesus of the moderns and the eternal Christ of the ancients? Had he not resolutely sought, with the whole force and power of his genius, to mediate in the tremendous onslaught of reason against faith, of philosophy against theology, of nature against grace, of natural law

409

against the Gospel, and of history against the Idea? And had he not fought with increasing effort against the removal of God from the world, the exclusion of the world from the reality of God, a Godless world and a worldless God, the separation of the two natures, and the elimination of the God-man? Did he not defend the Trinity and the incarnation of God so unyieldingly against all attacks – even from theologians – that many accused him (a dreadful reproach!) of crypto-Catholicism?[120] On Göschel's statement, '[o]nly in this revelation, only in *Jesus Christ*, does man know God, and he has no other name in which he ought to worship God apart from the name of the Son of man', Hegel remarked: 'But in how many textbooks of theology does one still encounter the doctrine of the incarnation of God, in how many does one still encounter philosophy?' (XXII, 310). And did not Hegel, who was a thoroughly candid and conscientious person, always profess to be a Christian, a Lutheran Christian? 'We Lutherans – this is what I am and intend to remain – have only the original faith' (XV, 178; *HP* 1, 73).

We can detect something stirring and trembling in this hard man, who was no lover of sentimentality either in philosophy or in his personal religiosity but who felt most deeply wounded as a Christian by the attacks on his Christian credentials, prompting him a year before his death to appeal with uncommon vigour to Christ himself against those who would deem him a heretic: 'This personal attack based on highly specialist external features of religion showed itself in the form of an enormous arrogance which would pronounce on the Christian credentials of individuals on the strength of its own absolute power, thereby stamping on them the seal of temporal and eternal damnation. Impelled by the enthusiasm of divine poetry, Dante presumed to take into his hands the keys of Peter and to condemn to damnation in hell many of his – albeit already dead – contemporaries, even popes and emperors. The disgraceful charge has been made against a recent philosophy that in it human individuals set themselves up as God; but we answer this charge, which is based on false logic, by stating that it is a quite different and real arrogance to behave as judge of the world, to pass sentence on the Christian credentials of individuals, and thereby to pronounce the most intimate rejection of them. The shibboleth of this self-made authority is the *name of the Lord Christ,* and these judges are assured that the Lord dwells in their hearts. Christ says (Mt. 7:20), "By their fruits ye shall know them", but the enormous insolence involved in rejecting and condemning other people is no good fruit. He continues: "Not everyone that saith unto me, *Lord, Lord,* shall enter into the kingdom of heaven. Many will say to me in that day, *Lord,*

---

[120]K. Rosenkranz: *op. cit.,* 407.

410

Lord, did we not prophesy in thy name? Did we not cast out demons *in thy name*? Did we not perform many great deeds *in thy name*? Then I shall confess to them: I never knew you. Depart from me, ye evildoers!"' (V, 23f; Foreword to the third edition of the *Encyclopaedia,* 1830).

Hegel intended to live as a Christian, and some day to die as a Christian. Unforeseen and suddenly, there crept up on him a reality concerning which he had constantly reflected and written anew ever since his Bern comparisons between Socrates and Jesus and especially since Jena, namely death. In 1830 it seemed that the troubled years around the turn of the century had returned. Folk had deceived themselves when in 1815 they believed that they could turn the clock backwards. While the *rector magnificus* Hegel festively conferred the prizes in the *aula magna* on 30 August 1830, a new revolution had just ended in Paris, Charles X had been dethroned and banished, and the crown had been offered to Duke Louis-Philippe of Orleans (cf. XXIX, 310). The elevation to the throne of the 'king of the French' was the signal for revolutions in Belgium and Poland, and for disturbances in Germany. Hegel, who as we have seen had from his absolute standpoint reckoned with no more genuine future, was deeply infuriated by this renewed bout of upheaval: 'Even so, at the present time the enormous interest in politics has devoured all other concerns, a crisis in which everything which formerly stood fast seems to be made problematic' (XXIX, 323). What should he do in the face of this abruptly erupting novelty of a history which was moving into a completely uncertain future? 'What never happened to him in forty years now happens to him for the first time: to the mute question posed by reality he must refuse the clear and definite reply of the Spirit. The one who had comprehendingly and affirmatively followed step by step as "secretary of the World Spirit" the process of revolution, the rise and fall of Napoleon, and the restoration of the old state order, now veils his countenance before history's new "jolt". He hears this jolt, but he can no longer see it, no longer interpret it.'[121] In the Prussian state journal of 1831, Hegel declared his own position with an essay on the Reform Bill before the English Parliament (VII, 281-323): against revolutionary innovations and the 'French abstraction', for the old English constitution.

While the future unexpectedly cleared fresh paths for itself in the history of the world, Hegel's end was nearer than he or anyone else anticipated. After the retreat of the cholera that had struck Germany in the same summer – Hegel had fled with his family to the countryside, where he celebrated his sixty-first birthday with Marheineke and others (XXIX, 347f; cf. Stieglitz's urging that

---

[121]F. Rosenzweig: *Hegel und der Staat* II, 237.

he should take issue more resolutely with his opponents, who were becoming increasingly vocal; (XXIX, 345f) – on 10 November 1831 he opened the lectures for the new semester with the philosophy of law and the history of philosophy. On the 11th, he spoke with especial vigour; it had gone 'particularly easily' for him, he said to his wife. On the 13th he fell ill, but on the morning of the 14th he was again significantly better. In the afternoon at five o'clock he departed painlessly in a smooth sleep, smitten, in the judgment of the doctors, by 'cholera in its most intense form'. In the words of his wife, he died like a 'saint': 'it was the slumber crossing of a transfigured person'.[122] The last work on his desk, which was intended for publication, remained a torso: it was the *Proofs for the Existence of God.*

Hegel had thus calmly passed away at the very summit of his life, without having struggled with death, without having seen the infirmities of old age or witnessed the down-turn in his fame, without having had any foreboding of the failure of his school 'Nothing in him was superannuated when he died,' says Kuno Fischer.[123]

There was tremendous surprise in Berlin. Overnight Germany had lost its leading philosopher, one of its great men. An epoch (Goethe was to die a few months later) had come to an end. Impressive funeral ceremonies were held in Berlin. As Hegel had wished, he was buried next to Fichte. The Rector of the university, Hegel's colleague, pupil and friend, Philipp Marheineke, the Professor of Christian Dogmatics, spoke the final words at the graveside: 'In company with our Redeemer, whose name he constantly glorified in all he thought and did, in whose divine teaching he recognised the deepest essence of the human spirit, and who as the Son of God gave himself into suffering and death, in order to return eternally as Spirit to his community, he too has now returned to his true home, and has penetrated through death to resurrection and glory.'[124]

Along with the young David Friedrich Strauss, who, having just arrived in Berlin, heard the news of Hegel's sudden death at Schleiermacher's house, many others took offence at these words. But do they not offer food for thought? Perhaps the last word has not yet been spoken on Hegel and on the Christian credentials of his philosophy.

---

[122]Quoted in K. Rosenkranz: *op. cit.*, 423.
[123]*Hegels Leben*, 201.
[124]Quoted from K. Rosenkranz: *op. cit.*, 563.

Chapter Eight: Prolegomena to a Future Christology

> 'The genuine refutation must penetrate the opponent's stronghold and meet him on his own ground; no advantage is gained by attacking him somewhere else and defeating him where he is not' (*SL*, 581).

1. Hegel *sub judice*

'Hegel denied the future, but the future will never deny Hegel.'[1] It should already be apparent from the preceding seven chapters that this statement is especially true of theology and Christology. If this eighth and final chapter bears the title 'Prolegomena to a Future Christology', it is well to remind the reader that according to its subtitle this whole book is meant to be understood in the sense of such prolegomena. From start to finish we have been involved in constant debate with both Hegel and Christology. Each of the seven chapters has worked its way like an inward-moving spiral through five interlocking layers of material, starting with Hegel's life and work, then focussing in turn on the general development of his thought, the contemporary intellectual milieu, and the unfolding of his Christology, and ending in theological debate. This kind of experimental and penetrating initiation and discussion has demanded great patience and many a deep breath from the reader – and, before that, of the author, who now looks back with no little relief at what he found to be well-nigh impassable mountains of material and thickets of problems – yet not, we hope, without bestowing on the reader a commanding view of Hegel's thought along with considerable insight into it. Thus our whole engagement with Hegel's philosophy, which has sought to 'penetrate the "opponent's" stronghold', has turned into a gradual and measured preparation for a future Christology which 'meets him on his own ground'. This final chapter in its turn, along with the Excursuses appended to it, does not intend to offer any definitive conclusions but simply to break more new ground by way of discussion.

'The future will never deny Hegel'? To begin with, however, it seemed that it might. Quite apart from his opponents, the parting title of the Italian liberal

---

[1] E. Bloch: *Subjekt-Objekt,* 12.

historian, Benedetto Croce, who was well disposed towards Hegel, ran as follows: *What is Alive and What is Dead in the Philosophy of Hegel.*[2] The debates which followed Hegel's death were at odds with his own expectations. For they were not debates conducted *on the basis* of his system, but debates *about the basis* of that system. They were embittered debates such as had been seldom experienced in the history of philosophy, and they were carried on from diametrically opposing standpoints: what was *vivo* for some was *morto* for others, and Hegel was glorified as pope of philosophy while at the same time being condemned as a most dangerous antichrist. To see what antitheses the deceased philosopher had harnessed and sheltered within himself we need only glance at the wide range of 'offspring' he produced who were often at daggers drawn with each other after his death. Just think of the disagreements between Marneineke, Feuerbach, Strauss, Kierkegaard and Marx!

Hegel's specialist knowledge and his idea of development exercised greater influence in fields other than philosophy, even though this influence often found no explicit mention or acknowledgement. This is true not only of historiography, ethnology and artistic and religious scholarship, but also of such seemingly remote fields as the art of war: General K. von Clausewitz, the author of the classic work on strategy, *Vom Kriege*, which appeared a year after Hegel's death, was a pupil of his and thought dialectically. In no field, however, were the effects of his philosophy greater than in theology. There was no significant theological movement in the nineteenth century which did not have some relation to him, whether positive or negative. The conflict about Hegel erupted in the domain of theology or, more precisely, of Christology. Now the young man who was to unleash the violent tensions which rocked the Hegel school arrived in Berlin just in time for the philosopher's funeral. At that juncture this later *Repetent* (coach) at the Tübingen seminary was himself still a Hegelian, and he observed in a letter to a friend that Marheineke would *surely* not have spoken the words he delivered at Hegel's graveside *in church*! The letter which immediately followed to the same friend contained the plan for *The Life of Jesus Critically Examined* which, on its appearance four years after Hegel's death, evoked equal measures of admiration and disgust. Even so, this was an epoch-making book, going through four reprints by 1840. *David Friedrich Strauss,* standing on the foundation supplied by Hegel's philosophy, resolutely took his place in the line of succession which passed through Semler, Reimarus, Lessing and

---

[2]*Ciò che è vivo e ciò che è morto della filosofia di Hegel.*

H. E. G. Paulus. He drew the strength needed for his historical adventure from Hegel's speculative Christology, considering that its speculative basis would preclude anyone's suffering any lasting harm. Strauss never ceased to enjoy exacerbating the mutual hostility between orthodox and rationalist theology, and he managed to subdue both these forces by refusing to explain away the gospel miracles in rationalist terms. He himself was wont to account for them on the basis of the myth-creating activity of the early Church. He thus radically questioned the reliability of the gospels, which had been naïvely taken for granted by rationalists like Paulus.

The first line leading from Hegel is that of historico-critical theology with its Christology of the *historical Jesus*. This line leads via Strauss and F. C. Baur to the later Tübingen school and to the liberal exegsis[3] which was not only surpassed but also continued by such great exegetes of our own century as Wellhausen, K. L. Schmidt, Dibelius, Bultmann and his pupils. The same line also leads to such figures as Bruno Bauer and Ernest Renan. The second line leading from Hegel is that of speculative theology with its Christology of the *speculative God-man*. It leads to Daub, Marheineke, Göschel and Biedermann,[4] finding an echo within Catholicism in Anton Günther and the 'Güntherians' (Knoodt, Baltzer, Veith, K. Werner and others). The latter led in its turn to the crisis within pre-Vatican I Catholicism which is already faintly audible in the only letter Günther ever addressed to Hegel, written in the year of the philosopher's death (XXIX, 309). After negotiations which stretched out over several years Günther was placed on the Index in 1857, and the *'Güntheriani'* were condemned by Vatican I. All of the various 'mediating theologians' tended to steer between these two extremes (I. A. Dorner was one who made a significant contribution to Christology). The severe debates on the *kenosis* doctrine which raged from Sartorius and Thomasius to Frank and Bensow[5] afford proof that even re-pristinated Protestant orthodoxy was unable to remain unaffected by modern problems.

Two other reactions to Hegel have had rather more momentous historical effects. First, there is the 'existentialist' theology which began with Kierkegaard and goes with a Christology of the *Christ contemparaneous* with us in

---

[3]The classical historical work on this development is Albert Schweitzer's *The Quest of the Historical Jesus*.
[4]The *Grundriss der Geschichte der Philosophie* (*History of Philosophy*), vol. 2, by the old Hegelian J. E. Erdmann, is still important for the history of the old Hegel school, which has unfortunately been too little researched (esp. in the 4th edition of 1896); cf. also W. Moog: *Hegel und die Hegelsche Schule*, 1930.
[5]cf. the short survey at the beginning of Excursus V.

faith.[6] The thread of this Christology has been picked up in the twentieth century in the dialectical theology of Karl Barth and Emil Brunner, who developed it further, making many changes in the process. Secondly, there is the phenomenon of theology as anthropology with its Christology of the *divine man*. As early as his letter to Hegel of 1828 Feuerbach saw the goal of 'the most recent philosophy' in the 'recent world period' as the 'casting from its sovereign throne . . . of the ego, the self in general, which, especially since the beginning of the Christian era, has ruled the world and understood itself as the only spirit in existence.' The issue of the hour is the 'secularisation of the idea, the *ensarkosis* or incarnation of the pure Logos' and the establishment of a kingdom 'whose founder . . . will be nameless' (XXIX, 245f). The path from Feuerbach leads to Karl Marx's critique of religion and to the most recent ideologies, such as dialectical or historical materialism, nihilism and existentialism.[7]

As far as Karl Marx was concerned, there could be no going back on Feuerbach's critique of religion and metaphysics. He therefore proceeded, with the aid of Hegel's spirit categories to transform the critique of heaven into a critique of the earth and the critique of theology into a critique of the economy. What Marx rejected was not the formal structure of movement (externalisation and return from alienation) but Hegel's blanket application of the abstract categories of logic to all externalisation and reification in general. K. Löwith makes the following observation as it were in Hegel's shoes: 'This criticism would have been of no consequence for Hegel himself, for the formal categories of logic are the "all-quickening spirit of all sciences"; they determine the content of the universal essence of things. Marx corroborates this against his will by clarifying the essence of economic relations with the aid of precisely these *spirit* categories taken over from Hegel. The difference between Marx and Hegel consists in the fact that the latter was sufficiently realistic only to reconcile and "sublate" the "contradictions", whereas the former, even when like Hegel he speaks of "sublation", in fact intends completely to eliminate them, dubbing this utopian pursuit "scientific socialism".'[8]

---

[6]Among recent monographs on Kierkegaard's debate with Hegel, leaving out of account the vast volume of works on Kierkegaard, the following are worthy of note: on Christology esp. H. Gerdes: *Das Christusbild Sören Kierkegaards verglichen mit der Christologie Hegels (und Schleiermachers)*; and among more general studies cf. M. Bense: *Hegel und Kierkegaard*; H. Radermacher: *Kierkegaards Hegelverständnis*; M. Theunissen: *Zur Auseinandersetzung Schellings und Kierkegaards mit der Religionsphilosophie Hegels*; H. Schweppenhäuser: *Kierkegaards Angriff auf die Spekulation*; E. von Hagen: *Abstraktion und Konkretion bei Hegel und Kierkegaard*.
[7]Leaving out of account the immense Marxist literature, the most thorough and stimulating account of the development of left-wing Hegelianism is offered by K. Löwith in his *From Hegel to Nietzsche*. Löwith here reckons Kierkegaard among the left-wing Hegelians and gives only a brief account of right-wing Hegelianism. A comprehensive intellectual history of Hegelianism in Germany has yet to be written.
[8]*Hegels Aufhebung der christlichen Religion*, 229.

The systematic mediation between and reconciliation of idea and history, faith and knowledge, and Christianity and modernity, which Hegel accomplished against the backcloth of an intensified Enlightenment, has always constituted a rock of offence for both theologians *and* philosophers. A crucial question must again be tackled here, one which this book has constantly sought to pose afresh, without adopting an arrogant, judgmental posture, in terms that do justice to Hegel: Is Hegel's philosophy Christian or not?

W. Oelmüller justifiably censures a recent critique of Hegel in the following terms: 'Recent philosophical and theological interpretations of Hegel written in the shadow of Lukács and Bloch and under the influence of the liberal-constitutional understanding of Hegel have frequently tended to side-step this rock of offence by representing him exclusively as an interpreter [*Hermeneutiker*] of his age and by treating as taboo the systematic pretensions of the *Philosophy of Religion,* the *Philosophy of Right,* the *Philosophy of History* and the *Aesthetics.* Alternatively, they simplify their debate with Hegel either – with the intention of being topical – by playing off the young against the old Hegel or – with the intention of compromising – by imputing a systematic uniformity and consistency and a philosophy of identity to the writings on the philosophy of religion which cannot be justified in the light of all of his utterances.'9
This exposition has not sought to evade the rock of offence, but rather, by interpretation and criticism, to make it stand out even more sharply. In this way both the young and the older Hegel have been taken equally seriously. Seeking not to fudge the issues, but to set the record straight, we have arrived at two important conclusions in this study: on the one hand, there is Hegel's basic *assertion* of an (albeit differentiated) identity, which he tenaciously maintained in the *Philosophy of Religion* and the *History of Philosophy;* on the other hand, however, we must not overlook the fact that, while his systematic thought was theoretically geared to differentiated identity, it was *in practice* marked by an inconsistency and vacillation which he himself neither intended nor desired.

In the first years after his death the conservative wing of the Hegel school, including the numerous right-wing Hegelians under the leadership of Marheineke, defended the proposition that Hegel was basically a Christian. But the opponents of this thesis were themselves no less numerous (Weisse, Bachmann, P. Fischer). Among their number was H. Ulrici, who shows how one could severely censure Hegel's brand of Christianity (his critique of Hegel's philosophy of religion[10] culminates in the accusation that Hegel presents us with a God who is 'six in one'[11]) and yet at the same time how one could be no less indebted to the secular *Zeitgeist.*[12] The period was often less concerned with impartial criticism than with vulgar polemic, an especially

---

9*Geschichte und System in Hegels 'Religionsphilosophie'*, 78.
10*Über Prinzip und Methode der Hegelschen Philosophie*, 245-277.
11*op. cit.*, 276.
12*op. cit.*, 291.

remarkable specimen of the latter being the anonymous pamphlet by the theologian Bruno Bauer, who himself shortly afterwards switched sides: *The Trumpets of the Last Judgment on Hegel the Atheist and Antichrist. An Ultimatum* (1841). Leaving out of account here the significant theological outsiders, Franz von Baader and Anton Günther, the contemporary critiques of two Tübingen theologians are still of interest for theology today. We refer to the critiques made by the Protestant C. A. Eschenmayer in 1834 and by the Catholic F. A. Staudenmaier in 1844. The latter was the first to venture upon a detailed theological debate with Hegel.

This was the result of Eschenmayer's examination: 'The whole character of Hegel's philosophy of religion can be expressed in the following brief propositions: it is nothing other than a logic intent on using Christian truths for the purpose of its own self-glorification; Hegel has a God without holiness, a Christ without love freely given, a Holy Spirit stripped of the office of illuminating and preserving the Word, a Gospel without faith, a fall without sin, evil without personal fault, reconciliation without forgiveness of sin, death without sacrifice, a Church without worship, freedom without imputation, justice without judgement, grace without redemption, dogmatics without revelation, this world without the hereafter, immortality without personal continuation, a Christian religion without Christianity and, generally speaking, a religion without religion.'[13]

At the end of his nine hundred-page work Staudenmaier recapitulates fifteen points against Hegel's philosophy of religion: 1) pantheism; 2) denial of the freedom of God in his revelation (false interpretation of the primal history, of the Old Testament and of the entry of Christianity into the ancient world); 3) dissolution of the Trinity into a process of development and cognition of the divine self-consciousness within the world and hence into a divine self-redemptive process; 4) positing the world as the real content of the Notion of God, thus sublation of God in the world and hence atheistic misunderstanding of God; 5) irreligious character of a system which, as part of natural religion, is a self-deification of man; 6) abolition of the mystery of the Trinity; 7) God's entering into sin by entering into finitude; 8) apotheosis of man who stands alone in the world; 9) subjection of the Church to the state; 10) understanding of revelation as self-deduction of substance and hence assimilation of religion to art; 11) assertion of a self-revelation of the Son already in pre-Christian religions; 12) denial of the immortality of the soul; 13) thus 'Hegel's philosophy constitutes a purely anti-Christian phenomenon'; 14) 'an almost word-for-word repetition of Sabellianism'; 15) 'Humankind is intentionally visualised without God.'[14]

Even recent critics of Hegel's Christian credentials remain to a large extent within this frame of reference. Right-wing Hegelians proper must be presumed to have died out (at any rate apart from the recently deceased C. G. Schweitzer) with George Lasson, the deserving editor of the *Philosophy*

---

[13] *Die Hegelsche Religionsphilosophie verglichen mit dem christlichen Prinzip*, 160.
[14] *Darstellung und Kritik des Hegelschen Systems*, 803-836.

of Religion and pastor of St. Bartholomew's in Berlin. Since the first half of the last century – in whose second half Hegel seemed largely forgotten and superseded (at least in Germany, though not so much in England, France and Italy) – there has been a fundamental change in the atmosphere of the discussion. 'Blasts of the trumpet', whether heralding judgment or glory, are no longer customary; a calmer and businesslike dialogue has set in; and the critics of our century tend to give a much more nuanced account of Hegel's teaching (with respect, for example, to pantheism, the immortality of the soul and the philosopher's supposed hybris) than was given by his contemporaries Staudenmaier and Eschenmayer. Leaping to conclusions with such verdicts as 'atheism', 'self-deification' and the like is avoided. Despite all the criticism which they have levelled at him, scholars have learned to illuminate Hegel's thought with great discrimination, interpreting it against the backcloth of the history of thought and endeavouring to criticise it within its own frame of reference.

Despite these qualifying factors, however, scholars have continued to adhere to the gist of the theological criticisms of the last century.[15] For our part, though, we can only identify with this criticism to the extent indicated. As we have seen, both the philosophical and the theological criticisms concentrate on Hegel's dialectic of God and the world tending toward identification. What is at stake here is Hegel's understanding of 'absolute Spirit', which, according to the problem-area under discussion, is termed absolute Idea, absolute Notion, absolute Self-consciousness, absolute Self or the like. Since it deals with universal and particular, abstract and concrete, subject and object, the basic issue can be posed at *each* of the countless stages of Hegel's dialectic of Spirit, since each of these stages must be understood as a realisation of the concrete-speculative process of differentiation and synthesisation of absolute Spirit. Even so, the question gains in intensity as the

---

[15]This is true of the following works written since the 1920s: W. Elert: *Der Kampf um das Christentum,* 21-35; J. Hessen: *Hegels Trinitätslehre,* 36-43; A. Schlatter: *Die philosophische Arbeit seit Descartes,* 172-186; W. Lütgert: *Die Religion des deutschen Idealismus und ihr Ende* III, 86-96; H. Ehrenberg: *Hegel,* 99-103; H. Groos: *Der deutsche Idealismus und das Christentum,* 108-116, 135-137, 202-208, 267-274, 324-329, 387-394, 424-503; E. Hirsch: *Die idealistische Philosophie und das Christentum,* 103-116; idem: *Hegels Verhältnis zur Reformation,* 27-49; T. Steinbüchel: *Das Grundproblem der Hegelschen Philosophie* I, 302-305; W. Schulz: *Die Grundprinzipien der Religionsphilosophie Hegels,* 178-237; H. U. von Balthasar: *Apokalypse der deutschen Seele* I, 562-619; G. E. Müller: *Hegel über Offenbarung, Kirche und Christentum,* 59f; K. Domke: *Das Problem der metaphysischen Gottesbeweise in der Philosophie Hegels,* 108-134; H. Niel: *De la médiation dans la philosophie de Hegel,* 351-353; I. Iljin: *Die Philosophie Hegels als spekulative Gotteslehre,* 340-382; K. Barth: *Protestant Theology in the Nineteenth Century,* 418-421; J. Möller: *Der Geist und das Absolute,* 209-218; E. Schmidt: *Hegels Lehre von Gott,* 255-258; P. Henrici: *Hegel und Blondel,* 165-188; 204-266; J. Splett: *Trinitätslehre Hegels,* 139-143; P. Tillich: *The Universal Synthesis: Hegel,* 115-123.

dialectic progresses, being posed with full clarity in the guise of 'absolute religion' and 'absolute knowledge'. It can be expressed here in both ontological and noetic terms as the *question of the identity of the identity and non-identity of finite and infinite Spirit, God and man (world)*. The question attains concrete form *à propos* the theological problems of the Triune God and his freedom, the creation, the incarnation and the consummation of the world. In a newspaper article written on the occasion of his eightieth birthday in 1969, Martin Heidegger made the following observation on a certain 'left-wing' interpretation of Hegel which deems itself competent simply to eliminate this dimension, so decisively important for Hegel himself: 'It is hard to extract this dominant thought of the present-day Hegel renaissance from the mill of dialectic. It is but an empty-running mill just because Hegel's basic position (that is, his Christian-theological metaphysics in which alone his dialectic has its element and support) is surrendered.'[16]

If a debate with Hegel's understanding of religion and Christianity is to be at all meaningful on his own terms, then it must not work from presuppositions which he had already dismissed, whether directly or indirectly, as starting-points for unravelling the historical *aporia* between Christianity and modernity. Thus, unless such a debate has already engaged seriously with Hegel's arguments, it cannot proceed from either of these two starting-points: a) an attitude of wholesale criticism deeming itself competent to unmask religion as false consciousness or ideology in the name of nature or society; b) an abrupt apology for religion deeming itself competent to bypass the *aporiae* of modernity and to justify religion, whether from the perspective of eternal being or in personal and existential terms.[17]

Wholesale criticism of religion in the name of nature. This ambiguous programme conjured up, for Feuerbach, a cosmos understood in evolutionary terms, sensual immediacy and the I-Thou relationship; for Nietzsche, the Dionysian primordial unity and the will for power; and, for Löwith, a speechless world sought for in sceptical resignation. Hegel himself subjected the alleged immediacy of nature (from which man's infinite value cannot be determined) to a caustic critique: 'Even if we cannot concur with Hegel's concept of mediation on the level of absolute Spirit, his critique of the abstract concept of nature and of the category of immediacy as a fundamental concept remains convincing.'[18]

Wholesale criticism of religion in the name of society. The revolutionary development of this programme against the background of socio-political alienation caused religion and the philosophy of religion to become superfluous for Marx as the 'opium of the people' and the spiritualistic *point d'honneur* of the intellectuals respectively. In view of the fact that the Marxist reconciliation of individual and society has come to

[16] *Neue Zürcher Zeitung* (21.9.1969).
[17] On what follows see W. Oelmüller: *op. cit.*, 80-86; and cf. *idem: Die unbefriedigte Aufklärung.*
[18] W. Oelmüller: *Geschichte und System in Hegels 'Religionsphilosophie'*, 85.

grief in both theory and practice, Marx's critique has been altered, relativised and in part explicitly liquidated by such advocates of Marxism as Lukács, Bloch, Adorno, Kolakowski, Gardavský, Machovec and Garaudy. Hegel himself criticised bourgeois society precisely as a system for satisfying immediate needs and natural interests: 'His whole philosophy proceeds from the fact that man lost his concrete freedom when, after his total rupture with all traditions, he "existed entirely through bourgeois society and used it as a means to accomplish everything". Hence as far as he is concerned the pressing need of the time is not a revolutionary break with previous history but rather a credible realisation of its substance in theory and practice.'[19]

A direct apology for religion from the perspective of everlasting being and of the eternal and the Absolute, as we find them in ancient and mediaeval metaphysics. This programme presupposes that man is both capable and in need of such a being and that Hegel, notwithstanding all his criticism, is, after all, the witness to and preserver of the metaphysics of the people of old. Yet notwithstanding all his invocation of this metaphysics, in his philosophy of religion Hegel's starting-point is not eternal being, but the historical world which was first summoned into existence by Christianity: 'His philosophy of religion is not a preservation and recollection of the metaphysics of the ancients, but an attempt, on the basis of his interpretation of the intensified *aporia* of Christianity and modernity, to apply the Christianity which had been handed down, an attempt of which Hegel himself says that it was being undertaken "in this way for the first time".'[20]

A direct apology for religion in terms of personal and existential finitude and individuality. Since the recent reception of Kierkegaard in the personalism and existentialism of the present century, this programme has been disentangled from its earlier legal and theological presuppositions. Understood in this way, the individual is anthropologised and ontologised so that this direct apology can easily be transformed into a wholesale criticism of religion. But we cannot dispose of Hegel with a string of reproaches culled from such criticism, for example, 'idealism', 'pantheism', 'atheism': 'The dialogue with Hegel's philosophy of religion conducted by the direct apology for religion in the name of personal and existential finitude and individuality usually anthropologises precisely that aspect of the individual subject which according to Hegel man must sublate if he wants to achieve his true freedom and supreme vocation, the aspect to which Kierkegaard wished to draw attention simply as a corrective of the age.'[21]

Poised in this way between a blanket criticism designed so to explain the living religious substance in man and society as entirely to compromise it and a direct apology affording it blanket justification, we shall continue along the lines to which we have hitherto adhered. That is, in critical dialogue with Hegel we shall formulate new questions – and perhaps new answers – for Christology, without surrendering the specifically theological starting-point given in the original Christian message. For all the criticisms to be made, our purpose is openly to take note of the positive possibilities of Hegel's philoso-

---

[19]*op. cit.*, 85.
[20]*op. cit.*, 86.
[21]*op. cit.*, 87.

phy, allowing it to provoke a critical reflection on our own christological tradition, so that perhaps we may acquire some impulses toward a more credible formulation of Christology's answer in the future.

This means that there can be no question of 'a jubilee essay' for 'Hegel the unconfuted world philosopher' on the occasion of his 200th birthday (as there was written by the old Hegelian Michelet for Hegel's 100th birthday in 1870). There can be no question of a renewal of Hegel's system or of his speculative method, or of any kind of rebirth of right-wing Hegelianism. Instead, we intend to do something which right-wing Hegelianism has by and large omitted to do, namely to undertake a renewed critical-constructive confrontation between Hegel and the original Christian message and between Hegel and the Christian tradition.

The questions posed to Hegel pervading all our chapters aimed to make it clear that his provenance lies in the Christian message, but not exclusively in the Christian message. Herein lies the ambiguity which hangs like a fog over the Christian credentials of his philosophy and which persistently resisted clarification to the very end of our investigation. Anyone who says that Hegel completely misunderstands the Christian message overlooks the genuinely Christian impulses and elements in his thought. Anyone who says that Hegel profoundly understands the Christian message overlooks the numerous heterogeneous impulses and elements in his thought. Hegel does not intend, as does the Christian theologian, to translate the Christian message into the terms of a new age, language and world. Or rather, he intends to do this too. Yet at the same time he intends to do more. As one who was, as we have seen, throughout his life caught up in the tension between Christianity and Hellenism, his intention is to pick up essentially different intellectual options (including, finally, those which originate with the Greeks) along with Christian ones, in order thus to erect his own system (or as he would say the system of Absolute Spirit) transcending the antithesis of Hellenism and Christianity. In Hegel there is 'a quite individual intertwining of admiration for the ancients with the consciousness of the superiority of the newer truth defined by Christianity and its reformational renewal'.[22]

If Hegel simultaneously understands and misunderstands the Christian message in this way, this is not simply due to the fact that an element of misunderstanding invariably accompanies all human understanding. Rather, it stems from the fact that Hegel here intends to understand and to misunderstand, to understand differently, and that he never made any secret of this intention. For this reason he dealt wilfully with Holy Scripture from the beginning, appealing to hermeneutical principles and to a hermenutical circle,

---

[22]H.-G Gadamer: *Hegel und die antike Dialektik*, 175.

in a way which was by no means simply wrong-headed but which presupposed a philosophical prior understanding deliberately witheld by Hegel from being measured against the text.

The upshot of O. Kühler's enquiry into the 'sense, meaning and interpretation of Holy Scripture in Hegel's philosophy', which is greatly disadvantaged by its exclusion of the *Early Theological Writings,* is that 'there is not question of a real significance of the Bible in Hegel's thought . . . in no way is Hegel really positively interested in the biblical texts'.[23] This judgment can only be accepted with the qualification that there might *in fact* be a greater openness to the biblical message in Hegel's thought than one might suspect on the basis of his hermeneutical principles. We should be paying less than sufficient attention to the actual genesis of his system if we were to hold with Kühler that from the start Hegel's philosophy could not be 'about the question of the sense and meaning of the Bible for Hegel's system as if it were a system which somehow derives its sense and meaning from the Bible and its message. The only question which remains to be resolved is the quite differently structured problem of the Bible's meaning within the parameters of the intrinsically and *a priori* certain principles of Hegel's system'.[24] Hegel assuredly no longer does what the rationalistic theologians of the Enlightenment still did. That is (at least if we leave his *Life of Jesus* and the section on Jesus' teaching in the *Philosophy of Religion* out of account) he no longer struggles with the meaning of the individual text of Scripture. And it seems clear why this is so – because he knows from the outset what it contains, what it *must* contain. Hegel approaches the Bible from the perspective of the speculative Notion with a view to elevating the Bible to the spirituality, purity and necessity of the speculative Notion. Hence Scripture *also* says what speculative thought says! Indeed *every* interpretation of the word of Scripture for this speculative thought seems to be justified from the word go, not least – as Hegel thinks – by the Bible itself. There are three biblical texts which he untiringly quotes: 'The letter kills, but the spirit gives life' (II Cor. 3:6), 'God is spirit and those who worship him must worship him in spirit and in truth' (Jn. 4:24), and 'the Spirit of truth will lead you into all truth' (Jn. 16:3). Thus to Hegel the free Spirit of God which 'bloweth where it listeth' seems to be nothing other than the absolute philosophical Spirit which develops of necessity, inspiration seems to be nothing other than speculation, exegesis seems to be nothing other than eisegesis.

Even so, all of this is only relatively correct. For a) Hegel's speculative philosophy was not forged exclusively in the context of abstract reflection; rather, the biblical message itself contributed in many ways to the formation of this speculative philosophy. And b) it may at any rate be asked to what extent the biblical message which contributed to Hegel's speculative thought manages to overleap the bounds of the system at important points.

It is not entirely easy to discover whether the impulses and intellectual options which govern this or that aspect of Hegel's thought are of Greek or Christian provenance. The reason why this issue is not easy to resolve is that nowhere more plainly than in Christology is the classical Christian tradition

---

[23]*Sinn, Bedeutung und Auslegung der Heiligen Schriften in Hegels Philosophie,* 91.
[24]*op. cit.,* 15.

itself determined and stamped not only by the original Christian message, but also at the same time by Greek intellectual options. It is therefore not out of the question that, in a confrontation with the Christian message, the discrimination of what is authentically Christian will by no means necessarily turn out in favour of the classical christological tradition and to the detriment of Hegel. The state of the problem precisely over this issue of Hegel's Christian credentials might well be more complex than that.

This factor alone is bound to provoke us to pursue further the confrontation of Hegel's philosophy with the classical Christian tradition at the central point of intersection provided by Christology. Our aim is to press forward from the perspective of the Christian message by means of critical reflection directed toward *both* camps to a better understanding of each. Previous theological discussion of Hegel has, in our opinion, suffered especially from too assured an 'assessment' of Hegel's problematic detachment from a Christian tradition itself apparently unproblematic, at any rate in comparison with Hegel. It has thus suffered from a failure to supplement all the justified theological criticism levelled at Hegel by submitting also the classical Christian tradition to criticism, in order to do justice – perhaps in different ways – to *both* sides and at the same time to secure once more a measure of breathing space and fresh understanding for the original Christian message in a new age and world.

We feel that these programmatic words written by H. Kimmerle hard on the heels of his review of the books on Hegel of G. Rohrmoser and H. Schmidt afford an explicit endorsement of our endeavour: 'In this exercise we must critically analyse the relationship of Hegel's thought to the Jewish, early Christian and ecclesiastical-theological tradition and contrast it with the view of these areas of tradition which we ourselves have acquired with the aid of historical criticism, in order to be able to separate what is genuinely Christian from a philosophical-speculative recasting of theology. If we see the issues aright, then what is at stake in a theological interpretation of Hegel is the most accurate possible grasp of how the contents of the Jewish, Christian, ecclesiastical and theological traditions have determined the concepts and systems of ideas which characterised Hegel's thought. It is imperative here, on the one hand, to acknowledge Hegel's correct understanding of the contents of this tradition. And it is equally needful, on the other hand, to notice his misunderstandings, whether these are to be explained in terms of the limitation of that particular period or to be traced to their origin in his own basic thought. Finally, we have to ascertain (corresponding to this understanding or misunderstanding) the material agreement or non-agreement of his thought with the ways of understanding the world and man to be found in the Bible and in the history of theology and the Church. This is a wide-ranging task awaiting Hegel scholarship, but it can hardly be said to have emerged from the whole gamut of Hegel studies as the chief need of the present moment. If theological interpretation of Hegel adopts this task, then it will contribute toward clarifying Hegel's concepts and making them more available to a contemporary theology, which is dependent on their proper application for the sake of its own most intimate concerns.'[25]

Hence, although it was already weighty enough in every respect, this book was not – as was intrinsically feasible – brought to a close with the preceding chapter (plus a brief epilogue). Precisely because it has hitherto proved impossible for this 'wide-ranging task of Hegel scholarship to emerge from the whole gamut of Hegel studies as the chief need of the present moment', we shall venture to set off on yet another marathon lap, even if with this decision the author's jubilation at successfully negotiating those thickets of problems and mountains of material has, alas, proved premature. It often happens on mountain hikes that new summits and expanses open up on our safe arrival at the peak which stands before us, bringing with them a fresh challenge to overcome all fatigue and difficulty. Even so, since we have no wish to come to grief at the very outset against the precipitous problems inherent in traditional Christology or against the unmanageable volume of literature devoted to this subject, the reader should pay heed to two points of method in the succeeding pages. First, we shall concentrate on the central problems of Christology. Secondly, we shall take some of the pressure off this chapter by consigning the more specialist concerns and reflections in the field of traditional Christology to a series of Excursuses. And all of this is meant to serve as prolegomena to a *future* Christology.

The differences which exist between Hegel's Christology and that of the original Christian message ought in no way to be blurred. It is, theologically speaking, quite impossible to minimise the irrevocable difference between God and man. From the *Phenomenology* onwards, through all phases of Hegel's development, we have been able to trace how internal philosophical criticism of ·his thought has itself unanimously upheld this principle against Hegel's speculative identity. Moreover, as we have likewise taken into account throughout this book, this principle must be theologically radicalised. To recapitulate what we have outlined earlier[26] in two brief slogans: in the *ontic* perspective we should see all God-world occurrence as based on God's free grace instead of on speculative necessity; and in the *noetic-ethical* perspective we should see all God-world mystery as based on trusting faith instead of on absolute knowledge.

There are two reasons why there is hardly any need for a lengthy demonstration that this is the case according to the biblical message: first, because it spontaneously catches the eye of anyone who gets to grips with Scripture and

---

[25]*Hegel-Studien* III, 368f.
[26]cf. esp. ch. 3, 6; 5, 4; 6, 2, 4, 6; 7, 6.

indeed has never been understood differently by the Christian Churches and theologies; and, secondly, because even Hegel himself saw this point very well, notwithstanding the fact that he had no intention of accepting it from the very start. This very 'alienness', 'objectivity', 'separation', 'opposition', 'antithesis' and 'heteronomy', this 'unhappy consciousness', this Lord God on the one side and man's need for help, passivity and dependence on the other – all this, according to Hegel, ought to be 'sublated' in a living unity. For this very reason he was able to do little with the Old Testament from the outset, since everything there – even the soil of the land – was 'conceded [by God] out of mere grace'. Hence at the beginning of his career he gave preference to Hellenism over Christianity because in the former 'synthesis', 'union' and 'independence' were humanely put into effect. Hence in the *Early Theological Writings* he usually prefers to speak of 'life' and 'love' rather than of 'grace' and 'faith', because the former expressions emphasise the unity of God and man and not the distance between them. Hence the 'forgiveness of sin' is merely an 'announcement' of forgiveness, because life itself is able to heal the wounds of the spirit without scars. Hence in the *Phenomenology* Hegel sublates both Enlightenment *and* faith, because faith is 'content without insight'. Hence in such works as the *Phenomenology* and the *Encyclopaedia,* in the lectures on the philosophy of history, art and religion, and in those on the history of philosophy, 'religion' appears as an imperfect 'penultimate' reality, because philosophy alone is competent perfectly to surmount the antitheses of grace and faith in the absolute Spirit and in absolute knowledge. Hence mysteries of faith are mysteries for the understanding but not for the reason, because speculative reason both can and must penetrate behind mysteries of faith. The sublation of faith and grace is consequently a central concern of Hegel's dialectic. This accounts for his neglect precisely of the 'Word' of God and for his relativising of subordination and superordination, of God's speaking and man's hearing, of the Lord's command and the servant's obedience. It accounts for his relativisation of reality in the provisional and still unknowing 'representation', which must be overcome! It accounts for the unmistakable stress in his syntheses on reason (against faith), on nature (against grace), on philosophy (against theology) and on natural law (against the Gospel). It accounts for the sublation of 'the truth' in knowledge (*Phenomenology*), for 'beginning' in being (*Logic*), of 'grace' in system (*Encyclopaedia*), of 'way' in right (*Ethics*) and of 'end' in the history of objective and subjective Spirit. And it accounts for the graceless necessity and dialectic of being which confront us on all the paths of world history in their various stages and forms as well as for the insight and historical science which annul faith at its root. Finally, it accounts for the sublation of absolute future into pure present.

In all these distinctions there is no need to stress yet again that Hegel's speculative dialectic would equip him to give an answer to every objection, to ward off every scruple, positively to incorporate every counter concept and somehow or other to affirm every antithesis. More particularly, there can be scarcely a single scriptural text (not even one about grace and faith) which Hegel would not be able to interpret speculatively at some stage or other of his dialectic. Even so, if we do not discern here a basic and thoroughgoing difference which only a spurious dialectic can resolve, then we must face up to the stark alternative of having understood *either* the biblical message *or* Hegel's system *or else* (should we persist in thinking ourselves to have understood both) of having failed to understand either in its *original* sense.

Our continuing concern for precise analysis requires that two important features of this basic divergence be taken into account:

1. In the first place there is the genuinely Christian starting-point of Hegel's existential way of thinking. In his examination of the ethical bases of Hegel's thought J. Flügge was right to point out his ethical 'earnestness' (which nevertheless looked with contempt at any moralising), his self-forgetful 'demeanour' which was at daggers drawn with the vanity of the educated, his 'conscientiousness', his 'hunger and thirst for the truth' and his 'sacrifice of the intellect'. Flügge follows his subject in describing Hegel's thought as 'worship of God', 'proof of God' and 'transformation of thought', remarking in this connection that: 'We could not examine here the question of whether Hegel fully understood the meaning of Christian worship. He certainly did not. Yet what is decisive in our context is that Hegel permits pure scientific thought to participate in the cult, indeed that for him it is only the performance of the spiritual cult which bestows on thought its scientific depth and its true content. It is equally decisive that Hegel confronts those who exclude pure scientific thought from the cult as one who takes the meaning of worship more seriously and understands it more comprehensively than they, and who could instruct them on this score.'[27]

2. In the second place there is the possibility of opening up Hegel's system of identity. Even though his doctrine and system contend for speculative necessity against all the 'contingency' of free grace, and for speculative knowledge against all the 'outwardness' involved in a faith directed toward Another, this still does not mean that his system is so closed and barred as to be incapable of being opened up. As we have repeatedly demonstrated, Hegel was himself unable to carry through in practice the claim of speculative identity to which he clung in theory. Nor could this be achieved by retrospectively adjusting Hegel's system; rather, we should have to work out a different

---

[27] *Die sittlichen Grundlagen des Denkens,* 118.

approach. Yet precisely because he never (even in his theoretical claim) understood identity as a simple and unmediated identity in the sense of vulgar monism and pantheism, but as a carefully defined and mediated identity, we may not airily dismiss the question whether it might not be possible to hold fast to Hegel's essential insights even when we abandon identity in the sense of the monism of Spirit which he proclaimed at the end and intended or presupposed at the beginning. At the level of religion – not of philosophy – Hegel himself, for all his unmistakable emphasis on unity, stoutly maintained that there is an ultimate difference. To cling to this ultimate difference, while not following Hegel in seeking to sublate it, would involve the abandonment of the claim made by his system (which, as has been pointed out, is ultimately an illusory claim anyway) to achieve absolute knowledge and absolute identity and thus the elevation of philosophy over religion.

E. Bloch plainly sets forth this difference in Hegel's thought which has often been overlooked by both Marxists and non-Marxists: 'It must be remembered, though, that Hegel never knows an ego without a counterpart. In his thought there is no subject without an object, the latter simply does not remain external or unpenetrated. In other words, the ego and its counterpart are dissolved together in the pure Self, something which for a long stretch (at the level of religion) does not occur, only leads to spiritual objectlessness for the first time at the end of the system in the philosophy of philosophy. As representation the Idea in Hegel's thought is admittedly a growing recollection, but in religion it remains entirely within the bounds of the Thou-relationship, in the specific subject-object relationship. Thus Hegel's strong religious emphasis on the subject must not be understood subjectively. Indeed, it occasionally returns to a particularly enhanced emphasis on the objective side of religion, and this by way of contrast to the disintegration of faith in mere feeling. Just as the latter already struck Hegel as a religiously warmed up emptiness, even though it had not yet reached the level of the drawing room chatter about "spiritual values". Hegel needed something substantial throughout, and this could most surely be provided by objects, and in the philosophy of religion this meant the supreme object, God . . . Hence in Hegel's religious dialectic the two dialectical moments of subject-object or object-subject do not look as though the subject is challenging the religious process without the counter ballast of objectivity. Reference has already been made above to the cult as the sphere in which Hegel wished to see the subjective side of Christianity preserved against mere subjectivism. Here too the counter reference of objectivity to inwardness turns into a mutual relation which defines subject and object in terms of each other . . . Hence Hegel is unmistakably wary of completely incorporating what is thought of as God in a purely human milieu. Important passages of Hegel's *Philosophy of Religion* force us to take note of this wariness, which presages a hostility on his part, in the very midst of his religious self-knowledge, to the ideas which would later be disseminated by Feuerbach . . . Not without reason could the right-wing Hegel school appeal to this primacy of God. He left God's throne unshaken by Prometheus and the father myth *hors de concours*.'[28]

---

[28] *Subjekt-Objekt*, 325-328.

Now if, as Bloch equally correctly observes,[29] 'Hegel's stress on the object in the sense of the Father and the supreme object' tended to increase even more in his later years, and if his lectures on the existence of God scarcely continue to emphasise the transposition of substance to the subject, being rather disposed to lay the accent on the divine aseity (that is, on God's being as dependent on himself alone), he did not stand alone on this path. Since we were obliged earlier to report much of an unconciliatory nature concerning Hegel's relationship with his former friends and kindred spirits Schelling and Fichte, it is in order to round off our picture in this final chapter in conciliatory vein by pointing out that, notwithstanding their continuing differences and despite the fact that Hegel himself would not have admitted it, he was in fact moving in the same direction that Schelling and Fichte had taken on turning away from their initial philosophy of identity.

Fichte's *The Vocation of Man* of 1800, written after the atheistic controversy, represents a breakthrough into a new dimension. E. Coreth comments: 'This very fact makes plain the existence of a concept of God here which has become in many respects deeper, fuller and livelier than before. On this level a breakthrough is now accomplished – for the first time in such explicit terms – to the core of religion, and its genuineness can surely scarcely be doubted. The texts in *The Vocation of Man*, along with the later and even more mature ones in the *Instruction to a Blessed Life*, speak too clearly for that. They express with warm intimacy, a personal religious sensitivity and experience, for example, in the words with which Fichte addresses God himself: "Sublime Living Will, known by no name and enveloped by no concept, I may surely lift up my mind to You, for You and I are not separated. Your voice resounds in me and mine re-echoes in You; and all my thoughts, if they are only true and good, are thought in You. I become fully comprehensible to myself and the world to me, in You, the incomprehensible, and in You all the riddles of my being are resolved and the most perfect harmony wells up in my spirit." Even so, God remains the incomprehensible. The "brooding intellect" does not grasp him; rather, "it depicts a contradictory monster, which it passes off as Your image." Only by an ethical disposition and humble sacrifice to God's will do we become truly conscious of him.'[30]

W. Kasper summarises Schelling's later philosophy as follows: 'Here God is no longer the calculable basic reality of thought and of the being which is expounded by thought; rather, he is the freedom above all being. The *a priori* science of being as a science of the being of being must confess itself to be a negative science incapable of grasping God. A way of thinking is being ushered in which aims to reflect critically on the relationship of being in general with the supreme being. Identity and indifference are turning into difference. The thus detached holy God (in the sense of the biblical *kadosh*) can only be experienced in the framework of human freedom as one who is absolutely free and incomprehensible in his freely chosen and freely offered compre-

---

[29]*op. cit.*, 327.
[30]*Vom Ich zum absoluten Sein*, 273; cf. also *idem*: *Zu Fichte's Denkentwicklung* and E. Hirsch: *Geschichte der neueren evangelischen Theologie* IV, 364-375.

hensibility, as one who is supra-historical in his historicity, as one who transcends being even while assuming being, and as one whom people cannot experience at will but only in amazement.'[31] Yet this does not involve a return to the Platonic God: 'Schelling does not project God beyond all being and essence to have him abide there in absolute motionlessness. That God trancends essence is for him a supremely positive statement which is identical with the freedom of absolute self-determination. Precisely because he transcends being, God is free to assume being, to enter into history while still remaining its absolute Lord, because he can freely determine his own being. Schelling's concept of God remains dialectical, but it is the dialectic of absolute freedom. In virtue of his freedom God is both the holy and the wholly other One, the non-objectifiable, inconceivable and nameless One who is divorced from all worldly being and yet at the same time the One who can be everything to us out of free love, who can unreservedly become our very life. He is not only always and eternally the same, not simply pure pastness. Nor is he only pure being in and for itself, not simply vague presentness, not a mere 'now'. Rather, as living free Spirit he is really the One who will be; he is not just *actus purus,* but also *potentia pura,* boundless novelty, surprise, geniality and future. He is the God who is able to be the free creator and Lord of history.'[32]

With all these fundamental reflections on Hegel criticism behind us, we have already indicated how we intend to develop our first topic – a consideration of Hegel's case with reference to a future Christology.

2. The Historicity of God

Where should the confrontation of Hegel's philosophy with classical Christology begin? Answering this question is not made easy by the fact that, on the one hand, Hegel's circular system itself on principle lacks a beginning, while, on the other hand, the person of Christ enjoys a universal significance for Christian theology. The only feasible way of giving a comprehensive answer would be to outline the whole of Christian theology in step-by-step confrontation with Hegel's system. Yet such a project is impossible within the confines of this book and would also be a tall order in the present intellectual situation.

Even so, there is one central point which not only gives concrete form to the twofold wider problem but also promises maximal contiguity between the vexed questions pertaining to both Hegel's philosophy and Christian theology. Oddly enough, this is the point on which, as we have seen, both theological and philosophical criticism have concentrated their fire: Hegel's dialectic identifying God and man, as occurs in the absolute Spirit. Or should it not be thought odd that the very Christian theology which has been swift to criticise

---

[31] *Das Absolute in der Geschichte,* 10f; cf. 181-215.
[32] *op. cit.,* 215.

Hegel has hitherto hardly paid serious attention to the fact that in criticising his refined unity it exposes itself to criticism, since it seems in its own Christology to presuppose the possibility and reality of just such a differentiated identity of God and man? For Hegel also appeals to the fact that this unity of God and man has been revealed in Christ. How can we then dispute the possibility of such a unity in the case of Hegel's philosophy, while at the same time presupposing it in that of our own Christology? Are we not obliged under these circumstances to modify either our own christological position or our criticism of Hegel?

This dilemma can perhaps be elucidated in the following way. The argument against the pivotal christological dogma of the incarnation and thus against the unity of God and man in Christ can be formulated as follows: 'We assert that there is absolutely no way in which the Infinite in itself can be finite, and least of all in which it can choose finitude *for itself*. However we might wish to express the unity of infinitude and finitude (thought of as inherent in the Infinite), the very idea is to be rejected.' Or the contradiction in the dogma about Christ might be formulated thus: 'The noetic-ontic equation of God and the creature occurs in two directions: God obtains characteristics which pertain to creaturely, finite being, and the creature is taken into the inner current of the divine life itself . . .'

Yet the arguments just quoted are by no means directed against the unity of God and man in Christ as presupposed by the dogma about Christ. On the contrary, they are advanced by Christian theologians and philosophers against *Hegel* and his unity of God and man in the Absolute.[33]

Let no one instantly retort that by the distinctions which it makes Christian theology has ensured the impossibility of such a parallel, for Hegel's thought too is highly differentiated at this point. Moreover, the history of Christology can show that there are crictical points in this history which have not been truly clarified to this day (cf. the Excursuses). These questions are not merely accidental but thoroughly fundamental in nature and are ultimately bound up with the Greek concept of God under whose influence classical Christology was developed. This becomes clearer when we consider this very question of the differentiated unity of God and man from another and more dynamic angle, that is, from the point of view of the concept of incarnation which was of pivotal importance for classical Christology. Oddly enough, Hegel's conception of God's becoming, of his self-externalisation into the world and of his suffering, has been found particularly offensive. Or, as we must ask once more, should it not be thought odd that the very theology which is bent on criticising Hegel has hitherto scarcely seriously noticed the fact that, in

---

[33]cf. H. Ogiermann: *Hegels Gottesbeweise,* 193; and E. Coreth: *Das dialektische Sein in Hegels Logik,* 189; cf. also 86, 115-118.

criticising the becoming and the suffering of God when these ideas crop up in Hegel, it exposes itself to criticism, since it seems to presuppose the possibility and reality of divine becoming and suffering in its own Christology? For Hegel also appeals to the fact that this divine becoming, self-externalisation, suffering and even death has been revealed in Christ. Thus is it not thoroughly irresponsible to challenge the possibility of this divine becoming, self-externa-lisation and suffering in Hegel's case while at the same time presupposing it in our own Christology? Would not the consistent advocacy of this point of view oblige us either to give up our own christological position or else to modify our criticism of Hegel?

It is conspicuous how Iljin's profound interpretation of Hegel, which we have so often quoted with agreement, becomes completely engrossed in this issue. Iljin's entire interpretation and criticism of Hegel ultimately boils down to this point: 'We thus come to the final conclusion that Hegel's original metaphysical conception does not tally with its implementation in practice: the heroic poem of victorious divine struggle turns into the infinite tragedy of divine suffering.'[34] He concludes from this: 'If God is really all-encompassing substance, then notwithstanding its greatness and its glorious energy this substance suffers from inner strife and its progress through the world testifies to a lack of true divinity.'[35]

But is it so certain that this argument is valid against Hegel? Or does it in fact strike home at the same time against the classical dogma about Christ? Can we from the perspective of Christology conclude so easily as Iljin: 'And if theodicy must accept that *God suffers,* that he is *helpless* in his suffering and that he has plunged into these sufferings *of his own volition,* then it has frankly failed as theodicy, for of the glory of God there would remain only divine suffering and misery . . .'?[36] After all that we have been able to establish, can we so easily say that 'Hegel *learned* the best part of his thought (i.e. the idea of the speculative-concrete) from the Gospel of Christ, but what he *taught* was not Christianity'?[37] And can we base this on the reason that the suffering Absolute is not absolute'[38] and that in this case '"man's limits" (would) at the same time be *God's limits*'[39]?

Let no one step in at this point, either, with the instant objection that Christian theology has employed clear distinctions to secure itself against misunderstandings and contradictions. For Hegel's dialectic too as we have said is highly differentiated. The history of Christology, however, can show that this issue forms the background of various crises and questions in

---

[34] *Die Philosophie Hegels als kontemplative Gotteslehre,* 380.
[35] *op. cit.,* 381
[36] *op. cit.,* 353.
[37] *op. cit.,* 418; cf. also 381.
[38] *op. cit.,* 382.
[39] *op. cit.,* 338.

Christology which have not been ironed out to this very day[40]. And at the same time the questionableness of purely philosophical criticism of Hegel becomes apparent here. For Hegel himself fully intended not to be a 'pure' philosopher. But does our criticism do him justice if it neglects the fact that he developed the Absolute's becoming, self-externalisation and overstepping of its limits not as an abstract theory, but in genetic and systematic connection with the Christian message?

If we do not intend to rest satisfied with previous criticism and previous information, then we must direct our attention, in the sense of the two-pronged critique demanded above, both to the problems of Hegel's under-standing of God in their general philosophical context and to the development of the vexed christological questions to which Hegel's philosophy stands in a peculiar relationship of tension. If this chapter is to avoid growing into a companion volume, then we can do no more than provide some footnotes on this twofold problem. Notwithstanding the necessity or usefulness of any backward and forward glances which we may take at Hegel in this section, we shall concentrate our thoughts so as to present the philosophical material as briefly as possible, eschewing the luxury of quoting from other authors or secondary literature. In the meantime the pertinent material from the history of doctrine will be accomodated in a series of short and measured Excursuses based on recent scholarship, a procedure which will have the advantage of taking some of the pressure off the main text. Thus we cannot aim to give a comprehensive historical account of either the philosophical problem of God or the doctrinal problem of Christology. Calling to mind the rough outlines of the prototypes to be encountered in the history of this topic, our aim will be to clarify the present *systematic* state of the christological problem with reference to Hegel. His concern, in which specifically theo-logical factors intersect with christological ones, is the dynamic unity in the living Godhead. The living God is for him the one who moves, changes and undergoes a history, who does not rigidly *remain* what he is, but *becomes* what he is. And he is the God who does not stubbornly remain within himself in a lofty posture of splendid isolation above the world, but who comes out of himself and externalises himself in the becoming of the world, a movement which comes to a climax when God himself becomes man. According to Hegel this God is the true, the Christian God; and so according to him the true God is the one who as infinite fullness comprehends all antitheses in unity in himself. He does not pallidly hover, severed from everything else as a grey Absolute, but lives in many forms as the one, all-encompassing Spirit. It is the God who does not

---

[40]cf. Excursuses I – IV.

suffer antitheses to congeal statically in themselves, but thrusts them out into the world, suffering along with them and reconciling them into unity; it is the God who, precisely in this externalisation into the world, which reaches its revealed pinnacle in the incarnation and the death on the cross, manifests the inmost depths of his heart. In brief, according to Hegel, the true God is the one who is both finite and infinite, both God and man in unity.

For its part, the christological problem, precisely in its classical form, stands intimately connected with the general philosophical problem, especially with the fundamental problems of being and becoming, unity and multiplicity, which had been high on the agenda since the beginnings of western philosophy. We aim to give a brief indication here of what this means for our understanding of the concept of God on which classical Christology is founded.[41]

1. To gain a broad view of the vexed question of being and becoming we must go back to the attempts of the pre-Socratics to explain the becoming and passing away of things, which so troubles experience, in terms of a primordial principle ($\grave{\alpha}\rho\chi\acute{\eta}$). Heraclitus provoked a lasting ferment by taking up some motifs from ancient lyrics to develop for the first time a radical philosophy of becoming according to which *everything* is fluid in the contradictoriness of all appearances. Yet Parmenides (before or after Heraclitus?) was the only one who dared to pronounce all becoming illusory and to ascribe to the one Being not merely unoriginateness and unchangeableness, but an absolutely rigid kind of immoveableness and unchangeableness: being is and cannot not be. It cannot be overlooked, however, that Parmenides's opposition to any kind of becoming exercised an almost ubiquitous influence, so that all future philosophy right up to Spinoza must largely be understood as an open or covert reaction to Heraclitus. With its conception of unchangeable substance, whether made up of elements or of atoms, the philosophy of nature (as represented by Empedocles, Anaxagoras, Leucippus and Democritus) concurred with Parmenides, as did Plato's ontology, which derived from him via the Eleatic school and the epistemological critique of the early Sophists. The atomists Leucippus and Democritus understood their atoms as unchangeable Eleatic blocks of being and accepted only local motion. Plato's theory of ideas, which tended to devalue a changing world of appearance – not, as with Parmenides, of illusion, Aristotle's *energeia* philosophy, which aimed to explain movement in terms of its notion of the motionless $\nu o \hat{\upsilon} \varsigma$, Plotinus's dynamic philosophy of emanation with its conception of the non-living

---

[41]For a better understanding of the drift of this discussion cf., in addition to the well-known histories of philosophy, J. Wahl: *Traité de métaphysique* and H. Heimsoeth: *Die sechs grossen Themen der abendlandischen Metaphysik.*

primordial One ($\tau\grave{o}$ $\check{\epsilon}\nu$) , and, dependent on all the foregoing, the metaphysics of mediaeval scholasticism – all of these systems were to a large extent constructed in the steps of Parmenides against a radical philosophy of becoming. The chief exceptions to this rule are supplied by the pantheistic Stoa, Scotus Eriugena, Eckhardt and the mystics who followed him, up to and including Nicholas of Cusa and Jakob Böhme. After Descartes developed his novel theory of motion, Leibniz joined with Hobbes under the influence of the natural sciences and especially of infinitesimal calculus to advocate a basically dynamic monadology. The young Kant was chiefly concerned with the becoming of the cosmos and Lessing with that of the history of the human race, while Herder was disposed to see the history of both nature and human-kind as a gigantic process of development. In the wake of Fichte and Schelling Hegel then moulded a consistent and comprehensive metaphysic of becom-ing, development, history and life, attempting to assimilate the whole of the antecedent intellectual development and paying particular attention to the concerns of Heraclitus, Eckhardt and Böhme. It is chiefly due to him that the nineteenth century became an historical century, with the philosophy of becoming exerting an especially strong influence on Nietzsche, Bergson, Whitehead and, finally, on Heidegger.

In the case of Eckhardt as of Böhme, of Nicholas of Cusa as of Giordano Bruno, of Malebranche as of Lessing, and in the case of Hegel himself, the multiform philosophy of becoming was overtly or covertly concerned with a living God. The mistrust felt by many Greek philosophers towards Heraclitus's philosophy of becoming had in the meantime permeated the understanding of God, often taking concrete form in the attitudes adopted on this subject. To preserve the inviolability of being, Parmenides had been obliged to declare the whole variety and motion of the world a human error; but his radical denial of becoming had not won the day. Plato in particular sought to overcome this denial. His only acquaintance with Heraclitus came via his teacher Cratylos and even then only through a forgery which distorted the original sense. In the solution which he proposed Plato was influenced not only by the Eleatic philosophy of being but also by Pythagorean dualism, thus opting for a momentous division of reality into the untrue, bad, disintegrated and sensual world of becoming and the true, good, unitary and spiritual world of being. Although the later dialogues do not preclude movement both within the world of Ideas itself (dialectics) and between the latter and the world of sense, the factor which decisively determined the future direction of thought was the separation ($\chi\omega\rho\iota\sigma\mu\acute{o}\varsigma$) between the changeable spatio-temporal reality of this world and the extra-spatial and extra-temporal eternal and unchangeable reality which transcends even heaven itself. Anaximander had understood the primordial principle as the boundless ($\check{\alpha}\pi\epsilon\iota\rho\sigma\nu$) and the divine ($\theta\epsilon\iota\sigma\nu$).

Xenophanes had already spoken, albeit in indefinite terms, of the one God, while Parmenides and Heraclitus had not thought of Being and Logos respectively as a personal God. For Plato himself, who subjected the discordant multitude of the Homeric gods to caustic criticism, the primordial principle was absolutely immovable and unchangeable. In the *Timaeus* he is acquainted with a demiurge which, while not the creator of the world, is certainly its architect. In this capacity it is subordinate to the Ideas, so that it is at least uncertain whether Plato regarded this demiurge as God in the strictest sense. In any case, for Plato the supreme principle is the spiritual sun depicted in the sixth and seventh books of the *Republic,* the Idea of the Good which stands at the apex of the pyramid of Ideas. Although Plato seems to make too little distinction between the supreme Idea and the other Ideas, the former nevertheless stands in the sharpest contrast to the God of Heraclitus and to some extent also to the God of the Stoics in its capacity as the divine, self-sufficient reality. That is, the supreme Idea is at odds with the God who is involved in becoming. Although Heraclitus curiously once more depicts him as separate from all else, this God is identical with the sequence of antithetical and warring elements and with the vigorously turbulent fire which as world-soul and reason ($\lambda\acute{o}\gamma o\varsigma$, $\delta\acute{\iota}\kappa\eta$, $\epsilon\acute{\iota}\mu\alpha\rho\mu\acute{\epsilon}\nu\eta$) presides over the eternally fluid universe and over the living antitheses of appearance in their mysteriousness and ambiguity. Many scholars also detect an incongruity in the thought of Aristotle between the all-attracting highest good and the unmoved First Mover. Although this divine $\nu o\hat{\upsilon}\varsigma$ is pure actuality, it is set so rigidly in a cast of immutability and it is so radically exclusive of any kind of movement that it knows only itself and tolerates no $\pi\rho\acute{\alpha}\tau\tau\epsilon\iota\nu$ or $\pi o\iota\epsilon\hat{\iota}\nu$ on anything else. Fear of becoming is only too apparent in this extreme transcendence of the immobile mover and in its thought of itself. Even in the case of Plotinus, the third star in this philosophical triumvirate, who to a great extent dynamically overcame Platonic rigidity by his system of levels of being which flow down from each other, the supreme principle of all being, the One, remains locked up in absolutely rigid immutability, so that Plotinus even denied him the predicate of life.

Hence while the three great representatives of classical Greek philosophy no longer had an Eleatic understanding of being, they did conceive of the divine in those terms. They now ascribed to the supreme principle of being not only unoriginateness and imperishability, but also the absolute immovability and immutability which Parmenides attributed to being as such. To this extent the Platonic Idea of the Good, the Aristotelian unmoved Mover and the Plotinian One match the Parmenidian being.

2. When we endeavour to glimpse the same set of problems from the perspective of *unity and multiplicity,* we find that in the thought of the great

Greek philosophers a sharp dualism tends to accompany an accentuated philosophy of being. There is no reason why in itself a philosophy affirming the primacy of being over becoming cannot definitively put the *unity* of antitheses in the foreground (Parmenides, Spinoza) just as well as can a philosophy affirming the primacy of becoming (Heraclitus: war as father of all things). But, generally speaking, we may say that a philosophy which puts the stress on becoming will be disposed to put it also on unity, so that we can discern an affinity between a philosophy of becoming and a philosophy of identity. In the end of the day this holds good even for Heraclitus, who wanted to establish unity in antitheses. (The expressions 'philosophy of becoming' and 'philosophy of identity' are used for the sake of simplicity, but in the absence of more precise definitions they are meant to denote only the *primacy* of becoming over being and of identity over duality.) By the same token, the philosophy of being is often inclined to sunder reality. Because its agenda had been dictated chiefly by Parmenides and the Pythagoreans, the classical Greek philosophy of Plato, Aristotle and Plotinus tended, notwithstanding all attempts at reconciliation, overwhelmingly to emphasise the factor of opposition. Of special interest to us here is its predilection for doing so where the relation between the primordial principle and the world is concerned.

In the later Plato the Ideas are present in things ($\pi\alpha\rho o\upsilon\sigma\acute{\iota}\alpha$), and the things share in the Ideas ($\mu\epsilon\theta\epsilon\xi\iota\varsigma$) by way of communion ($\kappa o\iota\nu\omega\nu\acute{\iota}\alpha$) and imitation ($\mu\acute{\iota}\mu\eta\sigma\iota\varsigma$), aspiring to them as their goal ($\tau\acute{\epsilon}\lambda o\varsigma$). Even so, as has already been noted, the sharp $\chi\omega\rho\iota\sigma\mu\acute{o}\varsigma$ between God's world of Ideas (the Idea of the Good) and the apparent world of sense (composed of evil matter) exerted by far the greater influence subsequently, causing Platonic philosophy to remain profoundly dualistic and permitting no *inner* ontic connection between Idea and thing. Plato's pronounced hostility to matter and sense is bound up with this factor. Aristotle succeeded in bringing Plato's transcendent divine Ideas down to earth and transferring them from heaven into the things of this world. Yet this only led to the distance between the first principle and the world becoming more unbridgeable still. Except for the divine impulse which set the world in motion, God and the world live alongside each other from eternity. Whatever may be said concerning the relation between efficient and final causality in Aristotle's God, this $\nu\acute{o}\eta\sigma\upsilon\varsigma$ $\nu o\acute{\eta}\sigma\epsilon\omega\varsigma$ thinks only itself. This God neither knows nor loves the world and we cannot trace back to him any causal operation, providence or gift of moral order and law. And all this because Aristotle believed that he owed it to the absoluteness of his God. For all such things would involve *passio* and *potentia* for his *actus purus*! And even Plotinus's divine One hovers in separation from the world. His God has no knowledge of the world. The world, having emanated from unity, is simply a falling away. Matter is something bad, and man must free himself from it.

437

This brief and perfunctory review should have made clear what is of decisive importance for our present purposes, namely that on account of their starting-point (that is the search by means of inferential logic for the primal cause of things), the classical Greek philosophers neglected both the living movement of God and the communion of an all-knowing and all-loving God with the world and humankind. While he was not, as in the case of the God of the Stoics, pantheistically identified with the world, the God of Platonism, Aristotelianism and neo-Platonism was infinitely remote from the world and truly rigidified in his infinitude. It therefore behoves us to keep this God in our mind's eye in order to get some inkling of the tremendous claim made by the Christian proclamation of a living God who is active in history. The very idea of a creator God, who directly and immediately intervenes as a living God in the being and becoming of the world (and of matter!), and who not only makes possible the world and its history but directs, knows and loves it and causes it to be good, stood in sharp contrast to the Greek conception of the rigid transcendence of an immutable God. Yet there was also another and completely different way in which the idea of a decisive revelation of God in this man Jesus, of some kind of identification of God with this one man, of 'the Logos become flesh', was bound to encounter resistance. The one who in purely transcendent absoluteness is infinitely alien to the world and man is supposed to reveal himself in a man, to identify himself with a man! The one who abides in unchangeable repose and who knows only himself, and that without motion, is supposed to humble himself to be a man, to assume human nature, to become 'flesh', that is, a wretched man!

The proclamation and theology of early Christianity had before it the immense task of unleashing the Judaeo-Christian belief in God, which was presupposed by belief in Christ, upon the Hellenistic world of thought. Although there was a tendency from the outset simply to preach the Christian message polemically *against* pagan philosophy, which at that time consisted in a syncretistic compound of the most diverse Platonic, neo-Platonic, Aristotelian and Stoic elements, nevertheless a positive debate conducted on the intellectual level of the day could in fact scarcely be avoided (above all by those who came to the Christian faith with a philosophical education behind them). The historical epoch and the Christian revelation itself seemed to join forces in demanding just such a debate: the claim of the Christian God would tolerate no other gods alongside himself. It was imperative to demonstrate that the Christian faith possesses the highest and purest understanding of the divine, and that the God of Israel and of Jesus Christ is the one true God. Not least on account of the contact of the biblical writings themselves with Hellenistic thought, the Old and New Testaments offered starting-points for

438

such an undertaking and for statements about God's essence – his uniqueness, omnipotence and eternity . . .

In the ensuing period we find that the Apostolic Fathers echo the New Testament in showing occasional connections with philosophical ideas, especially regarding the negative predicates of God: invisible, imperishable, untouchable, unbegotten, immutable, timeless, impassible. Even so, it was only after the influential Philo had blazed a trail in Hellenistic Judaism that the philosophical understanding of God was methodically adopted and consistently applied for the first time by the apologists of the second century. The latter thought in terms of the contrasting pairs measurable/immeasurable, comprehensible/incomprehensible, circumscribed/uncircumscribed, limited/unlimited and finite/infinite. In this way early Christian theology undoubtedly courted the grave danger of alienating the Christian message. It has frequently been pointed out how in its understandable polemic against pagan polytheism this theology made momentous concessions to the Platonic/neo-Platonic understanding of God and how it tended to see reconciliation and redemption more in the conquest of the Platonic dualism of God and world than in liberation from sin, guilt and law. It was as if the evil contradiction obtained between God and man as such and not between God and *sinful* man! It was as if for that reason reconciliation and redemption had taken place simply in virtue of God's entrance into humanity, hence on account of the bare fact of the incarnation rather than of the cross and resurrection! It was as if redemption should be expressed in pure ontological categories (nature, person, hypostasis etc.) and not primarily in historical categories, which is precisely what happened in the New Testament and in the first creeds! The changes produced by the introduction of Greek metaphysics into Christology can be illustrated by the example of the *apeiron* concept and of the conflict which raged about the axiom *'finitum non capax infiniti'*.[42]

Nevertheless, no one should fail to appreciate the challenge of the historical situation and the extremely significant achievement of the apologists, who had no wish to practise their theology outside the intellectual horizon of their environment and with no concern for the *aporiae* of contemporary reflection. Were they not obliged to engage in daring and unprecedented reformulation in order that the Christian message might be proclaimed in a manner intelligible to the Hellenistic world? The transcendent concept of God characteristic of so-called middle and neo-Platonism was clearly able to furnish acceptable and even useful insights for dealing with this difficult task, for it facilitated an effective presentation not only of monotheism but also of

---

[42]cf. Werner Elert: *Der Ausgang der altkirchlichen Christologie*, 33-70.

the supra-worldiness of the biblical God. In his essay on the philosophical concept of God in early Christian theology Pannenberg highlights the positive gains made by the Fathers, [43] correctly emphasising against Ritschl and Harnack that the inevitable appropriation of the Greek idea of God by no means meant simply the infiltration and ousting of the Christian by a 'deistic' notion of God. The questions which arose in connection with monotheism and the understanding of creation, with the ideas of God's otherness, spirituality, incomprehensibility, ineffability, immutability and simplicity, and with the notion that he is in a certain sense devoid of attributes, plainly demonstrate that the appropriation was by no means uncritical. We need only think of the stress on God's almighty freedom and on creation out of nothing. In principle at least Greek metaphysics was subordinated to the Christian faith.

Even so, Pannenberg himself draws our attention to the fact that the Church's critical penetration into and remoulding of the philosophical concept of God did not always go far enough. For the conception of God as a naturalistic world principle in the Greek sense and the conception of God as the free Lord of the world and its history in the Old and New Testament senses have tended to coexist in uneasy balance down the ages. All too often the predicates of God's changelessness, timelessness, simplicity, namelessness and lack of attributes have been used to pitch him into an unbridgeable remoteness, and have led to his free salvific activity not being taken with sufficient seriousness. Necessary changes in the philosophical concept of God either failed to materialise or else were not consistently carried through. Thus God's eternity was looked on too much as a Platonic timelessness and too little as a powerful, living contemporaneity with all time. His omnipresence was seen too much as a static extension throughout the universe and too little as almighty dominion over space. His goodness toward the world and man was regarded too much as a natural emanation of the Good and too little as the free self-giving in love and grace of the God who acts in history. His righteousness was viewed too much as a distributive and retributive justice based on a timeless concept of order and too little as the saving righteousness rooted in God's fidelity to his covenant and promises. His imcomprehensibility was pictured too much as the abstract absence of attributes in an anonymous ground of the world and too little as the otherness of the free God demonstrated in his acts. Thus while it is true that God appeared as the ground of the world, he was depicted too little as the one who is alive in a personal sense.

[43]'The Appropriation of the Philosophical Concept of God as a Dogmatic Problem of Early Christian Theology', *Basic Questions in Theology* II, esp. 140-173. cf. also Pannenberg: art. '*Gott*' (V: *Theologiegeschichte*) in *RGG* 2, 1717-1732.

The predicate of God's immutability affords a particularly dubious example of this dubious development. The Christian apologists Aristides, Justin, Athenagoras, Theophilus and Tatian already adopted the concept of immutability into Christian theology from Greek metaphysics.[44] The immutability of God was seen (this too being an aspect of the question of the primal ground of things) as closely bound up with his being without beginning and with his eternity: since God is without beginning, he is therefore eternal and immutable. And the apologists truly knew how to turn the concept of the immutability of God to good account; for with its aid they were able to demonstrate to Stoic pantheism that the changeable world may not be thought identical with the immutable principle of the world. They could show further that God does not arise and pass away like the things of this world, but is unoriginate and imperishable, that he is and works in the constancy and continuity of his being without any playful moods, and that he is and remains identical with himself, suffering neither physical nor moral change, which would indeed be bound to involve deficiency in God.

However, neither the apologists nor the Christian theologians who succeeded them were able to accept the immutability of God quite so wholeheartedly as did the Greek metaphysicians. The contrary testimony of Scripture was too strong, proclaiming (in contrast, say, to Aristotle) that God is by no means so immutable as to be forced to live eternally alongside the world. On the contrary, the living God of the Bible created the world out of nothing, knows it down to the tiniest detail and loves it. He preserves, accompanies and rules it, and constantly acts anew in freedom. These factors were already recognised by the apologists, who thereby gave proof that their adoption of the concept of the divine immutability was by no means uncritical.

And yet, in their dialogue with the pagans the apologists were obliged to give their primary attention to the topics of polytheism, cosmology, fate and resurrection, so that it is understandable that they hardly got to grips with the inner problems of Christology. This was not the least reason why they did not perceive the deeper difficulties involved in the concept of immutability. In fact, the total extent of the problems raised by this concept only became apparent at the time of the great christological controversies. Just as the axiom of God's impassibility lurked behind many of the christological difficulties which led some Fathers to arrive at unbalanced and onesided solutions, so the yet more widespread axiom of God's immutability in its turn lay behind this notion of the divine $\dot{\alpha}\pi\dot{\alpha}\theta\epsilon\iota\alpha$. In taking over this philosphi-

---

[44]On the immutability of God in the theology of the ancient Church, cf. Werner Elert: *Der Ausgang der altkirchlichen Christologie*, 41-43; W. Pannenberg: 'The Appropriation of the Philosophical Concept of God . . .', 131, 159f; G. L. Prestige: *God in Patristic Thought*, 6ff, 11.

cal truism the Fathers were not taking pains to listen to Scripture; insofar as they did so, they listened with Hellenistic ears.

This perfunctory account of the upheaval in early Christian theology, which involved – albeit only to a limited extent in both cases – the simultaneous Hellenisation of the Christian message and de-Hellenisation of philosophy, is not meant to imply that the Fathers either could or should have eschewed philosophical terminology. Rather, these historical footnotes aim soley to make the reader aware that a radical reshaping of the Greek terminology would still have been necessary even if the biblical message had been proclaimed in unabridged form. Such remoulding was requisite if full verbal expression was to be given to the God of the Bible who lives in history, and not simply to an intrinsically ambiguous primal ground of all existent reality deduced by logical inference. Such recasting would not have involved taking a negative short cut; rather, it would have been a concrete instance of excellent theological method.

But no such radical recasting was in fact achieved in the patristic period. By and large the early theologians took the basic starting-point of their system from philosophical thought, and the biblical statements were then fitted in to this alien structure. A critical questioning of philosophy would have required a greater distance from the intellectual starting-point of their age than was given to those who thought in Hellenistic categories. Thus the patristic age bequeathed an ultimate dissonance between elements of biblical and of philosophical provenance, along with an unbalanced tension potentially affecting Christology most of all. The problem still stood very much in the background for the apologists in their debate with paganism, but it was soon to be thrust into the centre of debate within the Church itself. For when the Fathers were obliged to explain, in terms of the Greek concept of God, the unity of Jesus with God, so strongly emphasised in the New Testament, the latent tension between the biblical message and Greek-Hellenistic metaphysics reached breaking point.

'The Word became flesh' (Jn. 1:14) or, to put it in the Pauline idiom, 'God was in Christ' (11 Cor. 5:19). How were such and similar statements to be expressed against the background of Hellenistic spirituality? Classical Christology was obliged to hold fast to both poles at the same time, equally emphasising Word *and* flesh, God *and* man, but overworking neither the unity nor the duality in the process.

The inevitable result of abstract emphasis on the factor of *unity* was banishment of the humanity of Christ into a kind of shadow existence. In this case Christ was not a real man with flesh and blood, body and soul, not a real historical figure. Rather, the only significant force in his person was God himself; a pure Absolute was at work in Christ which had not genuinely experienced finitude and suffering. This would mean that God did not really go out of himself in his grace, but remained within himself, absorbing everything. Even if Scripture did say that a true man suffered, this should be understood 'figuratively'. The correct interpretation of Christology according to this scheme was that the all-decisive element is the eternal divine Idea and its universal life. Ultimately, Monophysitism was lurking behind this conception of unity. Over against it, however, stood the irreversible axiom that the Word truly became *flesh*.

The inevitable result of abstract emphasis on the factor of *duality,* on the other hand, was that the humanity of Christ should lead an intrinsically independent existence, with God at work here and man at work there. On this view there appeared in Christ an *actus purus* which is basically in itself not passive, a God who does not himself suffer. This would mean that God did not really go out of himself in his grace, but that his gracious sacrifice was just a 'trick of the reason' in which he managed, despite all difficulties, to keep himself unsullied by real contact with the world. Even if Scripture did say that the Son of God truly suffered, this should be understood 'figuratively'. The correct understanding of Christology according to this scheme was that man alone suffers and not God. Ultimately, Nestorianism was lurking behind this conception of duality. Over against it, however, stood the irreversible axiom that the *Word* itself became flesh.

Yet it is easier to say what is false here than what is true. It was a long history which led from the New Testament to the refined conceptions of Monophysitism and Nestorianism. The road to the classical formula of Chalcedon is strewn with heresies – or so one might say if it were easy to determine in specific cases what is heresy and what is orthodoxy. But anyone who wishes to make a serious contribution to the discussion of this problem must have a thorough knowledge of this road to Nicaea and Chalcedon. The various christological models which emerged in the course of the first five centuries demonstrate the complexity of the problem and the difficulty of the solutions, both orthodox and heterodox, both those which deviated to the right and those which deviated to the left. At all events the first half millenium of the history of Christology shows that wherever a right turn was taken under the spell of the 'divinity' of Christ or a left turn out of concern for his 'humanity' (hence wherever theologians sought to break free from the polar tension) the absolutely transcendent and rigidly immutable God of Greek metaphysics will invariably be found either directly or indirectly in the background.[45]

Nowhere is this so clear as in the question of suffering. That Christ suffered both in body and soul and that he experienced both joy and sorrow, love and

---

[45]cf. Excursus I: The Road to Classical Christology.

wrath, could scarcely be disputed on the basis of the New Testament. Even so, this is precisely what happened! Not only did many outside the orthodox fold hold Christ's sufferings and death to be illusory, but even many orthodox Fathers believed it impermissible to predicate suffering of Christ, whether in the narrower sense of pain or in the wider sense of passions, emotions and impulses. The statements of the evangelists were very frequently weakened, restricted and reinterpreted. There was clearly a tendency to predicate painlessness and even emotionlessness of Christ, in short to ascribe ἀπάθεια or impassibility to him. This could even go so far as an unwillingness to allow that Christ truly digested and excreted food. What was the reason for all this? Behind the alleged impassibility of Christ stood the impassibility of God, a notion which was not based on the Bible but adopted as a self-evident philosophical axiom. The ultimate explanation is this: behind this picture of Christ we espy the immobile, emotionless countenance of the God of Greek metaphysics.[46]

Surprisingly the Christology of early scholasticism was scarcely influenced by Chalcedon, tending largely toward Nestorianism (*habitus* theory and *assumptus* theory) or, by way of reaction, toward Monophysitism, while the subsistence theory played a major role in the Christology of high scholasticism. And the doctrine of an exchange of the divine and human predicates in Christ, the so-called '*communicatio idiomatum*', got under way at an early stage, achieving great prominence in high scholasticism. All of these currents could have given rise to a fresh reflection on the concept of God implicit in classical Christology. After all, suffering and death were actually predicated of this God in accordance with the rules of the *communicatio idiomatum* with reference to Christ *in concreto*. This *communicatio idiomatum* did not aim simply to lay down the rules for logically unassailable linguistic expression but also to make a statement on reality itself; it did not intend just to prescribe a certain language, but to prescribe a certain language *cum fundamento in re*.[47]

At the same time an incentive was given for renewed reflection on the idea of becoming in God, a path which had largely been blocked from the outset for Christian theology under the influence of Greek metaphysics. And, in connection with this, occasion was offered for a critical examination of such mediaeval attempts at Christology as Aquinas's interpretation of the incarnation of God as *relatio relationis*. The fact that alternative conceptions of the spirituality and immutability of God could already be seen in the Old Testament was a particularly effective spur toward such rethinking.[48]

---

[46]cf. Excursus II: Can God Suffer?
[47]cf. Excursus III: The Dialectic of the Attributes of God.

Even if we were willing simply to put up with the *aporiae* emerging from classical Christology or simply to gloss them over, it would still prove unavoidable not to think beyond classical Christology. Or, to put it better, classical Christology itself compels us to think beyond it and to take it more seriously than it could take itself insofar as it was hampered by the Greek metaphysical concept of God. Consequently we should avail ourselves of this opportunity and take the trouble, while presupposing classical Christology's doctrine of the two natures, to think this notion further and to think it through consistently, even if we are convinced that – as will be demonstrated – an alternative way in to Christology is possible in principle and at the present time even requisite. So let us not avoid the risk of indicating, in three parallel trains of thought, some extremely important consequences of classical Christology for our ideas of God and Christ. We do so presupposing the results which have been brought together in the excursuses. And it should become evident in the process just how much Hegel's major intentions are brought to bear in a new way, albeit under decisively modified presuppositions.

1. We might begin by thinking further about the *aporia* of God's impassibility in the context of classical Christology and with reference to Excursus II.

As far as Greek metaphysics was concerned, suffering involves deficiency. In God, however, there is no deficiency, but rather fullness. This makes it impossible for Greek metaphysics to assert that there is suffering in God. In this sense can an $\dot{\alpha}\pi\dot{\alpha}\theta\epsilon\iota\alpha$, i.e. impassibility, or inability in God to suffer, be presupposed? There is absolutely no possibility for such an understanding of God to affirm suffering in God; it is not even posible for it to affirm the possibility that God suffers. On the contrary, everything seems to speak against such a view.

But is not too much asked of philosophy when it is obliged to pass such judgments about God? Can philosophy at best do more than speak of God in the abstract? Can it do more than produce *theologia negativa,* apophatic theology? How is one obliged to speak when as a Christian theologian one looks in terms of Christ on the God who 'was in Christ' and who 'was made flesh' in him? If we are already to speak here of suffering on God's part, then this must emphatically not be thought of as an *a priori* necessity either for some immanent world process, or for the inner-trinitarian life of God, or for some divine attribute or other. God is under no obligation to suffer, but he

---

[48]cf. Excursus IV: Immutability of God?

445

does so in his Son. This is a divine mystery which springs from God's free grace and can be known by humankind only by revelation and in faith.

Thus God suffers in his Son – not intrinsically, but *de facto*; not simply as God in himself, but in the flesh. But *he himself* suffers in the Son, and the suffering in the flesh is *his* suffering. He does not, as the philosopher might suppose, suffer on account of some deficiency of need for completion, for in this case he would not be God. He suffers from fullness, that is, from the fullness of love: 'For God so loved the world that he gave his only-begotten Son . . .' (Jn. 3:16).

This scriptural statement can also teach us that Father and Son must not be separated even with respect to suffering. The presuppositions with which it works flatly forbid classical Christology to avoid this difficulty by saying that it is not God as he is in himself who suffers, not the divine nature but only the person of Christ – as if scholastic thought posited a real distinction in Christ of his divine person from his divine nature! Nor may we say that only the Son suffers and not the Father. In that case we should only see what God really is in the Father. God would then remain aloof from everything, neither engaging with this dark history nor suffering, but remaining above it all in his untouched divine transcendence. Now Father and Son are certainly distinct, so that neither the Father nor the Spirit, but soley the Son is in the flesh. But ought God to be only figuratively present in the Son, as the Arians supposed in their zeal for the untouched transcendent God? Should he really not be one in essence (ὁμοούσιος) with the Father? But classical Christology saw things differently from the Arians. Notwithstanding their personal distinction, Father and Son are one (Jn, 10:30) and they work together (Jn. 5:17); everything which is the Father's is also the Son's and what is the Son's is also the Father's (Jn. 17:9f.; 16, 14). The fullness of the Godhead dwells bodily in Jesus (Col. 2:9); indeed, God himself was in Christ (II Cor. 5:19).

The Father did not, as the Patripassians supposed, become man, but remains 'God in the highest'. Yet the Father was assuredly not indifferent to the suffering of the Son. No apathetic father, he did not look passively on, but showed a vital concern and committed himself. Already in the Old Testament God revealed himself as the very opposite of an apathetic God. This is demonstrated in the most various ways by all of Yahweh's words and deeds as they were described from Genesis onwards. It can be said quite explicitly of the Old Testament God that he rejoices (Deut. 28:63; 30:9; Isa. 62:5; Wisd. 3:17), is grieved (Gen. 6:6) and experiences delight (Jer. 9:24), remorse (Gen. 6:6), vengeance (Deut. 32:35), wrath (Ex. 15:7), abhorrence (Lev. 20:23; Ps. 106:40), jealousy (Ex. 20:5; 34:14) and hatred (Deut. 12:31; Isa. 61:8). The opposite is assuredly plainly stated in other passages of Scripture as a safeguard against undue humanisation of God: God is not a man that he should repent (Num. 23:19; I Sam. 15:29; but cf. 15:11).

Even so, the first list of statements may not simply be explained away. It is noteworthy that the Septuagint tended to reinterpret the original text by weakening these statements as much as possible or even, in some cases, by eliminating them entirely. We obviously have to do here with anthropomorphisms and anthropopathisms, and parallels in the history of religions can easily be found. It would be superficial, however, to focus on this factor alone, as if those parts of the Old Testament which contain anthropomorphisms belong to strata of particularly poor quality. (Above all in the last century, scholars endeavoured to make out just such a case. A glance at the Prophets proves that this goes in the face of all the biblical data!) Again, it would be as if the God of the Old Testament were not a living God, but a mute force and an anonymous power, and as if the true God were not the God of Abraham, Isaac and Jacob, but Plato's apathetic divinity! 'The purpose of the anthropomorphisms is not to humanise God. On the contrary, they are meant . . . to bring God near to man as a *living personality* and to uphold and strengthen his religious life and feeling. He is not meant to conceive God as an abstract idea remote from him and unconcerned about him, but rather as a being who does not remain indifferent when he sins, punishing him yet also merciful when he repents and taking care of him in time of hardship.'[49]

The God of the New Testament most certainly does not appear as an apathetic God, but as a *'Dieu compatissant'*.[50] In this respect too the New Testament fulfils and outstrips the Old, so that classical Christology had every incentive to go on devoting consistent thought to this subject. Its own presuppositions should have prompted it to say to itself that God's own cause, indeed his very Son, was at stake in his revelation in Christ. Nor can he remain apathetic who 'spared not his own Son, but delivered him up' (Rom. 8:32; cf. Jn. 3:16). The New Testament would permit no one to penetrate behind Jesus

---

[49]P. Heinisch: *Theologie des Alten Testaments,* 33; ET Theology of the Old- Testament (tr. W. Heidt, 1950); cf. also P. van Imschoot: *Théologie de l'Ancien Testament* I, 29 and the various theologies of the Old Testament written by W. Eichrodt (I, 134-141; ET I, 210-220), L. Köhler (4-6), E. Jacob (28-32) and T. C. Vriezen (144-147; ET, 161-164). M. A. Beek, F. Michaeli, T. Vischer and F. Horst, who are quoted by these authors, consider that the anthropomorphisms and the 'humanity of God' which they herald are the basis of the Christian doctrine of the incarnation. Vriezen himself, however, is inclined rather to locate this basis in the fellowship of God and man which is attested in the Old Testament. On this subject cf. H. M. Kuitert's *Gott in Menschengestalt,* which seeks to combine the dogmatic with the hermeneutical approach in steering a middle path between total acceptance (anthropomorphitism) and total rejection (gnosis) of the biblical anthropomorphisms. Kuitert defines God's being and his adoption of human form as the being of a partner, in which context the incarnation appears as at once the climax of what has gone before and something completely new (cf. esp. 101-107, 215-223).

[50]P. van Imschoot: *op. cit.* I, 52.

or to bypass him in search of another more exalted and transcendent God. He who sees Jesus sees the Father, the true God (Jn. 14:9f.; cf. Jn. 8:19). The Son stands for the Father and pleads the Father's cause. Although the Father neither became human nor died on the cross, he is, as John constantly emphasises, 'one' with his Son.

Thus the Son reveals the Father in everything that he does. He reveals him in a special way in the negative abyss of his suffering and death, in which it was disclosed how 'the foolishness of God is wiser than men, and the weakness of God is stronger than men' (I Cor. 1:25). Only in terms of the cross, as it appears to faith in the light of the resurrection and of this new life with God, is it finally revealed who is the God of Abraham, Isaac and Jacob, and who is the God of Jesus Christ. The Christian conception of God appears in Christ's death on the cross, and theology proper is to be defined in terms of Christology. Christology is not only the theology of an incarnation which would anticipate the event of redemption and make the suffering and death of Jesus a mere appendix. The decisive element in Christology is that it is a reflection on this history of suffering and death which constitutes the central event of salvation, a reflection on the death and resurrection of Jesus whence we can look backwards to the beginning of the incarnation and forwards to the final consummation of all things. At the cross alone do we perceive the ultimate depth and the final seriousness of what occurred in the man Jesus and of its meaning for God himself: the suffering of Christ is the suffering of God and the death of Christ is the death of God. The latter proposition, however, can only be understood aright in the context of the statement that the resurrection of Christ is the resurrection of God.

2. We can extend the train of thought which we have pursued with respect to the possibility of God and apply it to the classical divine predicates. In our continued attempt to advance by consistently thinking through classical Christology in this direction, we may echo Excursus III by presenting the following account of the inner *Dialectic of the Attributes of God*.

It is possible, in the spirit of Greek metaphysics, to argue *a posteriori* from the world to God (*per modum affirmationis, negationis et supereminentiae*, as this method later came to be called) and then it can be said that God is God, that is, that he is one and simple, immutable and immeasurable, omnipresent, omniscient and almighty, eternal, spiritual and good. He is indeed *the* Simple, Infinite, Immutable, Immeasurable, Omnipresent, Omniscient, Almighty and Eternal, the Spirit and the Highest Good. He therefore is absolute perfection and needs no one and nothing, neither man nor the world which he has made. God is God. He needs nothing.

But is this understanding of God the whole truth? Or do we perhaps once again ask too much of philosophy by expecting it to pass definitive judgments here? How must the Christian theologian, as one who continues to look in terms of Christ at the God who 'was in Christ' and who 'was made flesh' in him, speak of God? Those Graeco-Christian metaphysical statements do not simply meet with denial when examined from the perspective of Christology. Even so, when looked at in these terms they do appear to be 'interwoven' with other factors in an unprecedented way. What is the concrete meaning of the statements that God identifies himself with this man and that he reveals himself in the 'flesh'? The Christ-event obliges us to formulate these statements as follows: the Perfect appears imperfect, the Simple compound, the Infinite finite, the Immutable mutable, the Immeasurable measurable, the Omnipresent here and not there, the Omniscient ignorant, the Almighty powerless, the Eternal temporal, the Spirit material and – to come to the climax of the paradox – the Highest Good seems to have 'been made a curse' (Gal. 3:13) and the Most Holy to have 'been made sin' (II Cor. 5:21).

This, then is how God appears when he identifies himself with man. But as Cyril of Alexandria constantly reiterated, God does not appear in this way as he is in himself but σαρκί, that is, through the flesh, in man. Even so, he still appears as very God. Man's salvation is entirely dependent on the fact that God himself does not hold aloof from this history and that it is God himself and not just a man who takes the stage in this man. Classical Christology gives us every incentive to go on devoting consistent thought here as well, and it urges us to avoid the trap of bypassing Christ in order to dream up a more exalted, pure and absolute God. The true, genuinely living and absolute God has shown who he really is in Christ. And it is in what he has *done* that he has shown who he really is. He did not do this under compulsion from another or under pressure from himself, not because he could not do otherwise or because it was rendered necessary by the dialectic of the Idea. How could such a course of action be necessary, bearing in mind that he is God? He did it because he willed to do so in perfect freedom and for man's sake.

We thus come to a history of great contrasts and antitheses. It is a deadly history, but a history of life because in this man we deal at the same time with God. This is a life which ends in death and in which the one in whom and with whom God was present appears to be forsaken by God, his unity with God thus seeming to have been severed: 'My God, my God, why hast thou forsaken me?' (Mk. 15:34). The man in whom God's finite rule seemed to have broken in comes to grief and dies, and God comes to grief and dies with him, becoming entangled in self-contradiction for the sake of godless humanity. But precisely because the death of this God-forsaken man at the same time involves the death of God, and because (to adapt Paul's phrase) the death of God is more lively than the life of people, for the believer this death is the death of death, new life comes from this death, sunrise from this sunset and victory from this defeat. What then is *ultimately* revealed in the cross, which in virtue of God's deed includes resurrection? Is God's enduring powerlessness disclosed in Christ's powerlessness? Is God bound to time because Jesus existed in time? Is God's blundering foolishness manifested in Jesus' foolishness and God's irrevocable death in Christ's death? If such were the case, then God would not be God. The true state of things is rather set forth in Luther's famous saying that God is revealed hidden under his opposite (*absconditas Dei sub contrario*). The resurrection is both hidden from and divulged to the believer in the cross. God discloses his spirituality confined in the flesh, his vastness in limitation, his eternity in temporality, his omnipresence in being here, his immutability in growth, his infinity in privation and his omniscience in silence. He reveals his omnipotence hidden in powerlessness, his simplicity in being poured out, his perfection in suffering, his righteousness in humiliation, indeed his holiness in the curse of sin, truth in condemnation, wisdom in foolishness and life in death. While it is true that God displays his humanity and fellow humanity in humanity, he does not thereby reveal his non-divinity but rather the deepest divinity of his Godhead. An 'astonishing exchange' (*admirabile commercium*), as theology put it early on.

By revealing his divinity in Christ not simply in the *doxa* of the 'form of God' (Phil. 2:6) but in the human *kenosis* of the 'form of a servant' (2:7), God manifested at the same time the abundance of his grace: 'but where sin increased, grace abounded all the more' (Rom. 5:20), and that 'by one man's obedience' (5:19). It was not simply in a mighty deed performed in his glory as creator, in which as the giver of life he could retain his own life, that God showed his greatest love, but rather in the self-sacrifice of the Son which became the self-sacrifice of the Father. For '[g]reater love has no man than this, that a man lay down his life for his friends' (Jn. 15:13). And the meaning of this for God himself is that 'God so loved the world that he gave his only-begotten Son ...' (Jn. 3:16). God was in fact able to give no more earnest, but also no more powerful confirmation of the love which is his essence than by the Father sacrificing the Son and the Son sacrificing himself. Faith here stands before the ultimate depth of God's love for man. Nowhere could the Eternal reveal his eternity more abundantly than in a temporal beginning, his omniscience more abundantly than in silence, and his omnipotence and wisdom more abundantly than in the powerlessness and foolishness of the cross. Nowhere could he display his lordship more abundantly than in servitude or his life more abundantly than in death. Indeed he could reveal his holiness nowhere more abundantly than in the sinner's shame and his divinity nowhere more abundantly than in this humanity and godlessness. For what concretely took place in the historical life, suffering and death is revealed to faith in the light of the consummation and future which began with Christ's

450

death and new life. That is, in the humiliation of the Son God did not reveal his lowliness, but his majesty, the superabundance of his majesty; in renunciation not his poverty, but the superabundance of his wealth; in the Godforsakenness of the cross not godlessness, but the superabundance of his inalienable divinity; in the death as a sinner not sin, but the superabundance of grace; and in disappearance not his transitoriness, but the superabundance of his presence as future.

Greek metaphysics was not aware of such a possibility. Its very starting-point would incline it to deny it. Indeed, the very possibility of an incarnation was bound to strike Greek metaphysics as indicative of a lack of divinity. In terms of God's revelation in Christ, however, it may be said that God is able to identify himself with a specific instance of suffering and death under Pontius Pilate precisely because he is not just any reality but purest reality, not just any *actus* but *actus purissimus*. He can afford a relativisation of this kind precisely because he is not just any Absolute but *absolutissimus*. It is permissible for him to enter into this wretchedness and humanity precisely because he is not just any vulgar deity or abstract philosophical God, but the true living God of the Old and New Testaments. He does this without abandonment or loss of self, his purpose being to confirm and reveal himself for the benefit of humankind. Only an *actus purissimus* of this kind has the power and ability to pour itself unexpectedly even into non-being, to bestow itself totally, without merit on the part of the recipient and without losing itself irrevocably, and to give itself into death without abandoning itself in death. Because God is an infinitely perfect being in himself, he was able to show himself in a state of infinite imperfection in man. The living God of the Old and New Testaments actually does what no abstract God (not even an abstract Absolute or an abstract *actus purus*) may deign to do lest his divinity be impaired. For Greek metaphysics was right in thinking that such a God would have good cause to fear a plunge into death from his transcendent pedestal. Thus 'the Godhead' was manifested 'bodily' in the depths of the flesh and not in a God who dwells in a spurious sublimity; and the πλήρωμα, the fullness of the Godhead, was revealed in the 'emptying' of his κένωσις (cf. Phil. 2:5-11; Col. 2:9).

Even this humiliation of God is already announced in the Old Testament when Yahweh constantly follows his people into all the lowly details of their lives, when nothing is too much trouble for him for the sake of his people, and when he as God is more human than men and women for the purpose of winning them for himself. The notion of a vicarious mediator is indeed contained in the Old Testament, being outlined in the Deuteronomist's picture of Moses and in the prophecy of the suffering and death of the Servant of God. Yet against this picture can be set other statements 'which express the idea that it was Jahweh himself who was "wearied" by his people (Isa. 7:13)

451

and who must "carry" the burden of his people's leadership (Isa. 43:3f). Oddly enough it is Deutero-Isaiah, the author of the Servant Songs, who also speaks in bold anthropomorphic terms of the vexation with which Israel burdened her God. What he says of the toil and trouble which the sin of his people gave Jahweh suggests the idea of a different Servant of God, the idea that God himself was to become the Servant for this people.'[51]

What occurs in Jesus in the New Testament does not take place of necessity, anymore than what occurs in the Old Testament, but out of unmerited grace: 'for us and for our salvation'.[52] Nor did this event occur to enrich God, but ourselves: 'Though he was rich, yet for your sake he became poor, so that by his poverty you might become rich' (II Cor. 8:9). None of this could be said of the graceless Absolute of metaphysics. It is not the case that the absolute God is *obliged* to act thus because it lies in his nature to do so. Nor is it the case that the absolute God is *unable* to act thus because it would contradict his nature to do so. What God does out of grace he does neither as a consequence of his rational nature nor in opposition to his rational nature, but he is nevertheless 'not a God of confusion but of peace' (I Cor. 14:33). God's stooping down to man in grace does not contradict his nature but is in keeping with it, yet he is not obliged to be in keeping with it: 'he acts neither on account of his nature nor against his nature, but in keeping with his nature'.[53] God is not *forced,* but he is able to do what he does in history; and he has a power and ability to perform these acts which are rooted in his nature. The nature of the living God is a nature which is capable of self-humiliation, even though not compelled to take this path, a nature which contains within itself the power for gracious self-externalisation.

The living Christian God is therefore a God who does not exclude but includes his antithesis. This quality does not, as Greek metaphysics would be bound to suppose, indicate any deficiency in God's nature, nor should it be understood as but an initial stage of his being to be perfected in a process of self-development. Rather, as a gracious power and a positive 'possibility' this facet of God's nature pertains to his full reality from the very outset. To express this thought yet again in concrete terms, God's life includes death and his wisdom embraces foolishness; his lordship includes servitude and his eternity embraces time; his immeasurability includes measurability and his infinity embraces finitude. The first term in all these pairs includes the second as a gracious positive 'possibility' and power. In the light of a consistent classical Christology this is the good dialectic of the divine attributes, a

---

[51]Gerhard von Rad: *Old Testament Theology* (Edinburgh and London, 1965) II, 404.
[52]*propter nos homines et propter nostram salutem.*
[53]*agit nec propter naturam, nec contra naturam, sed secundum naturam.*

dialectic which graciously includes as antithesis even finite and non-divine reality, resolving it in the divine superabundance which appears, however, as hidden under its opposite (*absconditas sub contrario*). We may indeed go further and speak of a goodness which, in the gracious and redemptive divine 'carrying', includes evil; a holiness, which in God's gracious and forgiving act of taking it on himself, includes sin; and a love, which in God's gracious and reconciling self-sacrifice, includes hatred. This dialectic of the divine attributes is not only good but at the same time makes good by embracing not just the non-divine and finite but even the anti-divine and futile (*nichtig*), sublating it in the divine superabundance as something which has been reversed into a 'happy fault' (*felix culpa*).

Thus in the light of classical Christology, God's nature appears from his way with the world or, as the ancients were fond of saying, *theologia* from the *oikonomia*. It is his concrete and not his abstract nature which is perceived on this way, a nature which must not ultimately remain ambiguous like the negative or positive divine attributes which metaphysics deduced by *a posteriori* reasoning, but a nature which is made perspicuous precisely through discord and strife. This, then, is the living God of the Old and New Testaments: infinitely exalted above all antitheses, in his abundant grace he includes all antitheses within himself in a dialectic which we may term the all-surmounting dialectic of grace. Thus this God, with whom being and action are congruous, shows himself in his *whole* nature and in his *every* attribute to be quite simply a mystery and paradox which no human categories or predicates can contain or define. We can plainly discern in him the mark of true divinity which was enuciated already by Nicholas of Cusa, the *coincidentia oppositorum* before which man's greatest knowledge can only be *docta ignorantia*.

3. If an undreamt-of *vitality* in the being of God was brought to our attention in the last section, then it might be useful now, in a third parallel train of thought linking up with Excursus IV, to give separate treatment to the principal *aporia* which forms the background both to the specific problem of the divine ἀπάθεια and to the general problem of the rigid divine predicates, namely the question of the *immutability of God and his involvement in becoming*. Our purpose here is to think these problems through as they work themselves out in classical Christology.

As far as Greek metaphysics was concerned, God's knowing or loving the world would already imply deficiency in the Godhead. The ancients therefore felt obliged to steer clear of ascribing to the Godhead any knowledge or love of anything other than itself. For many, even life in God would involve deficiency, therefore the predicate of life was widely denied him. Becoming, though, was almost universally regarded as an even more certain indication of deficiency, so that becoming could under no circumstances be predicated of the Godhead.

In terms of Greek metaphysics, *a posteriori* argument from the changeable world *per viam negationis, affirmationis et supereminentiae* must lead us to say that God *is*. He does not need to recover what he is, nor does he need to reach out to what he is not, for God does not need a process of realisation, self-becoming or involvement in the world. In God there is no deficiency and no unfulfilment, no transitoriness and no decay, nor desire and no striving after a goal. God is the infinite, imperishable, serene and eternal fullness, devoid of all deficiency and immutably and constantly faithful to himself. God therefore *is* and needs to become neither himself nor anything else.

These statements will not meet with outright denial even when judged in terms of the mode of thought advocated in these pages. We may, however, broach the question whether they represent the complete and final truth that has been vouchsafed to us. Once again it may be to ask too much of philosophy to expect it to say something other than this. But what should the Christian theologian, as one who looks in terms of Christ at the God who 'was in Christ' and 'was made flesh' in him, say of this metaphysical God? What would be the result of classical Christology's reflection on its own presuppositions here? Classical Christology laid great emphasis on the event of the incarnation and wished to understand it in terms of Greek metaphysics; in principle, as we have already stated, an alternative christological starting-point is possible. Now, according to this Christology, God identifies himself with this one man in such a way that the divine Logos *becomes* flesh and the Son of God *becomes* man. One can indeed say that he does not become himself; for the one who lives in an immutable fullness of perfection does not need to participate in becoming for the sake of his own self. Even so, he himself does become man in his Lord and Son, he does become the other in the other. By renouncing himself he brings the other to the level of his own reality, and by making the other his own in this way he becomes the other through self-externalisation. We are therefore bound to say that the one who is immutable in himself changes. Or ought he in fact not to have become? Ought nothing now to have happened to him? Ought he simply to have remained what and how he had always been? Was the incarnation then a mere illusion, since God's being adamantly refuses to countenance becoming? As far as Greek metaphysics is concerned it is monstrous to echo the creed by saying that 'transcendent being came down from heaven' (*ens transcendens – descendit de caelis*). 'The Son . . . came down from the Father . . . , though he never ceased to be with the Father . . . ; nor did he lose, what he was,

454

but *he began to be, what he was not*; in such a way, however, that he is perfect in his own nature and true in our nature'. [54]

Should not God's transcendence, immutability and unchangeability be subjected to a thoroughgoing reinterpretation? May we continue to interpret these concepts in isolated static terms instead of radically correcting them in terms of God's gracious activity? We are not concerned to provoke a decision for a philosophy of becoming against a philosophy of being. Yet, however we explain becoming as such and becoming as it refers to the divine, the necessity of God's becoming man according to classical Christology can never be demonstrated or deduced. God is not compelled to externalise himself in his Word and Son because either a world-historical hour or his own divine hour has struck; but he does so – as we can never sufficiently emphasise – in virtue of his free grace. Thus he does not engage in motion because he is *in potentia,* he does not participate in change because he is in need, and he is not involved in becoming because he seems imperfect. A faith of this kind would turn God into a pallid imitation of human wretchedness. If we wish to think christologically in the categories of Greek metaphysics, then we ought rather to say: precisely because God is *actus purus,* an abundant fullness devoid of wants and an immutable perfection, precisely because he is the exalted God and not a creature, he can enter into worldly change without surrendering his immutable divine perfection and can afford this descent into the depths which the world regards as a godless act without perishing miserably in the event of becoming different. God is under no obligation to do this, but he is able to do it. And although he is not obliged to do it, he wills to do it out of the extravagant abundance of his gracious love which intentionally identifies itself with man and his fate in this world.

Thus what is gratuitously affirmed of an abstract metaphysics' Absolute which knows no grace may not be gratuitously denied of the God who externalises himself in grace. This God is the God of the Fathers who has given a definitive and ultimately binding revelation of himself in Christ. It would be false speculation if this incarnation were to lead us to speculate about an incarnation *de jure*; for *de jure* God is under absolutely no obligation to become anything. And it would be an equally false mode of argument if we were to argue against a *de facto* incarnation; for *de facto* the Logos became man. This is a singular 'becoming' for which there is no ontological proof even in speculative perspective, no smooth transition from God's 'nature' to his

---

[54] *Fides Damasi (The Faith of Damasus)* ca. A.D. 500, *The Scources of Catholic Dogma,* tr. R. J. Deferrari, 16; cf. Denzinger-Schonmtzer: *Enchiridion Symbolorum,* 39: '*descendit a Patre, qui nunquam desiit esse cum Patre . . . , nec amisit, quod erat, sed coepit esse, quod non erat; ita tamen, ut perfectus in suis sit et verus in nostris.*'

being and doing, no logical inference from possibility to actuality.[55] Faith alone can attempt to explain the essence of the matter on the basis of God's own way. Because God in the Logos truly became man and because he is 'not a God of confusion but of peace' (I Cor. 14:33), faith is able to explain that this singular 'becoming' on God's part occurs not in unfaithfulness but in fidelity to himself and his nature. In the genesis and kenosis involved in becoming man God neither loses nor gains himself, but rather confirms and reveals himself as the one who he is. God sacrifices but does not discard himself in this singular 'becoming'. His becoming involves neither loss nor gain for his Godhead; rather, it takes place in the power of his Godhead. His singular act of becoming man is not a consequence of his being, nor does it run counter to his being; rather, it is in accordance with his nature. His being is so infinitely exalted as to endure this becoming, so that it both can and actually does become. In this sense God's factual becoming, which rests on his most free grace, is based on his divine nature. In its glorious freedom God's immutable and transcendent nature contains the 'possibility' of becoming. 'Possibility' here is not meant in the sense of unfulfilment or potentiality, but of power, superabundance and *omni-potentia*. God's being is in becoming.

We have briefly covered three lines of thought and have circled in a threefold inward movement in order to define more precisely the subject-matter of this entire section, namely *the historicity of God*. We have sought to explain this historicity of God from within the framework of traditional theology by attempting to draw the consequences from classical Christology's concept of God determined, as it was, by Greek metaphysics. To put it in a nutshell, the end result of this process is bound to be the 'sublation' of this metaphysical concept of God.

It may be freely admitted that the consequences of this rethinking reach far beyond the confines of classical Christology. Even so, in sounding out the possibilities latent in classical Christology we are aware of thinking in a direction which cannot be dismissed as a wrong turn taken by a solitary and perhaps lost hiker, at least in that many significant representatives of contemporary Catholic and Protestant theology are thinking along these very lines with greater or less consistency and lucidity. In Excursus V we intend to back up what has been said here by listing those theologians who have stimulated and confirmed us in our endeavour.[56]

It is of greater importance within our general frame of reference that in this rethinking we have manifestly walked in *Hegel's* footsteps. While the trains of

---

[55]*illatio a posse ad esse.*
[56]cf. Excursus V: Recents Attempts at a Solution of the Old Problems.

thought developed from classical Christology clearly led away from the Greek metaphysical concept of God, which proved too static o transcendent, they led at the same time toward Hegel's concept of God. The dialectical dynamism of the latter is manifestly better suited to express what must be stated by a classical Christology which has been thought through to the end.

This by no means implies a renewal of Hegel's *system*. For it has been our intention in all phases of this presentation to make it unmistakably plain that contemporary thought can under no circumstances go back on the universal criticism levelled by both Christians and non-Christians against Hegel's monism of Spirit, which is the very foundation of his system. Now Hegel certainly took cognisance of the difference between finite and infinite Spirit, between God and man, but he sought to sublate it in the absolute knowledge of absolute Spirit. After the unanimous criticism directed at Hegel on this point, however, the difference has been shown to be beyond the possibility of sublation. And we saw that theological criticism can only intensify this philosophical criticism. Thus our task is to counter a monistic dialectic of being in speculative necessity and an equally monistic dialectic of cognition in speculative knowledge (ontic and noetic-ethical perspectives tally with each other) by specifying theologically the difference, not just the neutral contrast between divine and human nature, but the sharp antithesis between the gracious and benevolent God and guilty and sinful man, between divine revelation and human unbelief.[57]

We shall do well not to emulate Hegel's assertion of speculative necessity against the 'contingency' of free grace and of speculative knowledge against the 'outwardness' of a faith directed to Another than ourselves. It is wiser instead to cling for the sake of both God and man to the irreversible divinity of God and humanity of man, thus refraining from sublating religion in a philosophy of identity. In this case we may recognise just how right Hegel was when, inspired by genuinely Christian motives, he attempted, as one who at once completed and overcame the Greek metaphysical concept of God, to take seriously the great themes of God's suffering, of dialectic in God and of God's involvement in becoming. He did so in a manner which has perhaps been equalled by no philosopher before or after him.

If we could now turn back to the beginning armed with the insights painfully gained during this study, then our whole exposition of Hegel's thought in general and of his conception of the Absolute in particular might well appear in another and more positive light. There are many statements which we might now be able to hear with different ears. A few brief quotations, starting with a handful from the *Phenomenology of Spirit*, the

---

[57]cf. esp. ch. 3, 6; 5, 4; 6, 2, 4, 6; 7, 6.

work which heralded at once Hegel's original intentions and the mature form of his thought, will make clear how the following notions can be better explained in terms of Hegel's philosophy than in terms of the Greek metaphysical concept of God:

1. The *suffering* of God: 'Thus the life of God and divine cognition may well be spoken of as a disporting of Love with itself; but this idea sinks into mere edification, and even insipidity, if it lacks the seriousness, the suffering, the patience, and the labour of the negative' (*PS*, 10).

2. The *dialectic* within God himself: 'The absolute Being which exists as an actual self-consciousness seems to have come down from its eternal simplicity, but by thus *coming down* it has in fact attained for the first time to its own highest essence . . . Thus the lowest is at the same time the highest; the revealed which has come forth wholly on to the *surface* is precisely therein the most *profound*. That the supreme being is seen, heard etc. as an immediately present self-consciousness, this therefore is indeed the consummation of its Notion; and through this consummation that Being is immediately *present qua* supreme Being' (*PS*, 460).

3. God's involvement in *becoming*: '*In itself*, that life is indeed one of untroubled equality and unity with itself, for which otherness and alienation and the overcoming of alienation are not serious matters. But this *in-itself* is abstract universality, in which the nature of the divine life *to be for itself*, and so too the self-movement of the form, are altogether left out of account' (*PS*, 10).

Hegel's late lectures on the philosophy of religion elaborate on these very motifs, which are presented on the level of religion in the fate of Christ. The significance of this 'monstrous and appalling idea' (XIV, 158) of the death of Christ is that it involves a 'divine history' (XIV, 164) and an 'externalisation of the divine' (XIV, 157), and 'the significance of history is that it is the history of God' (XIV, 166). That is to say 'that the negative, i.e. what is human, finite, frail and weak, is itself a divine moment, that it exists within God himself, that finitude, the negative and being-other do not exist outside God and do not hinder unity with God in virtue of their being-other. Being-other and the negative are known as a moment of the divine nature itself. The highest idea of Spirit is contained in this thought. In this way the outward and negative turns into the inward. On the one hand, the death [of Christ] means the stripping off of the human factor and the re-emergence of his divine glory; it is the stripping off of the human and negative. At the same time, however, this death is also itself the negative, the furthest extreme of what people *qua* natural beings are exposed to: this is therefore God himself' (XIV, 172; cf. 157f*).

Thus the publicly enacted death on the gallows of the cross, the 'civil disgrace . . . which is the basest thing we can imagine' is in a revolutionary

458

fashion turned into the most exalted thing we can imagine! The 'symbol of disgrace' turns into the 'banner whose positive content is at the same time the kingdom of God' (XIV, 161f*). 'God has died, God is dead – this is the most appalling thought, that everything eternal and true does not exist, that negation itself exists in God. Bound up with this are the most intense sorrow, the feeling of the complete absence of salvation and the surrender of everything of a higher order. Yet the course of things does not grind to a halt here, but a reversal comes about: God preserves himself in this process and the latter is but the death of death. God arises to life again, and [the negative] thus changes into its opposite' (XIV, 167; cf. 162-164*).

We repeat that all this does not mean that we intend to adopt Hegel's system, that is, the monism of Spirit with its ontic and noetic complusion. Nor do we intend simply to take the eclectic path of collecting and digesting individual elements of Hegel's thought, a procedure which both philosophers and theologians have often been content to follow. On the contrary, as was announced at the beginning of this chapter, we have attempted to 'penetrate the opponent's stronghold' and, regarding the central question of his theology and equally of the Christian revelation, 'to meet him on his own ground' (*SL*, 581). As Karl Barth asks concerning the theology which rejected Hegel, '[w]ho knows whether it was not in fact the *genuinely* theological element in Hegel which made it shrink back?' In this sense there might perhaps after all be some truth in the enigmatic final sentence with which Barth brings his moving account and criticism of Hegel's philosophy to a close, speaking of him 'as a great problem and a great disappointment, but perhaps also a great promise'.[58]

Where, after all that has been stated in this book, might we discern this promise? Set in the *aporia* between the metaphysical and the biblical conceptions of God, Hegel might well be better suited than anyone for the task of ensuring that our contemporary understanding of God does not lapse into either a primitive anthropomorphic biblicism or an (only seemingly superior) abstract Hellenism. More positively, Hegel might well help theology to avoid either cheaply and superficially harmonising the 'God of the Fathers and of Jesus Christ' with the 'God of the philosophers' (according to the wont of apologists and scholastics old and new) or else simply dissociating the two (according to the practice of Enlightenment philosophers and biblicistic theologians). Rather, his thought might prompt theology to *sublate* the 'God of the philosophers' in the 'God of the Fathers and of Jesus Christ' in the best Hegelian sense of the word, that is, negative, positive and supereminent sublation.

---

[58] *Protestant Theology in the Nineteenth Century*, 421.

By adopting this tactic it might prove possible to combine serious consideration *both* of the modern developments in our understanding of God (which have constantly been highlighted in this study) *and* of the decisive features of the biblical understanding of God in a new understanding of the *historicity* of God, which would show itself to the world and to men and women as primordial historicity and power over history. As the living God, by way of contrast with a God who exists in an unhistorical mode of being, God both has a history and himself creates history. Even if all the implications of and underlying reasons for this statement cannot be exhaustively stated within the framework of these prolegomena, it has perhaps become clear that our reflections are on the way to achieving an understanding of God which neither biblicistically disregards the perceptions of Greek metaphysics nor postulates the sort of metaphysical God who would be bound to earn Heidegger's reproach: 'One can neither pray nor sacrifice to this God. Man cannot fall to his knees in awe before the *causa sui,* nor can he make music and dance before him'.[59] In this way the very possibility of a future Christology can be shown to be conditional on the historicity of God. We aim to make this still clearer in the next section.

3. The Historicity of Jesus

Hegel's 'self-movement of the Notion was nevertheless the shrpest critique to have been levelled up to that time at Platonism or at the idea that nature (*Wesen*) is unchangeable, albeit a critique that itself originated within the Idealist camp. It criticised Platonism by abrogating (*aufheben*) the unchangeability of the Ideas and by introducing into them the possibility of becoming different, the dimension of time replacing that of timelessness.'[60] Now we noticed in our comparison of Hegel's understanding of absolute Spirit with classical Christology that there is the greatest propinquity between the problems which arise in connection with his philosophy and those which arise in connection with Christian theology. Hegel's philosophical thought (albeit not his system of the monism of Spirit) thus showed itself to be fitted (at all events more so than Greek metaphysics) to assist the expression of that concern of both Old and New Testaments which can today be termed the historicity of God. As at once the condition and the possibility of future Christology, this concept will serve to introduce our final section. A tentative attempt will here be made at shedding light on this idea of the historicity of God.

---

[59] *Idenität und Differenz,* 70; ET *Identity and Difference,* 72.
[60] E. Block: *Subjekt-Objekt,* 388.

After all that has been said in these pages (it needs to be surveyed yet again at this juncture) Christology in the future will obviously not insist on a return to a pre-Hegelian conception of God. It may, without any infidelity to its biblical origin, take seriously (albeit, as we have demonstrated, in critical vein) everything which has happened to affect our understanding of God since Copernicus's revolution in physics and Kant's in metaphysics.[61] Such a Christology may join Hegel in leaving behind the naïve and anthropomorphic idea of One who dwells in a literal or spatial sense 'above' the world, from whom the Son of God 'descends' and to whom he 'ascends'. It may do likewise with respect to the notion, characteristic of the deism of the Enlightenment, of One who exists in a spiritual or metaphysical sense 'outside' the world in an extra-mundane beyond, who admittedly created the world but by and large leaves it to its own devices, and who interferes in the world against and beyond all natural laws only occasionally, supremely in the sending of the Son. And a future Christology may join Hegel in thinking in terms of a unified understanding of reality in which the world is not without God nor God without the world, but in which God is in this world and the world in this God. Even so, this is a God who constantly eludes all the limiting definitions of human imagination and thought, a God who ought not to be understood as a 'supreme Being' above, outside and beyond and yet at the same time also alongside and over against this world, so that ultimately he exists as a mere part of reality as a whole, as finite alongside finite, as an addendum standing in competition with the world. Rather it is a God who can be understood as the Infinite in the finite, as the Absolute in the relative, and as the ultimate reality in the heart of things, in man himself and in world history; as the inscrutable and inexhaustible first cause, origin and meaning of all that is, as the this-worldly and other-worldly One (*der Diesseitig-Jenseitige*) and as transcendence in immanence.

Yet a future Christology will join with Hegel afresh in taking for its starting-point the fact that this God, as such a *coincidentia oppositorum*, is not just a rigidly static impulse toward motion which, as an immutable being, leaves becoming to the world and to human persons, keeping his distance from the suffering and death of man in unshakeable apathy. On the contrary, as a living

---

[61]On the development of the new understanding of God cf. the Introduction and ch. 1, 1 (background history and Enlightenment); ch. 2, 3 (Kant); ch. 3, 1 (Kant, Lessing, Goethe); ch. 4, 1 (Fichte, Schelling); ch. 4, 3 (modern atheism); ch. 4, 5 (philosophy of life and becoming and the new understanding of the world, authority, society and this-worldliness); and finally the specific contribution of Hegel himself, especially from the *Phenomenology* onwards (ch. 5, 1-3 and esp. 4), in his systematics (ch. 6, 1-6) and across he whole expanse of his understanding of history (ch. 7, 1-5 and esp. 6).

God of the kind presupposed by every Christology he is involved in vital motion, existing without either losing or acquiring being, but as a God who shares in becoming precisely by applying and confirming his being: a God who as One involved in becoming is also involved in coming, and who *qua* God in this world is capable of externalisation in this world and prepared for suffering in and with this world and for commitment to and with humankind. As far as Christology is concerned, it is vital that as One who exists in history God can be understood as One who also acts, reveals and speaks in history.[62]

Even so, along with this understanding of God a future Christology will at the same time learn from Hegel the negative point that, although this God exists within a unified reality that does not admit of two worlds or spaces, it is nonetheless impermissible to equate him with the world in such a way that the reality of God might be reduced to and dissolved in the reality of the world and God's place thus be usurped by man. Hegel's philosophy begins by teaching us not to separate God from man and ends by teaching us not to confound them. Even though every unhistorical scheme that works in terms of the contrast between immanence and transcendence (or between this world and the hereafter, history and supra-history or world and supra-world) has afforded sufficient proof of its insufficiency, the concept of historicity and worldliness still should never be willing to sublate the difference between God and man. The upshot of any blurring of this difference would be the reduction of Christology to a topsy-turvy dialectic of a-cosmic pantheistic and atheistic pan-cosmic monism.[63]

Thus the historical and actual God, who in virtue of his primordial historicity and power over history, renders possible the historicity and worldliness of the world, is not in any simple sense manifest or transparent in the·world and history. That is, he cannot be unequivocally perceived or grasped or speculatively known through the world and history. This is not to deny outright the possibility of knowing God in the reality of the world. Nevertheless, all knowledge of God gained through the world and history remains ambiguous and any concept of God deduced from these sources remains indefinite. We must take seriously the experience of atheism in acknowledging that God's presence in the world and history is in the first instance a questionable presence, one which seems to give more indication of his absence than of his presence, one which does not bestow on man the redemptive Word but leaves him in a solitude of oppressive silence. To put it in a nutshell, it is not the *Deus revelatus* who manifests the divinity of God in

---

[62]cf. ch. 8, 2 and the Excursuses.
[63]cf. ch. 6, 2; 6,4.

the worldliness of the world, but the *Deus absconditus* who thereby seems to give the worldliness of the world every reason for godlessness.[64]

The God of the world and its history is unambiguously revealed as the God of Israel and as the God of Jesus Christ, in whom God's silence, absence and claim (*Anspruch*) become his Word, presence and address (*Zuspruch*), and who is therefore the place where haziness takes on sharp contours and uncertainty turns into certainty. Yet the shadow cast by the cross of the living One causes us to subject all these statements to the eschatological proviso of the consummation which will fulfil the revelatory process and which, notwithstanding the manifold evidence of the dawn of the kingdom, is still awaited as a future event. The effect of the cross and of the divine future definitively inaugurated by Jesus' resurrection to new life is thus not to confer matter of fact knowledge on man, but rather to challenge him to a trusting faith and, in virtue of this faith, to love, to response and responsibilty, to eschatological hope and to involvement in the world here and now.[65]

Now less than ever can this God of the Christian revelation, presupposed in a fresh way by the Christology of the future, be restricted to the territory of the Church. On the contrary, he is even now displaying his reality in the secularity of the world through the community of believers. Not identical with the events of nature and history, he is the Absolute present in all the relativities of the world and man. Not only does he not abolish (*aufheben*) the worldliness of the world and the independence of man: on the contrary, he establishes these things and precisely in the worldliness of the world opens up to men and women fresh possibilities for inner, personal encounter with himself. Now less than ever can this God be taken as a matter of tradition, as a self-evident ingredient of one's world-view or as an ideological cement reinforcing an unalterable social status quo. On the contrary, his demand is for personal appropriation of the faith of the Fathers and for trust and love on the part of nature, rational and enlightened man, his aim being to see man committed as his free partner and an authorised representative for his fellow man. This God does not simply provide comfort as a projection of man's selfish need for a hereafter, but rather, as the Wholly Other bringing total transformation, he points us to the here-and-now. He is no longer just a God of the gaps, invoked when human enquiry and science run out of steam, and therefore increasingly superfluous as humankind makes more intellectual progress. He is no longer an entity that dispossesses man of what is most truly his own, that causes him to eke out a drowsy existence in this world in a state of pious passivity, an entity that is but a reflection of conscious-unconscious human anxieties and

---

[64]cf. ch. 4, 4.
[65]cf. ch. 3, 6; 5, 4; 6, 6; 7, 6.

longings, an opium for escaping reality and social responsibility, and therefore increasingly superfluous on the emotional level as man becomes progressively more human. On the contrary, this God is a God who is absolutely relevant to us in all the relativities of human life and common humanity, who, as the reality which upholds, preserves and embraces all things, is both infinitely remote from the superficial life of man and yet nearer to man's heart than he is to himself, and who is thus able to confer breadth, depth and ultimate meaning on the life of man and of humanity by liberating man for prayer, intercession and praise, for sacrifice and for all-embracing love. Thus this God does not exist behind the flux of history but is known as the God of history. Precisely as God of the beginning is he the God of the end, precisely as alpha is he the omega, and precisely as the creatively primordial One is he also the eschatologically future One, the coming One whom man and humankind, actively progressing in hope, may await as the One who will make all things new and who therefore already here and now demands that man and humankind rethink and return from the past to the future of the coming kingdom in which God will not only be in all, but will be all in all.[66]

This then is how the 'God of the Fathers and of Jesus Christ' appears when refracted through the experiences not just of the Hellenistic but also of the modern era. While a 'God of the philosophers and scholars' cannot be made to talk, neither can such a deity be rendered speechless; moreover, the good insights gained by the 'philosophers and scholars' of a new age enable him to be *understood* afresh, indeed perhaps even more originally than was possible with the insights of the Hellenistic period. Even the faith of the present day cannot get by without concepts, ideas, images and symbols; and it is precisely a post-Hegelian Christian understanding of God that will neither look down on images and symbols out of intellectual snobbery nor renounce concepts and ideas under the influence of agnosticism or mysticism. Least of all will it subordinate the primary witness of the original Christian faith to other Christian or secular traditions. The only thing that a Christian theology and proclamation bound to the original Christian witness should remember is that concepts, ideas, images and symbols of God may come and go, emerge and subside, just as the psalm says with reference even to the earth and the heavens: 'They will perish, but thou dost endure; they will all wear out like a garment. Thou changest them like raiment, and they pass away; but thou art the same, and thy years have no end' (Ps. 102:26f). Concepts, ideas, images and symbols of God change and fade away, but he himself remains the same. Faith likewise remains the same insofar as it cleaves to God alone amidst all

66cf. ch. 4, 5; 7, 6.

the change and fluctuation of concepts, ideas, images and symbols. To say this involves no neglect of tradition which, as should have been demonstrated in this study, both can and must assist in preserving the continuity and identity of the faith. Furthermore, tradition has much more of significance to offer for our contemporary understanding of God, and perhaps also for the current discussion of the problem of transcendence and immanence, than does many a superficial book on the question of God. And to this extent may all that has been said in this study about a post-Hegelian historical understanding of God be taken as the author intends it, that is, not in the least as a piece of demolition but as a modest experiment in the most solemn sense of the word, undertaken for the greater glory of God.[67]

It is imperative at this juncture to proceed yet further. If we aim in our understanding of God and hence also in Christology to plead resolutely for 'No going back behind Hegel', this as we have constantly stressed, does not mean 'No going beyond Hegel'. If we do not join the right-wing Hegelians in turning Hegel into the terminus of the history of thought beyond which there is no future, then precisely in the field of Christology we shall go beyond all that has been said thus far in forging a post-Hegelian link between the slogans 'No going back behind Hegel' and 'No going back behind Strauss'.

This link may astonish those who are only able to see in David Friedrich Strauss (the acquaintance of whose christological predecessors, especially Semler, Reimarus and Lessing, we have already made in the Introduction) one who in theological terms was a left-wing Hegelian (if not the very Antichrist!), and in historical terms an outright anti-Hegelian. Yet quite apart from the fact that these predicates stand in urgent need of precise definition, it is obvious that Strauss decisively combined the question of the historicity of *God* in the Hegelian-speculative sense with that of the historicity of *Jesus* in the historico-critical sense, so that the latter has since become one of the great, still unresolved issues of theology in the nineteenth and twentieth centuries. And if the primary *philosophical* source of the contemporary fashionable word 'historicity' has been shown to be Hegel's philosophy (and, indeed, its christological context), then the primary *theological* source is patently the research into the life of Jesus (*Leben-Jesu-Forschung*) which Strauss initiated for the nineteenth and twentieth centuries.

Here too the *fact* of 'historicity' was thought of long before the *word* itself came on the scene. Even so, it is conspicuous how at the same time as the philosophical concept of historicity was being developed in the thought of

---

[67]*ad maiorem Dei gloriam.*

Dilthey and York the same term was cropping up in Protestant theology in the sense of historical facticity (the historical by contrast to what is mythical, fictional and legendary); indeed, strictly speaking the concept of historicity was always related 'to a single problem, namely to the *historicity of Jesus Christ,* which became a critical issue for the modern history of religion and for biblical scholarship'.[68] The problem had become a burning one when David Friedrich Strauss applied the concept of myth to the gospels immediately after Hegel's death, and by the turn of the twentieth century it had reached a peak with renewed vigour, in liberal research into the life of Jesus. In 1892 Martin Kähler had written his justly celebrated essay with the enigmatic title *The So-called Historical Jesus and the Historic, Biblical Christ,* and then in 1909 the word historicity abruptly became 'a vogue word for the first time in German intellectual history'[69] in the controversy surrounding Arthur Drews's *Christusmythe,* a book which radicalised Strauss's position and created a sensation amongst the entire educated public in Germany. The first sentence of Drews's Foreword runs as follows: 'Since David Friedrich Strauss in his *Life of Jesus* (1835 to 1836) made the first pioneering attempt to explain the Gospel accounts and miracle stories in terms of myths and pious fiction, doubts about an historical Jesus have known no rest.'[70]

Thus the problem of the historicity of God, both in word and in fact, leads us to the problem of the historicity of *Jesus.* As the conclusively final step in our argument with Hegel we shall now attempt, against the backcloth of Strauss's dissociation of himself from Hegel, to round off our prolegomena to a future Christology with a brief contribution on the subject of the historicity of Jesus.

Closing the study in this way is meant to indicate that the theological argument with Hegel, understood as prolegomena to a future Christology, and especially what has been said here concerning the historicity of God, cannot be boiled down to an unhistorical repristination of classical Christology. In the immediately preceding pages we have clearly demonstrated the impossibility of such a course in view of the new understanding of the historicity of *God* to be gathered from Hegel. This impossibility will now be underlined by the new understanding of the historicity of *Jesus* to be learned from Strauss.

We have made every effort to display the potential of classical Christology, especially for our understanding of God, from the perspective of a fresh study of tradition, from that of the new contemporary christological projects,

[68]L. von Renthe-Fink: *Geschichtlichkeit,* 133.
[69]*op, cit.,* 133.
[70]Arthur Drews: *Die Christusmythe,* II (ET *The Christ Myth,* London, 1910).

and – finally and supremely – from that of Hegel himself.[71] Such considerations could go a long way toward affirming an awareness of a genuine continuity of Christian faith amidst all the discontinuity of theological solutions, and we have no intention of underplaying this factor in any way. At the same time, however, the impression should not be allowed to arise that the New Testament message of Jesus as the Christ can or may be expressed at the present day only with the aid of classical Christology or only in terms of the Chalcedonian doctrine of the two natures. The fresh attempts at solving christological issues to which allusion has been made already point far beyond Chalcedon, so that (to adopt a celebrated phrase of Karl Rahner) they tend to see the Definition of Chalcedon as more of a beginning than of an end. It would, moreover, be tantamount to carrying coals to Newcastle[72] or at any rate, with reference to Strauss, Ferdinand Christian Baur and what followed, to carrying sparrows to Tübingen,[73] if we should want to amass all the objections which have been somewhat monotonously urged again and again against the doctrine of the two natures since the Enlightenment and especially since the last century (Schleiermacher, Ritschl, Harnack, Schweitzer). It is therefore fitting to make only brief mention of the three roots from which stem the various objections to this doctrine:

1. With its terms and conceptions stamped by Hellenistic language and spirituality, the doctrine of the two natures is no longer understood *today* and is avoided wherever possible in practical proclamation.

Are such terms as hypostatic union, person, nature and consubstantiality still in any way accessible to people of the present day in their original meaning? For example, is it is still possible to employ the word 'nature' ($\theta \acute{v}\sigma \iota \varsigma$) meaningfully and to apply it universally for the purposes of the Church's proclamation when the contemporary use of language is borne in mind? Are there not better ways of describing the biblical figure of Jesus Christ than by asserting two 'natures' which must be thought of as somehow juxtaposed in one individual? Can both divine and human reality be subsumed under this one concept of 'nature'? Given the fact that divine and human reality are separated by an infinite qualitative distinction, is it admissible ontologically to coordinate them *de facto* from the very outset by applying one and the same concept to both, even if this is perhaps not explicitly intended?

2. The post-Chalcedonian history of doctrine bears witness that *even in*

---

[71]cf. 8, 2; Excursuses, I-IV and esp. V.

[72]lit. 'owls to Athens'.

[73]The author alludes to the diminutive form of the German *Spatz,* i.e. *Spätzle,* which in the Swabian dialect signifies both locally produced noodles and a term of endearment between sweethearts.

antiquity the doctrine of the two natures failed to resolve all difficulties: its sequel was the first great enduring schism within Christendom and it led to ever new logical *aporiae*.

According to the understanding of the non-Chalcedonian Orthodox Church, was not the idea of a personal union in two natures burdened with insoluble contradictions from the beginning? Can the person who shares in two natures really be understood as *one* individual? Can two intrinsically complete essential units ever form a unified whole? Is the vital unity of this one person upheld when, in the execution of Christology, either one nature is mixed with the other or, in the event of their remaining distinct, one (usually the divine nature) nevertheless outmanoeuvres the other and decisively determines the concrete image? Do we not have here the root of the constantly renewed struggles which broke out even after Chalcedon between unification and separation Christology, and of the permanently new bottlenecks and the permanently new endeavours to solve the problem?

3. Irrespective of whether it is seen as a falsification or distortion of the original New Testament message about Christ or, at the very least, as not the only or even best possible interpretation which may be put on it, the doctrine of the two natures is by no means identical with this original message.

An almost never-ending stream of concrete questions could be posed at this juncture. One would have to deal with the innumerable questions which historical research into the life of Jesus has set for classical Christology. We must return to these fundamental issues at a later stage.

Eschewing all dogmatic prejudice and all (equally dogmatic) antidogmatic emotion, a future Christology must sift these briefly listed fundamental objections anew in terms of the results attained in this study. The difficulties inherent in these objections are certainly not answered just by being stated: the questions at stake here are not simply rhetorical. Nor are these difficulties removed just by modifying the doctrine of the two natures, whether by the doctrine of the two states, a speculative theory of kenosis or a transcendentally established theory of incarnation. While these modifications do represent highly significant further developments within the system of the doctrine of the two natures, the question posed here concerns the *basic starting-point* of a systematic Christology.

Only a general answer can be given to this complex question within the framework of these prolegomena. What then is to be Christology's point of departure? It should not be disputed that we *can* start with the doctrine of the two natures, for this starting-point has its relative historical justification and was often the only real possibility for earlier epochs. But is it in principle the only possible starting-point? Given the cumulative force of the traditional difficulties, new historical experiences and the witness of the New Testament, are we not frankly obliged to start elsewhere, or at least to give serious consideration to a different approach? Chalcedon had indeed proceeded from the difference between divine and human nature in general, but had not Nicea thought much more in terms of the concrete unity of the historical man, Jesus? It is indeed possible to enquire about the realisation of the unity of God and man in Jesus and to understand the incarnation strictly as a unification and as the process of God's becoming man which is completed with the inception of the earthly existence of Jesus Christ. Would it not be equally possible, however, to proceed from the historicity and historical facticity of Jesus, from his historical Word, behaviour and fate, in order perhaps finally to understand from this vantage-point just how the reality of God is encountered in him?

The purpose of Christology is to explain what Jesus as the Christ means and is for contemporary man. But is this significance still so self-evident, indeed was it even so self-evident as far as the New Testament and especially the synoptic witnesses were concerned, that contemporary theology can simply proceed dogmatically from an established doctrine of the Trinity and presuppose the divinity of Jesus, i.e. the pre-existence of the Son, as a matter of course, so that it only remains to ask how this Logos who was pre-existent in the Trinity was able to assume and join to himself a human nature, in which process cross and resurrection must largely appear as little more than footnotes to the incarnation? Would it not be much more in keeping with both the New Testament witnesses and the historical thought of modern man to proceed from the man Jesus, his historical message and appearance, his life and fate and his historical reality and historical effect, in order to enquire about this man Jesus' relationship to God, about his unity with the Father? In short, is it not appropriate to eschew a Christology organised speculatively or dogmatically from above in favour of one worked out historically from below?

It is Hegel's own thought which impels us to state the issue in these terms. But it was David Friedrich Strauss who was responsible for the turn, immediately after Hegel's death, to the historicity of Jesus and consequently also for the turn from speculative Christology to historical research into the life of Jesus. With Strauss the split of Hegel's school into right and left became a fact. He was the first to give sharp expression to the thesis, which has gripped the attention of Christology right down to the present day, that there is a fundamental difference between the Jesus of history and the Christ of faith. In this he was concerned just as much with supplying a corrective to Hegel's speculative Christology as with the intricacies of the christological dogma itself. The relationship between Hegel and Strauss, we may add, is often oversimplified and even incorrectly presented.

Detailed treatment cannot be given here to the complex and in many ways contradictory personality and theological development of the theologian Strauss, who studied the Tübingen a generation after Hegel. Turning from supra-naturalism to Kant and thence to the philosophy of nature and finally via Schleiermacher to Hegel, he joined the staff of the Tübingen Seminary as *Repetent* a year after Hegel's death and in this capacity published the first volume of his *Life of Jesus Critically Examined* in 1835. By the time he issued the second volume in 1836, he had already been dismissed from his post. While at the time of his transition to Hegel he was able to preach and write in orthodox terms and even, paradoxically, to pen a prize-winning essay on the resurrection of the flesh for Tübingen's Faculty of Catholic Theology, he could drily observe in a letter of 8 February 1838 that 'I gave a fully convincing proof of the resurrection of the dead based on exegesis and natural philosophy, and while I was making the final point it dawned on me that there was nothing in the whole story'. With his *Life of Jesus,* however, the time for ambiguity was past. A vigorous rejection of his position ensued: in the appendix to his history of research into the life of Jesus, Albert Schweitzer lists a wealth of polemical treatises, most of which appeared independent of each other in the five years after the publication of Strauss's book. Forty-one of these items appeared under their author's name and nineteen anonymously, and Schweitzer's list takes no account of the unmanageable volume of essays which appeared in magazines etc.

The most penetrating account of Strauss's dazzling personality and theological work (let it be recalled that according to his own words an old scholar died off in him roughly every six years) would still be that of Karl Barth.[74] A. Schweitzer[75] and perhaps also E. Hirsch[76] unduly neglect the theological problems to concentrate too exclusively on Strauss's historico-critical side.

We must briefly take note of the following factors concerning the relationship between Hegel and Strauss and hence also the relationship between speculative Christology and historical research into the life Jesus:

1. Hegel's *Early Theological Writings,* especially his *Life of Jesus,*[77] together with the sections on the teaching of Jesus in his last lectures on the philosophy of religion,[78] show that the question of the historical Jesus was by no means foreign to him. Even so, the focus of Hegel's wider interests had tended increasingly to shift from the historical individual to the idea, to the realisation of the absolute Spirit in the appearance, death and resurrection of Jesus and consequently to speculative Christology.[79]

2. Strauss was certainly not investigating the question of the historical Jesus as a pure historian, as opposed to a speculative philosopher or theologian. He himself admitted that he was no historian and that his entire work originated

---

[74]*Protestant Theology in the Nineteenth Century,* 541-568; for the letter quoted above, see 546.
[75]*The Quest of the Historical Jesus,* 68-120.
[76]*Geschichte der neueren evangelischen Theologie* V, 492-518.
[77]Cf. ch. 2, 1-5, esp. 3.
[78]Cf. ch. 7, 4.
[79]Cf. ch. 5, 2-3; 6, 3; 7, 2-4.

in dogmatic interests. Even though he was more a passionate and shrewd dreamer and debater than a speculative thinker and constructive systematician, it is nevertheless patently obvious that in his historical examination of the life of Jesus, which was originally conceived as simply Part Two of a great three-volume work on Christology, Strauss both proceeded from and tended back in the direction of Hegel's speculative Christology. He pursued his historical criticism in the sense of Hegel's philosophy of history and religion and of its idea of the God-man. The qualifying factor was his conviction that the Idea does not pour out its fullness into a single historical individual, a point which his critical destruction of the history of Jesus was supposed to prove. He considered that humankind as such should accordingly take the place of the individual God-man, a view whose basis had already been supplied by the last part of Hegel's *Philosophy of Religion* and by his idea of universal Godmanhood.

Strauss was disposed to regard an enquiry into the mythical dimension of the gospels as occurring somewhere in between the opposing poles of the supra-natural exegesis of the ancient Church (represented in his own day in Ohlsen's commentary) and the new rationalist exegesis (especially that of H. E. G. Paulus): 'The exegesis of the ancient church set out from the double presupposition: first, that the Gospels contained a history, and secondly that this history was a supernatural one. Rationalism rejected the latter of these presuppositions, but only to cling the more tenaciously to the former, maintaining that these books present unadulterated, though only natural, history. Science cannot rest satisfied with this half-measure: the other presupposition also must be relinquished, and the inquiry must first be made whether in fact, and to what extent, the ground on which we stand in the Gospels is historical. This is the natural course of things, and thus far the appearance of a work like the present is not only justifiable, but even necessary.'[80]

Even though Strauss did not regard himself as an especially talented historian, yet he had the advantage over others of 'the internal liberation of the feelings and intellect' which 'the author early attained by means of philosophical studies'.[81] Given this philosophical foundation, Strauss had no fears for the dogmatic content and eternal truth of the Christian faith: 'The author is aware that the essence of the Christian faith is perfectly independent of his criticism. The supernatural birth of Christ, his miracles, his resurrection and ascension, remain eternal truths, whatever doubts may be cast on their reality as historical facts. The certainty of this can alone give calmness and dignity to our criticism, and distinguish it from the naturalistic criticism of the last century, the design of which was, with the historical fact, to subvert also the religious truth, and

---

[80] *The Life of Jesus Critically Examined* (tr. George Eliot, ed. Peter C. Hodgson, SCM, 1973), li (Preface to first edition); cf. the prior history of the mythical explanation from antiquity to the present in Strauss's Introduction, 39-92. The author has used the first edition of the *Leben Jesu*, and translations will be given from this edition in footnotes 83 to 90 below.
[81] *op. cit.*, lii.

which thus necessarily became frivolous. A dissertation at the close of the work will show that the dogmatic significance of the life of Jesus remains inviolate.'[82]

Already in *The Life of Jesus,* as subsequently happened in his *Doctrine of Faith* (1840-1841) and in his late work on *The Old and the New Faith* (1872), Strauss was found wanting as a systematician. The 'problem: to re-establish dogmatically that which has been destroyed critically',[83] which had originally been conceived as a large-scale Part Two and Part Three, was therefore dispatched briefly and above all negatively in an 'excursus' made up of a critique of dogmatic Christology presented in the form of a review which ranged from the orthodox system of the ancient Church and the challenges it faced via the Christology of rationalism, Kant and De Wette to the 'most recent philosophy' of 'speculative Christology'. Strauss gives a crisp and positive four page account of the latter, drawing on Hegel's *Phenomenology* and *Lectures on the Philosophy of Religion,* on Marheineke's *Dogmatics* and on Rosenkranz's *Encyclopaedia of Theological Sciences.*[84] Strauss concurs with the speculative Christology of the God-man, while making one radical correction which he labels as the 'key to the whole of Christology': 'In an individual, a God-man, the properties and functions which the church ascribes to Christ contradict themselves; in the idea of the race, they perfectly agree. Humanity is the union of the two natures – God became man, the infinite manifesting itself in the finite, and the finite spirit remembering its infinitude . . .'[85]

And what of Jesus? 'The subjective reason for the fact that the absolute content of Christology appears to be linked to the person and history of a single person is that by his personality and fate this individual became the occasion for the elevation of that content into the universal consciousness and that the spiritual level of the ancient world and indeed of the common people in every age is only able to contemplate the idea of humanity in the concrete figure of a specific individual.'[86] In those disrupted times this death of an individual who was revered as a divine emissary provoked 'the rapid formation of a belief in his revivification: *tua res agitur* was bound to occur to everyone.'[87] Thus mythologisation followed the death of Jesus: 'Just as the God of Plato formed the world by gazing on the Ideas, even so did the idea of humanity in its relationship to divinity hover unconsciously before the Church as it fashioned the image of its Christ under the impulse supplied by the person and fate of Jesus. Contemporary scholarship cannot continue for much longer to suppress its awareness that the relationship to just one individual pertains only to a provisional and popular form of this doctrine.'[88] Strauss's great work thus draws to a close with references to Schleiermacher and with some remarks on the preacher's dilemma, ending with a lengthy quotation from Hegel's *Lectures on the Philosphy of Religion,* according to which 'the sensual history of the individual . . . is simply the point of departure of the Spirit', a history which demands sublation and a 'going beyond sensual to absolute history' so that 'spiritual truth stands on its own ground'.[89] Hence Strauss's conclusion:

---

[82]*ibid.*
[83]*Leben Jesu* II, 686; ET, 757
[84]*op. cit.* II, 729-732; ET, 777f.
[85]*op. cit.* II, 734f; ET, 780.
[86]*op. cit.* II, 735f.
[87]*op. cit.* II, 736.
[88]*ibid.*
[89]*op. cit.* II, 737.

'Our age demands to be led in Christology to the idea in the fact, to the race in the individual: a theology which, in its doctrines on the Christ, stops short at him as an individual, is not properly a theology, but a homily.'[90]

3. There are three reasons why, although like Hegel he advocated a Christology from above, Strauss's influence led to a Christology from below. First, his whole presentation constitutes a thoroughgoing proof of the mutually refuting inconsistencies which abound in both the rationalist and the supranaturalist attempts to interpret the life of Jesus. Secondly, he followed Hegel's philosophy of religion in consistently applying the concept of myth not only to the beginning and end, but also to the whole life of Jesus. He thus explained the New Testament 'myths' as the result of early Christian ideas being vested in historical garb, a process which occurred in the unntentionally legend-producing consciousness of the early Church. Thirdly, at least in his early days when he stood under the influence of Hegel's speculative Christology, Strauss was uninterested in finding the historical kernel of the gospel accounts; indeed, he was basically uninterested in any kind of 'historical Jesus'. He alleged that there is a fundamental difference between the Christ of faith (the idea of the God-man) and the Jesus of history (the historical individual) and, finally, he substituted the idea of the unity of divine and human nature in humanity for the God-man Jesus Christ. All of these factors added up to an enormous challenge to historical scholarship to take a positive interest in Jesus' life, history, self-consciousness and person and a stimulus to carry out an examination of the life of Jesus of a kind which Strauss himself had completely neglected, that is, with the aid of literary and source criticism, the history of religions and the form-critical method.

One side of the nineteenth-century development took its point of departure from the lack of interest in the historical aspects of the life of Jesus which we have already encountered in Strauss and of which a philosophical parallel is to be found in Feuerbach. This tendency was clearly present in Bruno Bauer who switched over from being the confidant and manager of the Hegelian Right (he was editor of the short-lived *Zeitschrift für spekulative Theologie*) to being an outright denier of Jesus' existence as an historical person, explaining Christianity as an invention of the original evangelists. This trend eventually culminated in the total disintegration of the historical aspect of the life of Jesus – into an idea in Bauer and into a myth in Arthur Drews, who was still taken very seriously at the beginning of this century. However, this disintegration went on to provoke its own disintegration, so that no serious scholar has questioned the historical existence of Jesus since that time.

---

[90]*op. cit.* II, 738; ET, 781.

473

The sole apologetic device immediately available to the Right was the confrontation of the extreme (initially Hegelian) Left's disinterest in and disintegration of the historical Jesus with either Hegel's speculative idea of the God-man or the christological dogma of classical orthodoxy. As the century wore on, however, the broad stream of constructively-minded exegetes reacted by taking a lively interest in the historical factor and by subjecting it to a positive enquiry. With his correct classification of John as the latest of the evangelists, with his understanding of Jesus' eschatological expectation (which he did not define in political terms, as did Reimarus), and above all with his emphasis on the active function of the early Church in the formation of the tradition, Strauss himself had in fact made some important contributions to future development. On the debit side, not only did he overestimate the Old Testament motifs, but along with many others he was also wrong about the most important issue of source-criticism: as far as Strauss was concerned, Mark came after Luke.

If historical research into the life of Jesus now embarked upon an intensive treatment of Jesus' history and biography, his character and personality, his uniqueness and incomparability, its concern, notwithstanding many conflicts with traditional dogmatics, was not (as B. Slenczka has recently demonstrated convincingly against A. Schweitzer[91]) just with a critical destruction or even substitution of the christological dogma. With his Hegelian presuppositions, even Strauss himself had had no interest in the destruction of dogma. On the contrary, motivated as it was not only by historical, but also by theological and christological concerns, historical research into the life of Jesus aimed to demonstrate historically that faith in Christ is founded not on an idea, but on an historical fact, that the christological titles are rightly predicated of a single individual, that we should hold fast to a once-for-all revelation of God in the person of Jesus, and hence that the Jesus of history is after all identical with the Christ of faith. Looked at in this way, the issue at stake is not a blunt alternative of church dogma *or* historical research, or dogmatic Christology *or* the question of the historical Jesus, but rather an historical *interpretation* of the christological dogma and the resolution of its logical *aporiae*. Notwithstanding the great volume of pertinent criticism which it has levelled at the doctrine of the two natures, historical research into the life of Jesus does not in fact so much reject the dogma (or confession) in itself (and it has certainly taken little trouble to establish the function of the dogma) as call into question a particular understanding of dogma: as a formally and materially normative (i.e. legally enacted) and definitive (i.e. unhistorical) statement of doctrine (i.e.

---

[91]*Geschichtlichkeit und Personsein Jesu Christi,* esp. 118-126.

474

an absolutised law of faith). Such a legalistic understanding of dogma may not be identified without further ado with the idea of dogma espoused by the primitive or Reformation Church or with that held by recent Catholic or Protestant theology, but it may perhaps be equated with the view of dogma taken by Protestant orthodoxy and by post-Tridentine Catholicism. It is clear to the unprejudiced observer that historical research into the life of Jesus grew not only out of historical concerns, but at the instigation of a variety of interconnected motives.

R. Slenczka distinguishes three motives:[92]

1) *historical*, that is, the question concerning the 'historical Jesus' and the 'beginnings of Christianity',[93] concerning the continuity and discontinuity between the historical person of Jesus and the faith of the Church, concerning facticity and legitimacy;
2) *christological*, that is, interest in the person of Jesus and in certain statements made on this subject in the course of direct or indirect debate with christological dogma;
3) *hermeneutical-apologetic*, that is, the use of the question of the historical Jesus to substantiate the proclamation of Christ *vis-à-vis* both faith and unbelief.

Throughout the nineteenth century and especially from the 1860s onwards (the later Strauss, D. Schenckel, K. H. Weizsäcker, H. J. Holtzmann, T. Keim, K. Hase, W. Beyschlag, B. eiss) research into the historical Jesus made tremendous progress. For example, the earlier work of C. G. Wilke and C. B. Meisse was carried forward and the source question solved in principle on the lines of the priority of Mark and the two source theory (Proto-Mark and Q). At the same time the immensely assiduous labours of literary criticism released some astonishingly rich thoughts into the external and internal relationships between the New Testament writings themselves. Even so, the application of the originally Hegelian idea of development to the life of Jesus was shown to be bristling with difficulties.

Ferdinand Christian Baur was the founding father of the later, critical Tübingen school, as opposed to the earlier, supranaturalist school exemplified by Storr. He showed himself to be a direct disciple of Hegel by applying the master's idea of development to the history of dogma in general and to Christology in particular.[94] Baur departed from the habit, common to rationalists and supranaturalists alike, of examining the various items in the history of dogma in atomistic isolation by learning to interpret that history as a grand unified dialectical process of development. Notwithstanding the general rejection of the element of necessity in Hegel's system as

---

[92]*op. cit.*, 128-137, 296-302, 308f.
[93]*initia Christianismi.*
[94]See his first work on the history of dogma: *Die christliche Lehre von der Versöhnun* (1838).

well as of his three stage scheme, this innovation exerted a significant influence on all historians of dogma and dogmaticians who were stimulated by the Protestant Tübingen school, not least Ritschl and Harnack. At the same time, along with a penetrating critique of the authenticity of various Pauline epistles, Baur applied the idea of development to the gospels, adhering to Hegel's scheme to ascertain the existence of three basic historical tendencies: (a) Petrine Jewish Christianity (Matthew); (b) Pauline Gentile Christianity (Luke); and (c) the early Catholic Church. (Already hinted at in Mark, preparation is made in John for the resolution of the contradictions in early Catholicism.)

While, with the passage of time, historical scholarship on the life of Jesus softened the rigidities of Hegel's schematism, the influence of Schleiermacher's Christology of feeling and consciousness led to the ascendancy of the idea of Jesus' development. In particular this took the form of historico-psychological interpretation. Scholars concentrated on exhibiting Jesus' development, both outward (i.e. with respect to chronology and topography) and inward (i.e. with respect to the genesis of his religious, especially messianic, consciousness and of his motives), constantly seeking to conflate these two aspects into a synthetic portrait of Jesus' 'character', 'personality' and 'inner life'. On all sides there was an attempt to split up Jesus' life into distinct periods and to uncover his motives in each succeeding phase. Yet as Schweitzer concluded in his history of the research into the life of Jesus, this very undertaking of liberal scholarship came to grief: an outward, and above all an inward, psychological, 'development' on the part of Jesus cannot be read out of the gospels, but must at best be read into them. Schweitzer showed the root fault of liberal research into the life of Jesus to lie in the fact that its own unthought-through presuppositions caused it to produce a Jesus *modernised* in the light of bourgeois respectability and neo-Kantian moralism: '. . . the Jesus here portrayed can be imagined plunging into the midst of the debates in any ministerial conference.'[95]

With the work of Wilhelm Wrede, liberal scholarship on the life of Jesus seemed to end up in consistent scepticism. As an alternative to this, Schweitzer himself (in line here with Reimarus, the young Strauss, W. Baldensperger and J. Weiss) put forward the idea of *consistent eschatology:* not only Jesus' proclamation but also his entire conduct and fate must be understood in terms of his expectation of an imminent end.[96] Even though the detail of his own attempt to reconstruct the historical Jesus found little assent, Schweitzer had in fact brought to light the decisive feature of Jesus' proclamation of the kingdom of God by way of contrast to the portrait, sketched by liberal scholarship, of Jesus as a promotor of religion, as an extraordinary man and

---

[95] *The Quest of the Historical Jesus,* 207.
[96] On the theology of the future, cf. above ch. 7, 6.

as a celebrated ethical teacher of an internalised kingdom of God. Yet Schweitzer himself, who remained at heart a liberal Ritschlian, had no idea what to make of Jesus' eschatology for the present day. In later years he developed his doctrine of 'reverence of life' and gave an impressive practical expression of his understanding of Christianity through his work as a doctor in the jungle.

It required the colossal spiritual shock administered by the First World War (which provoked a simultaneous crisis in the diverse fields of politics, economics, culture and learning) to generate a crisis of liberal scholarship on the life of Jesus such as to lead to theology's becoming capable of a new understanding of the contemporary significance of the eschatological message. In the first edition of his *The Epistle to the Romans* (1919) the young clergyman Karl Barth began to answer idealistic moralism and pietistic individualism with a realistic and cosmic conception of the kingdom of God, inspired not least by German Idealism, but also by C. F. Blumhardt and religious socialism. In the second edition (1922) Barth intensified his attack on Schleiermacher and *Kulturprotestantismus* by expressing this idea of the kingdom of God in eschatological terms. This yielded a 'theology of crisis' set in an eschatological key. Impelled by the exigencies of preaching, Barth was concerned to reconnect the biblical message and especially Paul with the man of today, to go beyond historico-critical understanding in order to make possible a theological understanding of the text, and to hear the very call of God in the human documents. The matter at stake for this 'dialectical theology', the thing which caused it to react so sharply against the liberal tendency to put God and man on a par with each other and against the consequent attitude of anthropocentrism, was the infinite difference between man and the wholly other God – a difference which is abrogated solely in Christ, who himself, as a faith-paradox that cannot be inferred or proved by reason, can only be known in faith on the basis of revelation and cannot be 'sublated' by knowledge of any kind. Barth therefore radically disavowed any enquiry which would delve behind the kerygma and any recourse to an 'historical Jesus', since faith only remains faith when it renounces external legitimation.[97]

Behind Barth's change of mind (along with the criticism levelled at Christianity by Overbeck and Nietzsche and the influence wielded by Plato and Kant and by the Reformers and by Dostoyevsky) there stands above all

---

[97]On Barth's basic attitude see chiefly the Preface to the second edition of *The Epistle to the Romans* (tr. Sir Edwyn Hoskyns, OUP, 1933), and on his Christology see the exegesis: 29f, 98f, 275f etc.

Hegel's second great theological opposite, Soren Kierkegaard. His thought, particularly, made it possible for Barth to give a contemporary meaning to eschatology, to understand the kerygma as a revelation-event and, supremely, to interpret Christ as the absolute paradox of faith.

Although he eschewed the Dane's characteristic stress on inwardness, Barth nevertheless helped Kierkegaard achieve belated recognition long before Heidegger jumped on the bandwagon. Hegel's dialectic was an important influence on Kierkegaard's own existential dialectic, and he had developed many of his central concepts through debate with Hegel's philosophy. Barth now raided this conceptual store for his own thought, taking over the concepts of qualitative difference, paradox, incognito, decision, moment, contemporaneity and existence.

Increasingly worn out by his vocation of opposing the 'existing order' in Church and society by introducing Christendom to what it means to be a Christian, Kierkegaard rejected both the technique of proving Christianity in terms of the philosophy of history and also the science of speculative Christology: as 'God in time' and as 'God in the form of a servant', Christ is the 'absolute paradox' who cannot be reached by way of speculation; rather, he is a permanent offence to the understanding and can be apprehended by faith alone. At the same time Kierkegaard's background prompted him to reject the historical criticism of the New Testament: encountering it only in the form it took in the early Strauss and Bruno Bauer, he regarded this method as simply faithless. He explains how he would have Holy Scripture read in a meditation on Jas. 1: 22-27.[98] Just as a lover reads a love letter, so must I, alone with the Word of God and in the knowledge that it is personally relevant to me, not only read, hear, discuss and interpret the Word of God, but, above all, do it.

In *Training in Christianity,* surely his most significant writing after *Philosophical Fragments,* Kierkegaard makes clear his desire to introduce Christendom to what it means to be a Christian by helping the individual achieve his own Christian existence, a concern which he felt to be miserably lacking in Hegelian dialectic. It should occur in the believing encounter with Christ. In this respect Kierkegaard markedly differs from Barth in being vitally interested in the historical Jesus, albeit in a manner unencumbered with critical provisos: 'His definition of the "moment" in the *Philosophical Fragments,* the reduction of Jesus' significance for faith to the "world-historical *nota bene*" and the disavowal in *Training in Christianity* of proving Christianity in terms of the philosophy of history have caused us to overlook the fact that, within these purely abstract limits, Kierkegaard's faith in Christ lives entirely in relation to the "historical Jesus".'[99]

Even so, Christian existence does not mean the believing acceptance or intellectual clarification of historical, philosophical or dogmatic truths about Christ. On the contrary, Christian existence means to exist as a Christian. And the ardour required for such an existence is supplied by faith. The encounter with Christ occurs by faith alone, and by faith alone do I overleap the two thousand year-old 'ugly ditch' to become contemporaneous with him. And history – '. . . what does that prove? At the most it might prove that Jesus Christ was a great man, perhaps the greatest of all; but that He was . . . God – nay, stop there! This conclusion shall by God's help never be

---

[98] *For Self-Examination and Judge for Yourselves!* (tr. W. Lowrie, London, 1941), 36-50.
[99] H. Gerdes: *Das Christusbild Sören Kierkegaards,* 131.

drawn. If, in order to lead up to this conclusion, one begins with the assumption that Jesus Christ was a man, and then considers the history of the 1,800 years (the consequences of His life), one may conclude, with an ascending superlative scale: great, greater, greatest, exceedingly and astonishingly the greatest man that ever lived. If on the contrary one begins with the assumption (the assumption of faith) that He was God, one has thereby cancelled, annulled the 1,800 years as having nothing to do with the case, proving nothing *pro* nor *contra,* inasmuch as the certitude of faith is something infinitely higher.'[100] Hence: 'History you can read and hear about as referring to the past. Here, if you like, you can form your judgements according to the upshot. But Christ's life on earth is not a past event; in its time 1,800 years ago it did not wait, nor does it wait now, for any assistance from the upshot. An historical Christianity is galimatias and unchristian confusion . . . If thou canst not prevail upon thyself to become a Christian in the situation of contemporaneousness with Him, or if He in the situation of contemporaneousness cannot move thee and draw thee to Himself – then thou wilt never become a Christian.'[101]

If there is 'no going back on Hegel' regarding the historicity of God and 'no going back on Strauss' regarding the historicity of Jesus, there can accordingly be 'no going back on Kierkegaard' regarding the existential encounter with the New Testament message about Christ and the decisive function of faith.

In his polemic against liberal theology in general and Harnack[102] in particular Barth received unexpected support from the critical-exegetical camp as represented by Rudolf Bultmann.[103] While he acknowledged liberal theology's achievements in clarifying the historical picture and in training scholars to adopt a critical attitude in intellectual freedom and truthfulness, Bultmann reckoned liberal theology's reconstruction of a genuine portrait of Jesus on which faith might be based to have miscarried – and he was right! For all the results of historical scholarship are only relative, and the Christian faith may not be stripped of the element of offence. The wholly other God who is never something given in this world radically calls into question the whole man. As sinful man the latter is thus brought under God's judgment so as to discover his proper, true existence in Christ. In this sense Bultmann joined Barth in contending that faith is radically insecure. The subsequent difference between these two theologians have often prompted scholars to overlook the fact that they shared a common starting-point. This may well become increasingly obvious as the growing historical distance from the 1920s fosters a more balanced assessment of that period.[104] This common ground included

---

[100]*Training in Christianity* (tr. W. Lowrie, London, 1941), 29f.
[101]*op. cit.,* 68.
[102]cf. esp. the public correspondence of 1923 between Barth and von Harnack in the former's *Theologische Fragen und Antworten,* 7-31 (ET *The Barth-Harnack Correspondence*).
[103]See his 'Liberal theology and the most recent theological movement', *Faith and Understanding* I, 28-52.
[104]This fact was already lucidly emphasised by B. Fries in his *Bultmann – Barth und die katholische Theologie* (ET *Bultmann – Barth and Catholic Theology*, Pittsburgh, 1967).

THE INCARNATION OF GOD

the anti-liberal emphasis on the infinite qualitative distinction between God and man, the stress on the unworldliness and hiddenness of God and on the offence-provoking paradoxicality of his revelation, and the concentration of the Christ-event. Hence we find in both Barth and Bultmann contemporary existential understanding of revelation, which is not a timelessly valid truth, doctrine or system, but an event, an act and deed of God, indeed God's address, message and appeal, summoning and challenging man to response and decision: to faith, which rejects every kind of natural religion (whose aim is to have God at its beck and call) and which lives from the undemonstrability, unobjectifiability and paradoxicality of God and of his revelation.

Bultmann's agreement with Barth is not so very surprising when we recall the fact that completely new questions had been brought to the fore by the intellectual and historical upheaval associated with the First World War, and also by Rudolf Otto's rediscovery of the 'hóly' and the 'Luther renaissance' inaugurated by Karl Holl, and not least by the historical study of the New Testament sources themselves. While A. Schweitzer had neglected the source question, the work of H. Gunkel on the Old Testament and of J. Wellhausen on both Testaments was further developed in the years immediately following the Great War when several authors (especially Karl Ludwig Schmidt,[105] Martin Dibelius[106] and Rudolf Bultmann[107]) concluded almost simultaneously that the gospels are not to be thought of as scientific historiography but as the edificatory literature of the early Church, not as biographies of Jesus but as documents of faith. Thus even from a literary point of view the gospels are testimonies of faith, multi-levelled pieces of tradition culled and edited from various kerygmatic sources (sermonic, catechetical and liturgical), in whose emergence, formation and preservation the post-Easter believing Church (not to forget the evangelists themselves!) played an essential active part. They are witnesses to a proclamation which took place in the past so that proclamation might occur anew in the present and faith arise; hence they are kerygma. The person of Jesus is therefore no longer analysed simply on its own terms, but is interpreted in the context of the Easter event and the faith of the Church. In these sources Jesus is not described historically as a figure of the past, but rather proclaimed as the living Christ of faith, who continues to demand faith in the present.

The nineteenth century was obviously not just unaware of these problems. In the Foreword to the first edition of his *History of the Synoptic Tradition* Bultmann for his

---

[105] *Der Rahmen der Geschichte Jesu* (1919).
[106] *Die Formgeschichte des Evangeliums* (1919; ET *From Tradition to Gospel,* tr. Bertram Lee Woolf, 1933).
[107] *Die Geschichte der synoptischen Tradition* (1921; ET *The History of the Synoptic Tradition,* tr. John Marsh, 1963).

480

part gratefully commemorated the fact that Strauss, this 'late fruit of Romanticism', had followed Hegel in acknowledging the significance of the mind of the Church for the formation of the tradition. And we may refer in this context to the early debate which the important Tübingen Catholic theologian J. von Kuhn conducted with Strauss on this very subject.[108] Even so, the meaning and full implications of the fact that in the gospels history is transmitted only in the form of kerygma were first worked out by the form-critical school. In this sense we may with certain reservations follow James M. Robinson in his judicious account of the developments in the Bultmann school by talking of a post-Second World War 'new quest of the historical Jesus'.[109] The form-critical school systematically examined the pro-literary formation and the *Sitz im Leben* of the traditions recorded in the gospels, investigating the small units, the redactional framework and the synoptic categories, layers and tendencies. The form-critical method was therefore not only useful as a means of classifying the traditional material, but at the same time assisted in the investigation of the form and content of the tradition. In the most recent period scholars have sought to progress beyond the 'form history' of the small units to consider the whole of the gospel material from a comprehensive tradition-historial and redaction-critical standpoint.

These developments have to a large extent stood the earlier statement of the problem on its head: while it was formerly the done thing to discern theological interpretations in the historical sources, it is not fashionable to pick out historical source material from the kerygmatic texts. Bultmann's historical and philosophico-theological presuppositions had meanwhile impelled him to issue a radical demand in his *Jesus and the Word* (whose German original *Jesus* appeared in 1926): 'I do indeed think that we can now know next to nothing concerning the life and personality of Jesus, since the early Christian sources show no interest in either, are moreover fragmentary and often legendary; and other sources about Jesus do not exist.'[110] Under the influence of the early Heidegger's analysis of existence (*Dasein*) Bultmann now considered *existential interpretation* to be of decisive importance. For this, the quintessence of Christianity was not Jesus' life and personality but rather his proclamation. Hence Bultmann's stress on Jesus' words 'as his interpretation of his own existence in the midst of change, uncertainty, decision; as the expression of a possibility of comprehending this life; as the effort to gain clear insight into the contingencies and necessities of his own existence. When we encounter the words of Jesus in history, *we* do not judge

---

[108]J von Kuhn: *Von dem schriftstellerischen Charakter der Evangelien im Verhältnis zu der apostolischen Predigt und den apostolischen Briefen* (1836), incorporated in his *Leben Jesu* I, 452-488; cf. J. R. Geiselmann: *Der Glaube an Jesus Christus – Mythos oder Geschichte? Zur Auseinandersetzung Joh. Ev. Kuhns mit D. F. Strauss,* incorporated in Geiselmann's work on Kuhn's doctrine of tradition: *Die lebendige Überlieferung als Norm des christlichen Glaubens,* 1-47.

[109]J. M. Robinson: *A New Quest of the Historical Jesus.*

[110]*Jesus and the Word* (tr. L. P. Smith and E. H. Lantero, London 1935), 8.

them by a philosophical system with reference to their rational validity; *they* meet *us* with the question of how we are to interpret our own existence.'[111]

In the meantime, historical positivism had proved itself to be impossible. This was not just the result of the history of traditions approach. It was much more the fact that in the same period historical consciousness in general had undergone a transformation. The crisis of historicism (at any rate as it affected Troeltsch) made it clear that this was largely due to the questions posed by theology in general and 'historical Jesus scholarship' in particular. There was a growing awareness of the basic relativity of the knowing subject himself in his relation to the object of cognition, as awareness, that is, of historicity in the modern philosophical sense of the word. Thus it was that reflection on the *historicity of Jesus* (i.e. historical facticity as opposed to what is mythical, legendary and fictional), which had emerged in the wake of Hegel's fundamental reflection on the *historicity of God* (i.e. his having history and causing history as opposed to his existence in an unhistorical mode of being), was now inseparable from reflection on the *historicity of human existence.* This third dimension of historicity was already perceived by Hegel in the recollective self-knowledge of the human subject; it was radicalised in theological terms by Kierkegaard and Barth; Heidegger, following Kierkegaard, Dilthey and York, considered its philosophical first principles in his analysis of existence (*Dasein*); and, finally, Bultmann profitably employed it once more in the service of theology.[112] All in all this represents a remarkable mutual give-and-take on the part of both theology and philosophy, and it is well-nigh impossible to distinguish their respective contributions.

The new understanding of revelation brought about by dialectical theology, the form-critical and tradition-critical approach to the text and the new awareness of historicity form the presuppositions of Bultmann's existentialist interpretation of Scripture. The latter was already faintly present in *Jesus and the Word,* being demanded in principle and outlined in practice in the programmatic essay on *The New Testament and Mythology* and subsequently comprehensively executed in *The Gospel of John: A Commentary* and especially in *The Theology of the New Testament.* It is well to bear in mind that 'demythologisation' is merely the reverse side of this existentialist interpretation. Hence what Bultmann had to offer in positive terms was not a repristination of a mythical world picture (which was flatly impossible in view both of the natural-scientific world picture and the self-understanding of modern man), nor even – as with Strauss and many liberal exegetes – its

---

[111]*op. cit.*, 11.
[112]cf. ch. 7, 6.

482

elimination; rather it was an interpretation of the myths which the New Testament presents as objective notions, an explanation which seeks to uncover the underlying existentialist understanding. Even though Bultmann had no qualms about making statements concerning the 'what' and 'how' of the history of Jesus, as far as he was concerned the kerygma presupposes in principle only the 'that' of his having come. Thus faith is not based on an encounter with a past historical fact, but on an encounter with the contemporary Word, with the contemporary demand issued by the proclamation of Christ. Nor is this proclamation of Christ a message concerning the historical Jesus; rather, it focusses on Jesus' death and resurrection as a salvific event which is to be interpreted existentially. The first Christian theologians Paul and John already concentrated to a great extent on just such an existentialist interpretation; and in this respect Bultmann differed from the nineteenth century in regarding the transition from Jesus to Paul not as a sign of decadence, but as a necessary development within the tradition. Historical verification is unimportant for faith, whereas existential consummation is decisive.

We cannot here enter into the details of the debate surrounding Bultmann, demythologisation and existentialist interpretation.[113] A wealth of critical questions might be posed with respect to particular features of his system. For example, did he in his interpretation of the New Testament overrate the influence of *gnosis* and underrate that of the Old Testament (not to forget that of inter-testamental Judaism and Qumrân)? Was his form-critical method burdened with heterogeneous *a priori* statements? Did he allow the preconceived notions which he brought to the text to be corrected by the New Testament message in practice as he certainly intended them to be in principle, and did he let this message loose in its full force? Did he neglect the synoptic evangelists in favour of Paul and John? Was his historical scepticism justified and is faith really meant to be historically insecure as he and Barth demanded? Was the link between his hermeneutics and Heidegger's existentialist philosophy only formal, and not in many respects material also? Was the upshot of demythologisation and existentialist interpretation (which are certainly justified in principle) to drag the reality of God and the reality of the world into an anthropological bottleneck which led to the Christian faith's being not only spiritualised (in the neglect of living corporeality) but also 'privatised'? Did this not mean a reduction of the concrete history of humankind as perceived by the Bible and contemporary man to the historicity of human existence, of God's creation to human creatureliness, of the absolute future of the world to what befalls the individual in the present, and of the salvifically potent past to the present in which the individual believer is affected by the proclamation? We

---

[113]cf. the numerous essays in the several volumes of *Kergyma and Myth* (ed. by H. W. Bartsch), in the symposia *Il problema della demitizzazione* (ed. by E. Castelli) and *Kerygma and History* (ed. by C. A. Braaten and R. A. Harrisville). From the viewpoint of Catholic theology, cf. G. Hasenhüttl: *Der Glaubensvollzug. Eine Begegnung mit R. Bultmann aus katholischem Glaubensverständnis.* This study, which was applauded by Bultmann himself, has not been superseded by any of the more recent Catholic works on the same subject.

can and must discuss all these difficult and complex issues, and in the light of all that has been said above there can be no doubt that the most recent developments in theology have advanced beyond many of the existentialist impasses of Bultmann's kerygma theology.[114]

There is one reproach which it is absolutely impermissible to fling in Bultmann's face (even though the mistake has been made again and again right down to the present): that of having dissolved the historicity and revelation of God into the subjectivity of man. As far as Bultmann is concerned, the Christ-event is never reduced to a symbol or an idea: as kerygma it remains a fact and an event. He differed from liberal theology in holding that the revelation in Christ is an act of God which originates outside and beyond man: 'From the statement that to speak of God is to speak of myself, it by no means follows that God is not outside the believer. This would be the case only if faith is interpreted as a purely psychological event. When man is understood in the genuine sense as an historical being which has its reality in concrete situations and decisions, in the very encounters of life, it is clear, on the one hand, that faith, speaking of God as acting, cannot defend itself against the charge of being an illusion, and, on the other hand, that faith does not mean a psychologically subjective event . . . Are we not in danger of eliminating this "once for all" of Paul's (Rom. 6:10)? Are we not in danger of relegating the divine dispensation, the history of salvation, to the dimension of timelessness? It should be clear from what we have said that we are not speaking of an idea of God but of the living God in whose hands our time lies, and who encounters us here and now. Therefore, we can make our answer to the objection in the single affirmation that God meets us in His Word, in a concrete word, the preaching instituted by Jesus Christ . . . This living Word of God is not invented by the human spirit and by human sagacity; it rises up in history. Its origin is an historical event, by which the speaking of this word, the preaching, is rendered authoritative and legitimate. This event is Jesus Christ.'[115]

This means that, according to Bultmann, we should be careful not to contrast a Christology 'from below' with a Christology 'from above' in the manner of the last century, which often derived its Christology purely psychologically from man's religious consciousness or else deduced it directly from history with the aid of nothing more than historical method. Notwithstanding its radical involvement in history, a Christology from below is never tantamount to that 'reverence before history' which earned the reproach of Karl Barth. On the contrary, faced with the Jesus who both proclaims and is himself proclaimed, such a Christology finds itself confronted by the appeal of God in history, before which man cannot remain neutral. While heed must be paid to man's situation and understanding of reality prior to his hearing the Gospel, and while account must be taken of his changing world picture, a Christology from below will nevertheless never mean simply a Christology of human self-consciousness or of human piety, but rather a Christology of

---

[114]cf. e.g. ch 7, 6, and also the various commentaries on John's Gospel listed in Part IV of the bibliography.
[115]*Jesus Christ and Mythology,* 70f, 78, 79f.

divine revelation which radically lays claim to man's faith. Faith will not be regarded as merely a human attitude, a numinous feeling or a pious state of mind, but rather as a response to the God who acts in history as he is revealed in Jesus. In this sense we must give concrete emphasis here to the view that there is 'no going back behind Kierkegaard' (or Barth, or Bultmann).

Even though there has been a wide measure of agreement with Barth, Bultmann and Kähler with respect to the fundamental importance of faith, recent theologians have shown little inclination to emulate their position on one particular issue: their historically and theologically reasoned ban on enquiry behind the New Testament kerygma has not been followed. Did not Bultmann's existentialist depreciation of history in favour of the kerygma bring him astonishingly close to the idealist depreciation of history in favour of the Idea? Was there not a danger of the history of Jesus being dissolved into the history of the kerygma? When the younger F. Buri in complete self-consistency invoked Bultmann's authority for his demand to advance beyond demythologisation to dekerygmatisation,[116] even though Bultmann himself wished to do anything but say good-bye to the kerygma, history had in fact come full circle. For this process bears a certain similarity to the development from Hegel to Strauss, which Hegel himself would likewise certainly not have wished to see, but whose seeds were nonetheless to some extent contained within his system.

Why on earth should the historian – or the believer for that matter – meekly endure a ban on enquiry behind the kerygma about Christ into the history of Jesus, given the fact that the gospels themselves maintain that the Christ who is preached is identical with the man Jesus, in whose company some of the witnesses themselves had actually lived during his earthly ministry? How can a critically thought-out faith not have a burning interest in the question whether and, if so, to what extent, there is agreement between the apostolic proclamation about Jesus Christ and the historical reality of this Jesus, to whom faith is related even according to Bultmann? The reply to this question is not a matter of indifference to the historian, since it alone will enable him to explain the rise of Christianity. Nor is it a matter of indifference to the believer, since the answer to this question will alone decide whether the Christian faith is ultimately based on history, myth or misunderstanding. Scholars outside the Bultmann school took a different path from the beginning. This was the case in French and Anglo-Saxon exegesis, especially in the important works (which have sometimes had something of a *Life of Jesus* about them!) by

---

[116]'*Entmythologisierung oder Entkerygmatisierung der Theologie*', *Kerygma und Mythos* II, 85-101.

C.H. Dodd,[117] W. Manson,[118] T.W. Manson,[119] R.H. Fuller,[120] and V. Taylor[121] among others. In the German speaking countries strong methodological and material reservations about Bultmann's position have been registered not only by K. Barth,[122] but also by the systematicians H. Diem,[123] P. Althaus[124] and H. Ott,[125] and even by the form-critical exegets K. L. Schmidt,[126] J. Schniewind[127] and O. Cullmann.[128] Itis much more remarkable, however, that the members of the Bultmann school themselves were disinclined to follow the master, even though the latter set his face against the attempts made by his pupils to correct him on this score. They seemed to him, on account of their interest in historical phenomena, to have betrayed the concerns of existentialist interpretation.[129] In the ensuing period appeal was often made to the fact that, at an early stage, Bultmann himself spoke of a 'Christology implicit in Jesus' call for decision'.[130]

Ernst Käsemann signalled the change of direction in an address delivered to Marburg graduates in 1953 by working out afresh the historical continuity between the exalted and the earthly Jesus, a point which had been stressed by

[117] *The Parables of the Kingdom* (1935); *The Interpretation of the Fourth Gospel* (1953).
[118] *Jesus the Messiah* (1943).
[119] *The Sayings of Jesus* (1949); *The Servant Messiah. A Study of the Public Ministry of Jesus* (1953); 'The life of Jesus: Some Tendencies in Present Day Research', *in The Background of the New Testament and its Eschatology*, Cambridge, 1956.
[120] *The Mission and Achievement of Jesus* (1954).
[121] *The Life and Ministry of Jesus* (1954); *The Person of Christ in New Testament Teaching* (1958); *The Names of Jesus* (1953); *The Cross of Christ* (1956); *Forgiveness and Reconciliation. A Study in New Testament Theology* (1941).
[122] *Rudolf Bultmann. Ein Versuch, ihn zu verstehen* (1952; ET 'Rudolf Bultmann – An Attempt to Understand Him' in *Kerygma and Myth* II, 83-132).
[123] *Der irdische Jesus und der Christus des Glaubens* (1957; ET 'The earthly Jesus and the Christ of faith', in *Kerygma and History*, edd. Braaten and Harrisville, 1962.
[124] *Das sogenannte Kerygma und der historische Jesus* (1958; ET *The So-called Kerygma and the Historical Jesus*, Edinburgh,1959).
[125] *Die Frage nach dem historischen Jesus und die Ontologie der Geschichte* (1960).
[126] 'Das Christuszeugnis der synoptischen Evangelien' in *Jesus Christus im Zeugnis der heiligen Schrift und der Kirche* (1936), 7-33.
[127] 'Zur Synoptikerexegese', *Theologische Rundschau* 2 (1930), 129-189; 'Antwort an Rudolf Bultmann. Thesen zum Problem der Entmythologisierung', *Kerygma und Mythos* I, 77-121 (1948; ET A Reply to Bultmann', *Kerygma and Myth* I, 45-101).
[128] cf. his early and later essays on hermeneutics in *Vortäge und Aufsätze 1925-1962* and his *Heil als Geschichte. Heilsgeschichtliche Existenz im Neuen Testament* (ET *Salvation in History*, tr. S.G. Sowers, 1967).
[129] *Das Verhältnis der urchristlichen Christusbotschaft zum historischen Jesus* (1960; ET 'The Primitive Christian Kerygma and the Historical Jesus', in *The Historical Jesus and the Kerygmatic Christ*, edd. Braaten and Harrisville, 1964); 'Antwort an Ernst Käsemann', *Glauben und Verstehen* V, 190-198.
[130] 'Die Bedeutung des geschichtlichen Jesus für die Theologie des Paulus' (1929), *Glauben und Verstehen* I, 204 et passim.

the New Testament writers themselves. Käsemann's purpose was to preclude myth's usurping the place of history, holding fast to history as an expression of the *extra nos* of salvation! Other theologians have also learned to perceive anew the history which is contained *within* the kerygma of the gospels, a history in which, patently, these gospels themselves are supremely interested, in order thereby to gain a better understanding of the kerygma which is contained *within* the history.

Käsemann summed up his argument as follows: 'But conversely, neither am I prepared to concede that, in the face of these facts, defeatism and scepticism must have the last word and lead us on to a complete disengagement of interest from the earthly Jesus. If this were to happen, we should either be failing to grasp the nature of the primitive Christian concern with the identity between the exalted and the humiliated Lord; or else we should be emptying that concern of any real content, as did the docetists. We should also be overlooking the fact that there are still pieces of the Synoptic tradition which the historian has to acknowledge as authentic if he wishes to remain an historian at all. My own concern is to show that, out of the obscurity of the life story of Jesus, certain characteristic traits in his preaching stand out in relatively sharp relief, and that primitive Christianity united its own message with these. The heart of our problem lies here: the exalted Lord has almost entirely swallowed up the image of the earthly Lord and yet the community maintains the identity of the exalted Lord with the earthly. The solution of this problem cannot, however, if our findings areb approached with any hope of success along the ne of supposed historical *bruta facta* but only along the line of the connection and tension between the preaching of Jesus and that of his community. The question of the historical Jesus is, in its legitimate form, the question of the continuity of the Gospel within the discontinuity of the times and within the variation of the kerygma. We have to put this question to ourselves and to see within it the element of rightness in the liberal *Leben-Jesu-Forschung,* the presuppositions of whose questioning we no longer share. The preaching of the Church may be carried on anonymously; the important thing is not the person, but the message. But the Gospel itself cannot be anonymous, otherwise it leads to moralism and mysticism. The Gospel is tied to him, who, both before and after Easter, revealed himself to his own as the Lord, by setting them before the God who is near to them and thus translating them into the freedom and responsibility of faith.'[131]

It is remarkable that the very exegetes who were most keenly aware of the difficulties associated with a new round of historical Jesus research heeded Käsemann's call, and it is against this background that the American exegete J. M. Robinson has, so to say, pursued Schweitzer's history of 'life of Jesus' research into the most recent period, speaking of a '"post-Bultmannian" phase of post-war German theology.'[132] No more impressive confirmation of this statement can be produced than the long list of fascinating Jesus studies which have emerged from the most recent historical research.

---

[131]'The Problem of the Historical Jesus', in *Essays on New Testament Themes* (tr. W. J. Montague), 45f.
[132]*A New Quest of the Historical Jesus* (1959), 10; cf. also 12 – 19.

From within the Bultmann school itself we mention the works of G. Bornkamm,[133] H. Conzelmann[134] and H. Braun.[135] E. Schweizer[136] and K. Niederwimmer[137] have grappled positively with Bultmann's questions, and the same can perhaps be said of the account by M. Dibelius (reissued by W. G. Kümmel and still very much worth reading[138]). Independent paths have been taken by E. Stauffer,[139] X. Léon-Dufour[140] and L. Cerfaux.[141] Nor may we overlook in this context the intense efforts of J. Jeremias to establish the *ipsissima vox* of Jesus.[142]. Important specialist studies have come from the pens of E. Schweizer,[143] H. E. Todt,[144] B. vam Iersel,[145] E. Jüngel,[146] W. Kramer[147] and J. Blank.[148]

This development beyond Bultmann is corroborated by those recent *theologies of the New Testament* which clearly follow in his footsteps. For example, the most conspicuous and significant deviation in H. Conzelmann's *Theology of the New Testament* from that of his teacher Bultmann consists in the spacious treatment accorded to the synoptic kerygma,[149] which Bultmann had tended to neglect, and in the fresh interest shown in the question of the self-consciousness of Jesus.[150] It would be a fascinating exercise to compare the *Theology of the New Testament* written by this pupil of Bultmann with the one which has just appeared from the pen of his Marburg successor W. G. Kümmel. Given that Bultmann was wont to classify Jesus in terms of

[133]*Jesus von Nazareth* (1956; ET *Jesus of Nazareth,* 1960).
[134]The article '*Jesus Christus*', in *RGG* (1959) III, 619 – 653; ET pub. sep. as *Jesus*, tr. J. R. Lord, 1973.
[135]*Jesus* (1969; ET *Jesus of Nazareth* tr. E. R. Kalin, 1979).
[136]*Jesus Christus im vielfältigen Zeugnis des Neuen Testaments* (1968; ET *Jesus*, tr. D. E. Green, 1971).
[137]*Jesus* (1968).
[138]*Jesus* (3rd ed., 1960; ET of earlier edition: *Jesus,* 1939).
[139]*Jesus. Gestalt und Geschichte* (1957; ET *Jesus and His Story,* 1960).
[140]*Les Évangiles et l'histoire de Jésus* (1963; ET *The Gospels and the Jesus of History*, tr. John McHugh, 1968).
[141]*Jésus aux origines de la Tradition* (1968).
[142]*Kennzeichen der ipsissima vox Jesu* (1954; ET 'Characteristics of the *ipsissima vox Jesu*', in *The Prayers of Jesus*, 1967); *Die Gleichnisse Jesu* (6th edition 1962; ET *The Parables of Jesus*, tr. S. H. Hooke, 1963); *Die Abendmahlsworte Jesu* (3rd edition 1960; ET *The Eucharistic Words of Jesus*, tr. N. Perrin, 1964); *Das Problem des historischen Jesus* (1960; ET *The Problem of the Historical Jesus*, tr. N. Perrin, 1964).
[143]*Erniedrigung und Eröhung bei Jesus und seinen Nachfolgern* (1955; ET. *Lordship and Discipleship*, 1960).
[144]*Der Menschensohn in der synoptischen Überlieferung* (1959; ET *The Son of Man in the Synoptic Tradition,* 1965).
[145]*Der Sohn in den synoptischen Jesus-Worten* (1961).
[146]*Paulus und Jesus. Eine Untersuchung zur Präzisierung der Frage nach dem Ursprung der Christologie* (1962).
[147]*Christus, Kyrios, Gottessohn* (1963; ET *Christ, Lord, Son of God,* 1966).
[148]*Paulus and Jesus. Eine theologische Grundlegung* (1968).
[149]*Grundriss der Theologie des Neuen Testaments*, 115 – 172 (1967; ET *An Outline of the Theology of the New Testament*, tr. John Bowden, 1969, 'Part Two: The Synoptic Kerygma', 97 – 152).
[150]*op. cit.*, 143 – 159; ET 'The Question of Jesus' Understanding of Himself', 127 – 140.

the history of religions as belonging to Judaism, he would scarcely wish to have written Kümmel's sub-title himself: 'according to its major witnesses Jesus – Paul – John.'[151] Specialist Christologies of the New Testament are obviously important in this context, in particular those by G. Sevenster,[152] O. Cullmann[153] and F. Kahn.[154] And W. Marxsen's Bultmannian works on the question of the resurrection of Christ are of fundamental importance.[155] Finally, we ought to pay special attention in this list to the exceptionally stimulating early and later essays by E. Fuchs on the quest for the historical Jesus and on the christological problem. Strongly emphasising the history of Jesus, Fuchs has drawn attention in a new way to his behaviour as the appropriate framework within which to interpret his proclamation.[156] And the works of G. Ebeling, the systematician of the Bultmann school, have pointed in a forward direction, especially his penetrating discussion with Bultmann regarding the kerygma and the historical Jesus and his pertinent remarks of Christology.[157] The path from kerygma and faith to the historicity of Jesus has likewise been traced in such statements of the Catholic view point as those by R. Marlé,[158] F. Mussner,[159] R. Schnackenburg,[160] R. Geiselmann[161] and J. Blank.[162] It is also in order to refer to the essays edited by

---

[151] *Die Theologie des Neuen Testaments nach seinen Hauptzeugen Jesus, Paulus, Johannes* (1969; ET *The Theology of the New Testament According to Its Major Witnesses Jesus – Paul – John*, tr. J. E. Steely, 1974). On the problem of the historical Jesus, see 20 – 24 (ET, 22-27); and on the proclamation of Jesus according to the synoptic evangelists, see 24 – 85 (ET, 27 – 95).

[152] *De Christologie van het Nieuwe Testament* (1946; 2nd edition, 1948); cf. also *idem*: art. '*Christologie im Urchristentum*', in *RGG* (1957) I, 1745 – 1762.

[153] *Die Christologie des Neuen Testaments* (1957; ET *The Christology of the New Testament*, tr. S. C. Guthrie and C. A. M. Hall, 1963).

[154] *Christologische Hoheitstitel* (1963; ET *The Titles of Jesus in Christology*, 1969).

[155] *Die Auferstehung als historisches und als theologisches Problem* (1964); *idem*: *Die Auferstehung Jesus von Nazareth* (1968; ET *The Resurrection of Jesus of Nazareth*, tr. Margaret Kohl, 1970); *idem:* *Anfangsprobleme der Christologie* (1960; ET *The Beginnings of Christology: a Study in its Problems*, tr. P. J. Achtemeier, 1969); cf. J. Kremer: *Das älteste Zeugnis der Auferstehung Christi* (2nd edition, 1967); *idem*: *Die Osterbotschaft der vier Evangelien* (1968); K.Lehmann: *Auferweckt am dritten Tag gemäss der Schrift* (1968); F. Mussner: *Die Auferstehung Jesu* (1969).

[156] '*Zur Frage nach dem Historischen Jesus*', *Gesammelte Aufsätze* II, esp. 143 – 167 (1960; ET *Studies of the Historical Jesus*, tr. Andrew Scobie, 1964, 11 – 31); *idem*: '*Glaube und Erfahrung. Zum christologischen Problem im Neuen Testament*', *Gesammelte Aufsätze* III (1965), esp. 1-31, 433 – 470.

[157] '*Jesus und Glaube*', in *ZThK* 55 (1958), 64 – 110; *idem*: *Theologie und Verkündigung. Ein Gespräch mit R. Bultmann*, esp. 19 – 92 (1962; ET *Theology and Proclamation, a Discussion with Rudolf Bultmann*, 32 – 93); *idem*: '*Was heisst: Ich glaube an Jesus Christus*', in the book of the same name (1968), 38 – 77.

[158] *Le Christ de la foi et le Jésus de l'histoire* (1959); cf. also Part Two of Marlé's book, '*Bultmann et l'interprétation du Nouveau Testament*', from the 2nd edition of 1966.

[159] '*Der historische Jesus und der Christus des Glaubens*', in *Biblische Zeitschrift* N. F. 1 (1957), 224 – 252; *idem*: *Die Auferstehung Jesu* (1969).

[160] '*Jesusforschung und Christusglaube*', in *Catholica* 13 (1959), 1 – 17.

[161] *Jesus der Christus*, vol. 1 (1965).

[162] '*Zum Problem der neutestamentlichen Christologie*', in *Una Sancta* 20 (1965), 108 – 125.

H. Ristow and K. Matthiae[163] and by K. Schubert.[164] The most penetrating recent analysis of the theological and dogmatic implications of the older and the more recent historical Jesus research is that offered by R. Glenczka.[165]

The only way for an historically based Christology 'from below' to get to know its own starting-point, (i.e. the historical Jesus and his message) is by drawing inferences from the highly diverse proclamation of the New Testament witnesses. Even though the latter were in some cases actual eye witnesses, they spoke from disparate situations into disparate situations, so that the text of the New Testament as we have it abounds in contradictions of nuance and direction. The critical question thus arises within the Church's kerygma; indeed, it pervades the whole kerygma, whose historical relativity must be taken seriously. The varying and in part contradictory character of the Jesus tradition frankly forbids the cosy assumption that Jesus himself took pains to ensure an exact adherence to and transmission of his words and deeds. The state of the sources makes it impossible to advocate the historical reliability of the Jesus tradition as a whole. In fact, only a critical examination of the individual pieces of tradition can show up which portions represent interpretation, embellishment and, in some cases, even reduction by the post-Easter Church, and which represent the pre-Easter words and deeds of the Jesus of history. Despite all the difficulties, however, it remains true that inference from the kerygma is possible, justified and necessary: *possible* because there is a continuity between Jesus and the early Christian proclamation which outweighs all the elements of discontinuity; *justified* because the early Christian proclamation could only arise from and be understood in terms of Jesus' message and fate; and *necessary* because it is only in this way that the early Christian and hence also present day proclamation can be guarded against the suspicion that it is not based on an historical fact, but is rather a mere assertion, a product of faith, indeed a pure myth or apotheosis. This technique will not lead to a reconstruction of a biographical chronology, topography or psychology of the life of Jesus, but will cause the decisive characteristics and outlines of his proclamation and person to stand out in sharp relief. Such a result is entirely feasible, even if the so-called genuineness of each single saying of Jesus or the historicity of each individual report

---

[163] *Der historische Jesus und der kerygmatische Christus* (1960). In addition to the contributions of the authors already mentioned, cf. those by H. J. Schoeps, H. Gollwitzer, J. L. Hromádka, J. Leipolt, N. A. Dahl, E. Fascher, B. Reicke, W. Grundmann, O. Michel, H. Riesenfeld, H. Schürmann, L. Goppelt, G. Delling and E. Barnikol.
[164] *Der historische Jesus und der Christus unseres Glaubens* (1962), with contributions by F. Mussner, A. Stöger, W. Beilner and R. Haardt.
[165] *Geschichtlichkeit und Personsein Jesu Christi* (1967).

cannot be positively proved in detail. The hypercritical assumption that an authentic piece of tradition is *eo ipso* a great exception is just as unfounded as is the corresponding uncritical assumption that the authenticity of the tradition may be presupposed on principle.

W. G. Kümmel describes our task as follows: 'The scholar inquiring into the person and proclamation of Jesus will rather see himself confronted with the task of inquiring within the total stock of tradition for that stratum which can be demonstrated to be the earliest. Indispensable methodological aids in this task are the literary comparison of the parallel accounts of the gospels, the analytical delimitation of the individual piece of tradition, the form-critical distinguishing of various forms of narrative and discourse and their arrangement into the circumstances of emergence corresponding to them, the comparison of the ideas with the contemporary Jewish and Hellenistic thought-world, the exposure of special forms of discourse or ideas of Jesus or ways of behaviour typical of him, the excision of explicit Jewish or primitive Christian conceptions, and so on. Of course the decisive check on the correctness of such a setting apart of the earliest body of tradition can only be the proof that from the fitting together of the pieces of tradition thus gained a historically comprehensible and unitary picture of Jesus and his proclamation results, which also makes the further development of primitive Christianity understandable. Of course with the ambiguity of many arguments and the danger of the researcher's being bound to ecclesiastical, scientific-historical, or personal prejudices, it remains unavoidable that the opinions will always be divergent on the question of the antiquity of individual pieces of tradition and even of entire groups of traditions. But the uncertainty and need of correction of all such judgments must not allow any doubt to arise as to the necessity and importance of the question of the person and proclamation of Jesus in the context of New Testament theology. For "the Lord's position at the head of his community and his believers can and must also be expressed temporally" (E. Käsemann).'[166]

Thus there will be no question of a Christology 'from below' restricting its interest to 'Jesus as he really was', to an 'historical Jesus' of the past. It will not emulate the positivistic understanding of history by being satisfied with ascertaining facts and reconstructing causal connections, quite apart from the fact that in this case the sources preclude any biography which would psychologically analyse the subject or explain the course of events. Precisely a Christology 'from below' is interested in the Jesus who meets us today, within the horizon of the world, humankind and God, as the challenge to faith which he personally embodies. If the liberal 'life of Jesus' research was unable in practice to separate historical Jesus research from specifically christological questions, how much less can this be done today in view of the recent hermeneutical, exegetical-historical and theological-systematic state of the problem, according to which history can only be known in the kerygma and the kerygma can only be known in history.

---

[166] *The Theology of the New Testament*, 26f.

Research into the question of the historical Jesus is certainly incompetent to create faith or the certitude of faith, things which can be achieved only by the very Jesus who is the content of the Church's proclamation. Yet 'historical Jesus research' does enable us to scrutinise and verify the faith which has been handed down to us, so that it is purified from innocent superstition and from ideologies which serve as a cloak for vested interests, and so that uncritical credulity and critical scepticism can both be dislodged from their false security, thereby indirectly preparing the ground for renewed faith. Such research neither can nor will furnish proof for faith, yet neither should faith for its part wish to establish any historical facts. While a merely 'historical faith' does not work salvation, an 'unhistorical faith' can likewise be a sign of weak thought rather than of strong faith.

We are meant to perceive both the claim and the true meaning of this Jesus from his history, that is, from his word, behaviour and fate. From history he is meant to be known as the invitation, challenge and encouragement to believe in person, so that in and through his person the individual is placed before God himself in an unprecedentedly critical and promising way, in order that he may say his 'Yes' before God to Jesus' life and death. Christian faith is accordingly neither a mere acceptance of various facts or truths (believing this or that), nor is it the acceptance of a particular person's essential trustworthiness (believing this one or that one); rather, it is total reliance on a person: I believe *in* Jesus as the 'Christ'. Christian faith is therefore essentially faith in Christ, which in its turn is only meaningful and justifiable as faith in God. Christian faith means neither pure *theo*-logy (for faith in God remains ambiguous without faith in Christ), nor pure *Jesu*-ology (for faith in Jesus remains unfounded without faith in God). The structure of Christian faith is christological to the extent that, as far as it is concerned, to confess God also means to confess Jesus and, conversely, to confess Jesus also means to confess God. The same thing holds good of both faith in God and faith in Christ, namely that the decisive content of faith only becomes comprehensible when the decision to believe is taken. He who does the truth will also know it. Bearing these factors in mind we can, as has already been said, only speak of a Christotgy 'from below' in a qualified sense, using the term as a cypher (even if it goes without saying that we refrain from linking up either 'from below' or 'from above' with spatial conceptions).

Throughout this study we have sketched the grand route of Christology, how it stretched from the classical formulae to Hegel and from Hegel via Strauss to contemporary exegesis both Catholic and Protestant. Along with the arguments here adduced, it is this very process which urges us to adopt the historical starting-point 'from below'. To put it more precisely: the way in which we perceive Christology should follow the path from the history of

Jesus to the Church's confession of him as the Christ. At the same time this historical procedure will make it clear to the person of today, who thinks along historical lines, that the confession of Christ is not rooted in itself, so that it might be done away with as mere myth, illusion or ideology, but that, on the contrary, it is roooted in the history of this Jesus, who was born in Palestine under the Emperor Augustus, emerged into the public eye under the latter's successor Tiberius, by the authority of whose procurator Pontius Pilate he was ultimately executed. This approach consequently makes it as clear as daylight that, while Jesus himself was the occasion and cause, he was at the same time the content and criterion of the proclamation of and faith in Christ, so that the real and the cognitive bases of Christology coincide.[167]

This historical approach to Christology is not concerned merely with a decision for an exegetical as opposed to a dogmatic Christology: there are, after all, exegetes who (as in the case of Bultmann with his kerygma Christology) start 'from above', just as there are dogmaticians (such as A. Ritschl and W. Herrmann) who begin 'from below'. Nor is it a question of opting for a progressive as opposed to a conservative Christology: there are 'progressive' theologians (such as, despite all appearances, D. F. Strauss) who start 'from above', just as there are 'conservative' theologians (for example, P. Althaus) who begin 'from below'. Even so, it may be significant that, while in the heyday of dialectical theology Emil Brunner joined Karl Barth in constructing a Christology 'from above',[168] at a later stage of his dogmatic thought he proposed a Christology 'from below';[169] and that there is today a growing consensus, uniting theologians of highly diverse orientations and schools and embracing not only exegetes but also dogmaticians, in favour of starting 'from below'.[170]

The chief reason for the continuing apparent backwardness of Catholic dogmatics here can be traced back to a divergence in theological method which first became customary in the nineteenth century. The apologetic

---

[167]This connection has been precisely analysed by R. Slenczka (*Geschichtlichkeit und Personsein Jesu Christi*, 309 – 315), and G. Ebeling offers much food for thought on this subject in his *Was heisst: Ich glaube an·Jesus Christus*.

[168]*Der Mittler* (1927; ET *The Mediator*, tr. Olive Wyon, 1952).

[169]*Dogmatik* II: *Die christliche Lehre von Schöpfung und Erlösung*, 257 – 403 (1960; ET of earlier edition, *The Christian Doctrine of Creation and Redemption*, tr. Olive Wyon, 1952, 260 – 378).

[170]Among the systematic theologians who should be mentioned in addition to E. Brunner see, e.g., D. M. Baillie: *God Was in Christ* (4th edition, 1951); P. Althaus: *Die christliche Wahrheit* (4th edition 1958), 423 – 493; W. Elert: *Der christliche Glaube* (5th edition, 1960), 291 – 353; W. Pannenberg: *Grundzüge der Christologie* (1964; ET *Jesus – God and Man*, tr. Lewis L. Wilkins and Duane A. Priebe, 1968); F. Gogarten: *Die Verkundigung Jesu Christi* (1948); *idem*: *Jesus Christus Wende der Welt. Grundfragen zur Christologie* (1966; ET *Christ the Crisis*, tr. R. A. Wilson, 1970); G. Ebeling: *Theology and Proclamation*, 32 – 93; *idem*: *Was heisst: Ich glaube an Jesus Christus* (1968), 38 – 77.

Christology of fundamental theology does indeed tend to think 'from below', but its grasp of the historical and exegetical issues is for the most part unsatisfactory. The Christology of dogmatics meanwhile continues to think 'from above' without bothering its head about the state of the question, the methods or the results of modern exegesis. Given the intertwining of historical, hermeneutical-apologetic and theological-dogmatic perspectives and motives, this divorce will scarcely be maintained in the long run.

One point where Catholic dogmatic Christology has displayed an increasing openness to historical questioning is the issue of the knowledge and self-consciousness of Christ, which has been the subject of intense discussion since the middle ages and which has recently cropped up under the rubric of the 'ego' of Christ.[171] A thought-provoking survey of recent contributions to the christological debate in the *Herder-Korrespondenz*[172] (which, alas, appeared anonymously in keeping with the continuing custom of this periodical) explains how even for Catholic dogmatics the scope of the issues has in the meantime been considerably widened. The introductory sentences are particularly significant: 'Some years before the Second Vatican Council, Catholic Christology was brought to life by the debates concerning the ego of Christ. In the meantime, however, the controversy surrounding this specialist question has markedly subsided, and the thesis that Christ had a dual ego has found few adherents. It has, moreover, become increasingly apparent that the traditional basis shared by all partners in the discussion must be re-examined. After modern historical thought had been irrevocably granted admission into Catholic theology by the Second Vatican Council in its Constitution on Divine Revelation, it was no longer possible to continue the previous practice of keeping the traditional bases of Christology aloof from debate.'[173]
    Especially significant in this context are the courageous and constructive essays by the Dutchmen A. Hulsbosch (who has criticised the doctrine of the two natures),

---

[171]cf. the bibliographical survey offered by R. Haubst in his *Probleme der jüngsten Christologie* (1956), a work which was written against the background of the contemprary controversy between P. Galtier and P. Parente. Among recent works cf. B. Lonergan: *De constitutione Christi ontologica et psychologica* (1956); E. Gutwenger: *Bewusstsein und Wissen Christi* (1960); F. Malmberg: *Über den Gottmenschen* (1960), 89-114; K. Rahner: '*Dogmatische Erwägugen über das Wisen and Selbstbewusstsein Christi*' in *Schriften zur Theologie* V, 222-245 (1962; ET 'Dogmatic Reflections on the Knowledge and Self-Consciousness of Christ' in *Theological Investigations* 5, 1966, 193 – 215). An especially significant contribution has been made by H. Riedlinger in his *Geschichtlichkeit und Vollendung des Wissens Christi* (1966). This author explains the questionability of certain *theologoumena* (such as *scientia beata, infusa, acquisita*) which have become 'classic' and have found favour in Roman doctrinal pronouncements, while at the same time engaging in a critical and constructive discussion with the endeavours of M. Schnell, A. Loisy and M. Blondel. The latter, which have been stigmatised as 'modernist', nevertheless represent an early, though not invariably successful, attempt to do justice to the historicity of Jesus.
[172]'"*Geschichtliche" und "anthropologische" Christologie*' in *Herder-Korrespondenz* 21 (1967), 173 – 178. This article might be supplemented by C. Duquoc: *Christologie. Essai dogmatique. L'homme Jésus* (1968).
[173]*art. cit.*, 173.

E. Schillebeeckx (according to whom we only perceive the divinity of Jesus in his unique mode of being human), and P. Schoonenberg (who has criticised the traditional presentation of the motif of pre-existence).[174]

We heartily endorse the closing sentences of the above-mentioned survey: 'At all events, the progress made in Holland shows clearly enough which hour the clock has struck. The smouldering crisis over theological first principles can certainly no longer be quelled by raising a fire alarm and taking harsh counter measures. Since the very historical thought which has now been accorded irrevocable toleration is presently working like leaven through all departments of theology, including Christology, it will require the greatest prudence and patience to resalvage the old truth from the debris.'[175]

With reference to Catholic dogmatics as a whole it should be added that, so long as we avoid taking the trouble to come to grips with 'historical Jesus research' from the point of view of systematics (a task which admittedly demands considerable effort) then, while christological speculation, polished up with aid of various philosophical, psychological, sociological and other means, and the evolutionary understanding of the world, so popular among Catholics, might perhaps be able to glimpse the crisis over the bases of traditional Christology, they will hardly be able to find a cure for it.[176]

As far as possible none of the old schools or orientations should be artificially perpetuated or even formed afresh on account of this new approach to Christology. There ought to be no serious contemporay Christology 'from above' whose perspective would not oblige it to get caught up in the questions 'from below'. And by the same token there ought to be no serious Christology 'from below' which would be able to bypass the great concerns 'from above', that is, considering the Christ-event as a faith-eliciting act of God. Our purpose here has not been to dispute the 'from above' approach in principle, but only to reflect as seriously as possible on the historical and·theological issues which have surfaced in the course of this Hegel-centred account. Even so, it is our conviction that, in the course of modern development, the 'from above' approach has for many become simply inaccessible,

---

[174]All these essays were published in the *Tijdschrift voor Theologie* 6 (1960), 250 – 306; A. Bulsbosch: '*Jezus Christus, gekend als mens, belegen als Zoon Gods*'; E. Schillebeeckx: '*De persoonlijke openbaringsgestalte van de Vager*'; P. Schoonenberg: '*Christus zonder tweeheid?*'; cf. also the illuminating essays on Christology by H. Bortnowska, J. T. Nelis, C. van Gowerkerk and A. van Rijen; and for an interesting Protestant parallel cf. G. C. Berkouwer's starting-point against the background of the crisis of the doctrine of the two natures in his *De Persoon van Christus*, 12 – 43, esp. his remarks on 'Sticking to Chalcedon?', 65 – 76.

[175]*art. cit.*, 178.

[176]The increasing prevalence of the exegetical-historical approach to Christology in Catholic dogmatics is demonstrated in the recent work of K. Lehmann: *Auferweckt am dritten Tag nach der Schrift. Früheste Christologie, Bekenntnisbildung und Schriftauslegung im Lichte von I Kor. 15, 3 – 5* (1968). For the christological foundation of this change cf. the ecclesiological works of H. Küng, e.g., *Die Kirche*, 57 – 99 (1967; ET *The Church*, tr. R. and R. Ockenden, 1968, 43 – 79); of P. V. Dias: *Vielfalt der Kirche in der Vielfalt der Jünger, Zeugen und Diener* (1968), 91 – 148; B. Hasenhüttl: *Charisma – Ordnungsprinzip der Kirche* (1969), 19 – 45.

incomprehensible and unfeasible; and that both the perceptions of modern exegesis and the modern understanding of history, the world and existence urge us to begin 'from below'. This insight should not be countered by nothing better than a rigid insistence on the councils of antiquity, for while we have sought to give a positive appreciation of their answers, the fact of the matter is that their questions are in large measure no longer our own. We are today more aware than ever before of the time-conditionedness of those conciliar 'short formulae' which took shape, as we have seen, within a highly restricted hermeneutical horizon. Looked at in form-critical terms, the conciliar statements represent a further development (with similar or different conceptual means) of the credal formulae which already emerged in the New Testament, and for this reason they ought not to be neglected today as historical guidelines. But for this very same reason we ought also to beware of turning these formulae into 'principles' whence the whole of Christology is to be deduced and our understanding of Scripture to be rigidly cast along certain lines from the word go. On the contrary, a new age is entitled to demand the creation of new 'short formulae' of faith which, while obviously time-conditioned in their turn, will be at once accessible, comprehensible and feasible as far as contemporary man is concerned.[177]

At the same time, caution is called for when theologians want to find early predecessors for a Christology 'from below' and then cite Luther, as has constantly happened in Protestant theology from Ritschl to Ebeling and Pannenberg. We pointed out some parallels in mediaeval Christ piety[178] for the fact that Luther was supremely interested in the historical humanity of Christ. Even so, the Reformer's interest was soteriological and based four-square on the classical doctrine of the two natures; it was not a hermeneutical interest emerging from a grasp of historical problems. An enquiry of the latter kind only became possible after all in the context of the new historical consciousness.

We shall still do well to heed the words of W. Pannenberg (whose christological blueprint conbines a learned grasp of the tradition with a penetrating critique of classical Christology) about the latter's neglect of the historical particularity of the man Jesus of Nazareth: 'A Christology that takes the divinity of the Logos as its point of departure and finds its problems only in the union of God and men in Jesus recognises only with difficulty the determinative significance inherent in the distinctive features of the real, historical man, Jesus of Nazareth. The manifold relationships between Jesus and the Judaism of his time, which are essential to an understanding of his life and message, must appear as less important to such a Christology, even when it

---

[177]cf. K. Rahner: '*Die Forderung nach einer "Kurzformel" des christlichen Glaubens*', in *Schriften zur Theologie* VIII, 153 – 164 (1967; ET 'The need for a "Short Formula" of Christian Faith', in *Theological Investigations* 9, 1972, 117 – 126).
[178]cf. ch. 2, 5.

discusses the offices of Christ as well as his humiliation and exaltation. Certainly if one knows from the beginning that Jesus Christ is the Son of God, then these relationships with the Judaism of Jesus' time are not so crucial for the basic Christological questions. Then only the participation of the Logos in everything that belongs to general human nature is important, since our human participation in divinity through Jesus depends upon that. But no determinative significance can accrue to the historical particularity of Jesus, unless it be to his death as a payment that atones for sins. However, in this perspective even the problem of Jesus' death can become to a certain extent something supplementary. The problem of Jesus' death then primarily involves the question, Why must the man who is engaged by God also be subjected to the universal human fate of death?"[179]

A Christology 'from below' must not idle away its time sharpening its knives. It must get down to the matter in hand. In concrete terms this means, first, that despite the highly complex state of the problem, we must not get enmeshed in the (albeit necessary) methodological prolegomena! As has been demonstrated, the hermeneutical question is of pivotal importance for the historical problems, and it stands in need of further clarification; even so, it must not unintentionally become an end in itself and *de facto* turn into the more or less ultimate task of theology. Methodological questions are admittedly important, but it is imperative that the theologian should not run out of breath when still *en route* for his goal. Already in the prolegomena a Christology 'from below' must be strictly oriented to the matter in hand. That means the Jesus who was alive then and who lives now. Secondly, however justified may be our discourse about historicity in general, we must not lose sight of the concrete history of Jesus and his proclamation! It would be a wretched state of affairs if Christology no longer bothered with the texts of Scripture but contented itself instead with thoroughly abstract general theses. It is not enough to speak of 'happening' and 'event', for the concrete event and happening in the living concreteness of the history of Jesus must be made visible on the basis of the biblical witnesses.

Christology therefore cannot be too concrete or historical. Nor will it get involved in the dispute about the 'basic', 'primal' or 'central' datum of Christology. For the basic, primal and central datum is Jesus Christ himself, both the earthly, crucified Jesus and the risen Jesus of the Church's kerygma. Wherever one of these constitutive 'data' is lacking, Christology is impossible.

In the historical perspective demanded here Christology will have to deal with the following interlocking topics, in whatever form and sequence, as its biblical basis: Jesus' proclamation, Jesus' conduct, Jesus' fate, and Jesus' significance. We can basically only tell what questions lurk in these topics, and

---

[179]*Jesus – God and Man,* 34f.

indeed how these questions are to be posed in the first place, when we have developed some answers to them. Lest this demand for a concrete historical Christology should itself appear too abstract, we shall now venture (with all due reservations) to indicate in catchphrase form the questions with which a future Christology, critically and systematically adopting the results of biblical theology,[180] will have to deal under these rubrics, even though it will have to return different answers to them according to changing circumstances.

Space forbids us to do more in the following pages than simply to stake out the New Testament basis of the future Christology demanded here with the aid of a few background questions. Suffice it to say that the thought structure of such a Christology might be characterised as 'meta-dogmatic'. I borrow this concept, which must not be confused with 'un-dogmatic' or with 'anti-dogmatic', from my pupil Josef Nolte, whose long overdue fundamental critique of dogmatism in his extremely concentrated work *Dogma in History* rightly demands that contemporary theology adopt a meta-dogmatic way of thinking which would get to grips with the historicity of dogma. Anyone who fears that Troeltsch's 'everything is in the melting-pot' threatens such a meta-dogmatic Christology should be reminded that this meta-dogmatic way of thinking, whose formal aspect Nolte has developed in the course of hard toil and conceptual struggle, was already accomplished *in actu exercito* in my book *Die Kirche* (1967).[181] This was itself preceded by a volume along similar lines and with a like goal, intended to blaze the trail for its successor, namely *Strukturen der Kirche* (1962).[182] A future Christology must accordingly differ from the customary scholastic and neo-scholastic school Christologies as did my book *The Church* from the school ecclesiologies. Meta-dogmatic theology in this constructive sense therefore involves building, notwithstanding all demolition, and a shifting of the centre of gravity, notwithstanding all reduction. Thus precisely a meta-dogmatic way of thinking can express the originally decisive core of faith in Christ more concentratedly, richly and beautifully than can a dogmatic school theology, which only stays out of the melting-pot for one who, for whatever reasons, has long been accustomed to swaying in time with its rocking foundations.

a) *Jesus' proclamation.* Under this heading it would be fitting to explain how far the concrete historical situation (to be deduced primarily from the Church's kerygma) and the expectations which formed the backcloth of Jesus' ministry were significant for both his message and the Church's message about him. This situation included the people among whom he worked – no

---

[180]For the following pages, which ought properly to be developed in systematic terms, I am conscious of having received much exegetical stimulation from conversation with E. Käsemann and E. Fuchs and from the books on Jesus of Bultmann, Dibelius, Bornkamm, Stauffer, Schweizer and Niederwimmer.
[181]ET *The Church*, tr. R. and R. Octenden, 1968
[182]ET *Structures of the Church*, tr. S. Attanasio, 1964.

longer the Israel of the Old Testament (the Jewish state had lost its independence) and not yet Talmudic Jewry (Jerusalem and the second Temple were
not yet in ruins); it included the country in which he worked, comprising a
comparatively pure Jewish population in Judaea and elsewhere people of
mixed race, those in Samaria being separated from the cultic centre, Jerusalem, and those in Galilee being connected to it. It included the various
religious groups with which Jesus had to debate: the Pharisees, who demanded moral reform according to the law within the framework of what was
practicable (some more rigorous, others more lax); the radical Essenes, who
as the elect congregation dissociated themselves from other Jews, some of
them even migrating to the desert; the Zealots, who called for a political
revolution; the conservative Sadducees, who stood for the priestly establishment and for collaboration with the occupying power and its tool, the
Herodians. And then it included the various messianic conceptions corresponding to those groups; and finally it included the penitential and baptismal
movement of John the Baptist, to which Jesus himself was directly linked, as is
shown by his message and by his establishment of an intimate circle of
disciples.

What was Jesus' message against this background? Did it aim at moral re-
armament or at monastic asceticism, at political revolution or at conservative
churchiness? Still on the basis of the Church's kerygma, we could by way of
contrast work out the kerygma of Jesus himself in its continuity and
discontinuity – his publicly proclaimed message of the fulfilment of time and
the imminence of the coming kingdom of God, preached against an apocalyptic background. The content of his proclamation was neither himself nor a
theory nor a set of dogmatics, but the rule of God, which is not simply God's
perpetual dominion over the world as presupposed in Old Testament thought
and given with the creation, but rather the impending full realisation of the
eschatological dominion of peace, righteousness and fullness and of reconciliation between God and man. This is not, as many rabbis believed, to be built
up by faithfully fulfilling the law, but is rather achieved solely by the coming
God himself. It is not, as it was for broad sections of the people and for the
Zealots, an earthly political theocracy on the national level, but rather God's
dominion over a world renewed by him. It is not, as it was for many of Jesus'
contemporaries and also for the monastic order of Qumrân, a judgment of
vengeance against sinners, but rather on the contrary an event of salvation for
sinners. While being future it is not just a faraway event, but something which
erupts into the present in Jesus and his salvific acts. Then, finally, as the
consequence of the message of God's rule there is the demand for μετάνοια
– not acceptance of particular 'doctrines' or mysteries, not speculation
concerning the dates of the coming kingdom of God, but an acknowledge-

ment before the coming God that this time, here and now, is end time; not simply a matter of piously serving God in the Temple, of outward penitential practices or of getting baptised, but rather of the radical and total conversion of the whole person to God in trusting faith: an unconditional and unreserved readiness to fulfil not the letter of the law but the will of God, which does not decree negative denial of and ascetic monastic separation from the world (like Qumrân), but rather desires a new turning to the world in common humanity, thus not calling for force and coercion (the means favoured by the Zealots), but intending to be implemented through the active sacrifice rendered by an unqualified, boundless love at work in the everyday world, embracing even one's enemies.

On the basis of such a proclamation it is impossible to dodge the question of Jesus' authority. What is it, then, about the ultimately unguaranteed, faith-demanding authority of a man who, with his proclamation, casts himself in an astonishing freedom alongside and even against Moses (Sermon on the Mount), and who, with this claim of a kind unheard-of in Judaism, ceased to be a rabbi (whose authority is derived from Moses) or a prophet (who likewise stands under Moses), but who, on the contrary, even without using loaded messianic titles, simply exists and teaches 'with authority', and who precisely by so doing makes a *de facto* messianic claim: a claim to be the one whose Gospel is God's ultimately binding Word prior to the end, God's penetrating appeal for an unavoidable, radical decision for himself and his lordship and hence, without any reservations, for one's fellow man? Who is this, who, with such authority, dares to speak both as it were for God and in God's stead, and for men and women?

b) *Jesus' conduct.* It would be fitting here, again on the basis of the Church's kerygma, to set forth Jesus' characteristic conduct as the undetachable framework of his proclamation. He did not share the Baptist's ascetic lifestyle, and yet he provocatively lived in the unmarried state. He was neither a priest nor a scribe, but a 'layman' with lay disciples (even women!). At the same time, deeds of salvation, miracles and an immediate communion with God were reported of him. In the case of this enigmatic man there is at no time and in no place a contradiction between 'theory' and 'practice', word and deed, message and conduct, but these are fully and completely congruent at every juncture. He unconditionally and unimpeachably lived what he preached, and he not merely proclaimed but also fulfilled the will of God: by committing himself, in the face of the coming kingdom of God, in his whole existence for God, his lordship and the good of humankind – manifestly brushing aside the holy law of God and its stipulations when a concrete individual was at stake!. That this was so is clearly attested by the indisputable fact that he sided with the impious and lawless, those who were neither able nor willing to keep the law, to the great annoyance of the pious who were faithful to the law: he had fellowship, even table fellowship, with the despised, the outcasts and the oppressed, indeed even with the religiously degraded and depraved, so that he was regarded as a friend of notorious sinners, heretical Samaritans, taxgatherers (with their questionable business ethics), collaborators and prostitutes. All this represented an utmost intensification of God's demand, accompanied at the same time by a most prodigious augmentation of his grace! With his explosive message, Jesus was never concerned with a revolution for its own sake or at any price, but always with utterly concrete man, with the often so remote neighbour at whom God's will is constantly directed, working through the law and yet beyond its letter. Even though he lived on the whole in complete faithfulness to the law, when it seemed necessary to him for the sake of God and the good of man he scandalously brushed aside sanctified traditions, relativising the Temple cult by serving God in everyday things, daring even explicitly to announce to those who had fallen into guilt the forgiveness of their guilt.

Again, such conduct does not permit us to suppress the question of authority: What is it about the authority of a man who acts so differently from a teacher of law or of wisdom, or from a prophet for that matter? For although like the prophets he was indeed endowed with the Spirit, yet his immediacy to God was different in kind from theirs. He seems to outdo his opponents in intensifying God's demands with rigorous urgency and consistency, yet at the same time his generosity and liberality give offence when he humanely and rationally rejects all Jewish casuistry, himself living out a freedom, which provokes his strait-laced compatriots, and proclaiming forgiveness and reconciliation. He gives those who have fallen into guilt preferential treatment over those who have remained righteous. Such 'poor devils' as the lost and the poor he draws close to himself, yet he does not abandon them to a care based on an ambiguous pure fellow humanity, but rather places them under the forgiveness, mercy and grace of a God who lets the sun shine and the rain fall on good and bad alike, and who remains the father who will have all people given help, who loves sinners and who wills to fetch them home into the proclaimed coming Kingdom. Who then is this who dares in such a remarkable way to act on men and women as it were for God and in God's stead?

c) *Jesus' fate.* It would be appropriate under this rubric to give an account, based on the Church's kerygma, of the fate which resulted from this proclamation and conduct, a destiny which seems to be necessarily headed for catastrophe. Now in his incomprehensible freedom and independence Jesus by no means opposes the sacred law and the order which it represents, nor does he confront it with another law; yet not only does he interpret it differently from his contemporaries, but at decisive points he ignores it. Hence

501

things are bound to come to a head in a life and death conflict between him and the religious establishment, for whom the preservation of law, morality and order is a supreme and sacred duty.

Not only did Jesus hold with John the Baptist that physical descent from Abraham is ultimately incapable of guaranteeing salvation, but he said the same of the very law of God, which was the basis of the whole existence, morality and order of the people. There emerged here one making the *de facto* claim of being more than Moses, Solomon and Jonah, more than the law, the Temple and the prophets, and of proclaiming a God of sinners rather than a God of the righteous: it was an unparalleled challenge, provocation and even rebellion directed against the entire religio-social system and its representatives. Could the latter react otherwise than by liquidating the despiser of the law and its God and the seducer of the people? Better one than many. The proclamation of God's rule had thus reached its climax in the question: Is it to be absolute fulfilment of the law *or* in all things freedom for the cause of God and man? And Jesus had himself become the great sign of the time, the great demand for decision: here and now, before him, it is imperative to decide for or against God's rule, to take offence or to believe, to continue as before or to turn in one's tracks. Whoever says 'Yes' or 'No' to him already appears marked for God's eschatological judgment. In his person the future casts its shadow in anticipation, the old aeon seems already to be a thing of the past, and the *eschaton* of liberty, reconciliation, grace and love seems already to have dawned. And this in its turn must have prompted his opponents to ask: What is this man making of himself? The representatives of the system close their minds to him.

It would therefore be appropriate to set forth how Jesus lived, disputed, suffered and died. This Jesus, who wished to befriend the enemies of God and who in so doing proclaimed and revealed God in a completely novel way, was, as far as the hierarchs and their followers were concerned, no more and no less than a godless man. The system which made a simple identification of the law with God has its own thoroughly stringent logic: hostility to the law is godlessness. As a supremely dangerous foe of the law and seducer of the people as far as the Jews were concerned, and as a political rebel and enemy of Caesar as far as the Romans were concerned (this political implication was there), Jesus was to be arrested, condemned and executed. Now put to the final test, in the courtroom he unstintingly upheld to the bitter end the commitment which he had taken on himself for the love of God and the freedom of men and women: his death was the seal on his life and teaching. But the ones who had killed him were not simply certain guilty Jews or Romans acting as individuals; rather, those who had wrought his death were such persons acting as a product of the religio-political system. It was the law,

502

over which, appealing to the will of God and the good of man, he had placed himself in royal freedom, that killed Jesus.

For those who had entered into a personal relationship with him, God's very Word, will and love had taken on personal form in Jesus, and in him God's kingdom of reconciliation, peace, liberty and love seemed already to have arrived. And this was the man who was liquidated before the public gaze. A godless man in Godforsakenness on the cross: the God with whom he had authoritatively identified himself in word and deed, even though he occupied no office, had obviously abandoned him. Moreover, God seemed to contradict himself in this Godforsaken man, and with this death to have died his own death. As far as the world was concerned, this death meant that the game was up: Jesus' failure was obvious, his rejection was proved, and his opponents and their God seemed to be proved right. Even so, this godless one was in truth to be proved right, he was to be justified before God and man, powerlessness was to consummate his sovereign power. The Church's kerygma causes us to discern the aura of victory already in Jesus' cross. But why?

d) *Jesus' significance*. Working on the foundation of the Church's kerygma, it would be appropriate from the perspective of his proclamation and conduct to unfold the true significance of the Crucified One in the fate which befell him. How could a man, whose story, to public knowledge, ended in fiasco, acquire significance? How could a man who had absolutely failed be proved right after all? The faith of the Church asserts that Jesus' God, who himself died along with his Godforsakenness, actually did justify Jesus the Godforsaken and godless man.

However much embarrassment they occasion precisely at this point, it would be appropriate to explain the foundation of the Easter faith from the New Testament witnesses. After all, if this faith were founded on itself alone, it would in fact be baseless. Even so, the question of the resurrection is assuredly not a matter of establishing historical facts, as is the case with Jesus' death. Precisely here is faith less than ever a mere appendage to historical knowledge. For Jesus did not appear to the world in general, but only to his disciples in particular: it was he who provoked their faith, and their manifest unbelief did not turn into belief of its own accord. The witnesses to faith which have been handed down to us show many signs of having been embroidered with legend, and they contradict each other. A description or detailed account of the resurrection can be found in the apocryphal gospels, but not in the New Testament. The gospel narratives do not agree among themselves even in the ambiguous account of the empty tomb, but there is one point on which they do concur, namely that the Easter faith did not come about in virtue of any mental reflections or psychological developments undergone by.unbelievers; rather, it arose on the strength of the 'appearances' of the Crucified One,

503

which led to the disciples refinding their faith in Jesus and their courage to follow him: according to the unanimous witness of the gospels, these appearances were events in which, after Jesus' death, those, who from Peter to Paul were to become the witnesses and bearers of the early Christian message, knew Jesus as a speaking, living person; they were events which became of constitutive importance for the post-Easter proclamation of Christ, which in its turn was to be a grim matter of life and death for many of the proclaimers. Whatever real experience or, better, experience of the real, may be hidden beneath these accounts of the resurrection appearances permits a variety of modes of interpretation. Even so, they all express the decisive fact which alone can give a rational explanation of the resurrection faith: Jesus the Crucified One lives, and he was experienced as the Living One.

Thus what is decisive is not the 'how', 'when' and 'where', but the 'that' of new life, not the mode of the reality of the 'resurrection', but the identity of the Risen One with the earthly Jesus: Jesus, who died as a man forsaken by God, lives with God as the one who has been 'exalted' and 'glorified' by God. Thus Jesus was right after all, and he, not his opponents, is the victor. God is with him and God is really the God whom he preached, the God of the godless, the God of forgiveness and love. And this God justified the godless Godforsaken man; he confirmed his proclamation, his conduct and his claim to authority; he backed up his way of freedom, love and forgiveness; and he discovered the piety of the law, for through Jesus' death under the law he acquitted the lawbreaker and conferred life on him, so that he might live the life of God and so that (as his followers became increasingly aware through historical experience) those who cleave to him might be fundamentally freed from law, sin and death. In this way God proved himself to be Lord of life and death and the one who raises the dead and calls into being the things which are not. Before the horizon of apocalyptic the new life of Jesus appears as the anticipation of the new life of all humankind. Jesus' having come has thus been shown to be purely and simply *the* decisive event, *the* truly eschatological occurrence. In the light of the resurrection his entire earthly existence and his death on the cross themselves appear in a completely new light, for Jesus' coming under the curse of the law appears as the event of salvation: quite purely and simply *the* event of salvation, the end of the old and the beginning of the new age. The future has turned into the future of Jesus, and the future of Jesus is the future of all humankind in the kingdom of God.

It would be appropriate to go on to give an account of how the new life is ecstatically experienced 'in the Spirit': the Spirit of Jesus as the Spirit of freedom. Yet at the same time the experience of the Spirit does not permit us to forget that the possibility of new life was bought at the price of death and that the new way to God would not have been opened up without the sacrifice of life. The Church of believing men and women can therefore never forget that the Risen One is and remains identical with the Crucified One. The cross is not merely an example and model of Christian faith; on the contrary, it is the foundation and archetype of the Christian faith. It is the grand distinctive mark which radically distinguishes the Christian faith and its Lord from other religions and their gods. The fact that it is only through the cross that man in faith can share in the new life and the new freedom causes freedom to take on the aspect of obligation and life to become service of other people. Only from the perspective of the cross and in the act of taking up his cross as Jesus' disciple can man discover meaning in failure, only thus can he find the hope of a fulfilment of meaning in the meaninglessness of existence. Only through the cross can God be known as the God who has revealed himself anew in Jesus: not the God of the pious, but the God of a godless, the God of love, forgiveness, freedom, life and hope. In future we can only know the living Jesus along with knowing God, and we can only know the true God along with knowing Jesus. Jesus is 'one' with God, and he who sees him sees the Father. What holds good in view of Easter holds good already before Easter.

It would be appropriate also to expound how the Church, under the prompting of its Easter faith, engaged in a fresh definition and description of its relationship to Jesus and of Jesus' relationship to God. Our concern here would not only be with the continuation of Jesus' cause, but with the possibility of a new understanding of the past of the One who came and of the future of the One who is to come. It would be a question of solving the riddle of the person of Jesus, of understanding how certainty and confession came to take the place of presentiment and doubt, how the proclaimed Jesus emerged from the chrysallis of the proclaimer Jesus, and how the bearer of the message became himself the central content of the message, a message not only sparked off by the Easter faith but determined in its content thereby. It would be fitting in this perspective to narrate the Church's increasingly mature discernment and confession of Jesus' true significance for faith: in the course of a complicated process of tradition, which took place in the context of new needs and forms of worship, proclamation and church life, various exalted 'christological' titles were applied to Jesus, along with the concomitant conceptions of his way from God and to God.

Against the dual background of the expectation of an imminent end and the delay of the parousia, we should have to speak of the varying opinions which were held simultaneously in the early Palestinian church, in Hellenistic Jewish Christianity and in Hellenistic Gentile Christianity: well known titles which were current in contemporary thought (along with many notions which went hand in hand with them, such as pre-existence and post-existence) were applied to Jesus, only acquiring their specific meaning in the light of his concrete historical person. Jesus as the coming Son of man, the imminently expected Lord, the Messiah installed in the last times, the Son of David and vicariously suffering Servant of God, finally the contemporary *Kyrios* and the pre-existent Son of God and Logos: these are the most important of the titles which were applied to Jesus. Some of them presently passed out of usage (e.g., 'Son of man' in Pauline thought), while others gained a pivotal importance (e.g., 'Son of God' in the Hellenistic sphere) or even merged with the name 'Jesus' into a single proper name (as in the case of 'Messiah' rendered by the Greek 'Christ'). While all of these titles strike a different chord, in the end of the day they are interchangeable; and while they are well able to complement each other, despite all their internal discords they have only one clear point of reference: Jesus himself. For it was not these Jewish-Hellenistic titles which gave Jesus his authority; rather he, as the risen Crucified One and the crucified Risen One, gave them their authority. They did not determine what he was; rather, he himself, in his concrete historical existence, death and new life, determined how they are to be understood. At that time it was customary to dub many heroes and demi-gods 'Son of God'; hence what Jesus was can certainly not be derived from the concept 'Son of God' as such. On the contrary, the believer's task was to read the proper, decisive and incomparable meaning of 'Son of God' from Jesus' person and history in opposition to the multitude of 'Sons of God' who abounded in the syncretistic pantheon of Hellenistic religion. The decisive factor was not that precisely *this* term 'Logos' was applied to Jesus (John applied it, the others did not) but rather that this term 'Logos' was applied to *Jesus*. In view of this fact 'Logos' gained its precise sense of 'Logos made flesh'. In this way the most varied titles and mythical symbols were baptised in the name of Jesus, for the purpose of being of service to him and of explaining his unique significance for the people of that age, whether Jews or Greeks. They were understood not as instantly intelligible credentials, but as pointers to him, not as *a priori* definitions, but as explanations issued *a posteriori* in the light of the person of Jesus.

The ultimate task of Christology, the explanation of Jesus' significance *now* in terms of his significance *then,* must be borne in mind from the very beginning. Yet this would not be achieved by harmonising a single New Testament Christology from the diverse New Testament titles and images, as if Jesus' significance in the New Testament were exhibited only by one single Christology and not by many contrasting Christologies, as if instead of four evangelists we had only one, and as if instead of many apostolic letters we had only one New Testament dogmatics. Nor would it be achieved by merely analysing these diverse New Testament Christologies and unthinkingly repeating them for contemporary use, as if these titles and images were not stamped by a highly distinctive culture which, as far as we are concerned, is in many respects a thing of the past, and as if they had not changed in the meantime – which always happens when language is simply conserved.

On the contrary, we are faced with a difficult task which engages each succeeding age afresh: the translation without iconoclasm, for the sake of the contemporary significance of Jesus, of those titles and images into present-day terms and language. The purpose of this exercise is to ensure that faith in Christ remains the same and that the person of today is not prevented from accepting, understanding and living the proclamation of Christ by earlier concepts and images which cause unnecessary difficulties, and which are incomprehensible, under certain circumstances confusing, and at the present time even flatly misleading. A translation of this kind does not mean the abolition of old titles and confessions of faith, nor does it imply any disregard of the long christological tradition or even of the biblical origin. On the contrary, a serious translation of this kind can only take place when the theologian has minutely understood the original text and entered thoroughly into it, when he interprets and corrects the concepts and images of then and now in terms of the concrete historical Jesus, and when he achieves the greatest possible awareness of the entire christological tradition of two millenia with all its interpretative aids and its admonitions and warnings. We are thus obliged to accomplish a serious translation which goes beyond mere repetition and makes it clear that the one faith in Jesus permits many credal statements about him and that, while faith in Christ is one, Christologies are many, just as faith in God is one and theologies are many. The fundamental insight that no one ever puts the finishing touches to his God and his Christ prompts us to urge an attitude of modesty to theology in general.

These presuppositions enable, permit and even enjoin us at the present day once again to frame a witness which manages to stand on its own feet while at the same time being faithful to Christian origins. There is no need to be wary about ascribing new titles to Jesus: precisely such novel nomenclature can in many cases make it plain that the old titles were not the worst and that they often hit the nail on the head astonishingly well. Such a procedure can at any rate avoid the twin perils of turning Jesus at the present time into either (in docetic terms) a God disguised in human form, or (in ebionitic terms) into nothing more than the factor which sparked off the proclamation of Christ, into one whose messiahship is a mere cypher for a new understanding of the world and human existence. And such a procedure could make plain in a new way what is decisive from the very outset, namely that the historical Jesus is really the Christ precisely as the brother of man and the man for others (in the biblical sense of this term): in ultimate underivability ('pre-existence') and ongoing significance ('post-existence') he is *the* Word and Son of God and *the* Lord. In Jesus faith therefore has good cause and evidence for acknowledging that in him, his life, teaching, death and new life, we have to do with *God himself,* that the *vere homo* and the *vere Deus* meet in this person, that the humanity of our God is revealed in him, and that in him precisely as the *Word* of God *God truly became man so that man might become human.*

These remarks have already basically brought us beyond the prolegomena into the realm of Christology proper, and while this was not our aim, it was probably unavoidable. And thus we have now at long last arrived at the end of this book. Our mention of Hegel yet again at this point is more than a sign of politeness; rather, bearing in mind that his claim and his encouragement have prompted us to reflect on the historicity of God and the historicity of Jesus, it is an expression of gratitude. We are sorely tempted by way of a finale – to use a musical image – to pull out all the organ stops and let his great themes resound once more. Even so, Hegel had a personal aversion to summaries at the end of works, a dislike which sprang from the basic insight that the truth is the whole. And there are even symphonies, such as the Farewell Symphony composed around the time of Hegel's death two hundred years ago, which end on a note of restraint. It would thus be entirely in keeping with Hegel's thought for such an ending to be understood as a transition to a new beginning.

EXCURSUS I
THE ROAD TO CLASSICAL CHRISTOLOGY

Classical Christology presupposes an ontological understanding of incarnation and divine Sonship oriented to Greek metaphysics. After a very confused history, this Christology was given its first universally binding, if somewhat vague, expression at the First Ecumenical Council of Nicea in 325. This definition turned out to be both a summary of previous and a foundation of subsequent theology, but today even in the Catholic Church it is not accepted without question and in fact often hampers attempts at a fresh understanding. In this Excursus however we shall be dealing with a different theme, attempting a scrutiny of the classical christological tradition, which we need to appreciate before talking about it.

The strength of the Council of Nicea (which represents a first culminating point in the development of classical Christology) lies in the fact that it started out from the historical human being Jesus of Nazareth and described him from two different aspects as 'truly God' and 'truly man'. However differently they might be understood, these two aspects have been regarded from that time onwards as the poles to which any orthodox Christology must give adequate expression and they continued to make their impact throughout the centuries until they were adopted eventually as a basic formula by the World Council of Churches. The answer of Nicea could serve as a criterion precisely because of its indeterminacy, an indeterminacy both in regard to the content of the two components and in regard to their correlation with each other. The term ($\delta\mu oo\acute{v}\sigma\iota o\varsigma$) was not used in a technical sense and was not meant to impose the concept of ($o\grave{v}\sigma\acute{\iota}\alpha$) on to the concept of God, but only to clarify the statements about the Son in the New Testament: that the Son is not (as Arius maintained, in the light of middle-Platonism) part of created reality, but is on the same plane of being as the transcendent Father. There was no intention of going beyond Scripture or of giving a positive answer to the question of how Father and Son are related to one another. This indeterminacy of what would turn out to be, up to a point, a merely verbal solution (and here lies the weakness of Nicea) made it possible for diametrically opposed views to emerge from the welter of diverse interpretations. It called precisely for an explanation of how the one Jesus Christ could be both

509

truly God ('consubstantial' with God) and truly man and thus proved to be merely the first stage on a path which ended – again provisionally – with the classical formula of Chalcedon. But the Chalcedonian definition can be understood in its significance as a whole and in its distinctions only if we keep in mind at least in outline and schematically the different positions within the Christology of the early Church and especially the rejected attempts at a solution.

At the same time we shall not be able to avoid the use of the terms 'orthodoxy' and 'heresy', even though we have no intention of passing judgment on the belief or misbelief of individuals and groups. We are only too well aware of the fact that all historiography of heresy was formerly written from the standpoint of the victor and consequently as self-justification, and that the *audiatur et altera pars* was rendered impossible from the outset by the brutal destruction of almost all the heretical literature of the first century, leaving only a few fragmentary quotations in the works of their opponents. It is not our opinion anyway that heresy emerges simply from the struggle between a majority and a minority in the Church, with the victorious majority branding the defeated minority as heretics. The controversies in Christology in particular were not settled so casually. The question of who had the original Christian message behind them could not have been irrelevant for the formation of a majority and the outcome of the conflict. But it is certain that error and truth are never quite clearly distributed among individuals and that, as in orthodoxy there can be a great deal of error, so there can be a great deal of truth in heresy. And if, for instance, the teaching of the apologists represented a great liberation by comparison with pagan polytheism, it was at the same time a levelling down of the original message (out of the Christian message emerged a kind of Christian philosophy and higher wisdom teaching, a revealed 'doctrine' about God, Logos, world and man). Hence the terms 'orthodoxy' and 'heresy' should not be misunderstood as cheap labels.

In reality Christology developed in an extraordinarily complicated way in the midst of the tensions between Alexandria and Antioch, East and West Rome, Gaul (Lyons), Spain (Cordova) and Asia Minor (Cappadocia). What a confusion, often almost impenetrable (in philosophy, theology, politics of Church and state), of reciprocal positive and negative influences, actions and reactions, formation of fronts and changes of front, trends and schools! The one little word ($\delta\mu oo\acute{v}\sigma\iota o\varsigma$) – originating, paradoxically, in Gnosticism – illustrates vividly the state of affairs. A number of the persons involved in these controversies are themselves dubious and contentious characters (for example, Origen, Paul of Samosata, Cyril of Alexandria, and others). In this Excursus then there can be no question of entering into controversies in the history of theology about certain ancient theologians and christological conceptions (for example, F. Loofs's Spirit Christology or M. Werner's angel Christology). For all this the reader must be referred to the great works on the history of dogma by

L. J. Tixeront, T. de Régnon, J. Lebreton, J. Rivière and others and – on the Protestant side – by A. Harnack, R. Seeberg, F. Loofs, W. Koehler, M. Werner and A. Adam, as also to the numerous monographs on these subjects. Our aim then in this Excursus is to mark out (with inevitable over-simplification, but, we hope, without serious misrepresentation) points and lines of orientation, not for the study of the history of dogma but for systematic theology, which may bring out more clearly the problems of the Christ-dogma. In this respect we shall make use of the solid recent historical studies by A. Grillmeier, A. Gilg, J. Liébaert and B. Skard.[1] We shall rely on the latter works particularly for setting the various schools or heresies in their appropriate period (at the same time it should be remembered that the designations of heresies – like Monarchianism, Adoptionism etc. – are used by the different historians of dogma sometimes in a narrower and sometimes in a wider sense).

If we survey the vast struggle for a true Christology in connection with the doctrine of the Trinity, carried on within the Church during the first five centuries and linked at first with an external struggle against the aggressive imperial state, we may be surprised that Christianity did not perish like a good many religions and theories of salvation in the all-absorbing Hellenistic syncretism with all its deified human beings and its speculations about a divine Logos elevated above all flesh. This was connected, among other things, with the fact that an unswerving faith resisted the temptation (however enticingly plausible it might seem) rationally to dissolve the salvation-event in Jesus into one of two extremes: an unhistorical, eternal myth on the one hand, or an ultimately meaningless human historicity on the other. As opposed to this, the claim was upheld in the Church (as Irenaeus expressed it at an early stage) that Jesus of Nazareth as *vere Deus, vere homo* is 'one and the same'. In principle then two possibilities were rejected as heretical: either to take the path to the right and, fascinated by the 'divinity' of Christ, to neglect his human historicity; or to overlook God in him and, interested in his 'humanity' or humanness, to take the path to the left. Both to right and to left there can be discerned a fairly consistent path toward a greater sophistication of heresy; its stages can be marked out systematically almost century by century. While the subsequent heresy on the same path – to right or left – tried to demonstrate its ecclesial character as compared with earlier forms, it protected itself, revised its extreme positions and defined its views more precisely. At the same time however (as Athanasius's prudent approach to the Homoiousians showed at an early stage) it was also possible for progressive sophistication to bring about so close an objective convergence that the deviation became merely verbal and different formulae (like ὁμοούσιος and

---

A. Grillmeir: *Die theologische und sprachliche Vorbereitung der christologischen Formel von Chalkedon* (ET *Christ in Christian Tradition* I, tr. J. Bowdon, London, 1965, rev. edition, 1975); A. Gilg: *Weg und Bedeutung der altkirchlichen Christologie*; J. Liébaert: *Christologie*; B. Skard: *Die Inkarnation* (ET *The Incarnation*).

ὁμοιούσιος) in practice came to mean the same thing (an interesting example of the dubious verbal infallibility of conciliar statements and formulae at that time).

Leaving aside the multiple temporal and spatial intersections and entanglements, what are the essential *models* for the two paths? The chronological succession, deliberately simplified here, obviously cannot be understood without more ado as genetic dependence. Here we are not at all interested primarily in either the one or the other. Our real interest is in the objective connections of the theological problems and the individual christological conceptions (however they may be assessed) as possible christological models. For the rest, we shall relate them to what has been from the time of Irenaeus onwards (or John 1:14) the central concept of becoming man (or becoming flesh: σάρκωσις). How was the attempt made in the first centuries to solve the enigma of the person of Jesus?

1. First of all, how was the attempt made on the *right* to explain the enigma of the person of Jesus?

On this path the first radical attempt at christological interpretation is found in *Docetism,* spreading already in New Testament times and especially in the second century. 'Docetism' however is no more than a collective term for the very diverse, mostly gnostic groups and trends (Marcion stands out above all the rest), known mainly from the writings of their opponents in the Church and now no longer exactly comprehensible in detail. They can nevertheless be brought under a common denominator insofar as they attached the greatest importance to the divinity of Christ, but for that very reason denied that the Son of God had 'truly' come in the flesh. The unity of the person was thus safeguarded: Christ is the Son of God who 'apparently' (δοκεῖν) became man or at least only apparently suffered. The Docetists did not believe that God became *man.* At this point already we see in the background the transcendent-untouchable divinity who cannot be involved in matter, in corporeal reality, and who must remain remote from all the pain of this world, from becoming man and of course especially from suffering and death. Under no circumstances can *becoming* man be ascribed to this divinity.

In the third century we find as part of the same trend (at first with Praxeas and then with Sabellius, both in Rome) a new, moderate attempt at an explanation, that of *Modalism.* Scripture is no longer given short shrift. The Modalists insist (as against the Docetists) that Christ is also man and not merely apparently so. He 'appears' truly in the flesh, but this 'appearing' is transitory. The earthly life of Jesus is nothing but a transitory theophany of divinity in which the Father himself appears in the figure of the Son: Christ is the mask of God. Or, as Sabellius later expressed it, one and the same God appears in three different successive roles: one and the same God appears first as Father, then as Son, and finally as Spirit. Christ is thus the second 'mode' of appearance of the divinity. So, the unity of the person of Christ is assured and at the same time, against all ditheism and tritheism, monotheism (as Monarchianism) is decisively maintained. But this God, who appears on earth as Son, only skims over it lightly in passing and then retires again into his pure divinity. The Modalists do not believe that God truly became *man.* Their untouchable-transcendent divinity is capable only of a purely external incident of 'appearing', which in any case does not mean that God really *became* man.

After the 'Constantinian turning point', in the fourth century, there is a tightening in the development of Christology. It is significant of the new sophistication of heresy that Apollinaris of Laodicea, a pillar of orthodoxy and friend of Athanasius, could defend it for a long time without falling under suspicion. His theory was named after himself: *Apollinarianism.* He had no desire at all to be a Sabellian Modalist. For him the Son is different from the Father but equally eternal with the Father. He became truly and not merely apparently man. Against Arius, Apollinaris defended the true divinity of Christ, but, like the former, kept to the schema (prepared by the apologists and especially by the Alexandrians Clement and Origen and defended also by the Alexandrian Athanasius) of a Logos-*sarx* Christology, according to which the Logos is directly united with the flesh. In the view of Apollinaris, who at least later thought in terms of a trichotomy, the Logos assumed the body and soul of a man, but not the spirit – which is what properly constitutes man's nature. In Christ the divine Logos took the place of the human spirit-soul. At the expense therefore of the divinity of the Logos, Christ's humanity is essentially incomplete and must be so, since it is impossible for one person to emerge from two complete natures. Hence the Logos 'inhabits' the flesh. As opposed to the disjunction Christology of a Paul of Samosata, the unity of the person of Christ is saved, but obviously through a mingling of divinity and humanity in a vital-dynamistic unity of nature (here already we find the term 'one *physis*'); the Logos is the vital force and vital power, permeating and alone animating the flesh. Hence the Apollinarians did not believe after all that God truly became man: Christ's humanity lacks the properly human factor, the spirit. Here too the transcendent-untouchable divinity plays a part: properly speaking, there is no *becoming* man in the sense, that is, of the abasement and emptying of the Logos, of anything more than a splendid radiation of the Logos into the flesh.

The last phase of the christological struggle in the early Church was traced out by the demarcations of the Councils of Nicea and Constantinople, which decisively upheld the true divinity and true humanity of Christ. The extreme form of the Logos-*sarx* Christology was gradually superseded or complemented by the Logos-*anthropos* Christology. The pertinent question now is: *How* are divinity and humanity one? How are divinity and humanity related to each other in Christ? On the path to the right (with Eutyches and Bishop Dioscorus of Alexandria, among others) there is at first a keen interest in the *divine* nature; for it is a question of the encounter with God in Christ. At the same time the human nature is not mutilated (as it was with Apollinaris), but is whole and entire; nevertheless it falls into the background by comparison with the divine nature and is taken up into the latter. The iron becomes wholly and entirely glowing by the fire of divinity: a divinely glowing being, in which the humanity is absorbed. In reality there is only *one* nature – the divine – in Christ. This movement is therefore known as *Monophysitism.* Thus the unity of the person of Christ is again achieved by a mingling of divinity and humanity, in which (as always with this trend) the humanity comes off badly. It is not without reason that the Monophysites in particular are hostile to the title (θεοτόκος) or 'God-bearer' for the mother of Jesus. In the last resort the Monophysites do not take seriously God's becoming *man.* Their God lives on high, untouchable in his heaven, and his Son too is elevated as far away as possible into the divine heaven. Christ is lauded as God, but no one bothers much about the question of God's *becoming* man in the sense of emptying and abasement in suffering and death.

513

2. What are the explanations of the enigma of Jesus on the path to the *left*? In the first and second centuries the counterpart on the left to Docetism on the right is *Ebionitism* (the name is derived not from a person, but from the Hebrew word for 'the poor'). Originating as a Jewish Christian sect and later becoming gnostic-syncretist, it is also no longer exactly comprehensible. For the Ebionites Jesus was the Messiah, the Christ, but they were not faced with the problem of the Docetists: their Messiah was wholly and entirely human. But for that very reason he could not possibly be God. Thus the *unity* of the person is assured: Jesus is the Son of man and as Messiah he is the natural son of an earthly father. The Ebionites did not believe that *God* became man. Once again we find in the background the transcendent-untouchable divinity, whether understood in a Jewish or a Hellenistic sense. For the Ebionites no more than for the Docetists can *becoming* man be ascribed to God.

In the third century, on the path to the left, as the counterpart to Modalism, we find a modified Ebionitism. This is *Adoptionism,* maintained at first by Theodotus the tanner and by his student Theodotus the banker and later (at least according to his opponents) by the famous Antiochene, Bishop Paul of Samosata. On the left also there was no longer any attempt simply to trim Scripture: it was now 'interpreted'. The Adoptionists could take part with a clear conscience in the criticism of the Ebionites and acknowledge that Christ is also 'God'. That is, he became God. The Father filled with the power of the Spirit and accepted, adopted, as Son this incomparable human being who proved to be a model of human existence; when and how could be explained in a variety of ways (in addition to this powerfully ethical motif, Paul made use of the theory of an impersonal divine Logos). It is obvious that no adoration is owed to this 'Son of God'. In this way the unity of the person of Christ is assured and at the same time monotheism (in the form of Monarchianism) is victorious, but in the very opposite sense to that of Modalism. For, unlike Modalism, Adoptionism does not accept any 'appearance' of the divinity from above (as in modalist Monarchianism), but a becoming God from below as a result of man being filled with divine powers of the Spirit (dynamistic Monarchianism). The Adoptionists then do not believe that *God* truly became man. Their untouchable-transcendent divinity permits the ideal man Jesus no more than an affinity with divinity. This is very different from any *becoming* man on God's part.

For the fourth century the struggle about the true Christology became an international political controversy. The counterpart on the left to Apollinarianism was *Arianism*, by which it had been preceded and influenced and which for a long time, with imperial support, dominated the conflict. It is true that Arius follows exactly the trend that goes back by way of his Antiochene teacher Lucian to the latter's own teacher Paul of Samosata. But, unlike primitive Adoptionism, Arius, with the aid of middle-Platonic ideas of ascending stage of being, came much closer to orthodoxy. For him Christ is by no means merely a man adopted as God's Son. He is in fact Son of God before the creation of the World. But this means that the Logos was *created* by the Father before the world was created: there was a time when he did not exist; he was created as the great, divine, intermediate being and instrument for the creation of the world. Essentially different from the Father, he is dissimilar in every respect from the nature of the Father. He can be called 'God' only in virtue of the grace of the Father, which gives him as it gives us a share in the divinity. Since the Logos is not really God, but a creature and changeable, he can 'become'; becoming man and bearing humiliation can be expected of him. The Logos (for Apollinaris uncreated, for Arius created) takes the

with an explicit Logos-*sarx* theology. The Logos became flesh and is thus the redeemer and supreme model for all people. With Arius, as with Apollinaris, the unity of Christ is preserved by a 'mingling' of divinity and humanity. He does not believe that *God* really became man: this Logos lacks divinity (Logos-*ktisma* doctrine). Arius vigorously defends monotheism in the sense of Monarchianism. His God as transcendent-untouchable, as unbegotten, without beginning, as eternal, unchangeable substance, cannot have any Son properly speaking. Still less can he become man. Only a changeable creature can become anything. *Becoming* man, particularly in the sense of emptying and abasement, must be absolutely excluded from God.

In the fifth century, as the last phase on the path to the left, there followed the vigorous reaction of the school of Antioch against Alexandria, the centre of Monophysitism: here all kinds of contrasts in politics, philosophy, exegesis and theological method were involved. After the death of the much misunderstood Theodore of Mopsuestia, his disciple, Nestorius, Patriarch of Constantinople, became the leader of this movement. Hence we speak of *Nestorianism*. As opposed to the Alexandrian allegorical interpretation of Scripture, the school of Antioch started out with a straightforward exegesis of the Christ-image of the gospels and thus in fact from Christ's humanity. Christ's divinity was in no way denied; although Arius had been an Antochene, no one wanted to be an Arian. Yet, as opposed to Monophysitism, it had to be made clear that Christ's free will must remain intact, his human soul must be taken seriously, his humanity is not to be absorbed by the consuming fire of divinity, but must be separated from the latter. This is a Christology constructed symmetrically within the Word-man schema in which the unity is emphatically asserted but not secured (as in Alexandrian Christology) by a unique hypostasis of the Logos. The separation of the natures, understood in its extreme form, thus led to the division of the person into two subjects, exercising their exclusive divine or human powers, so that their unity could not be made credible: it was a disjunction Christology. A unity in Christ is attained, but in practice (within the schema of the 'indwelling') it is a purely accidental unity. As compared with the exaggerated unity asserted by the Monophysites, the internal-personal unity in Christ here becomes profoundly questionable. In the light of their starting-point it can be understood why the Nestorians wanted to substitute 'Christ-bearer' for Mary's title of 'God-bearer'. In the last resort they did not take seriously *God's* becoming man. The Logos remains ultimately untouchable in God, revealing himself in the *divine* in Jesus but not in the latter's humanity. for the Nestorians the divinity 'dwells' in the human temple and what might be called God's *becoming* man, his emptying and abasement, is only apparently involved.

Because the context of the problem changed considerably after 325, the *Council of Chalcedon* attempted to define more precisely the answer of Nicea, by starting out, not from the concrete unity of Jesus as an historical human being, but from the difference of the two natures or substances (first formulated by Melito of Sardis), of the divine and the human. This magnificently simple theological synthesis, more than any other, has determined the Church's Christology up to the present time; and yet in a variety of respects (not least in regard to the break in Church unity with the Monophysite Churches of Syria, Palestine and Egypt, and later the loss of these regions

515

associated with the beginnings of Christianity) it is a very problematic theological compromise formula:

'Therefore, following the holy Fathers, we all with one accord teach men to acknowledge one and the same Son, our Lord Jesus Christ, at once complete in Godhead and complete in manhood, truly God and truly man, consisting also of a reasonable soul and body; of one substance (ὁμοούσιος) with the Father as regards his Godhead, and at the same time of one substance with us as regards his manhood; like us in all respects, apart from sin; as regards his Godhead, begotten of the Father before the ages, but yet as regards his manhood begotten, for us men and for our salvation, of Mary the Virgin, the God-bearer (θεοτόκος): one and the same Christ, Son, Lord, Only-begotten, recognized in two natures (ἐν δύο φύσεσιν), without confusion (ἀσυγχύτως), without change (ἀρεπτως), without division (ἀδιαιρέτως) without separation (ἀχώριστος): the distinction of natures being in no way annulled by the union, but rather the characteristics of each nature being preserved and coming together to form one person and subsistence (ὑπόστασις), not as parted or separated into two persons, but one and the same Son and Only-begotten God the Word, Lord Jesus Christ' (*DS,* 301-302).[2]

The great minds of Christian antiquity had made their own contribution (sometimes positively, sometimes negatively) to the preparation of this formulary. It was a troublesome history with numerous transmutations of terms and ideas and a variety of (often very dubious) fluctuations.

The history of orthodoxy, beginning with the New Testament writings, is itself just as exciting as the history of heterodoxy. The starting-point of the Nicene formula *vere Deus, vere homo* may well have been in particular the dual way of considering Jesus 'according to the flesh' and 'according to the Spirit' as it is set out formally in Romans 1:3-4.

The Apostolic Fathers followed (for example, with the famous double origin Christ-formula of Ignatius of Antioch) and Irenaeus (in addition to the formula already mentioned, the soteriological perspective of his *anakephalaiosis* theory – equally stressed later only with Athanasius – is important), as also Melito of Sardis and Hippolytus of Rome. With the apologists (especially Justin), starting out from John's Prologue, Christology was developed with the aid of the Logos-concept and in this way the attempt was made positively to come to terms with Hellenistic philosophy. But few had so decisive an influence on the development of Christology as the Latin Tertullian who anticipated with amazing clarity many formularies established in Greek theology only after protracted struggles (for example, *videmus duplicem*

---

[2]H. Bettenson: *Documents of the Christian Church,* 2nd edition, 73; on the origin and theological analysis of the definition cf. I. Ortiz de Urbina: *Das Symbol von Chalkedon.*

statum, non confusum sed coniunctum in una persona, Deum et hominem Jesum), thus exercising an important influence not only on Augustine, but also on Leo the Great, and therefore indirectly on the Council of Chalcedon.

The third century opened with the Alexandrians Clement and Origen as the clearly dominant figures; Origen's Logos Christology formed the provisional (but not undisputed) culmination of the Christology of the early Church. But the controversies about this Alexandrian Logos Christology began mainly in connection with Arianism and were dominated on the orthodox side by the powerful figure of Athanasius of Alexandria, the guiding spirit of the Council of Nicea. Athanasius upheld as official teaching of the Church a form of the Logos-*sarx* Christology stressing particularly the unity of the subject, which is the Logos alone as bearer of all Jesus' intellectual vital functions; the *sarx* is merely the *organon,* the tool, of the Logos. Reaction to the one-sided Logos-*sarx* Christology took the form of the Logos-*anthropos* Christology of the Antiochene school, according to which the Logos was united to a complete human being with body and soul, thus seeming to imperil the unity of Christ and to lead to a disjunction Christology (which Theodoure of Mopsuestia, for instance, certainly did not want). To this Cyril of Alexandria responded with a corrected Athanasian Logos-*sarx* Christology, not always with a felicitous chance of terms ('one *physis*', for example): there was a renewed emphasis on the unity of Christ, which Cyril centred in the personal element while attributing duality objectively to the nature; Christ has his own human soul, but no human hypostasis; the Logos is united, not with an individual human being, but with a human nature which is merely the 'clothing' of the Logos. Out of the controversies (with Theodoret of Cyrus and Andrew of Samosata) resulting directly from Cyril's doctrine, and through the intervention of the Patriarchs of Constantinople Proclus and Flavian and the important influence of Latin theology (represented by Leo the Great), there emerged the compromise formula of Chalcedon.

The Council attempted to overcome the traditional dilemma: either an assumption of the individual human being Jesus (in the Antiochene sense), thus involuntarily sacrificing the complete unity of Christ with God, or the assumption of a complete unity by a single, that is, divine, hypostasis (in the Alexandrian sense), thus involuntarily sacrificing the complete individual humanity of Jesus. In this way the Council sought to take up the correct and permanent element of truth on both sides: on the Antiochene the real humanity of Jesus, on the Alexandrian the unsurpassable unity of Jesus with God. Nevertheless the solution remained problematic in as much as Chalcedon simply offered a compromise without a new starting point and (according to where the stress was laid) either the unity of Jeus with God or his true humanity was bound to be imperilled.

517

It was then a long and immensely varied history which led to the Chalcedonian definition. With it the ontological interpretation of biblical Christology through the medium of Greek metaphysics, which laid the emphasis not on happenings and events, but on being, was at any rate provisionally completed: not only had the conceptual framework changed, but the points of emphasis had been shifted and some perspectives altered. Hence it is doubtful whether many exegetes could subscribe in the light of the New Testament to the opinion of the historian of dogma, Alois Grillmeier, stated at the end of his penetrating study: 'The first impression thrust upon us is that of an intrinsic link between the two end-points. The Bible and Chalcedon are not opposed to one another. The formula of the "one person in two natures", who is Christ, has its clearly recognizable basis in Scripture. The whole history of the development of the christological formula is nothing but the history of essentially biblical patterns, among which John 1:14 occupies a predominant place. The tensions which could be observed already in the biblical manner of speaking continue throughout the whole history of the christological kerygma – up to our own time.'[3] The second Excursus may perhaps throw more light on this point.

EXCURSUS II
CAN GOD SUFFER?

Harnack's thesis – influenced by Ritschl – of the 'Hellenisation' of the Gospel, like the similar theories of the great historians of dogma, Loofs and Seeberg, cannot be taken over (particularly in Christology) without some correction. New philosophical terms were introduced into Christian theology, not only for the sake of metaphysical speculation, but also in order to understand better the concrete person of Jesus Christ (hence we find the word 'Logos' already in John's Prologue); and the process of establishing christological dogma, despite all alien influences, was continually given new directions in the light of the concrete Christ-image of the Scriptures and especially of the synoptic gospels. Recently, as we saw, not only in connection with the work of the apologists, but also in connection with early Christian dogma, there has been talk of a certain 'de-Hellenisation', insofar, that is, as the official doctrinal development of the Church became dissociated in the course of time, not from the biblical Logos idea, but from metaphysical Logos speculation as it went on from Justin to Origen. It is notable that the First

---

[3] A. Grillmeier: *Die theologische and sprachliche Vorbereitung der christologischen Formel von Chalkedon* I, 199; ET *Christ in Christian Tradition* 1,

Ecumenical Council of Nicea in particular appealed to John's Prologue but not to the speculatively over-burdened Logos idea. The term 'Logos' was deliberately avoided by the Council.

However, it would obviously be impossible to overlook the enormous influence of Greek philosophy on orthodox Christology. And it is also obvious that the more orthodox Christian theology made use of the Greek idea of God, the more it was imperilled not only by intellectualism and moralism but by the threatening loss of the soteriological factor and the exaggeration of the cosmological (understood in a Hellenistic-Platonic sense), by an open or concealed deism suspicious of any vital activity of God in the world, by a spiritualism aristocratically contemptuous of matter and flesh, by a dualism excluding any commonality between God and man.

As we observed, all the early heresies, in one form or another, to a greater or lesser extent, were tied to a philosophical notion of an absolute, transcendent-untouchable God which, particularly in the Hellenistic understanding of that time, largely represented an eclectic blend of Platonic-Plotinian ideas, Aristotelian logic and Stoic belief in providence (but without Stoic pantheism). In reality, however, even the different schools of orthodoxy, without dissolving the paradoxical tension of the christological statement in a one-sided heretical fashion, tended in the sense described above either to the right (especially the Alexandrians) or to the left (especially the Antiochenes); each side was thus faced with quite specific dangers and difficulties.

But, over and above these specific dangers, difficulties can be perceived with which *all* theological schools of orthodoxy had to struggle and which again evidently result from the philosophical idea of God. As already indicated, a contrast can be observed between the classical Greek idea of God and the biblical testimony with reference to all God's attributes, but especially his incomprehensibility and ineffability, immutability and simplicity, eternity and freedom. All these questions were bound to come to a head in Christology, since (as Ignatius of Antioch made clear with his famous 'double origin formula') in the *one* Jesus Christ the most clear-cut antitheses appeared in a unity: fleshly/spiritual, visible/invisible, unoriginated/born, perishable/imperishable, finite/infinite etc. And yet with no pair of opposites is the drama of the question so apparent or (particularly in the light of the gospels) so vivid as it is with the antithesis suffering/without suffering. The two recent accounts (Catholic and Protestant) of pre-Chalcedonian Christology, by Alois Grillmeier and Werner Elert, agree in regarding suffering, $\pi\acute{\alpha}\theta\eta$ (whether in the narrower sense of physical suffering and pain or in the wider sense of passions, emotions and instincts), as wholly and entirely a crucial difficulty for the Christology of the early Church. In this respect the question of physically painful or physically painless suffering was quite secondary; the primary question was that of suffering in any sense, that is, with reference to God himself: can *God* suffer? Can he suffer anything?

Within orthodoxy (unlike the Docetists, who radically denied Christ's suffering) it was impossible to dispute the fact that according to the gospels the *one* Jesus Christ suffered hunger and thirst, weariness and blows, joy and sadness, love and anger, and in the end troubles and pains, Godforsakenness and death. Not only with heterodoxy however, but also with orthodoxy, we encounter a variety of attempts to tone down, restrict, re-interpret and even profoundly to question these gospel statements. Over and over again in the patristic age we find an inclination to attribute to Christ an *apatheia,* an impassibility, as far-reaching as possible, either merely in the sense of painlessness or even of a general lack of feeling. What is the source of this peculiar phenomenon, so much the more peculiar since the gospels contain no statements on these lines but (like the epistles and the Johannine writings) are marked by an outspoken realism of suffering?

Obviously the focal points of the christological controversy were continually changing in the course of the progress of discussion and of the development of dogma; this also necessitated a number of changes of emphasis. While theology (in connection with the trinitarian discussion) was initially mainly interested in the pre-existent Christ and his consubstantiality with the Father, after the Council of Nicea interest was concentrated mainly on the Christ become man and the relationship between divinity and humanity in him. In this respect attention was first directed to the transition properly speaking from the pre-existent to the incarnate-that is, to the act of becoming man. But here too there emerged a further shift of emphasis: from God's Son's *becoming* man (becoming one, act of incarnation, uniting of the natures) to God's Son's *being* man (being one, state of incarnation, union of the natures); while Cyril still spoke of the 'Emmanual *from* two natures', the Council of Chalcedon spoke of the 'Christ *in* two natures'. But is this shift of emphasis from a mainly dynamically oriented to a mainly static Christology sufficient to explain the tendency to attribute impassibility to Christ? Actually the trend could be observed very much earlier, even with the apologists.

Grillmeier throughout his whole work has thrown a great deal of light on the close connection between the difficulties associated with Christ's ability to suffer and the denial (with Apollinaris and the Arians) or neglect (with, among others, some orthodox Alexandrians) of his human intellectuality, his human soul and the importance of these for salvation. Under these circumstances there was no genuine human medium of suffering, particularly of mental $\pi\acute{a}\theta\eta$. But this alone does not explain everything. For in the first place there is frequently a tendency to assert also an impassibility on the part of the body and a desire to free Christ from all corporeal $\pi\acute{a}\theta\eta$; Clement of

Alexandria, for instance, goes so far as to deny to Christ any real digestion or excretion. Secondly, there is often a tendency to attribute impassibility also to the *soul* of Christ by glossing over the passions and up to a point even asserting an immobility of his soul. It may also be asked whether it is merely the result of overlooking Christ's soul that some Fathers, like Athanasius himself, can regard Christ's fear as not real but only 'pretended', or do not take seriously the ignorance which Christ himself admitted.

Why then, even within orthodoxy, is there this dangerous tendency (contrary to all the statements of Scripture) to maintain an impassibility of Christ's body and soul, that is, of his humanity as a whole? Again Grillmeier and Elert agree in the statement that the inclination to attribute impassibility to the *humanity of Christ* arose out of the hope of protecting in this way the impassibility of the *divine Logos* himself: for *a God who bore suffering could not be truly God.* This principle of God's impassibility was taken for granted as the presupposition for the christological discussions of the first centuries.[1] However, the consequences of this assumption were very varied: some took the suffering seriously at the expense of the divinity; others took the divinity seriously at the expense of the suffering. For the leftward trend of heterodoxy Christ had obviously endured and suffered (as is utterly obvious from the gospel accounts), but for that very reason he could not be truly God like the Father (Ebionitism, Adoptionism, Arianism) or divinity and humanity must be rigorously divided and separated in Christ (Nestorianism). For the other – the rightward – trend of heterodoxy, Christ's divinity (this too based on an appeal to Scripture) was beyond discussion and for that very reason the ἀνθρώπινα (suffering being the most truly human reality) in the last resort could not be seriously attributed to him (Docetism, Modalism, Apollinarianism, Monophysitism). But the same assumption of God's impassibility caused dangerous tensions also within orthodoxy. Some were inclined to distinguish divinity and humanity in Christ so rigorously that suffering could only be on the part of the human nature without any intrinsic reference to the divine person (the Antiochene tendency); others toned down the suffering of body and soul in Christ to such an extent that it could no longer 'endanger' the divinity and impassibility of the Logos (the Alexandrian tendency).

It was however impossible to overlook the fact that in the New Testament the ἀνθρώπινα are predicated to the Son of God himself: 'That which was from the beginning, which we have heard, which we have seen with our eyes, which we have looked upon and touched with our hands, concerning the word of life . . .' (1 Jn 1:1); 'God sent forth his Son, born of woman, born under the

---

[1]cf. also G. L. Prestige: *God in Patristic Thought*, London, 1952, 6–9, 11.

law' (Gal 4:4; cf. Rom 1:3; 9:5); 'they crucified the Lord of glory' (1 Cor 2:8); 'you killed the Author of life' (Acts 3:15). Scripture speaks of 'the blood of God's own Son' (Acts 20:28), of the 'foolishness of God' and the 'weakness of God' (1 Cor 1:25). And finally there is the *locus classicus* (Phil 2:6-8): 'though he was in the form of God, he did not count equality with God as a thing to be grasped, but emptied himself, taking the form of a servant, being born in the likeness of men. And being found in human form he humbled himself and became obedient unto death, even death on a cross'.

Is it a question here only of an undifferentiated, unphilosophical mode of expression? Classical Christology repeatedly insists that in the redeeming èvent of Christ's life, suffering and death, everything depends on the one fact that, not only a man, but God himself, is involved: that the *Son of God himself* lived, suffered and died. Hence the very first Christian theologians, following the words of Scripture, did not hesitate to express this basic datum of Scripture in the strongest possible terms. Irenaeus speaks of the 'sufferings of my God' and of the 'blood of God'; Melito of Sardis, Tatian and others say that 'God suffered'. Later, Tertullian too speaks of the suffering and the blood of God and even of the 'dead God'; Gregory Thaumaturgus speaks similarly in his work on the 'Impassibility and the Passibility of God'. And the pillars of Nicean orthodoxy also, such as Athanasius, Cyril of Alexandria and Hilary of Poitiers, speak of the 'suffering God' or of the 'crucified God'.

But none of the statements of this kind (often kept up more as a matter of convention than as formal declarations) makes any difference to the fact that the suffering of the one and entire Christ was too frequently not taken seriously enough and the fear of infringing the principle of impassibility was stronger than the fear of mutilating the gospel image of Christ; far too often the statements about suffering were toned down or restricted without more ado to the humanity of Christ.

Meanwhile the great christological councils never failed, despite all their diversity of approach, to stress plainly the unity of the person of Christ. In this respect credit is due to the Alexandrian school for clearly reorienting an image of Christ far too symmetrically constructed from divinity and humanity on to the Logos as the sole sustaining hypostasis. Not only the letter of Cyril of Alexandria, approved by the Council of Ephesus (*DS,* 250-251), but also his anathemas, presented to the Council and from then onwards recognised as orthodox, clearly insist on the unity of Christ (*DS,* 253), the union in being (*DS,* 254), the impossibility of a division of the biblical predicates between the Logos and the man in Christ (*DS,* 255); after all this there follows the clear statement on the suffering of the Word of God: 'If anyone does not confess that the Word of God suffered in the flesh, was crucified in the flesh and tasted death in the flesh, let him be anathema' (*DS,* 264). The letter of Leo I to

Flavian, which was so important for the Council of Chalcedon, subsequently stresses very clearly the distinction of natures and operations. Nevertheless, nothing Nestorian may be read into this letter: there is nothing to suggest that perhaps only the flesh may have suffered. The Logos, who acts through the two natures (this is how the Chalcedonian definition must be interpreted), is and remains the subject of all action, since the humanity has no hypostasis of its own. Leo too stresses the unity of the person (*DS*, 293, 301) and predicates the crucifixion of the 'only-begotten Son of God'.

Yet it is striking that the decree of Chalcedon (which by no means represents the convincing conclusion to all debates) contains no statements properly speaking about suffering; a definition therefore had still to be provided. But in principle the decision had already been taken when, despite the emphasis on the duality of the natures, a human birth was ascribed to 'one and the same Son and Only-begotten God the Logos' and with the emphasis proper to the term θεοτόκος as used at Ephesus. Since human birth involves suffering, the Council of Chalcedon also attributes suffering implicitly to the divine subject. This is confirmed by the formal approval given by Popes John II (*DS*, 401) and Agapitus I, and eventually by the Second Ecumenical Council of Constantinople in 553 (*DS*, 432) to the vigorously disputed formula, 'One of the Trinity suffered' (whatever may be made historically of the papal approval of this council).[2] The same council (to a certain extent in contrast to the Tome of Leo) clearly declares: 'If anyone says that there was one God the Word who did miracles, and another Christ who suffered, or that God the Word was with Christ when he was born of a woman, or was in him, as one person in another, and not that there was one and the same Lord Jesus Christ, God the Word incarnate and made man, and that the miracles and the sufferings which he endured voluntarily in the flesh did not pertain to the same person, let him be anathema' (*DS*, 423). The same teaching is found at the Third Council of Constantinople in 680-681, with a stronger emphasis however on the duality of will and the mode of operation: 'Both the miracles and the sufferings we ascribe to one and the same, according to one or the other of the natures from which and in which he exists, as the admirable Cyril says' (*DS*, 557).

These post-Chalcedonian definitions (and with them a long series of formularies and anathemas) had proved necessary to interpret and define more precisely, to supplement and balance the Chalcedonian definition. This fact and the historical development behind it prove that the Chalcedonian

---

[2]cf. C. Moeller: *Le chalcédonisme et le néo-chalcédonisme en Orient de 451 à la fin du VI siècle*, 687-690. A. Grillmeier expresses doubts about Moeller's and E. Amann's questioning of the papal approbation, *Vorbereitung des Mittealters* II, 823.

definition may have provided the Church with important guidelines, but did not by any means solve all problems; this is clear not least from the breakaway of the Monophysite Churches, the first great and permanent denominational schism in the *oikoumene*. The question of Christ's suffering, which had been excluded at Chalcedon, broke out with quite extraordinary vehemence a few years after the Council, when Peter Fullo, Patriarch of Antioch, added the words 'who was crucified for us' to the Trisagion in the Good Friday liturgy: 'Holy God, Holy and strong, Holy immortal One'. From that time onwards the Theopaschite controversy dominated the sixth century (from 519 there was also the controversy about the expression 'one of the Trinity suffered') and in the seventh century developed into the Monothelite controversy. These disputes and disturbances shaking Church and Empire had broken out from *within* Chalcedonian orthodoxy, being the result of the confrontation of the dogmatic formula of Chalcedon with the Christ-image of the gospels.[3]

The post-Chalcedonian discussions and definitions showed that suffering cannot be restricted simply to the humanity of Christ and thus excluded from God's Son, without neglecting or even abandoning the unity of the person of Christ as it is presented to us in the gospels. But we have already drawn attention to the fact (brought out particularly clearly by Werner Elert[4]) that the question of suffering was decided in principle with the acceptance of the *Theotokos* formula into the Chalcedonian decree. Even to be born is to suffer. And if being born can and must be predicated, not only of the man Christ (as in Nestorius' *Christokos* formula), but of God himself the Logos made man (in the *Theotokos* formula of Ephesus and Chalcedon), then all other suffering described in the gospels can and must in principle also be predicated, not only of the man Christ, but of God the Logos himself. In other words, the one to whom Mary gave birth also died suffering on the cross. If (according to Nestorius) she gave birth only to the man Christ, then it is also only the man Christ who died suffering on the cross; but if (according to Ephesus and Chalcedon) she truly gave birth to God (the Son), then God (the Son) truly died suffering on the cross. Or yet again: the subject of the incarnation remains the subject of all that is related of the incarnate One in life, suffering and death. If the subject of the incarnation (according to Nestorius) is the man Christ, then suffering and dying also must be predicated of the man Christ; if the subject of the incarnation (according to Ephesus and Chalcedon) is not the man Christ (whose humanity is in fact without a human subject and who has

---

[3]On this cf., among others, the studies by W. Elert in *Ausgang der altkirchlichen Christologie,* in which he shows that Theodore of Pharan, the founder of Monothelitism, was not a Monophysite, but a Chalcedonian theologian.
[4]Cf. W. Elert: *Der Ausgang der altkirchlichen Christologie*, 92f; 113f.

his own hypostasis in the divine subject of the Logos), but God the Logos, then suffering and dying also must be predicated of God the Logos.

Because of the principle of impassibility, the Antiochenes were thus completely logical in opposing the *Theotokos* principle; and since they wanted at all costs to avoid the term 'God-bearer', they avoided also the expression 'God who was crucified and died'.[5] Anyone who accepts the *Theotokos* principle must in some way restrict the impassibility principle. But the question must be raised once again here: What is the source of the tendency to attribute impassibility to Christ? The answer is that the source is the principle of the impassibility of God himself. But what then is the source of the principle of God's impassibility?

On this point we can agree with Elert who, especially in his chapter 'The Suffering Christ, Image and Dogma',[6] has provided the most thorough investigation of this problem.[7] In his opinion, at the very beginning of Christian theology the principle of God's impassibility was not really substantiated from Scripture; it occurred more in the form of a self-evident axiom, taken over in practice from Plato's theory of God. Only too often, behind the Christ-image, we catch sight of 'the immobile, dispassionate countenance of the God of Plato, augmented by some features of Stoic ethics'.[8]

EXCURSUS III
THE DIALECTIC OF THE ATTRIBUTES OF GOD

Not only in ecclesiastical antiquity, but also throughout the middle ages, intense efforts were made to produce a theological description of the person of Christ. Mediaeval Christology had been prepared by the Theopaschite controversies, the conflict about the 'Three Chapters' and the Monothelite dispute, in which the antagonisms between unification and disjunction Christology – scarcely more than covered up by Chalcedon – broke out afresh and the 'two natures schema' was pushed through uncompromisingly in a Dyothelite sense: Christ has two different wills and operations (*energeiai*). In the West too at the same time all kinds of tensions and fluctuations emerged, as can be seen from the attitudes of Popes Vigilius, Pelagius I, Pelagius II,

---

[5]Cf. A. Michel: art. '*Idiomes*' in *DTC*, vol. VII, col. 598 and T. Camelot: *De Nestorius à Eutuchès* I, 219–221, 226f.
[6]W. Elert: *op. cit.,* 71-132.
[7]cf. also W. Pannenberg: 'The Appropriation of the Philosophical Concept of God as a Dogmatic Problem of Early Christian Theology', *Basic Questions in Theology* II, 159-165.
[8]W. Elert: *op. cit.,* 74; cf. 121f etc.

Gregory I, Honorius I, Martin I, and from the Lateran Synod of 649.[1] Subsequent Latin theology, however, was based on the strictly Chalcedonian Christology of Boethius, Cassiodorus, Gregory I and Isidore of Seville. In the eighth century extreme tendencies were found with the Spanish Adoptionists who placed an excessive emphasis on the duality of natures; but this emphasis should not be ascribed to the influence of the Chalcedonian definition.[2] In the ninth century on the other hand the main stress was laid on the unity of Christ by Scotus Eriugena, who relied for the most part on Maximus the Confessor, but had largely lost contact with the great christological controversies and had little influence on the scholastic development of Latin theology.

In the *early scholasticism* of the twelfth century,[3] when Greek was generally little known and reliance had to be placed on Latin translations of the Greek philosophers and theologians and also of the acts of the councils, the basic ideas and the essential formulae of Chalcedon continued to exercise an influence, mainly through the mediation of the *Quicumque* creed, of the Latin Fathers of the fifth and sixth centuries and the Latin translation of John Damascene's *De fide orthodoxa*. But 'the Council's definition of faith played scarcely any part in the lively christological discussions of the theologians'.[4] In their Christology neither Abelard with his school nor Peter Lombard, Robert of Melun, Praepositinus of St Victor, William of Auxerre, Anselm of Laon, Alexander of Hales, Bonaventure or Albert the Great quote any text from the Chalcedonian definitions; nor do they even mention the Council at all. Dogmas and councils can apparently be forgotten or passed over in silence. In early scholasticism only Walter of St Victor quotes the centrepiece of the Chalcedonian decree.[5] Naturally the subtleties of the post-Chalcedonian controversies are even less known. But there is an echo of Chalcedon in such expressions as 'the one Christ in two natures', 'one person in two natures', 'a giant in dual form', *'perfectus Deus, perfectus homo'*; in particular, any assumption of a transformation or blending of the two natures was excluded.[6]

At the same time (with Peter Lombard, for instance) there was an excessive emphasis on the duality of the natures. Peter Lombard adopted an obviously benevolent attitude toward the neo-Nestorian *habitus* theory, which went back to Abelard. According to this theory, the Son of God

---

[1]On this period cf. A. Grillmeier: *Vorbereitung des Mittelalters.*
[2]On this cf. J. Solano: *El Concilio de Calcedonia y la controversia adopcionista del siglo VIII en España.*
[3]On the Christology of early scholastiscism cf. L. Ott: *Das Konzil von Chalkedon in der Frühscholastik.*
[4]*op. cit.*, 921.
[5]*op. cit.*, 88f.
[6]*op. cit.*, 904-909.

assumed humanity merely externally as a garment. For Abelard, the proposition 'God is man, man is God' was merely a metaphorical expression, not to be understood literally. The logical conclusion of the *habitus* theory was the nihilianist proposition *Christus secundum quod homo non est aliquid,* according to which the humanity assumed as a garment is nothing essential or substantial in Christ; otherwise the Logos would have been changed. The school of St Victor (represented by Achard and Richard) and Gerhoh of Reichersberg especially attacked this neo-Nestorianism; the theory was condemned by Alexander III in 1177. A similar Nestorian tendency (within the Logos-man schema) appeared in the *assumptus* theory, according to which in the incarnation 'a man' is assumed and this *homo assumptus* becomes a human *suppositum* alongside the divine. On the other hand (often presupposing the *assumptus* theory) some Victorines like Hugo and Achard and the brothers Arno and Gerhoh of Reichersberg tended toward Monophysitism insofar as they simply identified the human attributes with the divine and thus ascribed divine wisdom, onmipotence and so on to the human nature.[7]

High scholasticism, following on Peter Lombard, also had to cope with with the *habitus* theory, the *assumptus* theory and the subsistence theory.[8] After its condemnation, the *habitus* theory was generally abandoned in favour of the *assumptus* theory which remained predominant up to the first decades of the thirteenth century. But by then Alexander of Hales, Bonaventure, Albert the Great and others had expressed misgivings in regard to it. Aquinas finally (the only representative of high scholasticism to draw on the documents of Chalcedon) rejected it categorically in his early *Commentary on the Sentences*; later he rejected it forthrightly as Nestorian heresy. The theologians of high scholasticism thus came to adopt the subsistence theory, founded by Gilbert de la Porrée, according to which the person of Christ, after the incarnation, no longer subsists merely in one (divine) nature but in two natures; the human nature too has its subsistence in the divine Logos. 'In the *Summa Theologica* Aquinas opposes to Monophysitism and also to Nestorianism decisive statements from the definition of Chalcedon. The significance for the history of theology of Aquinas's recourse to this definition of Chalcedon in order to repel the disjunction theory and Monophysitism can scarcely be exaggerated. A weightier or more relevant authority could not and cannot be brought to bear on the matter. Before and after Aquinas, we never find these principles quoted in high scholasticism as conciliar statements. And even for

---

[7]On these Nestorian and neo-Nestorian deviations cf. L. Ott: *op. cit.,* 909–921.
[8]cf. I. Backes: *Die christologische Problematik der Hochscholastik und ihre Beziehungen zu Chalkedon.*

Aquinas no further contribution to Christology emerged from the documents of Chalcedon. The comments in the *corpus articuli* do not indicate any direct influence of the Council.[9]

For the scholastics subsequently the problem of the unity of the person of Jesus Christ is expressed by the questions: Why is the human nature not a human person? What does it need to make it a human person? Some answer purely negatively: The human nature of Christ is not a human person because it lacks independence (Scotus) or because it lacks integrity (Tiphanius). Others probe more deeply and ask *why* it lacks independence and totality, to which they answer: The human nature of Christ is not an independent and completely human person because, although it has its own properly human existence, it lacks the specifically substantial mode of existence (Suarez speaks of a *modus subsistentiae*) or lacks any existence of its own at all, the latter being replaced by the divine existence of the Logos (most Thomists, following Capreolus, hold this view); there is also a midway solution (defended by Cajetan). It is obvious that these solutions depend on the general ontology of these authors (for example, on the distinction between essence and existence, being such and simply being; and in the light of this initial intuitive understanding of being as such).[10]
Scholastics hitherto have not reached any unanimous opinion on the question whether this one person has *one* actual existence (in scholastic terminology, *esse* as opposed to *essentia* or *natura*), that is, divine existence, or whether this person has *two*, a divine and a human.

Undoubtedly the scholastic formulation of the question goes deeper than that of Chalcedon. The question is no longer merely about person and nature, but (while affirming one person in two natures) about existence itself: that is, whether the human nature has its own existence or not. At the same time, however, it cannot be overlooked that the guidelines for the scholastic solutions are supplied not so much by the concrete Jesus Christ of the gospels, as by a variety of conceptual, logical and ontological reflections. If we want to proceed on these lines, it would be possible to probe even more deeply by asking about the being such of the two 'natures' themselves; by asking, that is, what personal unity (or unity in existence) means, not only in the abstract by heaping up further abstract predicates which add little more to our knowledge (*unitas personalis, substantialis, hypostatica* etc.), but what it means in the concrete – that is, for the two 'natures' – and then not simply in the light of a metaphysical system but in the light of the biblical statements themselves. If theologians start out by neglecting Scripture and taking it for granted that they know from common sense or their philosophical understanding what man is and what God is, and if they assume that in Christology, in order to

---

[9] *op. cit.*, 936.
[10] For a comprehensive survey of the individual scholastic attempts at a solution see A. Michel: art. '*Hypostatique*' in *DTC*, vol. VII: 1, coll. 510–541; cf. *idem*: art. '*Incarnation*' in *DTC*, vol. VII:2, coll. 1445-1539.

know what Christ is, we have only to bring together in faith these two known factors and link them with an equal sign (which is paradoxical in the last resort) – if then we start out from a concept of man and God assumed to be obvious, we ought really to wonder if we are quite certain that we know in the concrete what man is theologically and what God is theologically. There would in fact be another way open to theologians: to try to see in the concrete Christ what man is theologically and what God is theologically.

If we want to follow up this question, not only, as recently discussed, from the aspect of consciousness (that is, of the divine and human consciousness in Christ), but at the same time linking up with the classical tradition, then it would seem appropriate to make use of the theory of the *communicatio idiomatum* ('communion of properties') and in the light of that the interchangeability of predicates, which has always represented a touchstone of orthodoxy for the dogma of God's incarnation. The *communicatio idiomatum* follows directly from the personal unity of the one Jesus Christ and requires the attributes and operations of the two natures not to be divided between two subjects, asserting that the attributes and operations of the *human* nature must be predicated of the divine Logos and the attributes and operations of the *divine* nature must be predicated of that *same* self insofar as it is the personal power by which the human nature exists. Consistently, we ought therefore to say that *God* (not the divinity) is born, eats, sleeps, shows anger, pardons, suffers, dies... but also that this *man* (not the humanity) is omniscient, omnipotent, ubiquitous...

The theory of the *communicatio idiomatum* was used for the concrete description of the person of Jesus Christ long before it was considered more deeply and investigated systematically – in Greek theology by Origen, Ephraem, Athanasius, Cyril of Jerusalem and particularly by Gregory of Nyssa; in Latin theology by Tertullian, Arnobius, Hilary and particularly by Augustine.[11] The therory became relevant especially in the struggle against the Nestorian disjunction Christology. With the approval of the Fathers, Cyril of Alexandria established the theory of the *communicatio idiomatum* at the admittedly very controversial Council of Ephesus (*DS*, 255, 262, 263). The Council approved the title of God-bearer (*DS*, 250, 2520 which had been rejected by the Antiochenes. Subsequently the scholastics developed the theory down to the last detail and set up precise rules for its use.[12] The most important feature is that the rules apply to concrete, not to abstract, speech. We cannot simply say that the divinity (the Absolute) died, but only that God died; not that humanity (human nature) is omnipotent, but that this man is omnipotent. Negative statements are particularly dubious: it is wrong to say, for instance, that the Word of God did not suffer.

---

[11]On the history of the *communicatio idiomatum* cf. Petavius: *De incarnatione*, bk IV, chs. 14-15; A. Michel: art. '*Idiomes*' in *DTC*, vol. VII:1, coll. 595–602.

[12]cf., for example, Aquinas: *Summa Theologica* III, q. 16 a.4–5; in more detail Petavius: *De incarnatione*, bk. IV, ch. 16.

The scholastic theory of the *communicatio idiomatum* based on the doctrine of the two natures, was meant to achieve consistency when talking either of the unity or of the duality in Christ. At the same time it is unmistakably opposed (in mediaeval scholastic theology and in later Reformed theology as distinct from Cyril and, later, the Lutheran theology) more to an exaggerated unity than to an over stretched duality. With the doctrine of the two natures, however, the important thing is that statements about the unity are taken just as seriously as those about the duality and especially that what is considered is something concrete. What is it supposed to mean when we say that, despite his two natures, Christ is 'one', if we are merely repeating the same thing in different terms by giving to this unity a variety of explanatory names (substantial, hypostatic, personal unity)?

The consequences of such a *communicatio idiomatum* need to be considered afresh. It is not meant to be a mere grammatical or linguistic rule, but to express something about the reality of Christ himself. But what is it supposed to mean, for example, when, according to these rules, it can and must be said that God died? God *has* died? The *Immortal* died? In *Jesus Christ* God died? This dying then is not merely predicated of God; it is predicated of him because it *is* so. According to the rules the statement is supposed to be not merely logically correct but true. What then ought it to mean, precisely in the light of scholastic realism, that the *communicatio idiomatum* has not only a grammatical, or even a merely logical, but an ontological character?

EXCURSUS IV
IMMUTABILITY OF GOD?

Mediaeval theology, like that of the early Church, as a result of its dependence on classical Greek philosophy, was inclined much more to a metaphysic of being than to a metaphysic of becoming. And, as the notion of God's immutability, taken over from Greek meyaphysics, served the apologists and the later Fathers (especially Origen and Augustine) well in the struggle against Stoic pantheism and Gnostic and Manichaean dualism and for stressing the eternity and constancy of God, in the middle ages it was an important aid in resisting any kind of pantheism – as, for instance, in the statement of the Fourth Lateran Council about the *Deus incommutabilis* (*DS,* 800) and in modern times in the definition of the First Vatican Council referring to God as a *simplex omnino et incommutabilis substantia spiritualis* (*DS,* 3001). But, as we saw, the idea created a variety of difficulties for the apologists and the later Fathers in their Christology and it was the same with the scholastics when they came to reflect on the christological question. It was not least for this reason that the Johannine 'becoming man' and the Pauline

'self-emptying' (both understood ontologically from the earliest times) manifestly slipped well into the background in the course of centuries in favour of
other interpretations of the Christ-event, particularly the idea of an 'assumption' of the human nature.

The term 'assumption', however, can easily be understood as putting on
humanity like an article of clothing which remains purely external and does
not affect the person inwardly; the Logos would not need to become man or to
empty himself. But this was the way in which the 'assumption' of the human
nature was understood and repeatedly applied in a number of variations in the
early Church by some who upheld a disjunction Christology. In the middle
ages also the term was used similarly, especially by defenders of the *habitus*
theory, widespread in early scholasticism and later condemned, by going back
to Abelard who had treated the christological statement 'God is man' as a
figurative or metaphorical expression. The *assumptus* theory, maintained
until well into the period of high scholasticism, envisaged man's becoming
God more than God's becoming man, These difficulties arose out of a
particular metaphysical interpretation of God's immutability.

Aquinas not only rejected the *habitus* theory, but was the first to condemn
outright the *assumptus* theory and even to describe it as Nestorian. In his
doctrine of creation he tackled successfully the difficult task of qualifying the
one-sided transcendence of the Aristotelian 'unmoved Mover' in the light of
Aristotelian principles. In Christology he was faced with more serious
difficulties. After seeking in the light of Aristotelian metaphysics to understand the Christ-event as becoming man, the question arose as to how this
unmoving transcendent God of Greek metaphysics could *become* man.
Aquinas, here too basing himself on Augustine, produced the ingenious
solution which he had prepared in working out his theory of creation, making
use of the concept of *relatio rationis*.[1] This means that the divine Logos
remains unchanged in the incarnation; what is changed is the human nature,
which is taken up into the divine person. The human nature has a real
relationship – a *relatio realis* – to the Logos. On the other hand, the Logos has
only a conceptual relationship – a *relatio rationis* – to the human nature.
Aquinas gives the example of someone at first sitting on my left, then
changing his place to sit on my right, with the result that I am now sitting on
his left; but I have not changed my position, it is the other person who made
the move. I have not acquired any new reality, only a new conceptual
relationship. Hence, according to Aquinas, in the incarnation the human
nature (not of course pre-existing in time) is changed by being completely

---

[1] cf. Aquinas: *Summa contra Gentiles* II, 12 14; *Summa Theologica* I, q.13 a.7; also A. Krempel,
Doctrine de la relation chez St. Thomas, 563 570.

assumed into the divine nature. But the divine Logos remains completely unchanged in the incarnation.

This theory of the *relatio rationis* was not meant to raise doubts about the Logos *becoming* man, but to avoid the danger of reducing God to a process of becoming. It has the important consequence of bringing out clearly the fact that God in becoming man neither loses anything (becoming man means no loss to God) nor gains anything (becoming man means no gain to God), and anyway that becoming man is something different from the coming to be of man and the world. In God there is no movement in Aristotle's sense: no completion of what was hitherto incomplete, of what was *in potentia,* no actualisation as transference from pure possibility to reality. Is it permissible to lose sight of this consequence? It is scarcely possible to probe more deeply into the problems by questioning God's fullness of perfection either before or after his becoming man.

Would God be really God if in him there were imperfection needing to be perfected, a potency calling for actualisation? But, from the standpoint also of the Aristotelian-scholastic theory of God, the question might perhaps be raised in the opposite way. If according to this theory God is *actus purus,* purest reality, active *energeia,* whose being is operation, whose essence is action, must he not be understood as life at its most vital? But could not this divine life be understood, not in the light of potentiality, but in the light of supreme actuality, as becoming in an analogous sense? And then would not a real becoming man on the part of the divine Logos be conceivable? For classical Christology has always firmly maintained that the divine Logos *himself* became man. And at this decisive point the theory of the *relatio rationis* would not be adequate: a theory of a Logos remaining unmoved which was scarcely ever preached at all and certainly not at Christmas. For although this theory is able to explain that the Word of God in becoming man remained completely what it was – that is, God – it cannot show convincingly that the Word *itself* became man. For it is not flesh that became the Logos, but the Logos that became flesh. It is a question of the *self*-emptying of the Logos: not of an apotheosis of flesh, but of an *ensarkosis* of the Logos. Even though (according to this scholastic understanding) only the human nature is unchangeable in itself, nevertheless this changeable human nature is the Logos' own nature. Its history is the history of the Logos, its time his time, its dying his dying. According to scholastic theory the Logos himself assumed it and in this way emptied himself into it. If the Word had not himself become flesh and if this becoming did not affect the Word himself, the Word himself would not have become anything. He would then not have become man. How could the theory of an immutable Logos be compatible with the statements of the New Testament that the Logos himself is involved in becoming flesh (Jn.

1:14), that he emptied himself and humbled himself (Phil. 2:7-8), that he gave himself (Gal. 1:4; 1 Tim. 2:6), that he delivered himself up (Gal. 2:20; Eph. 5:2), that he offered himself (Heb. 7:27; 9:14), that he, the Son of God, became obedient (Phil. 2:8; Heb. 5:8)?

The dilemma cannot be overlooked, nor can it be simply dismissed as a 'mystery'. The mystery is to be sought in the fact that God, to whom the metaphysicians out of fear of imperfection have denied life and becoming, in fact lives, acts and becomes in perfection and from perfection. To accept this would however involve a revision of the static, Parmenidean understanding of God. It does not imply a simple decision for a philosophy of becoming as opposed to a philosophy of being. It means taking seriously the God who is wholly other, in whom being and becoming, remaining in himself and going out from himself, transcendence and descendence, are not mutually exclusive.

In this connection the question arises whether the Old Testament conception of God (presupposed in the New Testament) is in need of a similar revision or whether there is a possibility of understanding it in a different way. In the Old Testament too it is said that God, unlike the gods of Egypt, Babylon, Phoenicia and Greece, has neither beginning nor ending. Israel has no theogony. It is also expressly stated that, in contrast to the changing and passing world, God remains and remains the same (Ps. 102:25-27), and that his word and his decision also remain (Ps. 33:11; cf. Is. 31:2; 40:8; Jer. 4:28).[2] Over and above this, we read in the New Testament (presumably under hellenistic influence) of the Father of lights with whom there is no variation or shadow, as in the stars, resulting from change (Jas. 1:17; cf. 1 Pet. 1:24). But, in addition to such statements, there are many others which speak of God's repentance and change of plan, pardon and forbearance. It has already been pointed out that these passages are not to be understood or interpreted merely as anthropomorphisms and anthropopathisms, but that they must be taken seriously as expressions of the living reality of the God of the Old and New Testaments; of the God who can act and does act in ever-new ways, always and everywhere, in the freedom of his grace; of the God who can permit himself to repent and who can even permit himself to repent of his repentance.

When Scripture speaks of God's immutability, this is not to be understood in a metaphysical sense of a world-cause rigidly immobile by its very nature, but in the historical sense of his essential fidelity to himself and to his promises, guaranteeing permanence and continuity in his action. Neither do we find in Scripture an immutable divine staticism in the sense of classical Greek metaphysics, since the Old Testament in particular sees God's *intellec-*

---

[2] cf. P. Heinisch: *Theologie des Alten Testaments*, 38f (ET *Theology of the Old Testament*).

tuality as utterly different from the Greek metaphysical and especially the Aristotelian concept of νοῦς.

God's intellectuality is not denied, but not set off against matter in the Greek fashion. 'Hebrew does not oppose mind or spirit to matter, as Greek philosophy does, nor does it have any idea of a pure spirit, that is, of a substance purely spiritual and simple, excluding any composition. The term used to designate spirit (*ruaḥ*) signifies wind, breath or spirit and spirit is not understood as an immaterial and simpler substance, but as a concrete force represented as wind and contrasted with 'flesh' (Is. 31:3) only as that which is powerful and enduring (spirit) as contrasted with what is weak and perishable (flesh). God is not said to be, but to have, a spirit. The Hebrew does not speculate on the nature of God; he believes in God who has revealed himself and whose action is manifested in nature and in the history of Israel; for him it is sufficient to know that God is what he is and what he does for him and for his people. We must then not expect to find in the Old Testament a clear notion of God's spirituality.'[3]

Obviously this does not prevent further reflection on God's intellectuality. Even according to the Old Testament, God cannot be understood simply as a corporeal or material being. Not only is Yahweh seen as a *super*-human personality, there is also a deliberate reaction against any restriction or materialisation of God (in this connection we may recall the prohibition of images in the Decalogue). Precisely as a personal being God is utterly different from all created things and infinitely superior to all created beings in his omnipotence, eternity, ubiquity, perfection and immutability.

But, according to the Old Testament, God's intellectuality must be seen in his *vitality*. With reference to the anthropomorphic and anthropopathic expressions, 'an unprejudiced evaluation of the Old Testament's humanizing of the deity leads us to see that in fact it is not the spiritual nature of God which is the foundation of Old Testament faith. It is his personhood – a personhood which is fully alive, and a life which is fully personal, and which is involuntarily thought of in terms of the human personality . . . In this regard, some have even flatly asserted a kind of carelessness on God's part as to the manner in which he is revealed; and indeed, it is patent that those whose task it was to proclaim the divine will regarded it as far less damaging that men should have to grope in the dark on the subject of Yahweh's spiritual nature than that they should remain unconscious of the personal quality of his behaviour and operations. A doctrine of God as spirit in the philosophical sense will be sought in vain in the pages of the Old Testament. Not until John 4:24 is it possible to declare: "God is a spirit".'[4]

[3]P. van Imschoot: *Theologie de l'Ancien Testament*, 51f; also H.M. Kuitert: *Gott in Menschengestalt*, 56-77, 165-185
[4]W. Eichrodt: *Theologie des Alten Testaments* I, 134f (ET *Theology of the Old Testament* I, 211f).

As God's intellectuality cannot be understood statically, neither can his *immutability*. Particularly unsuitable for this mode of argument is the 'definition' of the name of Yahweh in Exodus 3:14, 'I am who I am', cited over and over again in Christian theology and understood in the light of Greek metaphysics: 'Nothing is farther from what is envisaged in this etymology of the name of Jahweh than a definition of his nature in the sense of a philosophical statement about his being (LXX ἐγώ εἰμι ὁ ὤν) – a suggestion, for example, of his absoluteness, aseity, etc. Such a thing would be altogether out of keeping with the Old Testament. The whole narrative context leads right away to the expectation that Jahweh intends to impart something – but this is not what he is, but what he will show himself to be to Israel. It has always been emphasised, and rightly so, that, in this passage at any rate, the (היה) is to be understood in the sense of "being present," "being there," and therefore precisely not in the sense of absolute, but of relative and efficacious, being – I will be there (for you). Undoubtedly the paranomastic relative clause (אשר אהיה) adds an indeterminate element to the protasis, with the result that the promise of Jahweh's efficacious presence remains at the same time to some extent illusive and impalpable – this is Jahweh's freedom, which does not commit itself in detail.'[5] Martin Buber translates Exodus 3:14: 'I shall be there as who I shall be there.'

Philosophical speculation therefore must not be permitted to introduce an alien element into the biblical image of God, if the peculiarity of the biblical God is to find expression at all: 'The living movement of God's dealings with men disappears when philosophical abstraction dictates the language to be employed. The prophets are concerned to portray the personal God, who woos his people with love, and cannot be indifferent or cold to their rejection of him. Hence they speak frequently and emphatically of his anger and jealousy, his love and sorrow; and it is easy to see that the values which lie hidden in such language ˌcan never be abandoned. "The repentance of God . . . grows into the assured conviction that human development is not for Him an empty, indifferent spectacle, that it is just this inner immutability of His being, which excludes that dull, dead unchangeableness which remains outwardly the same, however much circumstances may change . . . . His jealousy is meant to express that He is not an unconscious natural force, which pours out its fulness in utter indifference, but that human love possesses real value in his eyes. His fear indicates that He is a God who sets a definite aim before Him, who constantly keeps the development of the world within the limits of His eternal decrees, and that His wisdom does not tolerate the self-

---

[5] G. von Rad: *Theologie des Alten Testaments* I, 182 (ET *Old Testament Theology* I, 180).

assertion of short-sighted man. God's wrath and hatred . . . are standard expressions for the self-asserting majesty of his living essence" (H. Schultz). For this reason, God's kindness which bestows and blesses life can always stand side by side with his jealousy, the unchangeableness of the divine decree with his repentance, God's triumphing over the raging powers of this world with his fear, his beneficent power with his wrath. To draw all one's conclusions about the idea of God from the one class of statements only, without taking into account the other, would be manifestly mistaken; but it must be admitted that this is a mistake which Old Testament studies have not always managed to avoid.'[6]

Anthropomorphism then must be linked with the historicity of the Old Testament God: 'It is with the help of *anthropomorphism* that his unity becomes visible, that it leaps to the eye. The one object, the one life, the supreme, sovereign God, cannot possibly be manifested except through revelation: that is, by becoming man, entering into the mode of existence of human life, acting within the framework of human history, making himself known in events, so that man encounters – as it were – a greater fellow-man, a hand, a face. This "mythical" form of expression must be distinguished from mythology of religion; it is in fact the very opposite of the latter, being thrust on the sacred writers by the powerful impression of the *historicity* of existence in which God has become involved. Another way of putting it (even though the abstract terminology displaces somewhat the idiom of the Old Testament) might be this: God's transcendence forbids any kind of natural relationship, but nevertheless a perfect fellowship between God and man is possible; if we try to give a content to the term "fellowship" and a genuine and definite meaning to "perfect", we may escape from our theological abstractions back to the covenant and the relations between God and man existing *in the manner of men.*'[7]

With reference to the biblical image of God and that of the Church Fathers, N. Brox has recently drawn attention to the distinction (unclarified in patristic times) between the biblical and the hellenistic elements, especially in regard to God's immutability: 'the problem of this necessary preliminary penetration or questioning of philosophy, of its acceptance – only possible in a critical spirit – into the terminology of Christian theology, was neither readically grasped nor completely surmounted in patristic times.'[8]

---

[6]W. Eichrodt: *op. cit.* I, 138f; ET I, 216f.

[7]K. H. Miskotte: *Wenn die Götter schweigen*, 135f (ET *When the Gods are Silent*); cf. in this connection the informative work by P. Kuhn: *Gottes Selbsterniedrigung in der Theologie der Rabbinen.*

[8]N. Brox: *Antworten der Kirchenväter*, 144.

'Theology at this time took its systematic starting point largely and fundamentally in philosophical thought, since the latter had in fact developed a system and it was incomparably easier to cope with the multiplicity and variety of the biblical statements by an already existing system than by trying to discover a system in the biblical statements themselves. But in this way the content of the philosophical statements became predominant and the biblical statement was in fact ignored or – with a considerable effort – only subsequently introduced. Thus God came to be understood mainly as immutable by his very nature, but this immutability was seen, not in the biblical sense of God's fidelity to his free action, but in terms of the philosophical concept of the rigid immobility and complete facelessness of God. In this conception, together with the freedom of God's historical action as attested in the Bible, the contingency of mundane reality was also thrust completely into the margin: in philosophical thought there is no place for either of these things. In the Bible God's historical action and his creation are understood as absolutely free, contingent and consequently not essentially necessary action. That is why his difference from the world is seen precisely in his freedom, in his powerfulness in time and history, incalculable and unforeseeable by man. God cannot then be described – as in philosophy – as a kind of superlative of man's being and man's possibilities, revealed as such by an inference from what exists to what is in question. The God of philosophical theology always carries within himself the structures of non-divine reality and also those of human knowledge, while the biblical God carries within himself precisely the features, not of what is sought and known by inference, but of what is unforeseen and continually freshly and differently experienced.

'In patristic theology these features fade out to a large extent because of the persistence of philosophical ways of thinking. Similar conclusions can be drawn from the way in which biblical ideas like God's eternity, justice, incomprehensibility etc. are used, but given a predominantly philosophical content. The repression of the biblical testimony by a considerable injection of spiritualism derived from the hierarchically depotentialised model of the philosophical idea of reality and involving a distrust of matter had far-reaching consequences.'[9]

It may be asked whether in the light of such a conception of God we should consider afresh the problem of change and becoming in God.

Leslie Dewart demands a fundamental 'de-hellenisation' of Christian dogma for the sake of 'the future of belief'. This, he thinks, is more difficult than the hellenisation of Christianity was in the early Church: 'For hellenization introduced into Christianity the ideals of immutability, stability and impassibility as perfections that all Christians and Christianity as a whole should strive for, since these were the typical and central perfections of God himself.'[10] Unfortunately, Dewart does not examine more closely this central question of the hellenistic idea of God, but explains in a more general way how the hellenistic terminology of the traditional doctrine of the Trinity and the incarnation can no longer be understood in the intellectual climate of today.[11] The programme of a 'de-hellenisation' of Christian belief must be supported (and inciden-

---

[9]op. cit., 142f.
[10]Leslie Dewart: *The Future of Belief*, Burns and Oates, London, 134; cf. 200-215.
[11]cf. ibid., 135-150.

537

tally, it is also well under way also in Catholic theology with the decline of neo-scholasticism after Vatican II). But an intense effort on the part of the theologians will be necessary in order to find a better *positive* expression of the Christian faith.

EXCURSUS V
RECENT ATTEMPTS AT A SOLUTION OF THE OLD PROBLEMS

In studying the implications of classical Christology we found encourage-ment and confirmation in recent systematic attempts by leading Catholic and Protestant theologians at a solution of the old problems. With the aid especially of extensive quotations of the appropriate texts, we would like to draw attention to certain parallels, without explaining in detail to what extent the new initiative has been consistently maintained or how our own attempt differs from the others.

A critical examination of the *kenosis* theories of the nineteenth century would lead us too far.[1] These theories should be studied in the light of the older Lutheran theology which attempted an exegesis of Philippians 2:7, making use of the *communicatio idiomatum* in order to provide scope for the genuine humanity of Christ's earthly life. According to Martin Chemnitz and the Giessen theologians, the incarnate Son of God renounced the use of the attributes of the divine majesty during his earthly life; according to Johann Brenz and the Tübingen theologians, he continued to use them secretly.

In the nineteenth century discussion switched from the One who had become man to the One becoming man. *Kenosis* refers to the divine being of the eternal Son himself and consists in a 'self-limitation of the divine', according to Gottfried Thomasius. But differences arise in the interpretation of this 'self-limitation'. Thomasius himself holds that the Son in freedom and love renounces the attributes of divinity which relate to the world (omnipotence, omnipresence, omniscience), while retaining the immanent, inalienable attributes (power, truth, holiness, love). According to F. H. Frank it is a question of depotentialising the Son's consciousness, a conversion of the divine consciousness into the form of a developing, finite, human consciousness, but in such a way that the Son of man is and remains conscious of himself as Son of God. Finally, according to W. F. Gess, the Son also renounces both the immanent attributes and his eternal self-awareness. Similar attempts can be observed at this time also on the part of British and Russian theologians (particularly important among these being Sergius Bulgakov, following on P. Florensky and Vladimir Soloviev).

Paul Althaus is critical of the linking of christological dogma with a conception of the true humanity of Jesus understood in terms of empirical psychology. He observes:

---

[1] cf. the articles '*Kénose*' by P. Henry in the *Supplément* to the *Dictionnaire de la Bible* V, coll. 7–161, and '*Kenosis*' by P. Althaus in *RGG* III, coll. 1243–1246, and all the exegetical works on Philippians 2:5–11. In addition to H. Schumacher's detailed history of its interpretation, see especially E. Käsemann: '*Kritische Analyse von Philipper 2:5–11*' in *Exegetische Versuche und Besinnungen* I, 51–95; III:2 (1969), 133–326.

'It is outside the competence and the capacity of theological thought to make statements about Christ's consciousness of himself as human and divine. Theories of this kind must not be allowed to minimize the paradox of the incarnation. The tension of the profession of faith in Jesus Christ must be maintained at the highest level. The *whole* glory and power of God is there for us in the true, uncurtailed, unchanged humanity of Jesus. Christology must start out in its thinking from the cross: the full, undiminished divinity of God is active in utter powerlessness, in the death-agony of the Crucified, from which no "divine nature" may be removed. What Paul regarded as a saying of the Lord referring to his own life ("power is made perfect in weakness", 2 Cor. 12:9) we see in faith in Jesus Christ as a law of the life of God himself. With this insight of course the old version of God's immutability breaks down. Christology must take seriously the fact that God himself in the Son is actually involved in suffering and even there is and remains wholly God. This miracle of God cannot be rationalised by a theory which permits God to be present and active in Jesus Christ only as long as this presence does not burst through the limits of the human as we understand them. But neither can we attempt to show directly that the divinity is ontologically present in Christ's human existence. The divinity is present concealed under the human existence, open only to faith and not to vision, and therefore outside the scope of any theory. The fact that God enters into the hiddenness of his divinity under the humanity, this is what we mean by *kenosis*.'[2]

In recent Catholic theology it was Karl Rahner with his exemplary intellectual courage and the power of his penetrating thought who, here as elsewhere, opened up new avenues and confronted classical Christology with modern thinking.[3] The great mind behind this closely considered deepening of classical (Chalcedonian-scholastic) Christology, even to the details of its conceptual framework, is (while allowing for the influence of Heidegger) none other than Hegel. This fact is merely underlined by Rahner's occasional qualifications in regard to Hegel in a subordinate clause. Rahner is concerned to render theologically intelligible the conditions of the possibility of an incarnation of God on the basis of his own transcendental initiative.

a) From the aspect of *man*. The transcendental presupposition of an incarnation is the open transcendence of the human subject as intellectual

---

[2] P. Althaus: *art. cit., coll. 1245f.*
[3] Among Karl Rahner's contributions to the problems see his articles 'Jesus Christ' (systematic treatment) in *LThK*, vol. V, 1960, coll. 953–961; *'Der dreifaltige Gott als transzendenter Urgrund der Heilsgeschichte'* in *Mysterium salutis* II, 1967, 317–397, esp. 327–336; and his theological *meditation: Ich glaube an Jesus Christus* (1968). Among the many articles in *Theological Investigations* these are particularly valuable (the date given in brackets is that of the original publication in German): 'Current Problems in Christology' (1954) I, 149–200; 'Thoughts on the Theology of Christmas' (1956) III, 24–34; 'The Eternal Significance of the Humanity of Jesus for our Relationship with God' (1956) III, 35–46: 'On the Theology of the Incarnation' (1960) IV, 195–120: 'Christology within an Evolutionary View of the World' (1962) V, 157–192; 'Dogmatic Reflections on the Knowledge and Self-consciousness of Christ' (1962) V, 193–215; 'Christmas, 'Peace on Earth' (1966) VII, 132–135.

being to the absolute being of God (the nature of man as *potentia oboedientia-lis* for assumption by God): 'If the nature of man is understood entirely in this sense, existentially and ontologically as open (that is, neither possessing a definite limit nor demanding an absolute degree of fulfilment) transcendence (to be "personally" realised) to the absolute being of God, then the incarnation can be seen as the absolutely supreme (although free, in no way due, and unique) fulfilment of what "man" as such means ... Thus the incarnation would more easily and more intelligibly be protected against any miraculous or mythological interpretation. The true meaning of God-manhood in a general sense could be differentiated from and linked with the doctrine of an absolute God-manhood.'[4] Hence the '"humanity" of Christ is ... not merely ... an alien "instrument" taken up from outside, ... a uniform concealing' his divinity. In fact it reaches supreme fulfilment in its proper reality: 'difference from and unity with God increase in equal and not in inverse ratio'. And the Chalcedonian formula of 'two natures without confusion and without separation' thus becomes 'a general form of expression for the relationship between the intellectual creature and God in all (onto-logical) dimensions, which has its supreme and unique example in the hypostatic union'.[5]

b) From the aspect of *God.* The transcendental presupposition of an incarnation is the real possibility of the self-distinguishing of God (the coming to be of the Son in the 'immanent' Trinity) which outwardly ('economic' Trinity) is the possibility of the self-externalising of God in creation, the latter reaching its climax in the incarnation of the Son. 'Only in this way can the unity of the doctrine of the Trinity and of the incarnation be really made quite clear.'[6] Hence the Christ-event as God's self-giving self-externalising is the 'history of God himself'.[7] On the other hand the humanity transcending itself into the mystery of God is always God-manhood of which the qualitatively unique culmination is the God-manhood of Jesus Christ.

The dialectic of the inner-trinitarian self-distinguishing of God as presupposition of the incarnation: 'It is easy to see from all this that only a *divine* Person can possess as its own a freedom really distinct from itself in such a way that this freedom does not cease to be truly free even with regard to the divine Person possessing it, while it continues to qualify this very Person as its ontological subject. For it is only in the case of God that it is conceivable at all that he himself can constitute something in a state of distinction from himself. This is precisely an attribute of his divinity as such and his intrinsic creativity: to be able, by himself and through his *own* act *as such,* to constitute

---

[4]K. Rahner: *LThK*, vol. V, col. 956.
[5]*ibid.*
[6]*art. cit.*, col. 957.
[7]*ibid.*

something in being which by the very fact of its being radically dependent (because *wholly* constituted in being), also acquires autonomy, independent reality and truth (precisely because it is constituted in being by the one, unique *God*), and all this precisely with respect to the God who constitutes it in being. God alone can make something which has validity even in his own presence. There lies the mystery of that active creation which is God's alone. Radical dependence upon him increases in direct, and not in inverse, proportion with genuine self-coherence before him. Measured against God, the creature is precisely *not* to be reduced unambiguously to the formula of merely negative limitation. Our problem here is only the supreme application of this basic truth concerning the Creator-creature relationship (a truth which at least historically has never been reached in non-Christian philosophy). And it immediately follows once again that the purely *formal* (abstract) schema *nature-person* is inadequate. We must conceive of the relation between the Logos-Person and his human nature in just this sense, that here *both* independence *and* radical proximity equally reach a unique and qualitatively incommensurable perfection, which nevertheless remains once and for all the perfection of a relation between Creator and creature.'[8] 'The immanent self-utterance of God in his eternal fullness is the condition of the self-utterance of God outside himself, and the latter continues the former. It is true that the mere constitution of something other than God is the work of God as such, without distinction of person. Yet the ontological possibility of creation can derive from and be based on the fact that God, the unoriginated, expresses himself in himself and for himself and so constitutes the original, divine, distinction in God himself. And when this God utters himself as himself into the *void,* this expression speaks *out* this immanent Word, and not something which could be true of another divine person.'[9]

Incarnation as incarnation of God himself, in which God in the other nevertheless remains with himself: 'Nonetheless, it remains true: the Word *became* flesh. And we are only true Chrsitians when we have accepted this. It will hardly be denied that here the traditional philosophy and theology of the schools begins to blink and stutter. It affirms that the change and transition takes place in the created reality which is assumed, and not in the Logos. And so everything is clear: the Logos remains unchanged when it takes on something which, as a created reality, is subject to change, including the fact of its being assumed. Hence all change and history, with all their tribulation, remain on this side of the absolute gulf which necessarily sunders the unchangeable God from the world of change and prevents their mingling. But it still remains true that the Logos *became* man, that the changing history of this human reality is *his* own history: our time became the time of the eternal, our death the death of the immortal God himself. And no matter how we distribute the predicates which seem to contradict one another and some of which seem incompatible with God, dividing them up between two realities, the divine Word and created human nature, we still may not forget that one of these, the created reality, is that of the Logos of God himself. And thus, when this attempt at solving the question by the division and distribution of predicates has been made, the whole question begins again. It is the question of how to understand the truth that the immutability of God may not distort our view of the fact that what happened to Jesus on earth is precisely the history of the Word of God himself, and a process which *he* underwent. If we face squarely the fact of

---

[8]K. Rahner: *Theological Investigations* I, 162f.
[9]*op. cit.,* IV, 115.

the incarnation, which our faith testifies to be the fundamental dogma of Christianity, we must simply say: God can become something, he who is unchangeable in himself can *himself* become subject to change *in something else*.'[10]

With reference to the axiom of immutability, this means: 'It follows from this statement that the assertion of God's "immutability", of the lack of any relation between God and the world, is in a true sense a dialectical statement. One may and indeed must say this, without for that reason being a Hegelian. For it is true, come what may, and a dogma, that the Logos himself has become man: thus that he himself has become something that he had not always been (*formaliter*); and therefore that what has so become is, as just itself and of itself, God's reality. Now if this is a truth of faith, ontology must allow itself to be guided by it (as in analogous instances in the doctrine of the Trinity), must seek enlightenment from it, and grant that while God remains immutable "in himself", he can come to be "in the other", and that *both* assertions must really and truly be made of the same God as God.'[11]

Hence the incarnation is the self-emptying of God himself: 'the Absolute, or more correctly, he who is the absolute, has, in the pure freedom of his infinite and abiding unrelatedness, the possibility of himself becoming that other thing, the finite; God, in and by the fact that he empties *himself* gives away *himself, poses* the other as his own reality. The basic element to begin with is not the concept of an assumption, which presupposes what is to be assumed as something obvious, and has nothing more to do than assign it to the taker – a term, however, which it never really reaches, since it is rejected by his immutability and may never affect him, since he is unchangeable, when his immutability is considered undialectically and in isolation – in static concepts. On the contrary, the basic element, according to our faith, is the *self*-emptying, the coming to be, the κένωσις and γενέσις of God himself, who can come to be by *becoming* another thing, derivative, in the act of constituting it, without having to change in his own proper reality which is the unoriginated origin. By the fact that he remains in his infinite fullness while he empties himself – because, being love, that is, the will to fill the void, he has that wherewith to fill all – the ensuing other is his own proper reality. He brings about that which is distinct from himself, in the act of retaining it as his own, and vice versa, because he truly wills to retain the other as his own, he constitutes it in its genuine reality. God himself goes out of himself, God in his quality of the fullness which gives away itself. He can do this. Indeed, his power of subjecting himself to history is primary among his free possibilities. (It is not a primal must!) And for this reason, Scripture defines him as love' – whose prodigal freedom is the indefinable itself. What then is his power of being creator, his ability to keep himself aloof while constituting, bringing out of its nothingness, that which in itself is simply something else? It is only a derivative, restricted and secondary possibility, which is ultimately based on the other primal possibility – though the secondary could be realized without the primal.'[12]

It would be a particularly stimulating and fruitful enterprise to examine closely the immense work of Hans Urs von Balthasar with reference to its christological centre and at that point to its implicit understanding of God.

---

[10]*op. cit.*, IV, 112.
[11]*op. cit.*, I, 181, n.3.
[12]*op. cit,*, IV, 114.

Von Balthasar's knowledge of the Catholic (patristic, mediaeval and modern, both the systematic and the more existential, mystical and poetical) tradition, at a time when there are far too many 'latest fashions' in theology, can never be too much admired or over-estimated.[13] It may be connected not least with an understanding of the incarnation on the lines of Greek patristic thought that the theme of the kenosis of God and of an image of God seen in that light repeatedly occurs marginally in his work (he never fails to draw attention to the sayings of the Greek Fathers relating to these themes) and that in a later treatise (a large-scale theology of the *Triduum Mortis*[14]) he makes kenosis a main theme in the way that might be expected in the light of his *theologia crucis*.

In these closely reasoned comments (note for instance the brilliant concise survey, typical of von Balthasar's work, of the Christian theology and piety of the passion[15]) he occasionally includes bolder quotations from Origen, Cyril, Gregory of Nyssa, as well as Hilary and Augustine, which do not easily fit in with the pattern of Greek patristic thought, yet without overlooking the dilemma: 'But is this statement (about the incarnation as kenosis) intrinsically compatible with that about God's immutability – and thus also with the glory of the Son with God the Father? Looking back from the mature Christology of Ephesus and Chalcedon to the hymn of Philippians 2, without attaching too much dogmatic importance to the latter, we still cannot fail to see in its archaic language, stammering out the mystery, something that cannot really be perceived in the rigid formulas of God's immutability; we are conscious here of a residue of meaning that the German, English and Russian kenoticists of the nineteenth and twentieth centuries are trying to get at.'[16]

Subsequently von Balthasar deals with the theories of modern kenoticists[17] and then attempts to solve the dilemma by 'taking up a position midway between the two impracticable extremes: on the one hand an "immutability of God" which is such that the incarnation is regarded as exceptional, resulting in a merely external "addition"; on the other hand a "mutability of God" such that the Son's divine self-consciousness is "alienated" in a human conscious-

---

[13]The main achievements of H. U. von Balthasar should be noticed: the first amazing work of the young theologian was devoted to German Idealism (*Apokalypse der deutschen Seele* I, 1937); then came the different patristic studies (especially on Origen, Gregory of Nyssa and Maximus the Confessor); and see also the works on the theology of history (particularly *Das Ganze im Fragment*; ET *Man in History: A Theological Study*); finally the specifically christological articles in *Verbum Caro* (ET *Essays in Theology*) and the rich three-volume work on theological aesthetics, *Herrlichkeit* (ET *The Glory of the Lord*).

[14]H. U. von Balthasar: '*Mysterium Paschale*' in *Mysterium salutis* III:2, 133-326.

[15]*op. cit.*, 155-158.

[16]*op. cit.*, 146.

[17]*op. cit.*, 149-151.

ness for the period of the incarnation, which would affect the truth of "the lamb slain from the beginning of the world".[18]

Von Balthasar then sees the solution not so much in abandoning the idea of God of Greek metaphysics, which lies behind the Fathers' difficulties, but (following the Russian theologian Bulgakov) in an eternalisation of the historical event of the crucifixion, not only into the future, but also back into the past, to the dawn of creation and even into the eternal divine being of God, as described within the framework of trinitarian speculation: 'For here evidently two lines cross: the "slaying" is by no means to be understood in a gnostic sense as a heavenly sacrifice independent of Golgotha, but is the eternal aspect of the historical bloody sacrifice on the cross (Rev. 5:12), presupposed everywhere by Paul; nevertheless it designates a supra-temporal enduring state of the "Lamb", not only – as the "French School" described it – as the continuation of the "sacrificial state" (*état*) of the risen Christ, but as a state of the Son which is co-extensive with creation as a whole and thus affects in some way his divine being. Modern Russian theology – although not without gnostic and Hegelian temptations – has rightly placed this aspect in the centre. It might be possible to strip Bulgakov's basic view of its sophiological assumptions and to retain that idea – developed in a variety of ways – which we placed at the centre. The ultimate presupposition of kenosis is the "selflessness" of the divine persons (as pure relaions) in the innertrinitarian life of love.'[19]

It is notable, but not accidental in the light of the Greek starting-point, that von Balthasar repeatedly glances at Hegel. Although he includes in these passages a whole variety of positive remarks, for the most part he treats Hegel (as incidentally he does Luther) polemically as a 'temptation'.[20] Von Balthasar, however, leaves the last word on kenosis, not to the 'experiences of abandonment' of the mediaeval and early modern mystics,[21] but to Karl Barth's theology of the cross, to Barth who for his own part with reference to the kenosis theory learned from no one more than from Luther – and Hegel. But von Balthasar himself might also have been more open in regard to Hegel than he admits in his later work. In his *Rechenschaft 1965*, on the occasion of his sixtieth birthday, with reference to the divine-human character of truth, he expressly demanded an 'urgent discussion with Hegel': 'But that will be for others to undertake.'[22]

The fact should not be overlooked that in the same comprehensive work on dogmatic theology, *Mysterium salutis*, one of the two editors, Magnus Löhrer, had drawn attention at an early stage to the urgency of a 'new reflection' on God's immutability on the part of theology: 'There is a

---

[18]*op. cit.*, 152.
[19]*op. cit.*, 152f.
[20]cf. 161, 168.
[21]*op. cit.*, 179–181.
[22]H. U. von Balthasar: *Rechenschaft 1965*, 33.

prevailing impression that an unqualified statement about God's immutability takes too little account of a variety of theological aspects.'

Löhrer wants immutability to be understood not metaphorically as a static condition, but historically as God's unshakable fidelity: 'God's immutability, like other negative statements, should be understood as in patristic theology, primarily in its positive sense; as such it expresses mainly the free self-determination of God, who in his being and action is not exposed to any necessity on the part of what is not divine. In salvation history God's free self-determination is expressed in the fidelity with which he realises and maintains his decree of salvation, despite the infidelity of his human convenant-partner. This fidelity of God expresses a certain freedom of action and as such is quite different from metaphysical immutability. Moreover, the principle of God's immutability must be understood dialectically in the sense that it is clear in the light of the incarnation that God, remaining unchangeable in himself, really *comes to be* in the other. In Christology this principle must be developed and substantiated more closely in an interpretation starting out mainly with the idea of kenosis (Phil. 2:6-7) and in the light of this seeing God's incarnation as an actual event and not as a kind of subsequent unification of two natures. But the doctrine of God also is affected by this statement in the sense that it becomes clear in the light of the incarnation that God's immutability in himself need not exclude God's coming to be in the other.'[23] F. Malmberg[24] and R. Schulte[25] have expressed themselves in a similar way. In regard to the problems facing us here attention should be drawn to what Joseph Ratzinger has described as the 'law of disguise'.[26]

In Protestant theology no one has so impressively renewed classical Christology and given expression to it in its corrected form as Karl Barth. The classical Christian doctrine of reconciliation had perhaps never before been presented in such a comprehensive and polished, wide-ranging and profound christological concentration as it is here. Bringing a stupendous knowledge of theology and the history of dogma to bear upon the problems, he rejects the divisions hitherto customary in the Church's tradition: the separation between Christology and soteriology (including ecclesiology), between the doctrine of the person of Christ and the doctrine of the work of Christ, between the doctrine of the two natures of Christ and the doctrine of the states, between the doctrine of sin and the doctrine of reconciliation. The foundation of the doctrine of the Trinity is laid down already in the

---

[23]M. Löhrer: *Mysterium salutis* II, 311. J. Macquarrie adopts a similar standpoint in *Principles of Christian Theology*, 190f; cf. also the illuminating comments of P. Tillich on the 'living God' as 'eternal process' and on the 'polarity of dynamics and form' in God, in *Systematic Theology* I, 268ff, 272ff.

[24]F. Malmberg: *Uber den Gottn mschen*, 61-65.

[25]R. Schulte: art. '*Unveränderlichkeit Gottes*' in *LThK*, vol. X (1965), col. 537.

[26]J. Ratzinger: *Einführung in das Christentum*, 207-209 (ET *Introduction to Christianity*, London, 1969, 191-193).

'Prolegomena to Church *Dogmatics*',[27] and it is dealt with both in 'The Doctrine of God'[28] and in 'The Doctrine of Creation'.[29] The diversity of God and the world and also their reconciliation appear at the same time as description, representation and analogy of the diversity of Father and Son in the Spirit. Here too then we find a unity of 'immanent' and 'economic' Trinity. In a magnificent architectonic system, comparable to the systematic structures of German Idealism and influenced by these (more by Schleiermacher than by Hegel), three further volumes of the *Church Dogmatics*[30] describe the three forms of 'The Doctrine of Reconciliation', starting out first from the *vere Deus,* then from the *vere homo* and finally from the unity of the God-man. And on each of the three lines the advance is made in three stages: from Christology in the narrower sense by way of the opposite pole of sin and on to soteriology in its 'objective' realisation and in its 'subjective' appropriation ('The Doctrine of the Work of the Holy Spirit') firstly in the community and through the community in individual Christians. On the first of these three lines the incarnation is depicted as the humiliation of the true God for the exaltation of that man who wanted to exalt himself. Using a language more biblical than that of Rahner, Barth brings out forcefully the consequences of God's humble condescension where service proves to be dominion.

The *first* form of the doctrine of reconciliation: Jesus Christ is the true *God,* that is, the God who humbles himself and is thus the reconciling God, the Lord as servant and as high priest (*munus sacerdotale*). Against this Jesus Christ, the Lord who becomes a servant, man sins in pride. Against sin there is the achievement of reconciliation in Jesus Christ: man's pride encounters God's judgment, which takes place in man's justification. Justification is appropriated and realised through the work of the Holy Spirit. First in the community: through the Holy Spirit (as awakening power of the Word spoken by the Lord who became a servant and thus of the divine judgment which justifies man) the *gathering* of the community takes place. Then in individual Christians: them the Holy Spirit awakens in justification to *faith.*

The *second* form of the doctrine of reconciliation: Jesus Christ is the true *man,* that is, the man exalted and thus reconciled by God, the servant as Lord and King (*munus regale*). Against this Jesus Christ, the servant who is Lord, man sins in sloth. Against sin there is the achievement of reconciliation in Jesus Christ: man's sloth encounters God's direction, which takes place in man's *sanctification.* Sanctification is appropriated and realised through the work of the Holy Spirit. First in the community: through the Holy Spirit (as life-giving power of the Word spoken by servant who became Lord and thus of the divine direction which sanctifies man) the *upbuilding* of the community

---

[27]Karl Barth: *Church Dogmatics* I:1 and I:2; esp. I:1, 339–560; the basic christological principles are also to be found here in I:2, 1–202.

[28]*op. cit.,* II:1; II:2, esp. on 'The Election of God' (II:2, 1–506).

[29]*op. cit.,* III:1; III:2; III:3; III:4; esp. III:1, 42–94.

[30]*op. cit.,* IV:1; IV:2; IV:3.

takes place. Then in individual Christians: in sanctifying them the Holy Spirit quickens them in *love*.

The *third* form of the doctrine of reconciliation: Jesus Christ in the unity of both is *God-man,* that is, the guarantor and witness of our reconciliation, the prophet (*munus propheticum*). Against Jesus Christ, the witness and guarantor of reconciliation, man sins in falsehood. Against sin there is the achievement of reconciliation in Jesus Christ: man's falsehood encounters God's promise, which takes place in man's *calling*. The calling is appropriated and realised through the work of the Holy Spirit. First in the community: through the Holy Spirit (as the enlightening power of the Word who as God-man is guarantor of the promise and thus of the divine promise which summons man) the *mission* of the community takes place. Then in individual Christians: them the Holy Spirit enlightens in calling them to *hope*.

This, however, is the meaning of the incarnation of God for God himself: 'As God was in Christ, far from being against Himself, or at disunity with Himself, He has put into effect the freedom of His divine love, the love in which He is divinely free. He has therefore done and revealed that which corresponds to His divine nature. His immutability does not stand in the way of this. It must not be denied, but this possibility is included in His unalterable being. He is absolute, infinite, exalted, active, impassible, transcendent, but in all this He is the One who loves in freedom, the One who is free in His love, and therefore not His own prisoner. He is all this as the Lord, and in such a way that He embraces the opposites of these concepts even while He is superior to them. He is all this as the Creator, who has created the world as the reality distinct from Himself but willed and affirmed by Him and therefore as His world, as the world which belongs to Him, in relation to which He can be God and act as God in an absolute way and also a relative, in an infinite and also a finite, in an exalted and also a lowly, in an active and also a passive, in a transcendent and also an immanent, and finally in a divine and also a human – indeed, in relation to which He Himself can become worldly, making His own both its form, the *forma servi,* and also its cause; and all without giving up His own form, the *forma Dei,* and His own glory, but adopting the form and cause of man into the most perfect communion with His own, accepting solidarity with the world. God can do this. And no limit is set to His ability to do it by the contradiction of the creature against Him. It does not escape Him by turning to that which is not and losing itself in it, for, although He is not the Creator of that which is not, He is its sovereign Lord. It corresponds to and is grounded in His divine nature that in free grace He should be faithful to the unfaithful creature who has not deserved it and who would inevitably perish without it, that in relation to it He should establish that communion between His own form and cause and that of the creature, that He should make His own its being in contradiction and under the consequences of that contradiction, that He should maintain His covenant in relation to sinful man (not surrendering His deity, for how could that help? but giving up and sacrificing Himself), and in that way supremely asserting Himself and His deity. His particular, and highly particularised, presence in grace, in which the eternal Word descended to the lowest parts of the earth (Eph. 4:9) and tabernacled in the man Jesus (Jn. 1:14), dwelling in this one man in the fulness of His Godhead (Col. 2:9), is itself the domonstration and exercise of His omnipresence, i.e., of the perfection in which He has His own place which is superior to all the places created by Him, not excluding but including all other places. His omnipotence is that of a divine plenitude of power in the fact that (as opposed to any abstract omnipotence) it can assume the form of weakness and impotence and do so as omnipotence, triumphing in this form. The eternity in which

547

He himself is true time and the Creator of all time is revealed in the fact that, although our time is that of sin and death, He can enter it and Himself be temporal in it, yet without ceasing to be eternal, able rather to be the Eternal in time. His wisdom does not deny itself, but proclaims itself in what necessarily appears folly to the world; His righteousness in ranging Himself with the unrighteous as One who is accused with them, as the first, and properly the only One to come under accusation; His holiness in having mercy on man, in taking his misery to heart, in willing to share it with him in order to take it away from him. God does not have to dishonour Himself when He goes into the far country, and conceals His glory. For He is truly honoured in this concealment. This concealment, and therefore His condescension as such, is the image and reflection in which we see Him as He is. His glory is the freedom of the love which He exercises and reveals in all this. In this respect it differs from the unfree and loveless glory of all the gods imagined by man. Everything depends on our seeing it, and in it the true and majestic nature of God: not trying to construct it arbitrarily; but deducing it from its revelation in the divine nature of Jesus Christ. From this we learn that the *forma Dei* consists in the grace in which God Himself assumes and makes His own the *forma servi*. We have to hold fast to this without being disturbed or confused by any pictures of false gods. It is this that we have to see and honour and worship as the mystery of the deity of Christ – not an ontic and inward divine paradox – the postulate of which has its basis only in our own very real contradiction against God and the false ideas of God which correspond it it.'[31]

Barth is close to Heinrich Vogel and the latter's interpretation of the incarnation as representation: in the man Jesus God has taken our place.[32] Otto Weber has expressed himself sympathetically but critically in regard to Barth.[33] Noteworthy from the Lutheran standpoint are the comments of Paul Althaus,[34] Peter Brunner[35] and Werner Elert.[36]

Eberhard Jüngel's contribution to the debate is particularly significant in the present context simply because, as one whose background lies in the Bultmann school (more precisely, as a pupil of Ernst Fuchs) he has ventured to intervene in the controversy between Herbert Braun, the pupil of Bultmann, and Helmut Gollwitzer, the pupil of Barth, about the correct understanding of God. Solidly based on his work in hermeneutics, Jüngel has undertaken an amazing piece of bridge-building with his commonsense interpretative 'paraphrase' of some trains of thought in the 'responsible speech about the being of God' in Barth's *Church Dogmatics*. By adopting this approach Jüngel hopes that 'contemporary theologians will let themselves be encouraged . . . to listen seriously and cordially to one another and to

---

[31]*op. cit.*, IV:1, 186-188; cf. 183f; IV:2, 36-104.
[32]H. Vogel: *Christologie* I; *idem*: Gott in Christus, ch. VII, '*Das Werk des Sohnes*', esp. 624–756.
[33]O. Weber: *Grundlagen der Dogmatik* II, 172–189 (ET *Foundations of Dogmatics* II, 147–64).
[34]P. Althaus: *Die christliche Wahrheit*, 458–461, 472f.
[35]P. Brunner: *Die Herrlichkeit des gekreuzigten Messias*.
[36]W. Elert: *Der christliche Glaube*, 311-318.

combine the necessary criticism of other positions with the readiness to test critically their own starting-points'.[37] Progressing from God's trinitarian being-manifest to his being-objective (as being manifest, as sacramental reality, as anthropological existential), he comes to the third part which gives the whole book its name: 'God's being is in becoming'. This does not simply mean that God's being is *merely* becoming, but rather that God's being is *in* the deed, *in* the primordial decision, *in* passion: it is *in* becoming. Jüngel joins Barth in denying any self-contradiction on God's part in his passion. And he also joins Barth in his 'criticism of the traditional metaphysical concept of God according to which God cannot suffer without falling into conflict with his being'.[38]

What this perception entails for theology is that the 'ontological localisation of God's being in becoming is an attempt to *think out* theologically how far God is the living God. Without the courage to *formulate* the livingness of God, theology will finally become a mausoleum of God's livingness. The God who may be inspected within this mausoleum certainly deserved the protest of Herbert Braun – a protest which as such ought to be heard, however Braun's attempt to think the livingness of God may be judged.'[39]

If the historicity of God is considered in this way, then, despite all the differences, the parallelism with Hegel is obvious: 'But if God's being as subsistence is so thought of, that this being makes the event of revelation not impossible, but first and foremost possible, then the being of God as subsistence which is deduced from the event of God's revelation is itself thought of as event. And, indeed, as an event *granting* the event of revelation. God's independent being must thus be understood from the event of revelation as an event granting this event of revelation. God's being as subsistence is self-movement. As self-movement God's independent being makes revelation possible. Revelation as God's interpretation of himself is the expression of this self-movement of the being of God. Formulated differently: The grace of God's being-for-us must be able to be a "copy" [*Abbild*] of the freedom of God's being-for-himself, so that this freedom as the "original" [*Urbild*] of that grace becomes visible in that grace as the "copy" of this freedom. If revelation as God's *being*-for-us is to be taken seriously, then in Jesus Christ God's being must *become* visible and *be able* to become visible. This means, however, that both this becoming as well as this being-able to become must be understood from God's being itself, if indeed it is really true that *God* has revealed *himself.* Thus the historicality of God must be formulated *from God.* And on the other side, God's being must be formulated in view of this becoming and of this being-able to become if indeed it is really true that God has revealed *himself.* Thus at all costs we must formulate God's *historicality.*

---

[37] E. Jüngel: *gottes Sein ist im Werden,* 8; quoted from ET *The Doctrine of the Trinity: Being is in Becoming* (tr. Horton Harris, Scottish Academic Press, 1976), xviif.
[38] op. cit., 84.
[39] *op. cit.,* vii (Preface).

'Yet what help is the assurance that one must speak of God's being historically, when one *cannot* speak historically of God's being? It is still not achieved by applying historical predicates to the concept of God. History and the being of God are then again all too easily caused to be divided from one another. God's being is first then and only then really formulated historically when God's being as such is comprehended as historical being.

'In such comprehension, however, the all important thing is that history does not in any way become a general concept for the being of God. "God's being is historical" is and must remain a proposition of revelation. As a proposition of revelation this proposition is itself certainly an historical proposition. For revelation is an historical event or it is just not revelation. But revelation is just that historical event in which God's being shows itself as a being which is not only able to bear historical predicates, but demands them! In the historical event of revelation God's being is itself event, and indeed with the result that *human* language (and thus "anthropomorphic" language also; for human language even as the most abstract language – certainly hidden from itself – is "anthropomorphic") about God becomes not only appropriate, but necessary.'[40]

But, despite all the parallelism, in this thinking in the light of God's grace the radical difference from Hegel is no less obvious: 'In that we called God's being a being in becoming we understood that God can reveal himself. But that God does what he can, that he has reiterated himself in his revelation, this rests on no necessity. That is much more grace. Yet this grace is not strange to God's being. How otherwise would it be distinguished from necessity? God's grace is rather the reiteration of God's "Yes" to himself (which constitutes God's being) in relation to something other. In so far as this "Yes" in relation to something other than God first calls this "something other" into being, God's gracious "Yes" sets his being in relationship to the nothing. But in so far as this "Yes" of grace frees the creation which has been called into being from the threatening which comes through the nothing, God's gracious "Yes" exposes his being to the nothing. In the last resort, therefore, God's grace signifies God's own self-surrender. But if God's self-surrender is not also God's abandoning of himself, then God's self-relatedness wanted to prove itself precisely in God's relation to the nothing.'[41]

In connection with his book Jüngel developed his views further, particularly in their christological aspect, in two lengthy articles. In the lecture 'On the death of the Living God',[42] (which he described as a 'poster' heralding a larger work) he first of all brings out the Christian origins of the talk of the death of God, while invoking – in addition to Jean Paul – 'Hegel's talk of the death of God, which can be traced back by way of Tübingen tradition to utterances of Luther'.[43] This term therefore is used in modern atheism, not as a new 'invention', but as an old 'recollection', which however presents itself as a new theological task still to be mastered. After Jüngel has thus observed 'the

---

[40] *op. cit.*, 93f.
[41] *op. cit.*, 107.
[42] E. Jüngel: in *ZThK* 65 (1968), 93–116.
[43] *op. cit.*, 99.

homecoming of the talk of the death of God into theology',[44] he points, 'following Hegel's hint', to the 'christological origin of the talk of the death of God',[45] its theological possibility and necessity. He thinks that Luther was right as against Zwingli. For Luther the history of Jesus *'becomes* God's own history, the history involving his own being': 'It not only concerns God', but, as concerning him, it also 'starts out from him', so that 'God's being from the outset is ontologically projected toward this history'.[46] Consequently 'the true source of the talk of the death of God is the historical event of the historical death of Jesus of Nazareth'.[47] While this death of God in Jesus deprives death of its victory and turns it into a good deed for man,[48] for God, for God's *being,* it means: 'The essential act of death is essentially God's own act: not of course as alien reality, as that which alienates from God. *Nemo contra deum nisi deus ipse*! But in such a way that God himself in himself permits a negation which creates space in his being for other being. It was in fact for others, for *us*, that he went into death. The "No" of God to himself *is* his "Yes" to us. The essential act of which death is deprived exists in the being of the living God as providing an eternal place for those who are chosen and destined in Christ to exist in God's eternal being. God's being then can no longer be conceived as *omnino simplex esse*. God's eternal being is more differentiated and also more temporal than we are able to conceive.'[49]

A little later Jüngel expounded his ideas at greater length in a second article, 'The Dark Saying of the "Death of God"'.[50] In discussion with modern atheism and particularly with the American 'God is dead' theologians he lays greater stress on *life* from the death of God: the life of God and the life of man. Here Jüngel sees a dual task for theology. The first: 'On the one hand, theology must accept as justified and legitimate the charge of atheism raised originally against Christianity. That is to say, we may *not* continue to talk about God in such a way that the word "God" suggests something like the ancient "gods" or some kind of supreme being understood as transcendence or as majestic omnipotence. The God involved in the death of Jesus Christ is different. And it is quite impossible to understand what he is like without this involvement in death. The necessity of talking of the suffering and even the death of God and of thinking out God's divinity against this background means the end of all religious ideas of God and the end of all theistic talk of God.'[51] The second task: 'It consists in protecting the justified, theologically acceptable and legitimate charge of atheism, provoked by Christianity, from confusion with modern atheism now become

---

[44]*op. cit.*, 95–99.
[45]*op. cit.*, 99–105.
[46]*op. cit.*, 103.
[47]*op. cit.*, 104.
[48]*op. cit.*, 113–116.
[49]*op. cit.*, 111.
[50]E. Jüngel: in *Evangelische Kommentare* 2 (1969), 133–138.
[51]*op. cit.*, 138.

551

autonomous. The more similar two things are, the more carefully must they be distinguished. The fact that even faith must talk of the death of God cannot mean that faith must cease to talk precisely of *God,* although this is what the "death of God" theology demands. Gerhard Ebeling's words are relevant here: "We must not continue talk of God irresponsibly, but neither must we discontinue it irresponsibly." '[52]

Hence, according to Jüngel, future theology must abandon the alternative of an un-Christian theism on the one hand and of an un-Christian atheism on the other and the end of the statement about the death of God will be: 'God lives'.

Dietrich Bonhoeffer had recognised this new perspective of classical Christology in his letters from prison: 'The question is: Christ and the world that has come of age.'[53] The answer: 'the claim of a world that has come of age by Jesus Christ.'[54] In Jesus Christ the reality of God and the reality of the world are one. In the face of the inevitable total secularisation of modern life, which Bonhoeffer repeatedly describes, he tries not to reject or cancel the changed reality of the world become worldly, nor to add to it a dose of 'religion', but in the light of faith to interpret, sustain, endure it, positively to master it. For this there is necessary a non-religious, secular interpretation of the biblical terms. Non-religious, secular interpretation means christological interpretation, for which the code-word is John 1:14: 'The Word became flesh'.[55] The incarnation of God must be taken quite seriously and for Bonhoeffer this means in humiliation, in suffering. In the last weeks before his execution no idea made a greater impression on Bonhoeffer's mind than that of God's suffering, in which we are expected to participate. His doctrine of God therefore is essentially a *theologia crucis.* And what a strange harmony he found between the ejection of God from the world come of age, the autonomous, secular world, and the revelation of God in Christ, in whom God permits himself to be thrust out of the world and on to the cross. By his very powerlessness in the world, the living God of the Bible gains power and space. Man's Godforsakenness in the world has been endured and overcome precisely by God himself. It is only this suffering God who can help: that is, help the person who participates in faith in this suffering of God in the world. '"Christians stand by God in his hour of grieving"; that is what distinguishes Christians from pagans. Jesus asked in Gethsemane, "Could you not watch with me one hour?" That is a reversal of what the religious man expects from God. Man is summoned to share in God's sufferings at the hands of a godless

[52]*ibid.*
[53]D. Bonhoeffer: *Widerstand und Ergebung.* 218 (ET *Letters and Papers from Prison,* SCM, London, enlarged edition, 1971, 231).
[54]*op. cit.* 231; ET, 342.
[55]*op. cit.,* esp. 183–185; cf. 239–242 (ET, 285–287; cf. 359–362); cf. also the informative article by G. Ebeling: '*Die nichtreligiöse Interpretation biblischer Begriffe*'.

world . . . It is not the religious act that makes the Christian, but participation in the sufferings of God in the secular life.'[56]

God's suffering takes place in Jesus Christ: 'And we cannot be honest unless we recognize that we have to live in the world *etsi deus non daretur*. And this is just what we do recognize – before God! God himself compels us to recognize it. So our coming of age leads us to a true recognition of our situation before God. God would have us know that we must live as men who manage our lives without him. The God who is with us is the God who forsakes us (Mark 15:34). The God who lets us live in the world without the working hypothesis of God is the God before whom we stand continually. Before God and with God we live without God. God lets himself be pushed out of the world on to the cross. He is weak and powerless in the world, and that is precisely the way, the only way, in which he is with us and helps us. Matt. 8:17 makes it quite clear that Christ helps us, not by virtue of his omnipotence, but by virtue of his weakness and suffering.

'Here is the decisive difference between Christianity and all religions. Man's religiosity makes him look in his distress to the power of God in the world: God is the *deus ex machina*. The Bible directs man to God's powerlessness and suffering; only the suffering God can help. To that extent we may say that the development towards the world's coming of age outlined above, which has done away with a false conception of God, opens up a way of seeing the God of the Bible, who wins power and space in the world by his weakness. This will probably be the starting-point for our "secular interpretation".'[57]

In Jesus Christ the new image of God is revealed: 'Who is God? Not in the first place an abstract belief in God, in his omnipotence etc. That is not a genuine experience of God, but a partial extension of the world. Encounter with Jesus Christ. The experience that a transformation of all human life is given in the fact that "Jesus is there only for others". His "being there for others" is the experience of transcendence. It is only this "being there for others", maintained till death, that is the ground of his omnipotence, omniscience and omnipresence. Faith is participation in this being of Jesus (incarnation, cross, and resurrection). Our relation to God is not a "religious" relationship to the highest, most powerful, and best Being imaginable – that is not authentic transcendence – but our relation to God is a new life in "existence for others", through participation in the being of Jesus. The transcendental is not infinite and unattainable tasks, but the neighbour who is within reach in any given situation. God in human form – not, as in oriental religions, in animal form, monstrous, chaotic, remote and terrifying, nor in the conceptual forms of the absolute, metaphysical, infinite, etc., nor yet in the Greek divine-human form of "man in himself", but "the man for others", and therefore the Crucified, the man who lives out of the transcendent.'[58]

Bonhoeffer's christological ideas have frequently had a stimulating effect, and not least on John A. T. Robinson's influential book *Honest to God*.[59] Harvey Cox in his book *God's Revolution and Man's Responsibility* draws on

---

[56]*op. cit.*, 244; ET, 361.
[57]*op. cit.*, 241f; cf. 245–249, 153f, 265–267; ET, 360f; cf. 369f, 374f, 386.
[58]*op. cit.*, 259; ET, 381f.
[58]*op. cit.*, 259f; ET. 381f.

Bonhoeffer for his conclusions in regard to divine worship, to individual and social ethics, to social change.[60] In his book on Bonhoeffer,[61] in the chapter on the 'Christological perspective', Heinrich Ott also stresses the 'messianic suffering of Christ, the suffering of God in the world'[62] and goes on to compare Bonhoeffer's Christology with that of Teilhard de Chardin.[63] For Bonhoeffer the experience of Christ was that of the Crucified: 'Christ is God who suffers in the world and in whose suffering we as his community are expected to participate.' For Teilhard on the other hand Christ is 'primarily the Risen One who permeates everything with his presence and leads all reality to the future of his kingdom'.[64] For Ott this means that 'we are required to attend to the message of these two great Christians of our century, to reflect on their ideas interconnected over the distance of time, in order to recognize the one Christ, the Crucified and Risen, in the way he makes himself known today to his community and to his mankind'.[65]

In his book on Teilhard, S. M. Daecke compares Teilhard with Hegel in considerable detail, beginning with a chapter on the 'Death of God and the Worldliness of God' in Hegel:[66] 'The unity of God's and the world's reality comes about in Jesus Christ. In him God becomes "worldly". God in fact remains God and yet becomes man; he becomes immanent in the reality of the world, without however giving up his difference from the world, without becoming identical with the world. God's "worldliness", his "this-sidedness" and his immanence, have a christological basis: the eternal, heavenly, omnipotent God is identical with a temporal, earthly, powerless man. This unity of God's and the world's reality, the "worldliness" and "this-sidedness" of God, culminate in the death of the man in whom alone God became present and visible for us. The death of Jesus is the death of God. And it means the definitive unity of God's and the world's reality, the radical worldliness of God.'[67]

Daecke observes in Teilhard's thinking 'the unconscious resumption of Hegelian intentions':[68] 1. the conquest of dualism and the unity of reality; 2. the secularisation of god and the deifying of the world; 3. evolutionary thinking and God's becoming.

But, according to Daecke, Hegel is distinguished from Teilhard both by 'his spiritualistic understanding of God's and the world's reality as spirit'[69] and by

---

[60]H. Cox: *God's Revolution and Man's Responsibility*, ch. 4, 'Sacrament: Suffering with God in his World'.
[61]H. Ott: *Wirklichkeit und Glaubel I*, '*Zum theologischen Erbe Dietrich Bonhoeffers*' (ET *Reality and Faith: The Theological Legacy of Dietrich Bonhoeffer*, London, 1971).
[62]*op. cit.*, 327; ET, 373.
[63]*op. cit.*, 328–339; ET, 374–87.
[64]*op. cit.*, 339; ET, 387.
[65]*ibid.*
[66]S. M. Daecke: *Teilhard de Chardin und die evangelische Theologie*, 21-29.
[67]*op. cit.*, 21.
[68]*op. cit.*, 186–192.
[69]*op. cit.*, 193–195.

'unhistorical futurelessness'.[70] Daecke wonders whether Teilhard's differences from Hegel are sufficient to avoid the problems in which Hegel became involved.[71]

In this connection the 'theology of the pain of God', as developed by the Japanese theologian K. Kitamori, mentioned by Ott, is interesting. The dialectic of God's pain and love seems to Ott 'a new and fruitful approach, after the Western dogmatic tradition had understood God's innermost being as unfeeling, eternal blessedness'.[72]

A christological text of Kitamori's runs: 'The pain of God must ... be a fact other than that of the love of God. It is indeed the love for those who revolt against the love of God. It dissolves – as it were – in itself the immediate love of God as a mediating factor. Thus the pain of God rises higher than the love of God. Hence the pain of God can attest the love on the cross of Christ. It is the nature of love on the cross that it loves those who revolt against the love of God. The immediate (direct) love of God is nothing but law. The love of God ... revealed without the aid of the law is certainly the pain of God as gospel. Both the pain of God and the love of God on the cross are the love which loves man and overpowers the human sin that denies God's love: the love which is absolute affirmation as the negation of negation. Even if a human being might revolt against the immediate love of God, he cannot revolt against the pain of God, that is, the love on the cross of Christ. This in fact means the complete victory of the pain of God, the victory of the risen Christ. This victory then is nothing but the victory of love established by the pain of God. This victory of the crucified Christ is shown by his resurrection which overcomes the death on the cross. As Christ's death has his resurrection as its reverse side, so God's pain must have God's love as its reverse side.'[73]

We mentioned at an earlier stage Jürgen Moltmann's comments on the 'death of God', in which he was directly following Hegel and Bonhoeffer.[74] In his inaugural lecture at Tübingen, on 'God and Resurrection', Moltmann expressly raised the central question of where and who God is in the death of Jesus within the framework of the problem of theodicy. We may cite here an especially impressive passage: 'If God reveals something of his divinity in the raising up of the Crucified, where was he and who was he when that crucifixion took place? Did God merely permit it by keeping away from it? Did he hide himself when it happened? If the Easter faith transforms the cross of the Forsaken into an enigma, then obviously it is only the cross that can explain this Easter faith. The God who accepts him gives him up by forsaking him. The suffering and death of the Crucified at the hands of God then acquires the meaning of his surrender to the world, and in Jesus' self-giving is found the self-giving of God himself. God suffers in Jesus' suffering, in Jesus' death God himself tastes damnation and death. As Barth puts it, "God loses so that man may win". Thus in the cross the old image of God is changed, the

---

[70]*op. cit.*, 196–198.
[71]*op. cit.*, 198–200.
[72]H. Ott: *Wirklichkeit und Glaube*, 356; ET, 408.
[73]*op. cit.*, 357; ET, 408f.
[74]cf. chs. 4, 3 and 7, 6.

image of paternal authority or cold power, against which the question of theodicy rebels. "God is different." In the Crucified he gives up power and dominion, humiliates himself even to this death. Why and for whom does the Christ of God suffer? Contrary to what Georg Büchner says, this is the rock of Christian faith. For here, out of abstract superior power, the concrete suffering of God comes to be; and out of God's abstract immortality the "death of God" comes to be in Christ. As already in a hidden way in Job and in Isaiah's Suffering Servant, God is not now confronted by the human question of theodicy but is himself involved in it, is at risk in it: he is involved in a game in which the loser wins. But then the cross of the Risen One reveals who and where God is. Only on this assumption of "God in the face of Christ" – God, that is, not as a kind of heavenly partner but as the earthly and humane God in the Crucified – does the cross of Christ gain full juridical significance and meaning for the future within the framework of the question of theodicy. God is no longer the one accused in the human question of theodicy, the answer is in the question itself. The cross of Christ then becomes "Christian theodicy": a self-justification of God in which judgment and damnation are passed on God himself, so that man may live. This paradoxical sounding dialectic of the presence of God in the Crucified and Sacrificed is not a paradox closed up in itself, but an open dialectic. We encounter its openness to the future when we define the God who proves his power to the witnesses by the resurrection in terms of the God involved for all in the cross of Christ.'[75]

All this shows the fruitfulness of a renewed reflection on classical Christology even at the present time. Despite everything, this does not mean that we can dispense with further questioning, as we explained in the section on the historicity of Jesus. Is this classical Christology, particularly in its conceptual framework, in its ideological background and substratum, still generally intelligible today? Does it correspond to the New Testament message of Christ as perfectly as people thought it did for centuries? Do not fresh reflections, both Catholic and Protestant, on this Christology involve very considerable corrections? But is not even this renewed dogmatic Christology often very remote from the human reality of Jesus? Even in dogmatics ought we not to take the quest of the historical Jesus very much more seriously than we have done hitherto?

Allowing for all the necessary fresh understanding and transposition into the present time, *in the last resort* an enterprise of this kind is interesting only if the attempt is made to let the *whole* New Testament message find expression and to take it – certainly in its historical differentiation and detailed outline – really seriously. In

---

[75]J. Moltmann: *Perspektiven der Theologie*, 47f (ET *Hope and Planning*, 42f).

his reflection on the secular meaning of the Gospel,[76] van Buren cannot be accused of dispensing himself from coping with classical Christology.[77] It is particularly interesting to see how this 'secular' interpreter of the Gospel, in the wake of other scholars, is attentive, not only to the neglect of the human reality of Jesus,[78] but also to the problems of God's immutability and impassibility: 'The patristic idea of God coloured the whole development of classical Christology and has posed a problem for theology ever since. The Fathers insisted at all costs on the impassibility of God and his Word, for change was the mark of the imperfect, the sign of corruption and decay. This is a difficult presupposition with which to expound the biblical writings, however. On the one hand, the Fathers said that God was in Christ in an indissoluble union with Christ's human "nature". On the other hand, they said that Jesus Christ had actually suffered and died on the cross. If they had been more consistent in saying that God is unknown apart from his self-revelation and that we must begin with Jesus Christ in order to know anything about God at all, they might have been able to begin with the cross as the event of self-revelation of a God who is quite able to take suffering to himself and whose glory is so great that he can humble himself. Had this been done, the course of the development of classical Christology would have been quite different.'[79] Van Buren then is in many ways right in his criticism; in principle, too, he is right in his intention of making the Gospel intelligible for secular man – or, better, for the secular believer – today and of looking at the heart of the Gospel in the light of Christology. Neither can the advantage be disputed of philosophical linguistic analysis, from which modern theology (and philosophy) could learn a great deal with respect to clarity. What is problematic is only the way in which van Buren applies some very *a priori* principles of certain linguistic analysts to the New Testament message in order to reach a Christological synthesis (in itself a praiseworthy undertaking) between the theological 'right' and the theology of the 'left'. But – as always if the preconception brought in any case to the New Testament message is not, while making every allowance for justified 'demythologisings', corrected by that message, but used as a filter for it – the result is amazingly threadbare and insubstantial: Jesus is a man uniquely free for others, whose freedom became contagious.[80] This Christology, allegedly so radical, in the last resort, after a little reflection, may not seem very exciting or revolutionary particularly for the empirically thinking secular American with whom van Buren is assiduously concerned. In any case it is not something that he could not have discovered for himself after a little thought and without doing violence to the Gospel as a result of neglecting serious exegesis. Van Buren can no more appeal to Bonhoeffer (as he does at the opening of his book, in support of his enterprise) than to Barth and Bultmann, whom he also quotes, but much too superficially. On the contrary the Bonhoeffer quotation, which we quoted above in its full context, shows exactly what is theologically important in the modern secular world: 'And we cannot be honest unless we recognize that we have to live in the world *etsi deus non daretur*. And this is just what we do recognize – before God! God himself compels us to recognize it. So our coming of age leads us to a true recognition of our situation before God.'[81] However

---

[76]P. van Buren: *The Secular Meaning of the Gospel*, 1963; Penguin edition, 1968.
[77]*op. cit.*, 37-66.
[78]*op. cit.*, 51-53.
[79]*op. cit.*, 54.
[80]*op. cit.*, 171.
[81]D. Bonhoeffer: *Widerstand und Ergebung*, 241 (ET *Letters and Papers from Prison*, 360).

greatly Bonhoeffer was interested in the experience by faith of the world's reality, its presupposition for him was the unity of God's and the world's reality rooted in Jesus Christ. A Christology without theology is not a Christology at all. Faced with the choice between between Harnack's Gospel of the Father (to which Jesus Christ does not belong) and van Buren's Gospel of Jesus (in which the Father is absorbed), in the light of the New Testament and the modern world, Harnack is to be preferred. But we are not faced with this choice, neither in the light of the New Testament nor in that of the modern world. Some other way must be found to assist van Buren's positive intention to become effective.

Abbreviations

EKL   *Evangelisches Kirchenlexikon. Kirchlich-theologisches Handwörterbuch* (edited by H. Brunotte and O. Weber; Göttingen 1955).

D   H. Denzinger, *Enchiridion symbolorum, definitionum et declarationum de rebus fidei et morum* (Barcelona – Freiburg – Rome, 31st edition, 1960).

DTC   *Dictionnaire de Théologie Catholique* (edited by A. Vacant and E. Mangenot, continued by E. Amann; Paris 1903).

H   *Dokumente zu Hegels Entwicklung* (edited by J. Hoffmeister, Stuttgart 1936)..

LThK   *Lexikon für Theologie und Kirche,* vols. I – X (edited by J. Höfer and K. Rahner; Freiburg, 2nd edition, 1956–65).

N   *Theologische Jugendschriften, nach den Handschriften der Kgl. Bibliothek in Berlin* (edited by H. Nohl, Tübingen, 1907).

RGG   *Die Religion in Geschichte und Gegenwart. Handwörterbuch für Theologie und Religonswissenschaft* (edited by K. Galling, Tübingen, 3rd edition, 1957).

ThQ   *Tübinger Theologische Quartalschrift* (Stuttgart, 1819).

ZThK   *Zeitschrift für Theologie und Kirche* (Tübingen, 1891).

Other abbreviations used for Hegel's works appear below.

Bibliography

I. Works by G. F. W. Hegel

Küng's basic text is the Lasson-Hoffmeister critical edition, which is accepted today as definitive. In the German original, it was quoted with the volume number in Roman numerals, followed by the page number (e.g. XIII, 122) and this practice has been retained in the translation where passages are quoted for which no suitable English translation is available. In order to avoid misunderstanding, Küng has retained the accustomed earlier volume numbering, even when using newer Hoffmeister editions which bear different numbering. Thus even the Letters are quoted under the original numbering XXVII-XXX.

The lectures on aesthetics and on the history of philosophy which are lacking from the critical edition have been supplied from the Jubilee Edition of Hegel's Complete Works, edited by Hermann Glockner. These volumes are quoted as G number vol. followed by page number (e.g. GXIX, 343).

Finally, for the early writings, Küng has employed the familiar collections of Nohl (quoted as N number followed by page) and Hoffmeister (H page).

In order to facilitate the location of passages, there follows a list of the volumes used in the original, together with the English editions used in the translation (more precise bibliographic details are in the text itself).

1. From the Lasson-Hoffmeister Critical Edition

I   *Erste Druckschriften:* there are no English translations of these items.

II   *Phänomenologie des Geistes: Phenomenology of Spirit,* trans. A. V. Miller, Oxford, 1977.

III-IV   *Wissenschaft der Logik: Science of Logic,* trans. A. V. Miller, London, 1969.

V   *Enzyklopädie der philosophischen Wissenschaften,* comprising
1. *Logic,* trans. W. Wallace, Oxford, 1892, rev. edn. 1975 (*Wallace*).
2. *Philosophy of Mind,* trans. W. Wallace, Oxford, 1894, rev. edn. 1971 (*PM*).
3. *Philosophy of Nature,* trans. A. V. Miller, Oxford, 1970 (*PN*).

VI   *Grundlinien der Philosophie des Rechts: Philosophy of Right,* trans. T. M. Knox, Oxford, 1942, rev. edn. 1974 (*PR*).

VII   *Schriften zur Politik und Rechtsphilosophie*: selections in *Political Writings,* trans. T. M. Knox, Oxford, 1964, new edn. 1973; however not used in text.

VIII-IX   *Vorlesungen über die Philosophie der Weltgeschichte*: only the Introduction to the *Lectures on the Philosophy of World History,* trans. H. B. Nisbet, Cambridge, 1975, provides an E T corresponding to the German text (see p 320 note 6). Quotations from other parts of the *Lectures* have therefore only been referred to the Lasson-Hoffmeister text (*PWH*).

X Vorlesungen über die Ästhetik: only the first part of Vol. 1, *Die Idee und das Ideal*, is available in Lasson-Hoffmeister; see below under Glockner.

XII-XIV *Vorlesungen über die Philosophie der Religion*: there is no suitable ET. The one by Speirs and Sanderson is not based on the Lasson text.

XV *Vorlesungen über die Geschichte der Philosophie*: only the Introduction, System *und Geschichte der Philosophie*, is available in Lasson-Hoffmeister, but the ET is not based on this text; see below under Glockner.

XVIII *Jenenser Logik, Metaphysik und Naturphilosophie*.

XIX-XX *Jenenser Realphilosophie* I-II.

XXI *Nürnberger Schriften*.

XXII *Berliner Schriften*.

XXVII-XXX *Briefe von und an Hegel*.

(XXVII-XXX: There are no ETs of these items; but see the selection of letters in Kaufmann, *Hegel: Reinterpretation, Texts and Commentary*.)

2. From the Glockner Jubilee Edition

GXII-XIV *Vorlesungen über die Ästhetik* (Hotho edition): *Aesthetics*, trans. T. M. Knox, 2 vols., Oxford, 1975, referred to in the text where the translation corresponds to the German edition used (*A*).

GXVII-XIX *Vorlesungen über die Geschichte der Philosophie* (Michelet edition): *Lectures on the History of Philosophy*, trans. E. S. Haldane and I. H. Simson, 3 vols., London, 1892-6, repr. 1968; referred to in text where the citation is from elsewhere than the Introduction (see above) (*HP*).

3. Miscellaneous Collections

N *Theologische Jugendschriften*, ed. H. Nohl: *Early Theological Writings*, trans. T. M. Knox, Chicago, 1948, new edn. Philadelphia, 1971, covers most of the material; see also texts in H. S. Harris, *Towards the Sunlight*, Oxford, 1972.

H *Dokumente zu Hegels Entwicklung*, ed. J. Hoffmeister: there are no ETs of these items.

II. Literature on Hegel

Adorno, T. W., *Drei Studien zu Hegel* (Frankfurt, 1963).

Albrecht, W., *Hegels Gottesbeweis. Eine Studie zur "Wissenschaft de Logik"* (Berlin, 1958).

Antoni, C., *L'estetica di Hegel*, in *Giornale critico della filosofia italiana* 14 (1960).

Anz, W., art. '*Hegel*', in *EKL* II (Göttingen, 1958), 43-48.

Aspelin, G., *Hegels Tübinger Fragment. Eine psychologisch-ideengeschichtliche Untersuchung* (Lund, 1933).

Asveld, P., *La pensée religieuse du jeune Hegel. Liberté et aliénation* (Louvain Paris, 1953).

Axmann, W., *Die Frage nach dem Ursprung des dialektischen Denkens bei Hegel* (Würzburg, 1939).

Baader, F. v., *Revision der Philosopheme der Hegel'schen Schule bezüglich auf das*

THE INCARNATION OF GOD

Christenthum. Nebst zehn Thesen aus einer religiösen Philosophie. Sämtliche Werke, vol. IX (Leipzig, 1855), 289–436.

Über die Vernünftigkeit der drei Fundamentaldoctrinen des Christenthums von Vater und Sohn, von der Wiedergeburt und von der Mensch-und Leibwerdung Gottes. Aus einem Sendschreiben an Freiherrn Stransky auf Greifenfels. Sämtliche Werke, vol. X (Leipzig, 1855), 17–52.

Balthasar, H. U. v., *Apokalypse der deutschen Seele. Studien zu einer Lehre von letzten Haltungen,* vols. I–III (vol. I, *Der deutsche Idealismus*; Salzburg-Leipzig 1937–39).

Barion, J., *Dialektik der Natur und Geschichte,* in *Erkenntnis und Verantwortung (Festschrift* for T. Litt; Düsseldorf, 1960), 91–104.

Hegel und die marxistische Staatslehre (Bonn, 1963).

Barth, K., *Protestant Theology in the Nineteenth Century,* (London, 1972), ch. 10, pp. 384–421. Part of this was previously published as *From Rousseau to Ritschl* (London, 1959).

Barth, P., *Die Geschichtsphilosophie Hegels und der Hegelianer bis auf Marx und Hartmann. Ein kritischer Versuch* (Leipzig, 1890, 2nd edition 1925).

Bartsch, H., *Register zu Hegels Vorlesungen über die Ästhetik* (1844; reprinted Stuttgart, 1966).

Basch, V., *Les doctrines politiques des philosophes classiques de l'Allemagne* (Paris, 1927).

Bauer, B., *Die Posaune des jüngsten Gerichts über Hegel den Atheisten und Antichristen. Ein Ultimatum* (Leipzig, 1841).

Beerling, R. F., *De List der Rede in de Geschiedenisfilosofie van Hegel* (Arnhem, 1959; includes summary in English: 'Hegel and the Cunning of Reason').

Bénard, Ch., *L'estétique allemande contemporaine* (Paris, 1876).

Bense, M., *Hegel und Kierkegaard* (Köln-Krefeld, 1948).

Benvenuto, M., *Hegel, filosofo della religione* (Naples, 1953).

Bergh van Eysinga, G. A. van den, *Hegel* (2nd edition, ed. H. A. Ett; The Hague, 1960).

Beyer, W. R., *Zwischen Phänomenologie und Logik. Hegel als Redakteur der Bamberger Zeitung* (Frankfurt a.M., 1955).

Binder, J. – Busse, M. – Larenz, K., *Einführung in Hegels Rechtsphilosophie. Vorträge* (Berlin, 1931).

Bloch, E., *Subjekt – Objekt. Erläuterungen zu Hegel* (1951; enlarged edition, Frankfurt a.M., 1962).

Bodammer, Th., *Hegels Deutung der Sprache* (Hamburg, 1969).

Boehm, H.-G., *Das Todesproblem bei Hegel und Hölderlin* (1797–1800) (Diss. Marburg, 1932).

Bröcker, W., *Formale, transzendentale und spekulative Logik* (Frankfurt a.M., 1962). *–Auseinandersetzungen mit Hegel* (Frankfurt a.M., 1965).

Bruaire, C., *Logique et religion chrétienne dans la philosophie de Hegel* (Paris, 1964).

Bruijn, J. C., *Hegel's Phaenomenologie. Proeve van Tekstverklaring,* vols. I–II (Diss. Amsterdam, 1932).

Brunet, Ch., *L'ontologie dans l'"Encyclopädie" de Hegel,* in *Revue de métaphysique et de morale* 65 (1960), 449–462.

Brunstäid, F., *Untersuchungen zu Hegels Geschichtstheorie* (Diss. Berlin, 1909). *–Vorrede zu Hegels Philosophie der Geschichte,* abgedruckt in F. Brunstäd, *Gesammelte Aufsätze und kleinere Schriften* (ed. E. Gerstenmaier and C. G. Schweitzer; Berlin, 1957) 44–68.

BIBLIOGRAPHY

Buchner, H., *Hegel und das Kritische Journal der Philosophie,* in *Hegel-Studien* vol. III (1965), 95-156.
Bülow, F., *Der Entwurf der Hegelschen Sozialphilosophie* (Leipzig, 1920).
Burian, W., *Revolutionär und Kantianer. Ein Beitrag zur neueren Bestimmung des Einflusses der Französischen Revolution und der Gedanken Kants auf die geistige Entwicklung des jungen Hegel in der Zeit von Tübingen bis hin nach Frankfurt* (Diss. Paris, 1969).
Chapelle, A., *Hegel et la religion,* vols. I-II (Paris-Brussels, 1964-67).
Chevalier, J., *Histoire de la pensée,* vol. IV: *La pensée moderne: De Hegel à Bergson* (ed. L. Husson; Paris, 1966).
Clark, M., *Logic and System. A Study of the Transition from "Vorstellung" to Thought in the Philosophy of Hegel* (Löwen, 1960).
Copleston, F., *A History of Philosophy,* vol. VII: *From Fichte to Nietzsche* (London, 1963).
Coreth, E., *Dialektik und Analogie des Seins. Zum Seinsproblem bei Hegel und in der Scholastik,* in *Scholastik* 26 (1951) 57-86.
– *Das dialektische Sein in Hegels Logik* (Wien, 1952).
– *Hegel und der dialektische Materialismus,* in *Scholastik* 27 (1952) 55-67.
Cottier, G. M.-M., *L'athéisme du jeune Marx. Ses origines hégéliennes* (Paris, 1959).
Croce, B., *What is Living and What is Dead of the Philosophy of Hegel,* trans D. Ainslie, London, 1915, repr. New York, 1969.
– *Ultimi saggi* (Bari, 1935).
Danzel, W., *Über die Ästhetik der Hegelschen Philosophie* (Hamburg, 1844).
Dieter, Th., *Die Frage der Persönlichkeit Gottes in Hegels Philosophie* (Diss. Tübingen, 1917).
Dilthey, W., *Die Jugendgeschichte Hegels. Gesammelte Schriften* vol. IV (1905; Leipzig-Berlin, 1925), 1-187.
– *Fragmente aus dem Nachlaß. Gesammelte Schriften* vol. IV (1905; Leipzig-Berlin 1925), 190-282.
Domke, K., *Das Problem der metaphysischen Gottesbeweise in der Philosophie Hegels* (Leipzig, 1940).
Drescher, W., *Die dialektische Bewegung des Geistes in Hegels Phänomenologie* (Speyer, 1937).
Dulckeit, G., *Die Idee Gottes im Geiste der Philosophie Hegels* (Munich, 1974).
Dulckeit-von Arnim, Chr., *Hegels Kunstphilosophie,* in *Philosophisches Jahrbuch* 67 (1959), 285-304.
Ehrenberg, H., *Hegel. Der Disputation drittes Buch* (Munich, 1925).
Elert, W., *Der Kampf um das Christentum. Geschichte der Beziehungen zwischen dem evangelischen Christentum in Deutschland und dem allgemeinen Denken seit Schleiermacher und Hegel* (Munich, 1921).
Ephraim, F., *Untersuchungen über den Freiheitsbegriff Hegels in seinen Jugendarbeiten.* I. Teil (Berlin, 1928).
Eschenmayer, C. A., *Die Hegelsche Religions-Philosophie verglichen mit dem christlichen Prinzip* (Tübingen, 1834).
Fabro, C., *Giorgio G. F. Hegel, La dialettica. Antologia sistematica* (Brescia, 1960).
Fackenheim, E. L., *The Religious Dimension in Hegel's Thought* (Bloomington-London, 1967).
Fazio Allmayer, V., *Ricerche hegeliane* (Florence, 1959).
Fessard, G., *Deux Interprètes de la Phénoménologie de Hegel: J. Hyppolite et A.*

Kojève, in *Etudes* 225 (1947), 368–373.
–*La dialectique des exercices spirituels de St. Ignace de Loyola* (Paris, 1956).
–*Attitude ambivalente de Hegel en face de l'histoire*, in *Archives de philosophie* 24 (1961), 207–241.
Fetscher, I., *Das Verhältnis des Marxismus zu Hegel*, in *Marxismus-Studien* Series 3 (1954), 66–169.
Feuerbach, L., *Über Philosophie und Christentum in Beziehung auf den der Hegel'schen Philosophie gemachten Vorwurf der Unchristlichkeit* (Mannheim, 1839).
Findlay, J. N., *Hegel. A Re-examination* (London-New York, 1958).
Fischer, H., *Hegels Methode in ihrer ideengeschichtlichen Notwendigkeit* (Munich, 1928).
Fischer, K., *Hegels Leben, Werke und Lehre*, vols I-II (Heidelberg, 1901).
Flach, W., *Negation und Andersheit. Ein Beitrag zur Problematik der Letztimplikation* (Munich-Basle, 1959).
– *Hegels dialektische Methode*, in *Hegel-Studien* Beiheft I (Bonn, 1964), 55–64.
Fleischmann, E. J., *La philosophie politique de Hegel. Sous forme d'un commentaire des fondements de la philosophie du droit* (Paris, 1964).
– *Hegel's Umgestaltung der Kantischen Logik*, in *Hegel-Studien* vol. III (Bonn, 1965), 181–207.
Fleischmann, J., *Objektive and subjektive Logik bei Hegel*, in *Hegel-Studien* Beiheft I (Bonn, 1964), 45–54.
Flügge, J., *Die sittlichen Grundlagen des Denkens. Hegels existentielle Erkenntnisgesinnung* (Hamburg, 1953).
Foster, M. B., *Die Geschichte als Schicksal des Geistes in der Hegelschen Philosophie* (Tübingen, 1929).
Franchini, R., *Le origini della dialettica* (Naples, 1961).
Gadamer, H.-G., *Hegel und die antike Dialektik*, in *Hegel-Studien* vol. I (Bonn, 1961), 173–199.
Gans, E., *Vorwort zu Hegel, Grundlinien der Philosophie des Rechtes* (Berlin, 1833).
Garáudy, R., *Dieu est mort. Etude sur Hegel* (Paris, 1962); *Gott ist tot. Das System und die Methode Hegels* (Frankfurt a.M., 1956).
– *La pensée de Hegel* (Paris, 1967).
Gerdes, H., *Das Christusbild Sören Kierkegaards verglichen mit der Christologie Hegels und Schleiermachers* (Düsseldorf-Cologne, 1960).
Giese, G., *Hegels Staatsidee und der Begriff der Staatserziehung* (Halle, 1926).
Girndt, H., *Die Differenz des Fichteschen und Hegelschen Systems in der Hegelschen "Differenzschrift"* (Bonn, 1965).
Glockner, H., *Hegel.* Vol. I (Stuttgart, 1920, 2nd edition 1954); Vol. II (Stuttgart, 1940, 3rd edition 1958).
– *Der Begriff in Hegels Philosophie* (Tübingen, 1924).
– *Hegel-Lexikon.* Vols I-IV (Stuttgart, 1934).
– *Beiträge zum Verständnis und zur Kritik Hegels sowie zur Umgestaltung seiner Geisteswelt*, in *Hegel-Studien* Beiheft 2 (Bonn, 1965).
Görland, I., *Die Kantkritik des jungen Hegel* (Frankfurt a.M. 1966.).
Grégoire, Fr., *Aux sources de la pensée de Marx: Hegel – Feuerbach* (Löwen, 1947).
– *Etudes Hégéliennes. Les points capitaux du système* (Löwen-Paris, 1958).
Groos, H., *Der deutsche Idealismus und das Christentum. Versuch einer vergleichen den Phänomenologie* (Munich, 1927).

Gropp, R. O., *Zu Pragen der Geschichte der Philosophie und des dialektischen Materialismus* (Berlin, 1958).

Große Sowjet-Enzyklopädie, art.'Hegel' (Moscow, 2nd edition 1952; Berlin, 1955).

Günther, G., *Idee und Grundß einer nicht-Aristotelischen Logik.* Vol. I: *Die Idee und ihre philosophischen Voraussetzungen* (Hamburg, 1959).

- *Das Problem einer Formalisierung der transzendentaldialektischen Logik. Unter besonderer Berücksichtigung der Logik Hegels,* in *Hegel-Studien* Beiheft I (Bonn, 1964), 65-123.

Guerenu, E. de, *Das Gottesbild des jungen Hegel. Eine Studie zu "Der Geist des Christentums und sein Schicksal"* (Freiburg, Munich, 1969).

Guzzoni, U., *Werden zu sich. Eine Untersuchung zu Hegels "Wissenschaft der Logik"* (Freiburg i. Br.Munich, 1963).

Haag, K. H., *Philosophischer Idealismus. Untersuchungen zur Hegelschen Dialektik mit Beispielen aus der Wissenschaft der Logik* (Frankfurt a.M. 1967).

Habermas, J., *Theory and Practice,* trans. J. Viertel, Boston, 1973, London, 1974.

Hadlich, H., *Hegels Lehren über das Verhältnis von Religion und Philosophie.* I. *Teil* (Halle, 1906).

Haering, Th., *Hegel. Sein Wollen und sein Werk. Eine chronologische Entwicklungsgeschichte der Gedanken und der Sprache Hegels,* vols. I-II (Leipzig-Berlin, 1929/1938).

- *'Die Entstehungsgeschichte der Phänomenologie des Geistes',* in *Verhandlungen des dritten Hegelkongresses* (1934) 118-138.

- *Hegels Lehre von Staat und Recht. Ihre Entwicklung und Bedeutung für die Gegenwart* (Stuttgart, 1940).

Hagen, E. v., *Abstraktion und Konkretion bei Hegel und Kierkegaard* (Bonn, 1969).

Hartmann, E. v., *Über die dialektische Methode. Historisch-kritische Untersuchung* (Berlin, 1868).

Hartmann, K., *Sartre's Ontology: A Study of Being and Nothingness in the Light of Hegel's Logic* (Evanston, 1966).

Hartmann, N., *Die Philosophie des deutschen Idealismus 2. Teil: Hegel* (Berlin-Leipzig, 1929).

Haym, R., *Hegel und seine Zeit. Vorlesungen über Entstehung und Entwicklung, Wesen und Werk der Hegelschen Philosophie* (Berlin, 1857; Nachdruck Hildesheim 1962).

Heer, Fr., *Hegel. Auswahl und Einleitung* (Fischer-Bucharest 86; Frankfurt-Hamburg 1955).

Hegel-Jahrbuch (ed. W. R. Beyer; Meisenheim/Glan 1961).

Hegel-Studien (ed. F. Nicolin and O. Pöggeler, vols. I-IV; Bonn, 1961-67), Beihefte I - IV (Bonn, 1961-69).

Heidegger, M., *Hegel's Concept of Experience* New York, 1970.

- *'Hegel und die Griechen',* in *Die Gegenwart der Griechen im neueren Denken* (*Festschrift* H.-G. Gadamer; Tübingen, 1960) 43-57.

Heintel, E., *Hegel und die analogia entis* (Bonn, 1958).

Heiss, R., *Wesen und Formen der Dinlektik* (Cologne-Berlin, 1959).

- *Die großen Dialektiker des 19. Jahrhunderts. Hegel, Kierkegaard, Marx* (Cologne-Berlin, 1963).

Heller, E., *The Artist's Journey into the Interior and Other Essays* (New York, 1965).

Henrich, D., *Der ontologische Gottesbeweis* (Tübingen, 1960).

- *Anfang und Methode der Logik,* in *Hegel-Studien* Suppl. 1 (Bonn, 1964), 19-35.

– *Leutwein über Hegel. Ein Dokument zu Hegels Biographie*, in *Hegel-Studien*, vol. III (Bonn, 1965), 39–77.

Henrici, P., *Hegel und Blondel. Eine Untersuchung über Form und Sinn der Dialektik in der "Phänomenologie des Geistes" und der ersten "Action"* (Munich, 1958).

– *Hegel und die Theologie. Ein kritischer Bericht*, in *Gregorianum* 48 (1967), 706–746.

Hering, O. B., *Vergleichende Darstellung und Beurteilung der Religionsphilosophie Schleiermachers und Hegels* (Thesis, Jena, 1882).

Hessen, J., *Hegels Trinitätslehre. Zugleich eine Einführung in Hegels System* (Freiburg, 1922).

Hirsch, E., *Die Reich-Gottes-Begriffe des neuern europäischen Denkens. Ein Versuch zur Geschichte der Staats- und Gesellschaftsphilosophie* (Göttingen, 1921).

– *Die idealistische Philosophie und das Christentum. Gesammelte Aufsätze* (Gütersloh, 1926).

– *Fichtes, Schleiermachers und Hegels Verhältnis zur Reformation* (Göttingen, 1930).

– *Geschichte der neueren evangelischen Theologie im Zusammenhang mit den allgemeinen Bewegungen des europäischen Denkens*, vol. IV (Gütersloh, 1949, 2nd edition 1960) 447–490: Hegel.

Hocevar, R. K., *Stände und Repräsentation beim jungen Hegel* (Munich, 1968).

Hoetschl, C., *Das Absolute in Hegels Dialektik. Sein Wesen und seine Aufgabe im Hinblick auf Wesen und systematische Stellung Gottes als des actus purus in der Aristotelischen Akt-Potenz-Metaphysik dargestellt* (Paderborn, 1941).

Hoffmeister, J., *Hölderlin und Hegel* (Tübingen, 1931).

– *Goethe und der deutsche Idealismus. Eine Einführung in Hegels Realphilosophie* (Leipzig, 1932).

Hommes, J., *Krise der Freiheit. Hegel – Marx – Heidegger* (Regensburg, 1958).

Hotho, H. G., *Vorstudien für Leben und Kunst* (Stuttgart-Tübingen, 1835).

Hyppolite, J., *Les travaux de Jeunesse de Hegel d'après des ouvrages récents*, in *Revue de Métaphysique et de Morale* 42 (1935), 399–426, 549–577.

– *Vie et prise de conscience de la vie dans la philosophie hégélienne de Jéna*, in *Revue de Métaphysique et de Morale* (1936).

– *Genesis and Structure of Hegel's Phenomenology of Spirit*, trans. S. Cherniak and J. Heckman, Evanston, 1974.

– *Introduction à la philosophie de l'histoire de Hegel* (Paris, 1948).

– *Logique et existence. Essai sur la Logique de Hegel* (Paris, 1953).

Iljin, I., *Die Philosophie Hegels als kontemplative Gotteslehre* (Bern, 1946).

Jünger, F. G., *Vermittlung und Grenze. Zur Geschichte der Hegelschen Dialektik*, in *Merkur* 14 (1960), 201–225.

Kaminsky, J., *Hegel on Art. An Interpretation of Hegel's Aesthetics* (New York, 1962).

Kaufmann, W., *Hegel. Reinterpretation, Texts and Commentary* (Garden City, 1965 and London, 1966).

– *Hegel: A Reinterpretation* (Notre Dame, 1978)

Kern, W., *Das Verhältnis von Erkenntnis und Liebe als philosophisches Grundproblem bei Hegel und Thomas von Aquin*, in *Scholastik* 34 (1959), 394–427.

– *Hegel. Hegelianismus*, in LThK IV (Freiburg, 1960), 56–59.

– *Neue Hegel-Bücher. Ein Literaturbericht für die Jahre 1958–1960*, in *Scholastik* 37 (1962), 85–114, 550–578; 38 (1963), 62–90.

– *Hegel-Bücher 1961–1966. Ein Auswahlbericht*, in *Theologie und Philosophie* 42 (1967), 79–88, 402–418; 44 (1969), 245–267.

BIBLIOGRAPHY

- *Atheismus – Christentum – emanzipierte Gesellschaft. Zu ihrem Bezug in der Sicht Hegels,* in *Zeitschrift für katholische Theologie* 91 (1969), 289–321.

Kimmerle, H., *Zur theologischen Hegelinterpretation,* in *Hegel-Studien* vol. III (Bonn, 1965), 356–369.

- *Dokumente zu Hegels Jenaer Dozententätigkeit (1801–1807),* in *Hegel-Studien* vol. IV (Bonn, 1967) 21–99.

- *Zur Chronologie von Hegels Jenaer Schriften,* in *Hegel-Studien* vol. IV (Bonn, 1967), 125–176.

- *Zur Entwicklung des Hegelschen Denkens in Jena,* in *Hegel-Studien* Suppl. 4 (Bonn, 1969), 33–47.

Klaiber, J., *Hölderlin, Hegel und Schelling in ihren schwäbischen Jugendjahren (Festschrift* for the Jubilee of Tübingen University, Stuttgart, 1877).

Knox, J., *The Aesthetic Theories of Kant, Hegel and Schopenhauer* (London, 1958: first pub. 1936).

Koch, T., *Differenz und Versöhnung. Eine Interpretation der Theologie G. W. F. Hegels nach seiner "Wissenschaft der Logik"* (Gütersloh, 1967).

Kojève, A., *Introduction to the Reading of Hegel. Lectures on the Phenomenology of Spirit Assembled by Raymond Queneau,* ed. A. Bloom, trans. J. Nichols (New York, 1969).

Koyré, A., *Hegel à Jéna. A propos de publications récentes,* in *Revue d'histoire et de philosophie religieuses* 15 (1935), 420–458.

Kroner, R., *Von Kant bis Hegel,* vols. I-II (Tübingen, 1921–24; Nachdruck, 1961).

- *Culture and Faith* (Chicago, 1951).

- *System und Geschichte bei Hegel,* in *Logos* 20 (1931), 243–258.

- *Vom Sinn der Geschichte,* in *Erkenntnis und Verantwortung (Festschrift* for T. Litt, Düsseldorf, 1960). 194–206.

Krüger, H.-J., *Theologie und Aufklärung. Untersuchungen zu ihrer Vermittlung beim jungen Hegel* (Stuttgart, 1966).

Kruithof, J., *Het uitgangspunt van Hegel's ontologie* (Brussells, 1959).

Kühler, O., *Sinn, Bedeutung und Auslegung der Heiligen Schrift in Hegels Philosophie. Mit Beiträgen zur Bibliographie über die Stellung Hegels (und der Hegelianer zur Theologie, Insbesondere) zur Heiligen Schrift* (Leipzig, 1934).

Kuhn, H., *Die Vollendung der Klassischen deutschen Ästhetik durch Hegel* (Berlin, 1931).

Kym, A. L., *Hegels Dialektik in ihrer Anwendung auf die Geschichte der Philosophie* (Zürich, 1949).

Lacorte, C., *Il primo Hegel* (Florence, 1959).

Lakebrink, B., *Hegels dialektische Ontologie und die thomistische Analektik* (Cologne, 1955)

- *Anselm von Canterbury und die Hegelsche Metaphysik,* in *Parusia (Festschrift* for J. Hirschberger, Frankfurt 1965), 455–470.

Landgrebe, L., *Das Problem der Dialektik,* in *Marxismus-Studien* 3 (Tübingen, 1960). 1–65.

Lasson, G., *Hegel als Geschichtsphilosoph* (Leipzig, 1920).

- *Einführung in Hegels Religionsphilosophie* (Leipzig, 1930).

- *Hegels Religionsphilosophie,* in *Verhandlungen des zweiten Hegelkongresses* (1931), 183–193.

Lauener, H., *Die Sprache in der Philosophie Hegels mit besonderer Berücksichtigung der Ästhetik* (Bern, 1962).

Leese, K., *Die Geschichtsphilosophie Hegels auf Grund der neu erschlossenen Quellen untersucht und dargestellt* (Berlin, 1922).

Litt, T., *Hegel. Versuch einer kritischen Erneuerung* (Heidelberg, 1953, 2nd edition 1961).

Lorenzen, P., *Das Problem einer Formalisierung der Hegelschen Logik,* in *Hegel-Studien* Suppl. 1 (Bonn, 1964) 125–130.

Lotz, J. B., *Scholastische Urteilslehre und Hegelsche Seinsdialektik,* in *Scholastik* 36 (1961), 550–565.

– *Hegel und Thomas. Eine Begegnung,* in *Gregorianum* 48 (1967), 449–480.

Löwestein, J., *Hegels Staatsidee. Ihr Doppelgesicht und ihr Einflussim 19. Jahrhundert* (Berlin, 1927).

Löwith, K., *From Hegel to Nietzsche: The Revolution in Nineteenth-Century Thought* trans D. E. Green (New York, 1964, London, 1965).

– *Meaning in History: The Theological Implications of the Philosophy of History (Chicago, 1949).*

– *Hegels Aufhebung der christlichen Religion,* in *Hegel-Studien* Suppl. 1 (Bonn, 1964) 193–236.

Lukács, G., *The Young Hegel: Studies in the Relation between Dialectics and Economics,* trans. R. Livingstone (London, 1975).

– *Hegels Ästhetik,* in *G. W. F. Hegel, Ästhetik* (Edition F. Bassenge, Berlin-Weimar 1955).

Lunati, G., *La Libertà. Saggi su Kant, Hegel e Croce* (Naples, 1959).

Lütgert, W., *Die Religion des deutschen Idealismus und ihr Ende,* vols. I–III (Gütersloh, 1923–25).

Marcuse, H., *Hegels Ontologie und die Grundlegung einer Theorie der Geschichtlichkeit* (Frankfurt, 1932).

– *Reason and Revolution: Hegel and the Rise of Social Theory* (New York, 1941, 2nd edition London, 1955).

Marietti, A., *La pensée de Hegel* (Paris, 1957).

Marsch, W.-D., *Gegenwart Christi in der Gesellschaft. Eine Studie zu Hegels Dialektik* (Munich, 1965).

– *Logik des Kreuzes. Über Sinn und Grenzen einer theologischen Berufung auf Hegel,* in *Evagelische Theologie* 28 (1968), 57–82.

Marx, K., *Critique of Hegel's Philosophy of Right,* trans. A. Jolin and J. O'Malley (Cambridge, 1970).

Massolo, A., *Prime recerche di Hegel* (Urbino, 1959).

Maurer, R. K., *Hegel und das Ende der Geschichte. Interpretationen zur "Phänomenologie des Geistes"* (Stuttgart, 1965).

Mayer-Moreau, *Hegels Sozialphilosophie* (Tübingen, 1910).

McTaggart, J., *A Commentary on Hegel's Logic* (Cambridge, 1910).

Mehlis, G., *Die Geschichtsphilosophie Hegels und Comtes,* in *Jahrbuch für Soziologie* vol. III (1927), 91–109.

Merker, N., *Le origini della logica hegeliana (Hegel a Jena)* (Mailand, 1961).

Metzke, E., *Nikolaus von Cues und Hegel, Ein Beitrag zum Problem der philosophischen Theologie,* in *Kant-Studien* vol. 48 (1956–57), 216–234.

Meulen, J. van der, *Hegel. Die gebrochene Mitte* (Hamburg, 1958).

Michelet, C. L., *Hegel der unwiderlegte Weltphilosoph. Eine Jubelschrift* (Leipzig, 1870).

Möller, J., *Der Geist und das Absolute. Zure Grundlegung einer Religionsphilosophie*

BIBLIOGRAPHY

in *Begegnung mit Hegels Denkwelt* (Paderborn, 1951).
- *Thomistische Analogie und Hegelsche Dialektik,* in *ThQ* 137 (1957), 129-159.

Moog, W., *Hegel und die Hegelsche Schule* (Munich, 1930).

Müller, E. (ed.), *Stiftsköpfe. Schwäbische Ahnen des deutschen Geistes aus dem Tübinger Stift* (Heilbronn, 1938). Chapters on Hegel and Schelling by T. Haering.

Müller, G. E., *Hegel über Offenbarung, Kirche und Philosophie* (Munich, 1939).
- *Hegel über Sittlichkeit und Geschichte* (Munich, 1940).
- *Hegel: The Man, His Vision and Work* (New York, 1968). This ET is an abridged version of the original, *Hegel. Denkgeschichte eines Lebendigen* (Bern-Munich, 1979).
- *Fünf Ursprünge von Hegels Religionsphilosophie,* in *Studia Philosophica* 22 (1960), 60-82.
- *Origins and Dimensions of Philosophy. Some Correlations* (New York, 1965).

Mure, G. R. G., *An Introduction to Hegel* (Oxford, 1948). First pub. 1940.
- *A Study of Hegel's Logic* (Oxford, 1950, 2nd edition, 1959)
- *Some Elements in Hegel's Logic* (Oxford, 1958).
- *The Philosophy of Hegel* (London, 1965).

Nadler, K., *Der dialektische Widerspruch in Hegels Philosophie und das Paradoxon des Christentums* (Leipzig, 1931).

Negri, A., *Stato e diritto nel giovane Hegel. Studia sulla genesi illuministica della filosofia giuridica e politica di Hegel* (Padua, 1958).

Negri, E. de, *La nascita della dialettica hegeliana* (Florence, 1930).
- *Interpretazione di Hegel* (Florence, 1943).
- *I principi di Hegel* (Florence, 1949).

Nicolin, F., *Hegels propädeutische Logik für die Unterklasse des Gymnasiums,* in *Hegel-Studien* vol. III (Bonn, 1965), 9-38.
- *Unbekannte Aphorismen Hegels aus der Jenaer Periode,* in *Hegel-Studien* vol. IV (Bonn, 1967), 9-19.
- *Zum Titelproblem der Phänomenologie des Geistes,* in *Hegel-Studien* vol. IV (Bonn, 1967), 113-123.

Niel, H., *De la médiation dans la philosophie de Hegel* (Paris, 1945).

Nink, C., *Kommentar zu den grundlegenden Abschnitten von Hegels Phänomenologie des Geistes* (Regensburg, 1931).

Noack, L., *Der Religionsbegriff Hegels* (Darmstadt, 1845).

Noël, G., *La logique de Hegel* (Paris, 1933).

Oelmüller, W., *Hegels Satz vom Ende der Kunst und das Problem der Philosophie der Kunst,* in *Philosophisches Jahrbuch* 73 (1965), 75-94.
- *Geschichte und System in Hegels "Religionsphilosophie",* in *Philosophisches Jahrbuch* 76 (1968), 67-87.
- *Die unbelfriedigte Aufklärung. Beiträge zu einer Theorie der Moderne von Lessing, Kant und Hegel* (Frankfurt, 1969).

Ogiermann, H., *Hegels Gottesbeweise* (Rome, 1948).
- *Materialistische Dialektik. Ein Diskussionsbeitrag* (Munich-Salzburg-Cologne, 1958).
- *Hegelianische Dialektik heute,* in *Scholastik* 35 (1960), 1-26.

Oiserman, T. I., *Die Philosophie Hegels* (in Russian, 1956; in German, Berlin 1959).

Oosterbaan, J. A., *Hegel's Phänomenologie des Geistes en de Theologische Kenleer* (Haarem, 1953).

Ortega y Gasset, J., *Kant-Hegel-Dilthey* (Madrid, 1958).

Osculati, R., *Fenomenologia grazia. Il pieno compimento del soggetto umano in Hegel e nella teologia cattolica* (Rome, 1968).

Ott, E., *Die Religionsphilosophie Hegels in ihrer Genesis dargestellt und in ihrer Bedeutung für die Gegenwart gewürdigt* (Berlin, 1904).

Patočka, J., *Die Lehre von der Vergangenheit der Kunst,* in *Beispiel (Festschrift* for E. Fink; The Hague, 1965) 46–61.

Peperzak, A. T. B., *Le jeune Hegel et la vision morale du monde* (La Haye, 1960).

Plenge, J., *Hegel und die Weltgeschichte* (Münster, 1931).

Pöggeler, O., *Zur Deutung der Phänomenologie des Geistes,* in *Hegel-Studien* vol. I (Bonn, 1961), 255–294.

– *Hegels Jenaer Systemkonzeption,* in *Philosophisches Jahrbuch* 71 (1963–64), 286–318.

– *Die Komposition der Phänomenologie des Geistes,* in *Hegel-Studien* Suppl. 3 (Bonn, 1966), 27–74.

– *Hegel, der Verfasser des ältesten Systemprogramms des deutschen Idealismus,* in *Hegel-Studien* Suppl. 4 (Bonn, 1969), 17–32.

Popper, K. R., *The Open Society and its Enemies* (New York, 1945): vol. 1: *The Spell of Plato;* vol. II: *The High Tide of Prophecy: Hegel, Marx and the Aftermath.*

Przywara, E., *Thomas und Hegel,* in *Ringen der Gegenwart. Gesammelte Aufsäte* II (Augsburg, 1929), 930–957.

Puglisi, F., *L'estetica di Hegel e i suoi presupposti teoretici* (Padua, 1953).

Radermacher, H., *Kierkegaards Hegelverständnis* (Thesis, Cologne, 1958).

Reble, A., *Hegel und die Pädagogik,* in *Hegel-Studien* vol. III (Bonn, 1965), 320–355.

Redlich, A., *Die Hegelsche Logik als Selbsterfassung der Persönlichkeit* (Bremen, 1964).

Reese, H., *Hegel über das Auftreten der christlichen Religion in der Weltgeschichte. Ein Beitrag zur Geschichte der Religionsphilosophie* (Tübingen, 1908).

Régnier, M., *Ambiguité de la théologie hégélienne,* in *Archives de Philosophie 29* (1966), 175–188.

– *Les apories de la théologie hégélienne,* in *Hegel-Studien* Suppl. 4 (Bonn, 1969), 169–179.

Renthe-Fink, L. v., *Geschichtlichkeit. Ihr terminologischer und begrifflicher Ursprung bei Hegel, Haym, Dilthey und York* (Göttingen, 1964).

Reuter, H., *S. Kierkegaards religionsphilosophische Gedanken im Verhältnis zu Hegels religionsphilosophischem System* (Leipzig, 1914).

Reyburn, H. A., *The Ethical Theory of Hegel. A Study of the Philosophy of Right* (Oxford, 1921).

Riedel, M., *Theorie und Basis im Denken Hegels. Interpretationen zu den Grundstellungen der neuzeitlichen Subjektivität* (Stuttgart, 1965).

– *Hegels Kritik des Naturrechts,* in *Hegel-Studien* vol. IV (Bonn, 1967) 177–204.

– *Einleitung zu Hegel, Studienausgabe* vol. II (Frankfurt, 1968) 9–28.

– *Wissen, Glauben und moderne Wissenschaft im Denken Hegels,* in *ZThK* 66 (1969), 171–191.

Ritter, J., *Hegel und die Französische Revolution* (Cologne-Opladen, 1957).

Rohrmoser, G., *Subjektivität und Verdinglichung. Theologie und Gesellschaft im Denken des jungen Hegel* (Gütersloh, 1961).

Rondet, H., *Hégélianisme et Christianisme. Introduction théologique à l'étude du système hégélien* (Paris, 1965).

Roques, P., *Hegel. Sa vie et ses oeuvres* (Paris, 1912).

Rosenkranz, K., *Kritische Erläuterungen des Hegelschen Systems* (Königsberg, 1840; reprinted Hildesheim, 1963).
- *G. F. W. Hegels Leben. Supplement zu Hegels Werken* (Berlin, 1844; reprinted Darmstadt, 1963). This book is cited as 'Rosenkranz'.
- *Apologie Hegels gegen R. Haym* (Berlin, 1858; reprinted Darmstadt, 1963).
- *Erläuterungen zu Hegels Encyclopädie der philosophischen Wissenschaften* (Berlin, 1870).
- *Hegel als deutscher Nationalphilosoph* (Leipzig, 1870; reprinted Darmstadt, 1965); partial translation: *Hegel as the National Philosopher of Germany*, trans. G. S. Hall, (St. Louis, 1874).
Rosenzweig, F., *Hegel und der Staat*, vols. I-II (Munich-Berlin 1920).
Rossi, M., *Marx e la dialettica hegeliana*. Vol. I: *Hegel e lo stato* (Rome, 1960).
Rüfner, V., *Die zentrale Bedeutung der Liebe für das Werden des Hegelschen Systems*, in *Erkenntnis und Verantwortung* (*Festschrift* for T. Litt, Düsseldorf, 1960), 346–355.
Schaller, J., *Die Philosophie unserer Zeit. Zur Apologie und Erläuterung des Hegelschen Systems* (Leipzig, 1837).
Schilling-Wollny, K., *Hegels Wissenschaft von der Wirklichkeit und ihre Quellen*. Vol I: *Begriffliche Vorgeschichte der Hegelschen Methode* (Munich, 1929).
Schmidt, E., *Hegels Lehre von Gott. Eine kritische Darstellung* (Gütersloh, 1952).
Schmidt, G., *Hegel in Nürnberg. Untersuchungen zum Problem der philosophischen Propädeutik* (Tübingen, 1960).
Schmidt, H., *Verheissung und Schrecken der Freiheit. Von der Krise des antikabendländischen Weltverständnisses dargestellt im Blick auf Hegels Erfahrung der Geschichte* (Stuttgart-Berlin, 1964).
Schmidt-Japing, J. W., *Die Bedeutung der Person Jesu im Denken des jungen Hegel* (Göttingen, 1924).
Schmitt, R., *Christliche Religion und Hegelsche Philosophie* (Berlin, 1839).
Schmitz, G., *Die List der Vernunft* (Biberach/ Riss, 1951).
Schmitz, H., *Hegel als Denker der Individualität* (Meisenheim/ Glan, 1957).
Schneider, R., *Schellings und Hegels schwäbische Geistesahnen* (Würzburg, 1938).
Schoeps, H.-J., *Studien zur unbekannten Religionsgeschichte* (Göttingen, 1963), 255-284: *Die auss erchristlichen Religionen bei Hegel*.
Schrader-Klebert, K., *Das Problem des Anfangs in Hegels Philosophie* (Munich, Wien 1969).
Schüler, G., *Zur Chronologie von Hegels Jugendschriften*, in *Hegel-Studien* vol. II (Bonn, 1963) 111–159.
Schulin, E., *Die weltgeschichtliche Erfassung des Orients bei Hegel und Ranke* (Göttingen, 1958).
Schultz, W., *Die Grundprinzipien der Religionsphilosophie Hegels und der Theologie Schleiermachers. Ein Vergleich* (Berlin, 1937).
- *Die Bedeutung der Idee der Liebe für Hegels Philosophie*, in *Zeitschrift für Deutsche Kulturphilosophie* 9 (1943), 217–238.
- *Die Transformierung der Theologia crucis bei Hegel und Schleiermacher*, in *Neue Zeitschrift für systematische Theologie und Religionsphilosophie* 6 (1964), 290–317.
Schulz, R. E., *Interpretationen zu Hegels Logik* (Thesis, Heidelberg 1954).
Schulz, W., *Das Problem der absoluten Reflexion* (Frankfurt, 1963).

Schütte, H.-W., *Tod Gottes und fülle der Zeit. Hegels Deutung des Christentums,* in *ZThK* 66 (1969), 62–76.

Schwarz, J., *Die anthropologische Metaphysik des jungen Hegel* (Königsberg, 1931).
– *Die Vorbereitung der Phänomenologie des Geistes in Hegels Jenenser Systementwürfen,* in *Zeitschrift für Deutsche Kulturphilosophie* 2 (1936), 127–159.
– *Hegels philosophische Entwicklung* (Frankfurt, 1938).

Schweitzer, C. G., *Die Glaubensgrundlagen des Hegelschen Denkens,* in *Hegel-Studien* Suppl. 1 (Bonn, 1964) 237f.

Schweppenhäuser, H., *Kierkegaards Angriff auf die Spekulation. Eine Verteidigung* (Frankfurt, 1967).

Seeberger, W., *Hegel oder die Entwicklung des Geistes zur Freiheit* (Stuttgart, 1961).

Shepherd, W. C., *Hegel as a Theologian,* in *The Harvard Theological Review* 61 (1968), 583–602.

Simon, J., *Das Problem der Sprache bei Hegel* (Stuttgart, 1966).

Splett, J., *Die Trinitätslehre G. W. F. Hegels* (Freiburg-Munich, 1965).

Stace, W. T., *The Philosophy of Hegel. A Systematic Exposition* (London, 1924; new edition New York, 1955).

Staiger, E., *Der Geist der Liebe und das Schicksal. Schelling, Hegel und Hölderlin* (Frauenfeld, 1935).

Staudenmaier, F. A., *Darstellung und Kritik des Hegelschen Systems aus dem Standpunkte der christlichen Philosophie* (Mainz, 1844).

Steinbüchel, T., *Das Grundproblem der Hegelschen Philosophie. Darstellung und Würdigung.* Vol 1: *Die Entdeckung des Geistes* (Bonn, 1933).
– *Mystik und Idealismus bei Meister Eckhart und Hegel,* in *Universitas* vol. II (1947) 1409–1423.

Steininger, W., *Systematische Betrachtungen über den Begriff der Persönlichkeit Gottes in der Philosophie Hegels und seiner Schule,* in *Philosophisches Jahrbuch* 65 (1956–57) 182–231.

Stenzel, J., *Hegels Auffassung der griechischen Philosophie,* in *Verhandlungen des zweiten Hegelkongresses 1931* (Tübingen-Haarlem, 1932) 168–182.

Studies in Hegel, Tulane Studies in Philosophy 9 (New Orleans-The Hague, 1960).

Taminiaux, J., *La pensée esthétique du jeune Hegel,* in *Revue Philosophique de Louvain* 56 (1958), 222–250.

Theunissen, M., *Die Dialektik der Offenbarung. Zur Auseinandersetzung Schellings und Kierkegaards mit der Religionsphilosophie Hegels,* in *Philosophisches Jahrbuch* 72 (1964/65), 134–160.

Theyssèdre, B., *L'esthétique de Hegel* (Paris, 1958).

Tillich, P., *Perspectives on 19th and 20th Century Protestant Theology* (ed. C. E. Braaten, London, 1967), 114–135; *The Universal Synthesis: G. W. F. Hegel.*

Topitsch, E., *Die Sozialphilosophie Hegels als Heilslehre und Herrschaftsideologie* (Neuwied-Berlin, 1967).

Touilleux, P., *Introduction aux systèmes de Marx et Hegel* (Tournai, 1960).

Trott zu Solz, A. v., *Hegels Staatsphilosophie und das internationale Recht* (Göttingen, 1932, 2nd. edition 1967).

Ulrici, H., *Über Princip und Methode der Hegelschen Philosophie. Ein Beitrag zur Kritik derselben* (Halle, 1841).

Vancourt, R., *La pensée religieuse de Hegel* (Paris, 1965).

Vecchi, G., *L'estetica di Hegel. Saggi di interpretazione filosofica* (Mailand, 1956).

Vera, A., *Introduction à la philosophie de Hegel* (Paris, 2nd edition, 1864).

Verhandlungen des 1. Hegelkongresses, 22–25 April 1930, in The Hague (ed. B. Wigersma, Tübingen–Haarlem, 1931).

Verhandlungen des 2. Hegelkongresses, 18–21 October 1931, in Berlin (ed. B. Wigersma, Tübingen–Haarlem, 1932).

Verhandlungen des 3. Hegelkongresses 19–23 April 1933, in Rome (ed. B. Wigersma, Tübingen-Haarlem, 1934).

Volkmann-Schluck, K.-H., *Die Entäusserung der Idee zur Natur*, in *Hegel-Studien* Suppl. 1 (Bonn, 1962), 37–44.

Volpe, G. della, *Hegel romantico e mistico* (Florence, 1929).

Wacker, H., *Das Verhältnis des jungen Hegel zu Kant* (Berlin, 1932).

Wahl, J., *Le malheur de la conscience dans la philosophie de Hegel* (Paris, 1929, 2nd edition, 1951).

– *La logique de Hegel comme phénoménologie* (Les cours de Sorbonne; Paris, 1959).

Walentik, L., *Der Begriff des Endzweckes der Weltgeschichte bei Hegel* (Thesis, Wien, 1960).

Walgrave, J. H., *Rond de godsdienstfilosofie van Hegel*, in *Tijdschrift voor Philosophie* 18 (1956), 457–490.

Weil, E., *Hegel et l'État* (Paris, 1950).

– *La Morale de Hegel*, in *Deucalion* 5 (1955), 101–116.

– *Hegel*, in *Les philosophes célèbres* (ed. M. Merleau-Ponty; Paris, 1956, 258–265).

Wein, H., *Realdialektik. Von Hegelscher Dialektik zu dialektischer Anthropologie* (Munich, 1957).

Welte, B., *Hegels Begriff der Religion – sein Sinn und seine Grenze*, in *Scholastik* 27 (1952), 210–225.

Werner, J., *Hegels Offenbarungsbegriff. Ein religionsphilosophischer Versuch* (Thesis, Leipzig, 1887).

Wiehl, R., *Platos Ontologie in Hegels Logik des Seins*, in *Hegel-Studien* vol. III (Bonn, 1965) 175–180.

Wieland, W., *Hegel*, in *RGG* III (Tübingen, 1959) 115–119.

Wigersma, B., *Wordende waarheid* (The Hague, 1959).

Wolf, K., *Die Religionsphilosophie des jungen Hegel* (Thesis, Munich, 1960).

Wyneken, G. A., *Hegels Kritik Kants. Zur Einleitung in die Hegelsche Philosophie* (Greifswald, 1898).

Züfle, M., *Prosa der Welt. Die Sprache Hegels* (Einsiedeln, 1968).

III. Further Philosphical Literature

Bauer, G., *"Geschichtlichkeit". Wege und Irrwege eines Begriffs* (Berlin, 1963).

Betzendörfer, W., *Hölderlins Studienjahre im Tübinger Stift* (Heilbronn, 1922).

Binder, W., *Hölderlins Dichtung im Zeitalter des Idealismus. Antrittsrede an der Universität Zürich*, in *Neue Zürcher Zeitung* 22 May, 1965.

Biser, E., *'Gott ist tot' – Nietzsches Destruktion des christlichen Bewusstseins* (Munich, 1962).

– *Der totgesagte Gott*, in *Lebendiges Zeugnis* (1968), 53–66.

Bloch, E., *Das Prinzip Hoffnung*, vols. I-III (Frankfurt, 1959; new edition, 1967).

– Selections in *On Karl Marx*, trans. J. Maxwell, (New York, 1971).

Blumenberg, H., *Kant und die Frage nach dem "Gnädigen Gott"*, in *Studium Generale* 7 (1954), 554–570.

Bohatec, J., *Die Religionsphilosophie Kants in der 'Religion innerhalb der Grenzen der reinen Vernunft'* (Hamburg, 1938).

Böhm, B., *Sokrates im 18. Jahrhundert. Studien zum Werdegang des modernen Persönlichkeitsbewusstseins* (Leipzig, 1929).

Buber, M., *I and Thou,* trans. W. Kaufmann, (Edinburgh, 1970.)

Carové, F. W., *Rückblick auf die Ursachen der Französischen Revolution* (Hanau, 1834).

Coreth, E., *Vom Ich zum absoluten Sein. Zure Entwicklung der Gotteslehre Fichtes,* in *Zeitschrift für katholische Theologie* 79 (1957), 257–303.

– *Zu Fichtes Denkentwicklung. Ein problemgeschichtlicher Durchblick,* in *Bijdragen, Tijdschrift voor Filosofie en Theologie* 20 (1959), 229–241.

Delekat, F., *Immanuel Kant. Historisch-kritische Interpretation der Hauptschriften* (Heidelberg, 1963).

Descartes, R., *The Philosophical Works of Descartes,* trans. E. S. Haldant and G. R. T. Ross, 2 vols. (Cambridge, 1911–12).

Erdmann, J. E., *A History of Philosophy,* trans. W. S Hough (London, 1890–91).

Fichte, J. G., *Werke* (ed. F. Medicus, Leipzig, 1911; reprinted Darmstadt, 1962).

– *The Vocation of Man,* trans. W. Smith, (London, 1848).

– *The Popular Works of J. G. Fichte,* (London, 1873).

Fuhrmans, H., *Schellings Philosophie der Weltalter. Schellings Philosophie in den Jahren 1806–1821. Zum Problem des Schellingschen Theismus* (Düsseldorf, 1954).

Funkenstein, A., *Heilsplan und natürliche Entwicklung. Formen der Gegenwartsbestimmung im Geschichtsdenken des hohen Mittelalters* (Munich, 1965).

Gadamer, H.-G., *Truth and Method,* (New York, 1975).

Gandillac, M. de, *Pascal et le silence du monde. Cahiers de Royaumont. Philosophie* Nr. 1 (Paris, 1956).

– *La philosophie de Nicolas de Cues* (Paris, 1941).

Heidegger, M., *Being and Time,* trans. J. MacQuarrie and E. Robinson (London, 1962).

– *'On the Essence of Truth',* trans. R. F. C. Hall and A. Crick, in *Existence and Being,* ed. W. Brock (1951), 317–351.

– *'Letter on Humanism'.* in *Philosophy in the Twentieth Century,* eds. W. Barrett and H. Aiken, (New York, 1962), 270–302.

– *'The Word of Nietzsche "God is Dead"'* in *The Question Concerning Technology,* trans. W. Lovitt (New York, 1977), 53–114.

– *Identity and Difference,* trans. J. Stambaugh (New York, 1974).

– *Nietzsche,* 4 vols. (San Fransico and London, 1979–1987).

– *On Time and Being,* trans. J. Stambaugh (New York, 1972).

Heimsoeth, H., *Die sechs grossen Themen der abendländischen Metaphysik* (Stuttgart, 3rd edition 1958).

Hemmerle, K., *Gott und das Kenden nach Schellings Spätphilosophie* (Freiburg-Basle-Wien, 1968).

Hölderlin, F., *Sämtliche Werke. Grosse Stuttgarter Ausgabe,* vols. I-VIII (ed. F. Beissner, Stuttgart, 1943–68).

Hünermann, P., *Der Durchbruch des geschichtlichen Denkens im 19. Jahrhundert. Johann Gustav Droysen, Wilhelm Dilthey, Graf Paul Yorck von Wartenburg. Ihr Weg und ihre Weisung für die Theologie* (Freiburg-Basle-Wien, 1967).

Huonder, Q., *Die Gottesbeweise. Geschichte und Schicksal* (Stuttgart, 1968).

BIBLIOGRAPHY

Jacobi, F. H., *Über die Lehre des Spinoza in Briefen an den Herrn Moses Mendelssohn* (Breslau, 1785).
- *Wider Mendelssohns Beschuldigungen betreffend die Briefe über die Lehre des Spinoza* (Leipzig, 1786).
Kierkegaard, S., *Gesammelte Werke* (ed. Diederichs, Düsseldorf, 1950). The most extensive translations are those of W. Lowrie (London, 1939-44). A complete Princeton University Press edition is under production. Precise bibliographic references are given to works cited in the text *ad. loc.*
Kant, I., *Critique of Pure Reason*, trans. N. Kemp Smith (London, 1929; reprinted 1950).
- *Critique of Practical Reason*, trans. L. W. Beck (Chicago, 1949).
- *Religion Within the Limits of Reason Alone*, trans. T. M. Greene and H. H. Hudson (New York, 1960).
- *The Conflict of the Faculties*, trans. M. J. Gregor (New York, 1979).
Kasper, W., *Das Absolute in der Geschichte. Philosophie und Theologie der Geschichte in der Spätphilosophie Schellings* (Mainz, 1965).
Konrad, M., *Hölderlins Philosophie im Grundriss* (Bonn, 1967).
Korff, H. A., *Geist der Goethezeit. Versuch einer ideellen Entwicklung der klassischromantischen Literaturgeschichte*, vol. I-V (1923, Leipzig, 8th edition 1966).
Lefèbvre, H., *Dialectical Materialism*, trans. J. Sturrock (London, 1968).
Leibnitz, G. W., *Opera Omnia*, 6 vols. (ed. L. Dutens Genf, 1768).
- *Theodicy*, trans. E. M. Huggard (London, 1952).
- *The Philosophical Writings of Leibnitz* (selections), trans. M. Morris and G. H. R. Parkinson (London, 1973).
Lessing, G. E., *Sämtliche Werke*, 6 vols., ed. T. Knaur (Berlin-Leipzig).
- *Lessing's Theological Writings. Selections*, trans. H. Chadwick (London, 1956).
Löwith, K., *Heidegger. Denker in dürftiger Zeit* (Frankfurt, 1953).
Maier, H., *Politische Theologie? Einwände eines Laien*, n *Stimmen der Zeit* 94 (1969), 73-91.
Marx, K., *Early Writings* trans. T. B. Bottomore (London, 1963).
Mendelssohn, M., *Jerusalem: A Treatise on Religious Power and Judaism*, trans. I. Leeser (Philadelphia, 1852).
- *Morgenstunden oder Vorlesungen über das Dasein Gottes*. Part I (Berlin, 1785).
- *An die Freunde Lessings. Ein Anhang zu Herrn Jacobis Briefwechsel über die Lehre des Spinoza* (Berlin, 1786).
Michel, W., *Das Leben Friedrich Hölderlins* (1940; new edition Darmstadt, 1963).
Möller, J., *Die Geschichtlichkeit und Einheit der Wahrheit*, in *Die Wissenschaft und die Wahrheit* (Stuttgart, 1966), 185-200.
- *Geschichtlichkeit und Ungeschichtlichkeit der Wahrheit*, in *Theologie im Wandel* (*Festschrift* for the 150th anniversary of the Tübingen Catholic Theological Faculty; Munich-Freiburg, 1967), 15-40.
Nietzsche, F., *Complete Works*, 18 vols., ed. O. Levy (London, 1909-13).
Pannenberg, W., *Theologische Motive im Denken Immanuel Kants*, in *Theologische Literaturzeitung* 89 (1964), 897-906.
Pascal, B., *Pensées*, ed. Lafuma, trans. J. Warrington (London, 1973).
Redmann, H.-G., *Gott und Welt. Die Schöpfungstheologie der vorkritischen Periode Kants* (Göttingen, 1962).
Rousseau, J.-J., *Emile*, trans. B. Foxley (London, 1911, reprinted 1969).
- *The Social Contract*, trans. H. J. Tozer (London, 1895).

Rüttimann, J., *Illuminative oder abstraktive Seins-Intuition? Untersuchung zu Gustav Siewerth: 'Der Thomismus als Identitätssystem'. Als Beitrag zum Problem: Neu-Thomismus als Identitätssystem oder Thomismus als Analogiesystem?* (Thesis, Freiburg; Lucerne, 1945).
Schelling, F. W. J., *Werke.* Main vols. I-VIII; Supplementary vols. I-VI, ed. M. Schröter (Munich, 1927, 2nd edition 1958).
– *The System of Transcendental Idealism,* trans. P. Heath (Virginia, 1978).
Schlatter, A., *Die philosophische Arbeit seit Cartesius nach ihrem ethischen und religiösen Ertrag* (Gütersloh, 3rd edition 1923).
Schmitt, C., *Politische Theologie. Vier Kapitel zur Lehre von der Souveränität* (Munich-Leipzig, 1922, 2nd edition 1934).
Schulz, W., *Über den philosophiegeschichtlichen Ort Martin Heideggers,* in *Philosophische Rundschau* 1 (1953-54), 65-93, 211-232.
– *Die vollendung des deutschen Idealismus in der Spätphilosophie Schellings* (Stuttgart, 1955).
– *Der Gott der neuzeitlichen Metaphysik* (Pfullingen, 1957).
Schulze, W. A., *Kant und das Gebet,* in *Theologische Zeitschrift* 13 (1957), 61-63.
Schwarz, R., *Lessings "Spinozismus",* in *ZThK* 65 (1968), 271-290.
Siewerth, G., *Die Metaphysik der Erkenntnis nach Thomas von Aquin* (Munich-Berlin, 1933).
– *Der Thomismus als Identitätssystem* (Frankfurt, 1939).
– *Die Abstraktion und das Sein nach der Lehre des Thomas von Aquin* (Salzburg, 1958).
Spinoza, B., *The Chief Works of B. de Spinoza,* 2 vols., trans. R. H. Elves (New York, 1951).
Vogel, H., *Die Umdeutung der Christologie in der Religionsphilosophie Immanuel Kants,* in *Evangelische Theologie* 14 (1954), 399-413.
Wahl, J., *Traité de métaphysique* (Paris, 1953).
Windelband, W., *Über die Geschichtschreibung der Philosophie im 19. Jahrhundert,* in *Die Philosophie im Beginn des 20. Jahrhunderts* (*Festschrift* for K. Fischer; Heidelberg 1904-5), vol. II, 175-200.
Wittgenstein, L., *Tractatus logico-philosophicus* trans. D. F. Pears and B. F. McGuinnes (London, 1961, 2nd edition 1971).
Wolff, C., *Vernünfftige Gedancken von Gott, der Welt und der Seele des Menschen, auch allen Dingen überhaupt, den Liebhabern de Wahrheit mitgetheilet* (Halle, 1720).
– *Eigene Lebensbeschreibung,* edited with an essay on Wolff by H. Wuttke (Leipzig, 1841).

IV. Literature on Christology

Abelard, P., *Opera,* 2 vols., ed. Cousin (Paris, 1849).
– *Christian Theology* (selections), trans. J. Romsay McCallum (Oxford, 1935).
Adam, A., *Lehrbuch der Dogmengeschichte,* 2 vols. (Gütersloh, 1965-68).
Albright, W. F., '*Recent Discoveries in Palestine and the Gospel of St John*', in *The Background of the New Testament and its Eschatology* (*Festschrift* for C. H. Dodd; Cambridge, 1956), 153-171.
– '*Bultmann's History and Eschatology*', in *Journal of Biblical Literature* 77 (1958), 244-248.

BIBLIOGRAPHY

Althaus, P., *The So-called Kerygma and the Historical Jesus,* trans. D. Cairns (Edinburgh and London, 1959).
- *'Kenosis',* in *RGG* III (Tübingen, 1959), 1243–46.
- *Die christliche Wahrheit. Lehrbuch der Dogmatik* (Gütersloh, 4th edition 1958).
Altizer, T. J. J., *The Gospel of Christian Atheism* (Philadelphia, 1966).
- (ed.), *Toward a New Christianity: Readings in the Death of God Theology* (New York, 1967).
- and Hamilton, W., *Radical Theology and the Death of God* (Indianapolis-New York, 1966).
Arnold, F. X., *Das gott-menschliche Prinzip der Seelsorge und die Gestaltung der christlichen Frömmigkeit,* in *Das Konzil von Chalkedon III* (Würzburg, 1954), 287–340.
Backes, I., *Die christliche Problematik der Hochscholastik und ihre Beziehungen zu Chalkedon,* in *Das Konzil von Chalkedon II* (Würzburg, 1953), 923–939.
Baillie, D. M., *God was in Christ: An Essay on Incarnation and Atonement* (London, 4th edition 1951).
Baird, W., *'What is the Kerygma? A Study of 1 Cor. 15, 3–8 and Gal. 1, 11–17',* in *Journal of Biblical Literature* 76 (1957), 181–191.
Balthasar, H. U. v., *Science, Religion and Christianity,* trans. H. Graef (London, 1958).
- *Essays in Theology,* trans. A. V. Littledale (New York, 1964).
- *The Glory of the Lord: A Theological Aesthetics,* trans. E. Leiva-Merikakis (Edinburgh, 1982).
- *Man in History – A Theological Study,* trans. W. Glen-Doepel (London and Sydney, 1968).
- *Rechenschaft 1965. Mit einer Bibliographie der Veröffentlichungen H. U. v. Balthasars zusammengestellt von Berthe Widmer* (Einsiedeln, 1965).
- *Mysterium Paschale,* in *Mysterium Salutis,* vol. III: 2 ed. J. Feiner and M. Löhrer (Einsiedeln, 1969), 133–326.
Barnikol, E., *Das Leben Jesu als Heilsgeschichte* (Halle-Saale, 1958).
Barrett, C. K., *The Gospel According to St John* (London, 1955).
Barth, K., *The Epistle to the Romans,* trans. E. C. Hoskyns (London, 1933).
- *Church Dogmatics* (Edinburgh, 1936–69).
- *Protestant Theology in the Nineteenth Century,* trans. J. Bowden and B. Cozens (London, 1972).
- *Rudolf Bultmann – 'An Attempt to Understand Him',* in *Kerygma and Myth,* vol. 2, trans. R. H. Fuller (London, 1962). 83–132.
- *Theologische Fragen und Antworten. Gesammelte Vorträge* III (Zollikon, 1957). This the Barth-Harnack correspondence.
Baur, F. C., *Die christliche Lehre von der Versöhnung in ihrer geschichtlichen Entwicklung* (Tübingen, 1838).
Benckert, H., *Sive Deus sive Jesus,* in *Evangelische Theologie* 24 (1964), 654–669.
Benz, E., *Ecclesia spiritualis. Kirchenidee und Geschichtstheologie der franziskanischen Reformation* (Darmstadt, 1964; reprint of the 1934 edition).
Berkouwer, G. C., *The Person of Christ,* trans. J. Wriend (Grand Rapids, 1954).
Biehl, P., *Zur Frage nach dem historischen Jesus,* in *Theologische Rundschau* N. F. 24 (1957–58), 54–76.
Bilfinger, G. B., *De origine et permissione mali* (Frankfurt Leipzig, 1724).
- *Dilucidationes philosophicae* (Tübingen, 1725).

– *Varia,* 3 vols. (Stuttgart, 1743).

Bishop, J., *Die Gott-ist-tot-Theologie* (Düsseldorf, 1968).

Blank, J., *Zum Problem der neutestamentlichen Christologie,* in *Una Sancta* 20 (1965), 108–125.

– *Paulus und Jesus. Eine theologische Grundlegung* (Munich, 1968).

Boismard, M.-E., *St John's Prologue,* trans. The Dominicans of Carisbrooke (1957).

Boman, T., *Hebrew Thought Compared with Greek,* trans. J. L. Moreau (London, 1960).

Bonhoeffer, D., *Letters and Papers from Prison* (London, 1953; rev. edition 1967).

Bonsirven, J., *Theology of the New Testament,* trans. S. F. L. Tye (London, 1963).

– *Le témoin du Verbe* (Toulouse, 1956).

Bornkamm, G., *Jesus of Nazareth,* trans. I. and F. McLuskey (London, 1960).

Boros, L., *We are Future,* trans. W. J. O'Hara (New York, 1970).

Bortnowska, H., *Christus' nalatenschap in de wereld,* in *Tijdschrift voor theologie* 6 (1966), 225–237.

Braun, H., *Der Sinn der neutestametlichen Christologie,* in *ZThK* 54 (1957), 341–377.

– *Jesus of Nazareth,* trans. E. R. Kalin (Philadelphia, 1979).

Breton, S., *La pssion du Christ et les philosophies* (Teramo, 1954).

Brox, N., *Antworten der Kirchenväter,* in *Wer ist das eigentlich – Gott?* ed. H.-J. Schultz (Munich, 1969), 134–144.

Brunner, E., *The Mediator: A Study of the Central Doctrine of the Christian Faith,* trans. O. Wyan (London, 1939).

– *The Christian Doctrine of Creation and Redemption. Dogmatics,* vol. 2. trans. O. Wyan (London, 1957).

Brunner, P., *Die Herrlichkeit des gekreuzigten Messias. Eine vordogmatische Erwägung zur dogmatischen Christologie,* in his volume of essays *'Pro Ecclesia'* II (Berlin-Hamburg, 1966), 60–75.

Bulgakov, S., *Du Verbe Incarné. Agnus Dei* (Paris, 1943).

Bultmann, R., *The History of the Synoptic Tradition,* trans. J. Marsh (Oxford, 1963).

– *Jesus and the Word,* trans. L. P. Smith and E. Huntress (London, 1935).

– *The Gospel of John: A Commentary,* trans. G. R. Beasley-Murray (Oxford, 1971).

– *New Testament and Mythology,* trans. R. H. Fuller, in *Kerygma and Myth,* 2 vols., ed. Bartsch (London, 1953), vol. 1, 1–44.

– *Theology of the New Testament,* 2 vols., trans. K. Grobel (London, 1952–55).

– *Faith and Understanding,* trans. L. P. Smith (London, 1969).

– *History and Eschatology,* The Gifford Lectures for 1955 (Edinburgh, 1957).

– *The Historical Jesus and the Kerygmatic Christ,* ed. C. E. Braaton and R. A. Harrisville (Nashville, 1964).

Buren, P. M. van, *The Secular Meaning of the Gospel* (London, 1963).

Buri, F., *Entmythologisierung oder Entkerygmatisierung der Theologie,* in *Kerygma und Mythos* II (Hamburg, 1952), 85–101.

Camelot, T., *De Nestorius à Eutychès. L'opposition de deux christologies,* in *Das Konzil von Chalkedon I* (Würzburg, 1951) 213–242.

Canz, I. G., *Philosophiae Leibnitianae et Wolfianae usus in theologia, per praecipua capita,* 3 vols. (Frankfurt, Leipzig, 1733–35).

Cerfaux, L., *Christ in the Theology of St Paul* trans. G. Webb and A. Walker (New York, Edinburgh and London, 1959).

– *Jésus aux origines de la Tradition. Matériaux pour l'histoire évangélique* (Louvain, 1968).

Christian, C. W. and Wittig, G. R.(ed.) *Radical Theology: Phase Two, Essays on the Current Debate* (Philadelphia-New York, 1967).

Conzelmann, H., *Gegenwart und Zukunft in der synoptischen Tradition,* in *ZThK* 54 (1957), 177-296.

- *Jesus,* trans. J. R. Lord (Philadelphia, 1973).
- *Outline of the Theology of the New Testament,* trans. J. Bowden (London, 1969).

Cox, H., *God's Revolution and Man's Responsibility* (London, 1969).

- *On Not Leaving it to the Snake* (London, 1968).

Cullmann, O., *Christ and Time,* trans. F. V. Filson (London, 1951).

- *The Earliest Christian Confessions,* trans. J. K. S. Reid (London, 1949).
- *Zur Frage der Erforschung der neutestametlichen Christologie,* in *Kerygma und Dogma* 1 (1955), 133-141.
- *The Christology of the New Testament,* trans. S. C. Guthrie and C. A. M. Hall (London, 1959).
- *'Out of Season Remarks on the "Historical Jesus" of the Bullmann School',* trans. J. L. Martyn in *Union Seminary Quarterly Review,* vol. 16, (1961).
- *Salvation in History,* trans. S. G. Sowers (London, 1967).
- *Vorträge und Aufsätze 1925-1962* ed. K. Fröhlich (Tübingen-Zürich, 1966).

Daecke, S., *Teilhard de Chardin und die evangelische Theologie. Sie Weltlichkeit Gottes und die Weltlichkeit der Welt* (Göttingen, 1967).

- *Welcher Gott ist tot? Zum Wiederaufleben des Gesprächs mit Gott,* in *Evangelische Kommentare* 2 (1969), 127-132.
- *Was kommt nach dem "Tode Gottes"? Zum Wiederaufleben des Gesprächs mit Gott* (II), in *Evangelische Kommentare* 2 (1969), 187-192.

Dahl, N. A., *The Problem of the Historical Jesus,* in Kerygma and History, ed. C. L. Braaten and R. A. Harrisville (New York, 1962), 138-171.

Dewart, L., *The Future of Belief: Theism in a World Come of Age* (1966).

Dias, P. V., *Vielfalt der Kirche in der Vielfalt der Jünger, Zeugen und Diener* (Freiburg-Basle-Wien, 1968).

Dibelius, M., *From Tradition to Gospel,* trans. B. L. Woolf (London, 1934).

- *Jesus,* trans. C. B. Hedrick and F. C. Grant (first publ. in USA, 1949; London, 1963).

Diem, H., *'The Earthly Jesus and the Christ of Faith',* in *Kerygma and History* ed. Braaten and Harrisville (New York, 1962), 197-211.

Dodd, C., *The Parables of the Kingdom* (London, 1935).

- *The Interpretation of the Fourth Gospel* (Cambridge, 1953).

Dorner, J. A., *History of the Development of the Doctrine of the Person of Christ,* 2 vols., trans. W. L. Alexander and D. W. Simon (Edinburgh, 1859).

Drews, A., *The Christ Myth,* trans. C. Delisle Burns (London, 1910).

Dupont, J., *Essais sur la Christologie de Saint Jean. Le Christ, Parole, Lumière et Vie, la gloire du Christ* (Brussells, 1951).

Duquoc, C., *Christologie. Essai dogmatique. L'Homme Jésus* (Paris, 1968).

Ebeling, G., *'The Nonreligious Interpretation of Biblical Concepts',* in *Word and Faith* (London, 1963), 61-98

- 'Jesus and Faith', in *Word and Faith,* 201-46.
- *Theology and Proclamation,* trans. J. Riches (London, 1966).
- *Was heisst: Ich glaube an Jesus Christus,* in the book of the same title, (2. *Reichenau-Gespräch,* edited by the Evangelischen Landessynode in Württemberg; Stuttgart, 1968), 38-77.
- *Word and Faith,* trans. J. W. Leitch (London, 1963).

THE INCARNATION OF GOD

Eichrodt, W., *Theology of the Old Testament*, 2 vols., trans. J. A. Baker (London, 1961).

Elert, W., *Die Theopaschistische Formel*, in *Theologische Literaturzeitung* 75 (1950), 195–206.

– *Der Ausgang der altkirchlichen Christologie. Eine Untersuchung über Theodore von Pharan und seine Zeit als Einführung in die alte Dogmengeschichte*, posthumously edited by W. Maurer and E. Bergsträsser (Berlin, 1957).

– *Der christliche Glaube. Grundlinien der lutherischen Dogmatik* (Hamburg, 5th edition 1960).

Fries, H., *Bultmann-Barth and Catholic Theology*, trans. L. Swidler (Pittsburgh, 1967).

– *Theologische Überlegungen zum Phänomen des Atheismus*, in *Theologie im Wandel* (*Festschrift* for the 150th year of the Tübingen Catholic Theological Faculty; Munich-Freiburg, 1967), 254–279.

Fries, H.and Stählin, R., *Gott ist tot? Eine Herausforderung – Zwei Theologen antworten* (Munich, 1968).

Fuchs, E., *Studies of the Historical Jesus*, trans. A. Scobie (London, 1964).

– *Glaube und Erfahrung. Zum christologischen Problem im NT. Gesammelte Aufsätze* III (Tübingen, 1965).

Fuller, R. H., *The Mission and Achievement of Jesus. An Examination of the Presuppositions of New Testament Theology* (London, 1954).

Galtier, P., *Saint Cyrille d'Alexandrie et Saint Léon le Grand à Chalcédoine*, in *Das Konzil von Chalkedon* I (Würzburg, 1951), 345–387.

Gardavský, V., *God is Not Yet Dead*, trans. V. Menkes (Harmondsworth, 1973).

Geiselmann, J. R., *Der Glaube an Jesus Christus – Mythos oder Geschichte? Zur Auseinandersetzung Joh. Ev. Kuhns mit D. F. Strauss*, in *ThQ* 129 (1949), 257–277, 418–439.

– *Jesus der Christus. Die Urform des apostolischen Kerymas als Norm unserer Verkündigung und Theologie von Jesus Christus* (Stuttgart, 1951).

– *Die lebendige Überlieferung als Norm des christlichen Glaubens. Die apostolische Tradition in der Form der kirchlichen Verkündigung – das Formalprinzip des Katholizismus dargestellt im Geiste der Traditionslehre von Joh. Ev. von Kuhn* (Freiburg, 1959).

– *Jesus der Christus*. Part I: *Die Frage nach dem historischen Jesus* (Munich, 1965).

Gilg. A., *Weg und Bedeutung der altkirchlichen Christologie* (Munich, 2nd edition 1955).

Gogarten, F., *Die Verkündigung Jesu Christi. Grundlagen und Aufgabe* (Heidelberg, 1948; 2nd impression Tübingen, 1965).

– *Christ the Crisis*, trans. R. A. Wilson (London, 1970).

Goguel, M., *The Life of Jesus*, trans. O. Wyon (London, 1933).

Grässer, E., *Die falsch programmierte Theologie. Kritische Anmerkungen zu ihrer gegenwärtigen Situation*, in *Evangelische Kommentare* 1 (1968), 694–699.

Grillmeier, A. and Bacht, H. (ed.) *Das Konzil von Chalkedon. Geschichte und Gegenwart*, 3 vols. (Würzburg, 1951–54, 2nd edition 1959).

Grillmeier, A., *Christ in Christian Tradition*, vol. I trans. J. Bowden (London, 1965, rev. edition 1975).

– *Christ in Christian Tradition*, vol. 2:1, trans. P. Allen and J. Caute (London, 1987).

– *Vorbereitung des Mittelalters. Studie über das Verhältnis von Chalkedonismus und Neu-Chalkedonismus in der lateinischen Theologie von Boethius bis Gregor d. Gr.*,

BIBLIOGRAPHY

in *Konzil von Chalkedon* II (Würzburg, 1953), 791–839.
Grundmann, W., *Die Geschichte Jesu Christi* (Berlin, 1957).
Günther, E., *Die Entwicklung der Lehre von der Person Christi im 19. Jahrhundert* (Tübingen, 1911).
Gutwenger, E., *Bewusstsein und Wissen Christi* (Innsbruck, 1960).
Hahn, F., *The Titles of Jesus in Christology: Their History in Early Christianity*, trans. H. Knight and G. Ogg (London, 1969).
Hamilton, W., *The New Essence of Christianity* (New York, 1966).
Harnack, A., *History of Dogma*, trans. N. Buchanan et al, (London, 1894–99).
– *Sokrates und die alte Kirche*, in *Reden und Aufsätze*, vol. I (Giessen 1904), 27–49.
Hasenhüttl, G., *Der Glaubensvollzug. Eine Begegnung mit Rudolf Bultmann aus katholischem Glaubensverständnis* (Essen, 1963).
– *Die Wandlung des Gottesbildes*, in *Theologie im Wandel* (*Festschrift* for the 150th anniversary of Tübingen Catholic Theological Faculty; Munich-Freiburg, 1967), 228–253.
– *Charisma – Ordnungsprinzip der Kirche* (Freiburg-Basle-Wien, 1969).
Haubst, R., *Probleme der jüngsten Christologie*, in *Theologische Revue* 52 (1956), 146–162.
– *Vom Sinn der Menschwerdung. "Cur Deus Homo"* (Munich, 1969).
Heinisch, P., *Theology of the Old Testament*, trans. W. Heidt (Collegeville, Minnesota, 1950).
Heitsch, E., *Die Aporie des historischen Jesus als Problem theologischer Hermeneutik*, in *ZThK* 53 (1956), 192–210.
– *Über die Aneignung neutestamentlicher Überlieferung in der Gegenwart*, in *ZThK* 54 (1957), 69–80.
Hempel, J., *Gott und Mensch im Alten Testament* (Stuttgart, 2nd edition 1936).
Hendry, G. S., *The Gospel of the Incarnation* (London, 1959).
Henry, P., *Kénose*, in *Dictionnaire de la Bible, Supplément* V (Paris, 1950), 7–161.
Hoskyns, E. C., *The Fourth Gospel*, ed. F. N. Davey (London, 1947).
Howard, W. F., *Christianity According to St. John* (London, 1955).
Hulsbosch, A., *Jezus Christus, gekend als mens, beleden als Zoon Gods*, in *Tijdschrift voor theologie* 6 (1966), 250–272.
Iber, G., *Zur Formgeschichte der Evangelien*, in *Theologische Rundschau* N. F. 24 (1957–58), 283–338.
Iersel, B. Van, *Der Lohn in den synoptischen Jesus-Worten* (Leiden, 1961).
Imschoot, P. van, *Théologie de L'Ancien Testament*, 2 vols., (Paris-Tournai, 1954–56).
Jacob, E., *Theology of the Old Testament*, trans. A. W. Heathcote and P. J. Allcock, (London, 1958).
Jeremias, J., *The Parables of Jesus*, trans. S. H. Hooke (rev. edition London, 1963).
– *Characteristics of the ipsissima vox Jesu*, in *The Prayers of Jesus*, (London, 1967), 108–15.
– *The Eucharistic Words of Jesus*, trans. N. Perrin (London, 1966).
– *The Problem of the Historical Jesus*, trans. N. Perrin (Philadelphia, 1964).
Jüngel, E., *Paulus und Jesus. Eine Untersuchung zur Präzisierung der Frage nach dem Ursprung der Christologie* (Tübingen, 1962).
– *The doctrine of the Trinity: God's Being is in Becoming*, trans. H. Harris (Edinburgh, 1976).
– *Vom Tod des lebendigen Gottes. Ein Plakat*, in *ZThK* 65 (1968), 93–116.

581

- *Gott - als Wort unserer Sprache*, in *Evangelische Theologie* 1 (1969), 1-24.
- *Das dunkle Wort vom "Tode Gottes"*, in *Evangelische Kommentare* 2 (1969), 133-138, 198-202.

Jungmann, J, A., *Die Stellung Christi im liturgischen Gebet* (Münster, 1925).
- *The Defeat of Teutonic Arianism and the Revolution in Religious Culture in the Early Middle Ages*, in *Pastoral Liturgy* (London, 1962), 1-101.

Kähler, M., *The So-called Historical Jesus and the Historic Biblical Christ*, trans. C. E. Braaten (Philadelphia, 1964).

Käsemann, E., *The Problem of the historical Jesus*, in *Essays on New Testament Themes*, trans. W. J. Montague (London, 1964), 15-47.
- *New Testament Questions of Today*, trans. W. J. Montague and W. F. Bunge; (London, 1969).
- *Essays on New Testament Themes*, trans. W. J. Montague (London, 1964).
- *Jesus Means Freedom*, trans. F. Clarke (London, 1969).
- *Perspectives on Paul*, trans. M. Kohl (London, 1971).

Kerstiens, F., *Die Hoffnungsstruktur des Glaubens* (Mainz, 1969).

Kittel, G., (ed.), *Theological Dictionary of the New Testament*, 10 vol., trans. G. W. Bromiley (Grand Rapids, 1964-76).

Koch, G., *Die Zukunft des toten Gottes* (Hamburg, 1968).

Kramer, W., *Christ, Lord, Son of God*, trans. B. Hardy (London, 1966).

Kremer, J., *Das älteste Zeugnis der Auferstehung Christi. Eine bibeltheologische Studie zur Aussage und Bedeutung von 1 Kor. 15, 1-11* (Stuttgart, 2nd edition 1967).
- *Die Osterbotschaft der vier Evangelien* (Stuttgart, 1968).

Krempel, A., *La doctrine de la relation chez S. Thomas. Exposé historique et systématique* (Paris, 1952).

Kuhn, J. E. v., *Von dem schriftstellerischen Charakter der Evangelien im Verhältnis zu der apostolischen Predigt und den apostolischen Briefen*, in *Jahrbücher für Theologie und christliche Philosophie* 6 (1836), 33-91.
- *Das Leben Jesu wissenschaftlich bearbeitet* I (Mainz, 1838).

Kuhn, P., *Gottes Selbsterniedrigung in der Theologie der Rabbinen* (Munich, 1968).

Kuitert, H. M., *Gott in Menschengestalt. Eine dogmatisch-hermeneutische Studie über die Anthropomorphismen der Bibel* (Munich, 1967).

Kümmel, W. G., *The Theology of the New Testament According to its Major Witnesses. Jesus-Paul-John* (London, 1974).

Küng, H., *The Church*, trans. R. and R. Ockenden (London, 1968).

Lehmann, K., *Auferweckt am dritten Tag nach der Schrift. Früheste Christologie, Bekenntnisbildung und Schriftauslegung im Lichte von 1 Kor. 15, 3-5* (Freiburg-Basle-Wien, 1968).

Léon-Durfour, X., *The Gospels and the Jesus of History*, trans. J. McHugh (London, 1968).

Liébaert, J., *Christologie. Von der Apostolischen Zeit bis zum Konzil von Chalcedon (451), mit einer biblisch-christologischen Einleitung von P. Lamarche*, in *Handbuch der Dogmengeschichte*, vol. III.1a, ed. M. Schmaus and A. Grillmeier (Freiburg-Basle-Wien, 1965).

Lightfoot, R. H., *St John's Gospel: A Commentary* ed. C. F. Evans (Oxford, 1956).

Löhrer, M., *Dogmatische Bemerkungen zur Frage der Eigenschaften und Verhaltensweisen Gottes*, in *Mysterium salutis* II (Einsiedeln-Zürich-Cologne, 1967), 291-314.

BIBLIOGRAPHY

Lonergan, B., *De constitutione Christi ontologica et psychologica* (Rome, 1956).
Macquarrie, J., *Principles of Christian Theology* (New York, 1966).
Malmberg, F., *Über den Gottmenschen* (Freiburg-Basle-Wien, 1960).
Manson, T. W., *The Sayings of Jesus, as Recorded in the Gospels According to St Matthew and St Luke Arranged with Introduction and Commentary* (London, 1949).
– *The Servant-Messiah. A Study of the Public Ministry of Jesus* (Cambridge, 1953).
– *The Life of Jesus: Some Tendencies in Present Day Research*, in *The Background of the New Testament and its Eschatology* (*Festschrift* for C. H. Dodd Cambridge, 1956), 211–221.
Manson, W., *Jesus the Messiah* (London, 1943).
Marheineke, P., *Die Grundlehren der christlichen Dogmatik als Wissenschaft* (Berlin, 1827).
– *Einleitung in die öffentlichen Vorlesungen über die Bedeutung der Hegelschen Philosophie in der christlichen Theologie* (Berlin, 1842).
Marlé, R., *Bultmann et l'interprétation du Nouveau Testament* (Paris, 1955, 2nd edition 1966).
– *Le Christ de la foi et le Jésus de l'histoire*, in *Etudes* 92 (1959), 65–76.
Marsch, W. D., *Zukunft* (Stuttgart-Berlin, 1969).
– (ed.), *Diskussion über die 'Theologie der Hoffnung' von Jürgen Moltmann* (Munich, 1967).
Marxsen, W., *The Beginnings of Christology*, trans. P. J. Achtemeier and L. Nieting (Philadelphia, 1969).
– *Die Auferstehung als historisches und als theologisches Problem* (Gütersloh, 1964).
– *The Resurrection of Jesus of Nazareth*, trans. M. Kohl (London, 1970).
McCool, F., *The Oxford Congress on the Four Gospels*, in *Biblica* 38 (1957), 486–498.
Meinertz, M., *Theologie des Neuen Testaments*, 2 vols., (Bonn, 1950).
Metz, J. B., *Theology of the World*, trans. W. Glen-Doepel (London, 1969).
– *The Church's Social Function in the Light of Political Theology*, in *Concilium*, vol. 6, No 4, (1968), 3–11.
– *Political Theology* in *Sacramentum Mund*, vol. 5 (London, 1969), 34–38.
– *Die Zukunft des Menschen und der kommende Gott*, in *Wer ist das eigentlich – Gott?* ed. H. J. Schultz (Munich, 1969), 260–275.
– *"Politische Theologie" in der Diskussion*, in *Stimmen der Zeit* 184 (1969), 289–308.
Michel, A., *Hypostatique (Union)*, in *DTC* VII:1 (Paris, 1922), 437–568.
– *Idiomes (Communication des)*, in *DTC* VII:1 (Paris, 1922), 595–602.
– *Incarnation*, in *DTC* VII:2 (Paris, 1923), 1445–1539.
Miskotte, K. H., *When the Gods are Silent*, trans. J. W. Doberstein (London, 1967).
Moeller, C., *Le chalcédonisme et le néo-chalcédonisme en Orent de 451 à la fin du VIe siècle*, in *Konzil von Chalkedon* I (Würzburg, 1951), 637–720.
Moltmann, J., *Theology of Hope*, trans. J. W. Leitch (London, 1967).
– *Hope and Planning*, trans. M. Clarkson (London, 1971).
– *The Future as a New Paradigm of Transcendence*, in *The Future of Creation*, trans. M. Kohl (London, 1969), 1–17.
– *Politische Theologie*. Guest Lecture on the occasion of the 42nd Postgraduate Medical Seminar at Tegensburg, 15 May 1969.
Mühlen, H., *Die abendländische Seinsfrage als der Tod Gottes und der Aufgang einer neuen Gotteserfahrung* (Paderborn, 1968).

583

Murchland, B. (ed.), *The Meaning of the Death of God. Protestant, Jewish and Catholic Scholars Explore Atheistic Theology* (New York, 1967).

Mussner, F., *Der historische Jesus und der Christus des Glaubens,* in *Biblische Zeitschrift* N. F. 1 (1957), 224–252.

- *Die Auferstehung Jesu* (Munich, 1969).

Nelis, J. T., *Het getuigenis van de oerkerk over Jezus en zijn msterie,* in *Tijdschrift voor theologie* 6 (1966), 238–248.

Niederwimmer, K., *Jesus* (Göttingen, 1968).

Ortiz de Urbina, J., *Das Symbol von Chalkedon. Sein Text, sein Werden, seine dogmatische Bedeutung,* in *Das Konzil von Chalkedon* I (Würzburg, 1951), 389–418.

Ott, H., *Denken und Sein. Der Weg Martin Heideggers und der Weg der Theologie* (Zürich-Zollikon, 1959).

- *Die Frage nach dem historischen Jesus und die Ontologie der Geschichte* (Zürich, 1960).

- *Reality and Faith: The Theological Legacy of Dietrich Bonhoeffer,* trans. A. A. Morrison (London, 1971).

Ott, L., *Das Konzil von Chalkedon in der Frühscholastik,* in *Das Konzil von Chalkedon* II (Würzburg, 1953), 873–922.

Ouverkerk, C. van, *Christus en de ethik,* in *Tijdschrift voor theologie* 6 (1966), 307–317.

Pannenberg, W., *Gott (V: Theologiegeschichte),* in *RGG* II (Tübingen, 1958), 1717–1732.

- *The Appropriation of the Philosophical Concept of God as a Dogmatic Problem of Early Christian Theology,* in *Basic Questions in Theology,* vol. 2 (London 1970), 119–183.

- *Jesus – God and Man,* trans. L. L. Wilkins and D. A. Priebe (London, 1968).

- *Basic Questions in Theology,* 3 vols., trans. G. H. Kehm (London, 1970).

- *Dogmatische Erwägungen zur Auferstehung Jesu,* in *ZThK* 65 (1968), 105–118.

Petavius, D., *Dogmata theologica,* 8 vols., ed. Vives, (Paris, 1865–67).

Peterson, E., *Theologische Traktate* (Munich 1951), 45–147: *Der Monotheismus als politisches Problem* (1935).

Pfaff, C. M., *De praejudiciis theologicis* (Tübingen, 1718).

Prat, F., *The Theology of St Paul,* 2 vols., trans. J. M. Stoddard, (London, 1926).

Prestige, G. L., *God in Patristic Thought* (London, 1936).

Procksch, O., *Theologie des Alten Testaments* (Gütersloh, 1950).

Rad, G. v., *Old Testament Theology,* 2 vols., trans. D. M. G. Stalker (Edinburgh, 1962–65).

Rahner, K., *Theological Investigations,* vols. 1–9 (London, 1963–71).

- *Jesus Christus,* in *LThK* V (Freiburg, 1960), 953–961.

- *Der dreifaltige Gott als transzendenter Urgrund der Heilsgeschichte,* in *Mysterium salutis* II (Einsiedeln-Zürich-Cologne, 1967), 317–397.

- *Ich glaube an Jesus Christus, Theologische Meditationen* 21 Einsiedeln, 1968).

Ratschow, C. H., *Jesusbild der Gegenwart,* in *RGG* III (Tübingen, 1959), 655–663.

Ratzinger, J., *The Theology of History in St Bonaveintura,* (Chicago, 1971).

- *Introduction to Christianity,* trans. J. R. Foster (London, 1969).

Reimarus, H. S., *The Goal of Jesus and his Disciples,* trans. G. W. Buchanan (Leiden, 1970).

BIBLIOGRAPHY

Reuss, J. F., *Verteidigung der Offenbarung Johannis gegen Johann Salomo Semler* (Frankfurt-Leipzig, 1772).

Riedlinger, H., *Geschichtlichkeit und Vollendung des Wissens Christi* (Freiburg-Basle-Wien, 1966).

Riesenfeld, H., *The Gospel Tradition and its Beginnings: A Study in the Limits of 'Formgeschichte'* (London, 1957).

Rijen, A. van, *De christen in de wereld,* in *Tijdschrift voor theologie* 6 (1966), 318-333.

Ristow, H. and Matthiae, K. (ed.), *Der historische Jesus und der kerygmatische Christus* (Berlin, 1960).

Ritschl, A., *The Christian Doctrine of Justification and Reconciliation,* vol. 3 only, ed. H. R. Mackintosh and A. B. MacAuley (Edinburgh, 1902).

– *A Critical History of the Christian Doctrine of Justification and Reconciliation,* vol. I only, trans. J. S. Black (Edinburgh, 1872).

– *Geschichte des Pietismus,* 3 vols. (Bonn, 1880-86).

Roberts, H., *Jesus and the Kingdom of God* (London, 1955).

Robinson, J. M., *A New Quest of the Historical Jesus* (London, 1959).

Robinson, J. M. and Cobb, J. B. (ed.), *The Later Heidegger and Theology* (New York, 1963; reprinted Connecticut, 1979).

Robinson, J. A. T., *Honest to God* (London, 1963).

Sartorius, C. F., *Compendium theologiae dogmaticae* (Tübingen, 3rd edition 1777).

Sauter, G., *Zukunft und Verheissung. Das Problem der Zukunft in der gegenwärtigen theologischen und philosophischen Diskussion* (Zürich-Stuttgart, 1965).

Schillebeeckx, E., *Persoonlijke openbaringsgestalte van de Vader,* in *Tijdschrift voor theologie* 6 (1966), 274-288.

– *God the Future of Man,* trans. N. D. Smith (London and Sydney, 1969).

Schmaus, M., *Katholische Dogmatik,* 4 vols., (4th edition 1948).

Schmidt, K. L., *Der Rahmen der Geschichte Jesu. Literarkritische Untersuchungen zur ältesten Jesus-Überlieferung* (Berlin, 1919; reprinted Darmstadt, 1964).

– *Das Christuszeugnis der synoptischen Evangelien,* in *Jesus Christus im Zeugnis der Heiligen Schrift und der Kirche* (Munich, 1936), 7-33.

Schmithals, W., *Jesus und die Weltlichkeit des Reiches Gottes,* in *Evangelische Kommentare* 1 (1968), 313-320.

Schnackenburg, R., *Logos-Hymnus und jhanneischer Prolog,* in *Biblische Zeitschrift* N. F. 1 (1957), 69-109.

– *Jesusforschung und Christusglaube,* in *Catholica* 13 (1959), 1-17.

– *The Gospel According to St John,* vol. 1, trans. K. Smyth (London, 1968).

Schneider, J., *Die Frage nach dem historischen Jesus in der neutestamentlichen Forschung der Gegenwart* (Berlin, 1958).

Schniewind, J., *Zur Synoptiker-Exegese,* in *Theologische Rundschau* 2 (1930), 129-189.

– *A Reply to Bultmann,* in *Kerygma and Myth,* ed. H. W. Bartsch (London, 1953), vol. 1, 45-101.

Schoonenberg, P., *Christus zonder tweedheid?,* in *Tijdschrift voor theologie* 6 (1966), 289-306.

Schubert, K. (ed.), *Der historische Jesus und der Christus unseres Glaubens* (Wien, 1962).

Schulte, R.,*Unveränderlichkeit Gottes,* in *LThK* X (Freiburg, 1965), 536-537.

Schultz, H. J., *Auch Gott ist nicht fertig. Etwas Laienprosa* (Stuttgart-Berlin, 1969).

– (ed.), *Wer ist das eigentlich – Gott?* (Munich 1969).

Schumacher, H., *Christus in seiner Präexistenz und Kenose. Nach Phil 2, 5–8*, 2 vols., (Rome, 1914, 1921).
Schweitzer, A., *The Quest of the Historical Jesus*, trans. W. Montgomery (London, 1911; new edition 1954).
Schweizer, E., *Lordship and Discipleship* (London, 1960).
– *Jesus*, trans. D. E. Green (London, 1971).
Seckler, M., *Das Heil in der Geschichte. Geschichtstheologisches Denken bei Thomas von Aquin* (Munich, 1964).
– *Kommt der christliche Glaube ohne Gott aus?*, in *Wer ist das eigentlich-Gott?* (Munich, 1969), 181–192.
Seibel, W., *Das Christusbild der liberalen Leben-Jesu-Forschung*, in *Stimmen der Zeit* 163 (1959), 266–278.
Semler, J. S., *Abhandlung von freier Untersuchung des Kanon* (Halle, 1771–75).
– *Beantwortung der Fragmente eines Ungenannten insbesondere vom Zweck Jesu und seiner Jünger* (Halle, 1779).
Sevenster, G., *De Christologie van het Nieuwe Testament* (Amsterdam, 1946; 2nd edition 1948).
– *Chrisologie des Urchristentums*, in *RGG* I (Tübingen, 1959), 1745–62.
Skard, B., *The Incarnation*, trans. H. E. Jorgensen (Minneapolis, 1960).
Slenczka, R., *Geschichtlichkeit und Personsein Jesu Christi. Studien zur christologischen Problematik der historischen Jesusfrage* (Göttingen, 1967).
Solano, J., *El Concilio de Calcedonia y la controversia adopcionista del siglo VIII en España*, in *Konzil von Chalkedon* II (Würzburg, 1953), 841–871).
Sölle, D., *Christ the Representative: An Essay in Theology after the 'Death of God'*, trans. D. Lewis (London, 1967).
– *Atheistisch and Gott glauben. Beiträge zur Theologie* (Olten-Greiburg, 1968).
Stauffer, E., *New Testament Theology*, trans. J. Marsh (London, 1955).
– *Jesus and His Story*, trans. D. M. Barton (London, 1960).
– *Die Botschaft Jesu damals und heute* (Bern, 1959).
Storr, G. C., *Dissertatio de sensu historico* (Tübingen, 1778).
– *Neue Apologie der Offenbarung Johannis* (Tübingen, 1783).
– *Doctrinae christianae pars theoretica e sacris litteris repetita* (Stuttgart, 1793).
Strauss, D. Fr., *The Life of Jesus Critically Examined*, trans. G. Eliot (London, 1892).
Strolz, W., *Menschsein als Gottesfrage. Wege zur Erfarung der Inkarnation* (Pfullingen, 1965).
Surjanský, A. J., *De mysterio Verbi incarnati ad mentem B. Joannis Apostoli libri tres* (Rome, 1941).
Taylor, V., *Forgiveness and Reconciliation. A Study in New Testament Theology* (London, 1941).
– *The Names of Jesus* (London, 1953).
– *The Life and Ministry of Jesus* (London, 1954).
– *The Cross of Christ* (London, 1956).
– *The Person of Christ in New Testament Teaching* (London, 1958).
Teilhard de Chardin, P., *The Future of Man*, trans. N. Denny (London, 1964).
Thielicke, H., *The Evangelical Faith*, 2 vols., trans. G. Bromiley (Edinburgh, 1974): on the theology of the death of God, see vol. 1, part 2, 219–404.
Thomas von Aquin, *Summa contra Gentiles*. Dominican edition (London, 1923–28).
– *Summa theologiae*. Blackfriars edition 60 vols. (London and New York, 1963–76).
Tillich, P., *Systematic Theology*, 3 vols. (London, 1953–64).

Tödt, H. E., *The Son of Man in the Synopic Tradition,* trans. D. M. Barton (London, 1965).

Tromp, S., *De Revelatione Christiana* (Rome, 6th edition 1950).

Vahanian, G., *The Death of God. The Culture of Our Post-Christian Era* (New York, 1961).

Valensin, A., *A travers la Métaphysique* (Paris, 1925).

– *Panthéisme,* in *Dictionnaire apologétique de la foi catholique* III (Paris, 1916), 1303–33.

Vogel, H., *Christologie,* vol. I (Munich, 1949).

– *Gott in Christo. Ein Erkenntnisgang durch die Grundprobleme der Dogmatik* (Berlin, 2nd edition 1952).

Vriezen, T. C., *An Outline of Old Testament Theology* (Oxford, 1958, revised edition 1970).

Weber, O., *Foundations of Dogmatics,* 2 vols., trans. D. L. Guder (Grand Rapids, 1983).

Weismann, C. E., *Institutiones theologiae exegetico-dogmaticae* (Tübingen, 1739).

Weiss, J., *Jesus' Proclamation of the Kingdom of God,* trans. R. H. Hiers and D. L. Holland (London, 1971).

Wikenhauser, A., *Das Evangelium nach Johannes* (Regensburg, 1948).

Zahrnt, H., *The Question of God: Protestant Theology in the Twentieth Century,* trans. R. A. Wilson (London, 1969).

– (ed.), *Gespräch über Gott. Die protestantische Theologie im 20. Jahrhundert. Ein Textbuch* (Munich, 1968).

– *Es geht um die Existenz Gottes,* in *Die Zeit,* 4 April, 1969.

Index of Names

Abelard, P. 63 282 378 526 527 531
Acapitas I, Pope 523
Achard of St. Victor 527
Actemeier, P. J. 489n.155
Adam, A. 511
Adorno, T. W. 20 192f 196 205n.15
    205n.16 261 279 295n.60 421
Akbar, Emperor of Hindustan 14
Albert the Great 270 282 378 526 527
Albert, H. 295n.60
Albrecht, W. 251n.5 349n.47 355n.48
Alembert, J. L. d' 164
Alexander III, Pope 527
Alexander of Hales, 282 378 526 527
Altenstein, K. F. v. Stein z. 289 313
    409
Althaus, P. 486 493 538 548
Altizer, T. J. J. 170 171 172 173
Amann, E. 523n.2
Ammonius Saccas 378
Anastasio, S. 498n.182
Anaximander 378 435
Anaximenes 378
Anaxogoras 378 434
Andersen, W. 401n.112
Andreä, J. V. 307
Andrew of Samosata 517
Angelico, Fra 98
Angelus Silesius 3
Anselm of Canterbury 9 286 355
    374n.49 378
Anselm von Havelberg 257 331
Anselm of Laon 526
Antoni C. 334n.31
Anz, W. 22n.35 393n.76
Apollinaris of Laodicea 513 514 520
Aristides 441

Aristotle 7 36 89 256 257 259 262n.33
    269 270 272 283 284 378 397 434
    436 437 441 532
Arius 509 513 514 515
Arno of Reichersberg 527
Arnobius 529
Arnold, F. X. 4
Aspelin, G. 24n.2
Asveld, P. 24n.2 28 62 104 133
Asverus, 294
Athanasius 511 513 516 517 521 522
    529
Athenagoras 441
Athenagoras, Patriarch of
    Constantinople 63
Augustine 63 72 98 252 257 258 281
    282 283 299 331 409 517 529 530
    531 543
Augustus, Emperor of Rome 327 493
Axmann, W. 24n.2

Baader, F. von 105 418
Bach, J. S. 99 255
Bachmann 418
Backes, I. 527n.8
Bacon, F. 378
Bahrdt, C. F. 11 17 79 99
Baillie, D. M. 493n.170
Bakunin, M. 21
Baldensperger W. 476
Balthasar, H. U. von xv 110n.23
    147n.3 403n.114 403n.115 419n.15
    542–544
Baltzer, E. W. 415
Bañez, D. 3
Barion, J. 268n.39 290n.57

Barlach, E. 99
Barnikol, E. 490 n.163
Barth, K. xiv 1 11n.14 19–20 22n.35
  76n.19 147n.3 228n.28 269 283 391
  393n.76 398–399 416 419n.15 459
  470 477–478 479–480 482 483 485
  486 493 544 545–548 549 555 557
Barth, P. 320n.6
Bartsch, H. 333n.31
Bartsch, H. W. 483n.113
Bassenge, F. 333n.31
Bauer, B. 313 349n.47 415 418 473
  478
Bauer, G. 386n.54
Baumgarten, A. G. 77
Baumgarten, S. J. 11
Baur, F. C. 1 313 415 467
  475–476
Bayle, P. 12 164
Beck, L. W. 42n.46 45n.54
Beckmann, M. 99
Beek, M. A. 447n.49
Beerling, R. F. 20 320n.6 325n.16
  327n.23
Beilner, W. 490n.163
Bellarmino, R. 3
Bénard, C. 334n.31
Benckert, H. 267n.38
Beneke, F. E. 312n.1 313
Bengel, J. A. 53 282
Benjamin, W. 295n.60
Bense, M. 416n.6
Bensow 415
Bentham, J. 305
Benvenuto, M. 349n.47
Benz, E. 331n.27
Bergson, H. 435
Berg van Eysinga, G. A. van den
  22n.35
Bernard of Clairvaux 97 98
Bernardino of Siena 6
Berkeley, G. 8 378
Berkhof, H. 401n.112
Berkouwer, G. C. 495n.174
Bérulle, P. de 3
Bettenson, H. 516n.2
Betzendörfer, W. 24n.2 53
Beyer, W. R. 21 244
Beyshlag, W. 475

Biedermann, A. E. 415
Bilfinger, B. 35 36
Binder, J. 290n.57
Binder, W. 110n.22
Biser, E. 172
Bishop, J. 170n.37
Blake, W. 98
Blank, J. 488 489
Bloch, E. 1 21 22n.35 161 192 193 205
  223f 231f 250n.5 255f 261n.27 264
  268n.39 272f 284n.54 294n.58
  295n.60 306 315 334 338 347
  374n.49 399 404f 407n.119 413n.1
  417 421 428f 460n.60
Blondel, M. 191n.1 419n.15 494n.171
Blumenberg, H. 76n.19 87f 287
Blumhardt, C. F. 477
Bodammer, T. 191n.1 193n.4 334n.31
Bodin, J. 164
Boethius 526
Bohatec, J. 77–86
Böhm, B. 63n.12
Böhme, J. 45 53 185 186 262n33 362
  378 380n.51 435
Bök, A. F. 34
Boisserée, M. 267
Bolland, G. J. P. J. 20
Bonaventure 281 331 526 527
Bonhoeffer, D. 552–554 555 557
Bornkamm, G. 488 498n.180
Boros, L. 399n.109
Bortnowska, H. 495n.174
Bosanquet, B. 20
Bossuet, J.-B. 13331
Bowden, J. 488n.149 511n.1
Braaten, C. A. 483n.113 483n.123
  483n.129
Bradley, F. H. 20
Braun, H. 393n.76 488 548 549
Brentano, C. 181
Brenz, J. 538
Brinkley, A. B. 391n.71
Bröcker, W. 251n.5 262n.33 334n.31
Bromiley, G. W. 170n.37
Brox, N. 536f
Bruaire, C. 20 251n.5 349n.47
Bruijn, J. C. 191n.1
Brunet, C 268n.39
Brunner, E. 416 493

Brunner, P. 548
Bruno, Giordano 7 46 186 225 250
  378 435
Brunstäd, F. 20 320n.6
Buber, M. 237f 535
Büchner, G. 556
Buchner, H. 145f 147n.3 148n.4
Buddeus, J. F. 10
Buddha 305
Bulgakov, S. 538 544
Bülow, F. 290n.57
Bultmann, R. 90 266 393n.76 397n.89
  398 399 401 415 479–485 486 487
  488 489 493 498n.180 548 557
Burckhardt, J. 324 330 390
Buren, P. van 170n.37 171 556ff
Buri, F. 485
Burian, W. 76n.19
Buridan, J. 378
Burke, E. 43 294
Busse, M. 290n.57

Caird, E.20
Cajetan de Vio, T. 528
Calvin, J. 6 98 257 282 283 296
Camelot, T. 525n.5
Campanella, T. 378
Camus, A. 288
Canz, I. G. 10 35 36
Capreolus, see Johannes Capreolus
Carganico 314
Carové 293
Carpov, J. 10
Carriera, R. 99
Cart 61
Cassiodorus 526
Castelli, E. 483n.113
Cerfaux, L. 488
Chadwick, H. 10n.13
Chagall, M. 99
Chamberlain, H. S. 115
Chapelle, A. 20 349n.47
Charlemagne 330
Charles Augustus, Grand Duke 144
Charles V 330
Charles X, King of France 411
Chemnitz, M. 538
Chevalier, J. 22n.35

Christian, C. W. 170n.37
Chrysostom, J. 114
Clark, M. 251n.5
Clausewitz, K. v. 414
Clement of Alexandria 283 513 517
  521f
Clement IV, Pope 114
Cobb, J. B. 393n.76
Cocceius, J. 283
Coletti, L. 24n.2
Come, A. B. 393n.76
Comte, A. 304 324f 330
Condorcet, A. Marquis de 323 331
Confucius 305
Conzelmann, H. 266 588
Copernicus 7 228 461
Copleston, F. 22n.35
Coreth, E. xiv 21 148n.5 232 251n.5
  260n.23 261 262n.33 349n.47 429
  431n.33
Corinth, L. 99
Cotta, J. F. 35
Cousin, V. 294 314
Cox, H. 399 553f
Cratylos 435
Croce, B. 20 23n.2 334n.31 347
  374n.49 413f
Cullmann, O. 399 486 489
Cusanus, see Nicholas of Cusa
Cyril of Alexandria 449 510 517 520
  522 523 529 530 543
Cyril of Jerusalem 529

Dahl, N. A. 490n.163
Daecke, S. M. 170n.42 173n.57
  399n.99 554f
Damasus I, Pope 455n.54
Dante, A. 410
Danzel, W. 334n.31
Darwin, C. 1 272
Daub, K. 267f 415
Deferrari, R. J. 455n.54
Delekat, F. 76n.19 77
Delling, G. 490n.163
Democritus 272 378 434
Denny, N. 399n.99
Denzinger 455n.54

Descartes, R. xii 4 7 8 164 186 195
204 252 288 378 435
Dewart, L. 537f
Dias, P. V. 495n.176
Dibelius, M. 415 480 488 498n.180
Diderot, D. 8
Diem, H. 486
Dieter, T. 275n.48 349n.47
Dilthey, W. 20 23n.2 24n.2 27 34
60n.2 62 103 132f 139 192 386 388
390 391 395 465f 482
Dikel, A. xv
Dioscorus of Alexandria 513
Dodd, C. H. 486
Domke, K. 275n.48 349n.47 355n.48
419n.15
Dorner, I. A. 415
Dostoyevsky, F. M. 165 288 477
Drescher, W. 191n.1
Drews, A. 466 473
Droysen, J. G. 390
Dulckeit-v. Arnim, C. 334n.31 346
Dulckeit, G. 22n.35 349n.47
Duns Scotus 378 528
Duquoc, C. 494n.172
Dürer, A. 97

Ebeling, G. 393n.76 489 493n.167
493n.170 496 552
Eckhart 2 45 105 186 257 262n.33 355
374n.49 435
Ehrenberg, V. 175 419n.15
Eichhorn, J. G. 34
Eichrodt, W. 447n.49 534n.4 536n.6
Elert, W. 419n.15 439n.42 441n.44
493n.170 519 521 524 525 548
Empedocles 378 434
Endel, Nanette 107 142
Engels, F. 254
Ephraem the Syrian 529
Epictetus 305
Erasmus 12 63 97
Erdmann, J. E. 415n.4
Eriugena, see Johannes Scotus
Eriugena
Ernesti, J. A. 11 34
Eschenmayer, C. A. 349n.47 418 419
Eusebius of Caesarea 297 298

Eutyches 513 525n.5
Eyck, J. van 98 335

Fabro, C. 268n.39
Fackenheim, E. L. 349n.47
Faltot 33
Fascher, E. 490n.163
Fazio-Allmayer, V. 290n.57 320n.6
Fessard, G. 20 191n.1 320n.6
Fetscher, I. 191n.1
Feuerbach, L. xii 1 2 8 48 67 71 93
136 171 192 232 238 305 313 408
414 416 420 428 473
Fichte, I. H. 200
Fichte, J. G. 24n.2 32 36 37 42 50 52
60 66 69 89 103 105 107 109 119
144 145 146 147 148f 150 151f 153
154 155 165–167 168 170 175 178
187–189 195 202 204 205 225 250
252 270 271 275 282 289 293
314n.3 323 349 378 412 429 435
461n.61
Ficino, M. 7 378
Filson, F. V. 399n.97
Findlay, J. N. 22n.35 170n.37 251n.5
Fink 32
Fischer, K. 19n.27 22n.35 23n.2 25n.5
107n.13 250n.5 268n.39 374n.49
412
Fischer, P. 417
Flach, W. 251n.5 268n.39
Flacius Illyricus, M. 81
Flavian, Patriarch of Constantinople
517
Flechsig 244n.2
Fleischmann, J. 251n.5 262n.33
290n.57
Florensky, P. 538
Flügge, J. 20 22n.35 197n.8 229
355n.48 427
Forberg, F. K. 165
Foster, M. B. 290n.57 320n.6 374n.49
Franchini, R. 268n.39
Frank, F. H. R. 415 538
Franz, H. 393n.76
Francis of Assisi 6 98
Freud, S. xii 239 305
Friedrich von Spee 3

Frederick William II, King of Prussia 12
Frederick William III, King of Prussia 166
Fries, H. 170n.37 479n.104
Fries, J. F. 313
Fritzsch 99
Fuchs, E. 489 498n.180 548
Fuhrmans, H. 20n.29 155n.22
Fulda, H. F. 191n.1
Fuller, R. H. 486
Funkenstein, A. 331n.26

Gabler, G. A. 158n.24
Gadamer, H.-G. 56n.63 96 191n.1 240n.47 241 258f 263 422n.22
Galileo 7 164 272
Gallitzin, A. von 141
Galtier, P. 494n.171
Gandillac, M. de xii 7n.6
Gans, E. 290n.57 313 320n.6
Garaudy, R. 21 22n.35 62n.5 170n.37 172 232n.32 421
Gardavský, V. 170n.37 232n.33 421
Gassendi, P. 378
Gauvin, J. 191n.1
Gehlen, A. 295n.60
Geiselmann, J. R. 481n.108 489
Gentner, M. xv
Gentile, G. 20
Gerdes, H. 349n.47 416n.6 478n.99
Gerhoh of Reichersberg 2 527
Gerson, J. 378
Gerstenberg, H. W. von 44
Gesenius, W. 318
Gess, W. F. 538
Ghert, van 248
Gibbon, E. 50 92 323
Giese, G. 290n.57
Gilbert de la Porrée 527
Gilg, A. 511
Giotto, B. di 98
Gimdt, H. 147n.3 155n.22
Glen-Doepel, W. 399n.107
Glockner, H. 20 22n.35 24n.2 104n.6 105n.10 147n.3 192n.2 315 333n.31
Gobineau, J. A. 115

Goethe, J. W. von 8 19 102 103 132 144 146 147 148 152 166 179n.65 185 186 225 229 243 255 306f 314 323 340 346 412 461n.61
Goeze, J. M. 16
Gogarten, F. 493n.170
Gogel 107
Gollwitzer, H. 490n.163 548
Gontard, S. 107
Goppelt, L. 490n.163
Gorgias 378
Görland I. 76n.19
Görres, J. von 313
Göschel, K. F. 313 409 410 415
Grässer, E. 401 402
Greco, El 98 193
Green, D. E. 488n.136
Greene 76n.19
Grégoire, F. 274n.46 290n.57
Gregory the Great 282 526
Gregory of Nyssa 281 529 543
Gregory Thaumaturgus 522
Griesinger, G. F. 24
Grillmeier, A. 511 518 519 520 521 523n.2 526n.1
Groos, H. 349n.47 403n.116 419n.15
Gropp, R. O. 374n.49
Grosz, G. 99
Grotius, H. 12 97 378
Gründer, K. 290n.57
Grundmann, W. 490n.163
Grünewald, M. 97 99
Guereñu, E. de 196n.12 109 133n.35
Gunkel, H. 480
Günther, A. 4 415 418
Günther, E. 13n.19
Günther, G. 251n.5 262
Guthrie, S. C. 399n.97 489n.153
Gutwenger, E. 494n.171
Guzzoni, U. 251n.5 259 260n.23

Haag, K. H. 260n.23 261n.28 268n.39
Haardt, R. 490n.164
Habermas, J. 290n.57 295n.60 299
Hadlich, H. 349n.47
Haering, T. 20 24n.2 34 39 43n.49 45 51 62 62n.8 89 92n.30 104 105 108n.14 118n.31 132 133 139f

Haering, T. (*cont.*)
147n.3 150n.9 151n.10 155n.22
175n.59 176 191n.1 200 268n.39
290n.57
Hagen, E von 349n.47 416n.6
Hahn, F. 489
Hahn, J. M. 53
Haldane 374n.49
Hall, C. A. M. 399n.97 489n.153
Haller, A. von 59
Haller, K. L. von 141 294
Hamann, J. G. 46 187 313 323 349
385
Hamilton, W. 170n.37 171 173
Händel, G. F. 99
Harnack, A. von 63n.11 440 467 476
479 511 518 558
Harris, H. 549n.37
Harris, H. S. 47n.56
Harrisville, R. A. 483n.113 486n.123
486n.129
Hartmann, E. von 260 268n.39
Hartmann, K. 251n.5 262n.33
Hartmann, N. 20 22n.35 24n.2 147n.3
250n.5 268n.39 374n.49
Hase, K. 475
Hasenhüttl, G. 170n.37 483n.113
495n.176
Haubst, R. 286n.55 494n.171
Haym, R. 19n.27 23n.2 42 184 191n.1
200 388
Heath, P. 153n.15
Heer, F. 20 22n.35 257 280 331f
Hegel, C. 23 24 33 107 408
Hegel, J. 24 107 144 250
Hegel, K. 250 320n.6
Hegel, M. (von Tucher) 248f 250 268
412
Hegel, T. I. C. 250
Heidegger, M. 170 191n.1 192 195
222 223 261 262 386 391–396 398
401 420 435 460 481 482 483
Heidt, W. 447n.49
Heimsoeth, H. 434n.41
Heine, H. 165
Heinisch, P. 447n.49 533n.2
Heintel, E. 349n.47
Heiss, R. 22n.35 268n.39
Heller, E. 334n.31

Helvetius, C. A. 8 378
Hemling 335
Hemmerle, K. 20n.29
Hempel, C. xv
Henning 313
Henrich, D. 32n.16 40n.44 251n.5
260n.23 261n.24
Henrici, P. 21 22n.35 191n.1 232
385n.53 419n.15
Henry, P. 538n.1
Heraclitus 187 378 397 434 435 436
437
Herbart, J. F. 60 313
Herbert of Cherbury 164
Herder, J. G. 42f 44f 46 47 50 103
147 187 323 385 403 435
Herrmann, W. 493
Hessen, J. 22n.39 349n.47 419n.15
Hiers, R. H. 398n.92
Hilary of Poitiers 522 529 543
Hildegard of Bingen 332
Hinrich 314
Hinzen, U. xv
Hippel, T. G. von 39
Hippolytus of Rome 516
Hirsch, E. 20 22n.35 42n.46 109f
147n.3 148n.5 165n.32 314n.3
419n.15 429n.30 470
Hobbes, T. 8 12 97 178 299 378 435
Hočevar, R. K. 177n.63
Hötschl, C. 22n.35 349n.47
Hoffmann, E. T. A. 348
Hoffmeister, J. 19n.27 20 23n.2 24n.2
108f 146 159 178 179 182 184
190n.1 200 244n.2 246 268n.39
289n.57 312n.1 315 320n.6 374n.49
Hofmann, J. C. K. 282
d'Holbach, D. 8 165 378
Hölderlin, F. 31 32 33 34 40 43 44 45
47 53 60 102 103 104 107 108–110
112 119 133 137 146 147 348 409
Holl, K. 480
Holland, D. L. 398n.92
Holtzmann, H. J. 475
Homer 243
Hommes, J. 290n.57 320n.6
Honorius I, Pope 526
Hooke, S. H. 488n.142
Horace xiii

Horst, F. 447n.49
Hoskyns, E. 477n.97
Hotho, H. G. 193 313 318ff 333n.31
  334f
Hromádka, J. L. 490n.163
Hudson 76n.19
Hünermann, P. 390n.68
Hugo of Strassburg 282
Hugo of St Victor 282 527
Hulsbosch, A. 494
Humboldt, W. von 289 313
Hume, D. 8 12 76 378
Huonder, Q. 349n.47 355n.48
Husserl, E. 21 262
Hyppolite, J. 20 24n.2 191n.1 200 203
  212 251n.5 320n.6

Iersel, B.van 488
Ignatius Loyola 3 191n.1
Ignatius of Antioch 516 519
Iljin, I. 20 22n.35 197f 232 250n.5
  253f 262f 268n.39 274n.46 275n.50
  276 295n.59 326n.17 326n.19
  326n.20 326n.21 326n.22 345
  349n.47 389f 419n.15 432
Imschoot, P. van 447n.49 534n.3
Innocent III, Pope 114
Irenaeus of Lyons 282 511 512 516
  522
Isidore of Seville 114 282 526

Jacobi, F. H. 32 39 42 44 46 103 104
  166 249 268 270 378
Jacobs 249
Jakob, E. 447n.49
Jansen of Ypres 257 287
Jaspers, K. 191n.1 192
Jean Paul (Richter) 165 185 348 550
Jeremias, J. 488
Jeremias, J. F. W. 11
Joachim of Fiore 331
John II, Pope 523
John Capreolus 528
John Damascene 526
John of the Cross 3
Johannes Scotus Eriugena 2 435 526
Joseph II, King of Germany 12

Julian of Toledo 378
Jügel, E. 399 488 548–552
Jünger, F. G. 268n.39
Justin Martyr 63 281 441 516 518

Kaan, A. 191n.1
Kähler, M. 466 485
Kalin, E. R. 488n.135
Kaminsky, J. 334n.31
Kant, I. xiv 14 17 19 24n.2 32 36 37f
  39 41 42 44 45 46 50 51 52 60 66
  74–90 91 92 95 97 99 100 102 105
  109 111 112 113 117 118 119 120
  123 124 132 134 135 136 137 138
  143 145 146 147 148 151 152 157
  165 166 175 178 186 193 195 202
  203 204 205 225 228 250 252 256
  257 262 269 275 282 287 305 323
  336 340 349 350 354 362 374n.49
  378 380n.51 403 435 461 470 472
  477
Käsemann, E. 486f 491 498n.180
  538n.1
Kasper, W. 20n.29 155n.22 260n.23
  429f
Kaufmann, W. 22n.35 23n.2 238n.46
Keckermann, B. 282
Keim, T. 475
Kehm, G. H. 399n.103
Kemp Smith, N. 76n.18
Kepler, J. 269
Kern, W xiv xv 21 21n.33 22n.35 62
  136f 159 160n.28 170n.37 235–237
  320n.6
Kerstiens, F. 399n.101
Kierkegaard, S. 1 21 99 170 231 234
  257 281 347 349n.47 386 390f 409
  414 415 416n.6 421 478f 482 485
Kimmerle, H. 147n.3 158n.24 175n.58
  424f
Kitamori, K. 555
Klaiber, J. 24n.2 53
Klein, W. xiv
Kleist, H. von 193 348
Klopstock, F. G. 26 42 43 100
Knebel, K. L. von 244
Knoodt, P. 415
Knittermeyer, H. 166n.34

Knox, I. 334n.31
Knox, T. M. 23n.2 47n.56 90n.29
    111n.24 111n.25 177n.63 289n.57
    333n.31
Koch, G. 399
Koch, T. 21 22n.35 251n.5 252n.8
    260n.23
Koehler, W. 511
Kohl, M. 485n.155
Köhler, L. 447n.49
Kojève, A. 20 191n.1 222 223 391n.71
Kolakowski, L. 421
Konrad, M. 110n.22
Korff, H. A. 110n.22 146 147n.3
    346n.40
Koyré, A. 191n.1
Kramer, W. 488
Krempel, A. 531n.1
Kroner, R. 20 22n.35 24n.2 147n.3
    232 250n.5 268n.39 275
Krüger, H.-J. 24n.2 62 66 93n.31
    103n.2
Kruithof, J. 151n.5 260n.23
Kühler, O. 349n.47 423
Kuhn, H. 334n.31
Kuhn, J. von 481
Kuhn, P. 536n.7
Kümmel, W. 488f 491
Küng, H. 290n.57 495n.176
Kuitert, H. M. 447n.49 534n.3
Kym, A. L. 374n.49

Lacorte, C. 24n.2 27f 34 42n.47
    49n.58 53 61
Lakebrink, B. 349n.47 374n.49
LaMettrie, J. O. de 8 164 378
Landgrebe, L. 268n.39
Lantero, E. H. 481n.110
Laplace, P. S. 7
Larenz, K. 290n.57
Lasson, G. 20 146 175 190n.1 250n.5
    268n.39 315 320n.6 326.18
    333n.31 349n.47 418f
Lauener, H. 191n.1 193n.4 334n.31
Lavater, J.K. 103
Lebreton, J. 511
Leese, K. 20 320n.6

Lefèbvre, H. 21
Lehmann, K. 489n.155 495n.176
Leibniz, G. W. 4 7 8 9f 35 36 50 53
    76 86 103 142 186 225 252 257 269
    284 322 327 332 378 382 435
Leipoldt, J. 490n.163
Leitch, J. W. 399n.98
Lenin, V. I. 21 254
Leo the Great 517 522 523
Léon-Dufour, X. 488
Lessing, G. E. 8 10n.13 14 16f 19 26
    44 50 59 66 83 91 97 100 102 103
    104 105 132 147 148 186 229 349
    403 414 435 461n.61 465
Leucippus 378 434
Leutwein 32 33
Lewis, D. 170n.37
Liébaert, J. 511
Link 175
Lipsius, R. A. 378
Litt, T. 20 22n.35 232 274f
Livy 326
Locke, J. 8 378
Löffler, J. F. C. 30
Löhrer, M. 544f
Loisy, A. 494n.171
Lonergan, B. 494n.171
Loofs, F. 510 511 518
Lord, J. R. 488n.134
Lorenzen, P. 251n.5 262
Lotz, J. B. 268n.39 349n.47
Louis XIV, King of France 12 207
Louis XVI, King of France 43
Louis-Philippe, Duke of Orleans 411
Löwenstein, J. 290n.57
Löwith, K. 246n.4 253n.9 306n.74 307
    320n.6 330f 349n.47 385 393n.76
    416 420
Lowrie, W. 478n.98 479n.100
Lübbe, H. 295n.60
Lucian of Antioch 514
Ludovici, A. M. 55n.62
Lukács, G. 1 21 24n.2 42 61 62 142
    222f 334n.31 340 347 417 421
Lunati, G. 320n.6
Lütgert, W. 419n.15
Luther, M. 2 5f 12 28 98 99 163 193
    243 257 281 282 287 307f 368 409
    450 480 496 544 550f

Machiavelli, N. 299
Machovec, M. 421
Macquarrie, J. 391n.70 545n.23
Maier, H. 296.n 60 300
Maimon, S. 270
Maimonides, M. 378
Malebranche, N. 8 186 378 435
Malmberg, F. 494n.171 545
Mann, T. 142
Manson T. W. 486
Manson, W. 486
Marcion 512
Marcuse, H. 21 22n.35 251n.5
   290n.57 295n.60 320n.6 388
   391n.71
Marheineke, P. K. 313 349n.47 411
   412 414 415 417 472
Marietti, A. 22n.35
Marlé, R. 489
Marsch, W.-D. 21 22n.35 24n.2 62
   112n.26 116n.30 290n.57
Marsh, J. 480n.107
Martin I, Pope 526
Marx, K. xii 1 8 21 67 93 171 179
   191n.1 192 223 226 231 232 238
   254 290n.57 295 303f 305 313 330
   386 390 414 416 420f
Marxsen, W. 489
Masereel, F. 99
Massolo, A. 24n.2 62
Matisse, H. 99
Matthiae, K. 490
Maurer, R. K. 191n.1 320n.6
Maximus the Confessor 526 543n.13
Maxwell, J. 399n.100
McHugh, J. 488n.140
McTaggart, J. 21 251n.5 271n.41
Medicus, F. 165n.31
Mehlis, G. 324f
Melanchthon, P. 282 296
Melito of Sardis 515 516 522
Mendelssohn, M. 44 50 52 69f 92 103
   115
Menken, G. 282
Merker, N. 24n.2 147n.3
Metz, J. B. 295n.60 300 399
Metzke, E. 374n.49
Meulen, J. van der 251n.5 268n.39
   273n.43

Michaeli, F. 447n.49
Michaelit, I.D. 11
Michalson, C. 393n.76
Michel, A. 525n.5 528n.10 529n.11
Michel, O. 490n.163
Michel, W. 110
Michelangelo 98
Michelet, J. 313 374n.49 386f 422
Mill, J. S. 304
Miller, A. V. 190n.1 250n.5 271n.42
   274n.47
Miller, J. P. 10
Miskotte, K. H. 536n.7
Moeller, C. 523n.2
Mohammed 305
Molina, L. de 3
Möller, J. 21 22n.35 191n.1 232 233
   251n.5 268n.39 349n.47 355n.48
   395f 419n.15 .
Moltmann, J. 1 170n.37 172 307n.76
   309n.77 399 400–402 555f
Monrad, C. 374n.49
Montague, W. J. 487n.131
Montesquieu, C. 26 47 52 323
Montgomery, W. 398n.93
Moog, W. 415n.4
Mosheim, J. L. von 10 34
Mühlen, H. 170n.37
Müller, E. 24n.2
Müller, G. E. 22n.35 334n.31 349n.47
   419n.15
Murchland, D. 170n.37
Mure, G. R. G. 22n.35 251n.5
Mussner, F. 489 489n.155 490n.164

Naber, A. xiv
Nadler, K. 20, 232n.34 349n.47
Napoleon I 42 149 190 207 244 250
   411
Negri, A. 24n.2 27 61
Negri, E. de 20 24n.2
Nelis, J. T. 495n.174
Nestorius 515 524 525n.5
Newmann, J. H. 281
Newton, I. Sir 7 8 86 164 269 272 378
Nicholas of Cusa 2 7 99 186 257
   374n.49 435 453

INDEX

Nicolin, F. 147n.3 169n.36 191n.1
200n.11 246n.4
Niebuhr, B. G. 289
Niederwimmer, K. 488 498n.180
Niel, H. 20 22n.35 104 232 274n.46
419n.15
Niethammer, F. I. 243 244f 248 249
252 267
Nieting, L. 489n.155
Nietzsche, F. xii 1 2 55 67 110 164
169 172 173 192 193 241 288·305
306n.74 347 379 391 392f 416n.7
420 435 477
Nikolai, F. 11 103
Nink, C. 21 191n.1
Nisbet, H. B. 320n.6
Noack, L. 349n.47
Noël, G. 251n.5
Nohl, H. 20 23n.2 47 62 75 90 94 111
112 116n.29 117
Nolde, E. 99
Nolte, J. xv 116n.20 498
Novalis, 42 144 348

Ockenden R. 495n.176
Odgen, S. M. 393n.76
Oelmüller, W. 334n.31 347n.41 348
349n.47 417 420n.17 420n.18
421n.19 421n.20 421n.21
Oetinger, F. C. 53 187
Ogiermann, H. 232 268n.39 275n.48
349n.47 355n.48 431n.33
O'Hara, W. J. 399n.109
Ohlert 313
Ohlsen 471
Oiserman, T. I. 22n.35
Oosterbaan, J. A. 191n.1
Origen 98 282 283 510 513 517 518
529 530 543n.13 543
Orosius, P. 331
Ortega y Gasset, J. 320n.6
Ortiz de Urbina, I. 516n.2
Osculati, R. 191n.1
Osterwald, J. F. 10
Ott, E. 349n.47
Ott, H. 393n.76 486 554f
Ott, L. 526n.3 27n.7
Otto, R. 480

Otto of Freising 331
Ouwerkerk, C. van 495n.174
Overbeck, F. C. 141 477

Pannenberg, W. 399 440 493n.170 496
525n.7
Paracelsus 53 186
Parente, P. 494n.171
Parmenides 186 378 397 434 435 436
437 533
Pascal, B. xii 3 7 8 163 164 168 257
409
Patočka, J. 334n.31
Paul of Samosata 510 513 514
Paulus, H. E. G. 248 267 269 408 415
471
Pelagius I, Pope 525
Pelagius II, Pope 525
Peperzak, A. T. B. 20 24n.2 61 62
76n.19
Pericles 294
Perrin, N. 488n.142
Petavius D. 3 529n.11 529n.12
Peterson, E. 299f
Peter Fullo, Patriarch of Antioch 524
Peter Lombard 282 378 526 527
Pfaff, C. M. 10 34
Philipps 141
Philo of Alexandria 362 378 439
Picasso, P. 99
Planck, G. J. 12 50
Plato 32 39 45 63 70f 89 252 255f
257f 262 293 362 378 392 393 397
434 435 436 437 447 472 525
Plenge, J. 320n.
Plotinus 252 255f 378 397 434 436
437
Ploucquet, G. 35 53
Pöggeler, O. 116n.29 145f 147n.3
191n.1 200 251
Polybius 326
Pomponatius 378
Popper, K. R. 290n.57 294
Porphyry 378
Praepositinus of St Victor 526
Praxeas 512
Prestige, G. L. 534n.43 521n.1
Priebe, D. A. 493n.170

597

Proclus 378
Proclus, Patriarch of Constantinople 517
Protagoras 378
Proudhon, P. J. 330
Przywara, E. 20–21 232
Pufendorf, S. 378
Puglisi, F. 334n.31

Rad, G. von 452n.51 535n.5
Radbertus 378
Radermacher, H. 416n.6
Rahner, K. xv 1 399 494n.171 496n.177 539–542 546
Raimundus Lullus 378
Raimundus of Sabunde 378
Ranke, L. von 324 390
Raphael 98
Ratzinger, J. 331 545
Raumer, K. G. von 267 317
Reble, A. 246n.4
Redlich, A. 251n.5 262n.33
Redmann, H. G. 76n.19 86
Reese, H. 320n.6 349n.47
Régnier, M. 349n.47
Régnon, T. de 511
Reicke, B. 490n.163
Reimarus, H. S. 13n.19 14f 17 18n.26 50 66 75 79 82 97 100 133 398 414 465 470n.75 474 476f
Reinhardt, C. F. 42
Reinhardt, F. V. 17f
Reinhold, K. L. 32 37 144 145
Reitzenstein, R. 266
Renan, E. 21 415
Rendell Harris, J. 266
Renthe-Fink, L. von 386f 387n.59 388 388n.61 466n.68 466n.69
Reuchlin, J. 115 378
Reuss, J. F. 35
Reuter, H. 349n.47
Reyburn, H. A. 290n.57
Richard of St. Victor 527
Riedel, M. 147n.3 246n.4 290n.57 296f 349n.47
Riedlinger, H. 494n.171
Riesenfeld, H. 490n.163
Rijen, A. van 495n.174

Ristow, H. 490
Ritschl, A. 398n.91 440 467 476 493 496 518
Ritter, H. 312n.1
Ritter, J. 24n.2 176f 290n.57 299
Rivière, J. 511
Robert of Melun 526
Robespierre, M. 43 299
Robinet 378
Robinson, E. 391n.70
Robinson, J. A. T. 188n.70 553
Robinson, J. M. 393n.76 481 487
Rohrmoser, G. 21 22n.35 24n.2 62 90 93n.32 177 191n.1 222 223 290n.57 424
Rosenkranz, K. 19n.27 22n.35 23n.2 24n.4 29n.12 31 32 38 39n.40 39n.42 75 104 111 159 177 178 181 184 191n.1 206n.17 246 252n.8 260 268n.39 313 314n.2 334n.31 410n.120 412n.122 412n.124 472
Rosenzweig, F. 24n.2 62 108 290n.57 411n.121
Rösler, C. F. 34
Rossi, M. 24n.2 61 290n.57
Roscelin of Compiègne 378
Rouault, G. 98 99
Rousseau, J.-J. 11 16 34 39 40 42 44 45 50 52f 61 63 72 76 85 147 178 293 364 378
Rüfner, N. 235n.44
Rupert of Deutz 282 331

Sabellius 512
Saint-Simon, C. H. Graf von 304
Sanderson 349n.47
Sartorius, C. F. 35 415
Sartre, J. P. 262 288
Sauter, G. 399n.101
Savigny, F. C. von 289 294
Scaliger, J. J. 115
Schäzler, C. von 4
Scheeben, M. J. 4
Schell, H. 494n.171
Schelling, F. W. J. 20 23n.1 24n.2 32 33 34 37 38 39 40 41 44 47 53 60 61 62 66 89 102 103 104 105 106 107 109 119 133 141 143 144 145

Schelling, F. W. J. (*cont.*)
  146 147 148 149 150 151 152–154
  155 157 158 163 175 177 178 179
  187–189 190–192 207 208 225 249
  250 252 260n.23 269 270 271 273
  275 314 316 323 336 340 348 349
  378 390 409 416n.6 429 430 435
  461n.61
Schenkel, D. 475
Schelsky, H. 295n.60
Schillebeeckx, E. 399 402f 495
Schiller, J. C. F. von 25 26 42 43 44
  45 50 52 60 76n.19 103 108 111
  144 146 166 205 323 336 340 403
Schilling-Wollny, K. 104n.6 147n.3
Schlatter, A. 419n.15
Schlegel, A. W. 145
Schlegel, F. 42 141 144 145 336 348
Schleiermacher, F. 145 149 153 165
  240 289 301n.72 313 314 314n.3
  349n.47 412 416n.6 467 470 472
  476 477 546
Schmidt, E. 20 22n.35 251n.5 268n.39
  349n.47 419n.15
Schmidt, G. 245 246n.4
Schmidt, H. 21 22n.35 24n.2 62
  116n.30 142n.45 290n.57 320n.6
  524
Schmidt, H.-J. xv
Schmidt, K. L. 415 480 486
Schmidt-Japing, J. W. 22n.35 24n.2
Schmithals, W. 401 402
Schmitt, C. 299f
Schmitt, R. 349n.47
Schmitz, G. 320n.6
Schmitz, H. 179 268n.39
Schnackenburg, R. 266, 489
Schneider, R. 24n.2 53 62
Schniewind, J. 486
Schnurrer, C. F. 32 34
Schoeps, H. J. 349n.47 490n.163
Schonmetzer 455n.54
Schoonenberg, P. 495
Schopenhauer, A. 25 192 193 252 305
  312n.1 313 323 347
Schoreel 335
Schrader-Klebert, K. 260n.23
Schröckh, J. M. 26
Schubarth 314

Schubert, K. 490
Schüler, G. 23n.2 48n.57 61n.3 93n.33
  111n.25
Schulin, E. 320n.6 324
Schulte, R. 545
Schultz, H. 536
Schultz, H. J. 296n.60 399n.101
Schulz, R. E. 251n.5
Schulz, W. 20n.29 22n.35 251n.5 301
  349n.47 393n.76 419n.15
Schulze, W. A. 76n.19 86n.23
Schumacher, H. 538n.1
Schürmann, H. 490n.163
Schütte, H.-W. 173n.57
Schütz, H. 99
Schütz, P. 399n.101
Schwarz, J. 24n.2 147n.3 185 268n.39
Schwarz, R. 103
Schwegler, A. 32 32n.16
Schweitzer, A. 13n.19 18n.26 398
  415n.3 467 470 474 476f 480 487
Schweitzer, C. G. 385 418
Schweizer, E. 488 498n.180
Schweppenhäuser, H. 349n.47 416n.6
Scobie, A. 489n.156
Seckler, M. 88f 170n.37 331
Seeberg, R. 511 518
Seeberger, W. 290n.57 320n.6
Semler, J. S. 11 13f 16 34 35f 50 82
  91 97 100 414 465
Seuse, H. 186
Sevenster, G. 489
Shaftesbury, A. A. C. Earl of 44 45
  52
Shakespeare, W. 25
Shepherd, W. C. 349n.47
Sibree, J. 320n.6
Sigrist, R. xv
Simon, J. 191n.1 193n.4 334n.31
Simon, R. 13
Simson 374n.49
Skard, B. 511
Slenezka, R. 474 475 490 493n.167
Smith, L. P. 481n.110
Smith, N. D. 399n.108
Smith, W. 149n.8 166n.35
Socrates 25 29 50 54 59 63–66 70f 74
  89 305 329 369 370 378 411
Solano J. 526n.2

Solger, K. W. F. 313 340 348
Sölle, D. 170 172 173
Soloviev, V. 538
Sophocles 26
Sowers, S. G. 399n.97 486n.128
Spalding, J. J. 11
Spaventa, B. 20
Spears 349n.47
Spencer, H. 304 305
Spener, P. J. 6 34
Spengler, L. 307n.76
Spinoza, B. de 8 12 39 44 45 46 97
    103 104 105 109 119 132 148f 151
    152 186 225 229 262 267 305 378
    380n.51 434 437
Splett, J. 21 22n.35 24n.2 106n.12 124
    126 159 177n.62 184n.67 191n.1
    251n.5 268n.39 349n.47 380n.51
    419n.15
Spranger, E. 116n.29
Stace, W. T. 22n.35
Stahl, F. J. 294
Stählin, R. 170n.37
Staiger, E. 24n.2 44n.50
Stapfer, J. F. 77 86
Staudenmaier, F. A. 4 22n.35 268n.39
    349n.47 418
Stauffer, E. 488 498n.180
Steely, J. E. 489n.151
Steinbüchel, T. 21 22n.35 106 147n.3
    374n.49 419n.15
Steininger, W. 349n.47
Stenzel, J. 374n.49
Stewart, J. 61 111
Stieglitz 411f
Stirling, J. H. 20
Stöger, A. 490n.164
Stolberg, F. L. Graf von 141
Storr, G. C. 34 35–37 53 58 63 409
Strauss D. F. xi 139 192 225f 313 398
    412 414 415 465f 467 469–475 476
    478 479 481 482 485 492 493
Strolz, W. 393n.76
Suárez, F. 3 528

Taine, H. 21
Talleyrand, C. M. 42
Taminiaux, J. 334n.31 340

Tatian 63 441
Taylor, V. 486
Teilhard de Chardin, P. xii 173n.57
    399 554f
Terburg, G. 336
Teresa of Ávila 3
Tertullian 516f 522 529
Teyssèdre, B. 334n.31
Thales of Miletus 378
Theodore of Mopsuestia 282 515 517
Theodore of Pharan 524n.3
Theodoret of Cyrus 282 517
Theodotos the Banker 514
Theodotos the Tanner 514
Theophilus of Antioch 441
Theunissen, M. 349n.47 416n.6
Thibaut, A. F. J. 267
Thielicke, H. 170n.37 171 172
Thiersch, F. 249
Thomas Aquinas 9 20 88 98 175n.39
    159n.26 235n.44 257 258 269 270
    272 281 282 284 286f 296 331 378
    527f 529n.12 531f
Thomassin d'Eynac, L. 3
Thomasius, C. 538
Thomasius, G. 415
Thorwaldsen, B. 99
Thucydides 326
Tiberius, Emperor of Rome 493
Tieck, L. 144 348
Tietze, W. xv
Tillich, P. 1 419n.15 545n.23
Tiphanus, C. 528
Tixeront, L.-J. 511
Tödt, H. E. 401n.112 488
Topitsch, E. 290n.57
Touilleux, P. 22n.35
Trendelenburg, A. 260
Troeltsch, E. 395 482 498
Trott zu Solz, A. von 290n.57
Turgot, A. R. J. 330f
Turrettini, J. A. 10

Ulrich of Strassburg 282'
Ulrici, H. 260f 417

Vahanian, G. 170n.37 171
Valla, L. 97 332

Vancourt, R. 20 349n.47
Vanini 378
Varro, M. T. 269
Vasquez, G. 3
Vecchi, G. 334n.31 346n.39 347
Veith, L. 415
Velásquez, D. R. de Silva 98
Venturini, K. H. 17
Vera, A. 20
Vico, G. B. 323 331
Vigilius, Pope 525
Vincent of Beauvais 269
Vischer, F. T. 334n.31
Vischer, T. 449n.49
Vogel, H. 76n.19 548
Volk, H. xiv
Volkmann-Schluck, K.-H. 273n.43
Volpe, G. della 23n.2 24n.2
Voltaire 8 12 16 39 60f 72 164 323
    331 385
Voss, J. H. 243
Vriezen, T. C. 447n.49

Wacker, H. 24n.2 76n.19
Wagner, R. 347
Wahl, J. xiv 20 22n.35 23n.2 112n.27
    113 191n.1 204n.13 251n.5 262
    434n.41
Walch, C. W. F. 10
Walch, J. G. 10
Walgrave, J. H. 349n.47
Wallace, W. 20 268n.39 274n.47
Walter of St Victor 526
Weber, C. M. von 348
Weber, O. 548
Wegscheider, J. A. L. 318
Weil, E. 22n.35 290n.57 294
Weismann, C. E. 34
Weiss, B. 475
Weiss, J. 398 476
Weisse, C. H. 417 475
Weizsäcker, K. H. 475
Wellhausen, J. 415 480
Welte, B. 191n.1 233–235 349n.47
Werner, J. 349n.47

Werner, K. 415
Werner, M. 311
Werner, Z. 141
Werenfels, S. 10
Wette, W. M. L. de 472
Whitehead, A. N. xii 435
Whittemore, R. C. 274n.46
Wiehl, R. 191n.1 251n.5 262n.33
Wieland, C. M. 26 42 52
Wieland, W. 22n.35
Wigersma, B. 20 273n.43
William of Auxerre 526
William of Occam 378
Wilke, C. G. 475
Wilkins, L. L. 493n.170
Wilson, R. A. 493n.170
Winckelmann, J. J. 44 52 336
Windelband, W. 374n.49
Wittig, G. R. 170n.37
Wolf, F. A. 289
Wolf, K. 24n.2 62 105
Wolff, C. 4 9 10 18 35 35n.27 35n.28
    36 50 53 76 270 282 288 296 351
    378
Woltemar 69
Woolf, B. L. 480n.106
Wrede, W. 13n.19 18n.26 398n.93
    470n.75 476
Wünsch 29
Wyneken, G. A. 374n.49
Wyon, O. 493n.169

Xavier, F. 14
Xenophanes 378 436

York von Wartenburg, P. Graf 386
    388 390n.68 391 466 482

Zahrnt, H. 173 188n.70
Zeno 378
Zinzendorf, N. L. Graf von 6 115
Züfle, M. 191n.1 193n.4 334n.31
Zwingli, H. 6 551